Tokens of Exchange

Post-Contemporary Interventions Series Editors: Stanley Fish & Fredric Jameson

TOKENS of EXCHANGE

The Problem of Translation in Global Circulations

Edited by Lydia H. Liu

DUKE UNIVERSITY PRESS   Durham & London   1999

© 1999 DUKE UNIVERSITY PRESS

All rights reserved

Printed in the United States of America on acid-free paper ♾

Typeset in Quadraat by Tseng Information Systems, Inc.

Library of Congress Cataloging-in-Publication Data appear

on the last printed page of this book.

CONTENTS

Lydia H. Liu *Introduction*

The problem of translation has become increasingly central to critical reflections on modernity. What it means is that we can no longer talk about translation as if it were a purely linguistic or literary matter; nor can we continue to acquiesce to the material consequence of what anthropologists have termed "cultural translation," practiced for centuries by missionaries, ethnographers, travelers, and popular journalists in the West and subsequently adopted by scholars from other parts of the world. The universalizing tendencies of modernity have always called upon the service of the translator to spread its gospel elsewhere. (We might as well take the religious trope literally here, because the Christian missionaries were the self-appointed pioneers in these processes.)

Universalism thrives on difference. It does not reject difference but translates and absorbs it into its own orbit of antithesis and dialectic. For that reason, any articulation of cultural difference or alternative modernity must be treated with caution, because such articulations are themselves embedded in the process of global circulations that determine which elements count as difference and why they matter. The fact that one can speak about a varied range of modernities suggests an extraordinary faith in the translatability of modernity and its universal ethos. Can that faith be questioned? If so, on what ground?

The acceleration of globalization after the cold war demands that we grasp and contextualize the present forms of global circulation by reflecting on the earlier universalizing processes and related phenomena. This book is a collective effort to center the economy of symbolic and material exchange among peoples and civilizations in a study of the universalizing processes of modernity in the past and present. It is centrally concerned with the production and circulation of *meaning as value* across the realms of language, law, history, religion, media, and pedagogy and, in particular, with significant moments of translation of *meaning-value* from language to language and culture to culture.

There is good reason to believe that a new expectation is emerging from the recent theoretical work on translation. This expectation can be formulated in terms of such questions as How do signs and meanings travel from place to place in global circulations? Can a theory of translation illuminate our understanding of how meaning-value is made or unmade between languages? Is translatability a value in itself or a product of repeated exchange and negotiation in the translation process? What do we stand to gain or lose when we take up a position for or against the commensurability of verbal or nonverbal signs in multilinguistic or multisemiotic situations?

Undoubtedly, these questions bear a material relationship to the contemporary developments in information technology and the rise of a global media culture in the twentieth century. Such developments have been forcing upon us the need to imagine new ways of talking about language, communication, translingual exchange, global circulation, and so on. However, the spread of information technology does not automatically explain how meanings circulate *meaningfully* among the world's diverse groups, societies, and nations. We intuitively grasp the fact that meanings usually get around and circulate beyond their original point of eruption and that what is said in one context can be taken to mean very different things in different places. However, that intuition does not and cannot take us very far, especially when the idea of "the different" also travels, and sometimes faster than our intuition can catch up. Like all tautological expressions, the idea of "the different" often hinges on the act of translation just as much as does the idea of "sameness," being two sides of the "same" coin. And it seems unlikely, either now or in the near future, that we will derive an intuitive understanding of how one language functions vis-à-vis another language(s) outside what is normally taken as the realm of translation, be it literal, figurative, metonymical, or subversive translation. At each turn, we find ourselves at the mercy of the "translator" among us and in us.

Nevertheless, the problem of translation can be rethought within a new set of parameters that addresses itself to an economy of meaning-value and (often unequal forms of) transcultural exchange. The task of the theorist then is to analyze the intellectual and material conditions under which the *reciprocity of meaning-value* or the denial thereof occurs at significant moments of cultural encounter.

Two parallel historical developments have driven the intellectual agenda of this book. First, translation has been indispensable to the processes of global circulation of colonial language theories, universal history, scientific discourse, material culture, and international law for the past few hundred years. Second, colonial encounters between European and "other" languages have helped define the unique intellectual contour of Western philosophical thinking about language, difference, culture, and alterity. That contour has been revised but not significantly changed, notwithstanding the various claims to the contrary. Deconstruction, for example, has tried but not succeeded in leading Western theory out of its own self-referential mode of thinking about the limits of the thinkable despite its implicit reference to the *radical difference* of other languages and other writing systems. The occasional pointing toward the "other" histories and "other" languages often amounts to little more than a synecdochal gesture, whereas the repeated, violent encounters between the civilizations of "the East and the West" in the past few hundred years remind us that the fantasizing of an absolute other as if the two had never met is itself a form of violence.

The history of colonialism also reminds us how pervasive the work of translation has been in molding and continuing to mold people's deictic conception of the self, other, and difference, so much so that the self is already inhabited by the other before people become aware of it. The argument of "hybridity" or "interculturality" may help explain some of the consequences of colonial encounter, especially the formation of colonial identity and subjectivity, but seems to lose intellectual rigor when it comes to conceptualizing translation as a theoretical problem and social practice. In other words, we need to develop a whole new set of linguistically sophisticated and historically nuanced approaches to do a better job analyzing the processes of colonial exchange.

Contemporary studies of the European empires, the former colonies, and so-called contact zones have greatly enriched our understanding of the historical processes mentioned above. As the editor of this book, I am interested in exploring the possibility of pushing the insights of that scholarship in a new direction by tackling both the familiar and not so familiar modes of value exchange in global circulations. What I mean by the unfamiliar mode is the largely submerged and undertheorized forms of exchange such as the invention of "equivalent" meanings between languages, struggles over the commensurability or reciprocity of meanings as values, and the production of global translatability among different languages and societies in recent times. The emphasis on meaning-value, equivalence, (in)commensurability, and (non)reciprocity comes from my own dissatisfaction with genealogical and sociological studies of colonial institutions and symbolic power from which we learn so little about the subtle intellectual mechanisms of colonial circulation.

This book continues to discuss knowledge/power relations but considers a very different set of problems from those that usually inform Foucauldian postcolonial studies. As stated at the outset of this introduction, we hope to answer the question of how meaning circulates *meaningfully* among the world's diverse languages and societies, and how cultural difference has become a problematic and is translated as such in this context. Above all, we are interested in the processes whereby translation has helped universalize the "modern" by rewriting and reinventing it in the diverse languages and societies of the world during the shared and much embattled moments of globalization.

Hence, we seek a critical alternative to the studies of colonial metropoles, local resistance, cultural hybridity, and so on by proposing two sets of critical interventions in contemporary theory. These consist in historical analyses that focus on (1) how the circumstantial meeting of languages and peoples produces and contests the *reciprocity of meaning-value* between those same languages and cultures so that translation becomes a cognitive possibility, and (2) how *reciprocity* becomes thinkable and contestable as a problem in translingual and transcultural exchanges when predominantly unequal forms of global exchange characterize the material and intellectual conditions of that exchange. We pay close attention to the granting or withholding of reciprocity of meaning-value among languages and societies and treat the distribution of such values as a key mechanism in global circulations and relations of power.

I use the word "token" in the title to capture the range of our collective enterprise. The trope encompasses not only verbal and symbolic exchange but material circulations as well. It suggests that, like verbal signs, objects also constitute representations and that their tangible material existence participates in its own signification rather than exists outside it. On the global scale of signification, I take translation as a primary agent of token making in its capacity to enable exchange, producing and circulating meaning as value among languages and markets. In this sense, tokens and their exchange-value represent my way of talking about the circulation of the sign, text, works of art, commodities, philosophy, science, pedagogy, and social practice discussed in this book.

Specifically, our point of departure is to place the study of China and East Asia in a global context and, equally important, to examine global processes in East Asia. The double emphasis on the global enables our authors to depart from the regional or area studies approaches that tend to isolate East Asia as an object of research in American academia. What it means is that "national" histories and world history must be approached with absolute attention to the types of epistemological *translatability*—which is often taken for granted—that have been constructed among the various languages and scholarships in modern times.

This approach takes us, on the other hand, beyond the traditional field of historical linguistics and its studies of translation and etymology, because our goal lies not in the documentation and description of how a national language or culture has undergone changes by interacting with other languages and cultures, but rather in a rethinking of the very notion of self-sufficient national languages and cultures.

We do so by trying to recapture a sense of the *radical historicity* of constructed —and often contingent—linguistic equivalences and nonequivalences that have emerged among the world's languages and societies in recent times. Such equivalences and nonequivalences in turn constitute the very identity of each national language and national culture. The emphasis on the *interactive and conflictual processes* rather than identities—again, not to be confused with the notion of hybridity or interculturality—may help fill some major gaps of knowledge in contemporary scholarship. I believe that these gaps are there and have remained somewhat invisible because topics like this tend to fall through the cracks of well-established disciplines of national histories and world history and between East and West.

As the editor of this book, I have refrained from rehashing the familiar postcolonial and poststructuralist concerns and focus instead on the issues of coauthorship, circulation, contestation, and the question of equivalence and reciprocity in relations of unequal exchange. By sustaining a focus on China's interactions with the colonial and other forces over the centuries, I eschew the "broad sampling method" commonly adopted in edited volumes on transnational studies. The argument behind that decision is that the assemblage of diverse local histories (Asian, African, Latin American, etc.) in a book such as this would have weakened its intellectual potential by implicitly endorsing a pretheorized, geographical notion of the global. The very openness (and endless multiplication) of "local regions" underlying the broad sampling approach often suggests a large measure of theoretical closure.

With this book I would like to theorize the global in the local with some degree of discursive concreteness, tracing the world-making implications of local cultural processes over a long span of history. To that end, the limits of contemporary theory must be pushed on the following fronts: (1) the possibility of mutual intelligibility (or nonintelligibility) of languages, that is, the historical condition of translation; (2) moments of linguistic equivalence in relations of unequal exchange; (3) the question of coauthorship and agency with respect to such relations; and (4) the success or failure of modern regimes of knowledge in achieving universal status in translation.

This book consists of fourteen essays divided under four major headings. My own contribution, "The Question of Meaning-Value in the Political Economy of the Sign," begins with a discussion of the colonial legacy of value in the eighteenth century and raises the question of inequality in "equal" linguistic exchange. I go back to Marx's theorizing of the universal equivalent in the context of his labor theory of value and exchange-value and then to Saussure, who sees linguistics and political economy as parallel systems of "equivalence in difference." This discussion is followed by a critical reevaluation of Baudrillard's and Bourdieu's recent engagement with Marx and Saussure and reflects on how the problem of signification at linguistic and economic levels can be brought into fruitful dialogue with the theory of translation. My argument is that the equivalence or nonequivalence of meaning much discussed in translation theory participates in the same process of social exchange that produces the reciprocity and nonreciprocity of value in economic and other symbolic realms.

These initial ruminations are followed by three essays grouped under part 1, "Early Encounters: The Question of (In)commensurability." All three chapters are devoted to the question of cultural and linguistic (in)commensurability and struggle over cultural supremacy which first emerged during the Jesuit missionary encounter with the Chinese scholarly community in the seventeenth century. Roger Hart's work reflects critically on the legacy of linguistic incommensurability and cultural relativism in the history of science and, specifically, examines the ways in which Jacques Gernet and Jean-Claude Martzloff have interpreted the work of the Jesuit missionaries in seventeenth-century China. This critique is followed by Hart's own reflections on the Jesuit translations of European mathematics and Christian doctrines. He argues that translation served as an important patronage strategy in this period and was a crucial resource for the converts as active agents manipulating the meanings of the translated text.

Whereas Hart's emphasis is theory and language, Qiong Zhang's essay takes a focused look at the Jesuits' work on religion, especially their preoccupation with neo-Confucian spirituality. She shows how Matteo Ricci and the other missionaries took qi to represent the core of Chinese medical, cosmological, metaphysical, and moral discourses and sought to reorganize and command the discursive field of this indigenous concept. Translation became their standard means to fashion new meaning-value by strategically producing Christian theological readings of classical Chinese texts. The missionaries began by building up semantic equivalences between qi on the one hand and "soul," "air," "pneuma," and so on on the other. These equivalences led them to take a position on the Confucians' studies of certain classical texts for evangelical purposes and were also responsible for some of the most enduring forms of contested commensurability that continue to haunt scholars and the lay public today.

By the nineteenth century, the thesis of (in)commensurability began to take what Haun Saussy in his essay calls the "grammatical" turn. If seventeenth- and eighteenth-century studies of the Chinese language had more or less concentrated on its system of characters with its mix of phonetic and semantic clues, Wilhelm von Humboldt, Schleicher, William Dwight Whitney, and the other nineteenth-century linguists saw in the language no longer a bounty, but a lack. Exploring the conceptual realm in which these nineteenth-century comparative linguists worked, Saussy provides us with a historical argument as to why the Chinese language lost its grammar and with respect to what. His study raises some fundamental issues about comparative scholarship in general: Are the facts about the object of study neutral givens, or are they produced by interaction between the investigator and the object? If the latter, the comparatist's task is then to be redefined as the exploration of interactions, which is far more interesting than the evaluation of similarities and differences.

One of the main threads connecting part 1 to parts 2 and 3 is persistent attention to the role Western missionaries have played as linguists, translators, diplomats, and medical and cultural workers. Part 2, "Colonial Circulations: From International Law to the Global Market," turns to the second major phase of East-West contact and conflict, also known as the arrival of capitalism and imperialism (with major involvement of the Protestant missionaries). The authors in this group examine the spread of international law and the modern global market to East Asia, treating them as two related forms of colonial circulation in the nineteenth century. My own essay places the question of universalism in the context of the circulation of international law in the nineteenth century, focusing on the 1864 Chinese translation of Henry Wheaton's *Elements of International Law* initiated by the American missionary W. A. P. Martin. This study is closely paired with Alexis Dudden's account of how Martin's translation was interpreted and appropriated by Japan in subsequent years and changed its terms of dealing with China and other nations. Both essays interrogate the historical role that the Chinese translation of the American legal text played in helping to universalize the Western law of nations in East Asia and in the simultaneous rise of Japanese imperialism in the nineteenth century. By treating the history of international law and colonial historiography as one and the same process, we raise the question of when and how a universalistic understanding of international law began to shape the historical real during nineteenth-century imperialist expansions.

That historical real thrived on a material network of transportation and communication that James Hevia takes up in his study of the circulation of looted objects through a global network of exhibitors, art dealers, art historians, and curators. Hevia draws our attention to the significant transvaluation of the meanings of "pillage," "booty," "spoils," and "plunder" when such activities were described in campaign and newspaper accounts as "looting" and the objects seized as "loot." He argues that those were not interchangeable terms. The word "loot" was itself a loanword from Hindi or Sanskrit in the eighteenth century whose modern circulation was firmly embedded in the new lexicon of empire and colonialism. In a comparative analysis of two Euro-American looting episodes that occurred in Beijing in 1860 and 1890, Hevia thoroughly unravels the meaning of "loot" associated with international law, European military traditions, and the representations of the looted objects as these objects circulated through a variety of sites, such as auctions in China and Europe, public and regimental museums, international expositions, and the collections of British and French monarchs.

Andrew Jones's essay treats a related but different order of material and technological circulation: the invention of the gramophone and the rise of the global popular music market. The early music industry, Jones argues, embodies an internationalization of social relations transforming everyday life simultaneously in the metropolis and in colonial urban centers. The story of the gramophone in China, which is well told by Jones, challenges our theoretical assumptions about imperialism and colonial modernity. What we discover here is not the usual narrative of advanced European technologies being imported into a backward colonial periphery whose identity is belatedly defined in terms of its impossible yearnings for modernity. Rather, Jones argues that the record industry grew and thrived only insofar as it originated and invested in international (and domestic minority and immigrant) markets. London and New York were as much participants in the condition of colonial modernity as such cities as Shanghai and Calcutta.

Part 3, "Science, Medicine, and Cultural Pathologies," introduces a group of studies that investigate how science, medicine, and cultural pathologies produced racialized knowledge about culture, sexual essentialism, and nationalist agenda through translation and the circulation of cultural images. Larissa

Heinrich's research on medical portraiture in the nineteenth century establishes a crucial linkage among missionary medical work, the "Sick Man of Asia," and racialized representations and translations. She gives a detailed analysis of the medical portraiture done by the Chinese artist Lam Qua at the request of the missionary doctor Peter Parker and reflects on the broader implications of such scientific and visual translations of Chinese illness and deformity. Her work suggests that the pathologization of the Chinese race by the West must be reevaluated against the complex expressions of illness through the eyes of Lam Qua, Lu Xun, and other Chinese artists and writers.

Tze-lan Deborah Sang takes up the discourse of homoeroticism in modern Chinese translations of Western scientific theories of sexuality. Her essay examines a broad range of diverse Chinese interpretations from 1912 to 1949 of the works of Havelock Ellis, Iwan Bloch, Krafft-Ebing, Freud, and Edward Carpenter. Focusing on female same-sex love and its inclusion in public discourse, Sang argues that Chinese women's increasing participation in social and public life in modern times meant a simultaneous expansion of male scrutiny into a formerly private realm of female experience. In the past, Chinese men had been content to contain female homoeroticism within women's quarters rather than prohibit it, but modern male intellectuals of the May Fourth period no longer regarded it as an inconsequential part of women's domestic seclusion and began to regulate, stigmatize, and prohibit female same-sex love by the "scientific norms" of human sexuality.

Nancy Chen focuses her attention on the development of psychiatry and psychiatric institutions in China that began as a form of specialized medicine introduced by missionary practitioners but grew into larger programs of national order and discipline by the mid–twentieth century. She describes these processes as a series of translingual practices that occurred over the past century when the institution of psychiatry itself experienced several ruptures in its political organization and social meanings of practice. Psychiatry in contemporary China, Chen argues, is situated at particular intersections among cultural meanings of madness, international and national classification categories for mental illness, and evolving institutional practices. With a double emphasis on fieldwork and historical research, Chen's work effectively brings out significant moments of cultural translation to show in what ways this profession and its institutions are integral to national platforms for mental health, social order, and, more recently, to a globalizing discourse of modernity with shared categories from the *Diagnostic and Statistical Manual of Mental Disorders* and the *International Classification of Disorders*.

The three essays in part 4 turn to language and linguistic work as an institution in the production of universal knowledge through translation. The individual research represented here ranges from the invention of Basic English to global English-language teaching. Q. S. Tong's research uncovers the forgotten story of I. A. Richards's passionate, evangelical efforts to promote and teach Basic English in China in the 1930s–1940s and the 1970s. Richards's interest in China was sustained by his vision of Basic English as the most suitable candidate for the official language of the "World Government," in place of Esperanto. Emphasizing the politicoeconomic implications of Basic (British, American, scientific, international, and commercial), Tong shows how this influential movement was conceived as part of a Western global agenda for cultural domination. He argues, however, that cultural domination is a more enduring and more subtle form of domination than the other forms we know and, therefore, must be thoroughly scrutinized and given a more nuanced account than confining it merely to the experience of the former "colonies."

Tong's critical study of Basic English as institution is followed by Jianhua Chen's analysis of the circulation of the keyword "revolution" among Chinese, Japanese, and English at the turn of the century. Chen analyzes how the classical ideographic compound *geming* was resurrected, reconstructed, and incorporated into the diverse syntax of world revolution via the Japanese *kanji* term *kakumei*. His research centers on the lives and activities of three prominent reformers and revolutionaries at the turn of the century: Wang Tao, Sun Yat-sen, and Liang Qichao, each of whom appropriated or contested the availability of "revolution" for what they understood to be the true meaning of *geming*. This volatile engagement with the translation of "revolution" registers a full range of historical meanings of the time, stretching from moderate social reforms to late Qing intellectuals' call for the violent overthrow of the Qing regime in order to rebuild China as a new nation-state.

Wan Shun Eva Lam's essay concludes this volume by reconsidering language, pedagogy, and translation, both critically and historically, in the new global condition of diaspora, massive migration, cross-cultural contact, and multiculturalism within national borders as well as the implosion of the "third world" in the first world countries. Her work complements the preceding essays, especially Tong's study of Basic English, by rethinking the question of cultural imperialism in today's global English-language teaching. Initiated by colonial domination in the past and propelled by commerce, science, and technology, the spread of English has been facilitated through instruction in the classroom, as witnessed by the rise of the ELT profession. In the case of Hong Kong, the long-practiced policies of creating and maintaining a small group of the local elite as "intermediate leaders" educated in a Western or modi-

fied Western system deny the validity and competitiveness of educational certification from Taiwan and Mainland China. Lam's study raises the following
questions for theorists and practitioners of ELT: Can a critical study of culture
counteract the forces of cultural imperialism? Can teachers go beyond cultural
facts or the simple comparison of facts to engage students in developing the
knowledge, skills, and moral responsibilities needed for cross-cultural understanding and interaction that involve critical self-reflections?

In a sense, all the essays here are involved in a collective rethinking of the
moral implications of any cross-cultural knowledge making in the past and
present. As bilingual teachers and scholars, we are engaged in a critical and
pedagogical translation of languages and cultures that demands a radical departure from the previous cultural translations we have critiqued in this book.
If the story of the past speaks effectively to the present moment, the message
that comes across in this book is that our scholarship is also part of a shared
daily struggle with racial and cultural prejudices and with the colonial legacy
of our own profession.

This book grew out of the many conversations I had with friends and colleagues
over the past few years and benefited from a number of graduate seminars I
taught at Berkeley. Li Tuo deserves the credit for encouraging me at all stages
of the work and giving me expert advice on how to turn an edited volume into
a coherent intellectual project. I am grateful to my contributors, whose faith
in the project inspired me to carry it through. In a few cases, it was by pure
accident that we discovered each other's work. The discovery brings joy and
surprise, because we have trained and worked in such different disciplines:
anthropology, history, literature, history of science, and pedagogy; nevertheless, a shared desire to rethink the problem of translation and cross-cultural
scholarship has led our work to converge at some point and led us to speak to
one another productively across the disciplinary divide.

I spent the year 1997–1998 on leave at the National Humanities Center in
the Research Triangle Park, North Carolina, where I was trying to finish a book
about missionary translations and publications in Chinese in the nineteenth
century, a project that received the generous support of a Guggenheim Fellowship and a Lilly Fellowship of Religion at the Center. My essay "Legislating the
Universal: The Circulation of International Law in the Nineteenth Century"
represents a portion of that work completed during the year in which I also
brought the editing of this collected volume to its final stage. I thank my fellow researchers, the library staff, and Kent Mullikin for the productive time
I spent at the National Humanities Center. Others such as Judith Farquhar,

James Hevia, Arif Dirlik, Gang Yue, and Jing Wang made my stay in Chapel Hill a pleasurable experience. I am grateful to Kai-wing Chow, Ban Wang, Paula Zamperini, and the two anonymous reviewers for their kind support of this project; and to Larissa Heinrich who proofread the manuscript and helped me compile the index. Kenneth Wissoker has been a wonderful guiding spirit throughout, and I thank him and his staff at Duke University Press for making this happen.

The following essays previously appeared in journals, whose permission to reuse the materials is gratefully acknowledged. Roger Hart's essay was first published in *positions: east asia studies critique* (spring 1999) of Duke University Press under the title "How to Do Things with Worlds." An earlier version of James Hevia's contribution with the title "Loot's Fate: The Economy of Plunder and the Moral Life of Objects from the Summer Palace of the Emperor of China" was published in *History and Anthropology* 6, no. 4 (1994): 319–45 by Harwood Academic Publishers. The illustrated materials that appear in this volume are provided courtesy of the Bancroft Library of the University of California at Berkeley, the East Asian Library of UC Berkeley, and Yale University Medical Historical Library.

Lydia H. Liu   *The Question of Meaning-Value*

in the Political Economy of the Sign

Troubled by the uncertainty of commensurability among languages, translators and their critics have a tendency to approach the issue as if the problem
resided in the *inherent* properties (value) of individual languages. This seems
to suggest a level of intuitive comprehension of value in languages and cultures, although such intuition seldom succeeds in discouraging people from
pursuing the possibility of equivalence, finding common ground, or achieving
optimal pairing of meanings, and so on. But before dismissing it as harmless
intuition too quickly, we might benefit from a heightened awareness that the
persistence of this way of thinking has, as a rule, prevented an otherwise fruitful
discussion of the dynamic process of meaning-making that often takes place
between or *among* languages as well as within a single language. If meaning is
thus studied as a problem of exchange and circulation, not entirely bound to
the evolutionary process of a homogeneous language or culture, we must, then,
raise some new questions about language and translatability. For instance, *Can
the achieved or contested reciprocity of languages be plotted as the outcome of a given economy
of historical exchange?*

Questions like this can, perhaps, take us a step further toward overcoming
the circularity of commensurability and incommensurability in translation
theory. At the least, the theorist will be less inclined to insist on the plenitude
of meaning and begin to articulate the problem of translation to the political
economy of the sign. As I have argued elsewhere, Walter Benjamin's "Task of
the Translator" and Derrida's reading of the same in "Des Tours de Babel" are
among the few bold attempts in the twentieth century to rethink the problem

of meaning outside the purview of semantics and structural linguistics. Their notion of complementarity, which refuses to privilege the original over the translation, enables a powerful critique of the metaphysical ground of traditional semantics that has long dominated the translation theories of the West. Derrida's attack on Western metaphysics, in particular, has helped clear the philosophical ground for useful critical work, but one of the questions on which the notion of complementarity remains vague is how hypothetical equivalence is established, maintained, or revised among languages so that meaning, which is always historical, can be made available or unavailable to the translator. I wonder whether hypothetical equivalence does not already inhabit the idea of complementarity itself in a subtle but potent form.[1]

Hence, I would like to sketch out a number of intersecting areas for a preliminary rethinking of the production of meaning as value in circulatory relationship with other meanings (as no value can exist by itself). This tentative reworking of meaning-value may lead us to see that the much contested notion of translatability is often a displaced global struggle (displaced onto metaphysics) over the reciprocity of meaning-value among historical languages. I have suggested in the introduction that there are at least two basic questions we need to think about in order to resist such metaphysical displacements and pursue a fruitful study of translatability as a theoretical and historical problem. First, how does the circumstantial encounter of cultures produce and contest the reciprocity of meaning-value between their languages? Second, how does reciprocity become thinkable as an intellectual problem when predominantly unequal forms of global exchange characterize the material conditions of that exchange? Inasmuch as the historical (re)distribution of meaning-value constitutes a major aspect of global circulation, it is of paramount importance, I argue, to pay attention to the granting and withholding of reciprocity of meaning-value by one language vis-à-vis another.[2] (This struggle is proverbial in bilingual situations where a bilingual speaker always learns to deploy the languages he or she knows strategically under varying circumstance. He or she then becomes one of the physical sites of the processes I am trying to describe in this essay.)

One interesting consequence of recent world history is that we can afford not to marvel at the miracle of universal communicability. The argument of untranslatability need not contradict this description, because the suspicion of the circulation of meaning and anxiety to exert control over it may be yet another way of endorsing translatability and the plenitude of meaning. Moreover, such posited translatability among the world's languages is never simply a linguistic matter. Like many of the other events that have shaped the modern world, global translatability has inhabited the same order of universalistic aspirations as the invention of the metric system, modern postal service, international law, the gold standard, telecommunication, and so on. The significance of this event is yet to receive the kind of attention it deserves. The fact that we do not normally perceive things in this light goes to show that the mutual intelligibility of languages has been naturalized more than anything else by common dictionaries, repeated acts of translation, and received theories of language that are conceptually and structurally incapable of comprehending the monumental significance of this recent happening. The first step toward reconceptualizing translatability as a historical event is, therefore, to integrate the problem of translation into the general interpretation of so-called civilizational encounters and their intellectual and material outcomes.

From Counterfeit to the Colonial Legacy of Value

Let us examine briefly a moment of "civilizational encounter" in the early eighteenth century, when the modern notion of forgery was still in the process of forging a historical bond between published writing and minted coin. Evidently, fake writing and counterfeit money were widely engaged in the production and circulation of value between Europe and the other civilizations at this time, but, in the business of forgery, no one could beat the record of George Psalmanazar (1679–1763), the notorious imposter of his time or any time. Psalmanazar fabricated a native Formosan (Taiwanese) identity for himself in toto in exchange for patronage by the Church of England.[3] In deciding to "go native" through his writing and other performances, he anticipated the modern anthropologist long before the invention of the discipline itself. A curious prefiguration of the problematic of value, the Psalmanazar story raises some fascinating questions about the meaning of authenticity, parody, and colonial identity, and, more important, the circulation of not just silver, tea, silk, and porcelain but of *meaning as value* between East and West.

Psalmanazar arrived in London in 1703 in the company of Alexander Innes, chaplain to the Scots regiment at Sluys, who introduced him to Bishop Compton as a native of Formosa.[4] The story he and his accomplice Innes told to their new friends in London was that, as a child, Psalmanazar had been abducted by some evil Jesuits from Formosa to Europe. (Psalmanazar was a pseudonym and his real name was well hidden, even after his death.) Their plot worked instantly. Despite the fact that Psalmanazar had authentic Caucasian looks, blond hair and blue eyes (as this episode occurred before the rise of scientific racism in Europe), the physiognomic evidence proved less persuasive than his extraordinary gift of the tongue and extravagant performance mimicking the so-called cannibalistic behavior of the native barbarians of the remote island.[5]

The British public bought Psalmanazar's story because their imagination had fed on nothing less than the similarly extravagant accounts given by the missionaries, sea captains, and merchants about exotic lands outside Europe. So when Psalmanazar claimed "We also eat human Flesh, which I am now convinc'd is a very barbarous custom, tho' we feed only upon our open Enemies, slain or made captive in the field," the sensational description merely confirmed what the British reader had been consuming all along thanks to the European colonial exploitation abroad and the rise of the popular book market at home.[6] For a period of four years, Psalmanazar was a resounding success. He was even invited by Oxford University to study a variety of subjects and give lectures on Formosan practices, including human sacrifice. When Father Fontenay, a Jesuit missionary who had just returned from China, confronted him at a public meeting of the Royal Society, Psalmanazar effectively rebutted his accusation of imposture.[7]

Had Psalmanazar's subsequent conversion and confession not abundantly redeemed his youthful sins, time and death would have absolved him of the remaining moral stigma attached to his imposture. Twentieth-century scholars take much less interest in establishing who this man really was than how his extraordinary career helps us glimpse the meaning of authenticity, authorship, ethnographic writing, and the European book market in the eighteenth century.[8] One cannot but be struck by Psalmanazar's uncanny understanding of the power of words and their purported face value. His best-selling book, *A Historical and Geographical Description of Formosa* (1704; 1705), attacked the order of what Saussure would call the signifier and signified to fabricate a society for which there was no referent. Even the pseudonym, Psalmanazar, has no corresponding real name that we know of. He took this pseudonym from 2 Kings 17:3 — Shalmaneser, one of a line of Assyrian kings by this name — and presented himself to British society as a Formosan pagan converted to Christianity.

More fascinating than the infinite regression of names and referents is Psalmanazar's invention of a fictitious Formosan alphabet and an equally fictitious Formosan currency of which he gives meticulous illustration and description in his book (see figures 1 and 2). The fake alphabet and fake money stand forgery on its head by exploiting the materiality of the sign whose value is the face value on paper (signifying Formosan alphabet and Formosan currency, respectively) and nothing more. The so-called referent turns out to be a phantom called up by Psalmanazar's writing.

Within the fabricated textual universe of his book, Psalmanazar the forger

The Formosan Alphabet

Name		Power		Figure			Name
Am̃	A	a	a͑o	ꭗ I	I	I	ꓲI
Mem̃	M	m̃	m	ꓩ ꓩ	ꓶ	ꓶꓶ
Neñ	N	ñ	n	u	ŭ	ᵾ	ᵾ U
Taph	T	th	t	ƌ	ᵬ	O	xı O
Lamdo	L	ll	l	ſ	ſ	ſ	ꓕ
Samdo	S	ch	s	ꞁ	ꞁ	ꞁ	ꓕ
Vomera	V	w	u	Δ	Δ	△	△
Bagdo	B	b	b	/	/	/	/
Hamno	H	kh	h	ꞁ	ꞁ	ꓴ	ꓴ
Pedlo	P	pp	p	ᴛ	ꭍ	Λ	Λ
Kaphi	K	k	x	ꭚ	ꭚ	Ꝩ	Ꝩ
Omda	O	o	ω	ꓷ	ꓷ	Ɔ	Ɔ
Ilda	I	y	i	o	◻	◻	◻
Xatara	X	xh	x	ƻ	ƻ	ꓥ	ꓥ
Dam	D	th	d	ꓳ	ꓳ	ꓳ	ꓳ
Zamphi	Z	tf	z	ᵬ	ᵬ	ꓴ	ꓴ
Epsi	E	ε	η	Ɛ	Ɛ	Ꞁ	Ꞁ
Fandem	F	ph	f	X	X	X	X
Raw	R	rh	r	φ	φ	Ꝗ	Ꝗ
Gomera	G	g	j	ꓶ	ꓶ	Ꝯ	Ꝯ

T. Slater sculp.

Figure 1. The Formosan Alphabet, in George Psalmanazar, *A Historical and Geographical Description of Formosa.* Courtesy of the Bancroft Library of the University of California at Berkeley.

rivals Psalmanazar the plagiarist. For the textual sources Psalmanazar relied on in writing his book had been culled from contemporary popular travel literature and the Jesuits' accounts of the Orient, including authors such as George Candidius, an early-seventeenth-century Dutch missionary to Taiwan, and the French Jesuit Louis le Comte, who was sent to China in the same year (1688) as Father Fontenay by Louis XIV.[9] Candidius's "Short Account of the Island of Formosa" was a major source of Psalmanazar's encyclopedic knowledge of that island.[10] Like Defoe's best-selling novel, *Robinson Crusoe*, which appeared fifteen years later, Psalmanazar's imaginative book *Historical and Geographical Description of Formosa* was written in the form of a first-person narrative that strove to cover the whole gamut of familiar ethnographic data about the exotic island: geography, climate, costume, architecture, religion, burials, language, and social customs and organizations. Susan Stewart observes that this book "fulfilled an ultimate Enlightenment dream—the dream of animation where logical consistency can itself produce a referent, a world engendered by reason alone, unencumbered by history, materiality, or nature."[11] But it seems

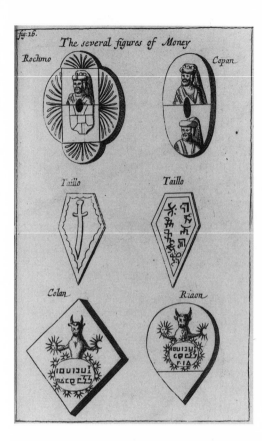

Figure 2. The drawing of Formosan money, in George Psalmanazar, *A Historical and Geographical Description of Formosa*. Courtesy of the Bancroft Library of the University of California at Berkeley.

to me that Psalmanazar's elaborate work reads more like a caricature of the Enlightenment dream and a parody of ethnographic imagination than their fulfillment.

Psalmanazar is a supreme parodist. His originality consists in casting himself as a native informant who testifies as he speaks and who goes so far as to use his adopted voice of authenticity to contest the reliability of Candidius's own text, calling the latter a forger. For instance, when some people objected that his extravagant description of human sacrifice in Formosa could not be substantiated by Candidius's report, Psalmanazar wrote in the preface to the second edition of his book that those sacrifices were not as strange as Candidius's own statement that women pregnant before their thirty-seventh year had their bellies stomped until they miscarried.[12] This turning of the tables on Candidius not only reverses the order of authenticity and forgery, referent and sign, true value and face value, but raises some fundamental questions about *meaning as face value* and *writing as parody of other writing*. Michel de Certeau once suggested in a different context that the act of making the sources one's own renders "the general process of fabrication visible: the interlinkage of the imaginary and the collection, in other words the labor of fiction within the library. That invention haunts the 'sources' is everywhere indicated by the citations, from the moment one opens the book. It is the law of the other in the narrative." [13] Psalmanazar's mock narrative inadvertently reveals to us to what extent the original text, Candidius's own "Account of the Island of Formosa," might have already produced *meaning as face value* and *writing as parody of writing* in the manner of Psalmanazar, who copied him in an ingenious and subversive way.

Psalmanazar's extraordinary career as forger, plagiarist, ethnographer/ native informant reminds us that the study of meaning in the political economy of the sign needs to be grounded in the actual history of the global circulation of meaning-value. That history is a history of colonialism whose exploitation of exotic difference has erected major obstacles against a historical understanding of difference. Like Psalmanazar, missionaries and orientalists have fabricated powerful fictions about other cultures and their languages. Those fictions, as Edward Said's critique of the Western philological construct of the Orient has made clear, have long inhibited a historical reassessment of the colonial encounter of languages and cultures.[14] The global romanization of the indigenous languages and dialects by missionaries and linguists in the eighteenth and nineteenth centuries was designed to do precisely what Psalmanazar's alphabet had envisioned for the Formosan language.[15] These universalist translations have produced "cultural difference" on the world map as an already translated fact and pretend to speak for that difference in a universalizing idiom.

The articulation of *difference as value* within a structure of unequal exchange thus simultaneously victimizes that difference by translating it as *lesser value* or *nonuniversal value*. To overcome this conceptual barrier, I propose that we substitute the notion of *competing universalisms* for cultural particularity to help understand the modes of cultural exchange and their genealogies beyond the existing accounts of colonial encounter. The ahistorical dialectic of the universal and the particular may, then, be understood as a recent historical manifestation of the will to the universal. As the studies contained in this volume demonstrate very well, the work of documenting and analyzing the various moments of competing universalisms deserves more scholarly attention than they have heretofore received.

The imperatives of competing universalisms demand that we reconceptualize the ways in which meanings circulate *meaningfully* from language to language and culture to culture. As a migrant deixis of potential value, meaning

acquires value in the process of exchange between actual signs. The circumstantial encounter of one sign with another (in a sentence) or another language
(in translation) decides the manner in which the actualization or sabotage of
meaning takes place. Thus, an original text may be "rewritten," "parodied," and
"manipulated" but not "distorted" by its being translated from text to text any
more than Candidius's Formosa was "distorted" by Psalmanazar's Formosa.
Derrida's critique of the myth of the transcendental signified can be evoked to
undo the commonsense understanding of translation as a transfer of the transcendental signified (authentic value) from one language system to another.[16]
An alternative formulation of meaning would do well by rejecting the metaphysics of signifier and signified on philosophical ground, though one needs
to remain vigilant about the deconstructionists' projection of a self-sufficient
intellectual realm of Western metaphysics and their possible recuperation of
an imperial view of value and global circulation.

William Pietz's study of the problem of the fetish, among other similar
works, is an important intervention in that regard. His research demonstrates
convincingly that the circulation of the notion of the fetish as "false value"
(parodied verbatim by our Psalmanazar) in Western philosophical discourse is
rooted in its own colonial past. In a series of fine studies of the discourse of
the fetish, Pietz analyzes the mercantile cross-cultural spaces of transvaluation among material objects of radically different social orders on the coast of
West Africa in the sixteenth and seventeenth centuries. He writes: "The mys-
tery of value—the dependence of social value on specific institutional systems
for making the value of material things—was a constant theme in transactions
on the Guinea coast during this period. The problem was especially expressed
in the category of the trifling: European traders constantly remarked on the
trinkets and trifles they traded for objects of real value [gold] (just as the socio-
religious orders of African societies seemed to them founded on the valuing
of 'trifles' and 'trash')."[17] Always initiated and formalized by the moments of
translation, these instances of colonial exchange are significant not because
they exemplify an earlier moment of civilizational encounters, but because they
articulate the condition of possibility of colonial history. Pietz goes on to show
how the earlier processes of colonial exchange set the stage for the Enlightenment discourse about value and the fetish, as, for example, when Kant formulated his aesthetic explanation for African fetish worship in 1764, deciding
that such practices were founded on the principle of the "trifling" (läppisch),
the ultimate degeneration of the principle of the beautiful.[18]

Kant's transcendental philosophy is profoundly indebted to the colonial
regime of anthropological knowledge. Emmanuel Chukwudi Eze's recent study

points out that, despite his cosmopolitan leanings, Kant never left his home-town Königsberg in his professional career and gathered his information about distant lands exclusively from seafarers and traveling merchants and from read-ing books such as Captain James Cook's *Voyages*. Out of this vast conglomer-ate of accumulated anthropological evidence, or "the labor of fiction within the library" in the words of Certeau, Kant derived a philosophical doctrine of "human nature" and assigned the "essence" of humanity to the self-image of eighteenth-century Europe: "white," European, and male.[19] (Psalmanazar was a mere caricaturist, not a philosopher; rather, he enacted the farce of what would be the philosopher's ethnographic "evidence.")

The tautology of the anthropological "evidence" turned out to circumscribe both Kant's doctrine of "human nature" and his aesthetic explanation of Afri-can fetish worship as the "trifling." Whereas the latter's "superstitious" under-standing of *causality* was held responsible for the "false" estimation of the *value* of material objects in African societies, the discourse of fetishism also articu-lated a colonial mercantile view of value that caused Europeans to conclude that non-Europeans tended to asign false value to material objects and, there-fore, false objective value to their own culture. From this view, according to Pietz, there "developed a general discourse about the superstitiousness of non-Europeans within a characteristically modern rhetoric of realism, which rec-ognized as 'real' only technological and commercial values."[20]

It bears pointing out, of course, that the circulation of meaning involves a great deal of coauthorship and struggle among the dominant and dominated groups over the meaning and distribution of universal values and civilizational resources. In order for the process of circulation to take place at all, the agents of translation on each side start out by hypothesizing an exchange of equivalent meanings, even if the hypothesis itself is born of a structure of unequal ex-change and linguistic currency. What this means is that we need to investigate further how a particular sign or object is made into an equivalent of something else during the process of circulation and how, theoretically speaking, this act of translation articulates the condition of unequal exchange.

The Question of Equivalence and Translatability

To study meaning as value is to place the problem of translation within the political economy of the sign. Contrary to forcing a parallel argument about verbal exchange in terms of its monetary counterpart, the linguistic and the economic — as well as their theoretical articulations — have long evoked each other and inhabited each other. In the *Grundrisse*, Marx draws an interesting comparison between translation and monetary transaction for the purpose of theorizing the problem of the universal equivalent that concerns both: "Language does not transform ideas, so that the peculiarity of ideas is dissolved and their social character runs alongside them as a separate entity, like prices alongside commodities. Ideas do not exist separately from language. Ideas which have first to be translated out of their mother tongue into a foreign language in order to circulate, in order to become exchangeable, offer a somewhat better analogy; but the analogy then lies not in the language, but in the *foreign quality of language*" (emphasis added).[21]

This is an important insight. The foreign quality (*Fremdheit*) of language describes a shared process of circulation in translation and in economic transaction, which produces meaning as it produces value when a verbal sign or a commodity is exchanged with something foreign to itself. (Here, the mutual articulation of the linguistic and the economic seems to suggest more than an analogous relationship between two separate spheres of activities. Marx's own analysis testifies against the fiction of a pure theory of political economy untouched by other social considerations. By the same token, we can no longer imagine a pure theory of linguistic exchange uncontaminated by economic models of exchange. See my discussion of Saussure below.)

Marx's insistence on the foreignness (*Fremdheit*) of language is central to his working out of a meaningful connection between linguistic estrangement (*Entfremdung*) and monetary alienation (*Entäußerung*) in *Capital*. As Marc Shell has pointed out, this move derives from Marx's preoccupation with the historical transformation of the commodity gold first into coin and then into paper money. "The act of monetary exchange, like the act of linguistic translation, depends on a socially recognized (*gültige*) universal equivalent, which seems to homogenize everything, or to reduce everything to a common denominator."[22] Gold became the universal equivalent by a social act (*Tat*) when this commodity began to assume the power to measure or purchase all the others. In this process, the foreignness of the other must be conquered in order for the other to assume exchange-value in the marketplace. (In that regard, the English language of the late twentieth century would be the closest analogue to the gold of the preceding era.)

But exactly how does Marx elaborate the problem of equivalence and exchange-value?

When considering the equation "1 quarter of corn = x cwt of iron" in *Capital*, Marx begins by asking: What does this equation signify? "It signifies that a common element of identical magnitude exists in two different things, in 1 quarter of corn and similarly in x cwt of iron. Both are therefore equal to a third thing, which in itself is neither the one nor the other. Each of them, so far as it is exchange value, must therefore be reducible to this third thing."[23] What is this third or common denominator that equates 1 quarter of corn to x cwt of iron or a potentially infinite number of commodities? The answer lies in abstract labor that produces exchange-value. Marx determines this exchange-value as a quantity of socially necessary labor-time (SNLT) required to produce one unit of any given commodity.

As we know, Marx's labor theory of value was a critical response to classical political economy, which takes "the economy" as a self-regulating market structure and constructs "trade" as an exchange of equivalents among individual traders. Marx considers the trading of commodities as a trade of "labor time." His notion of SNLT demystifies the notion of equal exchange by introducing human activity and its objectification into the analysis of commodity exchange in capitalist society. Because the SNLT is merely an average and not the quantity of actual labor time necessary for the production of the unit of the commodity being exchanged, there is no guarantee that such trade involves equal magnitudes of *actual* labor time. Such is the theoretical problem Marx raises and tries to resolve in *Capital*. As Jack Amariglio and Antonio Callari have pointed out, "In fact, these are trades of *unequal* magnitudes of *actual* labor time. But this inequality notwithstanding, for commodity circulation to take place, trade must be conceived by the agents of circulation — by individuals — as an exchange of equivalents. There is thus a contradiction: the same process of circulation is at once both an *unequal* exchange of quantities of actual labor time and an exchange of *equivalents*."[24] In other words, Marx derived an account of the exploitation of labor (extraction of surplus-value) by capital from an analysis of SNLT and, in so doing, reveals a fundamental inequality in "equal" exchange in capitalist economy.

Here we are less concerned with Marx's labor theory of value than with the significance of his formal analysis of commodity exchange which is not limited to the economic behavior of capitalist society. After all, Marx is centrally concerned with the problem of economic value as *social value*, that is, a problem of signification that overflows the exclusive realm of commodity production and exchange.[25] This is precisely where theorists of critical semiotics of our own time intervene to recast the study of the sign as a critique of the political economy of the sign. The problem of inequality in "equal" linguistic exchange also bears directly on our concerns with the reciprocity of meaning as value between historical languages in translation processes. But let us reflect more on the crucial connections that exist between the exchange of commodity and that of the sign in Marx.

In *Capital*, Marx argues that value "does not have its description branded on its forehead; it rather transforms every product of labour into a social hiero-glyphic. Later on, men try to decipher the hieroglyphic."[26] The word hiero-glyphic is interesting because it evokes "foreignness," "impenetrability," and "primitivity" typically associated with non-European cultures. Does this figu-rative turn of language comment on the situation of commodity exchange in colonial conditions? Marx does not ponder the question here, because he is more interested in explaining the abstract relationship between use-value and exchange-value than in the question of language, which he elaborates else-where. "As a use-value," he writes, "the linen is something palpably different from the coat; as [exchange] value, it is identical with the coat [*Rockgleiches*], and therefore looks like the coat [*sieht daher aus wie ein Rock*]."[27] The process of transformation that causes different things (the linen and the coat) to *look alike* is an abstraction process that eliminates difference or use-value for the commodities to become commensurate as exchange-value and be exchanged on that basis. Exchange-value is to political economy what simile, metaphor, or synecdoche is to the linguistic realm of signification, as both involve the making of equivalents out of nonequivalents through a process of abstraction or translation.

This is by no means a fortuitous rhetorical exercise in the service of theory, because the problem of signification within political economy is fundamen-tally connected with the economy of exchange within the linguistic realm.[28] As Thomas Keenan's rhetorical analysis of *Capital* shows convincingly, for Marx, exchange is "a matter of signification, expression, and substitution."[29] The process of signification and substitution (abstract labor for actual labor, etc.) is what allows commodities to be exchanged not as things but as values for other values, as amply illustrated by Marx in the classic case of how the linen becomes "coat-like or -identical" (*Rockgleiches*) in the exchange process. Not surprisingly, Marx uses the term *der Warensprache* or the "language of commodities" to talk about this process, and we are supposed to take his word figuratively and liter-ally. In *der Warensprache*, the commodity form, of which money is a pure form of general equivalent, bears out the mutual penetration of the problem of signi-fication within political economy and of the economy of exchange within the linguistic realm. Marx chose to verbalize the former in terms of the latter.

Saussure did the converse. If exchange is a matter of signification and sub-stitution, it is entirely possible to bring the economic system of significa-tion within the fold of parallel systems of signification such as language and other semiotic systems. After all, both use-value and exchange-value signify aspects of social value where a ground of "figurative equivalence" among different articulations of value, be it commodity value, linguistic value, or other, can be abstracted and theorized. In formulating a structural linguistics, Saussure pursued this ground of figurative equivalence in a direction very different from that of Marx. Although like Marx he understood political economy and semiology as mutually embedded systems of value and signification, Saussure reversed the order in which Marx had conceptualized the economic and the linguistic.

In *Course in General Linguistics*, Saussure begins by characterizing language as a social institution and conceives of semiology (language, symbolic rites, customs, etc.) as a science that studies the role of signs as part of social life. (Lévi-Strauss's important reconceptualization of social institutions and structures as communication systems drew inspiration directly from this formulation.) As a social institution, language must be analyzed with the same degree of rigor as is practiced in other sciences such as law and economics and in the history of political institutions.

Saussure emphasizes, in particular, the proximity of political economy and linguistics because, "as in the study of political economy, one is dealing with the notion of *value*. In both cases, we have a *system of equivalence between things belonging to different orders*. In one case, work and wages; in the other case, signification and signal." [30] This comes very close to the way Marx analyzes exchange-value in *Capital*. Whereas for Marx exchange-value can be analyzed and quantified in terms of abstract labor and labor time, Saussure sees an entirely arbitrary relationship between the signifier and the signified. Linguistic value remains for him a matter of internal relations within a linguistic community. "A community is necessary in order to establish values," says Saussure, and "values have no other rationale than usage and general agreement. An individual, acting alone, is incapable of establishing a value." [31]

According to Saussure, two basic conditions are necessary for the existence of any value and these are paradoxical conditions that require (1) something *dissimilar* that can be exchanged for the item whose value is under consideration and (2) *similar* things that can be *compared* with the item whose value is under consideration. To illustrate this point, Saussure goes on to consider the value of money by analogy:

To determine the value of a five-franc coin, for instance, what must be known is: (1) that the coin can be exchanged for a certain quantity of something different, e.g. bread, and (2) that its value can be compared with another value in the same system, e.g. that of a one-franc coin, or of a coin belonging to another system (e.g. a dollar). Similarly a word can be substituted for something dissimilar: an idea. At the same time, it can be compared to something of like nature: another word. Its value is therefore not determined merely by that concept or meaning for which it is a token. It must also be assessed against comparable values, by contrast with other words. The content of a word is determined in the final analysis not by what it contains but by what exists outside it. As an element in a system, that word has not only a meaning but also—above all—a value.[32]

In short, linguistic value expresses a horizontal relationship whose existence depends on the simultaneous coexistence of other values within the same system. Just as the signified, or the conceptual part of linguistic value, is determined by relations and differences with other signifieds in the language, so the signifier, or the material counterpart of linguistic value such as sound pattern, also relies on phonetic contrasts to allow us to distinguish among words and semantic units. When considered by itself, sound is merely something ancillary, a material the language uses. The arbitrary and differential relations of the sound pattern within a language are what assign linguistic value to a given sign. "It is not the metal in a coin which determines its value," argues Saussure. "A crown piece nominally worth five francs contains only half that sum in silver. Its value varies somewhat according to the effigy it bears." This structural understanding of value leads to Saussure's most uncompromising opposition to essentialism: "Linguistic signifiers are not in essence phonetic. They are not physical in any way. They are constituted solely by differences which distinguish one such sound pattern from another."[33]

Saussure makes a distinction between what he calls "conceptual aspects" (signified) and "material aspects" (signifier) of linguistic value. In this scheme of things, the meaning of a word is assimilated to the conceptual component of the sign that belongs to the vertical order of the signified and signifier, as set out in his famous diagram of the sign (see figure 3). But how does meaning or a concept operate in relation to linguistic value, which, according to Saussure, must be determined in horizontal relationship with other values in the same system? The answer is that a "particular concept is simply a value which emerges from relations with other values of a similar kind. If those other values disappeared, this meaning too would vanish."[34]

Saussure's constant recourse to on-the-spot "translation" and simultaneous failure to theorize his textual operation creates a logical impasse for structural linguistics. This causes no small degree of confusion when he tries to introduce some levels of distinction between meaning and value. In the quote above, Saussure equates meaning with value by saying that a "particular concept is

Figure 3. The diagram of the sign, from Ferdinand de Saussure, *Course in General Linguistics*, p. 116.

simply a value which emerges from relations with other values of a similar kind. If those other values disappeared, this meaning too would vanish." In the same space, however, he contradicts himself by arguing that value and meaning are not synonymous terms, one representing the horizontal order of differential relations with coexisting values and the other (meaning) comprising the concept along the vertical arrows of the signified and signifier.

A famous example he uses is the French word *mouton* and its English counterpart "sheep." By way of translation, Saussure decides that the two words may have the same meaning but do not share the same value. The difference in value, he argues, hinges on the fact that in English there is also another word, "mutton," for the meat, whereas *mouton* in French covers both. The differential relation of "sheep" and "mutton" in English, therefore, assigns a different value to each word that does not exist in French.

But if value is different, can meaning remain the same? Why should meaning be a fixed category a priori when the sound pattern and other properties of language are subject to the law of differential relations? How do we know that the French word *mouton* has the same meaning as the English "sheep" until we equate them through *selective translation* and vice versa? Is the reciprocity of meaning always guaranteed between the languages? Saussure treats meaning in translation as a given and deduces from it a radical theory of value but a very conventional theory of meaning based on intuitive translation.[35] His mode of analysis, which is ubiquitous translation, participates directly in what he says about signs and structural linguistics but is not registered as such. Saussure simply finds it expedient to utilize his vast knowledge of French, English, German, Greek, Latin, Portuguese, Czech, and even Sanskrit to illustrate a point or two in the course of demonstrating the general concepts of structural linguistics.

Recognizing the lacuna, Roman Jakobson made a deliberate attempt to integrate translation and translatability into his theory of semiotics. For Jakobson, translation exemplifies *equivalence in difference* that is operative in all semiotic and literary situations. In "On Linguistic Aspects of Translation," Jakobson argues: "Equivalence in difference is the cardinal problem in language and the pivotal concern of linguistics. Like any receiver of verbal messages, the linguist acts as their interpreter. No linguistic specimen may be interpreted by the science of language without a translation of its signs into other signs of the same system or into signs of another system. Any comparison of two languages implies an examination of their mutual translatability; widespread practices of interlingual communication, particularly, translation activities, must be kept under constant scrutiny by linguistic science." [36] Translation thus becomes the structural principle whereby signs are equated with other signs within the same code or between codes. This is a tantalizing thought, and could be used to explain Saussure's own mode of operation and bring some degree of self-consciousness into semiotic considerations of language. The observation that "any comparison of two languages implies an examination of their mutual translatability" possesses the best potential to develop into a major theoretical argument about translation.

Although that potential is eclipsed by the subsequent anecdotes Jakobson tells about translation, it is interesting to note that the majority of his anecdotes focus on grammatical gender as a point of comparison and translatability. For example, he points out that the Russian painter Repin was baffled by German painters' depiction of Sin as a woman because Repin was apparently unaware that "sin" is feminine in German (*die Sünder*); it is masculine in Russian (*грех*). Jakobson goes on to observe that a Russian child, while reading a translation of German tales, was astounded to find that Death, obviously a woman (*смерть*, fem.), was pictured as an old man (German *der Tod*, masc.). These anecdotes are well told and could be multiplied ad infinitum. But what do they tell us about translatability? Are we brought back to the argument that gender does not travel well across linguistic codes and that translation is impossible? If so, how do we translate gender into a noninflected language where this grammatical category is not available from the viewpoint of Indo-European languages?

Let us consider the gendering of the third-person pronoun in modern written Chinese to test this argument of untranslatability based on a synchronic comparison of linguistic difference. The original form of the written Chinese character for the third-person pronoun *ta* contains an ungendered *ren* radical (denoting "human"). For millennia, the Chinese had lived comfortably with the ungendered written form *ta* and other ungendered deictic forms, until the need to translate the feminine pronoun from European languages was suddenly thrust upon their attention in the early years of this century. Chinese linguists and translators proceeded to invent a written character that would be capable of translating the "equivalent" pronouns in the European languages. After many experiments, they settled on a character that replaced the radical *ren* in the ungendered *ta* with the radical *nü* denoting "woman" to form a new feminine pronoun in the language. That word has since become an inseparable part of the mainstream vocabulary of modern Chinese.

This process is fascinating in that the appearance of the feminine pronoun simultaneously converts the original ungendered *ta* into a *masculine* pronoun, even though the written form of the latter has not undergone the slightest morphological change and is still written with the same radical *ren*. Through the circumstantial contact with the Indo-European languages, the generic radical that denotes "human" now proclaims a masculine essence. In other words, the presence of a gendered neologism in the linguistic system has forced the originally unmarked pronoun to assume a masculine identity retroactively that is, nevertheless, contradicted by the etymology of its otherwise ungendered radical *ren*.[37]

Saussure would probably find in this a perfect example of structural differentiation, because the feminine and masculine pronouns in modern written Chinese have emerged in relation to each other as differential values. I am inclined to think, however, that translation played a pivotal role in the dual process of both introducing the structural differentiation of gender into the deictic category *and* making up equivalents where there had been none with reference to the gendered pronoun in Indo-European languages. Grammatical gender acquires translatability precisely in this limited, historical sense. Of course, my point is not to argue with Jakobson about the translatability or untranslatability of grammatical gender but to reflect on the historical making of hypothetical equivalence that is capable of producing shifting grounds of comparison and translatability.

Baudrillard's Quarrel with Saussure

Contemporary theorists attribute the theoretical impasse of Saussure's structural linguistics to a metaphysical conception of language.[38] Baudrillard, for example, reexamines the double condition of Saussure's theory of value and meaning as discussed above: "(1) the coin can be exchanged for a certain quantity of something different, e.g. bread, and (2) . . . its value can be compared with another value in the same system, e.g. that of a one-franc coin, or of a coin belonging to another system (e.g. a dollar)." Saussure sees a given coin as exchangeable against a real good of some value (bread in condition 1) while at the same time relating it to all the other terms in the monetary system (one franc or a dollar in condition 2). The economic exchange clearly evokes the distinction of the use-value and the exchange-value of the commodity. Although Baudrillard has no problem with the analogy of the economic and the linguistic, he questions the unexamined notion of meaning and its referent in structural linguistics on the one hand and that of use-value in Marx on the other:[39]

> As if articulating a theory of exchange-value, Saussure reserves the term *value* for this second dimension of the system: every term can be related to every other, their *relativity*, internal to the system and constituted by binary oppositions. This definition is opposed to the other possible definition of value: the relation of every term to what it designates, of each signifier to its signified, like the relation of every coin with what it can be exchanged against. The first aspect corresponds to the structural dimension of language, and the second to its functional dimension. Each dimension is separate but linked, which is to say that they mesh and cohere. This coherence is characteristic of the "classical" configuration of the linguistic sign, under the rule of the commodity law of value, where designation always appears as the finality of the structural operation of the *langue*. The parallel between this "classical" stage of signification and the mechanics of value in material production is absolute, as in Marx's analysis: use-value plays the role of the horizon and finality of the system of exchange-values. The first qualifies the concrete operation of commodity in consumption (a moment parallel to designation in the sign), the second relates to the exchangeability of any commodity for any other under the law of equivalence (a moment parallel to the structural organization of the sign). Both are dialectically linked throughout Marx's analyses and define a rational configuration of production, governed by political economy.[40]

Baudrillard attempts to unpack Saussure's notion of the signified in the same manner as Marx analyzed the commodity in *Capital*, although both Saussure's notion of the signified and Marx's idea of use-value come under attack.[41] He grapples with Saussure and Marx to develop a theoretical vocabulary that can explain the process whereby social privilege and domination are no longer defined exclusively by the ownership of the means of production but also by the mastery of the process of signification whereby equivalences and a hierarchy of values are established and maintained.[42]

The critique of the magical copula in sign production, or "the equal sign in 'A = A' " in Baudrillard's theory, merits special attention because this is where "metaphysics and economics jostle each other at the same impasses, over the same aporias, the same contradictions and dysfunctions."[43] The ideological form that traverses both the production of signs and material production, he argues, often comes with a logical bifurcation theorized in terms of use-value versus exchange-value on the one hand and signified versus signifier on the other. Baudrillard calls this double bifurcation magical thinking.

The binary thinking casts "use-value" and "signified" in the role of content, a given, need, and transcendental value, thus sealing them off from further inquiry and analysis, because the analyst has confined formal value and formal analysis to the domain of "exchange-value" and "signifier" alone. Marx has worked out a critique of political economy at the level of exchange-value but has not extended his theoretical rigor to a similar critique of naturalized use-value. For their part, Saussure and Benveniste have established that the sign presents itself as a unity of discrete and functional meaning, the signifier referring to a signified and the ensemble to a referent.[44] Baudrillard argues, however, that "the separation of the sign and the world is a fiction, and leads to a science fiction. The logic of equivalence, abstraction, discreteness and project of the sign engulfs the [referent] as surely as it does the [signified]."[45] Furthermore, he points out that the homology between the logic of signification and the logic of political economy rests entirely on this shared fiction. The latter exploits the reference to needs and the actualization of use-value as an anthropological horizon and, in so doing, precludes a consideration of their "formal" intervention in the actual functioning and operative structure of political economy. Of its linguistic homologue, Baudrillard writes:

> Similarly, the referent is maintained as exterior to the comprehension of the sign: the sign alludes to it, but its internal organization excludes it. In fact, it is now clear that the system of needs and of use value is thoroughly implicated in the form of political economy as its completion. And likewise for the referent, this "substance of reality," in that it is entirely bound up in the logic of the sign. Thus, in each field, the dominant form (system of exchange value and combinatory of the [signifier] respectively) provides itself with a referential rationale (*raison*), a content, an alibi, and, significantly, in each this articulation is made *under the same metaphysical "sign," i.e., need or motivation.*[46]

Before we consider the interesting implication of this critique for a theory of translation and global circulation, let us dwell further on Baudrillard's attack on the received communication theory as a part of his criticism of metaphysics.

Roman Jakobson's famous model of verbal communication serves as a point of departure for Baudrillard's reconsideration of the sequence of transmitter (encoder)–message–receiver (decoder). The universal sequence was originally schematized by Jakobson as shown in figure 4. Baudrillard regards this "sci-

```
┌─────────────────────────────────────────────────────────────┐
│                          context                             │
│       Addresser          message          Addressee          │
│                          contact                             │
│                          code                                │
│                                                              │
└─────────────────────────────────────────────────────────────┘
```

Figure 4. Jakobson's model of verbal communication, from "Linguistics and Poetics" in his *Language in Literature*, p. 66.

entific" construct as rooted in a *simulation model* of communication that allows neither reciprocal relation nor simultaneous mutual (especially conflictual) presence of the two terms. The artificial distance installed between encoder and decoder seals the full and autonomized "value" of the message, excluding, from its inception, the reciprocity and antagonism of interlocutors, and the ambivalence of their exchange. According to Jakobson's model, "what really circulates is information, a semantic content that is assumed to be legible and univocal. The agency of the code guarantees this univocality, and by the same token the respective positions of encoder and decoder." [47]

This critique of the simulation model of communication and structural linguistics brings Baudrillard to the point of a radical break with the received notion of linguistic exchange among his generation of French theorists. The idea of sign exchange-value, in particular, seems to offer a genuine possibility. Nevertheless, like Saussure before him, Baudrillard has excluded the problem of translation from the overall picture of sign exchange and theorizes the circulation of signs as if the world spoke a lingua franca of value and reciprocity. If the long history of mutual borrowing among the European languages and the hegemony of the metropolitan languages in the former colonies are somewhat responsible for his blind spot, it does not sufficiently explain why he reads Saussure the way he does.

Baudrillard takes Saussure to task for holding onto a metaphysical notion of meaning but fails to elaborate to what extent Saussure's modus operandi might be responsible for producing this metaphysics. Let us recall that in *Course in General Linguistics* Saussure renders the meaning of a sign *self-evident* independently of its history and of the translator's own selective appropriation of its meanings through a foreign equivalent. In Saussure's analysis of *mouton* and "sheep," the linguist adopts a circular procedure of glossing the meaning of "sheep" with that of *mouton* and vice versa, and decides that the two words have the same meaning but not the same value. That which his circular move fails to register, however, is an act of translation that actively produces the "same meaning" between the two words just as easily as it could have produced a different meaning in a different context (which Saussure has no way of explaining except by separating meaning from "value") to allow *mouton* to mean "mutton" and not "sheep." Due to the polyvalent etymology of these signs, the French *mouton* does not always have the same meaning as the English "sheep" until one has equated them through *selective* translation and already eliminated the other possibility, "mutton," and vice versa. Moreover, the etymology of the English "mutton" indexes another level of historicity having to do with the original translingual figuring of class relations between the French and the Anglo-Saxons after the Norman conquest of England. As Saussure's textual operation amply demonstrates, the talk of difference and equivalence hardly makes sense until the languages in question are brought together in a reciprocal, differential, and antagonistic relationship by translation, etymology, and history.

Baudrillard's engagement with Saussure and Marx suggests a parallel to what Pierre Bourdieu does with his own categories of symbolic goods, symbolic capital, *habitus*, field, symbolic power, cultural production, and so on.[48] As we know, Bourdieu also emphasizes an integrated understanding of the economic as a symbolic process and of the cultural as a material process. The mutual embeddedness of the economic and the cultural results in an extraordinary degree of interchangeability of linguistic and economic tropes in his language, which in turn feeds back into his understanding of the linguistic sign. Bourdieu writes: "Linguistic exchange—a relation of communication between a sender and a receiver, based on enciphering and deciphering, and therefore on the implementation of a code or a generative competence—is also an economic exchange which is established within a particular symbolic relation of power between a producer, endowed with a certain linguistic capital, and a consumer (or a market), and which is capable of procuring a certain material or symbolic profit."[49]

Bourdieu might not find himself operating in a world of metaphors, because the linguistic and symbolic are just as real as the economic and material. The strength of his position lies in his refusal to define the linguistic and symbolic as any less material than the other forms of capital. But when he goes on to speak of the *value* of utterances as regulated by the market and characterized by a particular law of price formation, there appears to be a curious tautological functionalism.[50] The *functional* problem of how a dominant language confers social distinction on the user of that language becomes the self-same point of departure and arrival of his reasoning. (Let us recall how Marx elaborated the

problem of signification and with what rigor he went about the whole analysis.)
Bourdieu asserts that all verbal expressions "owe some of their properties (even
at the grammatical level) to the fact that, on the basis of a practical anticipation
of the laws of the market concerned, their authors, most often unwittingly, and
without expressly seeking to do so, try to *maximize the symbolic profit* they can obtain from practices which are, inseparably, oriented towards communication
and exposed to evaluation" (emphasis added).[51]

That argument produces some extraordinary circular statements about capital, value, and exchange that cannot possibly go wrong because they participate in, and derive from, the perfect closure of Bourdieu's conceptual system.[52]
What we need to know is just how the value of an utterance functions with
respect to market prices and how meaning gets generated in the process of
symbolic exchange *within* a relation of power. The closure of Bourdieu's system
prevents him from giving a sustained look at the givenness of each of these
articulations with the kind of theoretical rigor exemplified by Marx in *Capital* or
Saussure in *Course in General Linguistics*. Saussure's elaboration of the meanings
of *mouton* and "sheep" is taken by Bourdieu to be a mere theoretical argument
about the arbitrariness of the sign and dismissed offhand, whereas we have
seen that Saussure's own analysis is much more nuanced and deserves serious
critical engagement.[53]

Reciprocity and Power in Cultural Translation

Translation need not guarantee the reciprocity of meaning between languages.
Rather, it presents a *reciprocal wager*, a desire for meaning as value and a desire
to speak across, even under least favorable conditions.[54] The act of translation
thus hypothesizes an exchange of *equivalent* signs and makes up that *equivalence* where there is none perceived as such. The invention of the third-person
feminine pronoun in modern Chinese is a case in point. Like the thousands
of loanwords and neologisms I have documented and analyzed elsewhere, the
existence of this word captures the invention of equivalents in a relation of unequal exchange between Chinese and European languages, and that exchange
is further complicated by the changing power relations between Chinese and
Japanese caused by the presence of the Western powers in Asia.[55] In contrast,
English and the metropolitan European languages have not experienced a similar need in modern times to adapt to the formal characteristics of the other
languages by eliminating, for example, one of its gender categories in a reverse
mode of operation. The point I am trying to make here is not merely contrastive
or comparative. In thinking about translatability between historical languages,

one cannot but consider the actual power relations that dictate the degree and magnitude of sacrifice that one language must make in order to achieve some level of commensurability with the other.

In colonial conditions of exchange, commensurability of meaning can sometimes be instituted and kept in place by law and brute military force. As my study of the missionary–Chinese translation of international law in "Legislating the Universal" shows, the so-called Chinese contempt for European "barbarians" arose out of a set of unique circumstances in which the British insisted on the translation of the word *yi* as "barbarian." The equating of the meanings of the two words by Britain's official translators became the cognitive ground on which a xenophobic Chinese "mentality" was first erected and then condemned, even though we know very well that the word *yi* had been previously rendered in English as "foreigner" or "stranger" in the eighteenth century and early nineteenth century.[56] After establishing the first level of commensurability between *yi* and "barbarian," the British felt insulted by the Qing government's use of that word in diplomatic communications and remonstrated against such "unequal" treatment of the British representatives by the Chinese official establishment. As the numerous dispatches between the two governments before the Opium War well testify, the linguistic crusade against the word *yi* became a counteroffensive led by the British to fight the Chinese government's prohibition of the opium trade. In the 1830s–1840s, the British protest against the Chinese use of *yi* escalated into a major diplomatic event and began to be centrally and thoroughly embroiled in the gunboat policy during the Opium War.[57] After the war had lifted the Chinese ban on opium trade, the British lost no time in banning the word *yi* from diplomatic communications by specific treaty provisions. The legal ban was so effective that it has made the word literally disappear from the languages of today's Chinese-speaking world.

The episode of the linguistic crusade against "barbarian" and the invention of the feminine pronoun in modern Chinese each tell a fascinating story about the politics of linguistic exchange and demonstrate that, in this general economy of meaning-value, (in)commensurability can be a contentious affair and impact the course of historical events. The reciprocity of meaning in the case of *yi* and "barbarian" simultaneously secures the nonreciprocity between *yi* and "foreigner," "stranger," or other earlier terms of equivalence. This process of meaning-making is guaranteed by a colonial regime of knowledge that recognizes as value only that which can help reproduce the colonial relations of power, hence the rhetorical value of *yi* and "barbarian" for making war. The circulation of other possible values and other meanings is effectively obstructed —

they are labeled "wrong translations"—when these do not otherwise participate in the production and reproduction of colonial relations.

Even as I emphasize relations of unequal linguistic exchange, I do not wish to suggest that this situation can be reduced to the mere "intentions" of the dominator and depict the dominated always as victims of the situation. To do so would be to underestimate the degree of coauthorship that has been going on between the dominator and the dominated. In the case of the neologism of the feminine pronoun, it was the Chinese linguists and translators, not Westerners, who were troubled by the "lack" of an equivalent pronoun in their own language and proceeded to invent one. The level of commensurability and reciprocity of meaning thus established between modern Chinese and European languages suggests nonreciprocity at yet another level, because few speakers of metropolitan European languages experience a similar need to reform their gendered deixis, except, perhaps, the feminist critics of our own time.

In the West, feminist critics attack the unmarkedness (universal availability) of the masculine pronoun for entirely different reasons from what I have in mind here. The majority of their criticisms borrow strength from the bourgeois discourse of human rights and equality rather than from a theoretical deconstruction of the gendering of deictic markers as a grammatical category. As a result, very few critics are concerned about the presence or absence of gendered equivalents in non-European languages or the possible "contamination" of those languages by Western forms of gender in the recent past. The poststructuralist critique of the unmarkedness of the masculine pronoun does not prevent the critics from taking the (gendered) grammatical categories of French or English as universal and using them as a philosophical basis for their argument. Interestingly, feminist critics in the Chinese-speaking world have themselves forgotten how the gendering of the pronoun in their own language occurred less than eighty years ago. When some decide to follow the new English way of writing the feminine and masculine pronouns with a slash in between, the gendering of these Chinese pronouns becomes twice universalized. This new moment of coauthorship leads to a foreclosure of the possibility of bringing forth an alternative way of doing feminist criticism in gender studies. The latter would require the feminist critic to grapple with the disjuncture of gendered and nongendered articulations of deictic relationships among different languages of the world, so that a new understanding of the grounds of reciprocity and power relationship among different feminisms could be envisioned.

What we observe in these processes is a powerful *coauthoring* of universal commensurability envisioned by the Chinese translators and the metropolitan theorists of universal language in a relationship of unequal exchange. That is to say, both the dominator and the dominated participate in the making of this miracle of universal communication but determine the outcome of such exchanges differently. In the global circulation of meaning as value, *hypothetical equivalence* is scrupulously and vigorously guarded and only occasionally contested by speakers of one or the other language. Equally worthy of attention is a condition of unequal exchange that produces and reproduces the condition of *hypothetical equivalence* and the colonial regime of knowledge. This paradox of equivalence and nonequivalence forms the cognitive basis on which cultural difference becomes articulatable ("A = A" or "A $\neq$ A," etc.). Such difference in turn becomes naturalized in our languages through repeated usage in everyday life, in the media, and in scholarly writings. The translator is thus able to manipulate difference, to dispense or withhold the reciprocity of meaning-value among the languages to make war or make peace.

Finally, the universalizing tendencies of the modern, which has grown to be the dominant universalism of our world, have worked toward erasing the traces of this recent happening so that we would all agree that modernity is inevitable, universal, and available to everyone. Suppose we treat text and textuality as a genuine historical event and not less than that, certainly not the reverse. The ultimate challenge for a new theory of translation would be to account for the philosophical connection between the universalizing logic of modernity and the invention of *hypothetical equivalence* among the world's languages.

Notes

Sections of this essay were presented at the Comparative Literature Colloquium of Cornell University in April 1998 at an event called "Borderless Wor(l)ds: A Roundtable on Translation at the Turn of the Millennium." I thank Emily Apter, Thomas Conley, Brett de Bary, and the graduate student organizers of the roundtable for the stimulating conversations that led to the strengthening of my thesis.

1   See my critique in *Translingual Practice*, 14–16.
2   James Clifford briefly discusses reciprocity and translation in his recent book *Routes*. He argues that " 'reciprocity' is itself a translation term linking quite different regimes of power and relationality. A capitalist ideology of exchange posits individual transactions between partners who are free to engage or disengage; a Melanesian model may see ongoing relationships in which the wealthier partner is under a continuing obligation to share. It is important to keep these different practices of reciprocity in view" (p. 175). Here, Clifford is more concerned with alternative models of reciprocity than with the articulation of the terms of reciprocity (that is, granting and withholding of meaning) between a capitalist ideology of exchange and the Melanesian model that seems to have enabled his comparison of these two in the first place. The articu-

lation of the terms of reciprocity, hence comparative relationality, is precisely what troubles me in cross-cultural studies.

3 The little we know about the biographical circumstances of this man comes from a few scattered contemporary accounts and Psalmanazar's own confessions published posthumously in *Memoirs of ****, Commonly known by the Name of George Psalmanazar: A Reputed Native of Formosa. Written by himself, In order to be published after his Death*. He was said to have come from France because he spoke Latin with a Gascon accent. His education at the hands of the Franciscans, Jesuits, and Dominicans gave him a good grasp of Latin, a smattering of theology, and a huge fund of general knowledge. For detailed treatments, see Susan Stewart, *Crimes of Writing*, 33–35. Also see Richard M. Swiderski, *The False Formosan: George Psalmanazar and the Eighteenth-Century Experiment of Identity*; Rodney Needham, *Exemplars*; and Frederic J. Foley, *The Great Formosan Impostor*.

4 The first name of Innes has been consistently misquoted as William by several generations of scholars. The main source of the error is Sidney Lee's article on Psalmanazar in the *Dictionary of National Biography*, in which the chaplain Alexander Innes is called William and the date of Psalmanazar's will is also given incorrectly. Foley, who did extensive archival research on the subject in the late sixties, has tried to correct this important detail, but for some reason his work is not read or cited by scholars who came after him. See Foley, 6 n. 2, and also Swiderski, 10–11.

5 For example, he would put on a show of eating raw meat and doing other shocking things to prove his authenticity to the public.

6 George Psalmanazar, *A Historical and Geographical Description of Formosa*, 2d ed., 112–13. His sensational description of child sacrifice in Formosa gave Swift the famous trope of cannibalism in *A Modest Proposal*, where his name is mentioned as "the famous Sallmanaazar, a Native of the Island Formosa, who . . . told my friend, that in his Country when any young Person happened to be put to death, the Executioner sold the Carcass to Persons of Quality, as a prime Dainty, and that, in his Time, the Body of a plump Girl of fifteen, who was crucified for attempting to Poison the Emperor, was sold . . . in Joints from the Gibbet" (Jonathan Swift, *A Modest Proposal*, 10).

7 The Psalmanazar–Fontaney confrontation took place at a session of the Royal Society on 2 February 1704 when Isaac Newton was serving as the president of the Royal Society. Psalmanazar began by asking Fontaney to whom Formosa belongs (because he had previously claimed that Formosa belonged to Japan). China, Fontaney replied. Psalmanazar wanted to know how Fontaney, who had, by his own admission, never been to Formosa, could be sure of this, and so on. For a detailed discussion of this meeting, see Swiderski, 27–35. The most damaging test of Psalmanazar's truthfulness was conducted by the astronomer Edmund Halley, who asked the Formosan, who had already mentioned the houses and chimneys of his native land, how long the sun shone down the chimney flue at certain times of the year. Psalmanazar slipped and was taken to task for having not even the most fundamental awareness of solar events in his "native" island. See Swiderski, 40–41.

8 The most sophisticated analysis of George Psalmanazar is found in Stewart's *Crimes of Writing*. See chapter 2, "Psalmanazar's Others," 31–65.

9 Candidius's book and Bernhardus's *Description of Japan* in Latin were the reference books given to him by Innes. See Foley, 21.

10   See George Candidius, "A Short Account of the Island of Formosa," 526–33.

11   Stewart, 54.

12   Ibid., 50.

13   Michel de Certeau, *Heterologies*, 139.

14   Edward Said, *Orientalism*.

15   Both Jesuit and Protestant missionaries designed the romanization systems for non-European languages and dialects, including Cantonese, Vietnamese, Fukienese, and indigenous Taiwanese (in spite of Psalmanazar's alphabet) to replace and contest the established universal script, that is, the written Chinese language.

16   See Jacques Derrida, *Positions*, 20.

17   William Pietz, "The Problem of the Fetish, 1," 6.

18   Immanuel Kant, *Observations on the Feeling of the Beautiful and Sublime*, 111, as quoted in Pietz, 9.

19   See Emmanuel Eze, "The Color of Reason: The Idea of 'Race' in Kant's Anthropology," in *Postcolonial African Philosophy*, 103–40.

20   Pietz, "The Problem of the Fetish, 2," 42.

21   Karl Marx, *Grundrisse: Foundations of the Critique of Political Economy*, 163, as quoted in Marc Shell, *Money, Language, and Thought*, 106.

22   Shell, 107.

23   Karl Marx, *Capital: A Critique of Political Economy*, 1: 127.

24   See Jack Amariglio and Antonio Callari, "Marxian Value Theory and the Problem of the Subject: The Role of Commodity Fetishism," 204. Their discussion of value in this article is part of a more extended treatment of how economic rationality, equality, and private proprietorship articulate the self-identity of individuals in the process of exchange.

25   For a juxtapositional reading of Marx's notion of value and contemporary French psychoanalytical theory, see Gayatri Chakravorty Spivak, "Scattered Speculations on the Question of Value," in *In Other Worlds*, 154–75.

26   Marx, *Capital*, 167.

27   Ibid., 143. The German quotes are from *Das Kapital: Kritik der politischen Ökonomie*, in Karl Marx and Friedrich Engels, *Werke* (Berlin: Dietz, 1984 [based on the Hamburg 1890 ed.]), 23: 66.

28   For a related study, see Donald N. McCloskey, *The Rhetoric of Economics*. McCloskey's analysis of rhetoric in economics is mainly concerned with how economists use rhetorical means to make arguments to achieve a certain end. This is not what concerns us here. We are talking about a two-way situation where the linguistic and economic penetrate *each other* at the rhetorical level and at the level of the basic conceptualization of value which is indispensable both to economic theory and to structural linguistics.

29   See Thomas Keenan, "The Point Is to (Ex)Change It: Reading *Capital*, Rhetorically," 174.

30   Ferdinand de Saussure, *Course in General Linguistics*, 80.

31   Ibid., 112.

32   Ibid., 113–14.

33   Ibid., 117.

34   Ibid., 115–16.

35 In this essay, I consider meaning and value together as a problem in the theoretical elaboration of translingual circulation. It is to be distinguished from "sound value," whose role in translation is not as central as the reproduction of "meaning value" in the host language.

36 Roman Jakobson, "On Linguistic Aspects of Translation," 233–34.

37 In 1920, an unsuccessful attempt was made to introduce sound differentiation between the feminine and masculine pronouns as well. For a detailed discussion of the gendering of the Chinese pronoun in the larger context of East-West encounters, see Liu, 36–39, 150–79.

38 Both Derrida and Baudrillard launched their respective theories by criticizing Saussure and his metaphysical conception of language. I choose to discuss Baudrillard here because he seems more attuned to what Saussure is trying to do in his own context than is Derrida, who is interested in Saussure's work insofar as the latter serves as a springboard for his critique of the privileging of the *phonè*, the *glossa*, and the *logos* in Western metaphysics. Saussure's other important contributions that deserve serious critique are passed over in silence. For Derrida's critique, see *Of Grammatology*, 27–73.

39 Baudrillard calls structural linguistics the "contemporary master discipline, inspiring anthropology, the human sciences, etc., just as, in its time, did political economy, whose postulates profoundly informed all of psychology, sociology and the 'moral and political' sciences" (Jean Baudrillard, *For a Critique of the Political Economy of the Sign*, 165 n. 3).

40 Jean Baudrillard, *Symbolic Exchange and Death*, 6.

41 Baudrillard, *For a Critique*, 148. For an informed discussion of Baudrillard's complex relationship to Marxism, see Douglas Kellner, *Jean Baudrillard: From Marxism to Postmodernism and Beyond*.

42 Baudrillard sometimes uses the word "sign value" interchangeably with the word "meaning value."

43 Baudrillard, *For a Critique*, 71.

44 Saussure locates the arbitrariness of the sign between the signified and the signifier. Benveniste modifies this schema by relocating the arbitrariness between the sign and that which it designates. "What is arbitrary," says Benveniste, "is that a certain sign, and not another, is applied to a certain element of reality, and not to any other. In this sense, and only in this sense, it is permissible to speak of contingency, and even in so doing we would seek less to solve the problem than simply to pinpoint it in order to set it aside provisionally. . . . The domain of arbitrariness is thus left outside the comprehension (logical intention) of the linguistic sign" (Emile Benveniste, *Problems in General Linguistics*, as quoted in Baudrillard, *For a Critique*, 151). See Roger Hart's discussion of Derrida's critique of Benveniste in this volume (pp. 50–52).

45 Baudrillard, *For a Critique*, 152.

46 Ibid., 153.

47 Ibid., 179.

48 In Bourdieu's earlier Algerian studies, structural linguistics was still very much part of his vocabulary as he was trying to develop a new set of analytical categories for anthropological work on a non-European society. For example, he would speak of the Kabyles' "grammar of honor" in a good old structuralist fashion when describ-

ing their elaborate code of honor. The "grammar of honor" is a linguistic trope, and much more. Within the specific theoretical context of Bourdieu's fieldwork, it acquires an ontological status and becomes the *conceptual equivalent* for what structural linguists and anthropologists take to be the totality of a social structure. Thus, "when they spontaneously apprehend a particular line of conduct as degrading or ridiculous," says Bourdieu, "the Kabyles are in the *same* position as someone who notices a language mistake without being able to state *the syntactic system* that has been violated" (emphasis added). Saussure's linguistic model resonates loudly in the form of a simile and conceptual closure. See Pierre Bourdieu, *Algeria 1960: The Disenchantment of the World, the Sense of Honour, the Kabyle House or the World Reversed*, 128.

49 See Pierre Bourdieu, "The Production and Reproduction of Legitimate Language," in *Language and Symbolic Power*, 66. This chapter was originally published as "La production et la reproduction de la langue légitime" in Bourdieu, *Ce que parler veut dire: L'économie des échanges*. The original French title of this book, emphasizing the economy of exchange, more directly spells out the theoretical emphasis of the author than does J. B. Thompson's English edition.

50 Ibid., 67.

51 Ibid., 77.

52 Another good example of this tautology is found in the following: "When one language dominates the market, it becomes the norm against which the prices of the other modes of expression, and with them the values of the various competencies, are defined. The language of the grammarians is an artefact, but, being universally imposed by the agencies of linguistic coercion, it has a social efficacy in as much as it functions as the norm, through which is exerted the domination of those groups which have both the means of imposing it as legitimate and the monopoly of the means of appropriating it" (Bourdieu, "Economics of Linguistic Exchanges," 652).

53 See Bourdieu, *Language and Symbolic Power*, 53.

54 The term "reciprocal wager" is taken from Baudrillard out of the immediate context of his discussion of the art auction. See *For a Critique*, 116.

55 See Liu, *Translingual Practice*.

56 For a critical analysis of *koutou* and other related constructions of Chinese contempt for the foreigner before and after the Opium War, see James Hevia, *Cherishing Men from Afar*, 229–37.

57 See Dilip Basu, "Chinese Xenology and Opium War."

PART 1

Early Encounters:

The Question of

(In)commensurability

Roger Hart   *Translating the Untranslatable:*

From Copula to Incommensurable Worlds

By adopting certain naïve presuppositions, studies of the asserted problems encountered in translations across languages have often reached dramatic conclusions about the fundamental differences between civilizations. These presuppositions are naïve in that they circumvent many of the questions that should properly confront historical inquiry, adopting instead simple formulas. For example, on what level of social organization should historical explanation concentrate—what are the significant units of society in analyses of historical change? Instead of determining the complex networks of alliances that dynamically constitute groupings within societies, in such studies the boundaries are already given—drawn along lines of languages or, more often, systems of languages that mark the purported divides between civilizations. What are the fracture lines in societies underlying antagonisms and conflict? Instead of analyzing complicated divisions along the dimensions of class, gender, status, allegiances, or competing schools of thought, all such differences are collapsed into a unity predetermined by the sharing of a single language (the same, that is, once all historical, regional, educational, and status differences are effaced). What kinds of relationships should historical analysis elucidate? With civilizations as the given units of analysis, such studies are typically content with assertions of similarities and differences. What is the relationship between thought and society? Instead of historicizing the role of ideologies, self-fashioned identities, and performative utterances in the formation of social groupings, individuals are instead reduced to representatives or bearers of entire civilizations. How does one understand thought through the transcriptions preserved in historical documents? Instead of explaining the dissemination of copies, commentaries, and interpretations of texts in their cultural context, such studies fix an original against which the correspondence of the translation can be compared. And what is the relationship between thought and language? Too often such studies implicitly presuppose a correspondence between words and concepts. After such a series of simplifying reductions, the conventional conclusions about civilizations are an almost inevitable result.

Rather than critiquing in a general fashion the aporias that inhere in claims made about civilizations in studies of translations, this essay illustrates these aporias through the analysis of selected studies. To accomplish this, I return to one of the most intensely researched examples of translations across civilizations: the Jesuit missionaries and their translations of European religious and scientific treatises in China in the seventeenth century. Admittedly, much of the historical literature on this episode hardly merits critique; I have chosen two exemplary studies of these translations that represent the best scholarship on the subject. I follow a tradition of applying historical research to philosophical problems, similar perhaps to what Pierre Bourdieu calls "fieldwork in philosophy." [1] I first outline the claims, presented in these two studies, of linguistic and conceptual incommensurability between seventeenth-century China and the West, claims that are based on the asserted difficulties of translating the copula and the concept of existence. I then turn to the theories of incommensurability that underwrite these studies, along with several related philosophical theories: Emile Benveniste's analysis of the copula *to be*, Jacques Derrida's critique of Benveniste, W. V. O. Quine's arguments on the indeterminacy of translations, and Donald Davidson's criticisms of assertions of conceptual schemes. Finally, as an alternative to incommensurability, I present an analysis of the translations by the Jesuits and the Chinese converts in cultural context.

China, the West, and the Incommensurability That Divides

Imagining China and the West to be two central actors in a historical drama, writers since the eighteenth century have sought symbols to distinguish the two.[2] Terms such as modernity, science, and capitalism headed the list of mutually incongruous candidates invoked to portray stark differences: China was identified often by mere absence (e.g., of science, capitalism, or modernity) or else designated by pejoratives (e.g., practical, intuitionistic, or despotic).[3] Anthropomorphized through the assignment of personality traits (pride, xenophobia, conservatism, and fear), China itself became the subject of a praise-

and-blame historiography of civilizations. In the period following World War II, Fairbankian historiography decried the lack of agency attributed to China, offering redress by assigning to China a limited capacity to respond to the West.[4] Joseph Needham proposed to restore for China its pride, correcting its slighting by making it an equal contributor among the tributaries that flowed into the river of modern science; his "grand titration" was to redistribute credit for scientific discoveries among civilizations.[5] Joseph Levenson projected Liang Qichao's thought onto a "mind of modern China" and psychologized China's historicist reaction against Western value.[6] These postwar approaches, then, focused on the ways that China had either responded to, contributed to, or rationalized away the West; the West remained for these writers conceptualized as essentially universal. Studies that emerged in the late 1960s and 1970s retained the China/West dichotomy but inverted the earlier triumphalist accounts of Western universalism, critiquing the exploitation, domination, and violence wrought by imperialism.[7] During the 1980s, a "China-centered approach" was articulated as an alternative that, however, for a field institutionalized under the rubric of "area studies," too often meant little more than a return to sinocentrism, with its attendant claims of particularism and Chinese uniqueness.[8] What these later approaches share with their predecessors, then, is a continued credulity toward an essential divide between China and the West.[9]

In this context, studies of the "first encounter" of these two great civilizations have acquired a particular urgency. Interpretive approaches have often been limited to two alternative models: conflict, opposition, and misunderstanding, or synthesis, accommodation, and dialogue.[10] But in recent years, relativism—again formulated within the context of an assumed plausibility of a divide separating China and the West—has become yet another important approach.[11] Theories of linguistic and conceptual incommensurability often underwrite this relativism, providing for relativism perhaps its most rigorous formulation. These claims of relativism and incommensurability have played an important role in encouraging the analysis of Chinese sources and viewpoints by positing a special Chinese worldview protected from pretentious dismissal by a historiography mired in universalism. Yet they have done so at the cost of further reifying China and the West and further radicalizing the purported divide that separates them. To elucidate the role played by claims about translation in theories of incommensurability, this section examines two important recent historical interpretations of this encounter: Jacques Gernet's *China and the Christian Impact* and a related analysis of the translation of Euclid's *Elements* by Jean-Claude Martzloff in his *History of Chinese Mathematics*.[12]

In probably the most sophisticated study of the Jesuits in China during the seventeenth century, Gernet's *China and the Christian Impact* adopts incommensurability between Western and Chinese concepts as the philosophical framework that is to explain the history of the translation and introduction of Christianity.[13] Against previous studies of the introduction of Christianity into China that had been based primarily on Western sources, Gernet proposes as a new approach the study of the "Chinese reactions to this religion." Previous approaches were often universalistic, assuming that "one implicit psychology— our own—valid for all periods and all societies is enough to explain everything." Gernet asserts that for the missionaries, the rejection of Christianity "could only be for reasons that reflected poorly on the Chinese." Later interpreters similarly have "a tendency to see the enemies of Christianity as xenophobic conservatives" while praising converts as open-minded. This thesis, Gernet asserts, "is contradicted by the facts."[14]

Gernet's defense of the Chinese rejection of Christianity is based on a claim of the fundamental incommensurability of languages and the associated Chinese and Western worldviews: "The missionaries, just like the Chinese literate elite, were the unconscious bearers of a whole civilisation. The reason why they so often came up against difficulties of translation is that different languages express, through different logics, different visions of the world and man."[15] Gernet outlines this theoretical framework in the final sections of his concluding chapter. He offers several examples of the difficulties in bridging "mental frameworks"; for example, "In trying to assimilate the Chinese Heaven and the Sovereign on High to the God of the Bible, the Jesuits were attempting to bring together concepts which were irreconcilable."[16] He discovers radical differences between Chinese and Western thought: "The Chinese tendency was to deny any opposition between the self and the world, the mind and the body, the divine and the cosmic. . . . For Chinese thought never had separated the sensible from the rational, never had imagined any 'spiritual substance distinct from the material,' never had conceived of the existence of a world of eternal truths separated from this world of appearances and transitory realities."[17] These differences (although still often conceptualized by Gernet as absences) are adduced as evidence that demonstrates the "radical originality" of China: "Ultimately, what the Chinese criticisms of Christian ideas bring into question are the mental categories and types of opposition which have played a fundamental role in Western thought ever since the Greeks: being and becoming, the intelligible and the sensible, the spiritual and the corporeal. Does all this not mean that Chinese thought is quite simply of a different type, with its own particular articulations and its own radical originality?"[18]

The philosophical framework of conceptual incommensurability that Gernet employs in this work is based on the linguistic theory of Benveniste: "Benveniste writes: 'We can only grasp thought that has already been fitted into the framework of a language . . . What it is possible to say delimits and organises what it is possible to think. Language provides the fundamental configuration of the properties that the mind recognises things to possess.' " [19] More specifically, Gernet asserts that the two fundamental differences between Chinese and Western languages are categories of thought that derive from language and the concept of *existence:* [20] "Benveniste's analysis illuminates two characteristics of Greek—and, more generally, Western—thought, both of which are closely related to the structure of Greek and Latin: one is the existence of categories the obvious and necessary nature of which stems from the use to which the language is unconsciously put. The other is the fundamental importance of the concept of being in Western philosophical and religious thought." [21] As I argue below, Gernet's examples—the translation of Christian terms—present special philosophical problems. So before exploring these, I will examine the translation of Euclid's *Elements* as a more concrete but related example for the comparison of Chinese and Greek thought and language.

The translation of Euclid's *Elements* into Chinese by Xu Guangqi 徐光啟 (1562–1633) and Matteo Ricci (1552–1610) in 1607 would seem ideal for an examination of linguistic incommensurability, given the extant historical documents. Jean-Claude Martzloff, perhaps the most eminent Western historian of Chinese mathematics, has written extensively on the translation.[22] He adopts Gernet's incommensurability in his explanation of the history of the translation, arguing that the Chinese had failed to comprehend the deductive structure of the *Elements* precisely because of linguistic incommensurability. Martzloff argues that the central problem was the difficulty of translating the copula, because of its absence in classical Chinese:

> In addition to the terminology, the even more formidable problem of the difference between the Chinese syntax and that of European languages had to be faced. The main difficulty was the absence of the verb "to be" in classical Chinese. The translators were unable to find better substitutes for it than demonstratives or transitive verbs such as *you, wu* and *wei.* . . . But often, the verb "to be" disappeared altogether, as in the following case:
> 圜者。一形於平地居一界之間。自界至中心作直線。俱等。
> [The] circle: [a] shape situated on flat ground (*ping di*) [sic] within [a] limit. [The] straight strings (*xian*) constructed from [the] limit to [the] centre: all equal.

Martzloff then offers for comparison Clavius's original:

Circulus, est figura plana sub una linea comprehensa, quae peripheria ap-
pelatur, ad quam ab uno puncto eorum, quae intra figuram sunt posita,
cadentes omnes rectae linae, inter se sunt aequales.[23]

He then links the copula to questions of existence, asserting that "one might
think that this type of phenomenon contributed to a masking of the conception, according to which geometric objects possess inherent properties, the
existence or non-existence of which is objectifiable."[24] Although Martzloff apparently borrows this framework from Gernet's *China and the Christian Impact*
and Benveniste,[25] in his argument he cites primarily A. C. Graham's " 'Being'
in Western Philosophy" as asserting that neither *you* 有, *wu* 無, nor *wei* 為 are
equivalent to the copula.[26]

In addition to Gernet's and Martzloff's assertions based on Benveniste, a
wide variety of arguments on the relation of language to thought has been presented in historical studies of China. Peter Boodberg suggests that "the great
semantic complexity of *tao* may have predetermined the rich system of associations surrounding *Tao* in its metaphysical and literary career."[27] Alfred Bloom
notoriously asserts that the lack of counterfactuals and universals in the Chinese language inhibited the ability of the Chinese to think theoretically.[28] Many
authors have presented claims that the Chinese language inhibited the development of science.[29] Until recently, such studies have rarely critically analyzed any
of the details of the theories they cite;[30] the following section, then, examines
Benveniste's claims about the copula.

The Philosophy, Language, and Translation of Existence

Benveniste's central thesis is that language and thought are coextensive, inter-
dependent, and indispensable to each other. "Linguistic form is not only the
condition for transmissibility," Benveniste asserts, "but first of all the condition for the realization of thought"; the structure of language "gives its *form*
to the content of thought."[31] Benveniste examines Aristotle's categories of
thought to assess whether we have "any means to recognize in thought such
characteristics as would belong to it alone and owe nothing to linguistic expression."[32] He concludes that Aristotle's categories were simply the fundamental categories of the language in which Aristotle thought: "the ten categories can . . . be transcribed in linguistic terms." "Unconsciously," Benveniste
argues, Aristotle "took as a criterion the empirical necessity of a distinct *expression* for each of his predications. . . . It is what one can *say* which delimits and
organizes what one can think."[33]

In "The Supplement of Copula: Philosophy *before* Linguistics," as an example of the paradoxes in claims that language governs thought, Jacques Derrida critiques Benveniste's assertion that the Greek language determined Aristotle's categories. It is Benveniste's own writings, Derrida asserts, that offer a "counterproof" against the assertion that *being* is nothing more than a category linguistically determined by the copula *to be*: Benveniste himself asserts that there is a meaning of the philosophical category *to be* beyond that expressed in grammar. For Benveniste argues, Derrida asserts, that (1) "the function of 'the copula' or 'the grammatical mark of equivalence' is absolutely distinct from the full-fledged use of the verb *to be*" in the sense of *existence*; and (2) "in all languages, a certain supplementary function is available to offset the lexical 'absence' of the verb 'to be,'" used grammatically as a mark of equivalence.[34]

Derrida then links this conflation of these two uses of *to be*—grammatical and lexical—to the history of Western metaphysics.[35] It is the "full-fledged" use that Heidegger wishes to recover when he suggests that *being* has become both compromised and effaced: "'Being' remains barely a sound to us, a *threadbare* appellation. If nothing is left to us, *we must seek at least to grasp this last vestige of a possession.*"[36] This nostalgia for a return to the use of *to be* as *existence* is echoed, Derrida asserts, by Benveniste: "It must have had a definite lexical meaning before *falling*—at the end of a long historical development—to the rank of 'copula.' . . . We must *restore its full force and its authentic function to the verb 'to be'* in order to measure the distance between a nominal assertion and an assertion with 'to be.'"[37] The copula thus transcends the grammatical categories of any particular language: in some languages it is denoted by only a lexical absence; on the other hand, the "full-fledged" notion of *to be* cannot be a category determined by language if it is still to be possible to return from the effaced use of *being* to its "full force" and "authentic function."

Derrida's critique of Benveniste exemplifies the aporias that Derrida suggests inhere in assertions that philosophic discourse is governed by the constraints of language. For the oppositions of linguistics, "natural language/ formal language, language system/speech act, insofar as they are productions of philosophical discourse, belong to the field they are supposed to organize."[38] Derrida thus inverts Benveniste's claim, asserting that "philosophy is not only *before* linguistics in the way that one can be *faced* with a new science, outlook, or object; it is also before linguistics in the sense of preceding, providing it with all its concepts."[39]

Among the claims for radical differences among languages, the absence of the copula has seemed to be both the most concrete and the most significant, for the copula has seemed to be the most plausibly connected with philosophically important consequences. Derrida's criticisms point to two fundamental problems in Gernet's and Martzloff's applications of the theories of Benveniste: (1) although the existence of the copula seemed to mark an important difference between the Indo-European and Chinese languages, Benveniste's claim is, rather, that the copula exists in all languages, and (2) the correlation between the copula and the metaphysics of existence results from the conflation of two separate uses of the same lexical term.[40]

If the linguistics of the copula does not demonstrate that radical differences exist between languages—much less between the thought expressed in those languages—the general question remains: To what extent can differences in thought be shown to result from differences in language? Derrida offered one answer: The concepts from linguistics that are to provide the basis for comparison are themselves constituted by the philosophy they purport to analyze. Quine offers a different critique: To compare systems of thought, we must first have solved the problem of translation. Against the views of Ernst Cassirer, Edward Sapir, and Benjamin Whorf that differences in language lead to fundamental differences in thought, Quine objects that we cannot, in principle, provide translation rigorous enough to assess such grand philosophical theses. He concludes that it is not that "certain philosophical propositions are affirmed in the one culture and denied in the other. What is really involved is difficulty or indeterminacy of correlation. It is just that there is less basis of comparison—less sense in saying what is good translation and what is bad—the farther we get away from sentences with visibly direct conditioning to nonverbal stimuli and the farther we get off home ground."[41]

If Quine's argument, based on the indeterminacy of correlation, concludes that it is impossible to rigorously compare differing conceptual schemes, Davidson, in "On the Very Idea of a Conceptual Scheme," warns that the notion of a conceptual scheme is itself ultimately unintelligible.[42] Davidson's argument is presented against the conceptual relativism of Quine, Whorf, Thomas Kuhn, and Paul Feyerabend.[43] Davidson notes the following paradox: The demonstration that two conceptual schemes are incommensurable requires the solution of the purported incommensurability in a frame of reference that incorporates both; assertions of conceptual schemes are always framed in a language that purports to explain that which cannot be explained.[44] The differences, he notes, "are not so extreme but that the changes and the contrasts can be explained and described using the equipment of a single language." Davidson thus argues that "we cannot make sense of total failure" of translation, whether based on a plurality of imagined worlds or incommensurable systems of concepts employed to describe the same world.[45] He concludes that "no sense can be made of the idea that the conceptual resources of different languages differ dramatically."[46]

Davidson's central argument is against the assertion of conceptual schemes by showing that they are unintelligible, that is, their very formulation is para-doxically circular. But in the course of his argument, Davidson also offers the following deflationary aside: "Instead of living in different worlds, Kuhn's sci-entists may, like those who need Webster's dictionary, be only words apart."[47] If Davidson is right that assertions of incommensurable conceptual schemes cannot be formulated coherently, then the question remaining for us to answer becomes How are claims of different worlds constructed from differences in words? It is precisely because of the impossibility, suggested by Davidson, of describing radically different conceptual worlds that such claims must defer by analogy to *other* radical differences. Thus, for example, Kuhn explains the purported incommensurability of scientific paradigms through analogies to differing linguistic taxonomies. Feyerabend explains incommensurability be-tween "cosmologies" through analogies in forms of art. Whorf explains differ-ing linguistic systems through examples from science. Quine explains differing conceptual schemes through analogies in physics.[48] And Martzloff and Gernet explain the incommensurability of thought through analogies to linguistic dif-ferences, via Benveniste's copula.

How are incommensurate worlds, then, created from words? The process of translation would at first seem an unlikely tool, for the putative goal of trans-lation is to establish equivalences between two languages. However, it is this assumption that provides for these claims a crucial resource: the purported im-possibility of finding equivalent words then itself serves as a sign of radically different worlds.[49]

The differences that appear in Martzloff's examples are not between Cla-vius's Latin version and Ricci's Chinese translation — no unmediated compari-son is possible — but instead between the untranslated Latin, the translation that Martzloff provides of Ricci's Chinese into English, and ordinary expres-sions of English. Clavius's Latin represents an uncorrupted original by remain-ing untranslated and dehistoricized: effaced are the problems of translation from Greek to Latin to French and English, the complex history of the transla-tion and editions of this text,[50] and in particular Clavius's redaction that altered and deleted much of the structure of the proofs.[51] Martzloff's translations convey the radical otherness of classical Chinese by employing techniques of defamiliarization similar to those used elsewhere to demonstrate (again, in English) the purported awkwardness of Chinese monosyllabism: "King speak: Sage! not far thousand mile and come; also will have use gain me realm, hey?"[52]

Indeed, Martzloff argues against "more elegant, more grammatical" renderings, stating that "English grammaticality tends to obliterate the structure of the Chinese and the connotation of the specialised terms."[53]

The differences Martzloff presents are the artifacts of these choices he makes in his translation. First, he insists on an extreme literalism in his selections of possible equivalents, for example "straight strings" for *xian* 線 and "flat ground" for *pingdi* 平地, with the latter marked by *sic* to emphasize the inappropriateness of what was, after all, his own choice. He marks articles with brackets. However, Martzloff's most jarring technique is his omission of the copula in English, a language in which the copula is denoted lexically.[54] Although Martzloff cites Graham as asserting the lack of the equivalent of the copula in classical Chinese, Martzloff notes, "We shall not retain [Graham's] English translations, since these translations introduce numerous elements which do not exist at all in classical Chinese (for example, the verb 'to be')."[55] Martzloff, however, then supplements English with a nonlexical symbol, the colon, to denote the absent copula: "Since ordinary words are not sufficient, we also use a punctuation mark" (in his earlier translations in French, Martzloff employed a question mark paired with an exclamation mark).[56] It is then senseless to correct Martzloff's translation. Whereas ordinary translation seeks to establish equivalences, Martzloff seeks to convey radical differences; but following these principles, an English translation of Clavius's Latin would be rendered equally bizarre, and thus Martzloff must leave the Latin untranslated. The extremes to which Martzloff takes the translation are necessary to evoke the linguistic differences that are to serve as an analogy for radical differences in thought.

If Martzloff's claimed linguistic incommensurability relating to *existence* is an artifact of his jarring omission of the copula in insistently preserving this "lexical absence" of classical Chinese in modern English and French that denote the copula lexically, is there any evidence to support claims of a radical incommensurability on the conceptual level? As noted above, Gernet's claims of conceptual incommensurability were based on his assertion, following Benveniste, of differences between China and the West in the fundamental "concept of being" and "the existence of categories" that unconsciously stem from the use of language;[57] Gernet adopts the claims of abstract differences in the concepts of *existence* and *categories* as a philosophical theory within which to frame his description of historical events. The critiques by Derrida, Quine, and Davidson suggested general philosophical problems with these claims; here instead I will seek historical explanations. That is, we must return to the debates on *existence* and *categories* not abstracted from but, rather, resituated within their historical context, and not as philosophy explaining history, but as philosophy inseparable from the history it was to explain. To do so, I reexamine one of the central texts analyzed by Gernet, Matteo Ricci's *Tianzhu shi yi* 天主實義 (ca. 1596), for evidence of the problem of the translation into Chinese of notions of *existence* and *categories*.[58]

The problem that confronted Ricci in the *Tianzhu shi yi*, it turns out, is not one of an impossibility of expressing the philosophical concept of *existence* in the abstract but, rather, debates about existence with specific referents—in particular, spirits and God. Chapter 4 begins with the following summary of the previous chapter:

中士曰：昨吾退習大誨，果審其皆有真理。不知吾國迂儒何以攻折鬼神之實為正道也。

Chinese scholar: Yesterday after I took my leave and reviewed your distinguished instruction, sure enough [I] understood that it all is true. I do not know why the deluded scholars of my country should accept as orthodox denials of the existence of spirits.

西士曰：吾遍察大邦之古經書，無不以祭祀鬼神為天子諸侯重事，故敬之如在其上、如在其左右，豈無其事而故為此矯誣哉？

Western scholar: I have comprehensively examined the ancient classics of your esteemed country. Without exception [these texts] take sacrifices to the spirits as momentous occasions for the Son of Heaven and the feudal lords; thus [they] revered these spirits as being above them and all around them. How then could it possibly be that there is no such thing and thus in this [they] acted deceitfully![59]

In the *Tianzhu shi yi*, there is no shortage of ways to express of spirits the predicate of *existence*: "Tang['s soul] continued to exist without dissipating" 湯為仍在而未散矣; "souls of the deceased exist eternally without extinction" 死者之靈魂為永在不滅; "the human soul does not dissipate after death" 人魂死後為不散泯.[60] Nor is there any shortage of debates on questions of the existence of spirits. In *Tianzhu shi yi*, the Chinese scholar summarizes contemporary Chinese positions on the existence of spiritual beings as follows:[61]

中士曰：今之論鬼神者，各自有見。或謂天地間無鬼神之殊[62]。或謂信之則有，不信之則無。或謂如說有則非，如說無則亦非，如說有無，則得之矣。

Chinese scholar: Among contemporaries that discuss the spirits, each has his own viewpoint. Some state that nowhere in the world are there things such as spirits. Others state that if one believes in them then they exist; if one does not believe in them then they do not exist. Others state that to assert they exist is incorrect; to assert that they do not exist is also incorrect; only to assert that they both exist and do not exist is to attain it [the correct viewpoint]![63]

The reply of the Western scholar proceeds from the claim that "all affairs and things that exist indeed do exist, [those that] do not exist indeed do not exist" 凡事物，有即有，無即無, and proceeds to the conclusion that spirits exist. Ricci's dispute with commonplace Chinese views is thus not that the spirits of ancestor worship do not exist; on the contrary, they exist eternally. Rather, there is a more important spirit that the Chinese must worship if they seek fortune and salvation. His defense of the existence of spirits is based on his own translation of an enigmatic phrase attributed to Confucius, interpreted through his knowledge of God:

故仲尼曰：「敬鬼神而遠之。」彼福祿免罪，非鬼神所能，由天主耳。而時人諂瀆[64]，欲自此得之，則非其得之之道也。夫「遠之」意與「獲罪乎天，無所禱」同。豈可以「遠之」解「無之」，而陷仲尼于無神之惑哉。

Thus Confucius states: "Respect the spirits, and distance them."[65] Happiness, fortune, and forgiveness of sin are not within the powers of the spirits, but up to the Lord of Heaven alone. Yet the trendy curry favor [with the spirits], desiring to receive this [happiness, fortune, and forgiveness] from them; but it is not the true way to obtain this. The meaning of "distance them" is the same as "if one sins against Heaven, there is no one to pray to."[66] How is it possible that "distance them" can be explained as "they do not exist," snaring Confucius in the deceit that spirits do not exist?[67]

What is superstitious about Chinese ancestor worship, then, is not belief in these spirits themselves but seeking favor by worshiping the spirits of ancestors rather than salvation by worshiping the Lord of Heaven. Ricci's answer indicates that the problem is not a lack of belief but, rather, that the Chinese concept of God has been effaced. Contrary to Gernet's claims, the translation of European treatises into Chinese provides no convincing evidence to demonstrate difficulties in expressing the concept of *existence*, whether of tangible or intangible objects. In historical context, these problems were not about the impossibility of translating the abstractions of modern philosophy into Chinese; they were debates about the existence of spirits and, in particular, the primal noun (God) and the primal verb (Being).

Similarly, differences in categories of thought—whether based on Benveniste's view that language dictates categories through an unconscious process or Kuhn's view that incommensurability results from mismatched taxonomies—do not provide a framework outside history available only to modern commentators. Instead, the claim of differences in taxonomies was itself a strategy in Jesuit propaganda. Ricci argues:

分物之類，貴邦士者曰：或得其形，如金石是也；或另得生氣而長大，如草木是也；或更得知覺，如禽獸是也；或益精而得靈才，如人類是也。

In dividing things into categories, the learned men of your noble country state: some [things] attain form, such as metal and stone; some in addition attain the energy of life and grow, such as grass and trees; some also attain the senses, such as birds and beasts; and some are more refined and attain consciousness and intelligence, such as man.

吾西庠[68]之士猶加詳焉，觀後圖可見。但其依賴之類最多，難以圖盡，故略之，而特書其類之九元宗云。

Our learned men of the West seem to have made even more detailed [categories], as can be seen from the following chart. Only its classes of accidents are most numerous and difficult to list completely, and therefore they are only summarized, emphasizing their nine major classes.[69]

Linguistic differences and conceptual differences do exist—as they do within civilizations, cultures, and subcultures—but this is very different from a theory of radical conceptual incommensurability split along a purported China-West divide. As an explanatory framework, conceptual incommensurability is at best inflationary: Does the rejection of Ricci's claims asserting the existence of spirits really require for its explanation a theory of incommensurability asserting the impossibility of the translation of concepts of existence? Does contesting Ricci's God and the evidence that he adduces for Him from the *Lun yu* really require for its explanation a theory of two radically different philosophical worldviews? Does the disbelief in the soul really require for its explanation assertions of the incomprehension of Western concepts and Scholastic philosophy? Worse, Gernet's thesis of incommensurability "is contradicted by the facts." The above examples suggest no insurmountable difficulties in expressing concepts of existence.

Gernet's claims themselves, like those of Martzloff, create the otherness of the world he purports to describe. These claims of differences derive their plausibility in the first place from the assumption of a Great Divide between China and the West. The complex similarities and dissimilarities between Jesuit doctrines and Legalism, Buddhism, Confucianism, Daoism, and popular religions are collapsed along a single radical China-West divide, which is then reinforced through the insistent, repeated assertion of difference: "The conclusion that emerges from the various texts which I have just cited is that Chinese conceptions are in every regard the opposite of those taught by the missionaries." [70] Counterexamples—the adoption of Western studies (Xi xue 西學) by Chinese converts—are themselves appropriated to further reproduce this divide: "What appeared to fit these traditions—or rather what could be easily integrated— was accepted; the rest was unacceptable"; "Chinese who sympathized with Christianity praised it in terms of Chinese philosophy and attributed their own conceptions to it." [71] Through links forged by tracing linguistic continuities, this break between cultures then becomes the suprahistorical break between civilizations;[72] the rejection of Jesuit doctrines is inflated to represent the rejection of "the European vision of the world." [73]

The import for research on China of this barrier constructed by incommensurability was that—against dismissals common in the received historiography that narrated the inexorable triumph of Western universals—relativism protected the assertions of the Chinese protagonists. Relativism insisted not just on equivalence but on the impossibility in principle of any comparison. Elevated to the status of an equal, the claims and allegations of the Jesuits' Chinese opponents came to merit historical analysis. This, then, is the central contribution resulting from Gernet's adoption of relativism and incommensurability: his insistence on understanding the arguments of the Chinese opponents of the Jesuits and their converts through the analysis of Chinese primary materials. For this, *China and the Christian Impact* has been justly recognized as seminal.

Yet one consequence of this very relativism was that it effaced the social and political context it should have analyzed; it is important here to see what this framework of incommensurability must, by construction, leave out. When social and historical context is shifted into the realm of discourse, rejections of Jesuit doctrines are explicable only by assertions of the impossibility of translation between two radically different worldviews; individuals are deprived of agency in deciding what is determined by these conceptual structures. Yet how can we be assured that the difficulty is one of translation if the existence of the referent of the term—whether *spirits* or *God*—is itself in question? How does one determine whether the notion of *God* was correctly translated? Without a grounding in a truth external to the text, the only criterion for assessing the translations is comparisons with explanations and glosses in other texts; in short, we have returned to doctrinal disputes within Christianity of which the

Jesuits were themselves but one faction. And perhaps the most serious problem in Gernet's framework is the collapsing of the complex interactions between individuals and subcultures to two mutually exclusive poles, China and the West; the Chinese converts, belonging to neither, can only be minimized as transparent, passive translators.

The Contextual Turn

Historical studies framed within the linguistic turn have often displaced social context into the realm of discourse;[74] theories of incommensurability have been but one variant on this trend. One important alternative that re-places discourse in social context is suggested by Mario Biagioli's proposal of a "*diachronic* approach" to incommensurability by analyzing "its *emergence* in relation to the internal structure, external boundaries, and relative power or status of the socio-professional groups involved in the non-dialogue."[75] Biagioli's concern is to explain how phenomena that have been interpreted as linguistic incommensurability are in fact strategies adopted in social conflicts between groups that share the same language.[76] I take a related approach, showing how claims of purported difficulties in translations between different languages themselves served as resources in social conflicts. Claims about translation will not be conceptualized as disembodied philosophical theories that provide a framework external to history within which events are analyzed; instead, claims about translation will themselves be examined as in need of historical explanation. That is, instead of accepting claims made by historical protagonists about translation, whether its accuracy, difficulties, or impossibility, we must analyze, contextualize, and render historically intelligible these claims themselves. For example, in seventeenth-century Europe, theories about the translation and accommodation of the spoken word of God to the languages of the illiterate masses provided both important resources and alibis in debates over heliocentric theories;[77] theories about translations of the Bible and the Book of Nature were central sites of contest in debates over the legitimacy of Galileo's claims.[78] How, then, did claims about translation provide for the Jesuits and the Chinese converts important strategies in their proselytism?

To answer this question, first we must examine translations, conceptualized not as an impossibility demonstrated by posing against translations objections from biblical hermeneutics but, rather, analyzed as historical events.[79] Perhaps the simplest approach to translation, and the one adopted by the Jesuits and their converts most frequently (except for the translation of important theological terms), was the creation of neologisms. In some cases, they resorted to loanwords, neologisms created by transliteration:[80]

亞尼瑪〔譯言靈魂亦言靈性〕之學。於費祿蘇非亞〔譯言格物窮理之學〕中。為最益。為最尊。

The study of *anima* (translated, means soul or nature of the soul), within *philosophia* (translated, means the study of "investigating things and exhausting principles"), is the most beneficial and the most respected.[81]

Transliteration provided one possible translation for the term *God*. For example, in the first chapter of *Tianzhu shi yi*, titled "Lun Tianzhu shi zhi tian di wanwu, er zhuzai anyang zhi" 論天主始制天地萬物而主宰安養之 (Showing that the Lord of Heaven created heaven, earth, and the myriad things, and controls and sustains them), Ricci argues that there must be a creator of the heavens, and "Thus this is the Lord of Heaven, the One our Western nations term *Deus*" 夫即天主，吾西國所稱『陡斯』是也.[82] A transliteration for *Deus* was, in fact, the choice for the translation of the term God into Japanese. This historical possibility of creating neologisms by semantically neutral transliteration undermines theories of incommensurability that assert radical impossibilities based on nothing more than the absence of lexical terms.[83]

Another approach was loan translations: the creation of semantic neologisms by combining characters. This was the approach most often employed by the Jesuits and their converts. The following examples will serve as a very small sample: in theology, terms for omniscience (*zhi zhi* 至智), omnipotence (*zhi neng* 至能), and infinite goodness (*zhi shan* 至善);[84] in Aristotelian philosophy, terms for cause (*suoyiran* 所以然), active cause (*zuozhe* 作者), formal cause (*mozhe* 模者), material cause (*zhizhe* 質者), final cause (*weizhe* 為者), the four types of causes—proximate, distant, universal, and special (respectively, *jin* 近, *yuan* 遠, *gong* 公, *si* 私);[85] substance (*zilizhe* 自立者), and accident (*yilaizhe* 依賴者);[86] and in Euclidean geometry, point (*dian* 點), line (*xian* 線), and surface (*mian* 面).[87] A very different strategy of translation adopted by the Jesuits and their converts was the selective omission of doctrines that would have subjected them to even harsher attacks: the Jesuits often omitted mention of the Trinity, revelation, and, with the exception of baptism, the sacraments;[88] they also frequently failed to mention the crucifixion of Jesus.[89]

For the translation of the most important terms in the most important subject, Christian theology, the Jesuits used semantic extension, borrowing and redefining terms from Buddhism and Confucianism. From Buddhism the Jesuits appropriated terms that had been employed as equivalents for Sanskrit: for Heaven, *tiantang* 天堂 (Sanskrit *devaloka*, mansion of the gods); for Hell, *diyu*

地獄 (Sanskrit *naraka*); for Devil, *mogui* 魔鬼 (*mo* for the Sanskrit *māra*); for angels, *tianshen* 天神 (Sanskrit *deva*; Protestant translators later employed *tianshi*); for soul, *linghun* 靈魂.[90] But it was from Confucianism that the Jesuits borrowed their most crucial terms. As Gernet notes, "The first missionaries were especially delighted to find in the Classics—the works venerated above all others among the literate elite—the term 'Sovereign on High' (*shangdi*), invocations to Heaven and expressions such as 'to serve Heaven' (*shi tian*), 'to respect' or 'fear Heaven' (*jing tian, wei tian*)."[91] For example, the overall project of the Jesuits was described by Xu Guangqi as "self-cultivation and serving Heaven" (*xiu shen shi Tian* 修身事天).[92] And among the terms translated, the one of the utmost significance for the Jesuits was God. Instead of the transliteration of Deus, early translations made use of several choices: *Tianzhu* 天主 (a term that appears in Buddhist texts), *Shangdi* 上帝 (a term that appears in several early Chinese texts, including the *Li ji* 禮記, *Shi jing* 詩經, *Shu jing* 書經, *Mo zi* 墨子, and *Shi ji* 史記), *Tiandi* 天帝 (a term appearing primarily in Buddhist texts but also in *Zhan guo ce* 戰國策), and *Shangzun* 上尊.[93]

Different choices in translation provided the Jesuits and their converts with different opportunities. Phonemic and semantic neologisms necessitated lengthy explanations and commentaries; examples include treatises explaining the concept of anima and the soul.[94] But borrowings from Buddhism and Christianity provided important additional opportunities. The borrowing of terms from Buddhism was the result of an attempt by the Jesuits in the early years of the mission in China to represent themselves as similar to the Buddhists. But in later years, their use of Buddhist terms also provided the Jesuits with the claim that their doctrines corrected Buddhist distortions. For the Jesuits, Buddhist theories were doubly false: Buddhist doctrines were perversions of Indian beliefs that were no longer accepted in India, doctrines that had in fact originated in the false beliefs of Pythagoras.[95]

The Jesuits' strategy in China was focused, as in Europe, on gaining patronage with the monarch. The official Confucian orthodoxy provided crucial opportunities for this project and, conversely, for the elite literati-officials who collaborated with the Jesuits. For the Jesuits and the converts, the problem in the choice of the proper term for God was not a lack of possible equivalents but, rather, the opportunities offered by each that entailed complex strategic implications and consequences—social, political, philosophical, and philological. (The conflict over these choices led to the Rites Controversy, with the use of *Tian* and *Shangdi* being forbidden by the pope in 1704.)[96] Claims made by the Jesuits and their converts about translation served as an important means of legitimation. As Gernet notes:

The missionaries also often resort to another idea: namely that part of the ancient Chinese tradition had disappeared in the Burning of the Books ordered by the first of the Qin emperors in 213 BC and that it was precisely that part that set out the thesis of an all-powerful, creator God, the existence of heaven and hell and the immortality of the soul; the teaching of the missionaries fortunately made it possible to complete what had been lost in the classical traditions of China. This is, indeed, pretty well the thesis put forward by Ricci in *The True Meaning of the Master of Heaven*, where he explains to a Chinese man of letters why it is that the Classics make no mention of paradise and hell.[97]

For the Jesuits and their converts, translation was not theorized as introducing new knowledge but, rather, as a recovery of knowledge that had been lost from the Chinese tradition.

The most important opportunity offered by translation was in the selection among possible equivalents for the term God: ambiguities in translation were a crucial resource to camouflage ambiguities in the loyalty of elite literati-official converts toward the Ming dynasty. These elite converts were central in the dissemination of Western studies in China, not merely as the object of Jesuit proselytism strategies but in translating Western studies into the language and literary style of the elite, helping to legitimate it, and building their careers on its advocacy.

The most important among these converts was Xu Guangqi; his success in patronage exemplifies how problems of translation permitted the converts to produce documents that could be read by both the Jesuits and the Ming imperial court as expressions of loyalty and faith.[98] Xu had been trained in the Hanlin Academy to write memorials to the Ming court on issues ranging from taxes to water conservancy, from military proposals to astronomy; as Ray Huang notes, "Because [the Ming] empire was created to be controlled from the center by documents, field experience or lack of it made very little difference."[99] In his memorials Xu repeatedly risked his career for the Jesuits, while at the same time fashioning himself as a statesman with novel practical solutions to Ming dynasty crises. Probably the most important example is Xu's explicit defense of the Jesuits in "Bian xue zhang shu" 辨學章疏 (Memorial on distinguishing learning):[100]

則諸陪臣所傳事天之學。真可以補益王化。左右儒術。救正佛法者也。蓋彼西洋鄰[101]近三十餘國。奉行此教。千數百年以至於今。大小相卹。上下相安。封疆無守。邦君無姓。通國無欺誑之人。絡古無淫盜之俗。路不拾遺。夜不閉關。至于悖逆叛亂。非獨無其事。
無其人。亦并其語言文字而無之。

Thus the learning of serving Heaven transmitted [by the Jesuits] can truly be used to supplement the moral influence of our sovereign, aid Confucianism and correct Buddhism. Thus in the West there are more than thirty neighboring kingdoms which implement this doctrine. For over a thousand years up to the present, the large and small help one another; the superior and the inferior live together in peace; borders require no defenses; dynasties exist without change; countries are entirely without cheats or liars; ever since antiquity there has been no lasciviousness or thieving; people do not pick up objects lost on the roads; and doors are not locked at night. And as for disturbances and rebellions—not only are they without such affairs and without such persons—there are not even words or written characters to denote such things.[102]

For Gernet, this passage is evidence of a Chinese "ancient mental framework" incommensurable with Western thought: "For Zhang Xingyao and Xu Guangqi, the ancient mental frameworks remain unchanged despite their conversions: orthodoxy must contribute towards the universal order and is recognisable by its beneficial moral and political effects."[103] Yet the content of this passage reflects not the workings of a mental framework but, rather, the intended audience; it is, after all, a memorial on political policy for the Ming imperial court. What Gernet ignores is evidence from other sources that can equally support the claim that Xu adopted the Christian faith: Xu's extant letters show, as Fang Hao notes, "many places that express the sincerity of his religious beliefs."[104] In particular, Xu's eleventh extant letter to his family shows that not only did he have his father-in-law converted, Xu was also worried that his father-in-law had not been given absolution before his death.[105] Questions about Xu's beliefs, then, cannot be answered a priori on the basis of differences in language or worldview; instead, it is precisely these questions that were central matters of debate among the historical protagonists. If instead of theorizing translation as an impossibility we seek to understand the process by which translation did occur, this passage is representative of that process. Xu's novel solutions—military, moral, mathematical, and astronomical—appealed to a desperate Ming court that promoted him to one of the highest posts;[106] in turn, Xu's success helped legitimate the Western studies that he advocated.[107] And in this passage, Xu's most dramatic evidence that this constructed world of the Western Other offered solutions to Ming dynasty crises was a lexical absence: the word for *rebellion*. Here again, as was the case with Martzloff and Gernet, fantastic claims about the radically different Other are betrayed by assertions of the absence of words.

Conclusions

Relativism and the incommensurability—linguistic or conceptual—on which it was based required for its initial formulation the assumption of a radical divide between two imagined communities, China and the West. Differences in languages then served as a natural symbol for this presumed divide, both by paralleling political boundaries and by providing compelling metaphors for the suprahistorical continuity of civilizations. This use of languages as emblems for civilizations could, however, with equal ease be used to support either universalistic or relativistic conclusions: differences in languages, through purported hierarchies constructed for languages (e.g., their precision and scientificity, or the development of alphabetization) have been linked to other civilization-defining teleologies (e.g., science or capitalism);[108] on the other hand, differences in language have also provided important metaphors to construct relativism's radically different Other.

For the purposes of this latter relativism, features of languages were further essentialized and radicalized: the difficulties of translation came to represent impervious barriers; mutual intelligibility came to represent an essentialized, systemic unity; diachronic continuities came to represent suprahistorical self-identity. The enormous diversity of strains of thought collapsed into an essentialized China provided crucial alibis in the forging of continuities and discontinuities on which the claims of incommensurability depended. On one hand, this diversity provided a wealth of examples to demonstrate the opposition between China and the West; yet this same diversity could always provide examples to explain the acceptance of Western doctrines in China as nothing more than the acceptance of the Chinese tradition.

Historically contextualized, in their translations the Jesuits and their converts adopted for their own religious concepts terminology appropriated from Buddhism. They created neologisms from terms in the Confucian tradition. Their neologisms provided the opportunity for explanations and commentary. Jesuit doctrines were then claimed to be the recovery of the lost meanings of the Confucian classics destroyed in the Qin burning of the books. But most important, problems in translation served as an important patronage strategy of the converts. By introducing ambiguities in the translation of terms such as *serving Heaven* and *Sovereign on High*, the converts produced documents that could be read by both the Chinese court and the Jesuit missionaries as expressions of allegiance. Translation was thus not an obstacle to dialogue but a crucial resource; the Chinese converts were not transparent scribes but active agents manipulating these translations for their own self-promotion.

Notes

I would like to thank Steve Angle, Mario Biagioli, Yomi Braester, Paul Cohen, Benjamin Elman, David Keightley, Ted Porter, Roddey Reid, Haun Saussy, and Wen-hsin Yeh for detailed criticisms. Two anonymous reviewers offered important suggestions. Versions of this paper have been presented at Berkeley, MIT, Stanford, the Association for Asian Studies, and the Mathematisches Forschungsinstitut Oberwolfach (Germany); I would like to thank all those who offered comments. *Positions* kindly published an earlier version of this paper. Finally, I owe special thanks to Lydia Liu for criticism, encouragement, and advice.

1   See Pierre Bourdieu, " 'Fieldwork in Philosophy,' " in *In Other Words: Essays Towards a Reflexive Sociology*, 3–33.

2   Two important early examples are Georg W. F. Hegel, *The Philosophy of History*, and Max Weber, *The Religion of China: Confucianism and Taoism*.

3   For critical analyses of works asserting that China did not have science, see Nathan Sivin, "Why the Scientific Revolution Did Not Take Place in China—Or Didn't It?", and Roger Hart, "On the Problem of Chinese Science."

4   For examples, see Ssu-yü Teng, John K. Fairbank, E-tu Zen Sun, Chaoying Fang, et al., *China's Response to the West: A Documentary Survey, 1839–1923*, and Edwin O. Reischauer, John K. Fairbank, and Albert M. Craig, *A History of East Asian Civilization*. For a critical analysis of Fairbank's and related works, see Paul A. Cohen, *Discovering History in China: American Historical Writing on the Recent Chinese Past*, chap. 1.

5   Needham proposes a retrospective competition between the West and China, fixing dates of discovery through a "grand titration" that compares "the great civilizations against one another, to find out and give credit where credit is due, and so . . . to see why one combination could far excel in medieval times while another could catch up later on and bring modern science into existence" (Joseph Needham, *The Grand Titration: Science and Society in East and West*, 12).

6   Joseph Levenson, *Liang Ch'i-ch'ao and the Mind of Modern China*, and *Confucian China and Its Modern Fate*. I am indebted to Wen-hsin Yeh for her suggestions on these and other points.

7   For examples, see the early issues of *Bulletin of Concerned Asian Scholars* (1968–), esp. James Peck, "The Roots of Rhetoric: The Professional Ideology of America's China Watchers"; John K. Fairbank and James Peck, "An Exchange"; and Joseph Esherick, "Harvard on China: The Apologetics of Imperialism." For an analysis of these and other studies critical of imperialism, see Cohen, chap. 3.

8   The China-centered approach is advocated in Cohen, chap. 4. It should be noted that Cohen explicitly asserts that China should not be treated in isolation (196). Cohen's China-centered approach, in fact, decenters China: the approach he advocates "disaggregates China 'horizontally' into regions" (following G. William Skinner); it "dis-

aggregates Chinese society 'vertically' into a number of discrete levels"; and it encourages interdisciplinary theoretical analyses (186). For a criticism of sinocentrism, see Philip Huang, "Theory and the Study of Modern Chinese History: Four Traps and a Question."

9 An important exception to these examples is the work of Benjamin Schwartz. See "The Limits of 'Tradition Versus Modernity' as Categories of Explanation," and *In Search of Wealth and Power: Yen Fu and the West*, chap. 1.

10 Important studies include Jonathan D. Spence, *The Memory Palace of Matteo Ricci*; Charles E. Ronan and Bonnie B. C. Oh, eds., *East Meets West: The Jesuits in China, 1582–1773*; John D. Young, *East-West Synthesis: Matteo Ricci and Confucianism*; and David E. Mungello, *Leibniz and Confucianism: The Search for Accord*, and *Curious Land: Jesuit Accommodation and the Origins of Sinology*. For important criticisms of the received historiography, see Lionel M. Jensen, *Manufacturing Confucianism: Chinese Traditions and Universal Civilization*.

11 For example, see *Journal of Asian Studies* 50, no. 1 (February 1991), which is dedicated to the issue of relativism, and esp. David D. Buck's summary, "Forum on Universalism and Relativism in Asian Studies: Editor's Introduction," 29–34. For Philip Huang, "culturalism" and the resulting relativism is one of his "four traps" (Huang, 192–201). For collected essays on the debates on relativism, see Martin Hollis and Steven Lukes, eds., *Rationality and Relativism*, and Michael Krausz, ed., *Relativism: Interpretation and Confrontation*.

12 Jacques Gernet, *China and the Christian Impact: A Conflict of Cultures*, originally published as *Chine et christianisme: action et réaction* (1982); Jean-Claude Martzloff, *A History of Chinese Mathematics*, originally published as *Histoire des mathématiques chinoises* (1987).

13 Gernet, *China and the Christian Impact*, and Spence, *Memory Palace of Matteo Ricci*, are generally recognized as the two seminal works describing this period. For two important critiques of Gernet's book, see Paul Cohen's review in *Harvard Journal of Asiatic Studies*, and Howard L. Goodman and Anthony Grafton, "Ricci, the Chinese, and the Toolkits of Textualists."

14 Gernet, 1–2.

15 Ibid., 2. For criticisms of assertions that individuals are the bearers of whole cultures, see Johannes Fabian, *Time and the Other: How Anthropology Makes Its Object*.

16 Gernet, 193.

17 Ibid., 201.

18 Ibid., 208.

19 Ibid., 240. Gernet cites Emile Benveniste, "Catégories de pensée et catégories de langue," reprinted in *Problèmes de linguistique générale*.

20 These two claims are in fact related, for Benveniste's central example of categories of thought is based on the copula.

21 Gernet, 240. Gernet quotes Benveniste's assertion that the existence of the verb *to be* in Greek made possible the philosophical manipulation of the concept, with the result that the concept of *being* became central in Greek thought.

22 In addition to Martzloff, *History of Chinese Mathematics*, 111–22, 273–77, 371–89, see his "Matteo Ricci's Mathematical Works and Their Influence"; "Eléments de réflexion sur les réactions chinoises à la géometrie euclidienne à la fin du XVIIe siècle:

le *Jihe lunyue* de Du Zhigeng vu principalement à partir de la préface de l'auteur et de deux notices bibliographiques rédigées par des lettres illustrés"; "La géométrie euclidienne selon Mei Wending"; and "La compréhension chinoise des méthodes démonstratives euclidiennes au cours du XVIIe siècle et au début du XVIIIe." For a more detailed study of the translation that supersedes Martzloff's work, see Peter M. Engelfriet, "Euclid in China: A Survey of the Historical Background of the First Chinese Translation of Euclid's Elements (Jihe Yuanben, Beijing, 1607), an Analysis of the Translation, and a Study of Its Influence up to 1723."

23   Martzloff, *History of Chinese Mathematics*, 116–18. Martzloff's French original: "Le cerle? Une forme située sur la terre plate (*ping di* 平地) (sic) entre de la limite! Les 'fils' (*xian* 線) droits construits de la limite au centre? Tous égaux!" (*Histoire des mathématiques chinoises*, 103). *Sic* is in the originals, both English and French. Martzloff (118) quotes from Clavius, *Euclidis Elementorum*, bk. 1, def. 7.

24   Martzloff, *History of Chinese Mathematics*, 118. In the original French edition, Martzloff states directly that the central problem is of "the concept of existence": "Ce type de phénomène rendait pour le moins hasardeuse la transmission du concept d'existence si important en mathématiques (parallèles, constructions géométriques, raisonnements par l'absurde dans lesquels on prouve qu'un certain objet mathématique n'existe pas)" (Martzloff, *Histoire des mathématiques chinoises*, 103).

25   It should be noted that a recent article by Martzloff, "Space and Time in Chinese Texts of Astronomy and Mathematical Astronomy in the Seventeenth and Eighteenth Centuries," instead asserts that it was a commensurability between the European and Chinese concepts of space and time that led to the rapid acceptance of Jesuit astronomy (67). Yet the incommensurability thesis remains in Martzloff's claim that the Chinese and Europeans had "fundamentally different orientations" (82–83). Gernet, in "The Encounter between China and Europe," argues that the commensurability that Martzloff argues for is only apparent.

26   A. C. Graham, "'Being' in Western Philosophy Compared with *shih/fei yu/wu* in Chinese Philosophy." Graham's conclusions are in fact in many ways the opposite of Martzloff's. Martzloff also cites Gilles Granger, *La théorie aristotélicienne de la science*.

27   Peter A. Boodberg, "Philological Notes on Chapter One of the *Lao Tzu*," 601.

28   Alfred Bloom, *The Linguistic Shaping of Thought: A Study in the Impact of Language on Thinking in China and the West*. For a critical review, see Kuang-ming Wu, "Counterfactuals, Universals, and Chinese Thinking—A Review of *The Linguistic Shaping of Thought: A Study in the Impact of Language on Thinking in China and the West*."

29   For a recent summary, and one further example, of these arguments, see Derk Bodde, *Chinese Thought, Society, and Science: The Intellectual and Social Background of Science and Technology in Pre-Modern China*.

30   Two important recent studies are Huan Saussy, *The Problem of a Chinese Aesthetic*, and Lydia H. Liu, *Translingual Practice: Literature, National Culture, and Translated Modernity—China, 1900–1937*. In their first chapters both works provide critical discussions of much of the literature on philosophy and translation.

31   Emile Benveniste, *Problems in General Linguistics*, 56, 53; originally published as *Problèmes de linguistique générale* (1966–74).

32   Ibid., 56.

33 Ibid., 60, 61; emphasis in original.

34 Jacques Derrida, "The Supplement of Copula: Philosophy *before* Linguistics," in *Textual Strategies: Perspectives in Post-Structuralist Criticism*, 114. Cf. Boodberg's discussion: "*(d)jwer* (modern *wei*, graphs: 唯, 惟, or 維), a copula-like particle common in the language of the *Shih* and *Shu*. If this be the lost Chinese verb 'to be' . . ." (603).

35 In this sense, grammatical peculiarities of the Indo-European languages have influenced the development of philosophy within those languages by the conflation of *to be* and *existence*.

36 Martin Heidegger, *An Introduction to Metaphysics*, 58–61, quoted in Derrida, 118, with Derrida's italics.

37 Benveniste, *Problems in General Linguistics*, 138, quoted in Derrida, 119, with Derrida's italics.

38 Derrida, 82.

39 Ibid., 98.

40 It should also be noted that elsewhere in his argument asserting that language determines categories of thought, Benveniste uses the example of science and the Chinese language to argue against linguistic incommensurability: "Chinese thought may well have invented categories as specific as the *dao*, the *yin*, and the *yang*; it is nonetheless able to assimilate the concepts of dialectical materialism or quantum mechanics without the structure of the Chinese language proving a hindrance. No type of language can by itself alone foster or hamper the activity of the mind. The advance of thought is linked much more closely to the capacities of men, to general conditions of culture, and to the organization of society than to the particular nature of a language. But the possibility of thought is linked to the faculty of speech, for language is a structure informed with signification, and to think is to manipulate the signs of language" (Benveniste, *Problems in General Linguistics*, 63–64).

41 Willard V. O. Quine, "Meaning and Translation," in *On Translation*, 171–72.

42 Donald Davidson, "On the Very Idea of a Conceptual Scheme," in *Inquiries into Truth and Interpretation*.

43 Benjamin Whorf, "The Punctual and Segmentative Aspects of Verbs in Hopi," in *Language, Thought, and Reality: Selected Writings of Benjamin Lee Whorf*; Thomas S. Kuhn, *The Structure of Scientific Revolutions*; Paul Feyerabend, "Explanation, Reduction, and Empiricism"; Willard V. O. Quine, "Two Dogmas of Empiricism." Davidson argues that Quine's conceptual schemes constitute yet a "third dogma." For Quine's response, see "On the Very Idea of a Third Dogma."

44 This is precisely the contradiction found in Martzloff: his assertion of incommensurability between Chinese and Latin itself requires a solution to the problem of incommensurability in a firm ground for philosophical translations among Greek, Latin, English, Chinese, and French, a solution that could not have existed four hundred years ago at the time of the translation.

45 Davidson, 184, 185.

46 Davidson, *Inquiries into Truth and Interpretation*, xviii. More precisely, Davidson states, "Our general method of interpretation forestalls the possibility of discovering that others have radically different intellectual equipment. But more important, it is argued that if we reject the idea of an uninterpreted source of evidence no room is left

for a dualism of scheme and content. Without such a dualism we cannot make sense of conceptual relativism" (xviii).

47 Davidson, "On the Very Idea of a Conceptual Scheme," 189.

48 See Kuhn, *Structure of Scientific Revolutions;* for a later formulation, see his "Second Thoughts on Paradigms."

Paul Feyerabend, in *Against Method,* 170–226, offers as an example of incommensurability two contrasting forms of Greek art that he identifies as cosmologies A and B. A is the "archaic style" in which a "paratactic aggregate" forms a "visual catalogue" through the placement of standard figures in varying symbolic positions; for example, death is the standard figure drawn horizontally (Feyerabend cites Emanuel Loewy, *Die Naturwiedergabe in der älteren Griechischen Kunst).* In B, art is arranged so that the underlying essence is grasped through representations that trigger illusions (e.g., two-dimensional drawings). Feyerabend then defines incommensurability: "A discovery, or a statement, or an attitude [is called] *incommensurable* with the cosmos (the theory, the framework) if it suspends some of its universal principles" (215).

Whorf asserts, for example, that the adoption of Western science entails the adoption of the Western system in its entirety: "That modern Chinese or Turkish scientists describe the world in the same terms as Western scientists means, of course, only that they have taken over bodily the entire Western system of rationalizations, not that they have corroborated that system from their native posts of observation" (214).

Quine's famous analogies are from boundary-value problems in physics: "The totality of our so-called knowledge or beliefs . . . is a man-made fabric which impinges on experience only along the edges"; "total science is like a field of force whose boundary conditions are experience" (Quine, "Two Dogmas," 42, quoted in Davidson, "On the Very Idea of a Conceptual Scheme," 191).

49 Arguably, it is the purported correlations of words with things that underwrites claims of deep ontological differences. Claims of radical differences are based on the assertion that one language fails to have a word for a particular phenomenon, not that the phenomenon cannot possibly be described.

50 John E. Murdoch, "Editions of Euclid."

51 On Clavius's mathematics and science, see James M. Lattis, *Between Copernicus and Galileo: Christoph Clavius and the Collapse of Ptolemaic Cosmology.*

52 The example is from August Schleicher, *Die Sprachen Europas in systematischer Uebersicht,* quoted in William Dwight Whitney, *Language and the Study of Language,* 331, quoted and criticized in J. R. Firth, "Linguistic Analysis and Translation," 76. For analysis of this translation, see Haun Saussy's article in this volume; I would like to thank him for bringing this passage to my attention.

53 Martzloff, *History of Chinese Mathematics,* 118.

54 For criticism of Martzloff's translations, see the review of his *Histoire des mathématiques chinoises* by Catherine Jami in *Historia Scientiarum.*

55 Martzloff, *History of Chinese Mathematics,* 273.

56 Ibid., 274. For the French, see n. 23 above.

57 Gernet, *China and the Christian Impact,* 240.

58 *Tianzhu shi yi,* in *Tianxue chu han* 天學初函 (TXCH); translated into English as Matteo

Ricci, *The True Meaning of the Lord of Heaven (T'ien-chu Shih-i)*. Several of the examples that I analyze are in fact cited or translated in Gernet, *China and the Christian Impact*, and provide important evidence against the conclusions he draws in the final chapter.

59 *Tianzhu shi yi*, 450; Ricci, *Lord of Heaven*, 34–36. In the following translations I have consulted Lancashire and Hu's translations, borrowing and making alterations where appropriate.

60 *Tianzhu shi yi*, 451–52; Ricci, *Lord of Heaven*, 176–77. Just as the asserted absence of a word precisely equivalent to the English verb *to be* is hardly evidence for broader philosophical conclusions such as conceptual incommensurability (as I have argued above), so too the translations I offer in this article of various Chinese phrases into English terms such as *existence, soul*, and forms of the verb *to be* are not meant to suggest a transparency of translation or to imply the exact equivalence of Chinese and English words or concepts (I would like to thank Marta Hanson for her suggestions on this point). The (im)possibility of translation cannot demonstrate either radical incommensurability or exact correspondence; these are questions not of linguistics but of philosophical interpretation and intellectual history.

61 For an important earlier example, see the chapter "Gui shen" 鬼神 (Ghosts and spirits) in Zhu Xi, *Zhuzi yu lei* 朱子語類 (Conversations with Master Zhu, arranged topically).

62 Reading *shu* 屬 for *shu* 殊 in the translation.

63 *Tianzhu shi yi*, 452; Ricci, *Lord of Heaven*, 178–79. This passage is also translated in Gernet, *China and the Christian Impact*, 68: "Some say that they definitely *do not exist*. Others say that they *do exist* if one believes in them and do not if one does not believe in them. Others say that it is just as false to say that they *do exist* as to say that they do not and that the truth is that they both do and at the same time *do not exist*" (emphasis mine). Gernet concludes that these debates were "hardly . . . to the missionaries' liking," but does not explain why this translation does not controvert his claims in his concluding section, "Language and Thought," and in particular his central assertion that "there was no word to denote existence in Chinese, nothing to convey the concept of being or essence, which in Greek is so conveniently expressed by the noun *ousia* or the neuter *to on*" (241).

64 Substituted for idiosyncratic variant.

65 The entire passage states: " 'Fan Chi inquired about intelligence. Confucius stated: 'Endeavor to make the people righteous, respect the spirits and distance them; this can be termed intelligence.' [Fan Chi also] inquired about benevolence. [Confucius] stated: 'The benevolent face difficulties first and obtain afterwards; this can be called benevolence.' "
樊遲問知。子曰：「務民之義，敬鬼神而遠之，可謂知矣。」問仁。曰：「仁者先難而後獲，可謂仁矣。」
(*Lun yu* 論語 [Confucian analects] 6.22, in *Shisan jing zhu shu* 十三經注疏 (SSJZS) [Thirteen classics with annotations and subannotations], 2: 2479). Thus, in the comparison, Confucius appears to be exhorting Fan Chi to concentrate on the affairs of the living rather than on spirits. See also *Lun yu* 11.12, in SSJZS 2: 2499.

66 *Lun yu* 3.13, in SSJZS 2: 2467.

67 *Tianzhu shi yi*, 1.468; Ricci, *Lord of Heaven*, 202–3.

68 Reading *yang* 洋 for *xiang* 庠 (academy).

69 *Tianzhu shi yi*, 461; Ricci, *Lord of Heaven*, 190; Gernet, *China and the Christian Impact*, 243.

70 Jacques Gernet, "Christian and Chinese Visions of the World in the Seventeenth Century."

71 Ibid., 15, 16.

72 For example, Gernet notes, "The difference between the philosophical ideas inherited from Ancient Greece and those of the Chinese emerges clearly here" (*China and the Christian Impact*, 210).

73 From Gernet's concluding sentence to "Christian and Chinese Visions of the World," 17.

74 The most sustained attempt to formulate such a theory is Michel Foucault, *The Archaeology of Knowledge*, originally published as *L'archéologie du savoir* (1969). For a critique, see Hubert L. Dreyfus and Paul Rabinow, *Michel Foucault: Beyond Structuralism and Hermeneutics*. The theoretical reformulation presented in *Archaeology of Knowledge* should be contrasted with Foucault's earlier historical works.

75 Mario Biagioli, "The Anthropology of Incommensurability," 184.

76 Incommensurability, Biagioli asserts, is often associated with instances of trespassing professional or disciplinary boundaries. He concludes against Kuhn that although the possibility of developing bilingualism is not logically wrong, the assumption is unwarranted in ignoring "the fundamental relation between social groups and cognitive activity" (ibid., 207).

77 Robert S. Westman, "The Copernicans and the Churches," esp. 90–91.

78 Mario Biagioli, "Stress in the Book of Nature: Galileo's Realism and Its Supplements." Biagioli argues that "Galileo's so-called mathematical *realism* was, in fact, a form of scriptural *fundamentalism*" (2).

79 For an important theoretical analysis of the problem of translation between Chinese and Western languages and a critical overview of theories on translation, see Liu, *Translingual Practice*, esp. chap. 1. These issues will not be further developed here.

80 For an analysis of translation and a discussion of terminology, see Theodora Bynon, *Historical Linguistics*, chap. 6; see also John Lyons, *Semantics*.

81 F. Sambiasi, "Ling yan li shao yin" 靈言蠡勺引 (Preface to "A preliminary discussion of anima"), in TXCH, 2.1127. The phrases in parentheses are commentaries, distinguished from the original text by half-width characters.

82 *Tianzhu shi yi*, 1.381; Ricci, *Lord of Heaven*, 70.

83 For examples of the translation of Christian doctrines into European languages, see Bynon, chap. 6.

84 "Tianzhu shi yi yin" 天主實義引, in *Tianzhu shi yi*, 1.370; Ricci, *Lord of Heaven*, 62.

85 *Tianzhu shi yi*, 1.390–91; Ricci, *Lord of Heaven*, 84–86.

86 *Tianzhu shi yi*, 1.406; Ricci, *Lord of Heaven*, 108. Hu and Lancashire note that the current terms are *ziliti* 自立體 and *yifuti* 依附體; see Ricci, *Lord of Heaven*, 108 n. 18.

87 For a comprehensive table of Euclidean terms translated by the Jesuits, along with their modern equivalents, see Engelfriet, 164–67.

88 Presumably, the most difficult of the sacraments to explain would have been the Eucharist: that bread and wine were in actuality the body and blood of Christ.

89 Yang Guangxian later accused the Jesuits of frequently failing to mention the cru-

cifixion, arguing that the Jesuits wished to deliberately conceal that the Lord they worshiped was nothing more than a criminal during the period of the Han dynasty.

90 These examples are from Lancashire and Hu, introduction to Ricci, *Lord of Heaven*, 35–36.

91 Gernet, *China and the Christian Impact*, 25.

92 Xu Guangqi uses this term to characterize the Jesuits' mission in China in a memorial to the Ming court. The phrase *Shi tian* appears in the *Li ji* 禮記 (Records of rites) (SSJZS, 2:1612); *xiu shen* appears in several passages from the *Li ji*, and most notably, *shen xiu* appears in *Da xue*. See Zhu Xi 朱熹 (1130–1200), *Da xue zhang ju* 大學章句 (The great learning, separated into chapters and sentences) in *Sishu zhangju jizhu* 四書章句集注 (Four books with collected annotations), 3.

93 *Tianzhu shi yi*, 359, 359, 366, and 369, respectively. Other terms were also used for God in more specific contexts, such as *Dayuan* 大元 (*Tianzhu shi yi*, 1.399; Ricci, *Lord of Heaven*, 96). Lancashire and Hu note that *Yuan* 元 was sometimes used by Ricci, along with *Yuan* 原, "to express 'source' or God as Creator" (Ricci, *Lord of Heaven*, 96 n. 32). As noted by Lancashire and Hu, these terms were sometimes preceded by a blank space to denote respect; the terms *Zhongguo* 中國 and *Zhonghua* 中華 were also preceded with a blank space (*Tianzhu shi yi*, 367). To denote this, I have capitalized these terms in pinyin; however, it should be noted that the addition of a blank space in the Chinese text is not used uniformly throughout.

94 F. Sambiasi and Xu Guangqi, "Ling yan li shao" 靈言蠡勺 (A preliminary discussion of anima), in TXCH.

95 For examples of Jesuit claims of Buddhist distortions, see Erik Zürcher, "The Jesuit Mission in Fujian in Late Ming Times: Levels of Response," 418 n. 3.

96 In 1704 Pope Clement XI banned the use of *tian* and *shangdi* as translations for God. See Lancashire and Hu, introduction to Ricci, *Lord of Heaven*, 20.

97 Gernet, *China and the Christian Impact*, 28.

98 It should be noted that the specific mechanisms of patronage in China are in many ways different from those found in Europe. Perhaps the most important differences are the examination system and the official bureaucracy and the way that these structured patronage in the Ming court.

99 Ray Huang, *1587, A Year of No Significance: The Ming Dynasty in Decline*, 50.

100 In Xu Guangqi et al., *Tianzhu jiao Dong chuan wenxian, xu bian* 天主教東傳文獻續編 (TZJDC) (Documents on the Eastern transmission of Catholicism, second collection), 1:25–26. In his introduction to this collection, Fang Hao 方豪 states that this reproduction is printed from a Ming edition preserved at the Vatican Library. Fang notes that there are many editions of this treatise, and many are incomplete. Fang offers several examples of editors that removed portions of the quotation cited (3–4); the edition copied by Wang Zhongmin in XGQJ omits parts of this passage (431).

101 Substituted for common variant.

102 This passage is translated in Gernet, *China and the Christian Impact*, 110; I have made minor alterations to his translation where appropriate.

103 Ibid., 110–11.

104 Fang Hao 方豪, *Zhongguo Tianzhujiao shi renwu zhuan* 中國天主教史人物傳 (Biographies of Catholics in China), 103.

105 *XGQJ* 2.492. For an English translation of these letters, see Gail King, "The Family Letters of Xu Guangqi."

106 Xu's career followed the pattern of exile and returns to power typical of the period; with the ascendance of Sizong in 1628, Xu returned to power. In the last year of his life, 1633 (Chongwen 6), he reached one of the highest posts in government, the Grand Guardian of the Heir Apparent, and Grand Secretary of the Hall of Literary Profundity (*Taizi taibao wenyuange daxueshi* 太子太保文淵閣大學士).

107 This argument is presented in detail in my manuscript "Proof, Propaganda and Patronage: The Dissemination of Western Studies in Seventeenth-Century China."

108 Important examples include Jack Goody, *The Logic of Writing and the Organization of Society*, and Bodde, *Chinese Thought, Society, and Science*.

Qiong Zhang *Demystifying Qi: The Politics*

of Cultural Translation and Interpretation in the

Early Jesuit Mission to China

In 1595, twelve years after the onset of their mission in late Ming China, the Jesuits formally discarded their monks' robes and began to "grow beard and hair and introduce themselves as Western literati."[1] This decision to change their identity came from their spiritual leader, Matteo Ricci (Li Madou, 1552–1610), whose reflections on the disparate roles of Buddhist monks and Confucian literati in Chinese society convinced him that the assimilation into the network of the Confucian scholar-officials was their one and only opportunity for a great enterprise in the empire. Ironically, however, among the three major Chinese religious traditions, Confucianism, especially the neo-Confucian orthodoxy that Ricci identified as the dominant ideology of the contemporary Confucian literati, was perhaps the least congenial to Catholicism in its spiritual orientation and conceptual framework. Whereas the Catholic ideal of salvation presumes the immortality of the soul, original sin, and a transcendental God as savior, the neo-Confucian orthodoxy was founded on exactly the opposite vision: the inseparability of soul and body, the innate perfectibility of human nature, and the unity of Heaven and mankind. Thus, Ricci and the other missionaries deemed it necessary to topple this basic structure of neo-Confucianism, or else they would not be able to start any enterprise in China at all.

This essay seeks to demonstrate the central role of cultural translation and interpretation as the Jesuits' strategy to resolve the tensions between their acclaimed accommodation to Confucianism and their intended goal of transforming it. In particular, it inquires into how the Jesuits located the problem of neo-Confucian spirituality on the plane of culture—the culture of *qi* in Chinese cosmological and medical discourses—and how they sought to reconstitute that culture by reinterpreting the teachings regarding *qi* and the human spirit in ancient Confucian classics and by forging a linguistic equivalence between the traditional Chinese cosmological and medical notions of *qi*, on the one hand, and air (one of the four Aristotelian elements) and *pneuma* or *spiritus* (in late Renaissance Galenic medicine), on the other, in their Chinese translations of Western learning. By highlighting the correspondence between their evaluations of neo-Confucian spirituality and Chinese culture and their manipulations of texts and words in their cultural translation and reinterpretation, this essay strives to probe the Jesuits' implicit understanding concerning the (in)commensurability of languages and cultures and to invite further inquiries into the epistemic-ideological complex that shaped the nature of translation during this earliest phase of Sino-Western cultural encounter.

Qi and the "Problem" of Neo-Confucian Spirituality

In the beginning, the Chinese concept *qi* was a great source of surprise and bewilderment to the early Jesuit missionaries. Apparently, however, it was not the semantic aspect of it that baffled them. On the contrary, they believed that they had mastered the Chinese character *qi* fairly well; it designates breath, air, gases, vapors, or anything gaseous in appearance. Thus they took it as the Chinese equivalent of the Latin term *aer* (air). Their first Chinese catechism, *Tianzhu shi yi* (The veritable record of the Lord of Heaven), a collaboration by Michele Ruggieri and Matteo Ricci, used *qi* to mean precisely air in an account of how God created the four elemental spheres: fire, air, water, and earth.[2] What astonished them was rather the total absence of *qi* in the Chinese world picture. To Ricci, who lavished praises on the extraordinary intellect, diligence, and self-discipline of the Chinese people, the efficiency of their government, and the affluent resources of their land, this undoubtedly betrayed the miserable backwardness of their learned cultural heritage. "To be honest," he wrote in a letter to the Jesuit general, Claudio Acquaviva, "if China was the entire world, I would not hesitate to call myself the greatest mathematician and even the greatest philosopher of nature, because all that the Chinese care about is moral philosophy and elegance of discourse, or, to be more accurate, literary style. All that they say is ridiculous and I am surprised at what little they know. For example, they believe that the sky is vacuous, with stars moving freely inside it. *They do not know anything about air, but have a theory of five elements which excludes air and includes metal and wood.* . . . Their silly ideas such as these are innumerable."[3]

Ricci's colleagues also experienced similar cultural shocks. Their early communications to Europe were inundated with exclamations that the Chinese did not even know that air is one of the four elements![4]

Soon, however, it was the reverse problem that began to bother them. As they came to know more about Chinese thought and practice, the Jesuits discovered that not only the concept *qi* was omnipresent in all sectors of Chinese culture, from elite to popular, but it constituted the very core of Chinese medical, cosmological, metaphysical, and moral discourses.[5] This discovery allowed Ricci to make sense of why, as he observed, the contemporary Chinese, particularly the Confucian literati, were so thoroughly this-worldly, believing in no personal god, the immortality of the soul, nor salvation and punishment in afterlife.[6]

Indeed, it could be argued that the very notion of *qi* emerged as a signal, as well as a cause, of a profound transformation from the theocentric world of the Shang (seventeenth–eleventh century B.C.E.) and early part of Western Zhou (1100–771 B.C.E.) to a humanocentric culture. The character *qi* had very little trace in China's earliest written records.[7] Xu Shen's etymological dictionary *Shuowen jiezi* (Explaining characters, composed ca. 100–121 C.E.) recorded two graphs related to it. The first pictograph (*qi*[1]) designated the "vapor of the clouds." The second (*qi*) had a rice component, conveying the image of nourishing vapors arising from boiling rice or grains.[8] The first graph suggests a connection between the early cosmological conception of *qi* and the ancient practice of cloud worship and divination through observing the movements of clouds (*wangyun*). The relatively early references to *qi*, found in *Guoyu* (Conversations from the states) and *Zuo zhuan* (Zuo's commentary on the Spring and Autumn Annals) indicate that the people of Western Zhou already conceived of the "six qi"—*yin*, *yang*, rain, wind, darkness, and light—as the operating powers behind natural order and transformation. In the south, where the culture of cloud worship was particularly strong, we find the first articulations of the metaphysical conceptions of *qi* and its two modes of being, *yin* and *yang*, as the prototypes of Dao or ultimate reality.[9]

On the other hand, the second graph of *qi* suggests the idea that human life depends on *qi* and that *qi* is the bond through which mankind exchanges energy with the environment.[10] The Chinese concepts of the human spirit or soul, *hun* and *po*, were both developed in reference to *qi* in this context. One of their earliest articulations, found in *Zuo zhuan*, refers to an episode in 535 B.C.E., when the people of the state of Zheng were greatly terrified by Boyou's ghost, which took many lives subsequently, until Zichan, prime minister of Zheng, appointed Boyou's son to succeed in Boyou's former position. In explaining his decision, Zichan goes into the issue of how spirits and ghosts are formed: "In man's life the first transformations are called *po* (the earthly aspect of the soul). After *po* has been produced, that which is strong and positive is called *hun* (Heavenly aspect of the soul). If he had abundance in the use of material things and subtle essentials, his *hun* and *po* will be strong. From this are developed essence and understanding until there are spirit and intelligence. When an ordinary man or woman dies a violent death, the *hun* and *po* [do not disperse immediately but] are still able to keep hanging about men and do evil and malicious things." [11] Here, Zichan considers the human soul (*hun* and *po*) and its various faculties not as an immaterial principle external to the body but as something dependent on and immanent in the body, capable of developing gradually in life through the nourishment of the body. Furthermore, the idea that *hun* and *po*, consequently, spirits and ghosts, are all *qi* of one form or another is also implicit in his images of *hun* and *po* as capable of dispersing or wandering about.

Be it the vapor of misty clouds or life-sustaining essence, *qi* had always meant more than simply matter. In the first instance, it invokes associations of the divine and unfathomable; in the second, human spirit and the principle of life. During the Warring States period (475–221 B.C.E.), through the Daoist philosophy of Zhuangzi, the Yin Yang cosmology attributed to Zhou Yan (305–240 B.C.E.?), the Jingqi Theory advanced in *Guanzi*,[12] and the medical philosophies of the *Huangdi neijing* (The Yellow Emperor's inner canon of medicine) emerging around the third century B.C.E., the term *qi* entered prominently into the philosophical vocabulary. The authors of the *Huangdi neijing*, in particular, developed a system of correspondence between the universe and the human organism, employing such key concepts as *qi*, *yin*, *yang*, and *wuxing*, or the five agents of metal, wood, water, fire, and earth. They regarded the human organism as a dynamic unity sustained by *qi*, which, in the forms of seminal essence, vital breath, body fluids, saliva, blood, and the pulses, circulates throughout the body, constantly interacting with, transforming into, and nourishing the body.[13] Their discussions on the controlling principles (spirit or soul) of the human being—*jing*, *shen*, *hun*, and *po*—reinforced Zichan's idea that all aspects of the human organism, from physical condition to mental activities and emotional states, are manifestations of the working of *qi*.

The Confucian School was not untouched by this wave of *qi*. In fact, Mencius not only embraced it in his moral philosophy but gave it a definitive twist that forecast much of its development in neo-Confucian thought. Like Confucius, Mencius looked on the individual's self-cultivation as the ultimate path to social peace and order. He believed that all people have the four beginnings of moral consciousness—humanness, rightness, propriety, and wisdom—which he referred to as the "Heaven-endowed nature." To him, exerting efforts to ceaselessly nurture and expand this nature is at once a moral and religious obligation of mankind.[14] Inspired by the theory widely endorsed at his time that human being is the conflux of a finer qi from heaven and a grosser qi from earth, he also added a physiocosmic dimension to self-cultivation. He defines qi as "that which fills the body" and subjects it to the control of the will: "Where the will arrives there the qi halts."[15] Whereas his contemporaries primarily spoke of a gross qi constituting the physical form and a refined qi controlling life and the mental faculties, Mencius ascribed a "flood-like qi" (haoran zhi qi) to moral virtues and interpreted self-cultivation as a process of transformation of physical qi into the "flood-like qi." In the following conversation, Mencius explains this transformation:

> "I am good at nourishing my 'flood-like qi.' "
> "May I ask what you mean by the 'flood-like qi'?"
> "A hard thing to speak of. It is the qi which is utmost in vastness, utmost in firmness. If you nourish it with integrity and do not interfere with it, *it will fill the space between Heaven and Earth.* It is a qi which unites rightness and the Way. Deprive it of these and it will collapse. It is born of accumulated rightness and cannot be appropriated by anyone through a sporadic show of rightness. Whenever one acts in a way that falls below the standard in one's heart, it will collapse."[16]

According to Mencius, the acquisition of this floodlike qi enables a perfected person (junzi) to exercise creative influences on the natural order, forming a triad with Heaven and Earth: "Wherever he has passed through, transformation follows; wherever he abides, his influence is of spiritual nature, flowing in the same stream as Heaven above and Earth below."[17] This image of the perfected person was mirrored in another Confucian classic, *Doctrine of the Mean*, where we read: "How great is the path proper to the sage! Like overflowing water, it sends forth and nourishes all things, and rises up to the height of heaven."[18]

However, it is through the works of Song Confucians that the conception of qi became a core component of Confucian moral, cosmological, and metaphysical discourses. Zhou Dunyi (1017–1073), to whom much of this development is indebted, laid out the groundwork of a qi-centered cosmology, taking the *Book of Changes* (Yi jing) as his point of departure. In the *Book of Changes*, it is written: "In the changes there is the Supreme Ultimate (taiji), which produces the two modes (yin and yang). The two modes produce the four forms (major and minor *yin* and *yang*), and the four forms produce the eight trigrams." [19] Zhou obviated the eight trigrams and included instead the five agents in his model of cosmic evolution, which he also refers to as the five qi: "When the five qi are distributed in harmonious order, the four seasons run their course." [20] Indeed, according to Zhou, in their final analysis, the Supreme Ultimate (*taiji*), *yin*, and *yang* are all qi.[21]

Zhou elaborated the idea in the *Book of Changes* that nature and mankind are generated by the transformation of qi.[22] Though human beings are part of the cosmic family sustained and nurtured by Heaven and Earth, they alone receive qi in its highest excellence, and therefore are most intelligent. Here lies the origin of human morals: "As the human being's physical form appears, his spirit develops consciousness. The five moral principles of his nature are aroused by, and respond to, the external world and engage in activity; good and evil are distinguished; and human affairs take place." [23] Zhou defined sagehood as sincerity, that is, being true to one's nature, and located the origin of that nature in the change and transformation of Heaven: " 'The Way of *tian* (Heaven) is to change and transform so that everything will obtain its correct nature and destiny.' In this way sincerity is established." [24] Thus in Zhou's thought we see Mencius's cosmic vision of the perfected person fully etched out with a renewed understanding of Heaven, human nature, and sagehood.

Zhou was, of course, merely a harbinger of a new era of flowering in the Confucian tradition, an era that saw the rise of the School of Principle (*li xue*) represented by Cheng Yi (1033–1107) and Zhu Xi (1130–1200), whose commentaries on the Confucian classics achieved the status of orthodox Confucian teachings by 1241; the School of Mind (*xin xue*) established by Lu Xiangshan (1139–1193) and Wang Yangming (1472–1529); and the School of Qi (*qi xue*) led by Zhang Zai (1020–1077), Wang Tingxiang (1474–1544), and Wang Fuzhi (1619–1692), to name some of the prominent currents. Although these schools were fundamentally divided on many issues to the extent that some consider it problematic to brand them under the umbrella of neo-Confucianism,[25] we can safely argue that there is a set of shared beliefs and understanding about the world, humanity, and the relationship of mankind to nature and to the ultimate source of all, Heaven, which cut across all these variants of Confucian tradition, and it is these shared values and ideals that constitute the distinctive features of a "neo-Confucian spirituality." This includes, first of all, the belief in the unity of being in the sense that all categories of existence from Heaven above to Earth below and from human beings, animals, plants, inanimate matter, to spirits and ghosts ultimately are originated in and manifestations of qi, hence the Chinese expression, *yi qi guan chuan* (the same qi runs through all).[26] Second is the belief in the unity of moral and spiritual nature with physical nature. The neo-Confucian philosophers regarded the human being as an organism with multidimensional natures. On the biological and psychological levels, they subscribed to the language and basic tenet of the medical tradition, describing the human being in terms of "qi, blood, perception, and feelings (qi, xue, zhi, qing)." Though recognizing human being's natural and cognitive faculties as forming an ascending order from the body, perceptive mind, intuitive knowledge, to discerning intellect (shenti, xinzhi, lingjue, shenming), they imposed no ontological divide between the physical and the mental, but rather regarded the spirit and the intellect as the "flower" and the "essence" of the body.[27] On the metaphysical level, they maintained that the human mind embodies an innate moral consciousness. It is this moral nature that constitutes the proper subject of Confucian moral cultivation. It is simultaneously human, as it constitutes human nature (xing), and divine, as it is what Heaven imparts to man as his destiny (ming). The conception of embodiment that connects all three—the innate moral consciousness, the human mind, and the body—dictates that moral cultivation must be, and can be, achieved within and through the cultivation of the total person.[28] Thus the neo-Confucian scholars often referred to their discourse on moral knowledge and practice as the "learning of the person, mind, nature, and destiny" (shen xin xing ming zhi xue). This unity of the moral and spiritual with the physical also underlies their conception of Heaven. Zhu Xi, for example, explicitly rejected both the idea that "there is a person residing in Heaven passing judgments on human wrongdoings" and that "Heaven is completely devoid of a mastering mind." He defined Heaven as "the great mass of qi which circulates ceaselessly," while at the same time he constantly spoke of the manner in which the "mind" of Heaven engendered the mind of human beings.[29] Thus, quite unlike the Catholic ideal of salvation which presumes an infinite ontological gap between God and the world, spiritual beings (angels) and corporeal substances, and soul and body, neo-Confucianism envisaged the entire realm of being as an organic unity and offered a path to spiritual union with the divine (Heaven) right here in this life.[30]

Reading between Text and Tradition

Indeed, the pivotal role of the cosmological and medical theories of qi in shaping the character of Chinese religion is in many ways comparable to the reverse effect of Platonic metaphysics in transforming the spirit of primitive

Christianity. The supreme deities *shangdi* (Lord-on-high), *tian* (Heaven), and *huangtian shangdi* (August Heaven Lord on High) in Chinese high antiquity, though not attributed any role in creation, were functionally similar to God in the biblical world. Conversely, before the early Church Fathers called upon Platonic conceptual categories to elucidate the intellectual basis of Incarnation, Trinity, and other mysteries of the Christian faith, Christianity had been likewise a this-worldly religion that promised resurrection of the total body through faith in God rather than salvation of the immortal soul in the world beyond.[31] However, at the end of their respective inculturations, both religions had become irreversibly something else.

The complex relation between the Confucian classical texts and the Song neo-Confucian commentary tradition was not lost on Ricci. Writing to the Jesuit General on 4 November 1595, he notes: "In the past few years, I had an excellent Chinese teacher expound the six classics and the four books to me, and I found that ideas such as the existence of a supreme deity, immortal soul, and Heaven are already present in those texts." [32] To Ricci, there were many discrepancies between the ancient Confucian teachings and their modern variants. He observed in his journals that in ancient times the Chinese used to worship a supreme deity and venerated various guardian spirits of the mountains, rivers, and the four quarters of the earth. However, "since corrupt human nature, unaided by divine grace, sinks ever lower, these unfortunate people little by little lost their first light, and they come to be so without restraints that they say and do whatever they wish, right or wrong, without fear. Thus, today, of those who have escaped idolatry, there are few who have not fallen into atheism." [33] Similarly, "the ancient literati seem to have been uncertain about the immortality of the soul and about its fate after death," whereas the recent Confucians categorically "assert that the soul dies with the body and explicitly deny the existence of a Heaven and Hell." The most serious error he detected in contemporary Confucian thought was the doctrine of "man forming one body with Heaven and Earth," which he attributed to Buddhist influence.[34]

Based on these comparative observations, Ricci decided to present Christianity as the religion that China had had in its high antiquity, the Way of the Confucian sages, which was lost to the later generations of Chinese due to the massive burning of books during the Qin (221–207 B.C.E.) and the corruption of Buddhist influence, but was kept intact and alive in the West.[35] Ricci's approach to Confucianism thus had two components: the appropriation of the classical texts and the rejection of their neo-Confucian traditions. Often referred to by historians today as the "Ricci method" or the method of "cultural accommodation," it is fully spelled out in a letter of 1609 that Ricci wrote to the Jesuit vice-provincial in Japan, Francesco Pasio:

> As your Reverence is aware, there are in this realm three sects. The most ancient is that of the literati, who now govern China and have always done so, the other two [Taoism and Buddhism] are idolatries which differ from each other but which are both condemned by the literati. The sect of the literati has little to say about the supernatural, but its moral ideals are almost entirely in accord with our own. Accordingly, I have undertaken in the books I have written to praise them and to use them to confute the other two sects. *I have avoided criticizing [the basic Confucian doctrine] but have sought to interpret it where it appears to conflict with our holy faith.* . . . I have had the others [in the mission] pursue my policy, for we would have more than we could manage if we were to take up the cudgels against all three sects. I have not failed, however, to dispute those new opinions of the literati in which they depart from the [Confucian] ancients.[36]

What is particularly worth noting in this revelation is that Ricci was well aware of the limitations of the textual basis for his acclaimed appropriation of classical Confucianism. The authors whom he referred to as "Confucian ancients" are by no means a homogeneous group, nor are the Five Classics and Four Books that make up the Confucian classical texts. Despite the remnants of a theistic religion preserved in the oldest documents in texts such as the *Book of History*, the *Book of Songs*, and *Spring and Autumn Annals*, the major portion of the classical texts was a composite of essays, records, and commentaries formed between the fifth and third centuries B.C.E., when the theories of qi, yin, yang, and five agents and a whole range of rationalistic discourses were already in full swing. Meanwhile, the Four Books that contained the teachings of Confucius, Mencius, and their disciples, though preoccupied with moral and political issues, also expressed a system of thought about the world, humanity, and nature that was incompatible with the conceptual framework of early modern Catholicism. Mencius's statement about cultivating the floodlike qi, for example, contains an unmistakably holistic conception of humans which contradicted the Catholic view of soul and body. When it comes to these basic Confucian teachings, Ricci emphasized that his method was not to directly criticize them but rather to overcome the conflicts through "interpretation." That Ricci heavily relied on interpretive strategies to cope with the problems inherent in Confucian classics is also testified to by a similar remark in his journals, where he says, "*I make every effort to turn our way the ideas of the leader of the sect of* the literati, Confucius, by interpreting in our favor things which he left ambiguous in his writings." [37]

However, appearing before his Chinese audience, Ricci presented his "interpretation" in an entirely different light. To them, he introduced himself as a scholar sincerely endeavoring to uncover the truths contained in the classics and portrayed the classics as timeless utterances of the ancient sage, which, having been handed down in written form, constituted a source of wisdom to be penetrated and appropriated by all people at all time:

> At a distance of a hundred paces, voices do not carry, but when [thoughts] are confided to writing for communication, then two men, although they live more than ten thousand miles apart, may converse, exchanging questions and answers, as if they were sitting face to face. I cannot know what kind of men there will be a hundred generations hence, who are not yet born, but because of the existence of this writing I can let those of ten thousand generations later penetrate into my mind, just as if they were of my own generation, and moreover, although the former masters of a hundred generations ago have already vanished, yet we, of these later days, because of the writings they left, still may hear their authoritative words, look up to their admirable behavior, and know about the (reasons of) order and disorder of those times, exactly as if we were living in that age." [38]

Indeed, to disqualify Zhu Xi's and other neo-Confucians' claim to authentic transmission of the Confucian Way and interject a Christian reading of the classics as the orthodox teaching, Ricci and his colleagues must first establish their right to interpret the classics as a group of foreigners. What Ricci says here is simply that "in the matter of comprehending classics all human beings are equal." He was confident that he and his colleagues had impressed the Chinese with their superior knowledge, intellectual capacity, and precision of reasoning;[39] therefore, the accentuation of reason in this context would, he hoped, allow their interpretation of the Confucian classics to supersede all that the neo-Confucian philosophers had offered.

As seen above, the theories of qi developed by the neo-Confucian philosophers had ample textual support in the classical texts as well, and thus to dismiss them is not a simple matter of introducing a new way of reading the text, but of engaging a subtle play with texts and contexts and with interpretations and ground rules for interpretation. The first Jesuit who systematically tackled this problem was Ricci himself in his major Chinese work, Tianzhu shi yi (The True Meaning of the Lord of Heaven, 1603).[40] The book was constructed in the form of eight consecutive dialogues between the Western scholar and his Chinese interlocutor. The goal of this work, as Ricci revealed to his superiors in Rome, was to demonstrate the basic truths of Christianity concerning the existence and property of God, the immortality of the soul, Heaven and Hell, and reward and punishment, and at the same time to destroy, *"at the very roots, with irrefragable arguments, the opinions of the Chinese which contradict those truths."* [41] The discussion on *qi* appears in chapter 4, "Exposing Various Errors Concerning Spiritual Beings and the Soul of Man, and Explaining Why the Phenomena of the World Cannot be Described as Forming an Organic Unity." In the Latin summary that Ricci sent to Rome accompanying the autographed copy of the first edition of this book, the entry on this discussion is entitled, "Confutatur opinio eorum, qui dicunt animam hominis esse aerem [Refutation of their opinion that the human soul is air]." This indicates that the extensive exposure to the Chinese understanding of *qi* he had had up till then did not change his initial understanding that *qi* is air. Rather, assuming that *qi*, to which the Chinese attributed so many mysterious qualities, could not have been any reality unknown to the Europeans but air, one of the four elements constituting the sublunar world, he considered his duty as primarily one of enlightening his readers with a bit of Aristotelian natural philosophy. In fact, Ricci already had introduced this elemental *qi* (air) in the previous chapter, where he gave a typical Aristotelian argument of why the soul, unlike the body, is immortal:

> *If you, Sir, wish to know why man's soul is not destroyed, you must first understand the things of this world.* For everything injured and destroyed there must be a reason. . . . Everything in the world comes into existence through the combination of the four elements: fire, air (qi), water, and earth. It is the nature of fire to be dry and hot, so that it is in conflict with water which is by nature cold and wet. Air (qi) is by nature moist and hot and is therefore the exact opposite of earth which is naturally dry and cold. Any two of these mutually antagonistic elements are bound to harm each other; and if they are combined in one thing, it is impossible for them to remain in harmony over a long period of time. . . . Thus, anything composed of the four elements is bound to be destroyed. The intelligent soul, however, is spirit and has no connection with the four elements. There is no reason, therefore, for it to be destroyed.[42]

In this argument, Ricci defined *qi* in Aristotelian terms, thereby placing it in the category of matter in diametrical opposition to spirit. Following up this discussion in the fourth chapter, Ricci takes issue with the neo-Confucian doctrine that all categories of existence ultimately are rooted in and manifestations of qi, maintaining that neither spiritual beings nor human soul are reducible to qi. It must be noted that because Confucius denounced inquiries into spirits and ghosts as futile and irrelevant,[43] there had been a strong tendency among the later Confucian scholars to shun such topics. On the other hand, the prominent presence of *guishen* (ghosts and spirits) in the classical texts, the Confucian rituals to venerate ancestral spirits, and the belief in spirits and ghosts being kept alive in popular religious practices altogether created a problematic that demanded a scholarly treatment. In their efforts to naturalize the supernatural, the neo-Confucian philosophers developed two theories to account for spiritual beings.[44] The first theory identifies the category of spiritual beings that were supposed to be wielding powers over mountains, rivers, and other natural phenomena as merely traces and manifestations of the spontaneous activities of the two modes of qi (*yin* and *yang*).[45] According to this theory, spirits are called *shen* on account of the liveliness of the expansion and going (*shen*[1]) of *yang*, and ghosts are called *gui* on account of the liveliness of the contraction and coming (*gui*[1]) of *yin*. Most pronounced in Zhang Zai's writings but also adopted by Cheng Yi, Zhu Xi, and other neo-Confucian thinkers, this interpretation echoed a passage in the *Book of Changes*: "The refined qi [integrates] to become things; [as it disintegrates], the wandering away of its spirit becomes change. From this we know the characteristics and conditions of spirits and ghosts."[46]

The other theory addresses the questions of whether ancestral spirits exist and whether, in general, the human soul continues to exist after death. Based on the medical view that the soul is the function of the refined qi (or *yang* qi), this theory asserts that after death the soul ceases to exist as the *yang* qi departs the body and disperses. Yet, this theory allows adequate room to accommodate observations and stories about appearances of ghosts. Zhu Xi, for one, retained Zichan's idea in the *Zuo zhuan* that when a person dies before his time, his soul may continue to hang about and do evil things, but Zhu Xi emphasized that even in such cases the soul eventually disperses.[47] As to the meaning of sacrifices, he speculated that, although the qi of the ancestors had long dispersed, its root was fastened to the qi of the living descendants; therefore, when a descendant performs sacrifices with sincerity, the concentration of his qi will help the ancestors' qi to reconvene, so that the qi of the departed and that of the living can respond to each other. "This is like the folds of waves (in the river): the water of the anterior and posterior waves is not the same water, and the posterior and anterior waves are not the same waves, but they belong to the same fold of waves and follow the same movement."[48] Thus, both theories reduce the presumably numinous qualities of the spiritual beings to the inherent properties and mechanisms of qi.

In his refutation, Ricci declares that nowadays "false doctrines are rampant everywhere defrauding and deceiving the people, and it is difficult to attack and destroy them in such a way as to eradicate them entirely. What must the zhengru [upright scholars] do? They must employ reason to condemn these heresies and to illuminate the true nature of spiritual beings."[49] Citing the episode about the appearance of Boyou's ghost in the Zuo zhuan (Zuo's commentary on the Spring and Autumn Annals), he accuses the suru (mediocre scholars) of the day, who denounced the continued presence of the soul, of having betrayed the true teachings of the ancients:

> Since the Zuo zhuan said that Boyou appeared as a ghost following his death, it is clear that in ancient times, during the Spring and Autumn period, people believed that the human soul was not dispersed and destroyed. Does not the mediocre scholar who regards diminishing the spiritual beings as his proper duty stand condemned by the Spring and Autumn Annals? When a person dies, it is not the soul, but the physical nature, the body, that dies. While a person is alive, his soul is like a fettered prisoner; after he dies it is like someone who leaves the darkness of prison and is freed from his manacles. He will understand the principles of things even more clearly. One should not think it strange that it should be superior to that of any ordinary person in the world. The superior man understands this truth and therefore does not look on death as an evil or as something to be feared; rather, he leaves this world, joyfully saying that he is returning to his hometown.[50]

As discussed in the first section, the episode about Boyou in the Zuo zhuan indeed reflected a popular belief in the existence of ghosts during the Spring and Autumn era (722–481 B.C.E.). However, the main thrust of the episode was Zichan's attempt to transcend that belief by offering a naturalistic explanation of such occurrences, and his account of why Boyou's soul did not scatter immediately after his death (as an exceptional case) was perhaps the earliest expression of a psychophysical conception of soul in Chinese history, one that was a most frequently quoted classical source on this subject by later medical authors and philosophers alike. It is interesting to note that, despite his general elitist bent, Ricci elected to invoke the popular religious belief, and not Zichan's sophisticated conceptualization, as the sagely way of the Confucian classics, the Spring and Autumn Annals. In place of Zichan's theory that the soul is immanent in the body and maturates through the nourishment of the body, Ricci offers to elucidate the sagely way by ushering in the Platonic prison metaphor, describing the body in terms of prison and shackles, and the soul a lone prisoner constantly yearning for freedom and intellectual perfection in the world beyond. It is only after such an elucidation that he turns to examine Zichan's conceptual scheme and its neo-Confucian developments. He lets the Chinese interlocutor summarize various theories that relate the spiritual beings and human soul to qi:

> The Chinese scholar: Those who assert that the soul is scattered and extinguished after death simply regard the soul as qi. The dispersal of qi can be either fast or slow. If a person dies before his time his qi continues to hold together and does not disperse immediately. Only after a long period of time has passed is it gradually dissolved. Men like Boyou of [the State of Zheng] are good examples of this. Further, the two kinds of qi, yin and yang, are the substance of all things and are everywhere present. There is not a thing in the world which is not yin and yang, and there is therefore not a thing which is not spiritual.[51]

Both opinions outlined here refer to classical sources, the first to Zichan's explanation of Boyou's instance, and the second to a statement in *Zhongyong* (Doctrine of the mean), which says, "[The spirits and ghosts] form the substance of all things and nothing can be without them."[52] In his counterargument, Ricci first defines the problem as one concerning the logic and principle of interpreting the classics above all else: "People who equate qi with spiritual beings and the human soul are confusing the true names by which categories of things are known. Those who seek to establish their teachings to guide others must provide an appropriate name for each category of things. In ancient classical texts different names are used for 'qi' and 'spiritual beings'; therefore, their meaning must be regarded as different. There are people who offer sacrifices to ghosts and spirits, but I have never heard of anyone offering sacrifices to qi. How come people today can mix up these two different names?"[53]

Here, Ricci proceeds from the premise that the classical texts, through which the ancient sages established their teachings for all generations to come, must have used appropriate names to distinguish different realities; therefore, as interpreters of the texts, we must assume that the realities designated by qi and *guishen* are different. His emphasis on precision of terms and one-to-one correspondence between name and reality certainly reflects the analytical bent that he inherited from the Aristotelian-Scholastic conceptual framework. In fact,

Ricci soon moves on to refute the neo-Confucian view that all categories of being are manifestations of *qi* and that they differ from one another only on account of the qualities (such as purity or turbidity) of the particular kind of *qi* they are endowed with, in the context of which Ricci produced a Chinese version of Porphyry's Tree of Predicables to show how, according to Western philosophy, the realm of being is dichotomized into the spiritual and material, and how the spiritual and material are further divided into their respective subcategories, and so on.

However, to believe that names and things should be related with such accuracy is one thing; to assert that the Confucian ancients also had entertained such a standard in their own way of thinking and writing is quite another. It is doubtful that Ricci really thought that they had. In his various personal writings, Ricci characterized Chinese thought, from ancient to modern, as fundamentally lacking clarity and logic. In a letter to Passionei of 9 September 1597, he says, "The Chinese have no knowledge of physics, metaphysics, and dialectic. . . . Just as Plato and Aristotle's philosophy was once in great demand in Italy, I am also well esteemed in China." [54] He entered a more systematic criticism in his journals: "The only one of the higher philosophical sciences with which the Chinese have become acquainted is that of moral philosophy, and in this they seem to have obscured matters by the introduction of errors rather than enlightened them. They have no conception of the rules of logic, and consequently, treat the precepts of the science of ethics without any regard to the intrinsic co-ordination of the various divisions of this subject. The science of ethics with them is a series of confused maxims and deductions at which they have arrived under the guidance of the light of reason." [55]

Such an impression about the "logical deficiency" in Chinese intellectual tradition can hardly support the premise of his argument that the Confucian ancients had distinguished names and realities with the same kind of comprehensiveness and precision that he projected on them. Furthermore, this premise also assumes that all categories of things and their respective names had been fully laid out in the Confucian classics, which contradicts another statement regarding the possible corruptions and incompleteness of the classics that he made in chapter 6 in his demonstration of the existence of Heaven and Hell. To compare the two very different images of the classics Ricci portrayed to his readers, we may quote that argument in full:

The Chinese scholar: Confucians regard the sages as authoritative examples [for the rest of mankind], and the sages used the classical texts and their authoritative commentaries as media of instruction; but in all our classical texts and their authoritative commentaries there is not a single mention of Heaven and Hell. Are you trying to say that the sages were ignorant of this teaching? Why is it concealed and not mentioned?

The Western scholar: The teachings handed down from the sages were geared to what people were capable of accepting; thus, there are many teachings which, though handed down for generations, are incomplete. Then there are teachings which were given directly to the students and which were not recorded in books or, if recorded, were subsequently lost. There is also the possibility that later, perverse historians removed parts of these records because they did not believe in their historical veracity. Moreover, written records are frequently subject to alteration, and one cannot say that because there is no written record certain things did not happen. Confucians today constantly misinterpret the writings of antiquity; and because they put greater emphasis on words than on content, therefore, although the essay flourishes, [the quality of] its content has declined. . . .[56]

If the classics could be treated with such a degree of flexibility to allow his introduction of "Heaven and Hell," his Chinese opponent, who is determined to defend the neo-Confucian doctrine that spiritual beings are nothing but qi, could easily avail himself of the same flexibility to claim We cannot conclude that the ancients did not identify spiritual beings as qi simply because such identification cannot be found in the classical texts, for, in the process of transmission, anything could have happened to their texts.

A more serious flaw in Ricci's argument, however, lies in the fact that his Chinese opponent did not have to make use of such an explanatory device at all. There are abundant classical sources that explicitly identified the human soul and spiritual beings as qi. Ricci dealt with only one of the more ambivalent remarks in *Zhongyong* attributed to Confucius, that "[the spirits and ghosts] form the substance of all things and nothing can be without them." According to the neo-Confucian reading, because *yin* and *yang* form the substance of all things, to say that spirits and ghosts constitute the substance of all things implies that they are *yin* and *yang*. Ricci retorts that what Confucius meant is simply that the virtues of the spiritual beings greatly affect things. Because things are devoid of intelligence, the Lord of Heaven commands the spiritual beings to guide them so that they can find their appropriate places in nature. "Therefore," he continues, "to say that spiritual beings form the substance of all things is just the same as to say that the sage ruler governs the country with his intelligence."[57] Ricci avoided other classical sources that were also frequently quoted by Zhu Xi and others, as they allowed him little room for interpretative manipulation.

For example, in the *Book of Rites*, the same text from which Ricci cited many passages to support his arguments in previous chapters,[58] we find:

> Confucius says: "Qi is the spirit in abundance, and the physical nature is the ghost in abundance. To take hold of both spirit and ghost is the highest goal of all teaching."
>
> The qi of the spirit ascends to heaven, while the physical form and its nature return to the earth.[59]

Obviously, for Ricci, what to select and deselect from the classical sources was no small matter, for he told his readers right after the aforementioned passage regarding the existence of Heaven and Hell that "according to the method of disputation in Western learned academies, *an orthodox book can prove the existence of a fact, but it cannot prove the nonexistence of a fact.*"[60] Simply turning this rule around, we have: The absence of a fact in classical writings cannot prove that a fact does not exist; however, the presence of it in classical writings can prove that it does exist.

The authority of classics is not all that Ricci depended on for compounding his refutations, after all. For, already in the opening statement of this book, Ricci introduced universal reason as the ultimate authority:

> That which is brought to light by the intellect cannot forcibly be made to comply with that which is untrue. Everything which reason shows to be true I must acknowledge as true, and everything which reason shows to be false I must acknowledge as false. Reason stands in relation to a man as the sun to the world, shedding its light everywhere. To abandon principles affirmed by the intellect and to comply with the opinions of others is like shutting out the light of the sun and searching for an object with a lantern.[61]

From this perspective, Ricci only needs to show that, according to reason, spiritual beings and the human soul cannot possibly be qi, which he does in the following:

> If qi is soul and the principle of life, then how can a living being die? When it does so, there is still abundant qi inside and outside of it. At what juncture is it deprived of qi? Why are we bothered by the possibility that it may die because it runs out of qi? Evidently qi is not the principle of life. In an ancient work, it is said: "A mistake of a hair's breadth will lead to an error of a thousand li." If one does not know that qi is one of the four elements and equates it with spirits, ghosts, and the human soul, it is still understand-

able. Having known this, one will have no difficulty explaining its essence and functions.[62]

Finally, Ricci is getting to the bottom of things: All such erroneous views about qi are rooted in ignorance. Once we know what qi is, we will know exactly what it can and cannot be:

> As a matter of fact, qi (air), along with the other three elements, water, fire, and earth, is what constitutes the bodily forms of all things, whereas the soul is the internal constituent of a human being and the master of the body. It is the agent that makes qi circulate throughout the body through respiration. Since human beings and birds and beasts all live within the space that is filled with qi, they can utilize qi to regulate the heat generated in their hearts through constantly drawing in fresh qi and breathing out warm qi. Since fish stay in water, and water is by nature very cold, capable of cooling down their inner heat from the outside, therefore, most of them do not use breathing to aid this process.[63]

Here, Ricci reminds his readers that qi is one of the four elements that make up the material world and has nothing to do with human spirit. He did not go into some of the more sophisticated Western physiological theories about the function of vital breath, but only touched on the mechanical aspect of respiration based on Aristotle's theory, according to which the role of qi in sustaining life is trivial indeed; for fish that can cool themselves with water, it is not even necessary.

Circumscribing Qi

In the example of Ricci's *Tianzhu shi yi* we have seen an interesting irony, one that persisted throughout the Jesuit campaign against neo-Confucianism: whereas neo-Confucian philosophy demystified the world by reducing all modes of existence, divine or human, spiritual or material, mental or physical, to the attributes and mechanisms of qi, the Jesuits sought to introduce the world of the numinous and supernatural—a personal god, the angels, and the separated souls—by remolding the Chinese psychophysical notion of qi into that of lifeless matter. All the major Jesuit apologetics against neo-Confucianism were in one way or another directed toward the deep-rooted Chinese "misconception" of qi: that qi, in its purity, can generate intelligence and, through its internal dynamism of yin and yang, can transform and produce all things; and all of their refutation fell back on some sort of "scientific account" of qi and its properties.[64] Meanwhile, a new culture of *qi*—the elemental and atmospheric air in Aristotelian natural philosophy and the vital breath or *spiritus* in late Renaissance Galenic physiology—was systematically introduced by the Jesuits to meet such a demand.

It must be noted that the transmission of Western learning, particularly in the areas of natural philosophy and science, constituted a phenomenal component of the Jesuit mission in China.[65] As Father Nicolas Standaert observed, this emphasis on learning and science was consistent with the Jesuit order's inherent drive to seek and find God in all things; furthermore, from the perspective of the dynamics of cross-cultural encounter, the Jesuits' concerted efforts to transmit European science also indicated an internal movement in China that encouraged and welcomed such efforts. Willard J. Peterson also pointed out that the Jesuit translations during the late Ming (i.e., up to 1644) formed a coherent representation of the Scholastic natural philosophy that was still being taught in contemporary universities in Europe but was about to be replaced; therefore, although "the Jesuits were not misrepresenting the prevailing tenor of contemporary European ideas, neither were they conveying to their Chinese readers the crucial elements of either substantive ideas or the method of the modern science which was emerging with such effect in Europe."[66] Bearing these general observations in mind, our primary interest here is to show that the site of translation was also the frontier of the Jesuit battle against Chinese thought and culture and that the apologetic agenda arising from the Jesuit understanding of the cultural foundations of Chinese religions informed their choice of what was to be given priority in the translation process and how to present it and relate it to its Chinese counterparts.

QI AS AIR

Back in 1595, Ricci wrote a treatise expounding the theory of four elements, entitled *Sixing lunlue* (Brief treatise on the four elements). Concerning the context and motive of this undertaking, Nicolas Trigault (1577–1628), who edited and elaborated Ricci's Italian journals into the Latin work, *De Christiana Expeditione apud Sinas as societate Iesu susceptua* (Rome, 1615), commented:

> With no foundation for their belief than antiquity, Chinese scholars taught that there were five different elements. None of them doubted this or ever thought of questioning it. These elements were: metal, wood, fire, water, and earth, and what is stranger still, they taught that these elements were derived from one another. They knew nothing about the air, as such, because they could not see it. To them, the space occupied by air was merely a

void. . . . Father Matthew paid little or no attention to their devotion to the authority of antiquity. He told them that there were four elements, no more nor less, possessed of contradictory qualities, and he taught them where each element was found. . . . Father Matthew wrote a commentary on this subject in Chinese, in which he did away with their five elements, as such, and established the four, to which he assigned locations, and of which he showed illustrations.[67]

For one reason or another, this treatise was not circulated in print.[68] In 1633, Alphonso Vagnoni published a two-volume work on this subject, *Kongji gezhi* (Investigation into the material compositions of the [sublunary] space), which he adapted from the commentated edition of Aristotle's *Meteorologica* issued by the Jesuit College of Arts at the University of Coimbra, Portugal (Lisbon, 1593; Lyon, 1594).[69]

The idea that all things in the universe are composed of four basic and mutually irreducible substances, or "roots," can be traced to Empedocles of Acragas (ca. 495–435? B.C.E.).[70] The pre-Socratic philosophers after him generally concurred that these four substances were the immediate constituents of all sensible things in the world and that they ultimately originated in primordial matter. It was Plato who first called these substances "elements." Meanwhile, a weightless, undefinable substance, ether, was added to the list as the fifth element, also known as the *quintessence* (the fifth essence). Aristotle synthesized these ideas into a systematic account of movement and change encompassing the heavens and the sublunar world. According to him, the universe is an enclosed, compact space with the earth at the center, surrounded by eight crystalline spheres, one stacked on top of the other, to which are attached the moon, the sun, the five planets, and the fixed stars, respectively.[71] He made a rigid distinction between the heavenly region and the sublunar world. The former is the perfect world of celestial bodies which, made of ether, are not susceptible to change and stay in eternal, circular motion. The sublunar world is composed of the four elements. They not only exist in the pure form of elemental spheres, filling the space below the moon in descending order from fire, air, water, to earth, but also mix in varying proportions to constitute all objects in the sublunar region, animate and inanimate alike. These four elements are distinguished from one another only by the combinations of primary qualities (hot or cold) and secondary qualities (dry or wet); thus earth is cold and dry, water cold and wet, air hot and wet, and fire hot and dry. Though basic constituents of things, the elements differ from the undifferentiated material substratum in that they are not indestructible; while they interact with each other, their contradictory qualities influence and corrupt each other, and, as a result, they collapse and transform into something else. Thus the sublunar world is the world of constant change and transformation. Aristotle treated the heavenly region in his *On the Heavens*, the mixed bodies on the earth in his *Physics* and biological treatises, and the elemental spheres, together with all atmospheric phenomena such as thunder, lightning, clouds, rain, wind, snow, hail, and comets, in his *Meteorology*, which is the source of Vagnoni's *Kongji gezhi*.

Vagnoni introduced the basics of Aristotelian theory on the four elements and the meteorological phenomena as the "orthodox teachings concerning nature and principle [*xingli zhenglun*]." [72] In addition to presenting the typical Aristotelian arguments concerning the total number and qualities of the elements, the shapes and thickness of each elemental sphere and their associated phenomena, he created two sections to address the Chinese views on the subject. The first is an examination of the Chinese theory of five agents (*xing*). I might note here that Vagnoni did not simply adopt the Chinese term *xing*, but coined a new term, *yuanxing* (primary *xing*), to render the Western concept of element. This indicates that from the beginning he was aware of the differences between the Aristotelian and the traditional Chinese ways of conceptualizing the constitution of the world. The tenor of the Aristotelian system is to locate the stable properties of things on the level of their constituents; thus, the elements are conceived as primary and constant substances with distinct qualities. Once these qualities are altered, the elements cease to be and the thing so composed undergoes change. The Chinese theory of five agents, on the other hand, is rooted in the tradition of the *Book of Changes*, which envisions the world as an ongoing process of transformation and interchange. The term *xing*, literally meaning "to act" and "to do" (as a verb) or "action" and "behavior" (as a noun), is used to designate and differentiate the basic phases, modes, and forces or agents of this process of transformation and interaction. First systematized by Zou Yan (between 350 and 270 B.C.E.), the theory of five agents also described them as possessing certain distinctive properties: water is "soaking, dripping, and descending"; fire, "heating, burning, and ascending"; wood, "accepting form by submitting to cutting and carving instruments"; metal, "accepting form by molding when in the liquid state, and the capacity of changing this form by re-melting and re-molding"; and earth, "producing edible vegetation." [73] However, unlike the elemental qualities defined by Aristotle, the properties of the five agents would only manifest at the juncture when these agents were in action or being acted upon and undergoing change. By the Han Dynasty (206 B.C.E.–220 C.E.), when the theory of five agents reached its finalized form, the five were related to one another in cosmogonic, mutual productive, and mutual conquest orders, which served as the basic models of interaction and cyclical movement for every conceivable category of things in nature, space, time, seasonal change, human body, and social affairs, the same way Aristotelian theory of four elements constituted the foundation of every area of premodern Western natural philosophy.[74]

The theories of four elements and five agents thus are mutually complementary in terms of perspectives, conflicting in overlapping areas, and competitive in view of their comparable roles in premodern European and Chinese learned traditions. The heading Vagnoni gave to this section, "Whether metal and wood are elements [yuanxing] or not?," certainly allows the possibility of drawing comparisons between these two systems without pushing the Chinese perspective out of the picture.[75] All he needed to do was determine whether or not metal and wood are elements according to his definition. However, his goal was clearly something else. He lets the Chinese interlocutor open the section by asking "In our country we also have a theory of five xing [agents] since antiquity. In addition to earth, water, and fire, we have metal and wood, making a total number of five. Is this similar to the theory you are explaining here?" In a manner reminiscent of Ricci, he first answers: "The theory of five agents held by the ancients is very different from that of today." He then explains that for anything to be qualified as an element, it must be an indispensable constituent of all things and should be pure and not containing mixtures of other elements. But this is not the case with metal and wood, for we see that a great many things do not contain metal and wood, such as human beings, worms, birds, and beasts; on the other hand, metal and wood in fact contain mixtures of water, fire, and earth. Like Ricci, he did not challenge the Chinese ancients but sought to detach them from the later tradition of the theory of five agents: "In the 'Councils of the Great Yu' [in the Book of History], water, fire, metal, wood, and earth are listed together with grain as the six treasuries of nature [liufu] only on behalf of their importance to human livelihood. This is also what is meant by [the five agents] in 'The Great Plan' [in the Book of History]. They did not say that these things are elements and sources of all things. It is only the later scholars [houru] who started to talk about the productive cycle of water → wood → fire → earth → metal."[76]

"This is not at all convincing," he continues. He poses a series of questions concerning this productive order: First of all, if wood contains fire and earth, why is it said that it is produced by water alone? Second, before fire and water is produced, how can wood grow all by itself, and, before earth is produced, where should wood be planted? Besides, if wood produces fire, then wood must be very hot. How can water, being cold by nature, produce wood, which is hot?

Metal is produced by earth; then how does it differ from wood? If they differ in that metal is born under the earth and wood grows above the earth, then should not all of them be produced by earth?[77] We can see from these questions that Vagnoni was constantly applying the Aristotelian definitions of the four elements to analyzing the relationships among the five agents. What began as a discussion of whether metal and wood are elements has turned into a systematic questioning of whether there are such things as the five agents at all. At the end of the section, he concludes: "The orders among these five things are so entangled and problematic that evidently the theory of five agents does not conform to principle and reason. Therefore, it is more appropriate to accept the four elements as we described above."[78]

The second of these added topics — "whether qi (air) is an element or not" — addresses what the Jesuits perceived as the greatest flaw in the Chinese world picture, namely, the idea of a vacuous space with stars moving freely inside it and the ignorance of qi (air) as an element that fills up the seemingly empty space surrounding the earth. Vagnoni's opening remarks immediately reveal this preoccupation: "In ancient times people may doubt the existence of qi simply because it is without color and cannot be detected through the five senses. This is a great mistake!" He produces six proofs to show that qi (air) exists: "First, if qi does not exist, then the space will be vacuous, how can earth rest in the center, how can all things grow, how can the sun, the moon, and the stars transmit their energy to nourish things on earth? All things need to be in contact with each other so that they can support and sustain each other. Vacuity is the greatest horror! Second, without anything to float on, the birds cannot fly, for in order to fly their wings must ride on qi, just as our hand has to be placed on top of water to keep afloat . . ." So he goes on.[79]

"Having proved that qi exists, we must now describe its form and qualities, so that people will not confuse it with other things."[80] Thus Vagnoni begins the following section, "On the Thickness of Atmosphere, Its Shape and Movements." He delineates the physical features of atmospheric qi as follows: The elemental sphere occupied by qi is about 250 li thick. It is divided into three strata: the upper stratum is close to fire, affected by the heat of fire, and therefore hot; the lower stratum is warm, as it is close to water and earth, both of which are warm due to constant exposure to sunlight; the middle stratum is far from both ends and so is very cold. The quality of qi differs from one stratum to another. Like the neo-Confucians, Vagnoni also characterizes the qualities of qi as pure (qing) or turbid (zhuo), albeit with a very different meaning. According to the neo-Confucian idea of qibing (endowment of qi), human beings are endowed with the purest qi and therefore are most intelligent among all living things. However, Vagnoni writes: "In the upper stratum, where wind and rain can not reach, the *qi* is purest (*zui qing*) and uninhabitable for human beings and other living things."[81] Besides the density or rarity of air, Vagnoni also uses "pure" and "turbid" to describe the inherent qualities of air—cleanness or putrefaction—and stresses that they do have a strong influence on human beings and animals:

> The purity or turbidity of *qi* is either due to the rays from the stars above or the influences of earth and water below. On the one hand, the rays from the stars carrying their energies to nurture things on earth necessarily mingle and clash among themselves while passing through the atmosphere, and since the substance of *qi* is soft and malleable, its original nature may be corrupted as a result. Light and afloat, the corrupted *qi* can then easily enter the body of humans and animals. On the other hand, soil and water also constantly emanate dry and moist *qi*, which carries their original qualities while joining the atmosphere. Therefore, we can infer that human beings' and animals' intelligence or stupidity, fair or ugly appearance, and their other physical traits have much to do with the regional *qi* which they breathe in.[82]

Vagnoni's account of how the physical qualities of air influence the qualities of human beings and animals offers simultaneously an alternative and a corrective to the Chinese idea of *qibing* by delimiting the influence of *qi* to human beings' and animals' postnatal growth through the channel of respiration alone. In his subsequent discussion on winds, he further elaborates the physical nature of such an influence, suggesting that wind can carry the air qualities of a certain locale and spread them to the people and living things along its way.[83]

Vagnoni's exposition of *qi*, grounded in the broader framework of the Aristotelian cosmic model, thus ushers in an entirely new, physicalist language of *qi*: *qi* as air, in which the only meaningful way to talk about *qi* is to describe its observable qualities such as warmth or coolness, wetness or dryness, density or rarity, and cleanness or putrefaction, as well as its physical functions and impact. After the definitive decline of Aristotelian theory of the four elements in Europe, the French Jesuits retained the interpretation of *qi* as air, though they upgraded it by incorporating, for example, Pascal's discovery of air pressure in 1648. Thus, in his *Xingli zhenquan* (Elucidating the true meaning of nature and principle, 1750), Alexandre de la Charme (1695–1767) suggests that one simple experiment will suffice to demonstrate that the so-called *yang qi* (refined, heavenly *qi*) has no spiritual qualities; like all other tangible objects, it is also corporeal and possesses a measurable weight: "If you infuse some quicksilver into a glass bottle and carry it to the top of a mountain, since quicksilver is heavier than the qi surrounding it, you will observe that the quicksilver sinks inside the bottle. When you bring it down to the foot of the mountain, since the qi surrounding the bottle is denser and heavier, you will observe that the quicksilver lifts up inside the bottle. This is a sure proof that qi is lighter at the top of the mountain and heavier at the foot of it." [84]

QI AS PNEUMA OR SPIRITUS

At the same time the Jesuit cosmological works brought qi from the position of the originator and transformer of the world down to that of an element filling up the sphere of about 250 li in height, their writings on the human being also reversed its role of the generator of the human spirit to that of a mere servant and instrument of the soul. During the late Ming period, the Jesuit works in this area introduced the basic late Renaissance orthodox doctrines in human psychology, physiology, and anatomy which synthesized Aristotelian and Galenic systems. Of these three subjects, human anatomy was least represented by the Jesuits. The only complete work on this subject was *Taixi renshen shuogai* (Summary of Western theories concerning the human body) by Johann Terrenz. Composed in 1625, this little treatise was not published until 1643, on the initiative of a Chinese doctor, Bi Gongchen, who acquired the manuscript from Johann Adam Schall von Bell and embellished the Chinese text before sending it to the printer.[85] According to Bi's preface, he was eager to read some Western accounts on the human body and asked Schall whether he knew of any such translations. Schall thus produced this manuscript, which he had kept for a long time after his friend Terrenz passed away, and told him that human anatomy "is one of the most active areas of research in Europe. There are many elaborate theories on this subject, engaging the greatest number of all publications [concerning the study of man]. However, we have been too busy translating works on our religion to cover this subject." [86]

Despite their tight schedule, the Jesuits managed to render two different versions of Aristotle's psychological treatise *De anima: Lingyan lishao* (Some cursory remarks on the soul, 1624) by Francesco Sambiasi (Bi Fangji), based on the *Conimbricenses* edition of 1617, Cologne, and *Xingxue cushu* (A brief outline on the study of human nature, 1623) by Giulio Aleni (Ai Rulue), based on the *Conimbricenses* edition of 1598, Coimbra.[87] The latter also contained an adaptation of the *Conimbricenses* on Aristotle's *Parva naturalia* (Short natural treatises), which, together with the related chapters in Schall's *Zhuzhi qunzheng* (A host of evidence that God rules),[88] formed a relatively detailed representation of the major concepts and theories of Aristotelian-Galenic physiology. Both groups of texts addressed the role of qi in the human body and its relationship to the soul. In his exposition of Aristotelian psychology, Aleni made significant modifications to his Latin text and added several sections to address neo-Confucian views of qi. He added a physiological reading of qi—qi as spiritus (jingqi)—to the purely physical one insisted on by Ricci and Vagnoni (qi as air), but he was trying to drive home the same point, namely, that however one understands qi, it has to be matter of one form or another, therefore it cannot possibly be the substance of the soul, which is purely spiritual.[89] It is in the physiological writings that we find the full context of this new interpretation.

The notion of spiritus (Latin) or pneuma (Greek) in premodern Western physiology originated in an understanding of air according to the Hippocratic School (fl. fifth–fourth centuries B.C.E.) that bears striking resemblance to the Chinese view of qi. For example, the author of the Hippocratic treatise "On Sacred Disease," in an attempt to drive superstition out of the medical profession, argues that all human mental and physical abilities, processes, and conditions can be explained in terms of natural causality. According to him, what seems to be most mysterious about human beings, their mental phenomena, are not mysterious at all: they are the functioning of the brain, and the brain is the interpreter of the intelligence inherent in air.[90]

Five hundred years later, this notion of air as possessing psychic qualities was still clearly present in the works of Galen (ca. 130–ca. 200 C.E.), who achieved the first medical synthesis of previous theories about the four elements, four qualities, and four humors. Galen subscribed to the Platonic tripartite model of the soul, distinguishing three separate faculties, each operating from their respective centers: the natural faculty, responsible for nutrition and growth, is located in the liver; the vital faculty, the principle of life, is located in the heart; and the psychic faculty, which controls mental activities and body movement, is located in the brain. However, he materialized the Platonic model of the soul by assigning to it an elaborate system of pneuma, taking hints from usages of the term by Aristotle and some of his disciples.[91] He conceived of two kinds of pneuma, vital and psychic—to which his followers added a third, natural or physical pneuma—to explain the functions of the vital, psychic, and natural faculties of the soul respectively, and often made no distinctions between them and the soul.[92] It is no wonder, therefore, that one of the major themes in the Christianization of Galen in the medieval Latin West was to purge Galen's materialist conception of soul and firmly establish pneuma (spiritus) as the physical instrument and agent of the immortal soul.

In rendering this reformed conception of spiritus, the Jesuits consistently adopted the term qi; thus they translated the natural or physical spiritus as *tixing zhi qi*, vital spiritus as *shengyang zhi qi*, and psychic spiritus as *dongjue zhi qi*. In his *Zhuzhi qunzheng*, Schall used the constitution of the human body as his fifth proof that there is a Divine Artificer who designed such a wonderful work.[93] He says, first of all, that the body has bones of all sizes, shapes, and solidity and over six hundred muscles of varying shapes and thickness, forming an optimal structure for all body functions. But then there should be innate heat for it to be alive, blood for it to be sustained, and qi for it to perform movements and sense perception. That is why when the Great Lord created man He prepared for him three principal organs to preside over the body. They are the heart, liver, and brain. All the other parts of the body follow their commands. By way of explaining the meaning of innate heat, blood, and qi, Schall introduced the three kinds of spiritus and their respective production processes.

At the first stage, food is cut and chewed in the mouth and turned to the stomach for digestion. The semidigested stuff is then filtered into fine and coarse portions. The former is stored in the cavity of the liver, where it is transformed into blood, and the latter is forwarded to spleen, gall bladder, and kidneys for the production of the other three humors (yellow and black biles and phlegm). The liver, by means of its refining power, produces fine essentials out of the blood, called *tixing zhi qi* (natural spiritus). "It is most tenuous, capable of penetrating all blockages in the blood vessels and entering the tiniest cavities," and is thus an ideal agent for conducting the blood through the veins to nourish the entire body.[94] At the second stage, part of the natural spiritus and blood ascends through a large vein to the heart, where it is fused with inhaled air and further refined into a dewlike substance. This is vital spirit (*shengyang zhi qi*), the primary function of which is to circulate around the body through the arteries to distribute the vital heat generated by the heart. At the final stage, a portion of vital spirit ascends through a large artery to the brain, where it is transformed into psychic spiritus (*dongjue zhi qi*) and, through the nerves, travels to the sense organs and limbs to enable sense perceptions and movement.[95] Aleni also presented these ideas in the third book of his *Xingxue cushu* and referred to the three kinds of spiritus altogether as *jingqi*. In the closing statements of the section, he reminded his readers once more that *jingqi* is a part of the body and servant of the soul: "All of the functions of the human body originate in the power of the soul; they make use of the five sense organs, other parts of the body, blood, and qi, just as human beings work with vessels and instruments."[96]

Conclusion

From today's perspective, the Jesuit discourse evolving around qi, the central concept of Chinese culture, stood at the beginning of a long and difficult path along which Westerners and Chinese struggled to comprehend, communicate with, and learn from each other. In a very concrete sense, the Westernization of the Chinese mind that resulted from the intensive maritime cultural contacts since the mid–nineteenth century expressed itself through the history of meaning-change of the term qi in modern Chinese philosophical and scientific literature. Meanwhile, Western missionaries and sinologists have slowly come to embrace a genuinely hermeneutical approach, and their efforts to recapture the cultural depth of qi through Western conceptual categories yielded a long sequence of approximate, tentative translations,[97] at the end of which came that meaningless yet infinitely meaningful transliteration qi (or Ch'i).[98] As we study the Jesuit discourse on qi against the background of these two later developments, we find in it an interesting combination of a drive to Westernize qi and an appearance of cultural hermeneutics.

From their apologetic writings to adaptations of Western learning, the Jesuit campaign to eradicate the culture of qi underlying neo-Confucian spirituality was conducted in the form of translating difference, either across time by introducing a new reading of ancient Confucian texts, or across cultural boundaries by transplanting an alien system of learned traditions. The epistemological prerogative that defines translation — the aspiration to approximate one set of ideas, concepts, and texts with another — was notably absent in their crosslingual endeavor. In Ricci's *Tianzhu shi yi*, the Confucian classics were, above all, symbolic resources of power and control rather than source texts to be fathomed and interpreted on their own terms. Similarly, in the Jesuits' uses of qi to render the Western concept of air and pneuma (spiritus), there were no conscious efforts to determine whether or not the chosen Chinese term qi, with all its native nuances and implications, was a good linguistic approximation. On the contrary, these translations exhibited a common pattern of proceeding, a movement from presuming such a linguistic identity toward fashioning a conceptual equivalence by trimming off qi its residual meaning in Chinese culture. If mistranslation and misrepresentation imply a violence to the source texts and the targeted readers, such a violence in this case was the intended goal from the very beginning. For all of us keenly interested in the "true meaning" of translation in the early Jesuit encounter with Confucian China, much can be learned from the spaces that we have thus far opened up between the Jesuit understanding of Chinese terms, texts, and traditions, and their conscious (mis)representation of that understanding in their Chinese writings.

Notes

The research for this paper was completed at Harvard under the supervision of my two dissertation advisors, Professors John E. Murdoch and Wei-ming Tu. I would like to thank both of them for their insights, criticisms, and thoughtful guidance. I also would like to acknowledge my gratitude to the Center for Chinese Studies at the University of California, Berkeley, for the postdoctoral fellowship that provided me with the time to write this article. All English translations cited are mine unless otherwise noted.

1   Matteo Ricci, *Fonti Ricciane*, n 429. For a biography of Matteo Ricci, see L. Carrington Goodrich and Chaoying Fang, eds., *Dictionary of Ming Biography, 1368–1644* (henceforth DMB), 1137–44.

2   Michele Ruggieri and Matteo Ricci, *Tianzhu shi yi*, chap. 4. For a brief biography of Michele Ruggieri, see DMB, 1148–49.

3   Matteo Ricci, letter of 4 November 1595, in *Opere Storiche*, 2:207; emphasis added. There are similar entries on this matter in Ricci's journals as well. In one of these entries, he hypothesized that the Chinese ancients had taken hints from the Buddhist theory of four elements (water, earth, fire, and wind), which, according to him, was itself a corrupt copy of the ancient Greek version, but the Chinese made it worse by "rather foolishly" altering its contents (Matteo Ricci, *China in the 16th Century*, 98–99, 327).

4   See, for example, Nicolo Longobardi's letter of 1598 in Samuel Purchas, *Hakluytus Posthumus*, 12:320.

5   For a few surveys of the conceptions of qi in traditional Chinese thought, see Benjamin Schwartz, *The World of Thought in Ancient China*, 179–84; Seoung Nah, "Language and the Ultimate Reality in Sung Neo-Confucianism"; and Cheng Yishan, *Zhongguo gudai yuanqi xueshuo.*

6   Ricci, *Fonti Ricciane*, n 176; *China in the 16th Century*, 93–97. See also *Opere Storiche*, 2:44, 48–49, 57, 69, 175, 185, 203, 216, 231.

7   Schwartz, 179.

8   Xu Shen, *Shuowen jiezi*, 14 and 148.

9   Li Qingming and Huang Yuren argue that the religious culture of cloud worship and cloud gazing prevalent in the Chu region was responsible for the emergence of the Daoist philosophy of Laozi and Zhuangzi that centered on the conceptions of qi, yin, yang, xu (vacuity), and wu (nonbeing). See Li and Huang, " 'Qi' yuan yitan."

10 Paul U. Unschuld suggests a third possibility, that the natural philosophical notion of qi perhaps originated with the medical doctors as a pathogenic concept, indicating the environmental influences (such as wind) on the human organism (*Medicine in China: A History of Ideas*, 67–73).

11 Cited with modification in Wing-tsit Chan, *Source Book in Chinese Philosophy*, 12.

12   The theory contends that human being is a composite of the essential or heavenly qi (*jingqi*) and the coarse, earthly qi (*xingqi*).

13   Yuan yang zhenren, *Huangdi neijing: Lingshu* (The Yellow Emperor's Inner Canon [of Medicine]: The spiritual pivot), chap. 30.

14   Meng Zi, *Mencius*, 7A/1.

15   Ibid., 2A/2; translation cited from Lau, 1:57.

16   Ibid.; translation adapted from Lau, 1:57; emphasis added. A similar reference to the "flood-like qi" is found in *Guanzi*, as A. C. Graham observed in his *Disputers of the Tao*, 103.

17   Meng, 7A/13; translation adapted from James Legge, trans., *Hanying sishu*, 517.

18   *Doctrine of the Mean*, chap. 27; translation cited from James Legge, trans., *Hanying sishu*, 53.

19   Translation cited with alteration in Chan, 267.

20   Cited in Chan, 463.

21   Ibid.

22   For example, the commentary on the hexagram *xian* asserts: "The two [modes] of qi move and respond to each other, thereby forming a union. . . . Heaven and earth exert their influences, and there ensue the transformation and production of all things."

23   Cited with modification in Chan, 463. The five moral principles are humanness, rightness, propriety, wisdom, and faithfulness.

24   Ibid., 465–66.

25   Benjamin Elman discussed some of the problems in identifying Confucianism and neo-Confucianism due to the fluidity with which these labels have been applied historically. See *From Philosophy to Philology*, xiii–xv, xxiv.

26   In "Language and the Ultimate Reality in Sung Neo-Confucianism," Seoung Nah argues that the conception of qi constituted the unifying thread for all Confucian schools developed in the Song period.

27   "That which is perceived is the principle in the mind; that which is capable of perceiving is the intelligence inherent in qi"; again, "The mind is the fine essential of qi" (Zhu Xi, *Zhuzi yu lei*, 85).

28   I owe this idea to an extended discussion with Professor Wei-ming Tu at Harvard University on a chapter of my dissertation dealing with the comparative features of premodern Chinese and Western approaches to human psychology. See also Tu, "A Confucian Perspective on Embodiment."

29   Zhu, 4; Chan, 643.

30   The neo-Confucian ideal of sagehood has been characterized as a spirituality grounded in the vision of the absolute as "transcendent immanent" or "immanent transcendent." See Wei-ming Tu, *Centrality and Commonality*; Rodney L. Taylor, *The Religious Dimension of Confucianism*; and Ch'eng Chung-ying, *New Dimensions of Confucian and Neo-Confucian Philosophy*, 1–61.

31   On the Platonic transformation of Christianity, see Krister Stendahl, *Immortality and Resurrection*; Andre-Marie Dubarle, "Belief in Immortality in the Old Testament and Judaism"; and Hans-Reudi Weber, "Biblical Understanding."

32   Ricci, *Opere Storiche*, 2:207.

33   Ricci, *Fonti Ricciane*, n 170.

34 Ibid., n 176.

35 The book-burning event in 213 B.C.E. was frequently used by the Jesuits and their converts as a pretext to introduce Christianity as the orthodox Confucian Way. For example, in his major Chinese work *Xingli zhenquan* (Elucidating the true meaning of nature and principle), Alexandre de la Charme (1695–1767) launched a systematic criticism of neo-Confucian discourse on nature and principle based on exactly this premise: "Just as China has the *Book of Poetry*, the *Book of History*, the *Book of Changes*, the *Book of Rites*, the *Spring and Autumn Annals*, the teaching of the Lord of Heaven also has the *Book of Poetry*, the *Book of History*, the *Book of Changes*, the *Book of Rites*, and the *Spring and Autumn Annals*. However, the classics of the teaching of the Lord of Heaven did not suffer the fire of Qin, therefore are complete, while all the Chinese classics, having gone through the destruction of the fire of Qin, are now damaged and incomplete" (*Xingli zhenquan*, fourth fascicle, chap. 2, sect. 7).

36 Ricci, *Opere Storiche*, 2:386–87; emphasis added.

37 Ricci, *Fonti Ricciane*, n 709; emphasis added. The Latin version of Ricci's journals, translated from the Italian original with supplements by his junior colleague Nicolas Trigault, contains a significant change on this point. Ricci emphasized both that the missionaries should use Confucius's authority to their own advantage and that they should interpret the ambiguities in Confucius's words in light of Christianity. Trigault omitted the second and justified the first by adding that Confucius's teachings were founded on the light of natural reason and that Confucius was cautious not to talk about things he did not know. See Ricci, *China in the 16th Century*, 156.

38 Matteo Ricci, "Shuwen zeng Youbo Chengzi" (Samples of Western calligraphy dedicated to Master Cheng Youbo), in Tao Xiang, *Sheyuan mocui*, second fascicle, pp. 10a–11a; translation in J. J. L. Duyvendak, "Review of Pasquale d'Elia," 394–95.

39 Ricci told his European correspondents that the Chinese always marveled at his extraordinary knowledge: "How come you know so much more than we do?" See, for example, *Opere Storiche*, 2:127, 178.

40 This is also the first of many Chinese works by the Jesuits that bear the title "Elucidating the True Meaning of . . ." Some later examples include Joseph Henri-Marie de Prémare (1666–1736), *Liu shu xiyi* (Penetrating the meaning of the six books), and *Rujiao shiyi* (The true meaning of Confucian teaching) (n.d.). See also note 35.

41 Ricci, *Fonti Ricciane*, n 709; emphasis added.

42 Matteo Ricci, *The True Meaning of the Lord of Heaven*, 149–51. Subsequent English translations are based on the Chinese text of this bilingual edition.

43 *Lun yu zhu shu* (Confucian analects), 7/21, 11/12, and 6/22.

44 For an overview of this subject by a Song neo-Confucian philosopher, see Chen Chun, *Neo-Confucian Terms Explained*, 142–68.

45 Zhang Zai's term: "*er qi liangneng* [the subtle operation of the two modes of qi]" ("Zheng meng" [Correcting Ignorance], in *Zhangzi quanshu*, 2:4a).

46 Cited in Chen, 147.

47 See Zhu, 47.

48 Ibid., 47–48.

49 Ricci, *The True Meaning of the Lord of Heaven*, 179; translation modified.

50 Ibid., 185; translation modified.

51 Ibid., 187; translation modified.

52 *Doctrine of the Mean*, chap. 16; translation cited from Chan, 102.

53 Ricci, *The True Meaning of the Lord of Heaven*, 188.

54 Ricci, *Opere Storiche*, 1:237.

55 Ricci, *China in the 16th Century*, 30.

56 Ricci, *The True Meaning of the Lord of Heaven*, 328–29.

57 Ibid., 190–91; translation mine.

58 For example, in chapter 2, he quoted two passages from the *Book of Rites*. See Ricci, *The True Meaning of the Lord of Heaven*, 124–25.

59 *Li ji zhengyi* (Expositions of the *Book of Rites*), in Ruan Yuan, *Shi san jing zhushu*, 2:1595, 1457.

60 Ricci, *The True Meaning of the Lord of Heaven*, 330–31.

61 Ibid., 69.

62 Ibid., 200; I translated this in consultation with Lancashire and Hu, 201.

63 Ibid.; my translation.

64 See, in particular, Julio Aleni (Ai Rulue) (1582–1649), *Sanshan lunxue ji* (Learned conversations at Sanshan), in Wu Xiangxiang, *Tianzhujiao dongchuan wenxian xubian*, 1:419–93; Ludovicus Buglio (Li Leisi) (1606–1682), *Budeyi bian* (Refutation of *Budeyi*), in Wu Xiangxiang, *Tianzhujiao dongchuan wenxian*, 225–332; and Charme, *Xingli zhenquan*. The Franciscan Brother Antonio Santa Maria Caballero (Li Andang) (1633–1669) also dealt with this theme in his book *Zhengxue liushi* (Touch stone of orthodox learning), in Wu Xiangxiang, *Tianzhujiao dongchuan wenxian sanbian*, 1:93–266.

65 For bibliographical surveys of the Jesuit-translated works, see Henri Bernard-Maitre, "Les Adaptations Chinoises d'Ouvrages Europeens . . . 1514–1688"; "Les Adaptations Chinoises d'Ouvrages Europeens . . . 1689–1799"; and Xu Zongze, *Ming qing jian yesuhuishi yizhu tiyao*. A list of reference materials and secondary studies on the Jesuit introduction of Western learning to China can be found in the relevant chapters in Erik Zürcher et al., *Bibliography of the Jesuit Mission in China*.

66 See Nicolas Standaert, "Science, Philosophy and Religion in the 17th-Century Encounter between China and the West," 251–68, and Willard J. Peterson, "Western Natural Philosophy Published in Late Ming China," 295.

67 In Ricci, *China in the 16th Century*, 327.

68 Bernard-Maitre, "Les Adaptations Chinoises d'Ouvrages Europeens . . . 1514–1688," 318.

69 Ibid., 348. For a biography of Alphonso Vagnoni (Gao Yizhi, Wang Fengsu, 1566–1640), see *DMB*, 1334–35.

70 G. S. Kirk et al., *The Presocratic Philosophers*, 286, 292–94.

71 The mathematical model of a geocentric, concentric cosmos was developed by Eudoxus of Cnidus (409–356 B.C.E.), an associate of Plato's Academy, but it was Aristotle who turned it into a physical model. The five planets known to the Greek ancients were Mercury, Venus, Mars, Jupiter, and Saturn.

72 Alphonso Vagnoni, *Kongji gezhi*, 856.

73 Colin A. Ronan, *The Shorter Science and Civilisation in China*, 147.

74 Ronan, 142–60.

75 Vagnoni, 849.

76　Ibid., 851.

77　Ibid., 851–52.

78　Ibid., 853.

79　Ibid., 893–95.

80　Ibid., 896.

81　Ibid., 897–98.

82　Ibid., 900–901.

83　For a review of premodern Western theories on how air and other environmental factors influence human beings' health, see Owsei Temkin, *Galenism*, chap. 1.

84　Charme, first fascicle, p. 3b.

85　For biographies of Johann Terrenz (also known as Johann Schreck, Deng Yuhan, 1576–1630) and Johann Adam Schall von Bell (Tang Ruowang, 1592–1666), see DMB, 1282–84 and 1153–57, respectively. According to Bernard-Maitre, *Taixi renshen shuogai* is adapted from Caspar Bauhin's (1560–1624) *Theatrum anatomicum* (Frankfurt, 1605). See Bernard-Maitre, "Les Adaptations Chinoises d'Ouvrages Europeens . . . 1514–1688," 338. It is a short treatise consisting of two chapters, the first describing various parts of the body—bones, nerves, fats, veins, skin, flesh, and the blood; the second dealing with the five senses, movement, and speech.

86　In Johann Terrenz, *Taixi renshen shuogai*, preface, 1b. Nancy Siraisi, *Avicenna in Renaissance Italy*, 325, points out that the most innovative areas of sixteenth-century medical science are anatomy and pharmacological botany, which corroborates Schall's evaluation of the role of human anatomy in contemporary European medicine.

87　For their biographies, see DMB, 2–6 and 1150–51, respectively.

88　According to Bernard-Maitre, this work is adapted from the first part of Leonard Lessius's *De Providentia numinis et animi immortalitate, libri duo adversus Atheos et Politicos*. See Bernard-Maitre, "Les Adaptations Chinoises d'Ouvrages Europeens . . . 1514–1688," 342.

89　Julio Aleni, *Xingxue cushu*, first fascicle, p. 7b. I gave a fuller account of this topic in my article, "Translation as Cultural Reform."

90　*Hippocratic Writings*, 249–50.

91　For an informative analysis of Aristotle's conception of pneuma, see his *Generation of Animals*, appendix B, 576–93; for his disciples' views on this, see Boyd H. Hill, "The Grain and the Spirit in Medieval Anatomy."

92　Temkin, 90.

93　Johann Adam Schall, *Zhuzhi qunzheng*, 521–29.

94　Ibid., 524.

95　Siraisi described how the core anatomical features of Galenic physiology were all called into question at the beginning of the sixteenth century (338–39).

96　Aleni, third fascicle, p. 2b.

97　Qi has been translated as fluid, matter, material force, matter energy, vital force, configurational energy, ether of materialization, psychophysical stuff, spirits, vapor, and more. See Nah, 3.

98　For example, Stephen Owen stressed the untranslatability of qi (among several other key Chinese concepts) and opted to leave it untranslated throughout his *Readings in Chinese Literary Thought*, 17.

Haun Saussy   *Always Multiple Translation,*

Or, How the Chinese Language Lost Its Grammar

If this were a "just-so" story, we would have to tell not only how the Chinese language lost its grammar but how it got it back. But then "it," the thing lost and found, would become the focus of a problem, for Chinese lost its grammar in one sense and recovered it in another. It was, to be more precise, a change in the accepted definition of "grammar," rather than new facts brought before an unchanging structure of assumptions, that revealed the error as such. Stories like this one reveal the history of linguistics to be discontinuous and improvised, an instance of "gypsy urban planning," to quote Umberto Eco's joke; and that realization should send us back to the tent makers, to the definers of the tacit body of theory that rings a scholarly discipline.[1]

   It is no longer current to say that Chinese "has no grammar," and it would be quixotic to argue against an idea so thoroughly discredited. The reason for looking into the history of the "error" is twofold: through it we may recover some of the conceptual context in which the great nineteenth-century comparative linguists discussed the Chinese language, and also gain some general lessons about the act of comparison. My examination of theories about the Chinese language leads to two recommendations for our own comparative work. We should, I think, always keep in mind two questions: First, are the facts about the object of study neutral givens, or are they produced by interaction between the investigator and the object? If the latter, the comparatist's task is then to be redefined as the exploration of interactions—which seems to me far more interesting than the evaluation of similarities and differences.[2] Second, when we have located an interaction, are we sure of having brought into play all the relevant centers of influence? Too often we in China studies tend to counterpose an unalterable China with a "West" fixed in the attitudes of the imperially expanding nations of Europe circa 1900. The dyad about which we then generalize makes for easy discussion, but it may, as I think is the case with the grammar controversy, leave out indispensable third parties. Translation similarly appears to involve two parties and no more: the source language and the target language. The history of ideas about Chinese grammar demolishes that simplification. Even the plainest typological contrasts, even the most obviously binary categorizations in this story emerge from multiple and layered interactions.

Interactions

Seventeenth- and eighteenth-century discussions of the Chinese language concentrate on what it, uniquely among living languages, possesses: the system of characters with its mix of phonetic and semantic clues. No one bothered to notice what rules bound these marvelous characters in sentences.[3] When the language began to be discussed from the point of view of grammar, in the early nineteenth century, the context predetermined scholars to see in Chinese no longer a bounty, but a lack. In this the passing of eighteenth-century sinophilia, as chronicled by Étiemble, joined with the replacement of general or universal grammar by historical and comparative philology as the central linguistic discipline to redescribe the knowledge of China that remained, as far as new sources of information are concerned, more or less stable between 1750 and 1820.[4]

To show what happens when we describe a language as founded on an absence, I can hardly do better than examine passages from the great American linguist William Dwight Whitney's cycle of lectures, *Language and the Study of Language,* first delivered at the Smithsonian Institution in 1864. (Whitney's debt to August Schleicher and Friedrich von Schlegel, which will become apparent below, reveals the geopolitical heritage of the differential description of grammars.) Whitney wants to impress on his audience the strict monosyllabic character of the classical Chinese language, which he says "may be in some measure seen by comparing a Chinese sentence with its English equivalent. The Chinese runs, as nearly as we can represent it, thus: 'King speak: Sage! Not far thousand mile and come; also will have use gain me realm, hey?' which means, 'the king spoke: O sage! Since thou dost not count a thousand miles far to come (that is, hast taken the pains to come hither from a great distance), wilt thou not, too, have brought some thing for the weal of my realm?' "[5]

The quoted sentence is almost the first in the philosophical book *Mencius*: *Wang yue: Sou bu yuan qian li er lai, yi jiang you yi li wu guo hu!* Whitney's choppy impersonation was obviously meant to startle his hearers. For a more decorous Victorian rendering of the philosopher's meaning, here is James Legge's translation, published three years before Whitney's lecture: "The king said, 'Venerable sir, since you have not counted it far to come here, a distance over a thousand li, may I presume that you are provided with counsels to profit my kingdom?' " [6] Now Whitney and Legge are inserting Mencius into different generic and institutional frames, and these frames determine what is noteworthy in a translation. Legge wants the king to speak in the fashion appropriate to a participant in philosophical dialogue—and so he does *chez* Legge, in a close match to the urbane conversation of Socrates and his Athenian friends as fluently Englished by Benjamin Jowett in the 1860s and '70s.[7] A common language and style forms a precondition (as well as an ultimate objective) for cosmopolitan philosophizing. To bring Mencius into the world of European thought speaking like a raw savage would only have put more barriers in the way of the mutual cultural recognition that Legge worked so hard to bring about.

But Whitney's purpose is not philosophical assimilation. If anything, the linguist needs to show Mencius as unassimilable to the common educated discourse. This is translation for the sake of difference. Why? Whitney's description of his own translation method as putting the original into English "as nearly as we can represent it" opens up a specifically ethnographic ambiguity. Word-for-word translation aims at a surpassing *nearness*, a one-to-one correspondence between signs of the original and of the rendition, no fuzziness or paraphrase permitted; but even with that the translator is unable to promise everything, only to depict "as nearly as we can" thought processes that must remain alien. The more convincingly the translator observes the protocols of "nearness," the more exquisite the reader's sense of strangeness, of distance from the original text. If Legge's policy tacitly anticipates the global common sense of Basic English, Whitney is opening the way to Benjamin Whorf; and these two styles of translation intend to make one another impossible.

The excessive "nearness" of the linguist's pidgin—its forcible transfer of not only the meaning but also the syntax of foreign sentences into another language—gives us a specific object of investigation, both morphological and historical: the "literal" translation. It was with deliberate perversity that Walter Benjamin declared "the interlinear paraphrase of the sacred text" the "archetype or idea of all translation" and cited Goethe's complaint about translators, that "they want to turn Indic, Greek, English into German, instead of Indicizing, Hellenizing, Anglicizing German. They have far more respect for the lin-

guistic habits of their own community than for the spirit of the foreign work." [8]
Benjamin and Goethe had at heart the interests of a cosmopolitan idea of the
German language, as a language that would live and grow in and through translations.[9] But that would have seemed dangerously romantic to the academic
linguists of the nineteenth century. Too great a degree of hospitality to foreign constructions signified a failure to acknowledge the special character and
genius of the home language. Ideologically speaking, this is the appearance in
linguistics of the chasm between democratic and conservative romanticism,
between aspirations to universal freedom and the legitimation of the traditional order, between the early Wordsworth, Coleridge, or Schlegel and their
later selves.

Unidiomatic translation, for most readers, hardly counts as translation;
even in the special case of sacred texts, the interlinear translation demands a
further translation to fill in the gaps. Pidgin translation exhibits its own incompleteness as an unequal relationship between normal speech in the target
language and the halting, misarticulated, or excessive speech of the source
language it paraphrases. Although these differences and asymmetries can be
described formally, the pidgin style comes into its own under the special conditions of the nineteenth century, conditions that may be marked out with
a sequence of proper names: Rousseau, Herder, Friedrich Schlegel, Wilhelm
von Humboldt, Franz Bopp. The procedures underlying it—calque, diglossia,
imperfect second-language acquisition—must be nearly as old as language
itself.[10] The Scythian policemen in Aristophanes' *Thesmophoriazousai*, to take
the earliest example I know, talk in "me Tarzan, you Jane" style, mangling the
verbs and cases of Greek—but always, as Dindorf first observed, in perfect
meter. Rousseau saw no reason why a savage should see his two feet as forming
a pair or falling under the scope of the single noun "foot." It is a pity Rousseau never attempted an extended description of the world from this refresh-
ing perspective—but to do so might demolish our concept of "language." The
translation of sacred texts, as Benjamin points out, required close comparisons
between the sentences of source and target languages. Those comparisons inspired compensatory gestures: so, for example, the Authorized Version of the
Bible produced under King James I uses italics for all English words that do
not correspond to terms in the original. But the age of linguistic typologies
and comparative grammar brought forth projects to which pidgin might contribute a steady underpinning and legitimation. Pidgin stands for—it makes
audible and visible—the incommensurability of languages. The discussion of
Chinese, that "grammarless" language, gives pidgin its greatest representational license.

To return, after this background sketch, to Whitney: His efforts on behalf of Chinese are not intended to expand the boundaries of English, but rather to show how little Chinese and other languages have in common. At this point in his lectures Whitney is going around the globe and classifying the different human languages for his audience. Coming to the languages of eastern continental Asia, he points out that

> the distinctive common feature of these tongues is that they are all mono-syllabic. Of all human dialects, they represent most nearly what, as we have already seen reason for concluding, was the primitive stage of the aggluti-native and inflective forms of speech. They have never begun that fusion of elements once independently significant into compound forms which has been the principal item in the history and development of all other tongues. The Chinese words, for example, are still to no small extent roots, repre-senting ideas in crude and undefined form, and equally convertible by use into noun, verb, or adverb. . . .
>
> Not very much requires to be said in explanation of the structure and history of a language so simple—a language which might be said to have no grammatical structure, which possesses neither inflections nor parts of speech, and which has changed less in four thousand years than most others in four hundred, or than many another in a single century.[11]

Pidgin translation is full of gaps—the hiccups caused by local, structural inequalities between English and Chinese. Whitney wants to persuade us that those gaps correspond to historical absences. Other languages have moved on from monosyllabism or, like English, back toward it, but the "scanty and crippled" [12] Chinese language stays right where it began, with no need, poten-tial, or opening for change. The rendering of Mencius into pidgin is thus an imaginative tunnel through which we journey back to a primitive state, the state at which all words are roots and nothing but roots. Formal parataxis is the representation in present speech of a history that should have taken place but never did, leaving the Chinese in "the primitive stage" preceding the fusions and inflections of actual linguistic history.[13] And because for us, who have a history, it is a journey backwards, the paraphrase affords us a historicizing ex-perience that would be unavailable to a Chinese reader, unless of course this reader had previously entered history by learning a language with morphology and a history of development. The historically determined translation therefore accomplishes an asymmetrical transaction: it shows us, who have more, gram-matically speaking, how much less the others have. Gaps in Chinese grammar ("no grammatical structure . . . neither inflections nor parts of speech") are as plain as the holes in a beggar's clothes, whereas the things Chinese speakers have that we English speakers lack (the tonal separation of otherwise identical syllables, for example, or a semantically based writing system with forty thousand distinct signs) become invisible, filtered out by the translator's technique.

Pidgin translation generally works only in this direction, from richer to poorer; it's a reverse Robin Hood. There are structural reasons for this. If we were trying to represent the word-for-word meanings of a language with finer grammatical articulations than ours, what would we put in the gaps between our own words? When translating from Chinese, Schleicher and Whitney insert a palpable absence or incorrectness to mark points of linguistic difference. But translation from a richer language stumbles on too many signs, outstripping the resources of linear speech, as in the examples from Whorf shown in figure 1.

Incommensurability arguments take quite different forms according to the language described and the language of the description. With isolating languages (if I may use a typology I will shortly move to criticize), the thoughts expressed by native thinkers are typically held to bypass some distinction thought essential in the investigator's language; with agglutinating languages or the more morphologically complex inflectional ones, the investigator notes subtleties or superfluities of thought.[14] In the latter arguments, the copious whirl of particles that must be laid out in translated equivalents becomes a quantitative basis for saying that we simply cannot make ours the thought processes of people with such exotically complex ways of saying things.

Translation, then, creates asymmetries and incommensurabilities while allowing us to think of these as intrinsic to the objects of study, not to the process. While purporting to give a view of Chinese "as nearly as we can represent it," Whitney, like any literal translator, is actually synthesizing a new language that has the properties it has only in relation to an earlier, in his case fuller, language. His Chinese is a dialect of English: only when set against English does it prove the incompleteness of the original; only the expectation of something else makes Chinese seem "scanty." To turn around the anthropological ambiguity alluded to earlier: If the "nearness" of the translation created, for Whitney's original hearers, an effect of distance, now we can say that the effect of distance itself could only be achieved with materials that lay close to home.

This is not to say that Whitney's description of Chinese is false, or merely parochial. It is not necessarily wrong to say that Chinese "possesses neither inflections nor parts of speech" and therefore "has no grammar"; but it is wrong to present these comparative judgments without also making explicit the standard to which Chinese is being held, thereby allowing the question to be raised

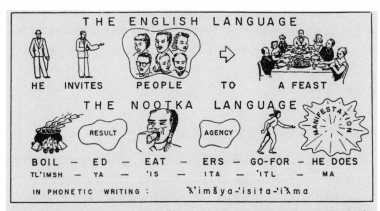

Figure 17. Here are shown the different ways in which English and Nootka formulate the same event. The English sentence is divisible into subject and predicate; the Nootka sentence is not, yet it is complete and logical. Furthermore, the Nootka sentence is just one word, consisting of the root *tl'imsh* with five suffixes.

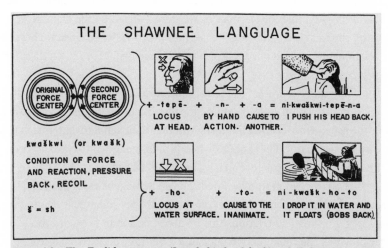

Figure 16. The English sentences 'I push his head back' and 'I drop it in water and it floats' are unlike. But in Shawnee the corresponding statements are closely similar, emphasizing the fact that analysis of nature and classification of events as like or in the same category (logic) are governed by grammar.

Figure 1. Pictorial representations of semantic and grammatical incommensurabilities, from Whorf, *Thought, Language and Reality*, pp. 235 and 243.

whether this is a meaningful standard of comparison. Had Whitney said *Chinese is poor (insofar as / in those respects in which / on the assumption that) English is rich*, he would have left us with the accurate depiction of an interaction instead of the tendentious description of an artifact of translation technique as the simple truth about Chinese.

Evolutions

The judgment on Chinese, then, in Whitney's case, resolves into a mirror effect of the pidgin-style translation into English. (Much of comparative literature reduces to mirror or seesaw effects.) But the remark that Chinese lacks a grammar has to be understood in a somewhat larger context. A contrast with English will not be adequate to reconstructing that context, nor can the consequences of the remark be discerned without introducing at least one more interacting element. To the poverty of Chinese corresponds not only the relative richness of the idiom—English or German or whatever—used by the translator, but above all the imagined glories of Sanskrit or proto-Indo-European. These are the relations into which our story of how Chinese lost its grammar dissolves; the primary facts of the case.

The "isolating" character of the early Chinese language, its monosyllabic cadence, and freedom from morphological markers are frequently remarked on by the nineteenth-century linguists, whether their scholarly interest in Chinese was active or not. The various divisions of languages into types according to their grammatical structure all have as their "degree zero" the Chinese language, the absence of grammar. Friedrich von Schlegel's essay of 1808, *On the Language and Wisdom of the Indians*, at one point divides all languages into those that show grammatical relationships by modification of the word roots, and those in which the roots remain unchanged but take on external affixes. Chinese is the paradigm of Schlegel's second type: "A noteworthy example of a language completely lacking inflections, where everything that other languages express through inflection is indicated by means of separate words that already have meanings of their own, is Chinese: a language that, with its unique monosyllabism, and on account of its thoroughness or rather complete simplicity of structure, aids us greatly in understanding the whole world of language." [15]

The system of two genera was too crude, inasmuch as it lumped together morphologically complex languages such as Turkish and Hungarian with the far simpler Chinese. Friedrich von Schlegel's brother August Wilhelm von Schlegel seems to have been the first to replace it with the subsequently classical scheme of three types: "languages with no grammatical structure, languages which employ affixes and languages with inflection." As before, Chinese is the primary example of the first type, a language "containing only one class of words, incapable of receiving either development or modification. It might be said that all its words are roots—but sterile roots producing neither plants nor trees. In these languages are found no declinations, no conjugations, no derivations, nor any word-compounds save by simple juxtaposition." [16]

Wilhelm von Humboldt's vast *On the Variety of Human Language Structures* proposes, "apart from the Chinese language which dispenses with all grammatical forms, three possible forms of language, the inflectional, agglutinative and incorporative." [17] For all the favorable things Humboldt found to say about the Chinese language in this book and in his letter to Abel Rémusat,[18] Chinese is, in the grand scheme of world languages, a pole to which all grammars are, qua grammars, to be contrasted. "Of all known languages, Chinese and Sanskrit stand in the most decisive opposition. . . . The Chinese and Sanskrit languages stand as the two extremes in the field of known languages, not perhaps comparable in their suitability for the development of the mind, but certainly so in the internal consistency and perfect execution of their systems." [19] "The development of the mind" connects Humboldt's anthropology with his linguistics. He insists that language is, rather than the expression of a prior thought, the organ through which thinking becomes possible. Because Chinese leaves so much of its grammar unexpressed in sound, realized only as relations of proximity and word order, Chinese occupies, in Humboldt's classification, the lower limit of the category "language": "It is hardly to be expected that an existing language family (or one language from such a family) should correspond in every point to the perfect form of language; in any case, such perfection lies beyond our experience. But the Sanskrit language family comes closest to this perfect form. In it the spiritual cultivation of the human race has reached its happiest development in the long series of its progresses. We can therefore establish the Sanskrit languages as a firm point of comparison for all the others." [20]

Under the conditions of nineteenth-century philology, then, to say that Chinese is a language without grammar necessarily involves it in a relationship with the supremely grammatical language, Sanskrit or Indic, and secondarily in a relationship with the languages that can claim a relation to Indic, the Indo-European family. That relationship can—must—be both direct and distant. Whitney's source for the *Mencius* example, August Schleicher's *The Languages of Europe in Systematic Review*, crowns this tradition by placing Chinese in a class of its own, the "monosyllabic language" as distinguished from the "flexional" and "agglutinating" languages. It is the book's organization that segregates monosyllabism even more strongly from the other two language types: the

Inhaltsübersicht.

Einleitung.

Figure 2. The "monosyllabic order of languages," that is, Chinese, inserted between the introduction and the main body of August Schleicher's *Languages of Europe in Systematic Review,* from Schleicher, *Die Sprachen Europas in systematischer Übersicht* (Bonn: König, 1850).

monosyllabic language, Chinese, appears only in the last section of the introduction, which is separated from the work proper by a second title (see figure 2). One of the three recognized language types is somehow not a part of the book that includes it in a "systematic review" of languages, European and other (the title is more restrictive than the work's actual contents). The opening pages of Schleicher's introduction explain this curious play of boundaries with a metaphor that gives a new weighting to the standard linguistic typology based on grammatical properties. In a language like Chinese

> the word is not in the least articulated; it is yet a strict unity previous to all difference, as is the *crystal* in the world of nature. These languages which express vocally meaning, but not relation, form the first language-class, which we may most suitably call the monosyllabic languages. . . . In the second class, that of the agglutinating languages . . . the word is articulated into parts (thus, a distinction from the first class), but these parts are not molded into a new whole, rather the word is still a collection of several indi-

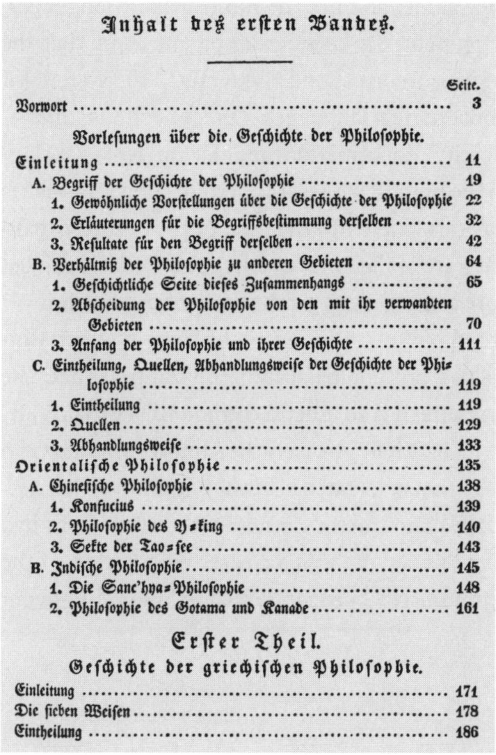
Inhalt des ersten Bandes.

Figure 3. "Oriental Philosophy," placed between "Introduction" and "Part One" of Hegel's *Lectures on the History of Philosophy*, from *Vorlesungen über die Geschichte der Philosophie*, ed. Karl Ludwig Michelet, in Hegel, *Werke* (Berlin: Duncker & Humblot, 1833), vol. 13.

> vidual lexical units (and this distinguishes the second from the third class). "The single, whole individual is still the ground [for several individual lexical units] rather than a subjective unity of members" as is the case, among natural organisms, for the *plants*. . . . The inflectional languages stand at the top of the ladder of language: here at last a genuine articulation of members develops in the organism of the word, the word is the unity-in-multiplicity of its members, corresponding to the *animal organism*, which has this same particularity.[21]

The unreferenced internal quotation comes from Hegel's *Encyclopedia*, the middle third of which, the *Philosophy of Nature*, seems to have given Schleicher a program to follow even to the uttermost details (see figure 3).[22] With this set of connotations at work, the tripartite division cannot be evenly balanced. It has to be scanned mineral // vegetable / animal, for both agglutinating and inflectional languages stand opposite Chinese as all live things are distinct from dead things. The contrast with monosyllabic languages relativizes the differences between the agglutinating and inflectional classes. Indeed, it puts them into a narrative relationship, for they alone, and not the monosyllabic languages, are capable of historical development: "It becomes apparent to us that the prehistoric development of languages corresponds perfectly to the system [of typology] and displays in the most perfect languages—the inflectional ones—the three periods of monosyllabicity, agglutination, and flexion. Not every language has worked its way up to the highest stages, the system shows us, just as not every organic substance has raised itself to the level of the animal organism; parts of the vocal substance are stalled at every stage and substage, just as parts of organic substance are at every stage of the scale of organic life." [23] Whitney, too, accepted this broad picture of linguistic history, in which Chinese was a relic of the very oldest past and could hardly be anything else because of its unalterable crystalline structure. It is so much a commonplace that Whitney's great enemy, Max Müller, repeats it in precisely the same terms; and Otto Jespersen, toward the end of the century, created a stir by suggesting that languages evolved not away from the condition of Chinese but toward it, as had English.[24] (One result of Jespersen's activity was a clearer recognition of the legitimacy of word order as a grammatical principle: that is how Chinese got its grammar back.) [25]

The Wobbling Pivot

What nineteenth-century European and American linguists had to say about Chinese has little to do with Chinese and a great deal to do with something few contemporary scholars of China learn about in their training—another sign of the "gypsy urban planning" under which we conduct our careers. If Indic was so important as to dictate the terms under which Chinese was studied and discussed for a hundred and more years, what accounts for its attractiveness? What projects did Sanskrit uphold? And what happened to them?

The split between Chinese and Sanskrit is nowhere made more insistently than in Friedrich von Schlegel's *On the Language and Wisdom of the Indians*. It is surprising that so insubstantial and topical a work should have had such lasting influence. But Schlegel established, as we have seen, the framework in which it was common knowledge that Chinese had no grammar and no history. We can now look for Schlegel's understanding of grammar and history.

Schlegel's praise of Sanskrit depends on a rejection of what he calls the Manchu language family (including predominantly Chinese). The two language families have opposite properties and distinct origins; indeed, property and origin here intertwine in truly mythic fashion. The Manchu-Chinese languages originate, Schlegel holds, in onomatopoeia and imitation, *Klangnachahmung*, and the Indic languages originate in *Besonnenheit*, understanding.[26] "Manchurian" languages have no structure because they are not principally products of mind, but rather of human animals subject to environmental stimuli; the structure of Indic languages derives from the "pure thought-world" of the first speakers, whose thoughts were "not in the form of pictures, but expressed themselves with immediate clarity." Rather like Revelation, which was supposed to have landed on certain peoples but not on others, this *Besonnenheit* grants the Indo-Europeans a "clear outlook," "exquisite feeling," "a sensitive and creative mind." It is never made clear how this correlates to Indic grammar—whether there is a causal relation one way or the other between them. Causality might detract from the purpose, after all. Schlegel wants to combat the idea, prevalent in France since Condillac and in England since Locke, that humanity had worked its way up from sense perception to naming of objects to grammatical categories. That way lies mechanism, materialism, and atheism. The completeness and exquisite organization of Sanskrit grammar—none of it "imitative"—is for Schlegel evidence of a separate creation. There are indeed languages that have developed in the way Locke and Condillac imagined them, and even in the way Rousseau and Herder imagined, but these are precisely not the languages we should study and imitate: "Many other languages appear to us, in truth, not as an organic artwork of meaningful syllables and fruitful nuclei, but as consisting for the most part of various sound-imitations and sound-plays, of raw emotional shrieks, signals, shouts, and directions, to which habit brought an ever more conventional understanding and arbitrary definition." [27] A language with a natural origin—imitation—stays in the realm of nature. The miraculous language begins, remains, and thinks in its own, properly supranatural realm.

This typological duality is founded on Schlegel's horror at the outcome of the French Revolution. What he calls Chinese is a language that Locke, Condillac, Rousseau, and de la Mettrie might have thought up, a mechanical system of signs founded on imitation, repetition, and reinforcement. And what he calls Indic is simply the spiritual converse of the mechanical languages. The center of the system of midcentury language typologies, Indic, turns out to be a reflection itself, the wishful projection of a disgruntled ex-republican.

Schlegel was a brilliant dabbler, but a real philologist was soon at work filling out the indications he had left. *On the Conjugation-System of the Sanskrit Language*, Franz Bopp's first publication, showed the original Indo-European tongue to have been a perfect language in the sense of Leibniz's or John Wilkins's philosophical projects, and sent down from the heavens by a benign personification as well. In Sanskrit conjugation endings Bopp sees the remnants of earlier

Indo-European pronouns. Nothing is wasted, nothing is meaningless: "When the Genius of the language has painstakingly and thoughtfully represented the simple concepts of persons with simple signs, and when we see that the same concepts are expressed similarly, with wise economy, in both verbs and pronouns—then it becomes obvious that the letter originally had a meaning, and that it remained true to its original meaning."[28] This is historical restitution in a different mode altogether from the crude primitivism of Whitney's Chinese, and it should be, because Bopp, in this a good disciple of Schlegel, treats the earliest form of Indo-European as the most perfect one. Chinese, and languages assimilated to it typologically or historically, does not start out as a structured whole but as a collection of isolated signs maintained as a set only by the coercive operations of culture.

Ancestors and Inheritors

Indic supplied Schlegel a historical story about transcendence; it also supplied him and many others with a brand-new pack of prestigious ancestors. The attempt to split Indic off from the merely natural "languages of imitation" could not stand up to critical examination. But the imagined community of Indo-Aryanism was a far more durable invention. As the memory of the revolutions and restorations in France faded, carrying with it the immediate polemical purpose of Schlegel's account of "Manchurian" languages, the idealized Indians remained. Whitney's account of his present moment calls on them to explain world history, curiously dissolving nations, empires, and enmities into a vast spreading of grammatical competence:

> One source of the special interest which we feel in the study of Indo-European language lies in the fact that our own tongue is one of its branches. . . . But we are further justified in our somewhat exclusive interest by the position which our languages, and the races which speak them, hold among other languages and races. . . . [The Indo-European race's] first entrance as an actor into what we are accustomed to call universal history . . . was in the far East, in the Persian empire of Cyrus and his successors. This founded itself upon the ruins and relics of more ancient empires and cultures, belonging to other peoples, in part Semitic, in part of obscurer kindred. . . . The Persian empire, in its conquering march westward, was first checked by one of these humble communities, the little jarring confederation of Greek states and cities, destined to become, notwithstanding its scanty numbers, the real founder of Indo-European preeminence. . . . Rome, appropriating

the fruits of Greek culture, and adding an organizing and assimilating force particularly her own, went forth to give laws to all nations. . . . And if Christianity was of Semitic birth, Greeks and Romans gave it universality. . . .

The Semites, inspired with the furious zeal of a new religion, Mohammedanism, broke from their deserts and overran the fairest parts of Asia and Africa. . . . They recoiled, at last, before the reviving might of the superior race, and the last and grandest era of Indo-European supremacy began, the era in the midst of which we now live. For the past few centuries, the European nations have stood foremost, without a rival, in the world's history. They are the enlightened and the enlighteners of mankind. . . . The network of their ability embraces the globe; their ships are in every sea between the poles, for exploration, for trade, or for conquest; the weaker races are learning their civilization, falling under their authority, or perishing off the face of the land, from inherent inability to stand before them. . . . They have inherited from its ancient possessors the sceptre of universal dominion . . . and they are worthy to hold it, since their sway brings, upon the whole, physical well-being, knowledge, morality and religion to those over whom it is extended.[29]

The idea that the Aryans acted as a people—at a time when, probably within hearing of the Smithsonian lecture hall, the Indo-European speakers of America were destroying each other over the question of how they should best conduct their "sway" over members of a fellow race—must have struck Whitney as inspiring, a compensatory adjustment. Worse would come in the name of pan-Aryanism. Of course, Indo-European philology does not reduce to an ethnic propaganda exercise (*pace* Bernal), nor did it contribute anything indispensable to the militarizations and dehumanizations of the past two hundred years. And yet, and yet . . . The phrase *corruptio optimi pessimum* (the worst thing is the corruption of the good man) comes to mind. Friedrich von Schlegel's influence on European thinking about tribes and selves is more subtle and insinuating than the classic racism of Gobineau, the racism of blame.[30] Does the praise of grammatical beauty create ugliness? Does the thought of noble ancestors prompt ignoble actions? Not necessarily, of course; but the observation of interactivity serves to point out what is at stake.

Notes

1 Umberto Eco, *Foucault's Pendulum*, 74–75.
2 By "interaction" I have in mind a loose analogy to the ways physicists have learned

to describe measurement since Einstein's relativization of space and time. For an intriguing set of papers on measurement, observers, and interaction, see Bryce S. De Witt and Neill Graham, *The Many-Worlds Interpretation of Quantum Mechanics*. A philosophical and literary study of such "general economies" is Arkady Plotnitsky, *Complementarity*.

3   On the tendency to give undue prominence to the sign rather than to the sentence, see my "The Prestige of Writing."

4   Étiemble, *L'Europe chinoise*.

5   William Dwight Whitney, *Language and the Study of Language*, 331. Whitney translates his version of Mencius from August Schleicher, *Die Sprachen Europas in systematischer Uebersicht*, 50–52, and Schleicher reproduces Stanislas Julien, *Meng Tseu vel Mencius*, 1. Schleicher translates: "König sprechen, Greis, nicht fern 1000 Meile und kommen, auch wollen haben zu Vortheil (ich) mein Reich (Fragepartikel)?" On Whitney's translation methods, see J. R. Firth, "Linguistic Analysis and Translation."

6   James Legge, trans., *The Works of Mencius*, bk. 1, pt. 1, p. 125.

7   Benjamin Jowett, trans., *The Dialogues of Plato*.

8   Walter Benjamin, "Die Aufgabe des Übersetzers," in *Gesammelte Schriften*, vol. 4, pt. 1, pp. 20–22; translation mine. For a full text, see "The Task of the Translator," in Benjamin, *Illuminations*, 80–82.

9   On the cosmopolitan-romantic ideal, see Antoine Berman, *L'Épreuve de l'étranger*.

10 On such processes, see Uriel Weinreich, *Languages in Contact*.

11 Whitney, 330–34.

12 Ibid., 257.

13 For similar statements, see Wilhelm von Humboldt, *Sur l'origine des formes grammaticales*, 102, 105, 147.

14 Examples: Herbert Fingarette, *Confucius — The Secular as Sacred*, on the claim that Confucius never conceived of moral choice; Chad Hansen, *Language and Logic in Ancient China*, maintaining that the Chinese language dictates an ontology of stuffs, not substances, individuals, or classes.

15 Friedrich von Schlegel, *Über die Sprache und Weisheit der Indier*, 45. On Schlegel and his influence, see Anna Morpurgo Davies, "Language Classification in the Nineteenth Century."

16 August Wilhelm von Schlegel, *Observations sur la langue et la littérature provençales*, cited in Theodor Benfey, *Geschichte der Sprachwissenschaft*, 366–67.

17 Wilhelm von Humboldt, *Über die Verschiedenheit des menschlichen Sprachbaues* (ca. 1830–1835; first publication, 1836), in *Humboldts Gesammelte Schriften*, vol. 7, pt. 1, p. 254.

18 Humboldt, "Lettre à monsieur Abel-Rémusat sur la nature des formes grammaticales en général et sur le génie de la langue chinoise en particulier" (1806), in *Humboldts Gesammelte Schriften*, 5:254–308. For a German translation of this letter with extensive commentary based on genuine sinological knowledge, see Christoph Harbsmeier, *Humboldts Brief an Abel Rémusat*.

19 Humboldt, *Über die Verschiedenheit*, 271, 274.

20 Ibid., 253.

21 Schleicher, 7–9; italics added.

22 For the quotation, see Georg W. F. Hegel, *Enzyklopädie der philosophischen Wissenschaften*,

Part 2: *Die Naturphilosophie*, sect. 343, "Die vegetabilische Natur," in *Werke*, 9:371; translation mine. See also *Hegel's Philosophy of Nature*, trans. Michael John Petry, 3:45.

23 Schleicher, 14–15.

24 "There is one language, the Chinese, in which no analysis of any kind is required for the discovery of its component parts. It is a language in which no coalescence of roots has taken place: every word is a root, and every root is a word. It is, in fact, the most primitive stage in which we can imagine human language to have existed. . . . All languages must have started from this Chinese or monosyllabic stage" (Max Müller, *Lectures on the Science of Language*, 273). For Otto Jespersen, see "The History of Chinese and of Word Order," in *Progress in Language*, 80–111.

25 See Aldo Scaglione, *The Classical Theory of Composition*, 337–49.

26 F. Schlegel, *Sprache und Weisheit*, 61, 63. *Besonnenheit* (understanding, reflection) was the middle term by which Herder threaded his way past the risky alternatives of the Berlin Academy's prize essay theme of 1770, "whether the origin of language was divine or human." See Johann Gottfried Herder, *Abhandlung über den Ursprung der Sprache; On the Origin of Language*.

27 F. Schlegel, *Sprache und Weisheit*, 66.

28 Franz Bopp, *Ueber das Conjugationssystem der Sanskrit-Sprache*, 147. "Bopp actually seems to have held that in the proto-language the primitive semantic elements were by and large expressed by separate morphemes. The morphology of a Proto-Indo-European word, Bopp believed, was a *representation* of the elements of its meaning. Obscured as this state of affairs was in the daughter languages, because of phonetic decay, it was nonetheless reconstructible by the comparative method" (Paul Kiparsky, "From Paleogrammarians to Neogrammarians," 338).

29 Whitney, 230–32.

30 On Schlegel as proto-racial thinker, see Martin Bernal, *Black Athena*, 227–39, and Edward Said, *Orientalism*, 98–99; on a linguistic controversy in which objections to racial ideology came to the fore, see Hans Aarsleff, "Bréal vs. Schleicher: Reorientation in Linguistics during the Latter Half of the Nineteenth Century," in *From Locke to Saussure*, 293–334.

PART 2

Colonial Circulations:

From International Law

to the Global Market

Lydia H. Liu   *Legislating the Universal:*

The Circulation of International Law in the

Nineteenth Century

Henry Wheaton's *Elements of International Law* was reissued in a centennial edition and published as part of the Classics of International Law series in 1936. In his introduction, the editor George Grafton Wilson brings up an interesting point about the circulation abroad of this American legal text in the past century. Wilson mentions, in particular, that *Elements of International Law* was translated into Chinese by W. A. P. Martin in 1864. "The edition published in China was quickly exhausted," writes Wilson. "The work had been received with much favour in Japan. An edition of this Chinese text reprinted and adapted for Japanese use was published in Kyoto, Japan, in 1865, and other editions were issued in the East."[1] The importance of the occasion is further noted in the official testimony of the American minister, Anson Burlingame, who wrote to the State Department in 1865: "The Chinese did not address me in writing, but called in person to mark their sense of the importance of the completion of the work, and when the Prince and suite kindly sat for their photographs, Fung Sun [sic], who had superintended the translation, desired to be taken with a copy of Wheaton in his hand."[2]

Moreover, the universal claim of Wheaton's book also finds support in the existence of other contemporaneous translations, such as the first French edition in 1848, which was followed by a Spanish-language translation in Mexico in 1854 and an Italian edition published in 1860. (The French text contained Wheaton's own corrections and additions shortly before his death.) Martin's Chinese translation appeared four years after the first Italian edition and two years before Dana's authoritative English edition in 1866, and so on. It seems to me that the extraordinary afterlife of Wheaton's 1836 book (multiple cross-textual editions) is very much indebted to the symptomatic circularity exemplified by those translations. Wilson cites the existence of the foreign-language editions as *evidence* of the universal value of Wheaton's text, but it requires the circulation of that book to prove the self-same universality.

Perhaps this situation can help us think about the historical making of universalism more than it reveals the inherent value of Wheaton's book or international law. To bring the familiar philosophical argument about universals and particulars into the fold of an earlier global and globalizing moment, I propose to analyze here the circumstances of the Chinese translations of international law. I argue that the coming into being of a global universal can be plotted as a series of *translated and contested* moments in colonial and cultural encounters in which the translator, who literally and figuratively plays the "diplomat," is a central agent.

The image of a translator as diplomat is useful also in the sense that a translated text relates to the original in more ways than a one-time deal. Negotiations go in multiple directions and produce changes in the original text as well. The various later editions of the "original" European and American texts of international law virtually *grew* in volume and reference matter over an extended period of time as the authors and editors incorporated additional tribunal cases and international resolutions into the original texts. It is not untypical of an editor to cite the existence of foreign-language translations to prove the universal value (not merely applicability) of a book. What it suggests is that later and *revised* editions can be just as illuminating as the original work in registering the process whereby, in this case, international law has been globalized and universalized over the past two hundred years.

I would like to emphasize that the *revised* editions of international law in the original language inhabit the same space of global production and circulation as its foreign-language counterparts and should, therefore, be brought to the foreground of historical studies. For that reason, it is important to keep a double focus in this study. On the one hand, the complex circumstances of the nineteenth-century Chinese engagements with international law must be carefully laid out and analyzed; on the other hand, these engagements need to be brought into a meaningful circulatory relationship with the contemporary reissuing of the *revised* editions of the same (?) text in the original settings of Europe and America. The double focus explains and can be explained by the global circulatory networks of translated knowledge in modern international relations, thus imbuing the whole problematic of universal and particular with a new significance.

The Question of Colonial Historiography

Anecdotes abound in the historical accounts of how China and East Asia made the entrance into the family of nations in modern history. One of those stories has acquired a near legendary status in the form of a prelude. It was Lord Macartney's royal diplomatic mission to the Manchu court in 1793 that posed the first serious challenge to the superiority of the Chinese civilization and its dominance over East Asia. In the eyes of the Europeans, Lord Macartney's mission exposed the profound ignorance of the Manchu court about the outside world because the court insisted on treating him as a tribute-bearer from England and tried to make him perform *koutou* in his audience with the Emperor Qianlong. In the end, the Macartney mission failed to achieve its goals after the emperor flatly rejected the British demands for establishing extensive trade relations with China. Until the recent publication of James Hevia's critical study, this well-documented legend of Sino-British diplomatic encounter has largely determined the tone with which most historians talk about the subsequent developments in Sino-Western relations in the nineteenth and twentieth centuries.[3]

The Macartney legend marks the beginning of what one might call "colonial historiography" in Sino-Western relations in West academia as well as in the works of some Chinese historians. A central argument in this shared historiography is that the cause of China's downfall in the nineteenth century was its own stubborn refusal to abandon the traditional sinocentric ways of thinking about the outside world and join the rest of world in free trade. Under the label of sinocentrism, this excessively psychologized cultural mentality becomes a self-explanatory mechanism and requires no further discussion.

Historians of international relations both before and after John King Fairbank have tended to fall back on the story of sinocentrism when they explain or cannot explain why the country was so prone to disastrous mistakes in handling "barbarian" affairs in the nineteenth century or why it "provoked" the kinds of punishment and retaliation by the Western powers that it did. Narratives of diplomatic history tell us repeatedly that the Manchus and Chinese were preoccupied with their ancient tributary protocols and consequently were unable to meet the challenge of modern European diplomatic usage. The resistance to British demands for trade and diplomatic representation is thus conveniently dismissed as a traditionalist's response to progress.[4] But Chinese resistance to Western imperialism need not be "traditional" to be meaningful any more than the "unequal treaties" have been traditionally Chinese. Conceptually, such trivialization of resistance is oddly unhistorical because it means that the survival strategies that the Manchu court and the Chinese official establishment had improvised and deployed on many occasions for the purpose of containing the encroachment of the Western powers were merely traditional responses to social change when they could have been understood as contemporary *face-to-face* and *day-to-day* struggles with global imperialist expansion, a very novel phenomenon of the time indeed.[5]

The dismissal of contemporary resistance as "traditional" lies at the heart of colonial historiography in the study of international relations and is by no means limited to Sino-Western relations. I argue that colonial historiography cannot be historical even by its own standard when it refuses to assign meaning to events or confront contemporary face-to-face and day-to-day struggles outside the evolutionary conceptual models of tradition and modernity, backwardness and progress, particular and universal, and so on. That does not mean, however, that colonial historiography has not played an important historical role otherwise. To British empire building and the imperial history of the West, colonial historiography has proved eminently useful, even indispensable when it grants, for example, universal validity to Euro-American international law and to modern diplomatic practice while translating everything else into particular, hence less significant and culturally specific moments. In this sense, the epistemological limits of the imperial history of the West are necessarily set and perpetuated by colonial historiography.

Marxist historiography, on the other hand, always emphasizes the importance of organized resistance to colonialism and imperialism and has done much toward historicizing the violent moments of encounter between the colonizer and the colonized. Because of its primary attention to the mode of production in explaining historical change, Marxist theory has, nonetheless, relied on a teleological view of history (the so-called transition from feudalism or the Asiatic mode of production to the capitalist mode of production) to characterize China's traumatic entrance into the modern international community.[6] This view of history has not been conducive to (1) a fundamental questioning of colonial historiography on the matter of universal history and international relations or asking questions such as how international law became universalized and in turn compelled a universalist reading of world history and international law itself; and (2) when it comes to conceptualizing the historical real, Marxist historians have tended to fall back on a set of historiographic approaches and assumptions about the value of the data and the ways of analyzing primary source materials which differ very little from that used in colonial historiography.

For example, the problem of *evidence* becomes intellectually meaningful only insofar as it enters into an argument about something else, be it an argument about imperialism or about national sovereignty. If the issue of "translation" happens to surface and meddle with the historian's handling of evidence, it is either disregarded or promptly relegated to secondary importance. This extraordinary naïveté in the construction of evidence often results in collusive readings of primary documents by taking them at face value—whether these come in Chinese, English, Japanese, French, or other languages—and therefore in misguided conclusions about diplomatic happenings, as if these events had taken place in a transparent mode of exchange.[7]

Linguistic Crusade against the "English Barbarian"

In the early phases of Anglo-Chinese diplomacy, Chinese-language documents were the originals that *actually* circulated between the two governments and were read in English only by the British government. This linguistic situation is presented by J. Y. Wong as an immediate challenge to those who study the diplomatic relations of the period, because "although the British government acted on these English translations and English originals, the Chinese government acted on neither. The Chinese government knew only the Chinese originals of their own despatches, and recognized only the Chinese translations of those prepared and presented to them by the British. Therefore, Western historians who have so far used only the English translations and English originals may have to reconsider their conclusions based on evidence of the despatches written in a language *that was not the medium of communication* between the British and Chinese diplomats."[8]

To put it more accurately, translation was the mode of exchange. As a regularly contested item in diplomatic intercourse, bilingual communication never went well and seemed to frustrate both parties. As far as the British were concerned, it simply posed too many threats and had to be brought under control. Therefore, Article 50 of the British Treaty of Tianjin made a special provision in 1858 that all British official communications to the Chinese authorities be written in English. They would be accompanied by a Chinese version for the time being, but the meaning as expressed in the English text should be held as authoritative. Within this time, the Chinese government was expected to provide a corps of competent interpreters. Article 3 of the French Treaty of Tianjin made a similar provision, and so on.[9]

Viewed in this light, the rhetorical strategy adopted by the British in a series of events that escalated into the first Opium War might acquire a new significance. As we know, the familiar quibble between Chinese officials and Western diplomats over the word "barbarian" had been the occasion of numerous clashes in the early phases of Anglo-Chinese diplomacy. The British had repeatedly protested against the Chinese use of the word *yi* and were determined to ban the expression from diplomatic intercourse. The ground of the perceived insult lies in the presumed equivalence of meaning between *yi* and "barbarian" and between *ying yi* and "English barbarian." It is useful to know that the equivalence thus established between the two words was a recent phenomenon or, at least, had not been in common usage before nineteenth-century European translators came along and insisted on "barbarian" as the exclusive signified of the Chinese word *yi*.[10]

If we look back to the eighteenth century or even the beginning of the nineteenth century, alternative translations of *yi* did exist. That word had been equated with "foreigner" or "stranger" in English. To give an example, among the official correspondences of the British East Indian Company I have examined is a translation of an official proclamation issued by the governor of Guangdong and Guangxi to the foreign business communities in China. Dated 20 August 1728, this English-language version had been supplied to the company by a Roman Catholic priest in Guangzhou (Canton), who had translated it from an earlier French version of the Chinese original.[11] Apparently, the European translator of the document did not have a vested interest in rendering *yi* as "barbarian" but used "stranger" and "foreigner" instead. Even as late as 1815, Robert Morrison of the London Missionary Society still thought it proper to render *yi* as "foreign" and glossed *yiren* as a respectable term for "foreigner" in the first Chinese–English lexicon published in Macao. After the fiasco of the Napier mission, however, Morrison decided to adopt a different translation of *yi*, now equating it with the English "barbarian."

Lord Napier arrived in China at the end of the monopoly of the British East India Company, bearing the official title of foreign superintendent to represent the British government. This change of hands meant that the Chinese Secretary's Office, which had previously served the needs of the company, would be converted into a government office. The Chinese secretary had always been a European man with some knowledge of the Chinese language who performed various translation tasks for European merchants. From 1834 on, this position began to be filled by missionaries and diplomats who received the official title of the Chinese Secretary of Her Majesty's Plenipotentiary.[12] Among those who occupied this position were Robert Morrison and his son J. R. Morrison, Karl Gützlaff, Walter Henry Medhurst, and Thomas Wade. (Wade became a sinologist after an illustrious diplomatic career in China and filled the first chair of Chinese at Cambridge University in the 1880s.)[13]

In view of the fact that all official diplomatic exchanges between the Chinese and British governments had to pass through the Chinese Secretary's Office between 1834 and 1860, the above-mentioned translators played a pivotal role in the crises that subsequently exploded in this critical period of Anglo-Chinese diplomacy. In fact, these translators were entirely responsible for making the word *yi* an exclusive equivalent of "barbarian" and fixing that equivalence as is still very much honored by Western historians. If the curious translation suggests a strange, masochistic self-image of the "barbarian" that the British insisted on projecting onto themselves by fantasizing a sinocentric worldview, I must point out that it has been one of the most tragic and costly fabrications in modern diplomatic history and continues to exist in the writings of today's historians and in the authoritative *Cambridge History of China*.[14]

Dilip Basu calls the nineteenth-century British translation of *yi* a respectable rhetoric for war. He sees a vital link between the new interest in the word *yi* and the misguided policy of Napier, whose armed expedition against China ended in his untimely death. Napier was outraged by the fact that his official title, foreign superintendent, had been rendered as *yimu* by the Qing government because the Chinese term had been explained to him as meaning "barbarian eye," a translation that might be attributed to the ridiculous incompetence of his language informant. Even Sir George Staunton noted at the time that *yimu* was no ground for dispute because the Chinese translation simply meant "foreign principal" and that *mu* ought to be rendered as "principal," not literally as "eye."[15]

Nevertheless, a general crisis began to build up around the so-called arrogance of the sinocentric attitude toward foreigners.[16] The British mounted one protest after another against the use of *yi* by the Qing government and remained absolutely convinced that their national honor was being insulted by the Chinese word. The crusade against *yi* thus became a counteroffensive against the Chinese prohibition on the opium trade, lending ample ammunition to the hostile exchanges between the two governments. After the British won the Opium War and lifted the ban on the opium trade, they lost no time in banning the word *yi* from the official language through treaty provisions. Article 51 of the British Treaty of Tianjin (1858) stipulates: "It is agreed that, henceforward, the character 'i' [barbarian], shall not be applied to the Government or subjects of Her Britannic Majesty in any Chinese official document issued by the Chinese Authorities either in the Capital or in the Provinces." (The ideograph for *yi* was inserted between "i" and [barbarian] in the original text of the Article.) [17] That ban turns out to be more successful than could have been imagined by its original architects, because the word *yi* has since been completely erased from the modern Chinese vocabulary.

Sir George Staunton and P. P. Thoms were among the few British men who voiced their disagreement with the translation and were critical of the political maneuver behind the uproar. Reflecting on Thoms's lost struggle against the rising tide of the linguistic crusade against *yi*, Dilip Basu observes: "Thoms's contestation was of no consequence. He noted that up to the time of Napier, no one complained about the term *yi* in Qing communications. He knew why. The communications mostly addressed commercial matters; they were respectful and elegant. Yet in 1836 no less an authority than Morrison or Gützlaff was translating the concept as offensive. He suspected that Morrison must have been acting '*under authority* (Thoms's italics) and not in compliance with his usual judgement.' He further noted that in the 'Correspondence relating to China' presented to both Houses of Parliament in 1840, the offensive terms occurred, in not a very long document, not less than twenty-one times." [18] Indeed, the sleight of hand in translation succeeded in arousing a general sentiment of hostility and public outcry against China, while at the same time the true evil of the opium trade, in which one of the Chinese secretaries, the missionary Karl Gützlaff, had a lucrative share, went unpunished. As late as 1852, Acting Imperial Commissioner Bo-gui in Guangzhou continued to be puzzled by Sir George Bonham's protest to his use of the character *yi* in official correspondences and wondered why the word would be a source of anger and dispute. Bo-gui was probably unaware of the fact that Her Majesty's Plenipotentiary was reading his dispatches in *English* translation supplied by the Chinese Secretary's Office.[19] And that document could have said only "barbarian." That was just a few years before the "English" meaning of all Chinese dispatches would be legally sanctioned by Article 50 of the British Treaty of Tianjin.[20]

In a sense, the colonial provisions in the British Tianjin Treaty are still being echoed word for word in colonial historiography. What counts as legitimate evidence in that scholarship has predominantly been the "English content" of the diplomatic dispatches and never their mode of translation or interaction. Yet the mode of translation is precisely where the historicity of so-called content is played out and where the circulation of meaning is made possible (figure 1).

EXHIBITION OF THE ENGLISH IN CHINA.

MR. FRISBY, our friend and correspondent, late Anglo-Chinese pundit of Canton, has favoured us with a most particular and lucid account of an exhibition now opened at Pekin; a show which has attracted all the mandarins and gentry, their wives and families, of the "flowery kingdom." Little think the sagacious English public who visit Mr. DUNN's Exhibition, Hyde Park Corner, to marvel at the pigtails and little feet of the Chinese, that a DUNN from Pekin—LI LI by name—has sojourned many years in England, for the express purpose of showing to his countrymen the faces and fashions of the barbarian English. But so it is. At this moment there is open in Flying Dragon Street, Pekin, an exhibition, called "THE BARBARIAN ENGLISH IN CHINA." There we all are, from high to low; numbered in cases as at Hyde Park-Corner, and a catalogue of our good and bad qualities illuminates the darkened mind of the curious.

Our dear friend the aforesaid pundit has translated this catalogue for *Punch*; and has, moreover, regardless of expense on our part, caused drawings to be made of our countrymen as they are presented by LI LI to the dwellers of the Celestial Kingdom. The prominent parts of this catalogue we lay before the reader; they will be found to beautifully harmonise with the skill which has displayed us in cases; wherein, sooth to say, we do appear with a certain Chinese air, which proves the national prejudices of the artist. Whether he has improved our looks or otherwise for the Chinese public, we leave to the opinion of the judicious and reflecting beholder. Our simple duty is now to lay before the render the Chinese catalogue, translated and enriched with notes, by our indefatigable and profound correspondent. The Exhibition is dedicated to the "Son

of Heaven," very vulgarly known as the Emperor. The dedication, however, we omit; as it tells us no more than that LI LI is, in his own opinion, a reptile, a dog, a wretch, a nincompoop, a jackass, when addressing the said "Son of Heaven;" that his "bowels turn to water" with dread, and his pigtail grows erect with amazement. It will be conceded that, allowing a little for oriental painting, the dedication in no way differs from many other such commodities of home manufacture. Leaving the preface, we begin with the

INTRODUCTION.

When your slave remembers that through the creamy compassion of the Son of Heaven, the Father of the Universe, and the Dragon of the World, the barbarian English were not, in the late war, seized, destroyed, and sawn asunder; that their devil-ships were spared, their guns respected, their soldiers mercifully permitted to retain their swords, and their sailors allowed to return to their barbarian wives and little ones,—when your slave remembers all this, his heart is turned to honey by the contemplation of your natural sweetness, whilst, in admiration thereof, his soul drops upon its knees, and prostrate, worships.

And when your slave further remembers, that in some leisure hour, you may—with a benevolence that is as broad as the earth, and as high as heaven,—vouchsafe to reign over and to comfort the aforesaid barbarians, your slave tremblingly takes hope that the samples of the people he has gathered together, with the subjoined faithful account of their manners and their doings, may find favour in the sight of HIM, who when he sneezes, arouses earthquakes; and when he winks, eclipses the moon.

| CASE I.—AN ENGLISH PEER. | CASE II.—SHAKSPEARE. |

He wears a garter about his leg: an honourable mark of petticoat government bestowed by the barbarian Queen. The Garter is sometimes given for various reasons, and sometimes for none at all. It answers to the peacock's feather in the "flowery kingdom," and endows with wisdom and benevolence the fortunate possessor. The Peer is represented at a most interesting moment. He has won half-a-million of money upon a horse, the British nobility being much addicted to what is called the turf, which in England often exhibits a singular greenness. The nobleman, however, displays a confidence always characteristic of the highly born. By winning so much money, he has broken the laws of the country, by which more than his winnings may be taken from him; but it will be seen that he has pens, ink, and paper before him, and is at the moment he is taken, making a new law for himself, by which he may, without any penalty whatever, protect his cash. It is the privilege of the nobility to have their laws, like their coats, made expressly to their own measure.

This is the national poet, which the barbarians would, in their dreadful ignorance, compare to Confutzee. It is melancholy to perceive the devotion paid by all ranks of people to this man. He was originally a carcase butcher, and was obliged to fly from his native town because he used to slip out at nights, kill his neighbours' deer, and then sell the venison to the poor for mutton. (All this I have gathered from the last two or three authentic lives lately written.) He went to London, and made a wretched livelihood by selling beans and wisps of hay to the horses of the gentlemen who came to the playhouses. Thinking that he could not sink any lower, he took to writing plays, out of which—it is awful to relate—he made a fortune. (It is, however, but justice to the barbarians to state that they give no such wanton encouragement to play-writers at present.) SHAKSPEARE, or SHAKSPEER, or SHIKSPUR,—for there have been mortal battles waged, and much blood shed, about the

Figure 1. "The Barbarian English in China," from the pages of *Punch* (no. 6, pp. 219–24). The satire is an imagined reversal of the actual "Chinese exhibition" of artifacts that took place in a building at Hyde Park Corner in London after the Opium War. That exhibition was organized by an American entrepreneur named Nathan Dunn.

Henry Wheaton's *Elements of International Law*, the first book of international law to be rendered into Chinese, was published in 1864 under the official auspices of Prince Gong and his newly established foreign affairs office called the Zongli yamen in Beijing.[21] The translation, known to the Chinese as *Wanguo gongfa*, stood at the head of several major translation projects initiated and brought to fruition by an American missionary named W. A. P. Martin. Martin (alias Ding Weiliang) was one-time president of the Imperial College appointed by Prince Gong.[22] Assisted by his Chinese colleagues, Martin was responsible for translating and publishing, besides *Wanguo gongfa*, T. D. Woolsey's *Introduction to the Study of International Law* (1878); Bluntschli's *Das Moderne Völkerrecht der Civilisierten Staten als Rechtsbuch dargestellt* (1879), rendered from Lardy's French version *Le Droit international codifié* of the same text; and W. E. Hall's *Treatise on International Law* (1903). Martin has also been credited with the translation of several diplomatic guide books such as *Le Manuel des lois de la guerre* (1881), compiled by the Institut de Droit International, as well as G. F. de Marten's *cours diplomatique* (1877).

These seminal translations, especially Wheaton's book, are often treated as the beginnings of a new chapter of China's foreign relations in world diplomatic history. Scholars argue that the official appearance of these texts marked a turning point in the Chinese government's dealings with the outside world after the 1860 crisis that led to the creation of the Zongli yamen.[23] Moreover, Japan and the future destinies of Taiwan and Korea were also implicated here because, as early as 1865, *Wanguo gongfa* traveled to Japan and the Japanese brought out a *kambun* transcription of Martin's translation in Kyoto within one year of the first Chinese edition. This and a new Japanese edition of *Elements of International Law* in 1876 unleashed a wave of interpretations and discussions of *Bankoku kōhō* that directly impacted the rise of Japanese imperialism, Sino-Japanese relations, and Korean-Japanese relations in the following years.[24]

But the relationship between a translated text and its application in diplomatic practice is never self-evident. Instead of assuming a direct or indirect relationship between text and practice, we must first examine how a translated text produces meaning—both intended and unintended meanings—*between* the discursive contexts of the two languages, for neither international law nor its application can possibly exist independently of translingual interpretation in diplomatic negotiations. The situation is doubly interesting when we consider how meaning becomes possible between those languages that had limited contact before and must learn to speak in each other's *political discourse* for the first time. Such was the difficulty that Martin and his Chinese colleagues faced when they first embarked on the ambitious translation of international law from English into classical Chinese in 1863.

The problem of translatability looms large in any such inquiry, but it would be futile to search for an ideal pairing of meanings when the matching of meanings is itself a historical phenomenon under investigation. The imagined *adequatio* of meanings as understood in traditional theories of translation is, therefore, a pseudoproblem as far as this study is concerned. Translatability means something entirely different here: it refers to the historical making of hypothetical equivalences between languages. These equivalences tend to be makeshift inventions in the beginning and become more or less fixed through repeated use or come to be supplanted by the preferred hypothetical equivalences of a later generation. As I have argued elsewhere, one does not translate between equivalents; rather, one creates tropes of equivalence in the middle zone of translation between the host and guest languages. This middle zone of hypothetical equivalence, which is occupied by neologistic imagination, becomes the very ground for change.[25]

Indeed, how are meanings initiated, legitimated, sabotaged, suspended, or put to practical use? I suppose that, even in cases where we need to consider how a text becomes involved in a larger diplomatic event, a question like this would suggest a more fruitful way of looking at the translation of international law in nineteenth-century China than a straightforward account of text and its application in diplomatic practice. Both text and practice must be subjected to the same process of rigorous interrogation. What this means is that the Chinese translation of Euro-American international law in recent history is no longer a mere textual event or a mere diplomatic event. There is yet a third dimension that one might tentatively call an epistemological event. This intellectual event crosses paths with the textual and diplomatic to produce a *triple event*. It is in the sense of a triple event that the translation of international law assumes the importance that it does in the present study. And I would like to emphasize that the rise of so-called global (and later national) consciousness in East Asia falls precisely within the historical parameters of this triple event.

By no accident did Martin take on the triple role of translator, diplomat, and missionary, which he played literally and conscientiously. Like the other Christian missionaries of his time, Martin attached a "higher" purpose to his secular translations, and he probably would have given an evangelical name to the epistemological aspect of the triple event in which he was engaged. Most likely he would have called it the Christian moral truth. Martin was an American Presbyterian missionary from Indiana who was appointed to China by the Foreign Mission Board. He and his wife sailed from Philadelphia on 23 November 1849 and reached Hong Kong on 10 April 1850.[26] Martin spent the first decade of his mission work in Ningbo, during which he occasionally offered diplomatic service to the U.S. government as an interpreter. Long before undertaking the official task of translating international law for the Manchu government, he had been employed by the U.S. minister William B. Reed to be an official interpreter for the American legation during the Tianjin treaty negotiations in 1858. After the next minister, John E. Ward, took office, Martin got himself hired again and interpreted for Ward during the Taku military confrontations between the allies and the Manchu government. These and the other diplomatic posts at the American legation were conducive to Martin's interest in international law after 1860, and, a few years later, he was to find a meaningful connection between his mission work and secular translations.

Protestant missionaries who went to China following in Robert Morrison's footsteps after 1807 adopted a typical method of proselytizing reminiscent of the strategies that the Jesuits had found practical in the seventeenth century. Fully aware of the fact that the mandarins were uninterested in the theological explanations of Christian truths, they decided to camouflage the religious doctrines with secular knowledge that they thought was either desired by or already inculcated into the Chinese elite. Martin read extensively about the work of the Society of Jesus in China under the Ming dynasty and greatly admired the Jesuit priest Matteo Ricci.[27] He liked to think of himself as a Protestant Ricci, whose example drove him to embark on the translation of international law. As one of the prominent missionaries of the nineteenth century, Martin produced work that embodies the evangelical traditions of both the past and his own time, which raises some new questions about the role of the missionaries in the secularizing and globalizing processes of the modern world.

In what seems to be the first mention of his translation, Martin wrote to his friend Walter Lowrie, a fellow Presbyterian missionary in Ningbo, in a letter dated 1 October 1863: "I was led to undertake it, without the suggestion of anyone," he says, "but providentially I doubt not, as a work which might bring this atheistic government to the recognition of God and his Eternal justice; and perhaps impart to them something of the Spirit of Christianity."[28] That sounds genuine enough but is not the whole story. Even at this initial stage, Martin did not make the decision by himself, as his biographer Ralph Covell seems inclined to believe.[29] In a memoir titled *A Cycle of Cathay* published many years later, Martin gives us more details about the circumstances of his translation and the reason why he chose the Wheaton book when he had first thought of translating Vattel (1714–1767). That was when he returned to China in 1862 after a furlough of two years back in America with his wife and children. This time around, Martin wanted to move north and open a mission in Beijing, but, due to the death of a colleague (William Culbertson) who had the editorial supervision of the mission press in Shanghai, he was temporarily detained in that city. "I employed a portion of my time in translating Wheaton's 'Elements of International Law,' a work that was to exert some influence on two empires as well as on the course of my own life," wrote Martin. "The want of such a book had early forced itself on my attention, and I was proposing to take Vattel for my text, when Mr. Ward recommended Wheaton as being more modern and equally authoritative." [30]

The timely intervention by John Ward is significant. The reader will remember that Martin had served as Ward's official interpreter during the Taku crisis and witnessed the military confrontations between China and the allies. Ward's opinion mattered to his former interpreter because it represented the official view of the U.S. government. Wheaton's *Elements of International Law* was endorsed for being "more modern and equally authoritative," but there is yet another reason not quite spelled out; that is, the author of the book was an American lawyer and diplomat who made no pretense of hiding the national interest of the United States. As early as 1855, the Department of State had sent a copy of Wheaton to the American commissioner in China, but the book never arrived. So William B. Reed, the American minister who first employed Martin as official interpreter, purchased another copy at official expense in 1857. [31]

In his preface to *Wanguo gongfa*, however, Martin does not and cannot spell out the interesting circumstances discussed here, which he occasionally mentions elsewhere or does not mention at all. For example, he offers an explanation in the preface that effectively erases the official policy implications in his choice of the text: "For the choice of my author, I offer no apology. My mind at first inclined to Vattel; but on reflection, it appeared to me that the work of that excellent and lucid writer might as a practical guide be somewhat out of date; and that to introduce it to the Chinese would not be unlike teaching them the Ptolemaic system of the heavens. Mr. Wheaton's book, besides the advantage of bringing the science down to a very recent day, is generally recognized as a full and impartial digest, and as such has found its way into all the cabinets of Europe. In England especially, it is employed as a text-book for the examination of candidates for the diplomatic service." [32] This quote immediately follows Martin's praises for Robert Hart, who, according to Wheaton's translator, overcame his national prejudices by endorsing "an American version of an American text-book." This might well have raised some eyebrows because Wheaton's book was an American version of international law and called for the author's defense of that choice. Thirteen years later when Martin issued a translation of Woolsey's *Introduction to the Study of International Law*, once again an American text, he found it necessary to defend himself from charges of "patriotic partiality."[33] His subsequent inclusion of Bluntschli, Hall, and others represented a corrective attempt to balance the patriotic partialities among the Western writers of international law. For example, when the Chinese translation of Hall's *Treatise on International Law* was presented to the public, Martin confessed that he introduced this British authority on the subject to "complete the list" of major international law texts.[34] Whether the list was complete or not, the national identity of the original authors casts a dubious shadow over the self-proclaimed impartiality of international law and shows that "authorship" in a broad sense does matter when the control over universal representation becomes a point of contention among the Western powers.

But back to Vattel, whom Martin briefly contemplated translating before changing his mind due to Ward's intervention. Vattel's *Le droit des gens* or *The Law of Nations* was not unknown to the Chinese at this time. As early as 1839, Imperial Commissioner Lin Zexu had requested the American medical missionary Peter Parker (1804–1888) to render three paragraphs of Vattel's book during the opium-suppression campaign in Canton. Lin's visit was recorded by Parker in *Tenth Report of the Ophthalmic Hospital* in 1839 as follows: "Case No. 6565. Hernia. Lin Tsihseu, the imperial commissioner. . . . His first applications, during the month of July, were not for medical relief, but for translation of some quotations from Vattel's *Law of Nations*, with which he had been furnished: these were sent through the senior hong-merchant; they related to war, and its accompanying hostile measures, as blockades, embargoes, etc.; they were written out with a Chinese pencil."[35] Parker's translation was later included in juan 83 of Wei Yuan's famous *Haiguo tuzhi* (An illustrated gazetteer of maritime countries), edition of 1852, with Vattel's name transliterated as Hua Da Er and the title rendered as *Geguo lüli* (Laws and regulations of all nations).[36] Immanuel Hsü rightly calls Parker's translation a travesty of Vattel's perspicuity because Parker did not seem to follow the original but simply paraphrased Vattel and added his own comments in a labored and nonliterary style.[37]

As Commissioner Lin had difficulty understanding Parker's translation, which bordered on the unintelligible, he sought the help of a Chinese interpreter, Yuan Dehui, who had studied Latin at the Roman Catholic School in Penang and had been a student at Milne's Anglo-Chinese College in Malacca. An interpreter of the Court of Tributary Affairs, Yuan had been sent to Canton in 1838 to purchase foreign books and temporarily placed on Commissioner

Lin's staff. It has been suggested that it was Yuan "who, in view of the impending trouble with the British, first called Lin's attention to the authoritative work of Vattel."[38]

Lin studied the translations by Parker and Yuan and followed the course of action discussed in them. One of the Vattel passages Lin had Parker translate reads: "Every state has, consequently, a right to prohibit the entrance of foreign merchandises, and the nations that are affected by such prohibitions have no right to complain of it, as if they had been refused an office of humanity. Their complaints would be ridiculous, since they would only be caused by a want of that gain, refused by a nation that would not suffer it to be made at its own expense."[39] Despite Parker's obscure rendering of the original text, Lin obtained some sense of what Vattel's international law was saying and followed the text to the letter by proclaiming opium a contraband in 1839 and demanding its destruction. He wrote to Queen Victoria requesting her to order the stoppage of opium traffic. "Suppose a man of another country comes to England to trade, he still has to obey the English laws," wrote Lin; how much more should he obey in China the laws of the Celestial Dynasty?"[40] Lin's use of international law in these transactions was strategic because the Vattel passages he had Parker and Yuan translate for him were strictly confined to the issues of how nations go to war and impose embargoes, blockades, and other hostile measures.

In other words, Lin treated international law as a mode of persuasion, not universal truth, which would enable him to argue against the harmful effects of the opium trade in a language he thought the British could understand. This "positive" use of international law bears some superficial resemblance to the argument Martin would advance twenty years later, when he wrote that his secular translation was intended to bring an atheistic government to the recognition of God and impart to it something of the Spirit of Christianity. Whereas Martin took a holistic view of his secular and religious work and would not commit himself to translating anything less than the whole text of international law, even if it was just a paraphrase of the whole text, Lin was unconcerned about the integrity of the text and its holistic values. When he proclaimed opium a contraband in 1839 and demanded its confiscation and destruction, he was strategically responding to the West's willful dismissal of the so-called traditional Chinese mode of persuasion during the government campaign against opium traffic.[41]

When neither the Chinese nor the Western mode of persuasion could produce the desired results, Lin resorted to force. As he issued the order to destroy the shipments of opium in Guangzhou, he was fully convinced of the moral and legal righteousness of his action even by the yardstick of Western international law. However, the Opium War followed an entirely different course of development that would hold international law up for ridicule. Britain declared war against China to seek compensation for the damages caused by Lin's confiscation and destruction of the commodity. The rest is a familiar story: Hong Kong became a British colony and five treaty ports were opened up along the Chinese coast. Indemnities were paid, and Lin too had to pay for the consequences of the war: he lost his post in the imperial government on charges of provoking the hostilities with the British. The historical irony is that China's entrance into the family of nations had logical connections with Britain's violation of international law during the Opium War. These connections should help us place Martin's translation of international law in a larger historical perspective.

Translating Elements of International Law

Twenty years after the first Opium War, when British Minister Frederick Bruce was informed of Martin's translation of *Elements of International Law*, he made a remark to Martin that once again spelled out the interconnectedness of the two events, namely, the West's violation of its own international law and China's simultaneous entrance into the family of nations. "The work would do good," Bruce said, "by showing the Chinese that the nations of the West have *taoli* [principles] by which they are guided, and that force is not their only law." [42] Bruce was admitting the fact that the Western nations went and conquered the rest of the world with weapons in one hand and the law (principles) in the other. Brute military force borrows the moral and legal authority of international law to justify their world taking as *œuvre civilitrice*. The act of justification in turn translates global killing and looting into a noble cause.

Bruce's endorsement of Martin's project suggests a need for *belated* justification for the British and other Western powers' violation of international law in the Opium War, the Arrow War, and other wars against China. The word "belated" is crucial here because it describes the circumstantial (not necessarily intended) meaning of Martin's work. After the various "unequal treaties" had been extorted from the Manchu government and ratified at gunpoint, they were now in need of being monitored and implemented faithfully by the Zongli yamen and the imperial court according to the requirement of international law. [43] In that sense, the translation was both belated and timely.

In spring 1863, when the Manchu court was having diplomatic difficulties with France, Wen-xiang, a leading minister of the Zongli yamen, asked the U.S. minister in Beijing, Anson Burlingame, to recommend an authoritative work on international law that would be recognized by all Western nations. Like John

Ward, Burlingame mentioned Wheaton's *Elements of International Law* and promised to have portions of the book translated. He wrote to Consul George Seward in Shanghai and was informed that by coincidence Martin was doing the work.[44] Burlingame gave Martin encouragement and assured him of his aid in bringing the work before the mandarins. In June of the same year, Martin headed north.[45] Further momentum was given to the arrangement when Chong-hou, who had been briefed on the translation by Martin at Tianjin in July 1863, offered to write to Wen-xiang to recommend his translation.[46]

On 10 September 1863, Burlingame formally introduced Martin to four members of the Zongli yamen with whom he had already become acquainted during the treaty negotiations in 1858.[47] Martin brought the unfinished translation of Wheaton to the meeting and showed it to the ministers. The ministers were impressed. Wen-xiang mentioned a selection of important passages translated earlier for the Zongli yamen by Robert Hart when Hart was the chief assistant to Horatio N. Lay, the inspector-general of Maritime Customs. "Does it contain the 'twenty-four sections'?" Martin recalls Wen-xiang asking. " 'This will be our guide when we send envoys to foreign countries.' "[48] The "twenty-four sections" refer to chapter 1 of part 3 of Wheaton's *Elements of International Law*, in which the rights of legations are discussed.[49] In reply, Martin said that his translation was incomplete and asked the Zongli yamen to appoint a competent official to assist him in a final revision and to print it at public expense.[50] Subsequently, Prince Gong appointed a commission of four men, all of high literary competence, one scholar working in the Hanlin Academy, to assist him in the completion of the translation.[51] In addition, Martin received five hundred taels to help cover the cost of printing and publication.[52] The work was done at the Yamen, and at the suggestion of Robert Hart, the newly appointed inspector-general, the book was printed for the use of the government.[53]

Martin dedicated the finished work to Burlingame, who, in Martin's words, "gloried in contributing something toward the introduction of international law into China"[54] (figure 2). The same can be said of Martin's own sense of achievement. But not everybody was as pleased. Several officials in the diplomatic establishment, Chinese as well as Europeans, questioned Martin's motivation. The French chargé d'affaires Klecskowsky regarded Martin as a troublemaker and is said to have complained to Burlingame, "Who is this man who is going to give the Chinese an insight into our European international law? Kill him—choke him off; he'll make us endless trouble."[55] Likewise, Samuel Wells Williams believed that the introduction of international law might stimulate China to reach the level of Western law and thus find a legal ground to abolish certain aspects of the "unequal treaties" such as extraterritoriality.[56]

Figure 2. The title page of the Chinese translation of *Elements of International Law*, 1864. Courtesy of the East Asian Library of the University of California at Berkeley.

The Chinese, on the other hand, were unconvinced that Martin's motives were disinterested benevolence and surmised that he wanted to make a name for himself after the illustrious example of Matteo Ricci.[57] If Prince Gong and Wen-xiang were the enthusiastic supporters of Martin's work, it was because the Zongli yamen wanted to use *Wanguo gongfa* as a practical manual for conducting diplomatic affairs with the Western powers. It would familiarize them with the protocols of the Western nations who had recently established legations in the capital after the crisis of 1860. The Zongli yamen desired to know what legal basis there was for the procedures that had been forced on them in the name of international law, such as unequal treaties, extraterritoriality, most-favored-nation treatment, tariff control, diplomatic representation, rights of war and peace, and more.

A good number of Manchu and Chinese officials felt ambivalent or downright hostile to Martin's translation. They distrusted the unspoken intention of his work "as Trojans did the gifts of the Greeks." [58] In response to such fear, Prince Gong memorialized the throne on 30 August 1864, arguing:

We, your ministers, find that this book of foreign laws does not entirely agree with our own laws, but there are in it occasional passages which are useful. For example, in connection with the case of Danish ships captured by Prussia outside of Tianjin, we used some sentences from the book, without expressly saying so, as arguments. The Prussian minister acknowledged his mistake without saying a word. This seems a good proof. He [Martin] says that this book should be read by all countries having treaty relations with others. In case of dispute it can be referred to. . . . We, your ministers, guarding against such frequent requests with books and possible attempts to make us follow them, have told him that China has her own laws and institutions and that it would be inconvenient to refer to foreign books. Martin, however, points out that although the Collected Statutes of the Great Qing Dynasty have been translated into foreign languages, China never attempted to force western countries to practice them. It cannot be that just because a foreign book has been translated into Chinese, China would be forced to practice it. Thus, he [Martin] pleaded repeatedly.[59]

Prince Gong built his argument on the basis of practical application, not on the universal value of Western international law. The case of Danish ships in Tianjin, which occurred as a result of Bismarck's war with Denmark in Europe, provided a useful occasion for the Zongli yamen to test the effectiveness of legal provisions as outlined in Wheaton's book. When the new Prussian minister to China, von Rehfues, arrived in China in a man-of-war in the spring of 1864, he found three Danish merchant ships off the port of Taku. He immediately seized them as war prizes. The Zongli yamen used the concept of maritime territory and the treaty provisions between China and Prussia to protest the extension of European quarrels to China. Prince Gong refused to grant an interview to the new Prussian minister and condemned him for the way he began his ministerial duties. The case was successfully resolved when von Rehfues relinquished the three Danish vessels, with a compensation of $1,500.[60]

Prince Gong's memorial proved effective. Martin's manuscript received imperial sanction and was allowed to be printed and distributed. But aside from one or two isolated cases of effective uses of international law whereby China was able to assert its sovereignty, how does the memorial articulate the cultural implications of the ministers' endorsement of Martin's translation? It is interesting to note that Prince Gong appealed to a vague notion of reciprocity at the suggestion of Martin himself. According to Martin, China had never attempted to force Western countries to practice its laws any more than the West intended to force its own laws on China. He does not, however, spell out the ground of such imagined reciprocity. As we know, the earlier translation of the *Daqing lüli* (Collected statutes of the great Qing dynasty) by George Staunton following Macartney's mission had occurred under conditions where there was absolutely no question of China's forcing the West to adopt its laws. The British man undertook the task in order to provide his own government with useful information about China.

By the mid–nineteenth century, when Martin undertook the translation of international law, however, the Western powers had already forced many of its demands and treaties on the Manchu government in the name of international law. So the alleged ground of reciprocity did not exist between the *Daqing lüli* and *Wanguo gongfa* to support Martin's argument of cultural relativism. Rather, as I argue in the next section, Martin's universalist agenda lies elsewhere. The fact that he pursued the translation at all may suggest a bona fide assumption of reciprocity and commensurability between English and Chinese. But reciprocity and commensurability are in every sense a *product* of deictic encounters between the two languages and not the other way around. This conception of reciprocity and commensurability opens up a hermeneutic space in which the significance of Martin's translation can be fruitfully grasped.

Insofar as Klecskowsky's insistence on "our European international law" affirms the brute instrumentality of that law, the French diplomat seems to flatly deny universal status to the same. Likewise, Martin's cultural relativism, even if it were just a pretense, suggests a very much circumscribed sense of how far international law can go to make universal claims outside the West. If international law was thus circumscribed and contested by the Manchus, Chinese, and Westerners, none of whom knew for sure whose interests this book would best serve, how do we go about identifying and analyzing a historical process that did seem to gesture toward granting universal recognition to international law in the years to come? This is the question the next section will try to answer.

Producing Universal Knowledge

The opening pages of *Wanguo gongfa* greeted its targeted audience, the Manchu-Chinese officials, with a loud and clear message about the place and placing of China on the new "scientific" map of the world (see figure 3). This map represents the two hemispheres printed back to back with brief geographic narratives set in the margins with names of the continents and oceans given in Chinese transliteration. The cartographic representation, which was not uncommon at the time, seeks to introduce a new order of universal knowledge

Figure 3. The Eastern and Western hemispheres of the world map printed in the Chinese translation of *Elements of International Law*, 1864. Courtesy of the East Asian Library of the University of California at Berkeley.

and global consciousness to the Chinese elite so that this ancient civilization would be persuaded to join the family of nations.

But the spread of universal knowledge also means overcoming the resistance of local languages at the textual level. Resistance was particularly strong in the mid–nineteenth century when hypothetical equivalence between English and Chinese had not yet been set in place and when there was a great deal of latitude as to what a word in one language might be taken to mean in the other. When Martin's manuscript was first presented to Prince Gong, the latter complained, "Examining this book, I found it generally deals with alliances, laws of war, and other things. Particularly it has laws on the outbreak of war and the check and balance between states. *Its words and sentences are confused and disorderly; we cannot clearly understand it unless it is explained in person* (added italics).[61] Prince Gong's reaction was, at best, ambivalent. He saw the usefulness of the book but thought it was poorly written. Although his criticism was directed at the level of words and sentences, it should not be taken merely as a commentary on literary style, but as a reaction to the relative absence of hypothetical equivalence between English and Chinese.

Martin's translations often employed neologisms at the expense of intelligibility. Some of the vocabulary seemed obscure at that time but has since grown self-evident. This is because the words have been gradually assimilated into the language as modern Chinese itself underwent massive changes through increased exposure to translations of European texts in the past century. This process suggests that translatability and intelligibility emerged during the first encounter of the languages, but the significance of this happening tended to escape the immediate historical context only to achieve some level of clarity later in the language of future generations. It is one of those historical happenings that cannot be tied down to its immediate sociological origins or explained by naïve recourse to contemporary events and individual biographies.

One of the key concepts to emerge in the political discourse of modern China can be traced back to the neologisms invented by Martin and the Chinese translators of *Elements of International Law*. The concept I have in mind is *quanli* or "right," which, like *zhuquan* (sovereignty) and many other nineteenth-century coinages, no longer strikes us as strange or un-Chinese, because they have been naturalized in the history of Chinese (and Japanese) political discourse and through repeated usage for the past 135 years. The situation was perceived differently, however, by those who lived during the mid–nineteenth century. This was duly documented by the translators themselves fourteen years after the fact because they continued to feel a need to defend their "unwieldy" coinage. In a headnote to the 1878 translation of Theodore Dwight Woolsey's *Introduction to the Study of International Law*, known in Chinese as *Gongfa bianlan*, Martin and his Chinese collaborators describe how they coined the neologism *quanli* to render the meaning of "right." Their tone was clearly apologetic:

> International law is a separate field of knowledge and requires special terminology. There were times when we could not find a proper Chinese term to render the original expression, so our choice of words would seem less than satisfactory. Take the character *quan*, for example. In this book the word means not only the kind of power one has over others, but something every ordinary person is entitled to. Occasionally, we would add a word *li* [to form a compound], as, for example, in the expression *quanli* meaning the born "rights" of the plebeian, etc. At first encounter, these words and expressions may seem odd and unwieldy, but after seeing them repeatedly, you will come to realize that the translators have really made the best of necessity.[62]

This is hardly surprising because, in the beginning of the nineteenth century when Robert Morrison first arrived in China, English and Chinese were still behaving like strangers to each other. Although Bible translations and religious tracts made some headway in the first half of the century, makeshift translations were the norm rather than the exception in political and philosophical discourse. It took a great deal of work for the first generation of translators, missionaries and their Chinese colleagues, to turn Chinese and English into mutual figures of interlocution at the expense of tolerable comprehensibility.

The Chinese noun *quan* thus underwent a drastic process of transvaluation through translation to be purged of some of its negative connotations often associated with *quanshi* (power/domination); likewise, the compound *quanli* took the word *li* (interest/calculation) out of its usual commercial context to be rendered pliable to suggest something positive within the context of international law. This positive meaning emerged entirely through the encounter with the English concept and introduced a new concept into Chinese political discourse. Some years later, the concept would take on a life of its own and garner increased respect, especially after the Sino-Japanese War when liberal political thinkers of the West began to be translated and popularized through Yan Fu's (1853–1921) writings and through Japanese translations.[63]

Still, it seems extraordinary that Martin should have been persuaded by his Chinese colleagues to pick two loaded (negative) characters to coin an equivalent compound for the English word "right." We must keep in mind that the word *quanli* possessed more ambiguity in the 1860s than it does now precisely because it was totally unfamiliar and hovered somewhere between Chinese and English. The "excess" meanings are entirely capable of reflecting back on the original English word "right" and glossing its meaning according to a different mode of association.

This translingual process may be glimpsed with some hindsight from an interesting glossary of Chinese–English bilingual terminology of international law called "Terms and Phrases" prepared by Martin and his Chinese colleagues many years after *Wanguo gongfa* had been issued. The text appeared as an appendix to their new translation of *Gongfa xinbian* (W. E. Hall's *Treatise on International Law*), published in 1903. In this authoritative glossary, the word *quanli* is rendered back into English as "rights and privileges," which I take to be a significant reverse translation of the Chinese neologism. The convoluted translation has the effect of reinterpreting the English word "right" with some translingual echoes of the original Chinese character *quan* suggesting "power," "privilege," and "domination."[64] The original English word "right," once put into circulation, cannot but be reinterpreted in light of other possible meanings and other possible associations that always come with the translation. At issue is not a matter of right or wrong, good or bad translation. The situation, I believe, is much more interesting and subtle than a simple judgment of that kind, because it poses the question of whether a translation could actually jeopardize the transparency and self-evidence of the original concept.

Let us explore this point a little further. We know that (human) rights discourse in Europe has figured prominently in the language of international relations and has been an inseparable part of international law since the Enlightenment. Kant, for example, called for a cosmopolitan order that would abolish war on the basis of moral practical reason, leading to the legal form of a federation of nations. In "Toward Perpetual Peace," Kant envisions a process by which all the peoples of the earth would enter into a universal community to the extent that "a violation of rights in one part of the world is felt everywhere. This means that the idea of cosmopolitan law is no longer a fantastical or overly exaggerated idea. It is a necessary complement to civil and international law, transforming it into public law of humanity."[65] Habermas marvels at Kant's miraculous foresight in a recent interpretation of this eighteenth-century dream of a family of nations and makes a point of glossing the notion of "public law of humanity" to mean *Menschenrechte* or human rights.[66] This meaning of "rights," as Habermas so acutely understands, places the discourse of human rights squarely in the historical unfolding of international law itself.

As I have argued throughout this essay, the historical unfolding of international law cannot but include the multiple translations and circulations of international law in the other languages. Habermas takes on a subject that has already been glossed again and again in Latin, English, French, Italian,

Chinese, Japanese, and many other languages in the past two centuries. Unaware of this always already translated history, he is doing to Kant's notion of "perpetual peace" what *Wanguo gongfa* did to Henry Wheaton's *Elements of International Law* and what Henry Wheaton had done to Heffter, the author of *Das europäische Völkerrecht*, in the nineteenth century, and so on ad infinitum. Namely, they all gloss the meaning of "law," "rights," and "human rights" with a specific historical and linguistic understanding of the stakes involved in each situated interpretation.[67]

Henry Wheaton, writing in English, refers the concept of human rights to the work of the famous German public law theorist Heffter, who introduced it to distinguish between two distinct branches of Völkerrecht. These are (1) human rights in general, and those private relations that sovereign states recognize in respect to individuals not subject to their authority; and (2) the direct relations existing between those states themselves. Wheaton cites Heffter to elaborate on these distinctions: "In the modern world, this latter branch has exclusively received the denomination of law of nations, *Völkerrecht, Droit des Gens, Jus Gentium*. It may more properly be called external public law, to distinguish it from the internal public law of a particular state. The first part of the ancient *jus gentium* has become confounded with the municipal law of each particular nation, without at the same time losing its original and essential character. This part of the science concerns, exclusively, certain rights of men in general, and those private relations which are considered as being under the protection of nations. It has been usually treated of under the denomination of *private international law*." [68] This provides a useful historical perspective for our understanding of human rights discourse in the past and the present. The concept of human rights is specifically glossed by Heffter as one branch of Völkerrecht, a commonly used German translation of the Latin *jus gentium*, like the French equivalent *droit de gens* or the English "law of nations" of the time. In this context, human rights has everything to do with an earlier understanding of private international law, and public law for that matter. This is what I meant by the always already translated reading of *Menschenrechte* in Habermas's recent writing about Kant. In Martin et al.'s translation of the above passage, the word "human rights" is rendered as *shiren ziran zhi quan*, literally "human natural rights." The clumsy phrase was the very first occurrence of the Chinese rendering of "human rights," which was later replaced by the neologism *renquan*.[69] Not surprisingly, this concept was first introduced as a term of international law and still plays a vital role in world politics today.

As I suggested above, the noun *quan* commands a broad spectrum of negative meanings associated with power, privilege, and domination in the Chinese usage, much like the word li that brings to mind interest, profit, and calculation. Lurking behind the renderings of "rights" and "human rights," these banished meanings can always come back and haunt the English translation and unwittingly contaminate the words "right" and "human rights" with the suppressed, other meanings. The subtext of "excess" signification thus glosses the self-evident meaning of the English word "right" with something more than what it ostensibly says. This is not to say that the translators were incapable of comprehending the true meaning of "right." On the contrary, the "excess" signification seems to heed the historical message of rights discourse in the practice of international law only too well, because it registers the fact that the law had been brought into China by the nineteenth-century representatives of European international law who had asserted their trade rights and the right to invade, plunder, and attack the country. Their language of rights cannot but convey a loud message of threat, violence, and military aggression to the Manchu government at the negotiation table and to the Chinese population at large.

Negotiating Commensurability

Martin and his Chinese colleagues undertook to create a preliminary level of hypothetical equivalence or makeshift translatability between the political discourses of two very different languages and intellectual traditions. They did so by negotiating a ground of commensurability between Chinese and Christian values, and that ground was where the intended readers were expected to get at the meaning of their translation. In the English preface to Wanguo gongfa, Martin argues for cultural commensurability on the basis of natural law, explaining why the Chinese are capable of comprehending the principles of Western international law: "To its fundamental principle, the Chinese mind is prepared to yield a ready assent. In their state ritual as well as their canonical books, they acknowledge a supreme arbiter of human destiny, to whom kings and princes are responsible for their exercise of delegated power; and in theory, no people are more ready to admit that His law is inscribed on the human heart. The relations of nations, considered as moral persons, and their reciprocal obligations as deduced from this maxim, they are thoroughly able to comprehend." [70]

Martin's understanding of commensurability between Chinese and Christian cultures carries strong connotations of natural law insofar as natural law is understood as the other side of the argument about positive law in Western theological/legal discourse. In the main text, Martin and his Chinese collaborators render "natural law" as xingfa and occasionally as ziran zhi fa. In contrast, "positive law" is rendered as *gongfa* (the same compound used to render "law of nations" and "public international law") and occasionally as *lüfa*.

This is significant because they are essentially calling on the key neo-Confucian notions *xing* and *gong* (glossed by the translators as "natural," and "positive" or "public," respectively) to create a philosophical ground of commensurability between two very different intellectual traditions. This move is strongly reminiscent of seventeenth-century Jesuit strategies when Roman Catholic missionaries attempted to introduce a ground of reconciliation between Confucianism and Christianity.[71]

However, Martin and his collaborators did not stretch the idea of natural law to make the moral principles of international law sound like the Confucian ethics of reciprocity. After all, they were trying to introduce new knowledge from the West. If one reads *xing* or *gong* with neo-Confucian philosophy in the back of one's mind, as Martin's readers would, the Chinese word certainly changes the meaning of "natural law"; but it is also true that the meanings of the Chinese words are simultaneously transformed by a process of translation that engages them in a deictic manner with the English concepts "natural law" or "positive law" in *Elements of International Law*.

What happens is that neither Chinese nor English can lay exclusive claim to the meanings of the translated terms because those meanings reside somewhere in between, like the neologism *quanli* (right) discussed above. Just as the neologistic use of *xingfa* and *gongfa* plucks the neo-Confucian concept *xing* and *gong* out of their familiar philosophical context, so do the same translations take the ideas of natural law and public law out of Wheaton's local engagement with Western legal discourses to create a broader and more "universal" basis for the global claims of international law than either tradition could have accomplished on its own.

The seventeenth-century Dutch theologian Hugo Grotius (1583–1645), whose work *De jure belli ac pacis* (On the rights of war and peace) lay the foundation for international law, made a crucial distinction between *jus naturale* (natural law) and *jus gentium* (the law of nations). *Jus naturale* was based on theological arguments about the rules of human conduct prescribed by God to his rational creatures and revealed by the light of reason universal to all. *Jus gentium* referred to the general or universal consent of nations to observe certain rules of conduct in their reciprocal relations. Those who endorsed natural law viewed nations and states as enlarged versions of moral beings (conveniently adapted by Martin to Confucian ethics) and thus treated international law as an extension of civil law.

In *Persian Letters*, for example, Montesquieu makes one of his fictional characters, Usbek, express this view in a letter to another character, Rhedi: "You would almost think, Rhedi, that there were two entirely different types of justice: one, regulating the affairs of private individuals, rules civil law; the other, regulating the differences that arise between nations, tyrannizes over international law; as if international law itself were not a kind of civil law, not indeed the law of a particular country, but of the world." [72] If Montesquieu puts the words of contemporary theory in the mouth of his fictional characters in *Persian Letters*, he gives a straightforward treatment of international law on the basis of natural law in *The Spirit of the Laws*, thus joining the rank of prominent international law theorists including Leibniz (1646–1716), Vattel, and the others.

Natural law and the law of nations represented two very different but related conceptualizations of the nature of human society and its ability to manage disputes and war among the nations. Grotius himself defined the law of nations in terms of a binding consent among all nations to observe certain rules of conduct in their reciprocal relations, and this term was used interchangeably with international law by most European theorists. After Bentham raised the objection that the law of nations sounded more as if it referred to internal jurisprudence than laws governing states, international law gradually replaced the law of nations as an umbrella term for the science, but the running theological debate about natural law and the law of nations continued unabated in the language of natural law and positive law (which partly explains why Martin and his collaborators considered the Chinese compound *gongfa* appropriate for rendering all three terms, the law of nations, positive law, and public international law, in *Wanguo gongfa*). As the Western powers sought to increase their colonies and conquer the rest of the world in the nineteenth century, the emphasis shifted more and more toward universal consent, treaties, balance of power, and international tribunals and away from commonly shared humanity or moral vision among the different nations. Thus, Henry W. Hallek, a well-known authority on international law of the nineteenth century, was able to give a supremely realistic picture of international law. He called it "the rules of conduct regulating the intercourse of states." [73]

However, the endorsement of a natural law position need not contradict such "realism" in the early nineteenth century. One of Martin's contemporaries and certainly a better known Protestant missionary of the time was a Prussian I mentioned earlier named Karl Gützlaff. Twenty years before Martin, Gützlaff had served as the official interpreter for the British government during the Opium War and helped negotiate the colonizing of Hong Kong and the opening of the five treaty ports. As early as 1838, Gützlaff had argued that, when the British demanded the right to free intercourse among all nations, they were not merely seeking material benefits, for Britain was acting in accord with international law. Chinese resistance to international trade amounted to defiance of God, who had decreed the brotherhood of all men. Those who denied their people access to truth and to the manufactures of the West were infringing on an inherent human right.[74]

The crude analogy Gützlaff makes between natural law and international trade puts a definitive historical spin on nineteenth-century discussions of natural law. Gützlaff's logic would sound familiar to his nineteenth-century European readers and not nearly as crude as it may seem now. He effectively exploited that logic with all its moral and religious implications to help justify the global expansion of the British empire. As a missionary, diplomat, and translator, Gützlaff wrote and published the above views at the height of Chinese resistance to British opium traffic and only a year before Lin Zexu's famous visit to Parker's clinic requesting a translation of Vattel. Lin, as I discussed earlier, had only those portions of Vattel translated that touched on the "positive" implication of Vattel's discussion of war, hostile measures, blockades, embargoes, and so on. The interesting contrast between Gützlaff's endorsement of natural law and Lin Zexu's "positive" use of international law in the opium dispute in 1839 is significant and reflective of the changing situation of universalism in the nineteenth century.

Henry Wheaton, an early-nineteenth-century theorist of international law, tried to tackle natural law in a critical review of earlier European theorists of international law in *Elements of International Law*. He did so with a view to adopting a more positive conceptualizing of modern states' relations. As a legal syncretist, Wheaton does not completely abandon natural law but attempts to imbue his notion of positive law with a vague notion of natural law. Thus, he defines international law among civilized nations (China being commonly viewed as semicivilized) as "consisting of those rules of conduct which reason deduces, as consonant to justice, from the nature of the society existing among independent nations; with such definition and modifications as may be established by general consent."[75] Note that the emphasis here is not on the moral being or reciprocal obligation so much as on a positive understanding of "general consent."

Wheaton calls international law (with Savigny) an imperfect positive law. It is imperfect "both on account of the indeterminateness of its precepts, and because it lacks that solid basis on which rests the positive law of every particular nation, the political power of the State and a judicial authority competent to enforce the law." He adds, however, "The progress of civilization, founded on Christianity, has gradually conducted us to observe a law analogous to this in our intercourse with all the nations of the globe, whatever may be their religious faith, and without reciprocity on their part." [76] Wheaton's argument about progress and universalism is very different from a universalist argument about international law that takes cultural commensurability as its chief point of departure.

Where Wheaton simply equates Christianity with the universal and refuses to consider reciprocity, Martin, his translator, talks about reciprocal obligations and the communicability of universal laws across cultures and languages. Is Martin trying to manipulate Wheaton's arguments to suit his own evangelical purposes? It seems to me that the situation is more complex than the translator's intentional use or misuse of the original text. For no translator can afford to do away with a certain assumption of linguistic or cultural commensurability between the languages he or she works with. Doing so would be tantamount to contradicting the act of translation itself.

Instead, Martin and his collaborators made a choice that most translators would have made under the circumstances; namely, *they turned the desired commensurability between English and Chinese into a condition of universality.* Neo-Confucian overtones notwithstanding, *xingfa* and *gongfa* were taken to signify "natural law" and "positive law." These neologistic compounds borrowed the universalism of neo-Confucian thinking to promote the translatability of international law. In that sense, the interjection of a notion of reciprocity and commensurability into Wheaton's argument by Martin and his collaborators did not help the cause of Confucianism so much as it did the universalist agenda of international law.

Both Wheaton and Martin lived at a time when the meaning of the universal in international affairs was undergoing fundamental changes. In his own way, Wheaton was very much in keeping with the global events that were shaping the modern world with unprecedented speed and that in turn informed his own explication of the principles of earlier and contemporary theories of international law. His reference to the "progress of civilization" as "founded on Christianity" in the above quote is by no means a simple statement of the author's religious faith but a reworking of natural law principles in response to the unfolding of world events. Thus, we are told:

> The more recent intercourse between the Christian nations in Europe and America and the Mohammedan and Pagan nations of Asia and Africa indicates a disposition, on the part of the latter, to renounce their peculiar international usages and adopt those of Christendom. The rights of legation have been recognized by, and reciprocally extended to, Turkey, Persia, Egypt,

and the States of Barbary. The independence and integrity of the Ottoman Empire have been long regarded as forming essential elements in the European balance of power, and, as such, have recently become the objects of conventional stipulations between the Christian States of Europe and that Empire, which may be considered as bringing it within the pale of the public law of the former.

The same remark may be applied to the recent diplomatic transactions between the Chinese Empire and the Christian nations of Europe and America, in which the former has been compelled to abandon its inveterate anti-commercial and anti-social principles, and to acknowledge the independence and equality of other nations in the mutual intercourse of war and peace.[77]

Interestingly, the reference to China did not exist in the first edition of *Elements of International Law* published in 1836, but found its way into the later, revised and more definitive third edition that appeared in 1846 (the same edition used by Martin for *Wanguo gongfa*), two years before the author's death. In this quote from the revised edition, Wheaton is clearly referring to the Opium War and the subsequent treaties and settlements that opened China to foreign trade, marking the beginning of what some have called semicolonial history in China. This is intensely ironic in view of what had happened to Lin Zexu and his tragic use of Vattel. Whatever might have brought the Chinese government to the negotiation table following the Opium War, this fact is used by Wheaton as *evidence* of the triumph of the principles of Christian nations' "particular" international law.

The evidence that Wheaton enlists to prove the universal principles of European international law can be read as doing something else in the context of the later editions of his book. What I mean is that the so-called evidence has been the outcome of what it is supposed to prove. The post-1836 editions of Wheaton's book underwent many revisions to accommodate a vast number of new treaties and tribunal cases as the Western nations, armed with gunboats and international law, went and conquered more territories and more people. Like foreign-language translations, these cumulative editions of international law in the original language represent repeated *deictic engagements* (one speaking to the other or vice versa) with other cultures and civilizations, though by no means on equal terms.

Of all the editions of Wheaton's book after the author's death, the 1866 edition edited by Richard Henry Dana was considered the most authoritative and was subsequently adopted for the centennial edition I mentioned at the outset of this essay. Wheaton's main text and Dana's copious notes both were frequently used as a legal ground for many of the important decisions concerning international disputes in the nineteenth century. For our purpose, this edition contains an interesting reference to Martin's 1864 Chinese translation. In an appended note, Dana calls special attention to the meaning of Martin's work:

> The most remarkable proof of the advance of Western civilization in the East, is the adoption of this work of Mr. Wheaton, by the Chinese government, as a text-book for its officials, in International Law, and its translation into that language, in 1864, under imperial auspices. The translation was made by the Rev. W. A. P. Martin, D.D., an American missionary, assisted by a commission of Chinese scholars appointed by Prince Gong, Minister of Foreign Affairs, at the suggestion of Mr. Burlingame, the United States Minister, to whom the translation is dedicated. Already this work has been quoted and relied upon by the Chinese Government, in its diplomatic correspondence with ministers of Western Powers resident at Peking.[78]

Dana's footnote captures a uniquely circular situation. Namely, Wheaton's original text calls for translation because it possesses an inherent universal value, but it takes the existence of foreign translations to substantiate its universal claim. To aspire to the condition of the universal, the text demands universal recognition and demands being translated.

I close this essay with Li Hongzhang's comment on the negativity of the universal in international law. Li was a prominent Qing official who signed the unequal treaties and handled numerous crises during the Taiping Rebellion, the Sino-Japanese War, and the Boxer Uprising. A controversial figure of his own time and today, Li's official career spanned most of the tumultuous years of Sino-Western relations. In 1901, at the age of seventy, Martin was preparing a new text for publication whereby he approached Li Hongzhang to write a preface for his translation of W. E. Hall's *Treatise on International Law*. Li complied and wrote the following:

> Dr. W. A. P. Martin has been in China for fifty years. He has successively filled the Chair of President in the Tung Wēn College and in the Imperial University. Last summer he was exposed to the dangers of the [Boxer] siege; but on escaping with his life, he at once resumed and completed the task of translating this book. In his preface, he states the causes of the siege but without a trace of resentment. In a note to the first chapter he speaks of the war with France; and adds that China's protection of French residents con-

trasted favorably with the way in which the French had treated the Germans. Proof that China had previously (to 1900) observed International Law in the spirit of peace. *If this book could be hung up at our city gates and obeyed by nations beyond the seas there would be an end of strife, and all the world would be at peace; a state of things which I agree with Dr. Martin in hoping for.* (emphasis added) [79]

Li's tongue-in-cheek endorsement of Martin's labor articulates the negative condition of international law in theory and practice. Perhaps the desire for an alternative universal could assert itself only through the negativity of this situation: Can international law rise above its brute realism and submit to the higher ideal of peace, not war?

Notes

This essay evolved over a period of four years and was presented in its various stages at the School of Oriental and African Studies of the University of London, the East Asian Studies Council at Yale University, the Duke School of Law, the Asia-Pacific Studies Institute of Duke University, the Cultural Studies Colloquium at the University of California, Santa Cruz, the Chinese Cultural Studies Colloquium of the University of Chicago, and at the 1998 Annual Conference of the Association for Asian Studies in Washington, D.C. In December 1997, I gave a version of this paper at an international conference held in New Delhi jointly sponsored by the Indian International Conference Center and the Center for Transnational Cultural Studies. Both there and elsewhere, I benefited enormously from the comments and criticisms provided by scholars who either read or heard me present the ongoing research. For their valuable input, I thank Paul Cohen, Catherine Admay, Martin Stone, Laura Underkuffler, Arif Dirlik, Leo Ou-fan Lee, Jonathan Spence, Anping Chin, Charles Taylor, Arjun Appardurai, Charles Laughlin, Kamala Visweswaran, Michael Hanchard, Dilip Gaonkar, Thomas McCarthy, Q. S. Tong, Michel Hockx, Gail Hershatter, and the others who have made a difference in my reconceptualization of the project.

    All English translations are mine unless otherwise noted.

1 In Henry Wheaton, *Elements of International Law*, 1936 ed., 16a.

2 Ibid. Fung Sun is probably a misspelling of Dong Xun.

3 James Hevia, *Cherishing Men from Afar*.

4 For a recent critique of this linear notion of time informing national histories, see Prasenjit Duara, *Rescuing History from the Nation*.

5 For a critique of the myth of China's rejection of Western science and technology, see Joanna Waley-Cohen, "China and Western Technology in the Late Eighteenth Century."

6 See the Marxist historian Hu Sheng, *Cong yapian zhanzheng dao wusi yundong* (From the Opium War to the May Fourth movement).

7 The ability to use foreign-language sources does not imply that one automatically engages the issue of translation affecting those sources.

8   J. Y. Wong, *Anglo-Chinese Relations 1839–1860: A Calendar of Chinese Documents in the British Foreign Office Records*, 7–8. The Chinese-language archives from the Chinese Secretary's Office between the years 1839 and 1860 are deposited in the Public Record Office in London under F.O. 682. The British Foreign Office records in English are classified as F.O. 17. Systematic comparison between the two sets of documents would help determine how the diplomatic exchange was conducted in this period of crisis.

9   Masataka Banno, *China and the West, 1858–1861: The Origins of the Tsungli Yamen*, 232. The French missionary translator for the French Treaty negotiations was notorious for adding his own words to the French version of the treaty stipulating that French missionaries will have the freedom to rent and purchase land and build houses in the Chinese provinces. See Hu, 176.

10   The changing etymology of *yi* within the context of the Chinese language has been studied by Chinese philologists as a separate problem. For a detailed analysis of *yi* and *dongyi* on the basis of classical textual studies and modern archaeological findings, see Pang Zhenggao, "Dongyi jiqi shiqian wenhua shilun" (A study of the prehistory of Eastern *yi* culture). The Chinese etymology, however, should not be confused with or be glossed in terms of the translation problem I am concerned with here. The latter has had its own interesting history, which ran parallel to the classical etymology of *yi* since the country's first contact with the West but did not significantly impact the meaning of *yi* until the early nineteenth century. Since then, the word has become obsolete in the living language due to the earlier diplomatic struggle and Sino-British treaties that banned its use.

11   See "Diary and Consultation of the Council for China," in "East India Company Factory Records (1595–1840)," British Library, G/12/27, Canton, 20 August 1728, 49–51.

12   The Chinese title adopted was *Zheng fanyi guan*, and after 1856 *Hanwen zhengshi*. See F.O. 682/1987/21 and F.O. 682/1992/25b, British Foreign Office records.

13   Wade is best known in the West as the chief designer of the Wade-Giles romanization system of Chinese. To the Chinese, he is remembered for the historical role he played in the negotiation of the unequal Sino-British Treaty of Yantai with Li Hongzhang in 1876.

14   Denis Twitchett and John K. Fairbank, eds. *The Cambridge History of China*; see *Late Ch'ing China 1800–1911*, vols. 12–13.

15   See Dilip Basu, "Chinese Xenology and Opium War," 9.

16   Anyone who has skimmed through the actual dispatches between the two governments in the British Foreign Office records will walk away with a different impression. The Qing officials displayed extraordinary patience and politeness toward the often rude words and insolent behavior of the British and the French.

17   *Treaties, Conventions, etc., Between China and Foreign States*, 1:419.

18   Basu, 10.

19   F.O. 23/75, British Foreign Office records, Xu Guangjin and Bo-gui to Bonham, 27 July 1852.

20   For the full text of this Article, see *Treaties, Conventions, etc., Between China and Foreign States*, 1:418; for a similar provision in Article 3 of the French Treaty of Tianjin (1858), see ibid., 816.

21 The Zongli yamen was established in 1861, the first centralized modern institution to handle foreign affairs. See Banno, *China and the West.*

22 The Imperial College, or Tongwen guan, was one of the first innovations to follow the Zongli yamen. It was one of the two main institutions attached to the Zongli yamen, the other being the Inspectorate General of Customs (Zong shuiwu si). The Tongwen guan was established in 1862 to train diplomatic interpreters. It soon expanded to include Western sciences taught by Western instructors. In the English Department, the first instructor was John Burdon, an Anglican, who later became the Bishop of Hong Kong. Burdon was followed by John Fryer, who soon made a name for himself as a translator of scientific books in Shanghai. When Fryer resigned, the post was offered to Martin at the recommendation of Burlingame and Thomas Wade (see W. A. P. Martin, *A Cycle of Cathay: or, China, south and north,* 296). This college was funded by the foreign customs revenue. When Robert Hart became the customs inspector-general, he gave strong financial support to the Zongli yamen and its college and acted as political advisor to Prince Gong.

23 See Immanuel C. Y. Hsü, *China's Entrance into the Family of Nations: The Diplomatic Phase, 1858–1880.* Hsü's study, though informative, was steeped in the shadow of John King Fairbank's work on Sino-British trade and diplomacy, which, until recently, has long dominated the study of international relations in the field of East Asia. See Fairbank, *Trade and Diplomacy on the China Coast: The Opening of the Treaty Ports, 1842–1854,* and Fairbank, ed., *The Chinese World Order: Traditional Chinese Foreign Relations.*

24 See John Peter Stern, *The Japanese Interpretation of the "Law of Nations," 1854–1874.* For a recent study, see Alexis Dudden's Ph.D. dissertation, "International Terms: Japan's Engagement with Colonial Control," and her contribution in this volume.

25 Lydia H. Liu, *Translingual Practice: Literature, National Culture, and Translated Modernity,* 40.

26 Ralph Covell, *W. A. P. Martin: Pioneer of Progress in China,* 27.

27 Ibid., 114.

28 Chinese Letters of the Board of Foreign Missions of the Presbyterian Church in the United States of America, 7, Peking, Martin to Board, no. 44, 1 October 1863, RBFMPC.

29 Covell, 146, quotes this letter but does not tell us that the American minister Ward also had a hand in this matter from the very beginning. See below.

30 Martin, 221–22.

31 Diplomatic Despatches, China Despatches, vol. 15, Reed to Cass, 31 December 1857, NARA.

32 W. A. P. Martin, translator's preface (in English), *Wanguo gongfa* (Public law of all nations), translation of *Elements of International Law,* 3.

33 W. A. P. Martin, English preface, *Gongfa bianlan* (An overview of public law), a translation of *Introduction to the Study of International Law,* by Theodore Dwight Woolsey, 2.

34 W. A. P. Martin, English preface, *Gongfa xinbian* (A new compilation of public law), translation of *Treatise on International Law,* by W. E. Hall.

35 First published in *Chinese Repository,* 8:634 (1840), as quoted in Hsü, 123.

36 *Haiguo tuzhi* was originally published in 50 juan in 1844. The edition in 60 juan appeared in 1849, and a third in 100 juan in 1852. Wei Yuan was also the author of *Shengyu ji* (Record of imperial military exploits) completed in 1842.

37 See Hsü's comparative analysis of the translated text and the original, 123–24.

38 See Chang Hsi-tung, "The Earliest Phase of the Introduction of Western Political Science into China (1820–1852)," 14.

39 E. Vattel, *The Laws of Nations* (New York, 1796), 97, quoted in Hsü, 123.

40 See Ssu-yü Teng and John K. Fairbank, *China's Response to the West: A Documentary Survey 1839–1923*, 26–27. Arthur Waley gives a very different translation of this letter in his book *The Opium War Through Chinese Eyes*, 28–31. Notably, whereas Teng and Fairbank continue the nineteenth-century tradition of rendering the word *yi* as "barbarian" rather than "foreigner" or "non-Chinese," Waley shuns the sensational "barbarian" and uses "foreigner" in his translation.

41 The irony is that James Matheson of Jardine and Matheson, the foremost among opium trading companies, evoked Vattel for his imperialist trade policy. Citing Vattel on the eve of the Opium War, Matheson, then a member of Parliament, argued that the arrogant Chinese people and their government must be made to follow the terms of free trade, by which he meant "All men ought to find on earth the things they stand in need of," by force if necessary. See James Matheson, *The Present Position and Prospect of Our Trade with China*, 7–20.

42 In Martin, *A Cycle*, 234. Hsü gives a similar quote by Bruce, which comes from a later source published anonymously in an article titled "The Life and Work of the Late Dr. W. A. P. Martin," *The Chinese Recorder*, 48.2 (February 1917):119. I suspect that this quote has been taken from Martin's earlier published memoir. See Hsü, 137, 239 n. 29.

43 These and other complex circumstances do not support Hsü's argument that Martin did the translation because he "was in sympathy with the Chinese need for a translation of a work on international law" (126).

44 Diplomatic Despatches, China Despatches, vol. 21, Burlingame to William Seward, 30 October 1863, NARA. Also see Martin, translator's preface to *Wanguo gongfa*, 2.

45 Martin, *A Cycle*, 222.

46 Ibid.

47 Covell, 146. The date given is based on W. A. P. Martin's "Peking News," *New York Times*, 8 January 1864. Hsü gives a slightly different date (11 September 1863) on the basis of Martin's "Journal of Removal to Peking," *Foreign Mission* 22 (February 1864):228. See Hsü, 128, 238 n. 28. For a discussion of the discrepancies among the sources, see Covell, 164 n. 102. Also see Chinese Letters of the Board of Foreign Missions of the Presbyterian Church in the United States of America, 7, Peking, Martin to Board, no. 44, 1 October 1863, and no. 71, 19 July 1864, RBFMPC.

48 Martin, *A Cycle*, 233.

49 Ibid., 233–34. Also see Hsü, 237–38 n. 16. On Robert Hart's translation, see Hart, "Note on Chinese Matters," in an appendix to Frederick W. Williams, *Anson Burlingame and the First Chinese Mission to Foreign Powers*, 285. Hart's translation cannot be found.

50 Martin, *A Cycle*, 234.

51 The appointed Chinese collaborators were He Shimeng, Li Dawen, Zhang Wei, and Cao Jingrong.

52 Covell, 146. Also see China Letters of the Board of Foreign Missions of the Presbyterian Church in the United States of America, 7, Peking, Martin to Board, no. 44, 1 October 1863, and no. 71, 19 July 1864, RBFMPC.

53 When Martin first arrived in Beijing, Robert Hart was out of town, but he soon wrote a letter to Martin from Tianjin, expressing pleasure at learning his intention to translate Wheaton. See Martin, *A Cycle*, 234.

54 Ibid., 235.

55 Quoted in ibid., 234.

56 Diplomatic Despatches, China Despatches, 22, S. Wells Williams to William Seward, 23 November 1865, NARA.

57 This was not groundless because Martin did ask for an official decoration during his meeting with the four members of the Zongli yamen on 10 September 1863. Later he recalls in his memoir, "They paid me in due time with substantial appointments, much better than empty honors, and titles and decorations were not forgotten" (*A Cycle*, 234). His biographer Covell comments in a footnote that Martin's request for a decoration is a less blunt request than it sounds in English and yet it is indicative of "Martin's increasing passion for official recognition" (164 n. 104).

58 Martin, *A Cycle*, 235.

59 *Chouban yiwu shimo* (A complete account of the management of foreign affairs), the Tongzhi period, 27:25–26. The translation used here is by T. F. Tsiang, with minor modification, in "Bismarck and the Introduction of International Law into China," 101.

60 For a detailed description of this incident, see *Chouban yiwu shimo* 26:29–38.

61 *Chouban yiwu shimo*, 27:26; as quoted in Hsü, 128.

62 See Martin, translators' headnote *Gongfa bianlan* (1878); my translation.

63 Yan Fu's formal training in Western science began in 1866 at the naval school of the Foochow Shipyard School. In 1877–1879, he was sent to England to study naval sciences, first at Portsmouth and then at Greenwich. The Sino-Japanese War marked a turning point in his career after his return from Europe, when he began the enterprise of translating eighteenth- and nineteenth-century European thinkers. *Tien-yen lun* (On evolution; Huxley's 1893 Romanes Lectures on "Evolution and Ethics") was his first translation, published in 1898. It was followed by his rendering of Adam Smith's classic text *An Inquiry into the Nature and Causes of the Wealth of Nations* (*Yuanfu*), John Stuart Mill's *On Liberty* (*Qunji quanjie lun*) and *A System of Logic* (*Mule mingxue*), Herbert Spencer's *Study of Sociology* (*Qunxue siyan*), Montesquieu's *Spirit of the Laws* (*Fayi*), and more. Nationalists and social reformers such as Liang Qichao, Cai Yuanpei, Lu Xun, Hu Shi, and Mao Zedong were all avid readers of his translations. Although Lu Xun and the others would later criticize Yan Fu's "conservative" politics in the Republic era, almost all of them grew up reading his translations. As Benjamin Schwartz has pointed out, Yan Fu was concerned with the secrets of Western military, economic, and political power in undertaking those translations; but, unlike some of his predecessors and contemporaries, he was profoundly interested in what Westerners had thought about these matters: "He is the first Chinese literatus who relates himself seriously, rigorously, and in a sustained fashion to modern Western thought" (Schwartz, *In Search of Wealth and Power*, 3).

64 See *Zhongxi zimu hebi* (Terms and phrases), in Martin et al., *Gongfa xinbian*.

65 Immanuel Kant, "Toward Perpetual Peace," in *Kant's Political Writings*, 108.

66 Jürgen Habermas, "Kant's Idea of Perpetual Peace, with the Benefit of Two Hundred

Years' Hindsight," in James Bohman and Matthias Lutz-Bachmann, eds., *Perpetual Peace: Essays on Kant's Cosmopolitan Ideal*, 124.

67 The standard German term for "international law" is *Völkerecht*. The ambiguity of this word is interesting because *Völker* also means "peoples" and *Recht* can be taken to mean either "law" or "right." In Kant's own writing, however, he glosses *Recht* as a German translation of Latin *ius* and often puts the Latin in parentheses after the German term. Martha Nussbaum argues that *ius* is best translated as "law" in the eighteenth-century context. See Martha C. Nussbaum, "Kant and Cosmopolitanism," in Bohman and Lutz-Bachmann, eds., *Perpetual Peace: Essays on Kant's Cosmopolitan Ideal*, 25–57, 51 n. 1.

68 Heffter, *Das europäische Völkerrecht*, as quoted in Wheaton, *Elements of International Law*, 1866, 16. This edition is based on the third edition (1846), which W. A. P. Martin adopted for his Chinese translation.

69 Martin, *Wanguo gongfa*, 1:9.

70 Translator's preface, in ibid., 1:1.

71 For an illuminating critique of the making and unmaking of commensurability in earlier cultural encounters, see the essays by Qiong Zhang, Roger Hart, and Haun Saussy in this volume.

72 Montesquieu, *Persian Letters*, 176.

73 Quoted in Wheaton, 1866, 23.

74 See Jessie G. Lutz, "Karl F. A. Gützlaff: Missionary Entrepreneur," 62.

75 Wheaton, 1866, 23.

76 Ibid., 21–22.

77 Ibid., 22. The Chinese translation of this passage has replaced the words "to abandon its inveterate anti-commercial and anti-social principles" with the phrase "loosen up its previous bans to have intercourse with the other nations." The phrase "the former has been compelled" is rendered as "China and the Christian nations of Europe and America have reached agreements" (see Martin, *Wanguo gongfa*, 1:12).

78 Wheaton, 1866, 22 n. 8.

79 Li Hongzhang, preface to Martin, *Gongfa xinbian*, np. The English translation used here is included in the original edition of *Gongfa xinbian*.

Alexis Dudden

Japan's Engagement with International Terms

The vast number of new terms in Japanese in the early Meiji period (1868–1912) invigorated dictionary crafters. Debates whirled over the viability of Japanese, and several thinkers suggested doing away with the language altogether. In 1872, educational reformer Mori Arinori pleaded with Yale professor William Whitney to help him create a new language for Japan because, as Mori saw it, Japanese was a "deranged Chinese" that was unusable in a modern nation.[1] The inaugural journal in 1874 of the Meiji Six Society (Meirokusha) featured a lead article by the progressivist Nishi Amane in which he, too, advocated writing Japanese in "Western letters" (yōji).[2] Even nativist Kurokawa Mayori argued for a contemporary resurrection of romaji (the practice of writing phonetic Japanese in the Roman alphabet) from its sixteenth-century Jesuit missionary roots to make Japanese more accessible to foreigners.[3]

Other linguistic convulsions, though seemingly less extreme, obscured the energy involved in their creation and mediation. Political and legal draftsmen, for example, concerned with a new place for Japan in the world, translated the terms of international law into Japanese, formulating the substantive terms necessary to engage Japan in the politics of colonial control.[4] Writing treaties and conducting diplomacy was not a new practice in Japan, but performing these transactions in the terms of international law inscribed a definitive change. By making the terms normative in Japanese, translators and diplomats articulated a new method of intercourse with the United States and Europe while simultaneously reordering the vocabulary of power in Asia.

As part of the process of creating a new terminology of exchange, noticeable verbal incursions frequently displayed themselves in Japanese diplomatic texts. Many of these invasions stemmed from the Meiji regime's numerous new diplomatic relations with the non-Chinese-character (kanji) world. French and English were the languages of international diplomacy, and the Japanese government often conducted its relations in these languages because it wanted to participate equally with "the Powers." [5] Such graphically apparent textual permutations intertwined with an even more jarring but less blatant transformation: the epistemological shift to the terminology of a sovereignty-based system of law. The Meiji refractors of international law exposed the inseparability of words and power. They created a lexicon that fluently enabled state aggrandizers to describe Japan's imperialist policies and wars as internationally legitimate.

When Dutch studies scholars Maeno Ryoka and Sugita Genpaku secretly dissected a corpse in 1771, they searched in Dutch texts for what they found lacking in Chinese books to aid in their experiment.[6] Understanding language as a technique for conducting scholarship was very much a part of the Tokugawa (1603–1868) intellectual environment. Several decades after their autopsy, however, quests for knowledge outside the kanji world gained a new dimension: to know those foreign regimes' mechanisms of power. Increasingly, Russians in the northern seas and lands challenged the Tokugawa regime's desire to harness Ezo into the shogunal realm.[7] In the early 1800s, a Russian ship returned several Japanese castaways who brought a Russian world map home with them. The moment catalyzed the Tokugawa government's interest in knowing the "many-nationed" world. "The West" was officially visible again, and the primary concern of many scholars became to describe the West—particularly military and governmental structures—as fully and as quickly as possible.

Beginning in the 1850s, Americans and Europeans demanded with threats of violence that the Tokugawa government sign treaties written in the vocabulary of international law. Terms such as "sovereignty" and "extraterritorial rights" appeared in the documents that representatives of the so-called first-rank nations brought with their gunboats. Almost a century earlier in the Enlightenment's wake, various European and American political theorists had begun reworking theories of jus gentium (law of nations) into a measurable discipline of positive law. In 1789, Jeremy Bentham renamed ideas of law and ambassadorial protocol previously explicated by thinkers such as Hugo Grotius, Samuel Puffendorf, and François de Callières: "The word international, it must be acknowledged, is a new one; though, it is hoped, sufficiently analogous and intelligible. It is calculated to express, in a more significant way, the branch of law which goes commonly under the name of the law of nations." [8]

Its explicators postulated international law as a science, an unattached body of knowledge that could be studied, taught, and expanded upon. In his 1836 tome *Elements of International Law with a Sketch of the History of the Science*, Brown University legal scholar and American diplomat Henry Wheaton asserted, "International law, as understood among civilized nations, may be defined as consisting of those rules of conduct which reason deduces, as consonant to justice, from the nature of the society existing among independent nations." [9] Legal draftsmen conceived of the terms of international law in a discourse integrally woven into prevailing European and American theories of civilization, theories that posited the independent nation as the perfect form of political achievement.

Although the authors of international law envisioned a limited field of practitioners—independent nations constituted the legal protagonists—they did not, by definition, render the field an already closed system. In his 1866 edited version of Wheaton's text, Richard Dana included a footnote articulating the ideal flow of this knowledge: "Already the most remarkable proof of the advance of Western civilization in the East, is the adoption of this work of Mr. Wheaton, by the Chinese government, as a text-book for its officials." [10] The prevailing racialist worldview that informed ideas of "Western" superiority undergirded how the authors of an international legal system envisioned its discursive unfolding.

When American and European commodores and merchants brought their documents of legal exchange ashore in Japan in the 1850s, Western studies scholars (*yōgakusha*) working for the Tokugawa regime investigated the meaning of the terms embedded in these texts. As revolutionary forces seeking to overthrow the shogunate were decrying as treacherous the government's negotiations with "the barbarians," scholars rendered preliminary definitions in Japanese for terms such as "independence." They ascribed new meanings to extant *kanji* and devised new compounds. Despite the revolutionaries' rallying call to "expel the barbarians," after the overthrow of the Tokugawa shogunate one of the first edicts by the new Meiji Council of State declared the nascent government's intention to conduct itself "according to international law" (*bankoku kōhō*).[11]

For centuries, rulers of countries of what is now East and Southeast Asia had manipulated the influence of Chinese emperors either by sending envoys to engage in subordinate exchanges with them or, like the Tokugawa shogun, by actively degrading them to elevate the claims of their own rule. In the early eighteenth century, historian and shogunal advisor Arai Hakuseki's concern for the terminology in naming the shogun vis-à-vis the Korean king revealed a desire to place Japan on a par with China by negating reference to China.[12] Nonetheless, whichever method of self-legitimation they performed, rulers conducted written legal exchanges with other foreign regimes in the region through the common currency of mutually intelligible *kanji* terms. The diplomatic agreements of harmony and friendship (*washin kyōyaku*) that defined centuries of protocol between Tokugawa and Yi rulers derived meaning from a shared formula of diplomatic discourse, the terms of which referenced a mutually comprehensible Chinese lexicon. Whether these contracts mentioned China or not, China's intellectual authority in the region was manifested through the continued use of legal terms derived from continental practice.

As part of the Meiji government's plan to describe anew Japan's place in the world, state aggrandizers decided to use a different legal discourse, a decision that intersected with the regime's overall aims. Japanese thinkers at the time reacted to what "the Powers" proclaimed as a "universal" form of mediation embodied in the treaties their envoys brought to Japan, and they determined that Japan would make use of these very forms. Self-determined universalistic ideas, including the concept of a sovereign state acting independently, were historically generated within the emerging dynamic of capitalist political economy.[13] The vocabulary of international law could not be separated, therefore, from the material conditions of industrializing capitalism. Nor, for that matter, were its terms meant to be distinct from such conditions. This discourse, like others generated within the capitalist dynamic, worked to render the new conditions of the social order normative and legal. In Japan, too, the Meiji internationalists rendered terms such as "sovereignty" and "independence" commonplace. By doing so, they reordered the intranation machinations of power in Asia for the twentieth century. Writing international law into Japanese was not simply an instrumentally responsive means to prevent Japan itself from being described in colonial terms. Rather, rendering the terminology of international engagement in Japanese reveals how the Meiji regime envisioned itself as a full participant in the industrializing, mass militarizing, nationalizing world.

Significantly, although the Japanese government made the terms of international law the new vocabulary of power within Asia, the science was first introduced to the *kanji* world in China. In 1862, bureaucrats at the Zongli yamen, the office established by the Qing court to cope with the dramatic incursion of Europeans and Americans in China, began to read parts of Henry Wheaton's *Elements of International Law.* The following year, Anson Burlingame, the American minister to China, introduced his missionary friend William Martin to members of the Zongli yamen because Martin had been working on a Chinese translation of Wheaton's text. William Alexander Parsons Martin, a missionary from Indiana, later recorded this moment: "The Chinese ministers expressed much pleasure when I laid on the table my unfinished version of Wheaton, though they knew little of its nature or contents."[14] Overall there was mild interest in the book among the Qing officials who were on good terms with Americans and Europeans, but they did not suggest using these different laws with their different terms for relations with other Asian governments. A copy of Martin's Chinese translation first reached Japan in 1865 and was republished several times there in different synopses and translations. In 1871, the Meiji government adopted the text that Shigeno Yasutsugu rendered into Japanese from the first parts of Martin's Chinese version of Wheaton as the official reference on the science. Similar to organizing an industrial fiscal policy and devising a conscript army, incorporating international law into its worldview meshed with the Meiji leaders' aspirations to remake society and Japan's place in the world.

Whether the scholars and theorists who fashioned Japanese terms for the vocabulary of international law redefined existing *kanji* or coined new combinations, they did not throttle their initial efforts by worrying if the Japanese renderings fully captured the original French or English or German. My inquiry is, therefore, fundamentally not concerned with origins. I am not proposing to discover singular moments when specific terms of European political thought were *finally* translated into Japanese in order to rectify the work of these translators and scholars.[15] Approaching translation from such a perspective often leads to discussions of mistranslation. And, although departures along these lines can produce rich essays about a particular language's past, they run the risk of doing battle with a universal language—a pre-Babelian ur-lexicon.[16] The mistranslation approach assumes an eventual *correct* translation, and it also effaces the productivity of meaning that preliminary renderings wrought. I am concerned instead, therefore, with how a particular vocabulary of power became "legitimate speech."[17]

Debates about Japanese renderings for abstract conceptual terms emerged as Western studies developed into a discipline and original texts became increasingly available. The renowned legal scholar Mitsukuri Rinsho alluded to this moment when he spoke at the opening ceremony of the fall term at the Meiji School of Law in Tokyo in 1887, particularly recalling his frustration at not having a book for his studies:

My grandfather was the Dutch studies scholar Mitsukuri Genpo, and ever since I was a little boy I also did Dutch studies. . . . Towards the end of the *bakufu* rule, however, when English studies came into fashion, I switched from Dutch to English studies. I worked diligently at English, but because

I didn't have [a textbook]—my school didn't have one either—I did it very haphazardly. . . . I wanted to go to the West very much.[18]

Mitsukuri described how he had accompanied the shogun's brother, Tokugawa Akitake, to the Paris Universal Exposition in 1867 and how that experience had qualified him as a French-language specialist to the new Meiji government:

I went to France. I became proficient at reading some French, and after a year I returned to Japan. The Meiji *Ishin* occurred very shortly after that. I didn't have even a smattering of knowledge about original legal texts, but in the second year of Meiji (1869), the government ordered me to translate the French criminal codes. . . . I didn't understand them. . . . There were no annotations, no glossaries, no instructors.[19]

He spoke at length about his translating efforts and humorously admitted his confusion to the students in the audience:

There were, in fact, many parts which I didn't understand. And even when I did understand, I was at a loss because there were no words to translate the terms. The words right (*kenri*) and obligation (*gimu*)—today you use these words with ease—but it was a great strain for me to use them in transla-tion. I didn't claim to have invented anything, however, so I wasn't able to get a patent. (Laughter. Applause.) Because the words *raito* (right) and *oburigeshyon* (obligation) were translated as *kenri gimu* in the Chinese version of *International Law* I took them, but I wasn't stealing anything.[20]

Above all, Mitsukuri passionately remembered the activity of translating:

The following year (1870), a man named Eto Shinpei was working as a com-missioner at the Council of State's Institutional Bureau. As soon as I trans-lated two or three sheets of the civil code, he rushed them off. . . . Debates about words and phrases were all there was. There were no debates about any other matters.[21]

Of course, Mitsukuri could be accused of hyperbole. The violent Conquer Korea Debates (Seikanron) of the early 1870s arose over a perceived terminological affront, making it a debate about words as well, but ultimately the arguments revolved around the dispossession of the former warrior class.[22] Mitsukuri's reminiscence of the early Meiji period was concerned with an equally crucial dispossession: the dispossession of legal terms. His speech illuminated a mo-ment in the creation of new terms, a vital aspect of Meiji intellectual activity. Mitsukuri's self-deprecating admonition to the young students who "use[d] these words with ease" brings into relief a landscape in which terms that totally transformed political interaction in Japan had become customary within the space of twenty years. Recently radical concepts such as "right" and "obligation" had fallen asleep in the language; they had become normative terms.[23]

Significantly, the first books in Japan concerning the practice of international law — "the epitome of Western political thought at the end of the Tokugawa regime" — appeared at this very time of "haphazard" language studies.[24] In 1862, the Tokugawa government sent Nishi Amane and Tsuda Mamichi to Leiden University, hoping that the knowledge they gained there would help resurrect the fraying regime. Nishi returned to Japan in 1866, and the notes he took during Simon Vissering's tutorials on international law formed the basis for the compilation of his *International Law* (*Bankoku Kōhō*), published by the *bakufu*'s Bureau of Translation and Foreign Affairs (Kaiseijo) in *kanbun* in 1868.[25] William Martin's Chinese translation of Wheaton's *International Law* had, however, reached Japan in 1865. At the same time that Nishi Amane's text was printed, Tsutsumi Koshiji published a synopsis of William Martin, *A Translation of International Law* (*Bankoku Kōhō Yakugi*), the first fully Japanese-language description of the science.[26]

Both Nishi and Tsutsumi understood the power involved in rendering alien terms meaningful. In the late 1850s, Nishi had worked as the *bakufu*'s interpreter during the treaty talks with Townsend Harris, negotiating in Dutch with Harris's interpreter, Harry Heuskins. Tsutsumi, in the opening statements to his book, introspectively noted that "a translator earnestly searches for the spirit" of the text.[27] Nishi and Tsutsumi wrote general descriptions of international law, a standard genre in Western studies. Neither explained how to use the terms of international law in practice.

At the time, the shogunate's hold on power had weakened drastically, and envoys from several of the "first-rank" nations tried to align themselves with various regional *daimyo*, particularly those critical of the *bakufu*. The lords, in turn, wanted to learn for themselves the terms of international law that the envoys used. In particular, after British ships firebombed Kagoshima in 1863 to avenge Charles Richardson's death, the Satsuma *daimyo* Shimazu Hisamitsu ordered Shigeno Yasutsugu, a teacher in the *han* Confucian academy, to negotiate with British representatives. When the talks ended, Shimazu (an outspoken advocate of "expelling the barbarian") ordered Shigeno to translate a complete Japanese version of Martin's Chinese rendering of *International Law*.[28] Shigeno was a Chinese studies scholar by training. In response to Shimazu's order, in 1869 he produced a facing-page publication juxtaposing his Japanese translation with the Chinese version to which he added Japanese readings for some characters as well as occasional sentence markers. Unlike Nishi and Tsutsumi, however, Shigeno did not attempt to describe the general features of international law nor its historical place in European thought. Rather, he offered working definitions in Japanese of the fundamental terms of international law. Shigeno's book elaborated how the terms of this law operated by explaining them with linguistic assistance from what had been the legal reference language in the region until that time. He did not include the Chinese version to imply that the new legal terms emanated from the continent. Shigeno made the terms practicable in Japanese by providing ready comparative explanations that were comprehensible to most educated members of his domain.

Factoring Legal Terms

In December 1905, during a discussion about privileges in Manchuria between Japanese envoys Komura Jutaro and Uchida Yasutoshi and Qing representatives led by Yuan Shikai, the Chinese officials raised concern over phrasing in a Japanese proposal. According to the Japanese minutes of the conversation, Yuan asked for clarification of the term "protest" (kōgi), as it was a term that "was not usually used" in China.[29] His interpreter Tang asked Uchida, "What is the meaning of kōgi?" Uchida responded in English, "Protest." Tang replied in English, "Have you this word?" "Yes," said Uchida. Tang inquired further, "Legally?" "Yes," said Uchida, "legally and diplomatically." Tang responded, "We have not had it. This is a new word." Returning to interpreted Japanese, another Chinese minister ruminated, "The British Ambassador Mr. Satow likes this term." Yuan Shikai added, "I learned this term from Mr. Satow." Komura Jutaro mused, "It puzzles me to learn that you do not like this term." The minutes noted general laughter.[30] By the early twentieth century, the Japanese government conducted foreign relations with all governments, including China, in terms that Japan formulated in practice not only with European and American countries but within and for the kanji world as well.

Meiji state aggrandizers, legal theorists, and translators not only created a new Japanese terminology, they also put that vocabulary into practice. According to the theory of international law that the Meiji draftsmen were writing into practice for Japan, only perfectly "sovereign" entities governed themselves "independently" of foreign power. The taxonomy of political descriptions in international law also included "semisovereign," "dependent," "principality under the suzeraineté," "protectorate," "vassal," and "tributary" to classify states that could enter into a variety of treaty relations with other states. Most of the concepts had been rendered into a variety of terms in Japanese, but for Japan to make treaties legally according to international terms, these words needed to exist outside dictionary encodings.

Japan's leaders created the opening for a new lexicon to accommodate new concepts. The Meiji government sanctioned Shigeno Yasutsugu's version of *Bankoku Kōhō*, adopting it in 1871 after Shigeno had become a member of the Bureau of Education. Both Shigeno's bitextual version and Tsutsumi Koshiji's initial Japanese-only version (1868) used Martin's Chinese translation of Wheaton's *Elements of International Law*. English studies developed to the extent that other versions such as Uryu Mitora's *Kōdō Kigen—Ichimei Bankoku Kōhō Zensho* (1868) directly translated Wheaton's English original.

As early as the 1930s beginning with Osatake Takeki, linguists and historians have compared the terms used in the Chinese and the Japanese translations.[31] Scholars generally have distinguished among the Japanese versions those authors who adopted the Chinese government's choice for the compounds and those who did not. Osatake, for example, drew notice to the "Confucian theoretical stance" in Uryu's use of *kōdō* ("official way") for "international law," differentiating it from Shigeno's reliance on *kōhō*. Analyses such as Osatake's offer insightful details of the various schools of thought participating on the discursive plane in which international law became Japanese. Unlike Osatake and others, however, I am focusing not on the degree to which several terms differed but instead on the act of rendering the terms into Japanese and putting them into practice. In the 1860s, the Qing regime chose not to make use of international law to write its policy with other Asian nations. Qing diplomats saw no need to so drastically rework the political order that continued to sustain the continental regime at the center of the *kanji* world. Conversely, the new Meiji government wanted to align its existing and not yet existing political relations according to these new legal concepts. As state theorists decided to use these terms for Japan's policies, Japanese policy writers and legal scholars created a new lexicon that displaced the norms that had long held. Ultimately, their collective action displaced the continent as the arbiter of power, determining in practice through revision and neologism what would eventually become a new political vocabulary in the *kanji* world.

On the plane of diplomatic technique, the purpose of Kuroda Kiyotaka's 1876 mission to Korea was to establish trade relations—not to wage war. Accompanying the sailors and soldiers, therefore, were numerous men of various ranks and functions from both the Foreign Ministry and the Bureau of Development (Kaitakushi). One of these men, Inoue Kaoru, appears in most discussions of the Meiji pantheon. Others, for example Moriyama Shigeru, are listed in histories as functionaries in the modern period.[32] Some, like Urase Hiroshi, appear only by happenstance: they were the scribes and translators. As Kuroda and his entourage waited to learn if they would be received in Seoul to establish new treaty relations, some of Japan's lesser emissaries had occasion to discuss aspects of the treaty the Japanese government sought with their Korean counterparts. On 2 February, Moriyama Shigeru, a secretary from the Foreign Ministry, wrote out the minutes of a conversation he had had that afternoon in Inchon with Yun Chasung, aide to the Yi court representative Sin Hon.[33] Moriyama noted that Urase Hiroshi was present as interpreter.[34] In the full dialogue he remembered when he transcribed it, Moriyama wrote that he had stressed to Yun that Korea would surely incur the enmity of the "nations" (bankoku) should its government refuse to trade, and then he threatened Yun specifically with the wrath of Russia, America, and France.[35] Moriyama explained that only by establishing this treaty as an "independent" and "sovereign" country could Korea survive.[36]

The confidence with which Moriyama recalled his words suggests the surety with which he might have uttered these new expressions of Japanese political practice. He wrote that he had said, "More than a fixed term 'emperor' (kō) or 'king' (ō), he is the sovereign (kunshu) of a country. The sovereign of a country namely makes that an independent [country]. And when you call [the country] independent, both emperor and king have comparably equal rights (dōtōhiken)." [37] Moriyama wrote that Yun then asked how that concept would be written into formal state correspondence, and that Moriyama obliged by writing out the following equivalences for him:

DaiNihonKokuKoteiChisho   ChōsenKokuōKeifuku
ChōsenKokuōDenka   DaiNihonKokuKoteiHeika

According to the legal theory that the Meiji men were beginning to practice, only "sovereign States" (defined by Wheaton and made Japanese by Shigeno as entities that "govern [themselves] independently of foreign powers" [38]) could freely make treaties with each other. On the one hand, this moment between Moriyama and Yun reveals one informal way that the new terms were written into legal form. It also reveals the Meiji government's new objective of extracting Chōsen from its sadae (literally, "serving the greater") relations with the Qing court. The ongoing debate about whether the Meiji government wanted Chōsen to be "independent" for the fictitiously altruistic equation that measured "all sovereign States [as] equal in the eye of international law" [39] or whether it was for the sheer power politics goal of displacing the Qing as the dominant force in the region will remain trapped in its internal logic of nationalist pride and hatred. Members of the Meiji government formulated Japan's new state relations with the Korean government from their inception at these treaty negotiations in an entirely new vocabulary. Mirroring the terms the United States and other "Powers" imposed on Japan two decades before, the Meiji government legitimated whatever subsequent course of action it wanted to pursue in Korea according to the accountable mean to which the "Powers" subscribed.

During the more formal negotiations over the Kanghwa Treaty, the Japanese negotiators inscribed Japan's new lexicon into official practice. The Meiji emperor's envoy Inoue Kaoru explained to Sin and Yun that the proposed treaty accorded with the larger international order, and although the terms were new to them, the treaty derived its legitimacy from this greater mean. According to the recorded minutes, when Yun asked to see the treaty, Inoue responded that the treaty he had was written in Japanese (kokubun) and that he would request a translation from the Bureau of Translation (Yakkan).[40] Inoue assured Yun that "this treaty makes your country independent [jishu] as well. It relies on the precedent of customary exchange among nations and is based on the just way of the world [tenchi no kōdō]." Next, the transcript credits the translator Urase Hiroshi with explaining the treaty "point by point," but Sin Hon responded by specifically requesting a kanbun text of the treaty.[41] Quibbling began about whether it would be sufficient merely to attach a translation of the treaty to the final version, until Kuroda interrupted, reiterating Inoue's claim of the "precedent" of international law and "the just way of the world."[42] Both Inoue and Kuroda's remarks may seem mechanistic, but their claims offer an indication that the Meiji men had located a new way to order their world that allowed them to define what they were doing as a departure from past practices.

The Meiji delegates explained the treaty's terms to the Yi representatives before and as they sealed the treaty. Sin Hon responded to Kuroda's assurance of the legality of the proposed treaty by saying, "Until now, our country has conducted exchange only with your country. We had no trade with foreign countries, and for this reason we are unfamiliar with the laws of exchange among nations [bankoku kōsai no hō]."[43] Despite whatever remained "unfamiliar" to the Korean men, two weeks later, on 26 February 1876, the representatives of the Meiji government Kuroda and Inoue sealed the Treaty of Peace and Friendship with the Yi delegates Sin and Yun.[44] As only "independent" governments could initiate and conclude treaties with each other according to international law, the first clause of the treaty announced that "Chosen being an independent state enjoys the same sovereign rights as Japan" (Chōsenkoku wa jishu no ho ni *shite Nihonkoku to byōdō no ken wo hoyū seri*). I have quoted the official translation to show that the Japanese expressions *jishu* and *ken wo hoyū* were used here to embody the concepts of "independence" and "sovereignty."[45]

The terms with which the Japanese government declared Korea "independent" reveal contradictory tensions pulling at Japan's desire for power. Linguistically, the terms also reveal the hazards of using redefined *kanji* words to express the new concepts. The literal translation of the compound the Japanese government chose for the Kanghwa Treaty—*jishu*—is "self-rule." The term in Korean (*chaju*) made sense in maintaining Korea within its *sadae* relations with the Qing, not the meaning the Meiji negotiators were trying to convey.[46] Japan designated Korea an "independent nation" because the Meiji regime was committed to writing all its foreign relations according to international law and only independent entities could contract legally.

Within the treaty that theoretically enabled Korea's "independence," however, the Japanese government impinged on that country's spatial boundaries. Korea's newly proclaimed independence enabled Japan to establish a colonial outpost on Korean soil. Article 10 of the Kanghwa Treaty introduced the even more "unfamiliar" international technique of extraterritoriality (*jigaihō*) to the Korean peninsula. Article 5 designated two new spaces (the treaty ports at Chemulpo [Inchon] and Mokpo) in addition to the area around the Sōryōkan in Pusan where Japan's domestic laws could be practiced legally inside Korea. In contrast to Japan's assertion of power, Article 3 of the treaty designated that for ten more years "official correspondence" from Japan to Korea would be written in Japanese with a Chinese translation attached, while Korea's communication to Japan would be written in Chinese. The Meiji internationalists were prepared to put the new terms of diplomatic exchange into practice within the *kanji* world. The Japanese government did not expect these terms to have currency in that region, however, until the Qing government acknowledged that the vocabulary had meaning in relations among countries within the region that had participated in its tribute order.

In 1882, after disgruntled and hungry Korean troops in Seoul killed about thirty Japanese soldiers and burned the Japanese legation building, Ito Hirobumi and Inoue Kaoru consulted the French legal scholar Gustave Boissonade on how to respond according to the principles of international law.[47] A decade earlier, the Japanese minister in Paris, Samejima Naonobu, had invited Boissonade to Tokyo to advise the Meiji government in drafting new legal codes for the new government.[48] Soon after his arrival, however, Boissonade's role broadened, and politicians and law students alike relied on him as an encyclopedia of civilized and modern European legal practices. Boissonade responded to Ito and Inoue's questions with a series of explanatory memos that elaborated the nature of relations between what were called unequal states. Ukawa Morisaburo, a student of French law, translated these essays, and his efforts offer glimpses at the lexical layers yielded by writing with the terms of the new legal vocabulary in the very documents that explicated the practices the words named. In his "Opinion Concerning the Chōsen Incident," Boissonade explained the rules of contracting with "semi-tributary states" (*han zokkoku*). In his translation, Ukawa juxtaposed a *katakana* word spelling, *shusurenti* (transliterating the French *suzeraineté* from Boissonade's original), next to the *kanji* compound, *kankatsuken*, to equate the term. In a separate essay of Boissonade's dated three months later, however, *suzeraineté* was written into *katakana* as *shūzurenute*, and *kankatsuken* had become *jōkuni no kankei* (relations with a higher/superior country).[49] Other French words such as *violation*, *réparation*, and *annexation*, also were transliterated into *katakana* and printed parallel to the *kanji* compounds that equated them. That there was not yet a "standard" term for "international" (still most often *bankoku* and occasionally the contemporarily preferred *kokusai*) underscores the newness of the concepts being used.

One of the reasons both Boissonade and his translator may have wavered in precisely naming Korea's place was that the concept of suzerainty was being used in a relatively new way among the "first-rank" nations at that time as well. In legal tracts throughout Europe and America, the term almost always appeared in its French form. Ito Hirobumi noted in his 1904 English-language memoirs that he had taken Hori Tatsunosuke's English–Japanese dictionary with him on his adventure to Europe in 1862: "We had only an English dictionary translated by Tatsunosuke Hori, before we went abroad. As there were very few who could understand English well at that time, many mistakes naturally found their way into this rare and costly book."[50] Although Hori's splendid dictionary included equivalents for a variety of "sovereign" and "sovereignty" words, there were no entries for "suzerain" or "suzerainty." More significantly, perhaps, Inoue Tetsujiro, Wadagaki Kenzo, Kodera Shinsaku, and Ariga Nagao's 1881 *Tetsugaku Jii* (Dictionary of philosophical terms), did not include the concept of suzerainty.[51] Their dictionary translated a variety of names of political organizations and relationships including "ochlocracy" into Japanese and included "international law" as *bankoku kōhō*, but it left blank the suzerain relationship encoded in that law. These reference books, along with the jumble of scripts in the translations of Boissonade's 1882 notes, suggest the arena of possibilities — even though several texts of international law had already been published — for creating and using new words in something as seemingly normative as intranation legal vocabulary. The translators remain largely unknown, but the terms they factored and used precisely captured one of the intellectual fields that Meiji aggrandizers had chosen to order Japan's new government in the world.

Universal Referents

In a remarkable maneuver of what Ito Hirobumi liked to call "diplomatic technique" (*gaikōjutsu*), one that indicated a clear break from past methods, Ito formally negotiated the terms of the Tientsin Convention (1885) with Qing representatives in English. Ito spoke in a language radically different not only from what the history of contact between Japan and the continent preconditioned, but also one with which the governments of both countries contended to prevent exploitative commercial invasions of their respective polities. In short, English was not a comfortable choice for Ito to have made. However, English was the European language he best knew. By speaking English, the Meiji emperor's ambassador plenipotentiary resolutely displayed the Japanese government's desire to transform how power was defined in Asia. Had Ito negotiated the Treaty of Tientsin in Japanese and attempted to use the new *kanji* expressions for "independence" or "sovereignty," for example, the Qing negotiators could have challenged the terms as meaningless misinterpretations of the *kanji*'s intended meaning—as defined by the Qing. Articulating the same words in a wholly alien language allowed the terms of international law to retain their authority. From a power politics perspective, English wielded a weighty force. More important, Ito made it clear that the language in which the new terms were articulated did not matter so much as whether the negotiated treaty spoke the terms of international technique.

In the Treaty of Kanghwa with Korea in 1876, the Meiji policy writers had indicated that Japan's government intended to use legal concepts new to the *tōyō* world (the "Orient") for *tōyō* practice. Japan would continue, though, as Article 3 of the treaty stipulated, to attach Chinese translations to its correspondence to make its interactions comprehensible in that world. In the spring of 1885 at Tientsin, however, Meiji envoys mouthed these legal concepts to Chinese representatives in terms that further attempted to dislodge a larger lexical order. The need for the meetings arose from a diplomatic impasse over attempts to resolve what both the Meiji and Qing representatives repeatedly euphemized as "the latest disturbance" in Korea.[52] Foreign Minister Inoue Kaoru had failed to reach an agreement with the Korean king over the stationing of Japanese and Qing forces in Seoul, and, in late February 1885, Sanjo's cabinet chose Ito Hirobumi as ambassador extraordinary to travel to the continent to negotiate what was arguably modern Japan's first disarmament treaty.[53] These negotiations resulted in a rare text prepared for the Meiji emperor. Ito Hirobumi's *Report* (*Fuku Meisho*) was unusual not merely because it was a bilingual text (Japanese/English), but because it was largely the Japanese half of the report that was the translated material.[54] The author of this manuscript (most likely Ito Miyoji) created a playbook-like effect to the official report, transcribing the minutes of Ito Hirobumi's meetings as fluid dialogue and noting each meeting's end almost in a curtain cue with descriptions of how, for example, the men adjourned to a dinner party.

Between 3 and 15 April 1885, Ito and Li Hongzhang held six meetings in Tientsin in a variety of spaces including Li's official residence, the Japanese consulate, and at the Qing government's marine office in the foreign settlement. The report noted Ito's daring diplomatic technique in a single sentence at the beginning of the first day's script: "The Minutes of the Conversation that follows, as well as those of subsequent ones, were taken down in English and afterwards translated into Japanese by Mr. Ito Miyoji." [55] Next, the men's words were recorded:

The Ambassador: (He spoke in English) . . .
The Vice-Roy: (He spoke in Chinese and his remarks were interpreted by Mr. Rahoroku in English.) . . .[56]

Only on the first day (and the only time in the recorded proceedings) was there any indication that the Qing representatives had even acknowledged the Meiji envoy's maneuver. The text read:

The Vice-Roy: . . . I must ask Your Excellency to be patient and conciliatory, and not to cast upon me too much difficulty (smiling).
The Ambassador (to Rahoroku, the interpreter): I will proceed to make a general statement of the points of my negotiation, through my Chinese interpreter and so I will not trouble you for the moment. The Ambassador then spoke in Japanese and his words are rendered into English as follows . . .[57]

Ito's action did not completely surprise the Chinese negotiators. They had been notified and brought along their own English-language interpreter. On the other hand, before this meeting, Chinese diplomats had not included English interpreters in negotiations with the Japanese; they either brought Japanese interpreters or no interpreter at all. The ingenuity of Ito's technique was further naturalized in this instance by his not dwelling on it, that is, by simply performing the negotiations in English and writing his action into practice.[58]

Ito Hirobumi clearly intended to conclude a treaty with Li that would read fluently with the Meiji government's new practice of international law. Throughout the negotiations, Ito invoked the term "law of nations" as a guiding referent in response to various points of contention. (Despite Bentham's efforts, this appellation continued to be used in English interchangeably with "international law" throughout the late nineteenth century.) Explaining the meaning of the second article in a draft of the treaty, for example, Ito said to Li: "It means simply the right of war which every independent nation enjoys. . . . Thus the present arrangement cannot affect in any way our right of waging war according to the Law of Nations. That clause may be modified thus: 'It is understood that the right of warfare according to the Law of Nations, shall not be affected.' " [59] Unlike the representatives of the Yi court at the Kanghwa Treaty negotiations, the Qing negotiators could not and did not plead ignorance of these rules. After all, Shigeno Yasutsugu had composed what became the Japanese government's new textbook standard from the Zongli yamen's version of the *Elements of International Law*. Throughout the negotiations, however, the Qing diplomats were insistent that the Japanese government recognize the Qing court's long-standing relations with the Yi regime. Li stated, for example: "There is a striking difference between the position of Japan and that of China towards Corea. To China, Corea is a tributary state and has the obligation to report to her every matter that takes place in her country. But Corea has nothing more than a treaty obligation towards Japan." [60] At Kanghwa, the Japanese delegates named Korea "independent," but at Tientsin the diplomats had not traveled with warships and had no stark displays of power politics with which to counter the Qing claims. The new legal terms that Ito wanted to write into practice in *kanji* to equate "Japan" and "China" in "independent" state relations with "Corea" had to be ignored or designated differently.

One of the very few discrepancies between the English and the Japanese texts of the *Report* is telling, considering Ito's dilemma. The Japanese words equate the English expressions, but in the Japanese text, the author included the following parenthetical note: "The modifications in wording [included] changing '*Dai Shin Koku*' (The Great Qing Realm) to '*Chūgoku*' (The Middle Kingdom [China]) and deleting the '*Dai*' (Great) from '*Dai Nippon Koku*' (The Great Japanese Realm) in the first clause. . . . As there was no difference in meaning, this does not appear in the English written text." [61] The author of this note was not devious. There is no substantial difference in the English meaning, and throughout the English version of the scripted dialogue "China" and "Japan" were used to designate the country names. Chūgoku is a different appellation for the entity of the continent, one that transcends dynastic labels without becoming entangled in the specific dimensions and relations of a legally diffuse but particular empire. The name, however, posits the centrality of the country vis-à-vis realms around it in its particular worldview. The term the Japanese wanted to use merely designated the regime's reign. Nonetheless, as a sovereign regime in the alien terms of international law, Chūgoku named an entity of similar composition to Nipponkoku.

The final treaty reads awkwardly in *kanji*. In both the Japanese- and Chinese-language versions, representatives of the two *daikoku* (great realms) sealed a treaty dated in the respective imperial calendars of each court, legalizing a troop withdrawal between Chūgoku (China) and Nipponkoku (Japan) in Chōsen (Korea).[62] Noticeably, unlike the Kanghwa Treaty, in the Japanese and Chinese final versions of the Tientsin Treaty any attempt to name Chōsen as "sovereign" or "independent" was absent. In the English version, however, the version that Japanese diplomats might have hoped would be read by "Great Power" officials along with the English-language report of the negotiations, Ito and Li agreed to a treaty between the distinct "two Great Empires" of "Japan" and "China" with respect to a distinct "Corea" according to international law. No mention of "Corea's" independence was made, but neither was there any allusion to the still murky point of the Yi court's tributary relations with the Qing.

From a balance-of-power perspective, the treaty negotiations in Tientsin were not about words but about the net reduction of the number of troops in Seoul. Even so, Michel Foucault's insistence that the *dispositifs* of power—those machinations of the elusive notion called power that make that notion productive rather than wholly repressive—is vital here.[63] Ito Hirobumi's decision to negotiate the treaty at Tientsin in English in order to articulate the terms of international law indicates that the Meiji government was determined to define power in a way that broke radically with continentally ordered terms.

A decade later, the truce meetings at the close of the Japan-Qing War (1894–1895) revealed how the lexical maneuvering at Tientsin (1885) was transforming negotiations of power within the *kanji* world.[64] Not only were the meetings conducted in English again, but also each piece of correspondence Li Hongzhang wrote to the Japanese negotiators during the talks at Shimonoseki included an English-language translation. Mutsu Munemitsu's son, Horikichi, worked as an English-language translator in the Foreign Ministry and transcribed the minutes of the meetings between Ito Hirobumi and Li Hongzhang just as Ito Miyoji had done a decade earlier at Tientsin. Introducing the proceedings Mutsu wrote:

> I was instructed by the Count to attend the meetings to take down the minutes of the proceedings which were conducted in the English language. Each

day when the meeting terminated it was my duty to transcribe the notes I had made at the conference and submit them to the inspection of our Plenipotentiaries . . . the faithful reproduction of what occurred was my essential aim and I have endeavored to place on record all such words and phrases as were actually employed by the representative negotiators without paraphrasing them into a more literary form. In view, however, of the fact that the present work is the only authentic record in existence of these memorable negotiations I venture to hope that it will not fail to attach to itself some historical value and will also serve as a book of future reference for the Department.[65]

Perhaps because the peace treaty itself was the victorious document, different from the negotiations at Tientsin, Mutsu Hirokichi's labors were not bound into a report to the emperor.

According to the *Report* from Tientsin, at the final meeting between Li Hongzhang and Ito Hirobumi, Li maintained that it was "customary with [his] Government that the Chinese text [was] prepared by [their] hands, leaving the preparation of the other text to the Plenipotentiary of the foreign Powers." Ten years later, on 30 March 1895 in Shimonoseki, however, Li and Ito sealed three different texts of a temporary armistice: Japanese, Chinese, and English. When a young Japanese man attacked and wounded Li later that same day and Li sent a note explaining that he would be absent from subsequent negotiations, he even included an English translation to that note.[66] Most noticeably, the Qing ambassador attached a complete English-language translation to his "vermilion paper" (*shusho*, i.e., official) response to the Japanese government's draft of the peace treaty.[67]

An English text encoding the terms of international law became the legal referent for the peace between Japan and the continent. On 17 April 1895, as ambassadors plenipotentiary of their respective emperors, Ito Hirobumi, Mutsu Munemitsu, Li Hongzhang, and Li Qingfang sealed the protocol note attached to the final peace treaty between Japan and China. In doing so they confirmed a radical departure from centuries of legal contract in the *kanji* world. Article 1 stipulated that an English translation be attached to the final Japanese and Chinese versions of the treaty; Article 2 further impressed the import of that translation, announcing that "should any differences in interpretation arise between the Japanese and Chinese texts, we agree to sanction the aforementioned English version." [68] That the Qing government concluded treaties by the end of the nineteenth century with delegates from London or Washington (or any European capital, for that matter) in English could be argued (somewhat paranoically) as a means of protecting the regime's interests from the cheating barbarians and their foreign words. Even if accurate, such an understanding would not explain how this practice came to order relations among places that shared a mutually communicable past.

It is precisely such a document as the Treaty of Shimonoseki with the Meiji government's decision to use a different language altogether that reveals the crucial connection between words and power.[69] By installing something as interventionary as English for the legally sanctioned referent language in Asia —a practice observed today—the Japanese government made it clear that the terminology of international law was the terminology of power it intended to use with all nations, whether the Qing wanted to use the new *kanji* renderings for these terms or not. The Imperial Japanese troops violently had used their guns and organized numbers to victorious effect against the Qing ranks. And while that victory was insufficient to garner the Liaotung peninsula as a war prize for Japan, ultimately it enabled the Meiji peace negotiators to displace the centuries of mutually recognizable terms with a wholly different argot, effectively delegitimating the continent as the arbiter of diplomatic discourse. The lexical technique performed at Shimonoseki, though yielding a prize less concrete than the 200 million taels in indemnity paid by the Qing, tangibly enabled the rewriting of the practice of intranation exchange within the *kanji* world.

Terms of War

Among the new laws that were weaving the Meiji government together with foreign regimes was the concept of the legally conducted and contracted war. Declaring and concluding large-scale violence and victory was not new; that these exploits could be defined as legal or illegal according to international law was.[70] The emperor Meiji's military's victories against Qing troops (1895) and Russian forces (1905) have long been held as the touchstones for modern Japan's proof of power to the world's so-called first-rank nations. Even scholars who offer more nuanced approaches toward the forms of international engagement in the twentieth century have not denied the brutish import wielded by Japan's victories in 1895 and 1905. E. H. Norman maintained that in spite of the Triple Intervention after the Qing war, the massive indemnity and "the diplomatic prestige which Japan gained were rich prizes for a nation which twenty short years earlier had just emerged from feudal isolation. The full recognition of Japan as a power on equal terms with the other nations automatically followed." [71] Whereas treaty revision was central to Norman's thesis, John Dower's focus on racialist perceptions asserted, "When Japan defeated czarist Russia with dramatic victories on both land and sea in 1904–5, her accomplishment not only stunned the West but also electrified nationalists throughout Asia."[72] Although not denying the necessity of military victory in the equation of power politics, I propose that the way Japan engaged discursively in these wars was also necessary to Japan's entrance into the arena of "first-rank" powers: the terms inscribed Japan's military victories as legal.

Creating such a perception required the technique of someone familiar with its terms. Ariga Nagao, a literature scholar in early Meiji days and one of the editors of Inoue's Tetsugaku Jii mentioned earlier, emerged in the 1890s and 1900s as Japan's leading scholar of international law. Ariga was born in 1860 in Osaka, and, after studying at Tokyo Imperial University, he went to Germany to study law. One of his first books was Studies of the Nation (Kokkagaku) and was published in January 1889 to anticipate the promulgation of the Meiji Constitution. The book was so successful that it immediately went into a second printing in March. In six sections Ariga described the elements of society he viewed as composing the new constitutionally grounded Japan. In the first section, "The Nation in Its Entirety," he defined his project: "In other words, national studies accords with the truth of a nation-state. . . . Studies of the nation may also be called sovereignty studies [kokkengaku]. Sovereignty is the power of a nation-state and the substance of the constitution."[73] In the final section, "Powers of the Sovereign in Diplomacy," Ariga explicated the three elements that made up the sovereign's rights in exchange among nation-states: sending emissaries, the right to declare war and conclude peace, and the right to contract treaties. The ability to execute these maneuvers ultimately established a nation-state as independent (dokuritsu).[74] Ariga used terms and concepts in Japanese (sometimes with German words such as Volksreicht spelled out in katakana and printed next to the kanji expression) that evinced a clear genealogy of nineteenth-century international legal theory.

When the Meiji government declared war on the Qing in 1894, Ito Hirobumi summoned Ariga Nagao. Unlike soliciting Gustave Boissonade's opinions in 1882, by enlisting Ariga, Ito indicated that practicing the terms of international law had increasingly become a "Japanese" endeavor. Ariga had become professor of international law at the Army College (Rikugun Daigakkō) in Tokyo in 1891.[75] Although he had not yet achieved status as Japan's premier scholar of international law, he occasionally met with government officials to discuss various points of law and law in translation.[76] Early in 1894, before the war broke out, Ariga wrote a treatise on the laws of war while teaching a class about these theories to a group of young officers headed for war. On 1 August, Ito queried him on the legality of the vocabulary of Japan's official declaration of war against the Qing. Beginning on 16 October 1894, Ariga's profession of international legal scholar melded with that of state employee: he departed for the battlefront with the Second Army to act as legal advisor to its commander, Minister of War Oyama Iwao. Throughout the winter, Ariga Nagao answered questions concerning the legality of the Imperial Japanese Army's actions during conflagrations at Xinjin, Lushun (Port Arthur), and Weihai.

Immediately after the war Ariga wrote an account of his actions, interspersing journalistic observations with official treaties and memoranda. Writing as international legal advisor to the army, Ariga encoded his own actions as Japan's to detail his nation's legally waged war. Initially, Ariga wrote in a European language (French) about the place of international law during the war between Meiji and Qing forces for consumption abroad and then translated the same text into Japanese several months later.[77] Creating the perception of a legally fought war required displaying that war in international terms to "Great Power" consumers. In the opening lines of both texts, he stressed that "the important point in the conflict between Japan and China . . . was found in the presence of two nations, one which did not observe the laws and customs of war, whereas the other, on the contrary, enforced their respect as strictly as possible." [78] Having inscribed Japan as the legal participant in the conflict, Ariga maintained that the invading Japanese armies observed the primary tenet of international law. He explained that occupation did not mean the right to rule but was de facto rule, and that "true sovereignty over the territory did not cease to belong to the occupied state." [79] He assured his readers in both tongues that although some Japanese soldiers and the "ignorant" Chinese did not readily understand the subtle distinctions made in international law along these lines, those in Japan's military command knew to "practice benevolent and humanitarian policy [in the occupied place] unparalleled even in the wars of Western countries." [80] Admittedly, Ariga's texts were not official government record as were the treaties and the reports to the emperor, yet his chosen terms were critical. Ariga embodied the connection between words and power both as advisor declaring when it was legal to fire and as propaganda scribe detailing how the Japanese Imperial Army's actions accorded to the terms of international law.[81]

To infer even slightly that those concerned with Meiji Japan's place in the world copied only the silhouettes of alien forms of knowledge would fail to explain how these forms took hold as forms of power. By definition, international law was/is a performative discourse in which representatives entitled to act with the sovereign rights of their country negotiate with similarly entitled envoys from a different place. The representatives mutually define one another, and, as such, it is very much a politics of display. A classification of the world into entities that were "completely sovereign and independent" and those in which sovereignty was "limited and qualified" undergirded the conceptualization and terms of the science.[82] As "limited and qualified" entities, non-fully sovereign regimes were definitionally dependent in some way on alien regimes for their own identities. It is, therefore, impossible to extract the nineteenth- and twentieth-century politics of colonial control from the functioning of this law. Examining how the terms of international law became the vocabulary of power in Asia penetrates tenacious legacies of Japanese imperialism. To make the terminology normative in Japanese, the Meiji regime rendered the lexicon meaningful in the kanji world. The government of Japan wrote treaties that declared its colonial policies legitimate according to an international standard. State aggrandizers inextricably fused the relationship of words and power by entwining military prowess with the ability to describe that force as legal. Engaging in the terms of international law did not cause Japan to become the imperialist nation it did. Fluently using the terms of this science, however, legitimated its imperialist claims.

Notes

Unless otherwise noted, all translations are mine.

1 Mori Arinori letter to William Whitney, 21 May 1872, collected in Kato Shuichi and Maruyama Masao, eds., *Honyaku no Shisō; Nihon Kindai Shisō Taikei*, 317. In 1798, Honda Toshiaki bemoaned the impenetrability of Japanese because kanji were too difficult to use in foreign exchange. At the time, Honda still envisioned a double order of diplomacy: one within the kanji world and one without. The Meiji decision to reorder Japan's relations with foreign countries according to international law lexically collapsed Honda's distinction. See Honda Toshiaki, "Kaihō Seiryō," in Tsukatani Akihiro, *Nihon Shisō Taikei*, vol. 44.

2 Nishi Amane, "Yōji wo motte Kokugo o Kaku Suru Ron," *Meiroku Zasshi*, no. 1 (March 1874).

3 See Kurokawa Mayori's grade-school primer *Yokobunji Hyakunin Isshu*. For a lavishly photographed and detailed, albeit cultural essentialist view (Nihonjinron), of these issues, see Kida Junichiro, *Nihongo Daihaku Butsukan, Akuma no Bunji to Tatakatta Hitobito*.

4 See Timothy Mitchell's lucid analysis of colonial politics in *Colonising Egypt*.

5 In 1874, the Department of Foreign Affairs of the Meiji government published its first English-language compilation of treaties signed between Japan and "the Powers." The preface to the fourth edition (1899) recorded the following printing history: "In order to afford an easy opportunity to consult the Conventional Arrangements regulating foreign intercourse of this Empire, a volume containing the Treaties and Conventions concluded between Japan and other Powers was first published by this Department in 1874; a revised edition was issued in 1884, with the addition of such Compacts

as had been newly concluded or had undergone modifications during the interval, and the later publication was followed by a supplementary volume in 1889" (Foreign Office, *Treaties and Conventions between the Empire of Japan and Other Powers*). I italicize the word "other" to emphasize that by 1899, the Meiji government considered Japan one of "the Powers." The texts were distributed to foreign legations in Tokyo, archiving the Meiji effort to render its foreign policy fluent in international terms.

6 The men referred to Gerard Dicten's *Ontleekundige tafelen* (1734), a Dutch rendering of Johann Adam Kulmus's *Anatomiche tabellen* (1722).

7 See Brett Walker, "Reappraising the *Sakoku* Paradigm: The Ezo Trade and the Extension of Tokugawa Political Space into Hokkaido."

8 Jeremy Bentham, *An Introduction to the Principles of Morals and Legislation*, 326 n. 1.

9 Henry Wheaton, *Elements of International Law: With a Sketch of the History of the Science*. Throughout I refer to the Carnegie Endowment's 1936 reprint of Wheaton's text. Edited by George Grafton Wilson, it fully replicates the original as well as the highly valued notes Richard Henry Dana added to the eighth edition (1866), and it is also available in most university libraries. See Dana, ed., *Elements of International Law*, 20.

10 See Dana, *Elements of International Law*, 19 n. 8.

11 Ordinance No. 98, 17 February 1868, collected in Naikaku Kanpōkyoku, ed., *Hōrei Zensho*, 1:45.

12 See Ronald Toby, *State and Diplomacy in Early Modern Japan: Asia in the Development of the Tokugawa Bakufu*, especially chap. 5, "Through the Looking-Glass World of Protocol: Mirror to an Ideal World," 168–230.

13 See Moishe Postone, *Time, Labour, and Social Domination: A Reinterpretation of Marx's Critical Theory*, 366–67.

14 W. A. P. Martin, *A Cycle of Cathay*, 233–34. See also Ralph Covell, *W. A. P. Martin: Pioneer of Progress in China*.

15 Evoking Jorge Luis Borges's notion of the "hypothesis" of a dictionary, Lydia Liu has beautifully critiqued the very assumption that there ought to be "equivalents" waiting to explain alien terms. See Liu, *Translingual Practice*.

16 For example, see Yanabu Akira, *Honyakugo Seiritsu Jijō* and *Honyaku no Shisō—Shizen to Nature*.

17 Pierre Bourdieu points out the futility of trying to understand "the power of linguistic manifestation linguistically." Doing so makes "one forget that authority comes to language from outside. . . . Language at most *represents* this authority, manifests and symbolizes it." By focusing on the translating and writing of a particular vocabulary, I hope to show how a specific use of terms describes the power of what Bourdieu calls "legitimate speech." See Bourdieu, *Language and Symbolic Power*, 109.

18 Quoted in Kato and Maruyama, 303–6. In his 1907 biography of Mitsukuri, linguist Otsuki Fumihiko (1847–1928), a descendant of the great scholar and adventurer Gentaku, quoted Mitsukuri's classmate Fujikura Kentatsu to describe the books the students brought to school: "The students brought whatever books they had to school. When one brought a book on physics, another brought an economics text. If one brought a geography, someone else brought a book on law. Military texts, histories—students brought these various books, and we would ask the teacher to instruct them" (Otsuki Fumihiko, *Mitsukuri Rinshō Kunden*, 32).

19   In Kato and Maruyama, 304–5.

20   Ibid., 305–6.

21   Ibid., 306.

22   See Harry Harootunian, "The Samurai Class During the Early Years of the Meiji Period in Japan, 1868–1882," 77–82.

23   Michel Foucault elegantly described "existing discourses" as "slumbering in a sleep towards which they have never ceased to glide since the day they were pronounced" (*The Archaeology of Knowledge and the Discourse on Language*, 123).

24   Seiyōbunmei no Yunyū Kenkyūkai, ed., *Yōgaku Jishi*, by Sawa Omi, 65.

25   Okubo Toshiaki ed., *Nishi Amane Zenshū*, 2:3–102. Thomas Havens mentions Nishi's *Bankoku Kōhō* in his biography of Amane, *Nishi Amane and Modern Japanese Thought*, 51–52.

26   Tsutsumi Koshiji, *Bankoku Kōhō Yakugi*, collected at the University of Tokyo.

27   Ibid., preface.

28   Shigeno Yasutsugu, *Bankoku Kōhō*, at Rikkyo University's Okubo Toshiaki Collection; a short segment of the second section is included in Kato and Maruyama. See also Yasuoka Akio, *Nihon Kindaishi*, 52–53; Numata Jiro comments briefly on this too, in "Shigeno Yasutsugu and the Modern Tokyo Tradition of Historical Writing," in W. G. Beasley and E. G. Pulleybank, eds., *Historians of China and Japan*, 264–87.

29   Gaimusho, ed., *Nihon Gaikō Monjo* 38, no. 1 (1936):371. (Hereafter NGM).

30   Ibid., 371–72.

31   Osatake Takeki, *Kinsei Nihon no Kokusai Kannen no Hattatsu*, 40–41.

32   See, for example, Yasuoka Akio.

33   NGM (1936) 9:44–49.

34   On 14 January 1876, Kuroda mentioned three Korean-language students from the Foreign Ministry who accompanied the mission: Urase Hiroshi, Arakawa Norimasu, and Nakano Kyotaro (ibid., 9:7).

35   Ibid., 47.

36   Ibid., 48.

37   Ibid.

38   Dana, 44.

39   Ibid.

40   NGM 9:87–92. Inoue's comments mentioned here are on 89.

41   Ibid., 90.

42   Ibid.

43   Ibid., 91.

44   Ibid., 114–20.

45   Ibid., 115; see also Foreign Office, 1. A variety of terms for "independence" and "sovereignty" were used until the vocabulary became more standardized. Since the early twentieth century *dokuritsu* and *shuken* have been the preferred terms.

46   My thanks to Andre Schmid for stressing this to me.

47   Ito Hirobumi and Hiratsuka Atsushi, eds., *Hisho Ruisan: Chōsen Kōshō Shiryō*, 2:182–241. (Hereafter HRCKS).

48   Okubo Yasuo, *Nihon Kindaihō no Chichi—Bowasonaado*, 77.

49   HRCKS, vol. 2, esp. 213–20.

50   Ito Hirobumi, *Marquis Ito's Experience*, 2–3.

51 Inoue Tetsujiro et al., *Tetsugaku Jii*. I am indebted to James Ketelaar for showing me this book.

52 On the evening of 4 December 1884, Kim Okkyun, Pak Yongho, and Hong Yongsik led members of their "progressive faction" (the Kaehwa'pa, also referred to as the "pro-Japan faction") in a coup attempt against the Min faction. Takezoe Shinichiro, the Meiji representative in Seoul, had promised Kim that should Kim's men go forward with their attempt to rout the pro-Qing Min faction from power, the two hundred Japanese troops in Seoul would assist. After the coup (known as the Kapsin Chongbyon) began, Takezoe forgot his promise. The coup failed drastically. In the subsequent three-day mayhem during which Takezoe not only fled for Japan with his "progressives" but even set fire to the Japanese legation building in Seoul, Qing, Yi, and Meiji soldiers confusedly volleyed bullets, causing casualties on all fronts. The Yi regime (with Qing backing) denounced Takezoe and accused Japan of trying to overthrow the legitimate Korean government. Inoue Kaoru, then foreign minister, initiated negotiations, but eventually the Meiji government decided it would have to send an imperial delegation to the Qing court.

53 NGM 18 (1936): 196–200.

54 *Report of Count Ito Hirobumi, Ambassador Extraordinary to His Imperial Majesty the Emperor of Japan of His Mission to the Court of China, 18th Year of Meiji/Ito Tokuha Zenken Taishi, Fuku Meisho.*

55 Ito Hirobumi, *Fuku Meisho*, 3 April 1885, 1.

56 Ibid., 1–2.

57 Ibid., 5–6, 12.

58 Telegrams were often sent between Japanese officials in a non-*kanji* language. Enomoto Takeaki, for example, dispatched a telegram to the Foreign Ministry detailing the proceedings of the first day's meeting. He wrote in English: "Negotiation was commenced yesterday at Li's office. On our side, Ambassador, myself and interpreter. On Chinese side, Li-Hung-Chang, Gotaicho and Zokusho" (NGM 18:237). Enomoto did not call any attention to the language used in the negotiations, mentioning only an "interpreter."

59 Ito, *Fuku Meisho*, 12 April 1885, 3.

60 Ibid., 4; the Japanese translation here when Li speaks is *wagakuni* (our country) for "China."

61 Ibid., 15 April 1885, 8.

62 I use the English names for the countries the way they appear in the *Report*.

63 Michel Foucault, "Truth and Power," in *Power/Knowledge: Selected Interviews and Other Writings 1972–1977*, 109–33.

64 This war is commonly referred to in English as the Sino-Japanese War, but I am purposefully skewing the translation to show how it was (and still is) perceived by the victors. I do the same for the Japan-Russia War (1904–1905). Notably, even though both wars engendered great suffering on the people of the Korean peninsula, as many battles of both wars were fought there, the place of Korea and its people continue to be effaced by the wars' labels.

65 The English-language transcript is in the archives of the Foreign Ministry in Tokyo and is also published in Morinosuke Kajima, *The Diplomacy of Japan 1894–1922, Volume*

1: *Sino-Japanese War and Triple Intervention,* 198–280. The transcript recorded in the NGM, 28, no. 2 (1936):380–436, was derived from the Japanese-language summary of the proceedings but does not mention that the negotiations were held in English.

66 NGM 28, no. 2, 330–31; see also Yasuoka, 287–88, for details on Ito Hirobumi's re-action to the sentence of life imprisonment for Li's attacker. Ito secretly sent a messenger to Judge Tsurugaoka Takutaro to try to persuade him to change his decision to the death penalty.

67 Ibid., 335–48.

68 Ibid., 366.

69 W. G. Beasley mentioned in a footnote that an English text was agreed to at Shimono-seki, but that "as a matter of national dignity it was the Chinese and Japanese texts that were signed" (W. G. Beasley, *Japanese Imperialism 1894–1945,* 58). By downplaying the importance of the linguistic maneuver, Beasley seems to accept the new Japanese action as standard practice, in effect naturalizing the use of English into the larger plane of diplomatic discourse. Notably, Akira Iriye makes almost the opposite argument from mine about this treaty, focusing attention on the fact that because Mutsu Munemitsu could "read and comprehend what the Chinese delegate Li Hung-chang wrote in Chinese . . . the episode revealed not so much a cultural sharing as a cultural dependence on China even while its military might was proving superior. Mutsu's example, which can be multiplied, suggests that no matter how much one was influenced by Western civilization, Chinese learning was still considered a prerequisite for Japanese leaders" (Akira Iriye, *China and Japan in a Global Setting,* 30). Of course, Chinese learning was still essential for educated Japanese, but this treaty reveals the Meiji government's decision to shift the universal referent of exchange not simply to English but to alien terms which the Japanese were putting into practice in Asia.

70 In the introduction to W. Michael Reisman and Chris T. Antoniou's recent book, *The Laws of War—A Comprehensive Collection of Primary Documents on International Laws Governing Armed Conflict,* the authors offer a very matter-of-fact treatment of these laws. In the nineteenth century, "a range of popular organizations and movements sought to condemn war, to temper its severity when it occurred and, even more ambitiously, to create international dispute mechanisms that might obviate it entirely. . . . The sources of the law of armed conflict, like international law of which it is a part, are . . . diverse. . . . Historically, much of the law of armed conflict on sea and land developed from practices that gradually were recognized as 'customary law' " (xviii–xix).

71 E. H. Norman, *Japan's Emergence as a Modern State,* in *Origins of the Modern Japanese State—Selected Writings of E. H. Norman,* 307.

72 John Dower, *War Without Mercy—Race and Power in the Pacific War,* 147.

73 Ariga Nagao, *Kokkagaku,* sect. 1, p. 8. My thanks to Yasuoka Akio of Hosei University for showing me this text.

74 Ariga, *Kokkagaku,* sect. 6, p. 296.

75 At military academies in all the "first-rank" nations there was a lecturer of international law.

76 Ito Miyoji, for example, mentioned Ariga Nagao in a letter (4 July 1889) to Ito Hirobumi discussing the English-language translation of the constitution. See Ito Hirobumi Kankei Bunsho Kenkyukai, ed., *Ito Hirobumi Kankei Bunsho,* 2:69.

77 Ariga Nagao, *La Guerre Sino-Japonaise au Point de Vue du Droit International;* Ariga Nagao, *Nisshin Sen'eki Kokusaihōron.*

78 Ibid., xi; 9.

79 Ibid., 173; 228.

80 Ibid., 176–77; 232–33. Ariga did not dwell on the Japanese Army's slaughter at Lu-shun in December 1894. For a critical discussion, see Inoue Haruki's new book, *Ryojun Gyakusatsu Jiken.*

81 Another scholar of international law, Takahashi Sakuei, was hired by the Navy as legal advisor during this war. Like his friend Ariga, Takahashi wrote a book detailing Japan's legal war. He, too, published his account in a European language (English), Sakuyé Takahashi, *Cases on International Law During the Chino-Japanese War.* Takahashi also compiled the section on legal matters for the official history of the war.

82 Dana, 44.

James Hevia   *Looting Beijing: 1860, 1900*

Plunder has long been a part of empire building and warfare in general. In the late nineteenth century, however, as European armies entered Asia and Africa, it took on special features. This was particularly the case for British military forces, where such activities were frequently referred to in campaign and newspaper accounts as "looting" and the objects seized as "loot." Intimately linked to British expansion in India, the word loot entered the English language from Hindi or Sanskrit in the eighteenth century.[1] In either its noun or verb form, it frequently replaced older English words such as pillage, booty, spoils, and plunder itself. Yet because it was firmly embedded in the new lexicon of empire, loot was not, strictly speaking, interchangeable with these terms. Insofar as it related to British imperial adventures in India, East Asia, and later, Africa, it evoked a sense of opportunity that empire building offered to the bold and daring. As such, loot simultaneously attracted recruits and operated as a kind of promissory note for a cross-section of the male population of Great Britain, particularly underpaid soldiers. It seems to have operated in a similar way for native troops who became part of the British imperial armies.

At the same time, however, loot could also signify the ethical ambiguities of empire building, particularly because the warfare in which the British engaged was usually justified on high moral grounds. It was others who broke treaties, defied laws, or perpetrated barbarous crimes; the British argued that they merely used warfare to teach the rules of civilized international relations to lesser powers. This was especially the case in China, where Great Britain and other Western powers claimed they went to war to enforce treaty rights or to punish the Chinese for transgressions against civilization.

Nevertheless, during the military incursions into north China by European forces in 1860 and 1900, warfare was accompanied by the plundering of Qing palaces, temples, and the homes of wealthy Manchu and Chinese residents of Beijing. In the first case, French, British, and Indian army troops were involved and their efforts were primarily limited to the Summer Palace or Yuanming Gardens northeast of Beijing. The second looting episode was part of the events surrounding the Boxer Uprising and the siege of the foreign legations at Beijing. Military forces from the United States, Great Britain, France, Russia, Germany, Austria, Italy, and Japan were involved in the plunder of Beijing and Tianjin, the towns and villages between them, and a number of other urban centers within a radius of two hundred miles of the capital. Any study of looting, therefore, must consider the challenge it posed to conventional ideologies of righteous warfare and the orderly exchange of property.

In order to address these issues, this essay deals with events in China in a context broader than these brief plundering episodes themselves. By exploring the legal niceties of loot and plunder, the British military traditions associated with looting, and the growth of a market in and knowledge about Chinese fine arts, I intend to situate the lootings of Beijing more firmly within the history of Euro-American empire building in the second half of the nineteenth century.

The Looting of the Yuanming Gardens, the Emperor of China's Summer Palace

On 7 October 1860, French cavalry swung northwest of Beijing in search of the main body of Qing imperial forces and found themselves at the gate of a large garden and pavilion complex later identified as the emperor's Summer Palace.[2] Soon afterwards the French were joined by British Indian Army cavalry units, including Sikh and Pathan irregulars of Fane's and Probyn's Horse, and British regular and Indian Army infantry regiments. Over the course of the next few days, these units ransacked and looted the Summer Palace in a wild, unregulated frenzy of destruction and theft.[3]

Yet, although all of the forces mentioned appear to have been engaged in the plunder, they did not all loot the same way. In general, European enlisted men sought out gems and precious metals such as gold and silver. Although their officers were not immune to such considerations, many of them also seem to have been interested in "curiosities" that might fetch a good price in European markets. In contrast, Indian Army troops seem to have been drawn to clothing, silks, furs, and jewels. Few seemed to have been interested in porcelain, unless of a large size, and as a result, vast amounts were destroyed in the search for more desirable objects. As looters loaded themselves down with as much as they could carry, the more resourceful commandeered caissons and wagons to haul as much as possible into their camps.

Although the sack of the palaces was a concern for the French and British leadership—the armies were, after all, in enemy territory—they handled matters quite differently. The French commander, General Montauban, seemed content to let the loot fever run its course. As the Count D'Hérrison, Montauban's interpreter, put it, "primitive human nature" had taken control of the men, making them selfish individuals rather than part of an army. Under the circumstances, officers must be "prudent and patient," waiting for the soldiers to fatigue themselves and return on their own accord to take up their "accustomed yoke."[4] As they waited for their army to exhaust itself, Montauban and his staff seem to have concerned themselves with picking out the right sort of Qing imperial objects to send to Napoleon III and the Empress Eugénie as trophies.

In contrast, the British Army, according to D'Hérrison, "arrived in squads, like gangs of workmen, with men carrying large sacks and commanded by noncommissioned officers, who brought with them, strange as it may seem, touchstones," the "primitive jeweler's tool."[5] Within forty-eight hours of the beginning of the sack, British looting became even more systematized. On 9 October, the commander, General Hope Grant, announced the formation of a prize committee, and indicated that all looted objects were to be turned over to this committee, with the exception of things bought from the French.[6] The items were to be put on display and auctioned off immediately for the "general benefit." Proceeds would be added to "treasure already seized" and distributed in three equal parts: one to officers, and two to noncommissioned officers and men.[7] This procedure of plunder, auction, and prize distribution requires some explanation.

BRITISH PRIZE LAW

From at least the reign of Henry IV (r. 1399–1413), an intricate pattern of legal codes had established that plunder taken in warfare was the legal property of the British sovereign. At his or her discretion, portions of the plunder could be awarded to the military forces involved.[8] For much of the seventeenth and eighteenth centuries, these rules tended only to apply to naval captures, but from the reign of George III forward a series of parliamentary laws created procedures for the disposition of plunder taken in land warfare.

As a kind of first principle, parliamentary acts involving prize were based on the notion that unless there was a promise that plunder would be equitably distributed among forces, armies would become undisciplined mobs. To avoid such a possibility, Parliament and military authorities treated plunder as the natural fruits of victory. They converted looting, with its threats to order, into prize, the lawful reward of righteous warfare, while transforming the stolen objects into private property. The procedures used by the British Army for legalizing plunder were as follows:

1   The Commander in chief appointed prize agents to organize and take charge of a prize commission. The commander also issued orders to members of the army, instructing them to hand over all loot to the commission.

2   The commission inventoried all plunder, arranged for its sale at public auction after the campaign, kept meticulous records of each sale, and created a prize roll indicating how much money was to go to members of each rank in the force.

3   All records of sales were forwarded to the Royal Hospital at Chelsea, which administered the allotment of prize money and kept records.

4   A notice was placed in the *London Gazette* announcing the allotment of prize money.

5   Soldiers or their heirs filed claims at Chelsea and produced proof that they were part of the campaign that had seized the prize.

6   Forms were created for such claims and standards established to prove participation in a particular campaign.[9]

Prior to the invasion of China in 1860, these procedures had been used most recently in the wake of the suppression of the 1857 rebellion in India (claims from which were still being processed when the British invaded China in 1860), and they were followed by auctions and prize distributions in both 1860 and 1900. Prize committees were created and, acting in the name of the crown, they called in loot. But instead of removing the loot to a new site for sale, the auctions were held immediately in the field (in 1860, at the Yellow Temple; in 1900, at the British legation). Items were sold to the looters themselves and the prize money apportioned on the spot.[10]

When the auction ended in 1860, for example, prize money totaling £26,000 had been realized. With Hope Grant and his two generals of division, Michel and Napier, relinquishing their shares, it was divided up among officers and men as follows: first-class field officers, £60; second-class field officers, £50; chaplains, £40; lieutenants, £30; ensigns, £20; sergeants and others, £7 10s.; privates, £5,[11] with none apparently issued to Indian troops.[12]

Although the processes of collection, auction, and redistribution of proceeds might seem unnecessarily involved, I argue that their importance lay in the way Chinese imperial objects were thereby organized into a moral order of law and private property, implicating them in a schema of values and concerns that neutralized the dangers they posed to order and discipline within the army. Such concerns are evident, for example, in Hope Grant's decision to violate the usual rules and hold the auction and distribution immediately in the field. In a letter to Secretary of State for War Sidney Herbert on 21 October, he explained that although he feared exposing "the English army to the demoralizing influence" of the plunder of palaces filled with "valuable works of Chinese art," his army had seen the French "laden with dollars and sycee [silver ingots]." He had thus ordered the auction and division of the proceeds so that his army would be satisfied and "have no reason to complain." Yet, it is also clear that these weren't his sole motives. "Without the prospect of such division," he added, "it would have been difficult to have prevented any but the best men from going to the palace without leave, to plunder for themselves." [13]

The orderly procedures of prize had, therefore, the useful effect of deflecting and channeling the potentially disruptive desires generated by the treasures of the emperor's palaces into the pacific feelings consistent with equitable distribution.[14] Moreover, because the distribution of prize money was done on the basis of rank and race, it also had the practical effect of reproducing the proper structure of the army, while maintaining a hierarchical distinction between British forces and India Army units. This last was no small concern; one-third of the expeditionary force was made up of South Asians. Among these, the cavalry regiments, "irregular" forces raised during the rebellion in India, were widely asserted to be virtual experts at looting. Thus, prize procedures helped to acculturate "wild" Pathans and others to the disciplinary regularities of their rulers. With the army now sealed off from the polluting effects of plunder, the lesson should have been clear: disciplined forces, not a mob of looters like the French, achieved righteous conquest.

Yet, if these were the general points that prize law affirmed and reinforced, there were other kinds of meanings attached to loot and looting that elevated plunder beyond the mundane routines and rituals of the British Army. First, and perhaps most important, loot stood as material proof of British superiority over the Chinese emperor and his empire. As Robert Swinhoe, a consul acting as an interpreter on Hope Grant's staff, so aptly put it, "Fancy the sale of the emperor's effects beneath the walls of the capital of his empire, and this by a people he despised as weak barbarians and talked of driving into the sea!" George Allgood, an officer on Hope Grant's staff, added that the humiliation of the "proudest monarch in the universe" would have an additional benefit. "The news of the capture of Pekin," he wrote, "will resound through Asia, and produce in India an excellent effect." [15] In these terms, loot bore the signs of the humbling of China's haughty monarch and mandarins and stood as an object lesson for others who might contemplate defying British power.

Such assertions of humiliation and dominance were especially pertinent to objects that could be identified as having a substantive connection to the emperor's rulership. These, in turn, can be divided into two groups: gifts previously given to Qing emperors by European monarchs and Manchu-Chinese symbols of imperial sovereignty. The first group included numerous mechanical clocks and watches, one of which was said to be the very timepiece presented by Lord Macartney to the Qianlong emperor, the cannon that Macartney had brought as a gift from George III, works of fine art such as an "extremely good French enamel" done by Petitot [16] and a tapestry from Louis XIV that now hangs in the Ashmolean Library, Oxford, after having passed through the Victoria and Albert Museum. [17] The latter category included imperial robes and armor, jade scepters, and several throne cushions, the "Cap of the Emperor of China," seals of the emperor, a carved screen "from behind the Emperor's throne," pages from the *August Court's Illustrated Catalogue of Ritual Implements* (*Huangchao liqi tushi*), which included hand-painted color drawings of court robes of emperors and empresses, various objects from the emperor's private quarters, such as a small jade-covered book said to be the sayings of Confucius, a Tibetan ritual vessel purportedly including the skull of Confucius, and a Pekinese dog, appropriately christened "Looty."

Much like the looted regalia of South Asian kings that Carol Breckenridge has described, imperial objects were sent to Queen Victoria, where they took their place with other symbols of the British monarchy. [18] A large collection was also sent to France. After appearing on exhibit at the Tuileries, these objects became part of Empress Eugénie's Oriental collection, where they presumably served a similar purpose as items given to the British monarch. [19] Other pieces were deposited in the officer's mess of various of the regiments involved. At these sites, Qing imperial objects were incorporated into regimental histories as trophies, material signs of successful campaigns, that also included the battle honors "Taku Forts" and "Pekin 1860" on the regimental colors. [20] As if to emphasize this triumph over the Chinese monarch, these and other Qing imperial objects also often carried the designation "From the Summer Palace of the Emperor of China."

If links to the emperor's person established one sort of value for looted objects, there were others as well. Although some, like Hope Grant, referred to Qing objects as art, more common in both campaign accounts and in London auction house records was their classification as "curiosities," a term rich in historical significance. It had referred, for example, to collections of objects brought to Europe from other parts of the world in the sixteenth and seventeenth centuries and displayed in "cabinets of curiosities."[21] In this setting, curiosities stood as "singularities" which, because "anomalous," defied classification.[22] By the end of the eighteenth century, the term was used to decontextualize South Pacific artifacts collected by the Cook expeditions and reorganize them into motifs that foregrounded a collector's claims of disinterested scientific inquiry.[23] With respect to things Chinese, the term curiosities had been applied to collections that appeared at shows held in London in 1842 and 1847,[24] and in the China section of the 1851 Crystal Palace exposition, where it seemed to denote the exotic and strange.

Though these various senses of the curiosity may have operated with respect to Summer Palace loot, they were given added weight by the fact that the objects themselves were not produced for export trade or gathered at one of China's treaty ports for a London show. They were, instead, royal exotica. For some, such as Garnet Wolseley, quartermaster of the British forces, this made them exceptional candidates for consideration as examples of the stagnation and backwardness of Chinese civilization.[25] Others seem to have considered the anomalous status of the objects something that enhanced their market value. Such calculations may have been supported by a rumor that one of the British officers was "understood to have an unlimited commission from Baron Rothschild."[26]

To summarize, objects looted from the Summer Palace in 1860 had a variety of meanings attached to them. They could signify the orderly reconstitution of the British Army and the disorderly conduct of the French, the humiliation of the emperor of China, the expanded sovereignty of British and French monarchs, the situating of things Chinese in a global discourse on the curiosities of non-European peoples, and, as commodities, the common sense of capitalist market exchange. These meanings adhered to the objects once they left China and began to circulate in an alien environment on the other side of the Eurasian land mass. In auctions, international expositions, and museum displays in Paris and London between 1861 and 1865, French and British collectors, art dealers, and the public in general had the opportunity to see and buy "Chinese curiosities" "from the Summer Palace of the Emperor of China."[27] Moreover, in many cases the latter epithet became part of the provenance of the items, making it possible to trace the travels and careers of some of the Qing imperial treasures down to the present.[28]

The Sack of Beijing, 1900

In August of 1900, after they had accomplished their military tasks, members of the eight armies that had invaded north China turned to looting and were joined by the diplomats and missionaries they had rescued. Almost all accounts agree that no one was immune from the loot fever. Speaking at a distance, the *Sidney Morning Herald* characterized the mad scramble for plunder as a "carnival of loot"; on the scene, W. A. P. Martin, a siege survivor, spoke of a riot "in the midst of booty." [29]

The rise in the number of looters was accompanied by an increase in the scale and duration of looting. In 1860, plunder had been limited to the Summer Palace and had occurred primarily over a two-to-three-day period. In 1900, all of Beijing, including the new Summer Palace, was fair game; plundering began in mid-August and stretched well into October. Outside of Beijing, it continued even longer as a part of punitive expeditions mounted in various parts of Zhili province (contemporary Hubei province and the municipalities of Beijing and Tianjin).

Quantitative differences aside, there were a number of notable similarities between 1860 and 1900. As before, there was an attempt to control or manage looting after the initial outburst of wild plunder. These efforts were reinforced by a general sense among some of the allied commanders that unless order was restored, the Chinese markets necessary for preserving order and maintaining a lengthy occupation of the city would not materialize.[30] As they had done before, the British Army took the lead in systematizing loot.[31] A Prize Commission was established, an auction market opened at the British legation, and prize shares determined by rank and by the distinction between British and Indian soldiers.[32] The American Army followed suit, but instead of creating a prize fund with auction proceeds, the commander, General Adna Chaffee, used the proceeds to pay a portion of the cost of the American occupation of Beijing in the coming months.[33]

Auctions continued well into the winter of 1900–1901 and included a much larger pool of buyers than in 1860. There were members of the diplomatic corps, foreign residents in Beijing and from other treaty ports, members of the eight allied armies, and eventually curio shop owners from Shanghai and Hong Kong, some of whom were reported to have commissions from European auction houses and art dealers.[34] Moreover, as replacement troops filtered in, they too had the opportunity to acquire valuable Chinese curios. By mid-October the British prize fund was reportedly more than $50,000.[35] In addition, as in 1860, armies collected trophies that were sent back to the home countries. In the British case, this included captured field guns sent to London, Edinburgh, Dublin, and Sidney.[36] For their part, the American forces shipped examples of Chinese weapons and a statue of the Chinese God of War, Guandi, to the recently established trophy room at West Point.[37]

In these and other ways, the meanings attached to Summer Palace objects were easily transposed onto 1900 loot. They could stand for the orderly reconstitution of armies (in this case, the British and American contingents), while highlighting the differences between disciplined and undisciplined armies. They could also act as signs of humiliation, of taste and discernment, of the triumph of civilization over barbarism, and of military trophy collecting.

Yet, as much as there were commonalities between the meanings attached to 1860 and 1900 loot, there were also a number of discernible differences. Perhaps the most significant of these was that objects taken in 1900 did not have attached to them the aura of a proper name such as "From the Summer Palace of the Emperor of China." Given the self-righteous conduct of Euro-American diplomatic and military personnel in China, particularly as it was articulated through rhetoric that demanded "retributive justice" for "savage" and "barbaric" Boxer assaults on Christian missionaries, this is something of a surprise. One would expect, in other words, to find references in auction or collection catalogues and on artifacts in museums to objects from the Forbidden City, or Beijing 1900, or the Boxer episode. But only a few such references seem to have surfaced in London then or later.[38] Nor were there sales of Beijing loot in London and Paris auction houses comparable to those of the 1860s. Moreover, no one like Garnet Wolseley emerged to ruminate on the absences and failures of Chinese civilization.

There were other sorts of differences between 1860 and 1900 as well. For example, it is possible to discern a more sophisticated approach to plunder among some of the looters. Though he makes light of it, George Lynch, a reporter on the scene, observed that "when offered a china cup or saucer, the correct thing to do is to look at the mark at the bottom as if one understood what it meant, and shake the head."[39] What people were looking for were imperial reign date ideograms that provided authenticity and enhanced the value of objects. Other looters, such as legation members and missionaries,[40] had first-hand knowledge of where to go for valuable things. These sites included not only the homes of the wealthy of the city but those of the Qing court nobility.[41]

The differences indicated above between looting patterns in 1860 and 1900 raise at least two issues: first, how to account for what appears to have been a more discerning sort of plunder; and second, how to explain the absence of a distinguishing designation on objects taken from Qing palaces and a host of other sites in 1900. To deal with these questions, it is necessary to explore certain developments in China, Europe, and North America over the four decades between the two looting episodes. These include the growth of a market for Chinese objects, a transformation in the understanding of oriental art, and changing Euro-American attitudes toward plunder in times of war.

Markets and New Knowledge

The Anglo-French invasion of north China in 1860 culminated in the ratification of the Treaty of Beijing. One of the provisions of the treaty allowed Western nation-states to establish diplomatic legations in the Qing capital. The foreign community grew over the next several years as a result, and Europeans and Americans gained unprecedented access to high-quality objects produced for the imperial court and the scholar-bureaucratic class. Ancient and contemporary porcelain, silk robes like those worn by royalty and officials, cloisonné, jade, paintings, and furniture could be purchased directly from the curio dealers in Liulichang and other parts of the Chinese city where Chinese connoisseurs themselves shopped. In addition, foreign art dealers began to appear at Beijing and in the major treaty ports, and at the Beijing legations, Chinese dealers sold their wares as a regular feature of Sunday afternoon tiffins.[42] These various sales venues were supplied by Chinese collectors, who were increasingly forced to sell off treasures because of warfare and political chaos in China. As foreigners bought up valuable collections, objects found their way into European and American markets. The volume of this traffic seems to have been so great that on her seventh visit to China in 1899, Eliza Skidmore declared that travelers could forget about finding valuable curios in Chinese markets; the best things were on sale in London, Paris, Dresden, Berlin, Weimar, New York, and Baltimore, not Beijing![43]

Meanwhile, as these developments in China linked Chinese fine arts to urban centers in Europe and North America, Summer Palace loot circulating in these two regions seems to have altered Euro-American connoisseurial attitudes toward Chinese objects.[44] One documented example of such an effect involved the American collector, Heber Bishop. According to the preface of a work he commissioned, Bishop claims to have first become interested in collecting upon finding a Qianlong-era carved jade vessel from the Summer Palace. He eventually bought it and several others he found for sale in Europe. Having exhausted the European markets, Bishop then went to Beijing in the 1890s, where he purchased a number of items,[45] including a large collection of jade that dealers had assembled at the request of court eunuchs as a gift for the empress dowager's birthday.[46] Bishop's coup may stand not only as a prime example of new interest in China's fine arts, but also as an indication of how new knowledge dovetailed with late-nineteenth-century markets and desires. Such changes were, in turn, related to the creation of new sites for producing and circulating knowledge about things Chinese in East Asia, Europe, and North America.

In China, these sites included the legations in Beijing and the ever growing number of treaty ports, where organizations such as the Peking Oriental Society, the Royal Asiatic Society, and the Society for the Diffusion of Useful Knowledge and libraries and newspapers contributed to opening China to careful and systematic analysis.[47] With native cooperation in many instances, some Europeans and Americans began to decode the meanings and ascertain the values of decorative arts, and they circulated their observations in new publications that appeared in the treaty ports.

Perhaps the most important of these productions were those associated with Chinese porcelain. By 1900, several works appeared that fundamentally altered the way porcelain was understood, represented, displayed, and sold at auction by art dealers. These works included Stanislas Julien's *Histoire de la fabrication de la Porecelaine Chinoise* (1856, a translation of the *Tao lu*), Octave Du Sartel's *La Porcelaine de Chine* (1881), Georges Paleologue's *L'Art Chinois* (1887), Fredrich Hirth's *Ancient Porcelain* (1888), Alfred Hippisley's *Catalogue of Chinese Porcelains* (1890, done for the United States National Museum), Ernest Grandidier's *La Céramique Chinois* (1894), and W. G. Golland's *Chinese Porcelains* (1898). There were also several publications by Stephan W. Bushell, including the catalogue of Heber Bishop's collection of Chinese jade (1900), all of which were highly significant in Great Britain and the United States.

While physician at the British Legation in Beijing from 1868 to 1900, Bushell collected and wrote extensively on Chinese art, particularly porcelain. Through his study of objects available in Beijing and his translation of the *Tao shuo* (*Pronouncements on Porcelain*, completed in 1891 and published posthumously in 1910), Bushell provided a classification scheme for organizing Chinese ceramics by date and historical type. In the former case, this included providing systematic translations of the Chinese dating ideograms to be found on the bottom of pieces. In the latter, it involved identifying previous errors in writings on Chinese porcelain, sorting out the best types of ceramics from particular eras, the evaluation of which was based on Chinese sources and the taste of Chinese connoisseurs, and attaching English or translated Chinese terms to the types.

Between 1897 and 1904, Bushell's classification scheme became the standard for public and private collections in Great Britain and the United States. This standardization was accomplished through a series of key publications under Bushell's authorship: the catalogue of the W. T. Walters collection in Baltimore in 1897 (printed in ten stunning volumes) and the subsequent publication *Oriental Ceramic Art* (1899), which brought to bear on the collection, in nine hundred-plus pages of text, the knowledge Bushell had accumulated over twenty-five years in China; the editing of Cosmo Monkhouse's *Chinese Porcelain* (1901); the cataloguing of the Victoria and Albert Museum's collection and the publication of a handbook on the collection in 1904; and the cataloguing of J. P. Morgan's collection for the Metropolitan Museum of Art.[48]

Coinciding with the creation of authoritative sources on Chinese art was the emergence of new venues for display, ones that extended the exhibitionary regime of the public museum and international fairs into the private sector. The Fine Arts Club of Burlington House in London was noteworthy in this respect. Their first exhibition of Chinese porcelain was held in 1878, and included a pale celadon glaze jar made in the reign of the Emperor Qianlong and a green glazed ridge tile from the Temple of Heaven in Beijing.[49] At the time, interest seems to have been limited, but in 1895 the Club held an exhibit exclusively devoted to blue-and-white oriental porcelain and followed it up the next year with one on colored Chinese porcelain.[50] Both the 1895 and 1896 shows were done under the aegis of Cosmo Monkhouse.

Thus, by the late 1890s, there were well-established routes of travel for Chinese art that connected Beijing and treaty ports to the fine arts markets in Europe and North America; an established body of standardized knowledge about various kinds of Chinese art, especially porcelain; and a growing number of authorities on and sites for displaying Chinese objects. Perhaps as a result of these developments, when collectors and connoisseurs consulted newly created written sources and took advantage of the opportunities to view Chinese art, they no longer spoke of things Chinese as curiosities. At the same time, however, they might also have fantasized with Eliza Skidmore about "some great political convulsion, the fall of dynasty, a foreign war with another sack of the palaces" [51] that would bring a new flood of Chinese art onto the market.

At the same time as the relationship between Euro-Americans and Chinese objects altered, questions were raised in Great Britain and in other parts of Europe concerning the legalities of plunder in land warfare. Although it did not outlaw plunder, an 1864 parliamentary commission on army prize investigated instances dating back to 1807, including the Napoleonic War campaigns and campaigns in India, and recommended that share allotments be made more speedily and that the scale of distribution be made more equitable among the ranks of soldiers.[52] That questions were being raised about prize is also evident in a 1903 War Office report on the practice. According to the findings of these investigators, prize was "a thing of the past." It had gradually been phased out between 1855 and 1903 and replaced by a cash gratuity for hardship and campaigning.[53] Though this does not mean that looting had ended, it does indicate that prior to 1900 some efforts were made to find an alternative to prize.

Problems involving the status of plunder and prize are also evident in military law of the second half of the nineteenth century. The War Office's *Manual of Military Law* (first edition 1884) in a section entitled "The Customs of War" acknowledges that the regulations therein were compiled for the use of officers and had no official authority. Nevertheless, the editors provided some sense of authority by consulting a host of publications on the laws of land warfare from Emmerich Vattel through Henry Wheaton (the latter of which contained a jumble of ambiguous rules and contradictory precedents; see the 1863 edition of *Elements of International Law*, 596–637). The issue of plunder was addressed in a subsection on "Property of the Enemy." It began by noting that the seizure of scientific or art objects was "incompatible with the admitted restrictions" of depriving the enemy of war-making resources and "could only be justified as a measure of retaliation." Within a page, however, the editors both acknowledged that officers should attempt to prevent pillage and noted procedures, identical to those found in prize law, for dealing with its results.[54] This seeming uncertainty and confusion over the status of looting is also evident in army regulations. The *Queen's Regulations* of 1868, for example, forbade plunder and indicated that officers had a duty to prevent it; further, no mention was made of prize money.[55] In contrast, the *King's Regulations* of 1901 contained a section on prize, noting that it is the property of the crown and therefore subject to acts of Parliament.[56]

The ambiguities and contradictions to be found in British military law and army regulations may also be indicative of international discussions over the legality of plunder. The result of these concerns is evident in the Hague Convention of 1899. In the sections of the final treaty dealing with rules of land warfare, plunder and the seizure of private property were outlawed without qualification.[57] All of the nations that invaded China in 1900 were parties to the convention, as was the Qing government.[58] Although these developments did not prevent an even more spectacular instance of looting Beijing, they may have been a contributing factor explaining why it is almost impossible today to identify objects looted in 1900. To explore this and other possible explanations for the absence of a designation like that to be found on 1860 Summer Palace loot, it may be useful to begin with a discussion of occurrences related to the disposition of the Forbidden City after the allied forces had occupied Beijing.

Civilization and Plunder

Soon after the legations were relieved and Chinese resistance ended, American and Japanese forces seized the gates of the palaces and the commanders of these forces sealed the entrances. The U.S. Army controlled the south gate of the city, the Japanese contingent the northern one. Until a resolution was made by the allied powers over the disposition of the palaces, the American and Japanese commanders seemed intent on preventing the sack of the site over which they assumed responsibility. As other parts of Beijing were plundered indiscriminately, representatives of the powers met around 21 August and agreed not to occupy the Forbidden City. Instead, they decided to hold a triumphal march through the center of the city to demonstrate to the Chinese the absolute power of the conquerors.[59]

Following the triumphal march, the palaces remained closed until September, when it was decided to allow in small parties of visitors. Written requests were made to the American and Japanese commanders, who then arranged the visits and issued passes.[60] Looting was strictly forbidden, and each party of ten people or fewer was accompanied by an American or Japanese officer. These tour groups appear to have been made up exclusively of officers from the various armies, diplomatic corps personnel, or people with connections to one or the other; all were gentlemen and ladies, in other words. Yet looting still occurred, but in an unusual way.

When visitors thought they were not being observed, they pilfered things that fit into their pockets or could be hidden under coats. According to one report, such sleight of hand was justified on the grounds that one could not pass through the Forbidden City without taking a souvenir.[61] Occasionally they were caught by either the accompanying officer or by Chinese attendants still in the palace complex. If the former, things were usually returned with a claim that the perpetrator was unaware that acquiring souvenirs was forbidden; if the latter case, there might be nasty altercations. All efforts to halt the activity proved futile. On 3 December, General Chaffee decided to close the palaces down.[62] Perhaps under these circumstances, looters were reluctant to draw attention to the objects they had stolen, either from fear of censure or fear that they might be forced to return them.

In other cases, some participants seem to have been bothered by the moral confusion looting posed to their triumph over Chinese barbarism. In his diary of the campaign, Major-General Norman Stewart noted that during the grand march through the Forbidden City, objets d'art "were lifted." Although he thought that it was perhaps best to keep "eyes front" and confine comments about such matters to the officer's mess, he was clearly disturbed by reports that even women from the diplomatic corps may have been involved. Moreover, even the orderly prize procedures of the British Army appeared to provide no solace, leaving him to conclude that he was "beginning to hate the sound of the word 'loot.' If you happen to pick up an article which seems good, and for which you have paid the price you are at once asked 'Where did you loot that?' Even those who ought to know better seem to doubt your honesty. *Life under such conditions is a bit degrading.*"[63]

Stewart's sense that the honesty and integrity of Europeans and Americans, even officers, was under scrutiny is borne out in other sources, some of which acknowledge participation in the opportunities available to obtain Chinese objects, while privately expressing moral doubts about the conditions of acquisition. In letters to his wife, Leslie Grove, a U.S. Army chaplain, at first expressed enthusiasm at being able to acquire valuable curios. However, as he became more fully aware of the extent of the looting, the American missionary involvement in it, and the degree to which plunder was made acceptable through prize sales, Grove found great cause for concern. Among other things, he told his wife that he would no longer buy at the British auctions and that he was certain the missionary complicity in looting would mean a severe blow to their cause.[64]

Such moral qualms may also have been connected to widely diffused negative accounts of looting. Newspaper reporters were present from the moment the allied armies landed at Dagu. Their accounts of looting not only appeared in their own newspapers, but were picked up by others in the treaty ports and in review magazines in Europe and North America. In addition, some accounts from 1860 were republished, including that of D'Hérrison. Even if these reports contained no aspersions, they gave a sense of the sheer breadth and scope of plunder. In other cases, writers were openly critical. *The Review of Reviews* noted, for example, that the news from China was "calculated to make Europeans hang their heads for shame."[65] The issue of shame was also raised by James Ricalton, a photographer on the scene, who attributed the following to Li Hongzhang, the eminent Qing official. As the story went, after consulting the "Mosaic decalogue," Li suggested that "the eighth commandment should be amended to read, Thou shalt not steal, but thou mayst loot."[66]

These and other reports of the behavior of the allied forces generated, in turn, defensive apologetics. Usually justifications included charges that the press greatly exaggerated matters, which only served to draw additional attention to the issue. Perhaps the best known of these was an exchange between Mark Twain and members of the American Board of Commissioners for Foreign Missions over missionary involvement in looting. It was triggered by an interview with the Reverend William Ament published in the *New York Sun* in which he justified missionary looting.[67] In "To the Person Sitting in Darkness" (1901), Twain questioned the moral logic of Ament, which led to interventions in support of the latter by Gilbert Reid and Judson Smith. In their responses, Reid and Smith claimed that missionary looting was "high ethics" — an argument that Twain almost gleefully shredded — and claimed that American missionaries had only looted to provide money for the relief of Chinese Christians.[68] Adolph Favier, the Catholic Bishop of Beijing, published a similar defense. In another instance unrelated to missionaries, Sir Claude MacDonald, the British minister in Beijing, justified the prize practices of the British Army; although he did not deny that looting had occurred, MacDonald argued that it was far more organized and limited than newspaper reports indicated.[69]

While some missionaries and diplomats literally wore the word loot as a badge of honor and were assailed on moral grounds, some critics such as John MacDonnell focused attention on the dubious legality of plunder, particularly that of the British Army. In a piece that appeared in the *Contemporary Review*, MacDonnell discussed the history of loot and prize law, arguing that rather than acting as a deterrent, laws, because they gave disproportionate amounts of the prize fund to officers, encouraged common soldiers to loot more. In addition, MacDonnell (virtually alone) drew attention to the fact that the "letter and the spirit of the Hague Convention" had been violated in China. As he put it, the theory of Hague was "all that could be desired," but the fact was that in dealing with "Oriental nations," when opportunity presented itself, "the old outrages were repeated." Those outrages, he added, were rooted in the practices of the British Army in India, which not only shaped prize law in the nineteenth century, but produced the most extreme examples of plunder to date.[70]

Linked to the arguments concerning the propriety of loot was one that helped to frame the issue in more global terms. In 1860, there were few if any voices raised over the plunder and destruction of the Summer Palace. In 1900, on the other hand, more than one observer/participant, as well as critics in the United States and Europe, noted that civilization was apparently only "skin deep" and that a bit of temptation easily led to a "retrogression to barbarism."[71] *The Review of Reviews* added that Europeans "have flung aside the garb of civilization and are acting like our piratical ancestors in the days of the Vikings." Seemingly supporting this contention, E. J. Dillon published an eye-witness account that provided graphic details on looting and numerous atrocities perpetrated against Chinese civilians by allied forces.[72] Dillon's reports of European barbarisms equal to those imputed to Chinese Boxers filtered through other sources as well,[73] suggesting what is perhaps one of the main reasons why objects seized in 1900 did not carry a designation of their source. Fortunately for the looters, however, the absence of the name Beijing 1900 probably had little effect on the market value of individual pieces once they made their way from China, through the network of relations established between treaty ports, to the Euro-American art market. At various sales sites, the objects could easily be organized into the categories established through the study of Chinese art in the previous decades. In 1900, those categories and the network of relationships linking Chinese objects to Euro-American markets appear to have been far more significant than the fact that an object had come from an imperial collection. Unlike in 1860, value, it would seem, no longer lay in historically disembodied singularities, but rather in the complex taxonomical relationship among highly differentiated things. The sea of words in which Qing imperial objects were now submerged provided a convenient cover not only for looting, but also for the fears of racial degeneration, of the fragility of civilization, and of barbarism within the civilized.

Such concerns were, however, not so easily repressed; they existed in a broader context of widely diffused apprehensions about atavistic primitivism in the last quarter of the nineteenth century. As a kind of repressed element within bourgeois sensibilities over the stark division between the civilized and the savage, such concerns focused not only on "racial" mixing,[74] but the possibility that contact with "inferior" civilizations or peoples would awaken latent desires or primitive remnants in the European psyche. As Patrick Brantlinger has pointed out, popular fiction and dissident literature during this period were rife with such concerns.[75] Thus, when a real event such as the sacking of Beijing exceeded rational expectations and seemed to converge with fiction, tropes from the latter were readily available for representing the meaning of European and American behavior in other than triumphalist terms. And, although there was not a thorough inversion of meaning, insofar as plunder could serve as a sign of degeneration, it was more difficult to construct the events of 1900 in the clear terms of European moral superiority that dominated constructs and rationales for the 1860 invasion.

If criticisms of looting and various efforts to obscure or justify it suggest a sense of unease with matters in China, they also point to the contradictions and hypocrisies evident in Euro-American attitudes toward and relations with the non-Western world. The absence of a sign of righteous conquest on objects plundered in 1900 equivalent to those taken from the Summer Palace forty years earlier serves, in the end, to highlight the moral ambiguities and ethical confusion Euro-American and Japanese violence against Chinese bodies and Chinese objects engendered. It is, therefore, something other than irony that the United States and the six European countries that invaded China in the summer of 1900 were among the first group of nation-states formally to ratify the Hague Convention. They did so on 4 September 1900, in the midst of the sack of Beijing, becoming the first signatory powers to violate the convention on the "Laws and Customs of War on Land."

Notes

1 According to Henry Yule and A. C. Burnell, *Hobson-Jobson*, "loot" was first used in 1788 but did not find acceptance in Great Britain until the period between the China War of 1841 and the Indian Rebellion of 1857.
2 Built primarily during the Qianlong reign (1736–1796), the Yuanming yuan, or Garden of Perfect Brightness, served as a haven outside of Beijing for the Qing court in the hot months of July and August. It was, however, not the only such site and is more properly thought of as one among other summer retreats used by the court.
3 It was also eventually destroyed as a "solemn act of retribution" for Chinese "treachery" by order of Lord Elgin; see Theodore Walrond, ed., *Letters and Journals of James, Eighth Earl of Elgin*, 366. The destruction of the Summer Palace was carried out by the Royal Engineers. See Whitworth Porter, *The History of the Corps of Royal Engineers*, 1: 514–15, which includes excerpts of a letter written by one of the participants, Charles "Chinese" Gordon.
4 Count D'Hérrison, "The Loot of the Imperial Summer Palace at Pekin," 625–26. D'Hérrison's memoirs, from which this is an extract, were translated in 1901 from a Paris reprint of *Journal d'un Interprète en Chine, par le Comte D'Hérrison*. The Smithsonian justified publication on the grounds that events in Beijing in 1900 mirrored those of 1860.
5 Ibid., 625.
6 See A. B. Tulloch, *Recollections of Forty Years' Service*, 118, and Robert Swinhoe, *Narrative of the North China Campaign of 1860*, 310.
7 See PRO, WO 147/2: 1–5.
8 On the history of prize, see C. J. Colombos, *A Treatise on the Law of Prize*.

9 See *Statutes of the United Kingdom of Great Britain and Ireland*, 54 George III (1814): v. 54, 328–51; 1, 2 George IV (1821): v. 61, 210–11; 2, 3 William IV (1832): v. 72, 236–59.

10 For sources describing the auction of 1860 see R. J. L. M'Ghee, *How We Got to Peking*, 294; Robert Swinhoe, *Narrative of the North China Campaign of 1860*, 311; Henry Knollys, *Incidents in the China War*, 193–94; George Allgood, *China War 1860*, 59; and Garnet J. Wolseley, *Narrative of the War with China in 1860*, 237–42.

11 The figures are from Knollys, 226–27, and *Illustrated London News* 5 January 1861: 7. Also see the discussion in Hevia, "Loot's Fate," n 17, concerning army salaries at this time.

12 Prize rolls for this campaign are not in the India Office record collection. There are, however, a substantial number of rolls and claims for various military operations that occurred in India before and after the China campaign, especially for 1857–1858. See, for example, the Deccan Prize Money rolls, dated 31 July 1832, in IOR, L/MIL/5/326, where Indian troops are included, but given a lower share.

13 See Knollys, 192, 226–27. Hope Grant's particular take on plunder was not unique to him. In a letter dated 8 December 1857 justifying a similar decision to apportion prize money in the field, G. Malcolm, commander of the Southern Mahratta Horse, noted that soldiers will maintain discipline when they understand that "booty" will be "fairly shared among them. Otherwise, they are libel to break ranks and plunder." See *Report of the Commissioners*.

14 See Hope Grant's General Order of 12 October 1860 in PRO, WO 147/2: 7.

15 Swinhoe, 311–12, and Allgood, 60.

16 Garnet J. Wolseley, *The Story of a Soldier's Life*, 1: 78.

17 Victoria and Albert Museum, Acquisition Records, the Crealock file. I am indebted to Verity Wilson for this source.

18 Carol Breckenridge, "The Aesthetics and Politics of Colonial Collecting," 203.

19 The collection was placed at the Château de Fontainbleau, where it remains to the present. See Colombe Samoyault-Verlet, *Le Musée chinois de l'impératrice Eugénie*.

20 In the mess of the Queen's Royal Regiment and of the Wiltshire Regiment are porcelain and silver trophies. On the former, see John Davis, *History of the Second Queen's Royal Regiment*, 5: 132, and Jock Haswell, *The Queen's Royal Regiment*, 103. On the latter, see Tom Gibson, *The Wiltshire Regiment*, 86. On battle honors, see N. B. Leslie, *Battle Honours of the British and Indian Armies*, 85–86.

21 See Krzysztof Pomian, *Collectors and Curiosities*; O. Impey, *Chinoiserie*; O. Impey and A. MacGregor, *The Origins of Museums*; and J. Ayers, "The Early China Trade."

22 See Barbara Kirshenblatt-Gimblett, "Objects of Ethnography," 392. Breckenridge, 199–200, makes a similar point about the "Oriental repository" kept by the East India Company in London to display curious artifacts from the East.

23 See Nick Thomas, "Licensed Curiosity."

24 On London shows, see Richard Altick, *The Shows of London*, 292–97.

25 For a discussion of Wolseley on Chinese curiosities see Hevia, 331–32.

26 See M'Ghee, 294.

27 On auctions and public display, see Hevia, 326–31, 341–42. Since the publication of this piece, I have learned from Regine Thiriez that there were approximately twenty-one sales of Summer Palace loot at the Hotel Drouot in Paris between 1861 and 1863.

28 In Hevia. Some of these items are identified as part of the collections of the Victoria and Albert Museum, the British Museum, and the Royal Engineers Museum in Chatham. I am grateful to Craig Clunas, Verity Wilson, Francis Woods, and Caroline Reed, curators at these institutions, for their cooperation and help. While I was researching this topic, Nick Pearce and Regine Thiriez were also tracking down Summer Palace loot in Great Britain and France. I am grateful to both of them for sharing their findings; see Pearce, " 'From the Summer Palace,' " and Thiriez, "The Rape of the Summer Palace."

29 The *Herald* is cited in Bob Nicholls, *Bluejackets and Boxers*, 111; for Martin, see *A Cycle of Cathay*, 134.

30 NARA, RG 395, 944, 12 September 1900. Also see George de S. Barrow, *The Fire of Life*, 64.

31 Norman Stewart, *My Service Days*, 241–42.

32 See PRO, WO 28/302, General Gasalee's Diary, 28–29. Also see Barrow, 64.

33 For sources related to Chaffee's decision see NARA, RG 203, entry 4, 54–56; Chaffee's letter of 8 March 1901 is in RG 395, 898, "Letter's Sent, 1900–1901"; in the NARA, Office of Finance, *Ledgers of Emergency Fund Account, 1898–1909*, the China Relief Expedition section indicated that loot went through one final transformation in Washington. In larger and bolder print over "Money received from auctions sales of captured property in China, Special order no. 36, Gen'l. Chaffee," is the name of the quartermaster reporting. Next to this name is the heading *Public Civil Fund, China.*

34 *The Celestial Empire*, 19 November 1900, 617.

35 This figure comes from the *Peking and Tientsin Times*, 18 October 1900. The final figures no longer seem to be extant. Although listed in the India Office catalogue, the prize rolls have been lost.

36 IOR, L/MIL/7/16765, 11.

37 NARA, RG 395, 944, circular 4, 24 September 1900. Wilber Chamberlain, *Ordered to China*, 119, mentions the war god, and something labeled as such is in Earl McFarland, *Catalogue of the Ordnance Museum*, 41, which also contains other Boxer trophy. Also see Lloyd Leonard, *Catalogue of the United States Military Academy Museum*, where the Boxer items are grouped together.

38 I have found only two references to sales of 1900 loot in England. One was in *The Celestial Empire*, 6 March 1901, which noted that a British private who had survived the siege had sold some items through the Stevens house. In 1913, Stevens sold a Chinese drum said to have been captured by the 39th Regiment at Beijing during the Boxer Rebellion. See National Art Library auction house catalogues, 23.zz.

39 George Lynch, *The War of Civilizations*, 170.

40 Various sources have specifically singled out Lady Claude MacDonald, wife of the British ambassador, as a looter; see Peter Fleming, *The Siege of Peking.*

41 At one of these, the Reverend Tewksbury of the American Board was said to have set himself up and auctioned off the contents. See Bertram L. Simpson, *Indiscreet Letters from Peking*, 374; Richard Steel, *Through Peking's Sewer Gate*, 56; and Martin, 135.

42 Archibald Colquhoun, *Overland to China*, 175–76. Also see Eliza Skidmore, *China the Long-Lived Empire*, 191.

43 Skidmore, 197, 200.

44 This argument has been put forward by Anna Cocks, *The Victoria and Albert Museum*, and Nick Pearce. Though Pearce's work on this issue remains unpublished, in a 1998 address at the International Convention of Asian Scholars, he reiterated the point.

45 Heber Bishop, *The Heber Bishop Collection of Jade and Other Hard Stones*, xiii.

46 Skidmore relates this story, but does not mention Bishop by name; see 198–99. Later, it seems to have taken on the quality of a legend; see Samuel Morrill, *Lanterns, Junks and Jade*, 136–37.

47 For an overview of the new network of knowledge production in China after 1860 see James Hevia, "The Archive State and the Fear of Pollution."

48 See the bibliography for references to some of Bushell's publications.

49 Burlington Fine Arts Club, *Exhibition of Japanese and Chinese Works of Art*, 34, 36.

50 Burlington Fine Arts Club, catalogues of 1895 and 1896.

51 Skidmore, 196.

52 See PRO, WO, 33/6337, and Parliamentary Papers for 1864. Also see the index to the latter under the entry "Prize Money, Prizes, Salvage, &c." for a list of acts of Parliament concerning prize.

53 PRO, WO 33/6338.

54 War Office, *Manual of Military Law*, 1887, 311–13. This is the 2d edition. The sections cited here are the same in the 3d and 4th editions of 1893 and 1899.

55 *Queen's Regulations and Orders for the Army*, 2:186.

56 *King's Regulations and Orders for the Army*, 50.

57 Charles I. Bevans, *Treaties and Other International Agreements of the United States of America*, 1:260.

58 Formal ratifications were delivered at the same moment the looting of Beijing was underway. See Carnegie Endowment, *Signatures*, 2–4.

59 See A. S. Daggett, *America in the China Relief Expedition*, 106; W. H. Carter, *The Life of Lieutenant General Chaffee*, 202; S. Butler, *Old Gimlet Eye*, 77; H. S. Landor, *China and the Allies*, 2:358; A. J. Brown, *New Forces in Old China*, 138; Martin, 139; and A. H. Smith, *China in Convulsion*, 2:727.

60 Because most people wanted to enter the palaces from the south gate, the Americans handled most of this. I have counted over 160 such passes; see NARA, RG 395, 898, which is the China Relief Expedition, Headquarters, general records: Letters sent, 1900–1901.

61 E. J. Dillon, "The Chinese Wolf and the European Lamb," 30.

62 For a report on thefts, see NARA, RG 395, 906, box 2 (27 October 1900) and box 3 (2 December 1900). On altercations, see Yamaguchi to Chaffee, 30 November 1900, RG 395, 906, box 3. Chaffee closed the south gate the following day; see RG 395, 898, no. 428. He reopened it two weeks later, apparently having received assurances that the plundering would cease. However, new regulations governing entrance to the city were issued on 14 February 1901 (see RG 395, 906, box 4), suggesting that the practice did not completely disappear, and further incidents were reported in March. See RG 395, 906, box 5, 5 and 20 March 1901.

63 Stewart, 252.

64 USMHI, Grove correspondence, letters of 22 August, 9 and 13 September, and 11 and 16 October 1900.

65 *Review of Reviews* 22 (1900): 52.

66 James Ricalton, *China through the Stereoscope*, 233.

67 The Sun interview appeared on Christmas Eve 1900 and was conducted by Chamberlain (212).

68 For the Twain-missionary exchange see Twain, "To the Person Sitting in Darkness" and "To My Missionary Critics"; J. Smith, "The Missionaries and Their Critics"; and G. Reid, "The Ethics of Loot" and "The Ethics of the Last War." See also *The Literary Digest* 23.2 (1901): 36–37; and William Ament, "The Charges against Missionaries."

69 *The Celestial Empire*, 22 April 1901, 4.

70 John MacDonnell, "Looting in China," 444–52, esp. 446–50. One of the few other references to the Hague Convention can be found in *Review of Reviews* 22 (1900): 52.

71 *Review of Reviews* 22 (1900): 52, and Robert Hart, *These from the Land of Sinim*, 88.

72 *Review of Reviews* 22 (1900): 52; 23 (1901): 44, 46; and Dillon, 1–31.

73 See, for example, Landor, 1: 364–65.

74 See Robert Young, *Colonial Desire*.

75 See Patrick Brantlinger, *Rule of Darkness*, 227–54.

Andrew F. Jones   *The Gramophone in China*

Sometime around the turn of the century, a young Frenchman named Labansat set up an outdoor stall on Tibet Road in Shanghai and began to play gramophone records for curious Chinese passersby. Labansat, whose career up to that point had consisted of operating a peepshow for Shanghai theatergoers, had recently purchased an imported gramophone from a foreign firm called Moutrie & Company. His new business gambit was simple and effective: when a sufficiently large crowd had gathered around the machine, he would ask each listener to pay ten cents to hear a novelty record called "Laughing Foreigners" ("Yangren daxiao"). Anyone who was able to resist laughing along with the chuckles, chortles, and guffaws emerging from the horn of the gramophone would receive his or her money back.[1]

Labansat himself, it seems, laughed all the way to the bank. By 1908, he had earned enough from this routine to establish China's first record company as a subsidiary of the multinational Compagnie-Generale Phonographique Pathé-Frères. With the help of a Chinese assistant from Ningbo and a French recording engineer, Labansat's new company, Pathé Orient (Dongfang baidai changpian gongsi), began to record Peking opera, sending the masters back to Paris for processing and manufacturing before selling the finished products to local Chinese. By 1914, the necessity for this last step was eliminated when Labansat established China's first recording studio and record-pressing plant in the French concession. By the 1930s, Pathé (which had recently become a subsidiary of another multinational, Electrical and Musical Industries) not only dominated the domestic Chinese record industry, but was also the hub of a distribution network that extended throughout Southeast Asia. Pathé had become a central player in the urban media culture of the Republican era, a pioneer in the transnational dissemination of Chinese-language popular culture, and the principal purveyor of an entirely new musical genre: Mandarin popular song.

Pathé, however important as the linchpin of a new industry dedicated to the production and consumption of the "decadent sounds" (*mimi zhi yin*) of jazz-inflected Mandarin Chinese pop, is only part of the story of the gramophone in China. Indeed, one of the central contentions of this essay is that the Chinese record industry itself is merely one piece in a *global* puzzle. Thomas Alva Edison invented his first tinfoil phonograph in 1877, but it was not until the turn of the century that the technology of sound recording yielded a new industry predicated on the industrial reproduction and mass-marketing of music. This new (and immensely profitable) industry was, from its very inception, transnational in character. Almost as soon as they were established, companies like Pathé-Frères (founded in 1897), The Gramophone Company (founded in 1898 in England), Victor Talking Machine Company (founded 1901 in New Jersey), The Columbia Graphophone Company (which entered the global market in 1902), and the German Beka-Record (1903) fanned out across the globe in search of new markets and new material, profoundly changing the nature of musical life in their wake. As one archivist of the early-twentieth-century recordings resulting from these efforts has put it, phonography in the colonies and elsewhere "altered the face of traditional music forever" at precisely the same moment that it was preserved for posterity on wax cylinders and shellac disks.[2]

It would be a serious mistake, however, to assume that traditional musics had somehow remained static or untouched by Euro-American influence before their fateful encounter with this new technology of sound inscription and playback. The century preceding the introduction and global proliferation of the gramophone had already witnessed another sort of musical upheaval. Like the one to which the bulk of this essay is devoted, this upheaval was global in nature. But instead of being implemented by a phalanx of newly minted recording conglomerates and their emissaries, it was a product of the complex encounter among the brass bands of imperialist armies, the religious hymns of colonial missionaries, and the musical practices of the various peoples they sought to quell and convert.[3] The incursion of these new musical genres, often utilized as technologies of colonial conquest and control throughout the nineteenth century, had already begun to erode what many nineteenth-century listeners had perceived as the radical incommensurability of European and other musical forms. Indeed, this incommensurability had led many early-nineteenth-century European listeners to deny non-Western sounds the episte-mological status of "music" per se.[4] By the turn of the century, however, brass instruments and the harmonium (an instrument often enlisted by missionar-ies to provide chordal support for choral renditions of translated Protestant hymns) had succeeded in introducing not only new musical forms (not the least of which being the distinctly European notion of functional harmony), but also new ways of integrating musical and social practice (choral song and the bour-geois recital, among others). A final and far-reaching aspect of this gradual and uneven process of encroachment and acculturation was the introduction of European musical notation to a variety of musical cultures it was ill-prepared (and often simply unable) to represent. Indeed, the forcible translation of non-Western music into the parochial representational economy of standardized notation—an economy that enforced functional harmony and the rational-ization of pitch at the expense of other musical values—could not help but impoverish the rich melodic, rhythmic, and timbral subtleties of these (often performance-based and improvisational) traditions.[5] More significantly, nota-tion also imposed constraints on what sorts of music could be composed and circulated in printed form.

Gramophone Culture

Recording, then, offered the prospect of an entirely different sort of musical transcription, one that in theory might liberate local performance from the straitjacket of the universalizing tendencies of notation. But phonography, the analogue "writing of sound," also imposed its own, equally far-reaching, con-straints. First, music was made to conform with the technical limitations of acoustical recording, effectively limiting the sort and size of ensembles and compositions that might be phonographically represented. The commodifica-tion of performance in the form of 78 rpm disks also mandated new, market-oriented constraints on musical production. Perhaps the most important con-sequence of these dual constraints was the emergence, in the United States and Europe as well as in China, India, and any number of other colonized nations, of a vast range of new urban popular musics. The extended compositional forms of European and other classical musics were not ideally suited to the two and a half minutes per side allowed for by the gramophone records of the era; popular songs and operatic arias could not only be recorded with greater fidelity than orchestral pieces, but also performed far more profitably in the urban record market.[6]

Even more striking is the way the gramophone brought about profound changes in the very nature and context of musical consumption. Indeed, the gramophone was one of the principal agents of the sort of "space-time compression" David Harvey identifies as characteristic of the condition of modernity.[7] The technology of sound recording and reproduction enabled both the preservation of individual musical performances, and thus previously unrepeatable moments in historical time, and their rapid and seemingly effortless diffusion across vast spaces. The power of the gramophone, as Jacques Attali points out, was that it could "stockpile" time and space in the form of musical representation and thus embody "the internationalization of social relations" already transforming everyday life in the early twentieth century.[8]

In practical terms, this meant that a heretofore unimaginable cornucopia of music, diverse in both historical and geographical provenance, was suddenly made available to the gramophone owner, regardless of whether he or she happened to live in New York or Shanghai, London or Calcutta. Yet although the easy availability of the Western musical repertoire to non-Western ears certainly spurred on the supplantation of indigenous music by European and American forms, the opposite is also true. And as I implied earlier, the gramophone—in freeing a variety of non-Western and folk musics from the tyranny of a European system of musical notation ill-equipped to represent their subtleties— actually spurred on an unprecedented proliferation of a variety of traditional, regional, and hybrid musical forms. This somewhat counterintuitive conclusion, of course, contradicts standard accounts of the complicity of modern communications technology with the forces of Western cultural imperialism.[9]

The advent of the gramophone also served to fundamentally alter the political economy and social meaning of musical consumption. The gramophone record "turned the performance of music into a material object, something you could hold in your hand, which could be bought and sold."[10] As such, it not only fundamentally altered the way musicians made their living, but also shifted the primary context of musical performance away from its traditional locales (aristocratic salons, concert halls, public festivals) and into the home.

Marketed in China and elsewhere as an indispensable accoutrement of the modern home and a marker of petit-bourgeois respectability, the gramophone was both a mechanical emblem of modernity and the principal engine whereby music became an object of private, individualized consumption as opposed to the focus of public gatherings.[11] Indeed, the domesticity of the gramophone is foregrounded in many Chinese print advertisements and calendar posters for gramophones, and is also an important aspect of the discourse on the gramophone and its uses in contemporary magazine articles and consumer guides.[12] The gramophone also frequently appears in urban popular literature of the Republican period as a signifier of middle-class leisure, urban sophistication, and domestic felicity.[13]

At the same time, the gramophone (and allied technologies such as radio broadcasting and sound films) brought music into a range of new, distinctly modern social spaces. The cinema is, of course, one such space. According to contemporary accounts, many cafés, restaurants, and nightclubs in Shanghai were also fitted with gramophones or wireless radios as a stand-in for live musicians. Record retailers, of course, offered customers the opportunity to preview new records, as did such Shanghai department stores as Wing On, Sincere, and Sun Sun. Dance music and the latest "screen songs," finally, often poured out into the streets and alleys from corner stores.[14] New listening habits and new musical tastes were one result of this expansion of musical space. New and more heterogeneous (in terms of both class and gender) audiences was another.[15] This unprecedented saturation of quotidian life in the modern metropolis by "gramophone culture" and its radiophonic and cinematic by-products meant that the financial and ideological stakes of controlling the means of musical production and distribution were very high. And for that reason, China's nascent "culture industry" became the site of fierce economic competition and intense cultural struggle throughout the Republican period.

These transformations took place in both the metropoles *and* the colonial urban centers. And significantly, they took place almost simultaneously in both places. The history of the record industry in Shanghai belies the assumption of "belated modernity" that all too often governs scholarly approaches to the question of cultural modernization in the Republican period.[16] The arrival of the gramophone in China cannot be understood in isolation from the history of global diffusion of capitalist modernity in the late nineteenth and early twentieth centuries. And precisely because the record industry was global in nature from the very beginning, Labansat's work with Pathé Asia, for example, is not merely another example of the introduction of advanced European technologies into a backward colonial periphery. The record industry grew and thrived only insofar as it invested in international (and domestic minority and immigrant) markets; London and New York were as much participants in the condition of colonial modernity as Shanghai and Calcutta.

Studying the historical diffusion of gramophone culture and its imbrication with colonial modernity, I argue, can also help us to place recent theoretical debates on the nature of transnational culture on firmer historical ground. Much recent work on global flows of capital and culture in our (post)modern and (post)colonial era is undergirded by the assumption that these remarkable developments are historically nonpareil. This oversight, I suspect, derives in part from a characteristically "postmodern" focus in the writings of Arjun Appadurai and other theorists on visuality and the ascendancy of "the image, the imagined, the imaginary . . . in global cultural processes."[17] At the same time, Appadurai's interest in (and perhaps unwitting reduplication of) contemporary culture's "nostalgia for the present" often causes him to lose sight of the historical role of commodities (such as the gramophone and gramophone records) in forging the networks of transnational exchange that constitute his primary analytical object.[18]

In (theoretical) practice, this means that the early history of these networks are almost invariably occluded from contemporary discourse on global cultural flows. Although Appadurai's seminal essay, "Disjuncture and Difference in the Global Cultural Economy," begins with a brief consideration of premodern global cultural contacts, he quickly launches himself into the task of constructing a "social theory of [global] postmodernity" without ever examining, or indeed mentioning, the crucial historical trajectory that lies between these two epochs.[19] In a more recent essay on transnational culture entitled "Here and Now," Appadurai accounts for this absence by positing a historical rupture between earlier modernities and the modernity we currently inhabit: "This theory of a break—or rupture—with its strong emphasis on electronic mediation and mass migration, is necessarily a theory of the recent past (or the extended present) because it is only in the past two decades or so that media and migration have become so massively globalized, that is to say, active across large and irregular transnational terrains."[20] Though I agree with Appadurai that the past few decades have brought an unprecedented intensification and "massification" of these global processes, I also believe that it is important to keep the continuities that bind us to earlier "transnationalisms" firmly in mind, if only because they serve to remind us of linkages between colonial power and capital that are by no means irrelevant to our current situation.

Indeed, something of the importance of earlier transnationalisms to our understanding of transnational culture in its contemporary form is suggested by the following facts. In 1931, the global record market was dominated by six multinational corporations. In the 1990s, six multinational corporations still account for more than 75 percent of global music production. And despite a tangled hundred-year history of mergers and acquisitions, the origins of the transnational corporations that currently control the market can be traced directly to such corporate ancestors as Pathé-Frères, Victor Talking Machine, and the Gramophone Company.[21]

The operations of these earlier transnational corporations in China and elsewhere cannot be divorced from the colonial contexts in which they took place.

In colonial Shanghai, almost all recording and production facilities (with one significant exception, which I discuss later in the essay) were owned by Pathé-EMI and RCA-Victor and located in the foreign concession areas. Profits, naturally, were funneled back to the metropoles. Management and technical expertise were supplied by foreign businessmen and technicians, whose knowledge of local music and local markets was supplied by Chinese "musical compradors." Raw musical material, in turn, was often supplied by small-time entrepreneurs and "pocketbook" record companies who signed "native" artists and rented the production facilities of the major labels in order to serve local markets. Not surprisingly, this patently exploitative situation engendered resistance. Indeed, at the same time that the gramophone became an emblem of modernity for the urban middle classes and an indispensable adjunct to the development of a new mass-mediated culture of consumption, it also became the target of anticolonial resistance on the part of both the emergent national bourgeoisie and leftist cultural insurgents.

The Music Goes Round

There is no better place to begin an examination of the global character of the record industry than with the story of a young American recording engineer named F. W. Gaisberg. Gaisberg began his career as an assistant to the German American inventor Emil Berliner, who perfected the gramophone in 1887. Berliner's gramophone differed from Edison's original phonograph in one essential respect: the wax cylinders Edison's machine used as a recording medium did not lend themselves to mass reproduction and repeatable playback nearly so well as Berliner's flat, shellac gramophone disks.[22] Berliner's gramophone, in short, paved the way for the development of a new consumer industry predicated on the mass production of music.

Berliner's bid to exploit the commercial possibilities of his invention resulted in the creation of two multinational companies. In 1898, Berliner sold the European rights to his patents to a London consortium called The Gramophone Company. In 1901, Berliner's interests, including a portion of The Gramophone Company, were taken over by the New Jersey–based Victor Talking Machine Company. Gaisberg, in his capacity as a representative of The Gramophone Company, spent the last year of the century traveling across Europe, opening agencies and recording such celebrated classical musicians as Fyodor Chaliapin and Enrico Caruso. In September 1902, he was sent still further afield, to Asia. Gaisberg's journey, which was undertaken to "open up new markets, establish agencies, and acquire a catalogue of native records," is documented in his autobiography, *The Music Goes Round*.[23] Equipped with a portable recording studio, Gaisberg visited Calcutta, Singapore, Hong Kong, Shanghai, Tokyo, Bangkok, and Rangoon, producing a grand total of seventeen hundred recordings of local music.

Gaisberg's modus operandi in Shanghai was typical of the journey as a whole. Having selected a sheet music dealer as the company's local sales representative—in this case, Moutrie & Co, the same outfit from whom Pathé's Labansat had purchased his first gramophone—Gaisberg found a musical comprador who would arrange a series of recording sessions with Chinese artists in Gaisberg's hotel room: "Wednesday, March 18th [1903]: We made our first records. About fifteen Chinamen had come, including the accompanying band. As a Chinaman yells at the top of his power when he sings, he can only sing two songs an evening and then he becomes hoarse. Their idea of music is a tremendous clash and bang: with the assistance of a drum, three pairs of huge gongs, a pair of slappers, a sort of banjo, some reed instruments which sounded like bagpipes, and the yelling of the singer, their so-called music was recorded on the gramophone. On the first day, after making ten records we had to stop. The din had so paralyzed my wits that I could not think."[24]

Despite Gaisberg's discomfort, he made another 325 records in Shanghai before moving on to Hong Kong. In Hong Kong, for reasons known only to his local comprador, Gaisberg occupied himself by recording two hundred songs sung by "teahouse girls," whose voices he likens (in terms remarkably similar to earlier European listeners) to "the sound of a small wailing cat."[25] All of these records were sent back to Europe for manufacturing and then sold to record buyers in the colonial treaty ports as well as to "the Chinese of America, the Malay States, and Australia."[26] This last point is particularly revealing, because it shows the extent to which the defining terms of Appadurai's theory of transnational culture—mediation and migration—were already shaping the development of a global media culture in the first decade of the century.[27]

If Gaisberg had been the only representative of a record company to visit Asia, his story might merely represent an interesting instance of transcultural contact and colonial miscomprehension of "native" musical forms. But as Pekka Gronow notes, Gaisberg was only the first of many emissaries dispatched to Asia to spur on the expansion of the industry.[28] In the next seven years, the subsidiaries Gaisberg had established in India and the Far East recorded over ten thousand titles. And by the time a recording engineer for Beka-Record GmbH named Heinrich Bumb arrived in Hong Kong in 1906 (just three years after Gaisberg's initial trip), a host of American, British, and German companies had broken into the business as well: "The Columbia Graphophone Company had just finished its latest recordings — said to be one thousand titles, for which fees of 50,000 dollars had been paid. 'Victor,' 'Grammophon,' as well as 'Zonophon-Records' and 'Odeon' were all represented in the colony." [29]

So rapid was the expansion of the industry into Asia and Latin America, in fact, that these regions soon came to represent more than one-fifth of world-wide record sales.[30] By 1907, Victor and the Gramophone Company found it necessary to divide their respective spheres of influence, with the former agreeing to restrict itself to North and South America, China, Japan, and the Philippines, leaving the latter free to operate anywhere else in the world.[31] By the middle of the next decade, this remarkable growth had rendered the industry's earlier, and distinctly mercantilist, system of production and distribution obsolete and inefficient. Rather than collecting raw musical materials in the colonies for manufacturing in the metropole and then shipping them back home with value added, companies such as Pathé-Asia began to import manufacturing equipment for local use. Between 1910 and 1931, most of the companies that had been able to weather the fierce internecine competition of the early years of the industry by way of consolidation into massive multinational concerns moved quickly to establish local manufacturing facilities and transnational distribution centers throughout Asia, Latin America, and Africa.[32] Shanghai was one such center.[33]

The Record Industry in Shanghai

The story of how Pathé Asia came to dominate the Shanghai record industry is symptomatic of these global trends. The corporate history is complex and more than a little confusing, but deserves comment. When Pathé opened its factory in Shanghai in 1916, the field was littered with competitors: Beka, Odeon, Columbia, Victor, and others. In 1925, Pathé's parent company merged with a London-based company, Columbia Graphophone. At the same time, Columbia Graphophone annexed its American counterpart, Columbia Phonograph, as well as the German Lindström concern (which included Beka-Record and Odeon). In 1931, finally, Columbia Graphophone and The Gramophone Company merged to form a new conglomerate, Electrical and Musical Industries.

In practice, this meant that Pathé-EMI had effectively swallowed almost all of its competition. Pathé's house label (which featured its famous rooster trademark) specialized in popular music and "screen songs" recorded by the most famous singers and movie actresses of the era. Popular music was also issued on the former Gramophone Company's flagship label, His Master's

Voice (HMV), using the famous dog-and-gramophone logo for which it had originally been named. In addition, the company released second-rate popular music and introduced new artists at cut-rate prices on its Regal (Lige) label. Beka (Peikai) and Odeon (Gaoting) continued to issue Chinese operatic music under their own trademarks, but were owned and operated by Pathé and beholden to its recording and manufacturing facilities.[34] In addition to Chinese records, the plant also manufactured music for the overseas Chinese, Vietnamese, Burmese, Laotian, Indonesian, Malayan, and Philippine markets. The entire operation, finally, was self-sufficient. The Pathé factory on Xujiahui Road employed more than three hundred workers operating twenty-four automated record-pressing machines, maintained a workshop for processing raw materials such as shellac, and was equipped with a press for printing record sleeves and labels. All of this added up to a production capacity of 2.7 million records a year.[35]

The merger with EMI left Pathé with only one serious multinational competitor for the gramophone business in China and Southeast Asia: RCA-Victor. Nippon Victor, a Japanese subsidiary of the American Victor Talking Machine, had established itself in Shanghai in the late 1920s. When Victor merged with the giant Radio Corporation of America in 1932, the company became the second multinational to establish a factory in China, albeit with only half the production capacity of Pathé-EMI. RCA-Victor issued a mixture of Chinese operatic, folk, and popular songs using the familiar dog-and-gramophone trademark pioneered by HMV, to which it was entitled by its earlier affiliation with The Gramophone Company. The company was called American Victory (Meiguo shengli) in Chinese, however, to distinguish it from HMV, which was referred to as Victory (Shengli) or transliterated as Victor (Wukeduo).

The vagaries of this tangled corporate history should not obscure the fact that in a very real sense the means of production were almost entirely in the hands of transnational capital. Indeed, the sole Chinese-owned company to possess production capacity—a venture called Great China Records (Da zhonghua changpian), to which I will return shortly—was established only with the aid of Japanese financiers. Pathé-EMI sat atop the heap, followed by RCA-Victor and Great China. The heap itself consisted of a host of locally owned "pocketbook" record companies (pibao gongsi). Equipped with little more than an office (and sometimes not even that), these companies negotiated recording contracts with local and regional musicians and rented studio and manufacturing time from the majors to produce their records.[36] Many of these companies specialized in traditional genres and catered to niche and regional markets. Some of the more interesting examples of this sort of enterprise include Great

Wall Records (Changcheng changpian gongsi), which recorded many of the era's most prominent performers of Peking opera (including Mei Lanfang), and Baige Records (Baige changpian), which catered to local fans of Shanghainese (huju) and yue-style opera (yueju).

Interestingly, provincial pocketbook companies were responsible for the mass-mediated proliferation of a variety of regional musics as well as the creation of new distribution networks in China's hinterlands. The importance of this development should not be underestimated, for much of this music was frowned upon by May Fourth–era music educators, barred from national music curricula, and effectively excluded from distribution in the form of sheet music and songbooks using European notation. Emei Records (Emei changpian gongsi) recorded Sichuanese opera (chuan ju), traditional art songs (qingyin), and folk music in Shanghai and shipped their products back to Sichuan. Lianxing Records (Lianxing changpian) distributed a variety of Fujianese local opera records in Xiamen and Fuzhou. Beihai Records (Beihai changpian) issued recordings of Peking opera and northern Chinese music for audiences in Hebei.[37]

Despite their commitment to a range of traditional musics shunned by the Westernized musical establishment of the treaty ports, none of these companies was able to extricate itself from the colonial economy in which all were enmeshed. Without access to production facilities of their own, they functioned, in effect, as "proletarian" subsidiaries of the transnational corporations. It should also be noted that though these pocketbook companies managed to provide consumers with a limited amount of local "software," the "hardware" upon which their business depended (gramophones and accessories such as replacement needles) was manufactured abroad by EMI and RCA and other multinationals and sold in China by their subsidiaries.

Indeed, one might argue that the pocketbook companies' position within the market was structurally analogous to that of the Chinese musical compradors who worked for European general managers within the Pathé-EMI and RCA-Victor organizations. A brief perusal of commercial directories and import and export manuals of the time reveals that all of the transnational record companies were managed by Europeans and Americans. Pathé, for instance, was managed by Labansat (in the capacity of managing director for the East) until the EMI merger, at which time he was replaced by a management team led by R. Degoy, R. L. Read, and H. L. Wilson. The only Chinese name to appear is Labansat's original Chinese collaborator, Zhang Changfu, who served as Chinese manager of Pathé Asia until 1928.[38] Although the precise nature of the balance of decision-making power within companies like Pathé remains somewhat unclear, it is safe to say that the foreign managers were responsible for all major business decisions and even attended to such tasks as approving song lyrics (which were translated into English for their benefit) before recording sessions. Chinese workers were relegated to providing musical expertise and negotiating with performers and local distributors.[39]

The company's internal hierarchy was complicated still further by the presence of other foreigners in nonmanagerial positions. These included French and English recording engineers and technicians responsible for the installation and upkeep of the company's manufacturing plant. More interesting, especially in light of Shanghai's multiple colonization and consequent status as global entrepôt, was the fact that Pathé's in-house studio orchestra throughout the 1930s and 1940s consisted primarily of White Russian emigrés, most of whom were both classically trained and fully conversant with the idioms of American jazz and Tin Pan Alley popular song.[40] Other record companies hired groups of Filipino musicians as well as local Chinese for popular music (as opposed to Chinese operatic) recording sessions.[41] Racial hierarchies held sway in this arena as well, as Chinese musicians, with the exception of female vocalists, were routinely paid substantially less than their foreign counterparts.[42] The profits accruing from all of these efforts, a substantial portion of which derived from their dealings with the Chinese pocketbook companies, were either funneled back into the business or remitted to parent companies overseas.

Anticolonial Resistance and the Native Bourgeoisie

Pathé-EMI and RCA-Victor, of course, were just two of the actors in a larger drama of imperialist economic exploitation in China. By 1918, more than seven thousand foreign companies had established a presence in China, and throughout the 1920s and 1930s, multinational corporations owned controlling stakes in a number of crucial industries, including shipping, coal mining, petroleum, chemicals, tobacco, textiles, and banking. China's balance of trade with the West and Japan was equally lopsided.[43] This dire situation provoked sporadic resistance on the part of both the Nationalist government and the national bourgeoisie. The efforts on the part of native elites to wrest control of the means of phonographic reproduction away from transnational conglomerates like Pathé-EMI are one example of this fight against imperialist economic domination.

I have already alluded to Great China Records. This company was brought into being by no less a personage than Sun Yat-sen, and explicitly conceived of as one part of a larger project of national industrialization.[44] While still in exile in 1916, Sun urged a group of Japanese businessmen to help finance the construction of a Chinese record factory in Shanghai's Hongkou district. The company, which Sun himself had christened, was established soon thereafter with a mixture of both Japanese and Chinese capital. In 1924, Sun even recorded two promotional disks of his own speeches, urging on the company, and, by extension, domestic goods and the national bourgeoisie who produced them, to ever greater success. By 1927, Great China was wholly owned by local capitalists. The company's facilities were limited, possessing just eight pressing machines to Pathé's twenty-four, but complete, and it issued records on three separate labels: green for modern songs, red for Peking opera, and blue for regional operas. Even so, the company was hard-pressed by its more amply financed foreign competitors, and the factory seldom operated at full production capacity. Some of this slack was filled by renting to pocketbook companies, but the company never really represented a serious threat to Pathé-EMI's domination of the record market.

A second example of this sort of nationalist resistance to foreign monopoly was a Hong Kong–based pocketbook company that worked in close collaboration with Great China in the early 1930s. New Moon Records (Xinyue liusheng ji changpian gongsi), founded in 1927 by a charismatic and musically inclined Cantonese businessman named Qian Guangren, is interesting in a number of ways. First, Qian, who was something of a self-styled intellectual, published his own trade magazine, *The New Moon Collection* (*Xinyue ji*). This document provides us with not only a rare and fascinating look into the business operations of a Chinese pocketbook record company, but also insights into the ideological positions and cultural sensibilities that informed those commercial activities.

What emerges most prominently from the magazine, both in Qian's own writings and in the advertisements and promotional materials that accompany them, is the explicit foregrounding of the company's nationalistic commitment to promoting the manufacture and consumption of domestic goods. The company recorded only with Great China, and this relationship became a prominent component of both their corporate identity and their marketing strategy. Certifications of the "domesticity" of New Moon's products are exhibited prominently on the inside cover of the magazine, and advertisements for the label (and its larger affiliate, Great China) feature slogans such as "There isn't a patriot who doesn't support Great China Records." In addition, almost every issue of the magazine features a polemic (usually penned by Qian himself) advocating the promotion of native industry and domestic goods.[45] By the early 1930s, this commitment had also led the company to pioneer the domestic manufacture of gramophone tone arms, needles, and other accessories.

Second, the magazine provides a window into the mass-mediated emergence of a distinctly regional, and unmistakably hybridized, popular culture in interwar Hong Kong. Despite New Moon's nationalist stance, its market and musical specialization was restricted to Hong Kong and its Cantonese-speaking environs. Many of the Cantonese opera singers whom Qian Guangren brought to the Great China recording studio in Shanghai were also stars of the nascent Hong Kong film industry.[46] Some of these legendary figures remain household words in Hong Kong today, including Xue Juexian (Sit Gok-sin) and the child prodigy Xin Ma Shisheng. Other recording artists for New Moon went on to fame in the Shanghai film industry, the most notable being the celebrated silent film actress Ruan Lingyu.

Perhaps even more interesting than New Moon's role in developing a stable of local Cantonese talent was the new genre of music that it produced for phonographic consumption. In addition to traditional operatic arias, Qian Guangren and his friends created a new hybrid genre that incorporated Cantonese folk melodies with new-fangled Western instruments such as guitar and saxophone. What is more, these songs were wedded to lyrics that fully reflected the polyglot colonialism of Hong Kong's linguistic idiom, rhyming Cantonese street slang and standard Chinese with fractured English and French phrases (see figure 1).[47] There are several questions and conclusions we can draw from this phenomenon. First, it prompts us to rethink the relationship between nationalism and regional identity in the 1930s. Second, it places into serious question the familiar proposition that the mass mediation of culture necessarily results in cultural homogenization. Finally, it should be noted that this sort of complex colonial transculturation was by no means unique to Hong Kong, but was also a salient characteristic of mass-mediated musical culture in Shanghai (and the other colonial entrepōts outside of China) as well.

Gramophone Culture and the Left

If Chinese businessmen were largely concerned with taking a piece of the business associated with this new gramophone culture away from the multinational companies who controlled it, the concern of leftist cultural workers was the "semifeudal, semicolonial" nature of gramophone culture itself. This is not to say that leftist critics were mere Luddites. As early as 1928, no less a figure than Guo Moruo had suggested the phonograph as a model for cultural production, urging leftist cultural workers to "be phonographs" that would objectively record the lives of the proletariat and play back what they found for the benefit of society at large.[48] For leftist musicians, then, the problem was not so much

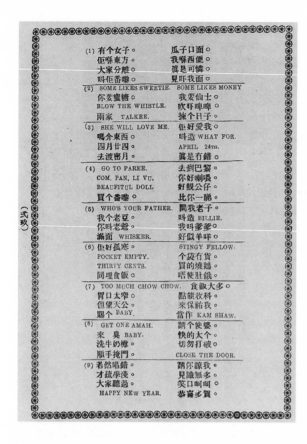

(弍玖)

Figure 1. "Shouzai Goes Dating," reprinted in *Xinyue ji* 2 (September 1930).

the gramophone itself, but the new urban media culture — born of the commercial interactivity of records, radio, musical cinema, and the popular press — in which it participated. That culture, they believed, was irredeemably tainted by its colonial decadence, its political escapism, and its association with both the "vulgar" commercial culture of the urban petit-bourgeois and imperialist economic domination. Their agenda, then, was to forge a new mass culture that would serve less as an object of private consumption than as a means for the mobilization of collective resistance against Japanese territorial encroachment and Western imperialism.

With the annexation of Manchuria in 1932 by Japan, leftists set about this project with redoubled urgency. To succeed, they needed to infiltrate both Chinese film studios and transnational record companies such as Pathé-EMI. The leftist composer Ren Guang was a central figure in this effort. Ren, who had spent the 1920s studying music in France and working for a French piano manufacturer in Vietnam, was hired as Pathé's musical director in 1928 to play the musical comprador role of his immediate predecessor, Zhang Changfu.[49] In the early 1930s, Ren began to involve himself in a number of left-wing musical organizations devoted to the proletarianization of Chinese music. It was through such study groups as the Soviet Friends Society (Sulian zhi you she) that he became friends with many of the most prominent leftist musicians and filmmakers of the era, including Nie Er, He Luting, and Tian Han. These figures, in turn, secured positions at Shanghai's major studios at the dawn of the sound era in 1932 and 1933.

Ren Guang thus became instrumental to the release of almost fifty leftist screen songs and national salvation anthems between 1932 and 1937.[50] This new music set itself in direct opposition to the modern songs that continued to dominate the market, replacing their Chinese melodies, jazzy harmonies, and melismatic female crooning with march rhythms, orchestral effects, and choral singing drawn from the example of Soviet mass music.

Many of these songs remain classics even today; some of the more prominent examples include leftist musician Nie Er's "March of the Volunteers" ("Yiyongjun jinxing qu"), which became China's national anthem, and Ren Guang's own composition, "Song of the Fishermen" ("Yuguang qu"). The commercial success of these songs, finally, allowed Ren to bring a number of his leftist colleagues, including Nie Er and later Xian Xinghai, into the company as the directors of Pathé's in-house Chinese music ensemble.

Ren's success as a comprador for leftist music rested on a pair of ironies. Although his efforts met with occasional resistance from his English and French managers, the relationship was smoothed by his fluency in the French language and his experience working as a manager of a French colonial enterprise in Vietnam.[51] More important, the colonial nature of the Pathé-EMI operation itself functioned as a sort of ideological shield against government censorship.[52] Much of the more overtly anti-Japanese material Ren was able to push through his foreign superiors could not have been released through pocketbook companies, who did not enjoy the extraterritorial status conferred on Pathé-EMI by Chinese authorities and the foreign-run Shanghai Municipal Council. Ultimately, the managers of Pathé-EMI were only too happy to exploit the limited but nonetheless lucrative market for this sort of music. The flow of leftist music into the mass media market was cut only after the military occupation of Shanghai in 1937, when Japanese military officials forced Pathé-EMI to fire Ren.[53]

That Pathé-EMI actually profited from the anticolonial critique launched by the leftists is the final irony with which I conclude this essay. Much of the force of this critique is summed up by a promotional image from a 1937 issue

Figure 2. "Damn! Those Foreign Devils Are Cheaters." A promotional still from a 1937 issue of *New China Pictorial*.

of a movie magazine called *New China Pictorial* (*Xinhua huabao*).[54] The magazine was the official organ of the leftist-controlled Xinhua Studio; the image in figure 2 is a still from a new film starring the most popular slapstick comedian of the day, Han Langen. Han, playing a country bumpkin, crouches in front of a gramophone being demonstrated to a Chinese crowd by a foreigner. The rhetorical force of the image is made clear by the appearance in the lower right-hand corner of what is indisputably the single most widely circulated trademark of the global gramophone industry, that of a dog listening to "His Master's Voice."[55] Han, and by extension the Chinese people, is likened to a dog, in a rhetorical move that subtly alludes to the probably apocryphal (but nonetheless pointed) anecdote about the municipal park in colonial Shanghai to which "dogs and Chinese" were not allowed entry. And in a masterful play on words (and images), the gramophone itself stands in for the voice of China's colonial masters. If that were not enough, Han's disingenuously naïve exclamation — "Damn! These foreign devils are cheaters" — steers the viewer of the photo toward a sharp awareness of the technologically mediated transcription, economic exploitation, and cultural dislocation that characterizes gramophone culture and the condition of colonial modernity in which it was embedded.

This scene, of course, is more than a little reminiscent of the anecdote with which I began this essay. We might even want to imagine the figure in the center of the photo as Labansat himself, demonstrating his new gramophone to curious Chinese passersby. In the first anecdote, audiences were encouraged to chuckle along with "Laughing Foreigners." In this case, however, Chinese viewers have the last, albeit bitter and even self-deprecating, laugh.

Notes

1   The record was recorded in Paris under the catalogue number 32606 by Pathé-Frères and was titled "Five Men Laughing." The men in question laugh, chortle, and guffaw throughout the two and a half minutes of the disk. See Li Qing et al., *Guangbo dianshi qiye shi neibu shiliao*, 137. Interestingly, one of the first gramophone records to arrive in India was "The Laughing Song," recorded by Burt Shephard for The Gramophone Company. See G. N. Joshi, "A Concise History of the Phonograph Industry in India," 148. The same record seems to have been part of the experience of listening to the gramophone in colonial Africa as well. Wole Soyinka, writing about the sorts of records he listened to as the child of a middle-class Nigerian household, recollects, "The voices of Denge, Ayinde Bakare, Ambrose Campbell; a voice which was so deep that I believed it could have only been produced by a special trick of His Master's Voice, but which father assured me belonged to a black man called Paul Robeson . . . Christmas carols, the songs of Marion Anderson; oddities such as a record in which a man did nothing but laugh throughout . . ." (Wole Soyinka, *Aké*, 108, cited in Michael Chanan's fascinating study, *Repeated Takes: A Short History of Recording and Its Effects on Music*, 90).

2   See Pat Conte, "The Fourth World: From Stone Age to New Age." Conte's article appears as the liner notes for *The Secret Museum of Mankind, Vol. 1: Ethnic Music Classics, 1925–1948*, a series of CD compilations of remastered 78 rpm records that document some of the diversity of traditional, folk, and hybrid popular styles recorded by the global record industry in the first half of the century.

3   Bruno Nettl's *The Western Impact on World Music* is a preliminary survey of this vast (and as yet relatively underexplored and undertheorized) topic. For a study of the role of brass bands in the musical life of the British colonies, see Trevor Herbert and Margaret Sarkissian, "Victorian Bands and Their Dissemination in the Colonies." For a detailed account of the history of Western musical incursion in China, see my "Popular Music and Colonial Modernity in China, 1900–1937," 17–67.

4   One famous example of this sort of miscomprehension is provided by the nineteenth-century composer Hector Berlioz, whose violent reactions to the Chinese and Indian music to which he was exposed at the Great Exhibition in London of 1852 are recorded at some length in his *Evenings with the Orchestra*.

5   For an illuminating discussion of the nature, history, and effects of notation, see
     Michael Chanan, *Musica Practica: The Social Practice of Western Music from Gregorian Chant
     to Postmodernism*, 54–80.

6   See Roland Gelatt, *The Fabulous Phonograph, 1877–1977*, 172.

7   See David Harvey, *The Condition of Postmodernity*, 240–41.

8   Jacques Attali, *Noise: The Political Economy of Music*, 95. For Attali, the introduction of
     recording heralded a transition in the political economy of music from a regime of
     "representation" to one of "repetition."

9   For a book-length account of the various debates around the issue of mass media and
     cultural imperialism, see John Tomlinson, *Cultural Imperialism*.

10   Chanan, *Repeated Takes*, 7.

11   Gelatt's study suggests that this emphasis on domesticity was an important aspect
     of the marketing strategy for the phonograph as early as the 1890s, and that there
     continued to be a great emphasis on disguising the machine as a piece of domestic fur-
     niture by way of "cabinetry and styling" throughout the teens and twenties (69, 191).

12   As the 1930 ad copy in a record trade journal indicates, the expansion of the media
     into private space was essential to the growth of the industry: "In the home . . . New
     Moon Records are the most elegant and proper sort of leisure product" (*Xinyue ji* 1
     [September 1929]: 39). Jiang Tie's 1932 consumer guide to the gramophone, *Liusheng
     ji*, includes a long section on its "Use in the Home." See also Ke Zhenghe, "Liusheng
     ji de liyong fa," and "Changpian de shiyong ji baocun fa."

13   One example is Xu Xu's 1930s novella *Wuti* (Untitled) in which a wealthy Shanghai-
     nese love poet issues the following complaint about his disaffected (but beautiful and
     artistic) wife: "She doesn't even like all the piano records I bought her anymore, hasn't
     listened to them in months, but when she goes out on the town and starts to discuss
     music with someone, she'll always brag about all the records we have at home, about
     how we stay up late together just to listen to them" (in *Xu Xu quanji* 4: 428). A sec-
     ond example, dating from 1943, is Zhang Ailing's short story "Huadiao" (A withered
     flower), in which an ironic assessment of the Zheng household's economic situation
     is offered by way of an inventory of their consumer goods and leisure activities: "It
     was hard to tell if the Zheng family was rich or poor. A house full of servants at their
     beck and call, living in a foreign-style building, but only two beds in the whole place,
     so that their daughters had to carry bedding down to the living room and spread it
     across the floor every night before they went to sleep. The few sticks of furniture in
     the living room were actually borrowed from other people. Only the wireless set was
     their own, and the cabinets of the gramophone were always stuffed full with all the
     latest popular records" (in Eileen Chang, *Chuanqi* [Romances], 360). In the 1920s,
     gramophones (and wireless radios) were more unambiguously playthings of the rich,
     as indicated in Zhang Henshui's description of the bedroom of a Beijing warlord's
     pampered concubine in *Tixiao yinyuan* (Fate in tears and laughter). In the concubine
     Yaqin's own words, as she attempts to overawe the visiting Shen Fengxi: "Sister, I
     want you to feel at home, so I've invited you into the bedroom. It's not easy for us to
     get a chance to visit, so don't leave just yet. You can eat here, chat, listen to the talking
     machine, or I can let you hear the wireless radio. Our wireless isn't the same as the

usual kind, because we can hear foreign opera singers sing, so it's just about as new and fresh as can be" (156).

14 Shui Jing, *Liuxing gequ cangsang ji*, 8, notes that in the 1940s almost every corner store in Shanghai's residential districts was equipped with a radio and a gramophone, and that such spaces became a prime site for popular music consumption.

15 It is no surprise, given both the industry's emphasis on domesticity and the expansion of musical space, that one frequently finds advertisements for gramophone records and radio equipment in the women's magazines of the period. See, for example, the string of RCA/Victor print ads that ran in the popular wartime journal *Nüsheng* (Women's voice).

16 I borrow the term from Gregory Jusdanis, *Belated Modernity and Aesthetic Culture: Inventing National Literature.*

17 Arjun Appadurai, "Disjuncture and Difference in the Global Cultural Economy," in *Modernity at Large: Cultural Dimensions of Globalization*, 31.

18 Ibid., 30. "Nostalgia for the present" is originally Fredric Jameson's phrase.

19 Ibid., 47.

20 Ibid., 9.

21 See Deanna Campbell Robinson, Elizabeth B. Buck, Marlene Cuthbert, and the International Communication and Youth Consortium, *Music at the Margins: Popular Music and Global Cultural Diversity*, 41. The six companies in question are Sony Music (which owns CBS Records, itself a descendent of Columbia Graphophone), Thorn-EMI (a product of the 1931 merger of The Gramophone Company, Columbia Phonograph Company, and Pathé-Frères), Bertelsmann Music Group (which owns the recording empire of what used to be known as RCA-Victor), WEA (a division of Time-Warner), Polygram Records (a German conglomerate that began international operations as early as the 1910s as the Polyphon Company), and MCA (an American major label recently purchased by the Japanese electronics firm Matsushita). For a brief review of the structure of the global record industry, see Rene Peron, "The Record Industry," 292–97.

22 The authoritative study of this first phase in the evolution of recording technology is Walter L. Welch and Leah Brodbeck Stenzel Burt's *From Tinfoil to Stereo: The Acoustic Years of the Recording Industry, 1877–1929.* For a comprehensive, if less technical, history of the recording industry, see Gelatt.

23 F. W. Gaisberg, *The Music Goes Round*, 48.

24 Ibid., 62.

25 Ibid., 63.

26 Ibid., 64.

27 As Gronow notes, this was also true of other national and ethnic groups. Columbia, for instance, was marketing Syrian and Arabian recordings "for the U.S. ethnic market" around the turn of the century. Nor should we forget that the sorts of recordings Gaisberg and others made in Europe were also targeted at immigrants to the United States of Italian, German, and Russian descent, among others. See "The Record Industry Comes to the Orient," 261.

28 Ibid., 251. Gronow is perhaps the foremost historian of the global record industry. See also Gronow's "The Record Industry: The Growth of a Mass Medium," 53–76.

29 Heinrich Bumb, "The Great Beka 'Expedition,' 1905–6," 731, cited in Gronow, "The Record Industry Comes to the Orient," 251.

30 A. G. Kenwood and A. L. Lougheed, *The Growth of the International Economy, 1820–1960*, 93. An interesting anecdotal testament to the growing importance of the Asian record market is supplied by the American arranger and composer Claude Lapham, who worked as musical director for Columbia Records in Japan in 1935: "For the Japanese are not only avid students of all jazz records but also of all symphonic ones; in fact, during the year of my contract with Columbia Records, more Beethoven symphonies were sold than in all of Europe combined. I also walked into a teashop one day and found a huge stack of every standard symphonic movement and string quartet" ("Looking at Japanese Jazz," 14).

31 John F. Perkins, Alan Kelly, and John Ward, "On Gramophone Company Matrix Numbers 1898 to 1921," 57. These sorts of arrangements, unsurprisingly, often followed the familiar pathways of colonial power. Companies tended to be stronger in markets where their own country's colonial interests were best represented: English companies dominated Indian and Egyptian markets, American concerns were stronger in Latin America and the Philippines, and Germans relied on record sales to Turkey and the Dutch East Indies. China, reflecting its partial and multiple colonization at the hands of several different countries, was a free-for-all: the Shanghai record industry was financed by English, American, French, German, and Japanese capital.

32 For details and dates, see Gronow, "The Record Industry Comes to the Orient," 252–70.

33 The scope of Pathé's operations provides some indicators of this decentralization of the record industry. By 1908, the company already maintained several factories throughout Europe as well as branch offices in Tokyo, Shanghai, Bombay, and Singapore. A factory in Latvia served the Russian market, and its Vienna facility catered to record buyers in the Balkan states, Syria, and Egypt. In Russia alone, recordings were made for nine different linguistic groups, and efforts were also made to break into the Afghan market. In 1914, it opened its first factory in the United States; 1916 brought the first Chinese record factory. The company was also especially strong in the North African and East African markets because of the French colonial presence in Algeria, Tunisia, Morocco, Somaliland, and Madagascar. The company also produced records for French colonial holdings in Southeast Asia (Indochina) and the Pacific (Tahiti). See ibid., 263–66.

34 Unaffiliated American labels like Brunswick (whose principal business was the manufacture and sale of gramophones) also remained in Shanghai after the merger, but concentrated on selling imports of American popular music. According to Ke Zhenghe, a contemporary commentator, recordings of the European classical repertoire issued by the German multinational Polydor and the American Columbia Records were also available in Shanghai in the early 1930s, but it is unclear whether or not these companies actually established agencies in Shanghai ("Changpian de piping," 17).

35 The ratio of domestic production to imported repertoire can only be estimated because of the paucity of available trade statistics and sales figures. I will, however, venture a few, tentative conclusions, based on Pekka Gronow's pioneering research on record export figures, as well as estimates of domestic production capacity garnered

from my own reading of the materials presented in Li Qing's history of the Chinese record industry. Bear in mind that some of what follows is merely guesswork. As many authors (including Gronow and Gelatt) note, 1929 represented a high-water mark for the transnational record industry in the interwar years. Gronow's figures indicate that record exports to China in 1929 amounted to 1.1. million records from Germany (887,000 units), the United States (215,000 units), and France (40,000 units). If we add to this figure U.S. imports to Hong Kong and Canton (366,000 units) and an estimated 500,000 units from the United Kingdom (a conservative estimate extrapolated from the fact that the U.K. exported over 600,000 units to India and 483,000 to Java in the same year), we arrive at a total of around 2 million records. Before the 1930s—which saw the modernization of the Pathé operation following its merger with EMI and the expansion of the RCA-Victor plant—domestic production capacity was almost certainly limited to about the same amount. Thus, it seems clear that imports surpassed domestic production by a considerable margin between 1916 (the year that the first domestic manufacturing facilities were established in Shanghai) and 1930. In the six years before the Sino-Japanese war, however, it appears that domestic products came to dominate the market. By 1932, domestic production capacity had mushroomed to 5.4 million records per annum (with Pathé-EMI accounting for a whopping 2.7 million records, RCA-Victor for 1.8 million, and Great China running a distant third at 900,000). Although precise figures are unavailable, we also know that a substantial portion of these records were produced for export to overseas Chinese and Southeast Asian markets. Gronow, for instance, notes that China exported almost 50,000 records to the Dutch East Indies (Indonesia) in 1929 alone. The total figure was certainly much larger. For Gronow's numbers, see "The Record Industry Comes to the Orient," 281–84. Estimates of domestic production capacity are extrapolated from Li Qing's description of the facilities maintained by the three majors in Shanghai (138–41).

36   For a detailed account of these local operations, see Li Qing, 141–43.

37   Other pocketbook companies include Asia Records, China Records, Harmony Records, Kunlun Records, Taiping Records, and Xingshi Records. The Hong Kong–based New Moon Records—which I discuss in more detail shortly in terms of its role in the anticolonial promotion of an indigenous Chinese record industry—should also be included in this group.

38   See *Commercial Directory of Shanghai*, 123–24. For later listings of record companies in Shanghai and their management personnel, refer to *Guide to China's Foreign Trade: Import and Export Annual 1933* and *Shanghai Hong List*. This colonial state of affairs persisted well after Pathé-EMI's move to Hong Kong in 1949 in the wake of the Communist revolution.

39   Sadly, both EMI and RCA-Victor have long since disposed of the kinds of archival materials that could elucidate exactly how business decisions were carried out in the 1920s and 1930s. Li Qing's work, however, presents a summary of much of this (now unavailable) material, as culled from documents confiscated from Pathé's offices in Xujiahui after the company left Shanghai for Hong Kong in 1949.

40   Interview with Yao Li, Hong Kong, 20 October 1995. See also Wong Kee-chee, "Shanghai Baidai gongsi de yange," 91. White Russian *women*, of course, are often portrayed

in accounts of the era's nightlife as low-class cabaret dancers and prostitutes. See, for instance, Marc T. Greene, "Shanghai Cabaret Girl," 25. As such writing makes abundantly clear, Russians were seen as the poor, and distinctly inferior, cousins of the American, English, and French colonizers who tended to dominate political and economic life within the precincts of the International Settlement.

41 The house band at the famous Paramount Ballroom (Baile men), for instance, was a Filipino outfit led by Gloria Andico. For a picture of the band, see the cover of *Yinyue shijie* 1.1 (August 1938).

42 See Li Jinhui, "Wo he Mingyue she," 240.

43 See Jonathan Spence, *The Search for Modern China*, 329.

44 I am relying here on the account of the company provided by Li Qing, 140–41.

45 See, for instance, Qian Guangren, "Tantan woguo jiben shuchupin yu xinxing gongye."

46 For recent work on the early Hong Kong film industry's relationship with the Mainland and the articulation of a regional identity in Cantonese cinema, see Fu Po-shek, "Framing Identity: Mainland Emigres, Marginal Culture, and Hong Kong Cinema, 1937–1941."

47 See, for example, the song "Shouzai paituo" (Shouzai goes dating) reprinted in *Xinyue ji* 2 (September 1930). This amusing send-up of middle-class courtship, colonial style, is brimming with Cantonese neologisms. The song was written and accompanied on the piano by Zhao Enrong and sung by Huang Shounian, a comedian apparently fluent in several languages. Interestingly (and quite ironically, given the popular and self-consciously colonial character of the song), the promotional blurb for this record invokes Cai Yuanpei's May Fourth–era dictum of "incorporating East and West" (*zhongxi hebi*) to create a new national aesthetic.

48 Guo Moruo, "Liusheng jiqi de huiyin" (The phonograph's echo), in *Moruo wenji*, 10: 345.

49 For a month-by-month chronology of Ren's life, see Qin Qiming, *Yinyue jia Ren Guang*; for a description of Ren's duties, see 9.

50 As estimated by Li Qing, 149. Something of the market dominance of nonleftist popular songs and traditional music, however, is suggested by the fact that these fifty songs represent only 5 percent of Pathé's domestic output between 1932 and 1949 (which numbered nineteen hundred titles in all).

51 Li Qing, 148.

52 See Qin, 31–32.

53 Ibid., 44. Ren Guang, fearing for his life, fled the "Paris of the East" for Paris, France. After a year in exile, he returned to China in 1938 to participate in anti-Japanese resistance efforts. He was killed in action in January 1941, a victim of "friendly fire."

54 See *Xinhua huabao* 2.1 (January 1937).

55 Indeed, it is "generally considered the most valuable trademark in existence" (Welch and Burt, 134, cited in Michael Taussig, *Alterity and Mimesis: A Particular History of the Senses*, 212). Taussig's illuminating study contains two chapters on "colonial phonography" and the appropriation of the HMV logo by the Cuna people of Panama in their textile designs.

PART 3

Science, Medicine, and

Cultural Pathologies

Larissa N. Heinrich   *Handmaids to the Gospel:*

Lam Qua's Medical Portraiture

> *"Influence" is a curse of art criticism primarily because of its wrong-headed grammatical preju-*
> *dice about who is the agent and who the patient: it seems to reverse the active/passive relation*
> *which the historical actor experiences and the inferential beholder will wish to take into account.*
> *If one says that x influenced y it does seem that one is saying that x did something to y rather*
> *than that y did something to x. But in the consideration of good pictures and painters the second*
> *is always the more lively reality.*
> —MICHAEL BAXANDALL, *Patterns of Intention: On the Historical Explanation of Pictures*

In the century and a half since Lam Qua (fl. 1830–1850) made the disturbing series of medical portraits that accompanied Reverend Peter Parker on
his fund-raising mission to medical schools and Protestant authorities in the
West, the paintings have been exhibited only once. Curators shy away from
their grotesque, unflinching portrayal of cysts, tumors, growths, and ampu-
tations juxtaposed with perplexingly serene human hosts: too unsettling, too
"inappropriate for public view." [1] Likewise, evaluations of Lam Qua for the
most part concentrate on his mastery of port scenes and commercial portraiture, only mentioning his medical portraits as a sort of curious afterthought,
despite the fact that they represent the largest unified body of extant works
by the artist (eighty-three pieces are in the collection of Yale Medical College
Library; another smaller group is at Guy's Medical Hospital in London; and
four paintings are housed at Cornell).

Yet precisely because of their medical content and the complexity of inter-
related fields they bring together (are they portraits? medical illustrations?

simple works of art? innovative or imitative? Chinese or Western?), this set of paintings is a uniquely valuable resource for research on the beginnings of modernity in China and, in particular, on the roots of the simultaneously racialized and pathologized Chinese identity that began to emerge during this time. First, as medical illustrations their subject matter is not limited to either the elite literati of Chinese painting nor to the wealthy *hong* merchants and foreign traders of typical commercial portraiture. Thus through them we have a rare opportunity to view representations of a range of classes and both genders from the poorest, uneducated servant to the wealthiest urban matron. Second, because in their capacity as medical illustrations the paintings were intended to accompany or illuminate a more discursive representation of illness, we may "read" the paintings in conjunction with their detailed textual counterpart— Parker's case journal—allowing us to attempt a level of evaluation much less feasible with undocumented portraiture. Finally, because these paintings were intended for use essentially as a kind of propaganda for the medical mission in China, they offer a valuable opportunity to look at how Westerners and Chinese might have conceived of—and attempted to shape—Chinese identity on the eve of the Opium War, when the balance of power concerning the development of "modernity" shifted decidedly westward. In short, Lam Qua's medical portraiture offers us an important ideological resource concerning visions of a newly emerging and increasingly racialized Chinese identity.

In this essay I provide rudimentary analyses of some of Lam Qua's more representative works of medical portraiture alongside entries from Parker's journal, suggesting the painter's visual contribution to the invention of the tenacious stereotype of the "Sick Man of Asia" (*dongya bingfu*). How did Lam Qua conceive of and create sickness and Chinese identity in his paintings? How did he interpret the specific ideologies that Parker called for in his intended use of the paintings? Barbara Stafford makes the point via Foucault that the very fact of making specific visual records of externally manifest ailments such as "blisters, blotches, eruptions, and tumors" was part of a uniquely modern obsession with cataloguing the "disfigurements punctuating the modern stigmatized skin." [2] How, I ask, did this peculiarly modern process of visualization get translated in a Chinese setting? In asking such questions, my hope is to lay a basic foundation for a more general examination of the role of visual images in creating the idea of a racialized Chinese identity in the modern era. Were there precedents, one might ask, for this kind of representation in China? Or, moving forward along the historical spectrum, were there ways that Lam Qua's paintings might have influenced or anticipated the way pathology and Chinese racial identity were interpreted after the Opium War, when Western medicine became an even more powerful vehicle for intellectual colonialism?

I draw for inspiration on observation of literary representations of illness and deformity that appear to an ever increasing extent in fiction of the modern period from Xiao Hong to Lu Xun to Yu Hua and that constitute a kind of trend in the "pathologization" of representations of this newly racialized Chinese identity. This pathologization demonstrates itself through a changing language of illness or symptomatology that reflects the increasing influence of Western medical ideology and debates about the nature of the self, and emerges when we examine the "etymology" of the various pathologies that appear in these works. Bridie Andrews gives an interesting example of one such etymology when she discusses the case of Republican-period definitions of tuberculosis. Pointing out how the term "tuberculosis" as employed in this period is the hybrid product of Western evangelizing activity combined with conventional Chinese understandings of tuberculosis (*feilaobing*), she notes that "it is no surprise that some of the new generation of writers [e.g., Lu Xun and Ding Ling] chose to capitalize on the disease's association with sensitivity and literary virtuosity" in their creation of certain famous tragic characters such as the tuberculine Sophie or the ill boy of "Medicine." [3] What Andrews is pointing out is that in literary representations of illness in the modern period by two of the most famous "social realist" writers, we can detect the clear influence of hybrid medical ideologies in the creation of a certain characterization or identity. By performing this analysis, Andrews makes it possible to trace some of the sources of these characterizations and thereby understand a little better how some of the most influential characters in modern Chinese literature were created. Her analysis also points up some of the links between a maturing sense of national identity and illness at the level of representation.

Likewise, it is the premise of this essay that a similar critique of representations of illness can apply in the case of graphic representations. Though a picture of a sick person — especially in the context of medical illustration, which may pretend to perform a number of nonartistic functions — offers us the illusion of one or another form of unmediated representation of illness, in fact, as with most "realism," anything we see has already been filtered through multiple cultural, technical, and personal channels. The early-nineteenth-century paintings of gross pathologies by the commercial painter Lam Qua for the medical missionary Peter Parker likewise confront us with a stark, undeniable dimensionality that suggests that they, like the literary figures, are a "real" record of real illnesses: straightforward likenesses of objectively definable pathologies (tumors, growths) that happen to share the frame with sensitive portrayals of their human hosts. Yet I argue that like the portrayals of consumptives in the stories of Ding Ling and Lu Xun, these portraits are in fact prismatic emblems of a certain historical moment, cultural time capsules in effect. Lam Qua's medical paintings are artifacts of modernity, situation-specific representations of an increasingly racialized Chinese identity that was also intensely pathologized.

Analyzing a selection of the Lam Qua medical portraits, I focus on how he uses composition and content to transmit a message about the "curability" of Chinese culture, simultaneously creating and pathologizing a protoracial Chinese identity, all in keeping with the propagandistic requirements of Parker's missionary ideology. Offering a brief comparison with photographs from an early-twentieth-century Western medical manual, I suggest that the association of sickness with Chineseness in general and the Chinese body in specific had, by the time of the photographs, evolved from being based in an abstract notion of "culture" and character to being based in a highly absolute, post-Darwinian understanding of race. I conclude that Lam Qua's paintings, like the Lu Xun fiction that came later, conflate illness with a nascent racialized Chinese identity, but in a way that is deeply idealistic, "curable" in effect, and therefore in telling contrast to the more fixed notions of Chinese identity that appeared as Western medicine and ideology of race in general began to take a stronger hold.

This study is essentially a rumination on what it meant to be and to become the Sick Man of Asia. Through an analysis of several representative paintings by Lam Qua, I look at notions of cultural/racial identity in a time when Western medicine had not yet fully matured to its role of providing a pretext for claims of Western cultural superiority. Observing a parallel phenomenon in literary representations of illness of the early modern period, I hypothesize a gradual "medicalization" of Chinese identity in visual representation that coincides with the emergence and establishment of the idea of a racialized Chinese self-identity. Lam Qua's medical portraiture, I conclude, represents but one stage in this process, and opens the way for further examination of the evolution of racial identity and representation in the colonial period and beyond.

Brief Background on Lam Qua

A commercial port painter, Lam Qua made his name painting likenesses in oil of visiting European tradesmen and wealthy *hong* merchants, as well as port scenes and copies of other portraits and pictures. In the most thorough and informative investigation into Lam Qua's background, training, development, style, and ouevre, Crossman's *Decorative Arts of the China Trade*, the author remarks that Lam Qua, "far more than a copyist . . . was . . . the most celebrated Chinese painter in the English style in Canton." [4] The first Chinese working in the Western manner to exhibit in America, over the course of his career Lam Qua also exhibited at the Royal Academy in London, the Pennsylvania Academy of Fine Arts, and the Boston Athenaeum, as well as other Western venues — "no mean feat," as Crossman points out, "for a Chinese who had learned to paint in a foreign style." [5] Some of his more famous sitters included Chi Ying, the signatory to the Treaty of Nanking, Commissioner Lin (Lin Chong), who was "responsible for the onset of the Opium War," as well as Peter Parker, Sir Henry Pottinger, and numerous other Western and Chinese dignitaries.

Lam Qua was probably the student of the famous Chinese coast painter George Chinnery, from whom he may have inherited "the fresh, fluid brush-strokes and use of the light so characteristic of Chinnery's painting." [6] Although there was reputed to be some conflict between the two artists as Lam Qua's clientele and reputation increased, Lam Qua's style in general belongs to the same genre as Chinnery's, the English "grand manner" best represented by Sir Thomas Lawrence, Sir William Beechey, and the like. However, it is also probable that Lam Qua, also known as Guan Qiaochang, was a member of a family of professional painters with the surname Guan, one of the most famous members of which, Guan Zuolin ("Spoilum"), was also known for his like-nesses in oil and rumored to have traveled extensively in the West. [7] Crossman hypothesizes that Spoilum was Lam Qua's grandfather; in any event, a familial relationship would imply that Lam Qua learned some aspects of Western-style painting with Spoilum and others in the manner of the guild system. [8] Lam Qua was also adept at various Chinese painting styles; he was reputed to charge less for these. [9]

Lam Qua produced excellent likenesses, convincingly real and successful in projecting a complicated sense of personality and even intimacy. One contemporary of Lam Qua's exalted the painter's skill in depicting a series about the stages of opium addiction, commenting that "the opium smoker's progress would not disgrace Hogarth, either for conception or handling; this series is painfully correct in all its details." [10] Regarding Lam Qua's skill in capturing a likeness, another writer remarked dryly, "His facility in catching a likeness is unrivalled, but wo [sic] betide if you are ugly, for Lam Qua is no flatterer." [11] Though allowing that his likenesses sometimes lack "that extra dash and verve more characteristic of the Englishman [Chinnery]," apologists occasionally measure Lam Qua's success by noting how on various occasions his work has been mistaken for that of Sully or Chinnery. Crossman notes, for example, that "a fine Lam Qua portrait of a Beekman of Philadelphia was long thought to have been a Sully."[12]

It is interesting to note that where Lam Qua's artistic successes with likeness are measured in these instances by his ability to imitate or "not disgrace" a Western painter, conversely, problems of dimension, vitality, distribution of color, and placement of landscape are consistently and frequently attributed to Lam Qua's (and other commercial painters') Chineseness. For example, as one contemporary comments, "Talented though he was . . . [Lam Qua] could never entirely eliminate his Chinese mannerisms." His works, the critic continues, "almost without exception speak of western art with a strong Cantonese accent."[13] This critic's comparison between what he perceives as an ethnically marked painting style and an ethnically accented voice is more than a wooden analogy. It reveals the author's awareness of qualitative stylistic differences in the works of other Chinese commercial painters (e.g., in use of perspective or shading) and reflects an intense concern of the time for establishing fundamental differences between Chinese and Western art, perhaps what one could call the "Chinese characteristics" of commercial artwork. Thus one might glean from such declarations a sense of urgency about distinguishing "authentic" Western oil paintings from well-realized Chinese reproductions, an urgency that perhaps stemmed from the larger epistemological issue of determining who gets to discriminate the "real" from the "counterfeit" in the debate about Chinese painters working in the Western styles. Because authenticity was defined, in this case, by its origins in the West, it must have been awkward indeed when a Sully was finally revealed to be none other than a "fine Lam Qua," for what was at stake was not only the authenticity of the painting itself, but the authenticity of the culture that the painting had managed to infiltrate.

The Medical Series

Lam Qua's skill at capturing likenesses was put to good use in the well more than one hundred paintings in different collections that make up the medical illustration series. In spite of their often uncomfortably detailed depictions of people with dramatically unusual pathological conditions, these paintings nonetheless represent one of the most significant collections of Lam Qua's work in existence.[14] At times hideous and beautiful, the portraits render gross pathologies that often enough invite reflection on one's own mortality, or in the longer view, on "an all-encompassing human vulnerability."[15] Others have had a somewhat less somber reaction to the paintings: on a yellowing scrap of paper taped to the inside of the wooden cabinet that houses the paintings at Yale, one viewer quips, "Peter Parker's priceless pictures:/goiters, fractures, strains & strictures./Peter Parker's pics prepare you/For the ills that flesh is heir to." [16] Solemn or inspired, no viewer of these paintings can be left unmoved.

The medical portraits, like Lam Qua's commercial portraiture, possess a vivid realism, individual personality, and diversified focus (between human and pathology) that distinguish them from more purely representational medical illustration; they are, in addition to representations of pathological phenomena, portraits of individual people. Layout and color emphasize this individuality. "The canvasses," one writer observes, "with their sparing use of white and their Rembrandtesque emphasis on flesh colors, tan backgrounds, and dark brown garments, are clever in conveying facial individuality." [17] They also contain the dashes of red around the mouth and face, as well as compositional qualities, which Crossman identifies as Chinnery's influence; those that also have landscapes use the bright, bold palette found in Lam Qua's commercial landscape paintings.[18] Meanwhile, within the paintings themselves, Lam Qua observes certain standard rules of triangularity that help to create a relationship between human subject and pathology, juxtaposing a bulbous red chin tumor, for example, with the cherrylike knot in a man's cap (figure 1), or creating a resonance between a woman's dangling goiter and the slope of her similarly dangling earrings (figure 2).

Like the commercial portraits, the majority of medical portraits are full or half-length where the illness allows, and are laid out according to basic symmetrical principles, with the subjects occupying the lower central portion of the frame and allowed plenty of surrounding background space within the frame. Males tend to face the viewer directly, whereas females are shown in profile or quarter-profile. Subjects stand, sit, or recline; pose against simple backdrops, including props such as a chair or a pillow; or share the frame with detailed, colorful landscapes. With one important exception that portrays a mother and child, the patients are all represented in isolation. The subjects are clothed or semiclothed so that instead of juxtaposing tumors or growths with their healthy counterparts in the paintings—a cancerous breast with the healthy one, for example—clothing is economically displaced to reveal, as a rule, only the afflicted area.

The medical portraits differ from Lam Qua's commercial portraiture in several crucial ways. First, the medical series, unlike typical commercial portraiture, was not painted for commercial profit. Rather, much has been made of how the medical portraits were a sort of donation to the cause of Peter Parker, and they may have been donated by Lam Qua in part due to a personal interest

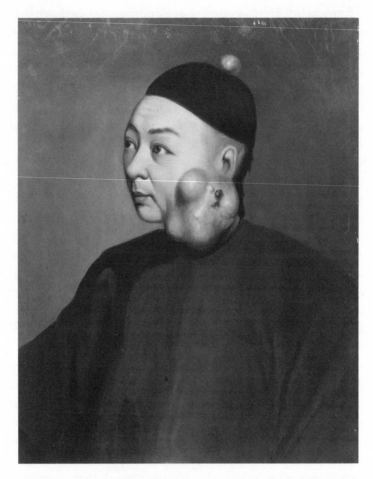

Figure 1. *Man with Facial Tumor*, by Lam Qua. Oil on canvas, 24 × 18 in., ca. 1830s. Courtesy of Yale University Medical Historical Library.

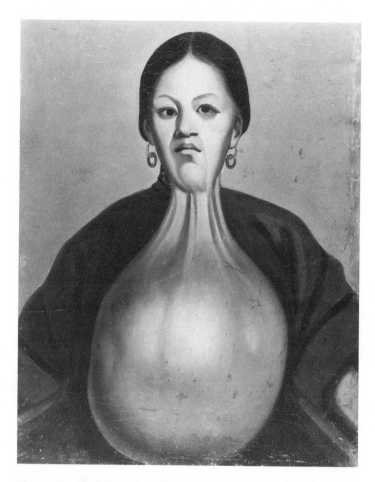

Figure 2. *Yang She*, by Lam Qua. Oil on canvas, 24 × 18 in., ca. 1830s. Courtesy of Yale University Medical Historical Library.

in medicine. Parker himself remarked on Lam Qua's intense interest in medicine: "[Lam Qua] is a great lover of the medical profession, and regrets that he is too old to become a doctor himself." [19] The series was probably also a sort of thank you for Parker's training of Lam Qua's nephew Kwan (Guan) A-to in Western medical techniques.[20]

Second, the subjects of Lam Qua's medical portraiture, unlike those of the commercial paintings, were of diverse class and gender backgrounds. Where Lam Qua's usual subjects included Western merchants, missionaries, and dignitaries, as well as local *hong* merchants and other Chinese subjects, such as the "private secretary to the governor of Canton," thanks to Parker's journal we know that many of the uniformly Chinese subjects for this unusual series of paintings came from diverse classes and social positions. Parker mentions, among others, the "son of a respectable tea broker in Canton"; "an artificial flower maker"; "Wang ke, aged 12 years . . . a slave . . . sold by her mother"; "a stone cutter"; "a gardener . . . accused as a smuggler"; "a shoemaker of Pwanyu"; and "a laborer of Tungkwan." Of particular note is that so many of Parker's patients, and therefore Lam Qua's subjects, were women — who otherwise rarely appear in his paintings. Unlike Lam Qua's commercial portraiture, then, these are not paintings of only wealthy Western males or powerful Chinese merchants. Rather, they are paintings of a mostly poor and otherwise almost completely unrepresented class of people whose only point of commonality, across the spectrum, is the fact of their afflictions.

Third, the medical portraits would have presented certain basic pragmatic challenges to Lam Qua that would not have confronted him (or his staff) when making what the sign outside his studio advertised as "handsome-face" commercial portraits. For one, the peculiar shapes, needs, and circumstances of the "sitters" for these paintings — not to mention the dual subjects of pathology and human host — meant that conventional modes of commercial portraiture, contrived to offer the subject the most "handsome" face possible in the quickest, most economical way and according to preset compositional conventions, could not, or would no longer, apply. Lam Qua would have to invent other ways of dealing with presentation that took into consideration, for example, how long or in what positions a subject might "sit" for a likeness. Entries from Parker's hospital journal confirm that patients had individual challenges that would have kept them from "sitting" for a portrait in the conventional way. He writes, for example, of Wang Ke-king, that *"when the man sits down, the tumor forms a circular cushion which elevates him six inches or more in his chair"* (figure 3). Of Yang She's goiter (figure 2), Parker notes that "It extended below the umbilicus, but not so far as to rest in the lap; consequently its weight was

Figure 3. *Wang Ke-king*, by Lam Qua. Oil on canvas, 24 × 18 in., probably ca. 1837–38. Courtesy of Yale University Medical Historical Library.

sustained by the attachement, and *the patient had to sit constantly in a bracing posture, to prevent its drawing down her head.*" [21] Thus, where a "normal" client could sit for several hours at a time in Lam Qua's studio, having his or her facial features added to a prepainted body, these sitters would have required innovative, deliberate arrangements of lighting, position, clothing, and overall composition.

However, perhaps the single most striking feature of the paintings as a body, given the extreme nature of their afflictions, is the unexpected lack of emotion to be found in subjects' faces. "Their faces are quite serene, with rarely a hint of pain, shame, or discomfort of any kind," Josyph writes. If the portraits communicate a sense of human-scale vulnerability, he continues, it is due to "the absence of any specific emotion by which the patient can truly be seen to own his disease." [22]

One possible explanation for this is simply that in the English grand style or contemporary styles of portraiture it was not customary to portray a subject's emotional state; on the contrary, the self or trappings of identity were projected out onto the attire and setting in which the subject was placed, so that emphasis on emotion would have fundamentally, even pathologically, altered the meaning and function of the painting. Thus, from a stylistic standpoint, the subjects' emotionlessness might be explained away by the use of the English grand style that so informed Lam Qua's other portraiture.

From a functional perspective, however, the tumor sufferers' impassive expressions might be explained by the concurrent development in the West of a genre of medical illustration that also portrayed individual patients who bore their stigmata with curious detachment. As Gilman writes, "The image of the identifiable patient as the bearer of a specific pathology arose in European medical illustration as an outgrowth of the medical philosophy of the *Ideologues*, who believed that only single cases could be validly examined and could serve as the basis of any general medical nosology." As an exemplar of this trend, Gilman singles out in particular Jean-Louis Alibert (1766–1837), who, with a monumental manual on skin diseases in the early 1800s, "began . . . a tradition of illustrating medical studies with images that were perceived as mimetic rather than schematic." [23] A notable feature of Alibert's careful illustrations was that his subjects, like Lam Qua's, also seemed to ignore the horrible affliction that was the point of the illustration to begin with. Barbara Stafford interprets these clinical studies, for example, as "*simultaneously dispassionate reproductions of fragmenting corporeal afflictions and moving images of individual Stoic heroism, transcending the tumor-burdened body.* . . . The disquieting and contradictory message of perfection overlaid with morbidity was that no one was secure" (emphasis added).[24] Thus, where the English grand manner may have contributed to the convention of modest expression in Lam Qua's medical portraiture, innovations in Western medical illustration may have provided a source for his creation of a new, Chinese Stoic.[25]

But another possible explanation for the expressionlessness of Lam Qua's subjects that bears investigating is simply that he strove to portray the vision of the Chinese patient that Parker wanted to communicate to his Western audience, the vision that Parker himself had of what it meant to be Chinese and to suffer from what seemed inconceivably horrible pathologies. For Parker, insensibility to pain was a crucial part of the romance (his own and that of the Chinese) of Chinese heroism against which his own tenuous position as Western medical missionary in China was defined. In instance after instance, Parker's journals reveal his fixation with—and awe of—what he perceived as a peculiarly Chinese ability to cope with extreme pain (anaesthesia had not yet been invented). For example, Parker writes of Woo She, who suffered from "scirrous breast":

> *Her fortitude exceeded all that I have yet witnessed. She scarcely uttered a groan during the extirpation,* and before she was removed from the table, clasped her hands, and, *with an unaffected smile,* cordially thanked the gentleman who assisted on the occasion. . . . *The natural amiableness and cheerfulness of this woman . . .* attracted the attention of many who visited the hospital during her stay. Surely, *natural sweetness of the temper exists in China* [emphasis added].[26]

Or in the journal entry regarding the case of Mo She, a woman suffering from the same condition as her friend Woo She, Parker explicitly links resistance to pain with acceptance of foreign medicine:

> This is the first instance of the extirpation of the female breast from a Chinese, and few operations could exhibit in a stronger light their *confidence in foreign surgery,* yet it was submitted to with the *utmost cheerfulness.*[27]

Or:

> No. 2214. Nov. 21st. Sarcomatous tumor. Lo Wanshun, aged 41. This interesting [woman], of the first society of her native village, had been affected with a large tumor upon the left side of her face. . . . *The patient endured the operation with fortitude, characteristic of the Chinese.* The loss of blood was considerable; she vomited but did not faint [emphasis added].

In Parker's journal mythology, over and over again, insensibility to pain, along with a tendency toward conspicuous demonstrations of gratitude and a willingness to tell friends about the new "foreign surgery," is portrayed as one of the more striking and peculiar aspects of Chinese identity, something constituting the elusive Chinese "temper" in Parker's world.[28] In making his argument for further funding of the medical mission, this receptive temperament is what Parker uses as evidence that the medical mission could succeed in converting the Chinese to Christianity, just as a "natural" insensibility to pain corresponds to an increasing "confidence in foreign surgery" among the Chinese heathen. Because Lam Qua's job was to illustrate this argument for Parker—to illuminate Parker's journal—it is not impossible to imagine that the surprising lack of emotion we see juxtaposed against the frightening presence of the tumors may to some extent represent the artist's efforts to portray the Chinese temper as Parker saw it.

Finally, what is especially extraordinary about this set of paintings as a whole is that, unlike the few nonmedical portraits by Lam Qua that earned him the distinction of being the "first Chinese working in the western manner" to exhibit in the West, this series achieved an impressive audience of Western medical, religious, and political authorities. Josyph summarizes as follows:

> During his trip to the United States and Europe in 1840–41 to raise funds for his medical mission, Parker displayed the portraits widely, allowing his most dramatic surgical cases to make their own eloquent plea. . . . Parker carried the banner for the American Board of Foreign Missions with zeal and was besieged with invitations not only to lecture and preach but also to meet with leaders in the political and business communities. Before returning to Canton in 1842, Parker had traveled to several cities throughout the United States, Great Britain, and France. He had also appeared before both houses of Congress and been introduced to the most eminent men of science, as well as such powerful figures as John Quincy Adams, Henry Clay, Daniel Webster, Presidents Harrison and Van Buren, the Archbishop of Canterbury, and the King and Queen of France. . . . Wherever Parker displayed them, the Lam Qua portraits brought attention to medical missions and the ability of simple surgical procedures to relieve human suffering.[29]

Several pieces reportedly even reached China, gazing for a time in strange benediction upon the visitors to the lobby of the hospital at Canton.[30]

In the heyday of the freak show and the grotesque and at the start of the Opium War, when China had moved from being a popular object of fantasy and affection to being the insidious enemy of the Western psyche, it is significant that Lam Qua's medical paintings reached such a diverse audience of influential people as part of Parker's missionary endeavor.[31] Unlike commercial portraiture of the China trade, which seems to have been accepted in Western curatorial settings only as a sort of exception to the rule, Lam Qua's medical portraiture achieved an unprecedented (if unconventional) success, marking him in this period as the native scribe to the diseased Chinese body as Parker and his cohort had begun to narrate it. Yet even more than a scribe, in the age before photography Lam Qua was also a kind of visual interpreter, bringing to bear within his medium all the troublesome and complicated questions of license and control that such a role entails.

Chinese Culture as Pathogen

Given the fact that these paintings are realistic likenesses of Chinese subjects in a clinical setting, it is tempting to assume that the Chinese identity written within is knowable as a finite, if fictional, entity after the fashion of post-Darwinian understandings of race. What constitutes "Chineseness" in the paintings may be read as self-evident, visible in the skin color or shape of eyes or color of hair of the patients that posed for Lam Qua. Meanwhile, the significance of more ineffable characteristics of cultural identity or habits (perceived and otherwise), such as resistance to pain or cultural habits or customs that lend themselves less readily to graphic representation, may be overlooked or subsumed under the rubric of a more modern understanding of the term "race." In Gilman's cursory reading of the paintings, for instance, the maturity of the notion of Chinese racial identity as a category within the paintings is simply assumed, to such a degree that Chineseness becomes almost secondary, a sign that enables the viewer to feel superior to the subjects rather than a questionable category in itself. Meanwhile, the unique individuality of each patient is significant only inasmuch as it lends to the scientific authority of the images. Gilman writes:

> In Lam Qua's paintings the patient becomes an extension of the pathology much as the English country gentlemen in Lawrence's paintings become representative of a class or an attitude toward life. In Lam Qua's paintings the patient "vanishes" since the patient becomes the perceived object shared between the physician-missionary, Peter Parker, who is lecturing about them, and his Western audience. The audience, whether of physicians or of Christian missionaries, has its belief system concerning the nature of the Chinese reified in the establishment of its sense of superiority to the patient. The patient bears a double stigma—first, the sign of pathology, and second, the sign of barbarism, his or her Chinese identity. Each patient must still appear

to be unique in order for the scientific value of the illustration to dominate. There is no attempt to present a schematisized image of the pathology independent of the image of the patient.

Although Gilman sees the patient's Chinese identity as half of a "double stigma" that directly contributes to reifying the Western audience's "belief system concerning the nature of the Chinese" when presented "scientifically," the specifics of what constitute this "Chinese nature" in this time period are not elaborated. For example, Gilman does not pursue the relationship of the pathology to the patient from which it is not "independent" beyond stating that one is an "extension" of the other. Instead, he focuses on pointing out the portraits' role in providing "the Western audience . . . with this sense of their own superiority to this Chinese inferiority." [32] His conclusion that the portraits "illustrate what happens when systems of representation meet and one is dominant over the other that is perceived by all involved to be weaker" ignores more profound questions of identity, function, and structure in favor of a different agenda of analyzing power dynamics.

But what constitutes Chinese identity in Lam Qua's paintings is much more complex and is probably based more substantially on the nineteenth-century theory of national character that Lydia Liu discusses in her book *Translingual Practice* than on the racially defined other that would seem to be at the heart of Gilman's reading. It is significant that only slightly after Parker wrote in his journals about "the natural sweetness of the Chinese temper" or about his patients' "fortitude" in the face of extreme pain, a whole genre of missionary travel-writing on the topic of so-called Chinese characteristics was born. Of Arthur Smith's work *Chinese Characteristics*, Liu writes, for example:

> Smith's book belongs to a special genre of missionary and imperialist writings that made a huge difference in modern Western perceptions of China and the Chinese, as well as the self-perception of the Chinese and the Westerners themselves. Some of the earliest efforts to theorize about Chinese character were written by American missionary S. W. Williams, who published *The Middle Kingdom* in 1848; British missionary Henry Charles Sirr, whose *China and the Chinese* came out in 1849; French missionary Evariste-Regis Huc, who brought out *The Chinese Empire* in 1854; and Thomas Taylor Meadows, who wrote *The Chinese and Their Rebellions* in 1856. [33]

Thus, though I agree that the paintings stigmatize Chinese identity through visual association with the gross pathologies, I would argue that what constitutes this Chinese identity here most likely owes less to race as a physically defined category than to the notions of so-called Chinese characteristics or even national character that pervaded Western portrayals of Chinese (and other groups) in this period. Representation of Chinese identity in these paintings casts a net wide enough to include those concepts that we might, retroactively, call culture: not race exactly, but a sort of composite protoracialized Chinese identity, made up of various social practices *as well as* stereotypes of certain physical characteristics. Historicized, protoracial Chinese identity in Lam Qua's paintings can be seen not only as something stigmatized through its association with gross pathology, as Gilman points out, but even more important, as something constructed to be the *cause and source* itself of the spectacular illnesses.

For Parker, a portrayal such as this would have been essential to his objective of attracting more funding and other support for his medical mission in Canton. His Protestant backers made it clear that their support was contingent on Parker's ability to prove that his practice as a missionary always took priority over his practice as a doctor; they were probably aware that missionary doctors often felt divided between their two professions.[34] The American Board of Foreign Missions wrote to Parker quite unambiguously: "The medical and surgical knowledge you have acquired, you will employ, as you have the opportunity, in relieving the bodily afflictions of the people. You will also be ready as you can, to aid in giving them our arts and sciences. But these, you will never forget, are to receive your attention only as they can be made *handmaids to the gospel. The character of a physician, or of a man of science, respectable as they are, or useful as they may be in evangelizing China, you will never suffer to supersede or interfere with your character as a teacher of religions*" (emphasis added).[35] This notion of "handmaids to the gospel" encapsulates what must have been a pivotal dilemma for Parker: on one hand, the challenge of attracting wary Chinese patients with the promise of radical cures and simple medical procedures (such as tumor removal and cataract surgeries), and on the other, the difficulty of simultaneously convincing the Board that its religious objectives, and not Parker's dramatic medical cures, remained a priority.

One way to interpret Lam Qua's paintings is to suggest that they respond to this dual challenge by presenting images in which the delicate portrayal of individual personality juxtaposed with gross physical abnormality produces an idea of Chinese identity as something inherently ill, something vulnerable to grotesque afflictions and in need of the simultaneous spiritual and physical cures that only Western spirituality, and its handmaid medicine, might provide. By linking pathology with personal identity, the images thus suggest that the cause of the strange growths lay within Chinese identity itself, and that as such,

Chinese identity, even more than the tumor or strange pathological manifestation, must be the true target of the missionary's radical surgery. Within such a framework, the shocking proportions of the pathologies not only represented a surgical or physical dilemma, but also came to stand for the enormity of the "cultural problem" that confronted the missionaries as they tried to proselytize in China.

Landscapes

Lam Qua's landscapes in particular provide a vivid example of how the paintings implicated this increasingly racialized Chinese identity as something inherently ill that could only be cured by the missionary. In these paintings, illness and health are encrypted within the natural environment, so that the invisible hand of the Western missionary doctor heals concentrically, removing the outward manifestation of pathology on the body, and in turn restoring the more global ecology of the natural world and, we may presume, the world's spirituality. By using compositional dynamics and structure to construct implicit metaphorical relationships among the pathology, the human body, and the natural environment, the paintings set up pathology as part of a larger holistic system that in many ways contains its own narrative.

One example of this type of painting is that of Akae, a thirteen-year-old girl (figure 4). In this painting we see a triple subject or triple focus: the girl, her facial tumor, and the complex (almost narrative) landscape against which she is painted. Akae stands slightly left of vertical center, holding what appears to be an empty sack in front of her. Her clothes are simple; she is barefoot; a pair of earrings mark her as female. The foreground of the painting is mostly bare, in contrast to the large triangular outcropping of rock that diagonally bisects the space behind her. Further up, in the upper left corner, a tree extends out from behind the outcropping and geometrically frames the head of the girl. From beyond the foot of the rock a harbor scene unfolds; a male figure walks past a boat as clouds billow up on the horizon. The tumor on Akae's face—the focus of the viewer's attention as guided by the architectural lines of the rock, the tree, and the horizon—seems almost incidental to the composition as a whole. Parker's journal entry reads:

> No. 446 Dec 27th [1836] . . . Akae, a little girl aged 13. As I was closing the business of the day, I observed a Chinese advance timidly to the hospital leading his little daughter, who at first sight appeared to have two heads. A sarcomatous tumor projecting from her right temple, and extending down

Figure 4. *Akae*, by Lam Qua. Oil on canvas, 24 × 18 in., probably ca. 1836. Courtesy of Yale University Medical Historical Library.

to the cheek as low as her mouth, sadly disfigured her face. It over hung the right eye and so depressed the lid as to exclude the light. . . . The child complained of vertigo, and habitually inclined her head to the left side. . . . From the first it appeared possible to remove it.

In typical Parker fashion, he goes on to describe the patient's stoic resistance to pain and her subsequent complete recovery:

On the 19th January, with the signal blessing of God, the operation was performed. The serenity of the sky after several days of continued rain, the presence and assistance of several surgical gentlemen, and the fortitude of a heroine with which the child endured the operation, call for my most heart-felt gratitude to the giver of all mercies. . . . The patient cheerfully submitted to be blindfolded & to have her hands and feet confined. The tumor was extirpated in eight minutes. . . . In fourteen days the whole except the fourth of an inch was entirely healed.

He goes on to thank Lam Qua in one of the only direct references to the painter:

I am indebted to Lam Qua, who has taken an admirable likeness of the little girl & a good representation of the tumor. The more interesting cases that have been presented at the hospital, he has painted with equal success, and uniformly says that as there is no charge for "cutting," he can make none for painting.

With the exception of the subject's being a lower-class female and that she "at first sight appeared to have two heads," the painting looks typical of many portraits or landscapes by Lam Qua and other commercial artists of this period. Even the palette, as Crossman notes, is the same used in Lam Qua's commercial landscapes.

Yet a closer look reveals it to be a more holistic environment, a painting of a whole interactive system rather than a set of accidental or conventional components. The outcropping of rock, for example, does not exist in a void but rather corresponds to, or echoes, the outcropping of flesh on the girl's face. Meanwhile, the primary elements of the landscape taken as a whole, as if corresponding to Parker's notation that the patient "habitually inclined her head to the left side," concentrate like the tumor on one side of the composition. The rock slopes upward at about a forty-five-degree angle; the tree hangs in a kind of aesthetic sympathy from above; the cumulous clouds billow atop one another with patches of light that suggest the fullness of the tumor. The tree, rock, clouds, and tumor all work together to emphasize fullness, roundness, hanging, solidity, extrusions. The girl's body becomes a microcosm of this natural grouping, the host of an implied landscape, the upright figure in a picture full of motion (up the grade of the rock, out over the figure on the limb of the tree, and billowing upward and away with the clouds).

In many ways this picture, more than a Taoist bodyscape or even the work of Vesalius or Alibert, brings to mind the masterful painting by Ren Bonian (1820–1857) known as Nu Wa. In this work, Ren ingeniously juxtaposes the divine form of Nu Wa with another, natural form: the rock with which she will (presumably) heal the world. Within the environment of the painting, Ren creates a careful complementarity of fields of black and white, of use of space, and even, argu-ably, of distribution of masculinity and femininity. This complementarity lends to the portrayal of a deeply dependent connection between the two forms; one is not meaningful without the other. Although Ren's painting works differently from Lam Qua's, the two pieces share an inventive internal dynamism whereby human and environmental phenomena implicate each other in the creation of the natural world of the painting. In short, in Lam Qua's painting, the self is conceived as resonant with nature, so that traces of pathology in the human body may also be found in the natural world. The whole landscape, the painting seems to suggest, and not just the little girl, will respond favorably to Parker's treatment.

The deliberateness of this type of landscape in Lam Qua's medical portrai-ture may be seen most clearly in the unique "before and after" paintings of the patient known as Po Ashing (figure 5). As in the painting of Akae, natural landscape in these paintings functions as a sort of sympathetic projection of the human landscape of Po himself; the state of the landscape also gives us some clue as to Po's internal (and by association, spiritual) state. As these are the only examples of medical portraits in the series that employ "before and after," they reflect usefully on the rest of the series (all "befores"), giving us some sense of how they were intended to function.

A painting of someone whom Parker refers to as "the first Chinese, so far as I know, who has ever voluntarily submitted to the amputation of a limb," the "before" picture shows Po seated on a chair against a dark backlit interior. His figure takes up most of the frame. His "good" arm rests on one knee, while the other arm is balanced over the other knee. He wears no shirt, only a hat and three-quarter-length trousers. He looks at the viewer confrontationally. Meanwhile, the "after" picture shows Po in profile, his direct gaze replaced by a full-on view of the site of the amputation. This time his torso is draped with a jacket open to one side, his queue is partially visible beyond the empty arm socket, and under the same hat he wears a mild, unconcerned expression. He

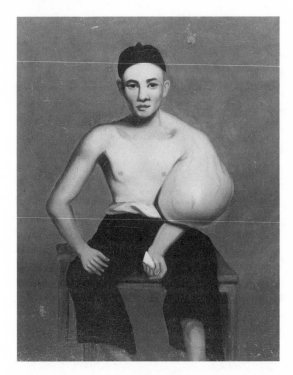

Figure 5. *Po Ashing (Before and After Surgery)*, by Lam Qua. Both paintings oil on canvas, 24 × 18 in., probably ca. 1836–37. Courtesy of Yale University Medical Historical Library.

shares the frame with a bright, uncluttered landscape background that juxtaposes a gently sloping hill and calm body of water in the left lower corner with a clump of bushes and a few scattered rocks in the lower right.

Compared to the painting of Akae, the "after" landscape of Po Ashing is much more open. The overpopulation of Akae's portrait, with its large rock outcropping and harbor scene, in Po's portrait becomes an expanse of open sky with a light blending of clouds, possibly how an "after" painting of Akae might have looked. Meanwhile, within the painting itself, the contrast of uncluttered light space (the sky and sea) with dark, defined solids (Po, the shrubbery) invoke Po's own astonishing calm in the face of the loss of an arm: the calmness of his expression seems to be mirrored in the serenity of the sea and sky that surround him. Further, as we also have the "before" painting for comparison, we know that not only the sea and sky but the entire natural environment has shifted to reflect Po's newfound freedom, his liberation from sickness. In the transformation of the claustrophobic darkness and confrontational attitude of the "before" picture into the lightness and calm of the "after" landscape we see the progression from sickness to a globalizable health.

Landscape in both the portrait of Akae and the "after" portrait of Po Ashing thus mirror the physical condition of the human subject and function metaphorically to enhance the sense of a narrative-like progression from a dark, encumbered self and environment to a spacious, light, calm one. The variously clear or turbulent sky that appears in other landscape portraits may thus be read either as a sign of what awaits the patient who submits himself or herself to Parker for treatment (the "after" to look forward to), or the externalized projection of the sickness in need of cure. In perhaps the most moving portrait of all, for example, a man's back faces us, its long perfection marred by a gargantuan open spinal tumor near the base (figure 6). Instead of looking at the man's face, which is turned away from us, we join the subject in gazing from within a darkened room out through the window, where a hint of blue sky is visible beyond a wall of clouds: the man's future if he is treated by Parker. In another painting, an upper-class married woman, whose hands are crossed on her lap in sympathy with her bound feet, looks calmly at the viewer from within another dark room (figure 7). On the right side of the painting, directly across from the growth that disfigures her face, blue skies beyond the clouds promise redemption and a reunion with the natural environment.

To generalize, against the backdrop of a culture that proscribed both amputation and autopsy, these landscapes suggest a novel conception of Chinese identity whereby even an amputee ("The first Chinese ever to submit voluntarily") may move from isolation and separation to harmony with nature, a

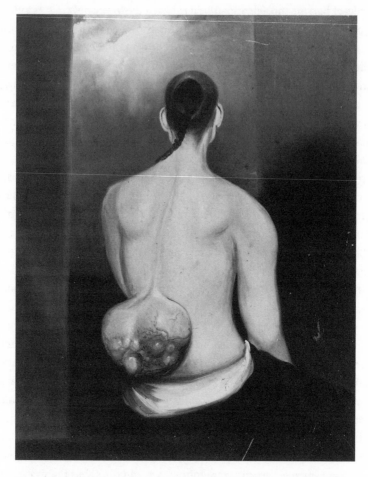

Figure 6. *Man with Spinal Tumor*, by Lam Qua. Oil on canvas, 24 × 18 in., ca. 1830s. Courtesy of Yale University Medical Historical Library.

Figure 7. *Woman with Facial Tumor*, by Lam Qua. Oil on canvas, 24 × 18 in., ca. 1830s. Courtesy of Yale University Medical Historical Library.

normal life. As Parker writes of Po Ashing, for example, "This patient perfectly recovered. In about one year after, he married, and by selling fruit, with one hand, he is able to obtain a livelihood." By opposing the tumor sufferer with the graphic sign of his or her cure, the paintings make explicit what is implicit in paintings where no landscape is portrayed: the possibility of a cure, the optimism of life without the terrible burden of these strange illnesses. Through these paintings we get a special glimpse into an ironic reconception of Chinese identity for this period: surgery as a means of becoming whole.

Counterexamples: Good Chinese vs. Bad Chinese

As I mentioned at the beginning of this essay, one aspect of these paintings that makes them unique among portraits and medical illustrations alike is the abundant text—Parker's journal—that accompanies them. A rich source of information about the subjects as well as Parker's attitude toward them, the journals represent the substance of what Parker most likely said when he presented the paintings along with his discussions and descriptions of his practice in Canton. For that reason, they are our best source for conjecture concerning how various paintings functioned or were intended to function, and to some extent may be usefully considered a part of the paintings themselves.

In the landscape paintings, we see how a "cure" becomes global and utopian: not just the individual patient's body, the compositions seem to say, but the whole environment (natural as a metaphor for spiritual) may be cured by Parker's hand. Similarly, it is also possible to see how some paintings construct Chinese identity ("culture") as an inherent obstacle to this cure in a way that betrays missionary frustration with Chinese resistance to evangelism. In the journals, for example, Chinese reluctance to accept Christianity is expressed in other language as resistance to the surgical knife; again and again, Parker relates stories of frustrated attempts to ply his trade on obstinate Chinese patients whom he believes are more handicapped by cultural prohibitions against Western surgical procedures than by the tumors, goiters, and fractures that afflict them. In Parker's time, this failure to accept Western medical treatment was literally a failure to open oneself up to the Christian god, for medicine was intended to be the vehicle of the Word. But even later, once the influence of missionary organizations in establishing hospitals waned, the attitude that Chinese were *culturally incapable* of acting in their own best interest persisted.[36]

Evidence of this nascent stereotype of a generic cultural obstinacy around surgeries can also be found in some of the Lam Qua portraits. For instance in the portrait we have seen of Wang Ke-king, "the son of a respectable tea broker resident in Canton," the figure stands along the vertical axis with his back to the viewer and his head turned slightly so that we can make out his profile and his almost cheerfully oblivious expression (figure 3). He wears a long white gown, coarsely detailed, which he lifts with his left hand to expose for the viewer an enormous pendulous growth that appears to be even larger and wider than the host torso itself (Parker records, "The weight is variously estimated from 60 to 100 pounds"). From beneath this growth project Wang's legs; his trousers lie in a heap around his ankles. Hanging the length of his body and tapering off toward the bottom edge of the frame is Wang's queue. The two white circular patches on the growth would no doubt have been explained by Parker to the viewing audience as examples of a form of Chinese medical treatment, about which Dr. William Henry Cumming remarked, "Chinese plaisters applied to two craters that have opened upon this mountain [are] as effectual probably in preventing Eruptions as would be a wire gauze hood over the top of Vesuvius to check a discharge of his artillery." [37] The background, a simple interior, is of the same luminous brown as the "before" picture of Po Ashing.

From Parker's journals we know that, unlike the majority of the paintings depicted in the medical series by Lam Qua, there is no implicit "after" in this painting — no utopia, no universal healing. This patient not only did not survive and go on to live a "normal" life, he never even accepted treatment from which he might have had a chance to "perfectly recover." Parker writes:

> Previous to the [bioptic] incision, the main objection to an operation . . . was the unwillingness of his wives; the removal now seems more formidable to the patient himself. Whether it shall be attempted or not depends upon his relations to determine . . . [the young man] is of a nervous temperament, all his motions quick, and very sensitive to the slightest touch.

Later, Parker makes a lengthy entry (worth reproducing in its entirety):

> On the 26th of March 1838 Wang Ke King was seized by a violent fever which terminated fatally in three days. I was not aware of his illness till his death was reported. Immediately repairing to his late residence, I was shown the way into his room, where his two youthful widows and a little daughter, clad in sack cloth, were upon their knees upon the floor by the side of the corpse, with incense and wax candles burning before them. After retiring from the room, it was explained to the father and brothers how desirable it was that the tumor should be examined, the service it might be to the living, and the inconvenience of putting the body & tumor into one coffin; they affected

assent, but must first consult the widows and mother. The father soon returned, saying it would be agreeable to him to have the examination, but the mother and wives of the deceased would not assent. "They feared the blood and that the operation might occasion pain to the deceased." After returning home, the kindness of a friend enabled me to offer a present of $50 to the family, provided they would permit the autopsy. A linguist was sent to negotiate with them, but in vain. Probably $500 would not have overcome their superstition.

Unlike Po Ashing or Akae, whose cases are distinguished in Parker's writing by their voluntary nature and their uncomplaining and even cheerful submission to the surgical knife, Wang Ke-king, by contrast, is portrayed as a somewhat helpless pawn, "nervous" and "sensitive," caught in the middle of an elaborate net of Chinese customs and superstitions that prevent him from receiving treatment. These customs and superstitions interfere at every juncture where there might be "desirable" application of Western science. Where Po agreed to be "the first Chinese to willingly submit" to an amputation, for example, at first it is Wang's wives' objection to surgery that prevents his going beyond the biopsy. After his death, proscriptions concerning autopsy, which was not legalized until 1913, filtered through the nexus of familial superstition concerning the afterlife and the proper treatment of the dead, further keep Wang's body from being usefully examined. As the microcosm of culture, it is ultimately the family, in particular the women, who are blamed for obstructing the advancement of Western "service . . . to the living": even a bribe of $50 is not sufficient to "overcome their superstition" (more likely than not, it was sufficient only to insult). Ultimately the combination of journal and painting present Wang to be as much the victim of his upper-class family's backward cultural practice as of the tumor itself.

Thus, in Lam Qua's portrait of Wang, the long, fine queue running the length of his body serves as the literal yardstick against which we measure not only the astounding dimensions of the tumor, but (we are meant to read) the extraordinary backwardness of the culture that would not allow Parker to operate on it.[38] As a most obvious outward marker of Chinese difference, the queue, which actually was commonly used as a sort of measuring tape in everyday life, forms a blunt visual equation with the huge tumor. In other words, it is clear this is a picture of an unnaturally large pathology that needs to be excised; but the question is, which one? Along with the plasters, which underscore by their diminutive size the inadequacy of traditional Chinese medicine to address the problem of the tumor, as well as even the white robe that quite possibly invokes the specter of death (it is the only portrait in the entire series that uses this color of clothing), the queue seems to symbolize the need for Chinese practical reform, the reform of the obstinate resistance to Western technology and spirituality that is the true object of Parker's ministrations.

A final example of Lam Qua's medical portraiture further illustrates how the portraits, read in conjunction with Parker's journals, pathologize Chinese identity. In the only picture to contain two human subjects, a painting that easily recalls the Madonna and Child, an upper-class woman is portrayed holding her young daughter on her lap (figure 8). In this portrait the child is in the center of the frame. Looking more like an adult in miniature, she sits somberly on her mother's lap, her left arm disproportionately foreshortened. Her well-dressed mother sits in a similar angle to the child, holding her somewhat stiffly, her arms posed geometrically around the child's body. The child's gangrenous feet, like Akae's facial tumor, seem to be almost an afterthought as they dangle in the lower left quadrant, echoing the drop of the mother's earrings. The motion of the painting flows in a crescent, beginning with the mother's hairpin, curving inward along the angle of her body, and ending finally at the child's feet.

Like the portrait of Wang Ke-king, this painting also depicts a subject whose illness, we read, could have been cured or at least treated more effectively with the early intervention of Western medicine. We know from Parker's journal entry, for example, that the family members concerned in the process of bringing in the patient for treatment, like Wang's family, showed some reluctance about accepting the principle of Parker's advice:

> Loss of both feet at the ankle, from compression. — March 8, 1847. Lu Akwang, an interesting little girl of Honan, 7 years of age. February 9, agreeably to a custom that has prevailed in China for thousands of years, the bandages were applied "a la mode" to her feet, occasioned her excessive sufferings, which *after the lapse of a fortnight* became insupportable, and *the parents were reluctantly compelled to remove the bandages,* when as the father represented, the toes were found discolored. Gangrene had commenced, and *when she was brought to the hospital,* March 8, it had extended to the whole foot. The line of demarcation formed at the ankles, and both feet were perfectly black, shriveled and dry, and nearly ready to drop off at the ankle joint. . . . The friends preferring it, *notwithstanding advice to the contrary,* they were furnished with the necessary dressings, and the child was treated at home, being brought occasionally to the hospital. The last time she was seen, the right stump had nearly healed over; the other was less advanced in the healing process [emphasis added].

Figure 8. *Child with Gangrenous Feet*, by Lam Qua. Oil on canvas, 24 × 18 in., ca. 1830s or possibly 1840s. Courtesy of Yale University Medical Historical Library.

In this passage Parker's language clearly demonstrates a critical attitude toward the patient's family; not only does he write that they were only "reluctantly compelled" to confront the problem initially, he takes special note of the time line of events concerning this particular case. The girl's "excessive sufferings," he writes, continue for "a fortnight," by which time "the toes were found discolored." However, it is another two weeks before the parents bring the girl to the hospital, by which time the gangrene "had extended to the whole foot." He then further criticizes the parents by recording how, "notwithstanding advice to the contrary," the family insists on treating the girl at home.

As in the case of Wang Ke-king, the locus of this critique lies within the family unit. Where he opens the passage discussing the larger problem of footbinding as a cultural phenomenon ("a custom that has prevailed in China for thousands of years"), by the close of the narrative the problem has become localized: this particular family's stubbornness, their "reluctance" to accept Parker's "advice" regarding proper treatment. Where cooperative parents such as Akae's father consistently earn Parker's effusive praise throughout his journals, the target of this critique of Chinese cultural practice, as in the case of Wang Ke-king, is the wealthy or upper-class Chinese family.

The portrait, therefore, like that of Wang Ke-king, is a critical one, less a portrait of the adverse effects of Chinese cultural practice at large than of the interference of a class-marked Chinese culture with Western healing paradigms. Like the queue in the picture of Wang, in this painting the additional presence of the mother acts as a sort of symbol of culture against which the gravity of the child's pathology is measured; the mother literally embodies a whole cultural equation to be read as "footbinding = Chinese = maternal = barbaric." The parents' significant role in Parker's journal in obstructing his better judgment regarding the girl's treatment is echoed in the mother's protective embrace. Thus, what fascinates about this painting is that "what understands itself to be maternal nurture is in fact represented as its opposite."[39] Further, if one accepts the compositional reference to the Madonna and Child and the sacrosanct relationship it subverts, the painting's impact becomes even more dramatic. Whereas on the one hand the painting presents a girl who must be cured of her *pathologic* condition, on the other it also portrays a mother who must be cured of her *cultural*—Chinese—condition.

In short, in Lam Qua's paintings we see both the creation and pathologization of an image of Chinese identity based on certain "Chinese characteristics": insensibility to pain, inadequacy of native medicine, practical inability to perform either amputation or autopsy, belief in the spirits of the dead, and superstition in general. Part of what was to become in the modern era the idea of the

Sick Man of Asia, a persistent romantic/imperialist stereotype about Chinese nationhood where national identity and race are always already pathological, these paintings not only fabricate a Chinese cultural identity that is fundamentally sick, they also describe a cure for it. For those "good" Chinese who accept the ministrations of the Western surgeon, the cure of a promised land, with its clear skies and reunion with nature, awaits. However, for "bad" Chinese, who either reject the doctor-missionary's treatment or who fail to escape from the web of Chinese tradition, the end is more grim. Either way, the paintings hint at a radical cure: the superimposition of a new and improved Chinese identity that can be had only through the ministrations of the medical missionary.

Parting Glances

As Walter Benjamin has pointed out, painting at the dawn of photography could still do what photography could not. It could, for example, provide motion, full color, or other manipulations of images. This may partly explain why Lam Qua's medical portraiture was so successful: painted in vivid color, full of personality, and freakishly grotesque, the paintings no doubt left a stronger impression on their nineteenth-century audience than they do even today. Although it would be difficult to quantify precisely the extent of this influence—that is something that needs to be the subject of further evaluation—nonetheless, taken as a historical artifact, Lam Qua's medical paintings allow us to make constructive hypotheses about the exchange and circulation of ideas concerning Chinese identity in a most formative era. In his portrayal of a seeming indifference to pain, for example, we may find an explanation for (or contributing factor to) the persistence of this stereotype among missionary doctors until well after the invention of anaesthesia (and arguably beyond). Whether due to British portrait-painting conventions or to Lam Qua's literal interpretation of Parker's observations, this aspect of his paintings, combined with Parker's explanations, would have left a strong impression indeed upon the minds of the influential medical men and prominent intellectuals who saw them. In other words, the question Lam Qua's paintings oblige us to ask is not *whether* these men were impressed by his depictions of sick Chinese, but *how* and *to what extent.*

Likewise, a premise of this essay has been to speculate on possible avenues by which Chinese intellectuals and literati of the modern period arrived at the notion of pathology as a convenient metaphor for Chinese national identity. What kind of visual images acted as sources for Lu Xun, for example, whose medical training in Japan no doubt contributed to the flourishing of medical imagery to be found in his short fiction and, indeed, throughout the body of his literary works? Similarly, how were ideas of pathology and Chinese identity translated by Parker and his contemporaries and then reinterpreted through the eyes of the Chinese practitioners who would soon become one of the target audiences for medical literature published by Western missionary doctors and surgeons? What was the relationship of Lam Qua's portraiture to the development of medical photography that followed, in China and elsewhere in the world? And significantly, how did the evolution of images relate to the evolution of the concept of race in the modern era?

Examples of medical photography from the early 1900s reveal that, by this time, constructions of Chinese identity in medical images had indeed evolved from the protoracial world of good and bad Chinese found in Parker's journals and Lam Qua's paintings to the post-Darwinian maturity of race as an absolute category. The black-and-white photographs that accompany the text of the early twentieth-century medical manual *Diseases of China*, for instance, bear an uncanny resemblance in composition and iconography to their oil-painted predecessors of seventy years before, yet depart in their use of certain representational conventions that are still current in medical illustration today. In these images, unlike in the Lam Qua portraits, all signs of context or individuality are systematically erased, the patient photographed naked against a blank background. Faces, clothing, landscapes, queues (generally), and all markers of individuality are replaced instead by a reductive caption that refers to the pathology but not to the human host, as in a pair of before-and-after pictures of a little boy with a misshapen clavicle bone which is marked only as "Sarcoma of Clavicle" and "Clavicle and Tumor removed." Very little is included in these images beyond the shade of skin and possibly hair or facial features of the patient. As the editors of the volume remark in their preface, the purpose of the book was to provide "a concise account of the special diseases . . . brought about by the hygienic habits and the racial peculiarities of the people of China." Thus, by the time of *Diseases of China*, the ultimate visual metonymy has occurred: the deformities in these photographs have come to stand for the Chinese race itself.

It is in these early-twentieth-century photographs, then, that the patient truly "vanishes" (as Gilman might put it), leaving behind only an unnerving collection of skin, hair, and instructive captions to guide us in our interpretation of their message about Chinese (and indeed all nonwhite) identity. The shift in representational meaning from Lam Qua's paintings to the photographs of *Diseases of China* stands for the shift into modernity, where modernity is characterized by new ways of looking, the application of new surfaces and boundaries,

Figure 9. *Man with Tumor of the Hand,* by Lam Qua. Oil on canvas, 24 × 18 in., ca. 1830s or possibly 1840s. Courtesy of Yale University Medical Historical Library.

and the imposition of new power dynamics. Lam Qua's paintings show Chinese identities constructed of disparate parts, the cocreation of Parker's ideological requirements and Lam Qua's artistic innovations. But the subjects of the later photographs reveal themselves to be the representationally racialized descendents of these composite identities, no longer requiring the legitimacy of the native interlocutor but rather depending on the truth-telling voice of the camera, as well as the cooperation of the new Chinese audience, for legitimacy. To what extent did this transition from cultural ("protoracial") to racial identity, from postrenaissance to scientific body, from painting to photography, mirror or conspire with the development of literary realism? What was the trajectory of this transition and how did it come about?

In one of Lam Qua's more haunting works, a man reclines along the horizontal length of the frame, leaning on a pillow (figure 9). His right hand, disturbingly deformed, contrasts in turn with the perfection of the left hand, which covers the face of the patient so that only an eyebrow and the high hairline indicative of the patient's (male) gender can be seen. No landscape complicates this picture with suggestions of a promised land. No facial expression or queue invokes the (imagined) peculiarities of Chinese culture. Yet by concealing the identity of the patient, the painting still conveys a strong message about the curability of Chinese culture. Undermining the painting's function as a work of portraiture, it becomes in one eloquent gesture a portrait not of individual identity but of hidden potential: the potential that surgery will not only reveal the latent integrity of the deformed hand (so that it will match the other), but that, by association, it will reveal the true nature of the sufferer himself. The true nature of Chinese identity, the painting seems to say, is merely waiting for the art of Parker's scalpel to describe.

Notes

I would like to thank the Pacific Cultural Foundation for a grant that led to the completion of this essay, as well as Wang Daw-hwan and the scholars of the medical history studies group at the Institute of History and Philology at Academia Sinica in Taipei, for all their assistance. I am also grateful to the two anonymous reviewers, as well as to Cheryl Barkey, Lydia Liu, Hajime Nakatani, Rachel Sturman, and Isaac Shou-chih Yan, for their patient editorial comments.

1 Peter Josyph, *From Yale to Canton*, 5.
2 Barbara Stafford, *Body Criticism*, 23.
3 Bridie J. Andrews, "Tuberculosis and the Assimilation of Germ Theory in China," 132.
4 Carl L. Crossman, *The Decorative Arts of the China Trade*, 77.
5 Ibid., 81.
6 Ibid., 96.
7 See Craig Clunas, *Chinese Export Watercolours*, for a hypothesis about the origins of the *qua* suffix used by various artists at this time.
8 See Joseph S. P. Ting's introduction to *Late Qing China Trade Paintings*: "Since it is a common practice for Chinese artists to carry on their family trade or skill for generations, it is possible that the Guan brothers [Lam Qua and his younger brother Ting Qua] and Guan Zuolin [Spoilum] might have come from the same family."
9 Sander L. Gilman includes this as evidence in his argument that Lam Qua generally considered Western styles superior; see "Lam Qua and the Development of a Westernized Medical Iconography in China."
10 Henry-Charles Sirr, *China and the Chinese*, 113.
11 Osmond Tiffany, *The Canton Chinese*, quoted in Crossman.
12 Quoted in Crossman, 72.
13 Henry Berry-Hill and Sidney Berry-Hill, *George Chinnery*, 39; and Robin Hutcheon, *Chinnery, the Man and the Legend*, 72.
14 See Crossman, 84: "These somewhat gruesome paintings of subjects with very noticeable pathological conditions [are] the most important single body of work by Lam Qua in existence." The collection comes as a shock to scholars of the China trade, Crossman adds, "because of the very nature of its most unusual subject matter."
15 Josyph, 5.

16 The poem in its entirety reads:

> Peter Parker's pickled paintings,
> Cause of nausea, chills & faintings;
> Peter Parker's putrid portraits,
> Cause of ladies' loosened corsets;
> Peter Parker's purple patients,
> Causing some to upchuck rations.
> Peter Parker's priceless pictures:
> goiters, fractures, strains & strictures.
> Peter Parker's pics prepare you
> For the ills that flesh is heir to.

17 Edward V. Gulick, *Peter Parker and the Opening of China*, 153.

18 See Crossman.

19 Cited in Gulick, 133.

20 Crossman, 87.

21 Quotes from Parker, unless otherwise noted, come from the looseleaf typewritten pages to be found among his papers housed in the Yale Medical College Library.

22 Peter Josyph, *From Yale to Canton*, 5. A more Orientalist interpretation may be found in Purcell, who reads the portraits as exotic and inscrutable. See Rosamond Wolff Purcell, *Special Cases: Natural Anomalies and Historical Monsters*.

23 Gilman, 63.

24 Stafford, 302.

25 A promising area of inquiry concerns the possible Chinese sources for Lam Qua's style. Wu Hung, in his essay on the "costume" portraits of Yongzheng and Qianlong, for instance, makes reference to " 'visage' portraits" of the emperor that employ "a pictorial style that rejects any depiction of physical environment, bodily movement or facial expression" ("Emperor's Masquerade," 27). See also Richard Vinograd's exceptional *Boundaries of the Self: Chinese Portraits 1600–1900*. Even the use of landscape in Lam Qua's portraits, which I discuss later, may be seen to share certain structural elements with Chinese portrait conventions.

26 Parker, page marked 48.

27 Ibid., 46.

28 On numerous occasions, Parker records detailed accounts of patients' expressions of thanks; for example, "[Leang A Shing] seems properly to appreciate the favor he has received, and was ready to tell others what has been done for him," and "[Woo Pun] evinces *unbounded* gratitude. He seems to regard the favor received, as conferring on him full liberty to introduce any and all his diseased friends" (ibid., 29 and 46, respectively, as marked on the typed manuscript).

29 Josyph, "The Missionary Doctor and the Chinese Painter," 56.

30 See Crossman.

31 See Colin Mackerras, *Western Images of China*, for a discussion of changing attitudes in the West toward China in this period.

32 Sander L. Gilman, *Disease and Representation*, 149.

33 Lydia H. Liu, *Translingual Practice*, 58.

34 Dr. William Lockhart's preface to "The Medical Missionary in China" is quoted in K. Chimin Wong and Lien-Teh Wu, *History of Chinese Medicine*: "If the medical missionary is ordained, either a good surgeon or a good pastor is spoiled. I have seen this in Protestant and Roman missions; a man attempts to follow two professions, and always fails signally in one, sometimes in both, and thus loses rather than gains influence and power for good" (238).

35 Cited in C. J. Bartlett, "Peter Parker," 407–11.

36 See, for example, W. Hamilton Jefferys and James L. Maxwell, *The Diseases of China*: "Combined with a *lack of ability* to remove even the simplest growth, the Chinese are as a race particularly unembarrassed by the mere presence of morbid growths which other races would find repellant indeed. To the Chinese a growth is painful or inconvenient, but seldom disfiguring" (451, my emphasis).

37 Quoted in Josyph, *From Yale to Canton*, 8.

38 Again, I use the term "culture" retroactively here.

39 I am indebted to one of the anonymous reviewers of this article for this observation.

Tze-lan Deborah Sang *Translating Homosexuality:*

The Discourse of Tongxing'ai in Republican China

(1912–1949)

Magnus Hirschfeld, the founder of the Institute for Sexual Research in Berlin, a key figure in the popularization of the theory of "the third sex" and activist for homosexual rights, visited China and gave thirty-five lectures (in German with Chinese interpretation) on sexology, including the issue of homosexuality, in the colleges and universities of major Chinese cities in 1931. Made a refugee by Hitler and his Institute for Sexual Research in Berlin destroyed by the Nazis, Dr. Hirschfeld was well-respected and heartily welcomed by his Chinese audience. The Chinese press "made almost daily announcements and reports of [his] lectures during [his] entire stay." [1]

Though perhaps unique in touring China, Hirschfeld was by no means the only European specialist on same-sex attraction to be introduced to China during the Republican decades. Among others translated or discussed were Havelock Ellis, Iwan Bloch, Richard von Krafft-Ebing, Sigmund Freud, and Edward Carpenter. Chinese terms were coined for Krafft-Ebing's and Ellis's medical theories of "homosexuality" as sexual "perversion" and "inversion," as well as for Carpenter's view of "homogenic love" as a superior sentiment. A wide spectrum of conceptions of same-sex desire and correlative value judgments existed in this translated material. The diversity suggests that multiple and competing, rather than uniform, alliances were formed between Chinese translators and Western sources. It is precisely in a moment of choice, when a Chinese translator had the freedom to cite and appropriate certain materials rather than others, that we witness the possibility of cross-cultural understanding and coalition, rather than bleak, whole-scale Western cultural imperialism and imposition in the name of universality. The Chinese translator's agency, perhaps like all forms of agency, is never uncircumscribed, but its existence and function are undeniable.

This formative Chinese discourse of homoeroticism revolved around the neologism tongxing'ai (also tongxing lian'ai and tongxing lian), literally "same-sex love." To define same-sex love, Chinese writers distinguished it primarily from "love between man and woman" (nan nü zhi lian'ai), "love between the opposite sexes" (yixing zhijian de ai), or simply, "love" (lian'ai, aiqing). Attraction between the two sexes was assumed to be the primary or default form of romantic and sexual attraction. Nevertheless, the fact that many Chinese writers took interest in novel theories of homosexuality from the West suggests that there was a convergence of local factors necessitating such discussion. Part of the necessity stemmed, actually, from the fact that love between man and woman was being defined, debated, and advocated as young people's right and desire in China. Chinese intellectuals' examination of opposite-sex love required an inspection of human affection and attachment in general, for analogy but also for distinction and contrast. The examination extended to, among other things, the friendship between man and woman and the love and friendship between persons of the same sex. In a sense, to establish love between man and woman at the center of human affection, Chinese intellectuals had to delineate its boundaries and define its peripheral or overlapping neighbors, including kinship, friendship, and "abnormal" forms of love.

Historical and social circumstances fueled Chinese intellectuals' curiosity for Western "modern science" and their own theoretical reflection on same-sex love. Due to centuries of sex segregation in the past, same-sex bonding was strong and prevalent in Republican China. In fact, close same-sex ties were so common in Chinese schools and colleges that Western discussions of homosexuality in school inevitably intrigued many Chinese intellectuals. An area of problematization and theorization may indicate discrimination, but it was probably also a privileged form of relationship. Same-sex love in the schools—between students, between student and teacher, and between teachers—was definitely for the Chinese translators as well as the editors and middle-class readership of urban publications a privileged relationship, given much more recognition and consideration than the same-sex relationships of the uneducated or those between adults above a certain age outside an educational setting.

Specific in focus and Western in origin, Republican Chinese translations about same-sex love reflect, nonetheless, major tensions in Republican Chinese society. In an important theoretical reflection on translingual practice, Lydia

Liu points out that it may be fruitful to consider translation in terms of "invention." She maintains, "Meanings . . . are not so much 'transformed' when concepts pass from the guest language to the host language as invented within the local environment of the latter." [2] If we agree with Liu, then details of Republican Chinese intellectuals' translation of homosexuality are important, for it is precisely through examining the formation and local significance of modern Chinese terms for rendering "homosexuality" from other languages that we may make major discoveries about Chinese views of sexuality. This essay is interested, then, in an emergent specialized discourse but also something more. It is an attempt to shed light on Republican Chinese politics of gender, desire, class, and subjectivity through an investigation of Chinese "same-sex love" as translingual practice.

The Significance of the Word Itself

Tongxing lian'ai, tongxing ai, tongxing lian — these terms differ slightly in flavor, but basically they are all composed of the words "same," "sex," and "love" to denote "same-sex love." Common in present-day Chinese parlance, these words have distinctively modern origins and rather short histories. Tongxing'ai (read doseiai in Japanese) was coined in Japan at the end of the Meiji and the early Taisho periods as Japanese intellectuals translated European sexology.[3] Because the process slightly predated Chinese intellectuals' interest in sexology, we have reason to believe that tongxing'ai was a direct adoption of the Japanese doseiai, based on which the Chinese then invented the variants tongxing lian'ai and tongxing lian.[4] Not only was "same-sex love" a new coinage, but its individual components were also neologisms or characters used in a fresh sense. Tong xing ("same," "sex") was a new construct, in that the character xing, prior to this century, had not meant sex but had been limited to denoting nature: the original state, truth, quality, or disposition of something. In Confucianism, xing is a specialized philosophical term, meaning "human nature." The canonical discussion of xing occurs in Mencius. In one instance, Mencius disagrees with the philosopher Gao Zi, who maintains, "Human nature consists of eating and sex." For Mencius, human nature is precisely men's moral capacities and tendencies beyond the desire for food and sex.[5] In other words, the orthodox meaning of the character xing has only a tangential if not reverse relation to sexuality. The link between gender and the traditional meaning of xing was similarly tenuous. A single character denoting gender does not exist in classical Chinese. Xing was chosen to be used as gender out of the need to translate the category gender in European languages. Like many other words, the unorthodox usage of *xing* was first started by Meiji Japanese intellectuals before it came to China.[6] By the 1920s, the modern usage of *xing* with the double meaning of gender and sexuality was well-established in Chinese (but not to the exclusion of its old usage as nature), making the character similar to the English word "sex."

Although not quite a neologism like *tongxing*, the compound *lian'ai*—"romantic love," "love affair," "falling in love," "being in love"—was a novel and exalted concept for Chinese youth after the mid-1910s through the 1920s.[7] May Fourth (1917–1927) intelligentsia advocated "free love" (*ziyou lian'ai*) between man and woman against Confucian morality and the traditional patterns of arranged first marriages (with the possibility of polygamy), which had dictated the proper segregation of respectable young women from men well before puberty, prohibiting courtship and the free congress of the sexes.[8] In May Fourth publications, there appeared endless discussions devoted to *lian'ai*: what romantic love is, in terms of its constituents, conditions and rules. How should young men and women proceed to learn to practice romantic love? Is friendship a prerequisite for love? What differentiates love from friendship? What distinguishes love from mere sexual intercourse such as is expected on the wedding night of a traditionally arranged marriage? Some said that romantic love was absolute; others maintained it was conditional and changeable. Some believed romantic love was a special modality of emotion distinguished from other kinds of affections; others declared there was no qualitative affectional difference between romantic love and fast friendship. Some put forth the formula that the ideal romantic love equaled the union of two people in both spirit and flesh; others claimed that "spiritual romantic love" was the most exquisite and highest kind, for it sublimated animal sex instinct and was sacred. In addition, there were those who doubted there was any such thing as "romantic love"; they argued that what was usually thought to be romantic love was no more than sex plus the basic feelings one human being has for another.[9]

It is of tremendous import, therefore, when this exalted, magical, discursive construct *lian'ai* was combined with the words "same-sex" to form the concept "romantic love between/among people of the same sex." The early Republican Chinese intellectuals did not translate "homosexuality" as "same-sex sexual desire" or "same-sex sexual intercourse," but as "same-sex *love*."[10] The neologism's difference from traditional Chinese categories of homosexuality is apparent, for the latter focused exclusively on the carnal and the sensual. In traditional language, some men could be described as "liking men's beauty and sex" or "preferring men's to women's beauty and sex" (*hao nanse*), and some women could be nicknamed a "mirror-rubbing gang" (*mo jing dang*).[11] With the category same-sex love, however, the emotional intensity and sympathy between two people was highlighted. According to the discursive construction of love in the May Fourth period, an erotic component can be taken for granted but is not supposed to be the only component in love.

Whereas love between young men and women may have been a difficult process or art that had to be "learned" in the 1910s and '20s, most educated youth were instructed in single-sex schools (including colleges and universities), where deep sympathy and intimacy—not limited to spiritual intimacy—between best friends often grew. Does this mean they all had same-sex romantic loves? Was it more natural for the Chinese youth of the time to fall in same-sex love than cross-sex love?

The thorny issue surfaced when the distinction between love and friendship was challenged. In the intellectual discussion on romantic love during the 1920s, although many assumed, as a matter of course, that love is a tangible entity that occurs between man and woman, there were radical thinkers who attempted to deconstruct love defined as such. They ask whether love is any different from friendship, and whether passionate love cannot just as well take place between same-sex friends.[12] In a 1928 debate between those who questioned and negated the existence of love and their opponents in New Woman (Xin nüxing, La Nova Virineco), one of the participants, Mao Yibo, writes in objection to the category love:

> I admit that there exists sexual friendship and that the most intimate relationship/friendship between man and woman is sexual friendship, but sexual friendship is not something limited to people of the opposite sexes. Even between people of the same sex, haven't there been cases in which, because of the seamless matching of beliefs, personalities and aspirations, the most intimate and passionate involvement took place? If this is true, why should we call some sexual friendships "love" but not others? How do we tell the difference between a cross-sex friendship and a same-sex friendship? Should we simply say, like Ellis, that the distinction [between love and friendship] is blurry? If a relationship of the same weight is called "love" if occurring between the opposite sexes, and "friendship" when between people of the same sex, I think such naming is not only "unwise" but also "superfluous."[13]

Mao Yibo objects to the reification of love as a higher category than friendship; he protests against the differential treatment of homo- and heterosexual bonds in May Fourth discourse. According to him, though heteroerotic friendship is privileged and crowned with the new title "love," homoerotic friendship is not accorded the same status. He believes that to be fair to both forms of the most intimate intersubjective bonding, they should be named the same. Understandably, though Mao Yibo's proposal is that both be called sexual friendship, in the sense of friendship with some degree of sexual involvement, some people's strategy to make the same point is to use the term "homosexual love" (*tongxing lian'ai*) in addition to "love," which, when not specified, means "heterosexual love" in May Fourth discourse.

If same-sex love was so common in the 1920s, to the extent that certain intellectuals openly protested the construction of male-female free love as the ultimate love, what did it mean to introduce into China at this historical juncture European sexology—such as Havelock Ellis's work—theorizing the pathology, neurosis, or abnormality of homosexuality? Did it help to advocate free association and love between the opposite sexes? Did it threaten to shift the center of many Chinese youths' emotional lives from a same-sex axis to a cross-sex axis? Did it function to intimidate those women who were gaining the possibility of economic independence through modern education and professional jobs from becoming life-long lovers with each other? [14] Were Chinese gay males affected by an unprecedented social stigma? [15]

It appears that all of the above happened to some extent, not instantly but gradually, not on a sweeping scale but first in small circles, over the course of the first half of twentieth-century Chinese history. The medical stigma on homosexuality in Republican China was moderate, however, and one cannot foretell from its mildness that the Chinese Communist Party, after 1949, would harshly denounce homosexuality either as Western capitalist corruption or a heinous feudalist crime. The ambiguity of the Republican Chinese attitude toward homosexuality is best illustrated by the partial history of translation reconstructed below.

Same-Sex Love in Urban Middle-Class Periodicals

When the subject of homosexuality first appeared in Republican China, it was not only a phenomenon catalogued in medical manuals for sex education, but was also represented in translated articles and discussions in major urban journals on women, gender, education, love, relationships, and sex. Journal articles on same-sex love are especially interesting, for the translators for journals could choose a broader range of Western sources for their endeavor than strictly medical genres and were more likely to show their own opinion through their selection.

The material that Chinese intellectuals chose to translate covered a fascinating variety. Contemporaneous with the dissemination of the Krafft-Ebing and Ellis schools of sexology that pathologizes homosexuality, many Chinese intellectuals took an active interest in Western gay liberation discourse. Iwan Bloch's less judgmental theory of inborn homosexuality received attention, for example.[16] The translations during the 1920s of Edward Carpenter's writings, which often idealize homogenic love in the advocacy of gay liberation, are especially provocative. They indicate a certain degree of open-mindedness and freedom of expression on the issue of homosexuality in China then. Granted these translations appeared in journals promoting "new knowledge," social reform, and progress, the journals were not in any sense underground or marginal. They were, on the contrary, well-known periodicals published by the most successful and prestigious publishing houses, such as the Commercial Press and the Kaiming (Enlightenment) Bookstore in Shanghai. I hesitate, therefore, to describe the translations as a counterhegemonic discourse. It would be more accurate to say that the literate, urban Chinese public in the 1920s had no definite opinion on the nature of same-sex love, and that there was much room for the maneuvers of Chinese intellectuals who had access to theories of homosexuality written in other languages.

A few months before the revolution that was to establish the Republic of China, in June 1911, *Women's Times* (*Funü shibao*), one of the pioneer women's journals based in Shanghai, published an article entitled "Same-Sex Erotic Love between Women" (*Funü tongxing zhi aiqing*).[17] Written by Shan Zai (pen name, gender unclear)[18] well before the advocacy of vernacular by the New Culturalists, the essay is in classical Chinese.[19] Shan Zai mentions many German and British sexologists by name, and whenever he includes terminology from European sexology, the words are in German rather than English. He may have consulted some work in German, such as the German edition rather than the English of *Sexual Inversion*, the second volume of Havelock Ellis's *Studies in the Psychology of Sex*, published in Germany in 1896 as *Das konträre Geschlechtsgefühl* (Contrary sexual feelings).[20] Moreover, in the article Shan Zai shows familiarity with the prevalence of female same-sex erotic love in Japanese schools, which indicates he probably either lived in Japan or read Japanese publications on the topic.

Shan Zai opens the essay thus: "When a woman falls in same-sex love with another woman, it is in fact the same as a man being fond of men's beauty and sex [*Fu nü yu nü tongxing zhi xiang lian'ai shi tongyu nanzi zhi hao nanse*]." The phrase *hao nanse*, or "[a man's] predilection for male beauty and sex" (as opposed to "female beauty and sex," *nüse*), is a well-established expression in traditional Chinese, comparable to "male homosexual preference" in late-twentieth-century parlance. Shan Zai, attempting to put forth and explain the novel idea of same-sex erotic love between/among women, uses the well-known male case as an analogy.

Shan Zai then moves on to say: "There are different kinds of motives and reasons for same-sex erotic love between women. Modern people study it from a medical perspective, and they have generally claimed that it arises from the inversion of erotic desire (*Inversion des Sexualtriebs*) [*qingyu zhi diandao*], and that it is a disease [*jibing*], or abnormality [*bianchang*]. When a woman lacks love for men, but feels erotic love for people of her own sex, this is a perversion of erotic desire [*qingyu zhi biantai*]." [21] In this passage, we encounter almost all of the key psychomedical neologisms—*qingyu zhi biantai* (perversion, abnormality, or metamorphosis of sexual desire), *diandao* (inversion), and *jibing* (disease)— that would later recur in modern Chinese medical discourse on homosexuality. Later in the essay, Shan Zai's invocation of names makes the origin of these words and ideas clear: it is German and British sexology of the late nineteenth and early twentieth centuries, particularly the work of Havelock Ellis. Prior to the arrival of European sexology, the Chinese indigenous concept of homosexual liking, such as "a man's passion for male beauty and sex," is basically neutral; it is the balanced opposite of "a man's fondness for female beauty and sex." [22] The term carries no negative value judgment, no comparison of homosexual taste to either disease or the perversion of an aim-specific, originary, "normal" erotic drive. Moreover, it is without dispute a notion dissociating sexual pleasure from procreation. Its limitation resides in its negligence of female-female attraction. Modern sexology bestows upon female homosexuality a visible status comparable to that of male homosexuality. However, the overall assumption about homosexuality is already negative.

Shan Zai is careful to differentiate between different kinds of female same-sex erotic love. "Those females who have inverted erotic desire," he writes, "would have no romantic feelings even if they see beautiful men. However, not all of those trapped in same-sex erotic love have behaved out of inverted erotic desire. Some of them do so because they want to satisfy their erotic desire but have no opportunity to associate with men, and still more indulge in this bad erotic affection out of the curiosity for pleasure. The reasons and motives for the same-sex erotic love prevalent among female students nowadays are difficult to ascertain, but they probably do not exceed the above reasons." [23] In other words, Shan Zai dutifully introduces the European sexological idea that some females are determined inverts; they are a special kind of women. Their same-sex erotic love can be distinguished from temporary kinds. Here the new idea "same-sex erotic love among women" (*funü tongxing zhi aiqing*) is a category of sexual pleasure and love relationship, containing also a (sub)category of personhood.

After having described same-sex erotic love among women in broad medical terms, Shan Zai comments on the common occurrence of this love in European history and literature as well as in non-European cultures. He mentions Sappho, "Tribadie," and Denis Diderot's La religieuse (The Nun). Interestingly, in this section Shan Zai's tone is considerably less judgmental. He says that there are many melancholic, romantic intricacies (qingjie zhi aiyan) in women's same-sex love fit for poets' and novelists' pens.

Then Shan Zai moves on to Japan's situation and ends the article by discussing the difficulties in "preventing" female same-sex love:

> Recently in the society of female students in Japan, same-sex mutual love is also prevalent. Educators are eager to extinguish it but do not have good methods. . . . To prevent this fashion [feng] by abolishing the dorms in women's schools or forbidding close female friends to sleep in the same room is easy to say but difficult to carry out. To instruct female students that, from medical and ethical perspectives, this is an unnatural and unethical behavior is also difficult, for we would have to tell young girls explicitly about the matter. Some educators have said that proper sex education can sweep away this bad fashion. But it is difficult to explicitly explain such a thing; therefore, nowadays no one is advocating this approach any longer. Indeed, to prevent same-sex romantic love among women, there is no other method besides cultivating women's moral character.[24]

The language here is fascinating. Female homosexuality in the schools is discussed as a "fashion" that might be "extinguished" and "prevented." The trope of "wind" — custom or fashion — presents female homosexuality as a changeable social practice rather than a fixed personal truth. However, this "fashion" acts like a most difficult epidemic. Though much anxiety over women's homosexual behavior and relationships is expressed, male homosexuality is conspicuously absent from this discussion of the necessity and strategies of preventing homosexuality. In other words, although European sexology on homosexuality instills a new awareness of women's homosexuality as a counterpart of men's, the new awareness turns immediately to regulate female desire but not male desire. In this case, sexology merely provides the necessary conceptual means for regulating female sexuality. As early women's journals in the late Qing and the Republican periods often had a large number of male contributors and readers,[25] Shan Zai's essay on female same-sex love in the schools may be a telling example of male anxiety over female sexuality, especially over female sexual pleasure dissociated from men and reproduction, in a modernizing society.

In December 1923, *The Chinese Educational Review* (published by the Commercial Press in Shanghai) put out a special issue, *Sex Education*. In it were thirteen articles. Among essays such as "Introduction to Sex Education," "The Movements of Sex Education in Europe and America," "Life between the Two Sexes and Education," "Analysis of the Male and the Female Sexes," and "Sexual Hygiene and Ethics during Puberty," we find an article entitled "Same-Sex Love and Education" by Shen Zemin. "Same-Sex Love and Education" (*Tongxing'ai yu jiaoyu*) is not Shen Zemin's original work; it is a translation of the chapter "Affection in Education" from Edward Carpenter's *The Intermediate Sex* (1908). In his afterword to the translation, Shen indicates why he considers Carpenter's critique of Victorian England relevant:

> Carpenter's essay is targeted at the education in England. But isn't the situation he describes common in the schools [including colleges] of China? . . .
>
> China is a place where "the gutter" pointed out by Carpenter is most prevalent. Emotion has been stunted in part by the common opinions in society, and in part by the traditional marriage institution. Now schools continue in doing such work.
>
> Shall we advocate the education of emotion or preserve "the gutter"? Why don't we gather courage to recall our own school days! We have all gone through life in the schools! [26]

Addressing probably adult educators, Shen pleads, via Carpenter, that they show tolerance and understanding for the same-sex affectional ties, often intense and romantic, developed between students or between student and teacher in schools. In the essay, it is maintained that true comradeship, friendship, and love between students have been unjustly equated with the "wretched" practices and habits that merely provide a sexual outlet. Serious attachments are forced, by indiscrimination, to "exist underground, as it were, at their peril, and half-stifled in an atmosphere which can only be described as that of the gutter." [27] It is imperative that the attachments be openly acknowledged and institutionalized, for affection is an educative force and school is the appropriate place for developing it. Carpenter does not explicitly state in the essay whether same-sex affection should last beyond school days, whether serious same-sex comradeship legitimizes same-sex sexual practice, or whether it may be an alternative to marriage. But we can easily gather from his other writings and his own life that he affirms lifelong same-sex unions. The translator, Shen Zemin, cautiously refrains from bringing up such issues in his afterword.

However, his evocation of past school days reads like a melancholic lament over some aborted friendship.

Toward the end of "Affection in Education," Carpenter distinguishes women's homogenic attachment from men's: "The remarks in this paper have chiefly had reference to boy's schools. . . . in girls' schools friendships instead of being repressed are rather encouraged by public opinion; only unfortunately they are for the most part friendships of a weak and sentimental turn, and not very healthy either in themselves or in the habits they lead to. . . . on the subject of sex, so infinitely important to women, there needs to be sensible and consistent teaching, both public and private. Possibly the co-education of boys and girls may be of use in making boys less ashamed of their feelings, and girls more healthy in the expression of them." [28] These are rather enigmatic remarks. What exactly is sensible knowledge about sex for women? Is Carpenter suggesting that girls by themselves cannot figure out what correct sex is? And what are the "unhealthy habits"? Because Carpenter does not go into detail, it is difficult to pin down his position. At any rate, one thing is certain: he sees "sentimentality" as a fault in girls' friendships, and he believes society is responsible for encouraging women to be unduly sentimental. Coeducation, according to him, can enhance the feelings in boys' friendships, whereas it reduces the emotionality of girls' friendships: a curious corrective proposal, for it implies that boys' friendships will strengthen in spite of the presence or availability of girls, yet girls' mutual love will lessen because boys, supposedly solid in intellect and knowledge, are around.

We may compare Carpenter on female friendship with Havelock Ellis on female homosexuality. Ellis's opinion was later translated into Chinese by Pan Guangdan. Ellis writes: "Among women, though less easy to detect, homosexuality appears to be scarcely less common than among men . . . the pronounced cases are, indeed, perhaps less frequently met with than among men, but less marked and less deeply rooted cases are probably more frequent than among men." [29] Their ideas, I would argue, are rather similar, in that female same-sex love is considered in many cases a mistaken passion. It is suggested that self-delusional female friendships are possible because society allows a greater measure of sentimentality in women than in men, and that these friendships may be revealed to be less "deeply rooted" when challenged than male homosexuality.

Shen Zemin makes no indication whether the critique of oversentimentality applies to female friendships in China, or whether the Chinese public in 1923 were similar to Victorians in encouraging women's intimate bonds but repressing men's. We have to seek comments on the local context in another essay, published earlier in the same year. In the May issue of *The Lady's Journal* (*Funü zazhi*), a person pen-named Yan Shi authored "The Segregation between the Sexes and Same-Sex Love" (*Nannüde geli yu tongxing'ai*).[30] Yan Shi (gender unclear) writes:

> Last semester we received fliers attacking the president of a certain women's normal college. Among other faults, the president was accused of ill management which led to the popularity of the habit of same-sex love among the students in that college. The question whether the president is responsible aside, the issue of same-sex love in itself is worth our careful discussion. It is a common phenomenon that same-sex love takes place between student companions in schools—whether in men's or women's schools. All of us who have had the experience of living in a school can observe it. It is not limited to any one school, although it may be more common in some schools than in others. However, people usually treat such things merely with ridicule, and no one seriously wants to study the matter or to think of some remedy. This is very strange.
>
> We should be aware that same-sex love is a perversion of love. It is harmful to young men and women. Those who experience strong same-sex love are often repelled by the opposite sex, and they refuse to lead a normal married life.[31]

If we can trust Yan Shi, same-sex love was equally common in Chinese men's and women's schools. The Chinese public's attitude toward both cases, according to Yan Shi, was laissez-faire and lacking in seriousness. There was ridicule instead of probing interest in causes or corrective measures, although students' same-sex love might sometimes be seized upon as a reason for attacking certain school authorities. Yan Shi's own attitude is that same-sex love is a serious ill caused by sexual segregation, so coeducation must be promoted. Yan Shi includes a passage he translates from Walter M. Gallichan's *The Psychology of Marriage* (1917) as his sociological authority. The article concludes with the assertion that only coeducation can prevent same-sex love.

Obviously, there is quite a gap between Shen Zemin's and Yan Shi's attitudes although both rely on Anglo-American authorities. Whereas Shen Zemin calls for open affirmation and institutionalization of the youth's same-sex attachment, Yan Shi denounces it as an obstacle in the path to normal marriage and a "perversion" (*biantai*), a novel concept in sexology and psychology.[32]

The Lady's Journal, a major intellectual forum then for Chinese discussions of issues of particular relevance to women (such as women's suffrage, the women's labor movement, women's education, coeducation, male-female socialization, new gender ethics, love, sex, marriage, motherhood, divorce) did not always publish negative theories about same-sex affection. In the June 1925 issue, an affirmative article, "The New Significance of Same-Sex Love for Women's Education" (*Tongxing'ai zai nüzi jiaoyu shang de xin yiyi*), appeared. It was translated by Wei Sheng (pen name) from a Japanese essay by Furuya Toyoko.

In the article, Furuya defines same-sex love as a form of spiritual love, which excludes "ugly" sexual intercourse between people of the same sex. Then she theorizes it as an intensified, modern modality of "adoration" or "friendship":

> Same-sex love in the sense I newly discovered is an emotional rapport between people of the same sex. Traditionally it has been called "adoration" if between the younger and the elder, and "friendship" if between equals.
>
> However, because the spirit of mankind has been incessantly progressing upward, feelings have reached amazing fineness and intensity in our century. If such feelings flourish between people of the same sex, they exert a determining influence on these people, sometimes to the extent of becoming the fundamental affection motivating their lives, dominating the entirety of their spiritual faculties. Therefore, we cannot call it by simple traditional terms such as "adoration" or "friendship." [33]

Furuya constructs an evolutionary theory of human emotions and identifies same-sex love as the most recent manifestation of human spiritual progress. In modern women's education, she maintains, same-sex love can work vitally. Love motivates female students to imitate admirable female teachers in character, behavior, and intellect. Therefore, mechanical, impersonal pedagogy must be forsaken, to be replaced by an education suffused with feelings and the interaction between personalities. Moreover, Furuya points out that love and comradeship between female students cultivate and purify sentimental faculties. Such love is abiding and continues even after the women are married and have children, which is proof of the love's purity and spirituality. These positions constitute her so-called New Culturalism of Education.

Significantly, Furuya mentions Edward Carpenter as one of the first people to point out the value of same-sex love in education. Furuya's own contribution, then, is to theorize specifically about the educative power of the female form, instead of subsuming it under the value of male same-sex love as Carpenter did. Other than that, she is similar to Carpenter in elevating the spiritual and eschewing the physical in the discussion of homogenic love in schools. She also follows Carpenter in arguing that the prevalence of homogenic love in modern civilization is due to an increase in the intermediate sex—a fact of evolutionary import. According to her, one of the major signs of modernity is that men and women are becoming similar in characteristics. As a result, masculine women may attract feminine women and vice versa. However, in the end Furuya reminds the reader that the attraction between women of opposite gender types is just one of the many possibilities of female same-sex love. This is an important moment in the text as it frees the imagination of the Chinese reader (who reads Furuya in translation) from the set pattern of masculine-feminine pairing. The reader may observe that the female student's fervent adoration for the female teacher described by Furuya is not so much about opposite-gender role playing as about identification.

That the Chinese intellectuals in the 1920s were particularly fascinated with female homosexuality is apparent in the appearance of another translation. The October 1927 issue of the journal *New Culture* published "Same-Sex Love among Female Students" (*Nü xuesheng de tongxing'ai*). It is a translation by Xie Se (pen name) of "The School Friendships of Girls," an appendix Ellis added to the revised and enlarged English third edition of *Sexual Inversion*.[34]

The editor of *New Culture*, "Dr. Sex" Zhang Jingsheng, was a controversial and notorious figure on the intellectual scene in Shanghai and Beijing in the 1920s for promoting sexual knowledge and the attainment of sexual pleasure and bliss, defined solely in terms of male-female intercourse.[35] As Peng Hsiao-yen has pointed out, Zhang appeared as a radical reformer of traditional Chinese sexual mores, deploring Chinese youths' ignorance of sexual techniques and lack of sexual energy. Further, Zhang promoted a female-centered utopia where beauty, art, and love would be the ruling values.[36] We can note, however, that Zhang was criticized by some of his contemporaries, most notably the contributors to the feminist magazine *New Woman*, for being male-centered, unscientific, and Taoist-superstitious about male and female sexualities. In his writings, Zhang encouraged men to derive pleasure with women from foreplay alone (*shen jiao, qing wan*) in a language that emphasized the conservation of semen in the interest of health, an advice that reminded Zhang's opponents of traditional Taoist sexual alchemy. Zhang also advocated female sexual climax by theorizing a temporal or direct cause-and-effect link between female climax, the emission of the egg, the perfect impregnation, and the generation of healthy, gender-distinct offspring. His opponents cried out against the theory as absurd. From my point of view, the theory is problematic mainly in that Zhang tried to legitimize female pleasure through reproduction and dichotomous gender ideals. His notion of "sexual beauty" (*xing mei*) is not just a theory about pleasurable intercourse but also an ideology of gender difference, dictating standards for women's femininity and men's masculinity. Finally, Zhang sought to dispel the value conventionally placed on women's virginity by arguing that a sexually experienced woman can give a man more pleasure than a virgin. The last—his promotion of women's freedom of sex in a rhetoric that defines women as objects rendering pleasure to men—was especially suspect and distasteful to the writers in *New Woman*.[37]

The article chosen for translation for Zhang Jingsheng's *New Culture*, "The School Friendships of Girls," turns out to be very ambivalent about educated young women's homoerotic activities. I shall give a rather detailed discussion of Ellis's essay's male voyeurism, anxiety over autonomous female sexuality, and phallocentrism to argue that it is precisely because the piece offers at once dangerous titillation and phallic assurance that it could be endorsed by Zhang Jingsheng as authoritative opinion on women's same-sex intimacy in schools. Moreover, the translator as well as the editor must have implicitly drawn many parallels between women's liaisons in schools in the West and in China to consider the discussion of situations in European and American institutions of particular interest.

Ellis recounts several studies on girls' school friendships of a particular kind, called "fiamma" in Italy, and "rave" or "spoon" in England. According to the researchers, these friendships are different from usual friendships in that they have many elements characteristic of the sexual love between man and woman, such as madness, passion, exclusivity, and jealousy. In Italian, the word *fiamma* refers both to such a relationship and to the beloved person, who ignites love in another and makes her assume the role of the active, pursuing lover. A flame most often breaks out from the attraction of physical beauty and elegance. It takes place between students who do not know each other rather than between familiar, constant companions. In a typical scenario, a boarder chances to see a day pupil or merely hears of her elegance, then falls in love and starts to court and woo her, in which process love letters play a central role.[38] Ellis writes: "Notwithstanding the Platonic character of the correspondences, Obici and Marchesini remark, there is really a substratum of emotional sexuality beneath it, and it is this which finds its expression in the indecorous conversations already referred to. The 'flame' is a love-fiction, a play of sexual love. This characteristic comes out in the frequently romantic names, of men and women, invented to sign the letters."[39] Although Ellis recognizes a sexual dimension in girls' school friendships, he automatically assigns the status of a play or fiction to these friendships. The unspoken assumption here is that, unlike girls' school friendships, the love between a man and a woman is nonfiction; it is real. He implies that a romance between girls is merely temporary staging, and that their amorous acts and speeches are mimetic rather than serious in intention and consequence.

Besides passing phallocentric judgment, Ellis toils to find unthreatening explanations for girls' school friendships, and he falls into a theoretical impasse. On the cause of the flame friendship, Ellis believes that the "intense desire to love a companion passionately is the result of the college environment," where girls far away from home "feel the need of loving and being loved." He emphasizes that the flame relationship is different from sexual perversion:

> While there is an unquestionable sexual element in the "flame" relationship, this cannot be regarded as an absolute expression of real congenital perversion of the sex-instinct. The frequency of the phenomena, as well as the fact that, on leaving college to enter social life, the girl usually ceases to feel these emotions, are sufficient to show the absence of congenital abnormality. The estimate of the frequency of "flames" in Normal schools, given to Obici and Marchesini by several lady collaborators, was about 60 per cent., but there is no reason to suppose that women teachers furnish a larger contingent of perverted individuals than other women. . . . The root is organic, but the manifestations are ideal and Platonic. . . . It may well be that sensual excitations, transformed into ethereal sentiments, serve to increase the intensity of the "flames." [40]

The passage is tellingly tortuous in logic. Ellis's predicament, briefly, is that if flames are real expressions of sexuality, then "60 percent" (of Normal school women as practitioners of flames) is too high a figure for an "abnormality." Therefore, Ellis must maintain that these friendships do not count as sexuality, and that genuine "perversion" is something else. It does not occur to him that he may solve the theoretical impasse by reconsidering and renaming the sexual feelings among women—whether short-lived or abiding—normal. Later on, he plainly contradicts his claim that flames do not indicate "congenital" sex instinct when he surmises that "organic" sensual excitations among girls are "transformed into ethereal sentiments." This amounts to his arguing, in spite of himself, that there exists a primal sexual impulse for the same sex that becomes suppressed later.

What Ellis obstinately regards as the only "normal sex-instinct" may in fact be engineered by socioeconomic factors. With a different set of socioeconomic factors operating, alternative manifestations of desire may naturally arise. Apparently, female teachers showed a higher than usual percentage of what Ellis calls "perversion" because they were educated women able to write each other love letters and, more important, to make their own living independent of men and outside conventional middle-class marriage.

In the article, Ellis cites his own informant, an Englishwoman familiar with the "raves" fashionable in English girls' schools. Her independent observations of the duration and causes of raves are enlightening: "That the 'raves' fell and act like a pair of lovers there is no doubt, and the majority put down these romantic friendships for their own sex as due, in a great extent, in the case of girls at schools, to being without the society of the opposite sex. This may be true in some cases, but personally I think the question open to discussion. These friendships are often found among girls who have left school and have every liberty, even among girls who have had numerous flirtations with the opposite sex, who cannot be accused of inversion, and who have all the feminine and domestic characteristics." [41] Compared with Ellis on flames, the Englishwoman is much more doubtful about the explanations of single-sex environment and gender inversion (i.e., lack of femininity).

The translator Xie Se is rather faithful to Ellis's essay. However, Xie Se departs from the original in two significant places. In rendering the title as female students' "same-sex love" rather than "friendships," he does not resist calling these women's school friendships homosexual the way Ellis does. Xie Se unambiguously locates frequently seen female romantic friendships within the sexual sphere, and within a homosexual spectrum. This shows that Xie Se's conception of homosexuality departs significantly from Ellis's. Unlike Ellis, Xie Se's notion of homosexuality does not pivot around gender inversion, nor does it theorize about the subject's orientation of desire. Xie Se focuses, rather, on the behavior and feelings actually manifested intersubjectively. Ellis's sense that a certain personal essence is the foundation for object choice is absent from Xie Se's creation of the category same-sex love out of this essay. Xie's attitude may reflect traditional Chinese understanding of the self, in which the self is seldom perceived as an autonomous, independent entity, but often as the site where a set of relations converge. The self takes shape in reference to others and within communities. Therefore, same-sex desire may not be said properly to "belong to" a subject.

When it comes to the notions of activity and passivity in sexuality, Xie Se again diverges from Ellis. The English original states that in a flame, one girl takes on a more active role while the other is passive. In the Chinese translation, these roles are reinscribed as "the role of a husband" and "the role of a wife." Xie Se derives the meanings of active and passive from conventional matrimony in China, collapsing sexuality into marriage. Compared with Ellis, Xie Se's attitude toward sex strikes us as a fascinating mixture of liberalism and conservatism, indicating the imprint of cultural difference.

So far in the five journal articles on tongxing'ai I have surveyed, tongxing'ai is primarily signified as a modality of love or an intersubjective rapport rather than as a category of personhood, that is, an identity. Moreover, the essays all focus on attachments in same-sex schools. All five recognize same-sex attachment, especially women's same-sex attachments, as a common occurrence in schools rather than an uncanny singularity. Two essays denounce homogenic love as perverse; two affirm its ennobling capacity or the crucial role it can play in the refinement of the young, and the last one is ambivalent. Ellis affirms the passionate emotional quality of female students' homoerotic love, and yet he also would like to believe it is merely a temporary phase.

Ironically, it is the denunciatory essays that entertain the idea that there may be same-sex lovers who resist usual marriage. The affirmative essays, by contrast, focus exclusively on the school phase and eschew the possible conflict between homogenic love and the conventional marriage expected of adults in many societies. Carpenter's essay avoids the question altogether and Furuya's asserts that homogenic love is purely spiritual, so it can coexist without conflict with the carnal, nuptial union between man and woman.[42] Ellis's essay, though seemingly neutral, achieves this neutrality only by seeing female same-sex love in the schools as a harmless rehearsal for cross-sex love and marriage. We may observe that in these five essays, homophobia—the attempt to detect improper beginnings and prevent grievous extremes—and a proto-awareness of the homosexual identity paradoxically go hand in hand, while to avoid arousing the public's apprehension, pro-gay writers tend to emphasize that passionate homogenic love is common to humanity, that it is not a peculiarity limited to a minority of people, and that such a universal emotion does not necessarily conflict with marriage.

During the 1920s, the most significant event in the Chinese translation of European writings positive about homosexuality was probably Qiu Yuan's (pen name, probably Hu Qiuyuan) rendition of Carpenter's "The Homogenic Attachment" under the title "On Same-Sex Romantic Love" (Tongxing lian'ai lun).[43] The translation was published in 1929 in two installments in the April and May issues of the journal New Woman in Shanghai. The translator explains in his first footnote, "Although my translation is bad, I hope it will make people become seriously interested in the issue [of homosexuality]. If people will not simply regard it as 'uncanny' or 'perverse,' or as some old thing such as 'fondness for male sensual beauty' [nanse] or 'women mirror-rubbing' [mo jing], I will feel content with my own effort."[44] Qiu Yuan assumes the pose of a humble enlightener facing a rather ignorant public. He intends to make readers realize that homosexuality is more than a matter of sexual pleasure as conceptualized in the past ("men liking male beauty and sex" or "women mirror-rubbing"). Second, he hopes to abridge most people's psychological distance to homosexuality by providing knowledge. Most important, he objects to the latest opinion that homosexuality is perverse (*biantai*). The translated sexological notion of homosexuality as a perversion was probably gaining circulation and that is why Qiu Yuan was compelled to openly acknowledge it and combat it.

The essay begins with an enumeration of brilliant examples of what Carpenter calls "homogenic attachments" in European history, literature, and art. Then the latest scientific discoveries about the subject by European doctors are summarized. First, homosexuality is not a morbid, degenerate, or neurotic condition; on the contrary, many of the most outstanding people in history have strong homosexual temperaments. Second, people with strong homosexual temperaments need not and cannot be "cured." Third, the homogenic attachment (homosexual love) can be found in a wide spectrum of people ranging from those who are attracted quite exclusively to people of their own sex—the "Urings"—to those who occasionally become attracted by an object of their own sex. We see, then, with the Chinese rendition of this essay, that not only did the idea of a healthy social spectrum ranging from mostly homosexual persons to mostly heterosexual persons become available to the Chinese reader, but the concepts of congenital homosexuality and homosexual identity without any pathological or inferior implication were also introduced to the Chinese public, maybe for the first time.

The essay contains other politically and philosophically interesting ideas. Via translation they also became available to the Chinese readership. One such idea is that the desire for physical contact and closeness is an integral dimension to spiritual comrade love; the spiritual should not be asked to be divorced from the physical. Another is that human sexuality should be freed from the reproductive imperative; this imperative is outmoded and meaningless in the modern age, though in the past national or tribal strength may have depended on population size. The value of a sentiment or attachment should be measured in other ways. The correct emphasis, though, Carpenter believes, is not on pleasure, but on sacrifice, courage, and unswerving devotion. Yet another interesting idea is that there exists an intrinsic connection between homogenic attachment and democracy, or between it and the women's liberation movement. It draws different classes together, and it forms comrade alliances among women to fight their sex's oppression. Carpenter's articulation of the relationship between women's liberation and homosexual love may have struck a sympathetic chord in some Chinese feminist readers of *New Woman*.

The translations during the 1920s surveyed above were later overshadowed by Pan Guangdan's translation, published in 1946, of Havelock Ellis's work *Psychology of Sex*. Although Ellis's book is not entirely on homosexuality, it has a long chapter on it, and Pan's lengthy annotations containing numerous references to homosexual people, writings, institutions, and theories in Chinese culture and history were especially valuable. Pan even wrote an appendix, "Examples of Homosexuality in Chinese Historical Documents." Besides listing examples of male-male love and instances of female-female love, Pan analyzes indigenous Chinese views of the causes of homosexuality. Not accepting "sexual psychology" wholesale, Pan instead raises questions about it. For instance, he doubts the applicability of Ellis's theory of sexual inversion to the adult men who liked boys in Chinese history, for the former showed no effeminacy. He believes that deeper or other causes of homosexuality are yet to be discovered.[45]

Pan Guangdan is now remembered as a pioneer who introduced European scientific interest in homosexuality into the Chinese context,[46] while the translators before him — Shan Zai, Xie Se, Shen Zemin, Wei Sheng, and Qiu Yuan — have been completely forgotten.[47] Several factors may have contributed to such a course of events: the earlier translators' imperfect command of English and other foreign languages, the obtuseness (i.e., flavor of foreign syntax) of their Chinese prose, the fact that they themselves did not become prolific scholars or writers, and the ephemeral quality of journal articles compared with books. Another crucial reason is that Pan Guangdan's erudition in Chinese homosexual culture and history is difficult for the others to match.

Nonetheless, I maintain that the translators before Pan Guangdan were, like Pan, serious about East-West parallels and comparisons. Above all, they chose foreign texts that seemed to them most useful and urgent for clarifying, justifying, or criticizing the prevalence of same-sex passionate attachment in Chinese schools (including colleges). On the one hand, there was a serious desire to regulate adolescents' and college students' sexuality. On the other hand, insofar as the problematized erotics in formal education was primarily an upper- and middle-class experience, the regulatory attention it received also signified social importance and privilege. The early translators' work in the 1920s, not polished in style or worth reprinting nowadays, nevertheless represented the moment when Chinese intellectuals first came into contact with modern European theories of homosexuality. Their pieces on *tongxing'ai* constituted the first modern discourse of homosexuality in China, where trite and novel concepts and foreign and local social phenomena were negotiated.

This discourse of *tongxing'ai*, to recapitulate, was not unified in character. Homosexuality was as a rule conceived of as a rapport, which admits contingency, interactive creativeness, and the individual value of a specific love object. But the idea of an unchangeable, innate homosexual temperament in the subject of desire (what we now call orientation) also appeared in the discourse. Homosexuality was affirmed by some as an ennobling sentiment, a consequence of and propelling force for human evolutionary progress. At the same time it was decried by others as dangerous, as the perversion of desire and gender. Female-female erotic love, especially, gained unprecedented attention in the translations. In quite a few articles, a strong anxiety is expressed over female but not male homosexuality. Female homosexuality in the schools is a fascinating modern phenomenon for both curious inspection and anxious regulation.

Two decades later, in the early 1940s, Pan Guangdan would describe the phenomenon of same-sex love in Chinese schools in the 1920s in relatively trivializing terms:

> Ellis's observation [that "many of us are unable to recall from the memories of school life and early associations any clear evidence of the existence of homosexual attractions, such rare sexual attractions as existed being exclusively towards the opposite sex" [48]] might be true of the situation in Europe and America, where social interaction between men and women and co-education became common at an early date. However, in the schools in China ten or twenty years ago, same-sex love between male students occurred quite a bit. Although it could not be said to form a "tradition" as in some English public schools, even the concrete examples which I can personally identify and remember were more than one. After co-education became popular in China, of course, such incidents have become fewer and fewer. Still, even in co-ed schools, we can find many instances of same-sex love between female schoolmates. Some women even make a mutual agreement not to get married, or to marry the same man in the future. Nonetheless, in the final analysis this is but the temporary expression of emotion. When time and setting change, and the women reach maturity, they will separate and follow the paths of heterosexuality and marriage. [49]

These remarks attest retrospectively to the prevalence of same-sex love in Chinese schools in the 1920s. Pan's argument, unlike the debates during the 1920s, fails to indicate the tension between seeing same-sex desire as a product of the environment or an immature phase, and regarding it as deeply satisfying, precious, or serious, however fleeting the passions may be. Pan's interpretation of same-sex love in the schools is dismissive compared with Qiu Yuan's or Shen Zemin's attitudes, although it is no more heterosexist than some other translators' agendas in the 1920s, such as Yan Shi's or Xie Se's. One may observe that in the transition from the 1920s to the 1940s, a liberal discourse that would celebrate homosexual love in and/or out of the school in Edward Carpenter's fashion became less audible in Chinese. The range of Chinese discourses on homosexuality narrowed after the 1920s, in which process Ellis's medical theory of homosexuality, premised on a dichotomy between sexual normality and deviation, gained hegemony through repeated citations and translations into Chinese.[50]

Republican Chinese "Same-Sex Love": A Discourse of Alternative Modernity

The Republican Chinese discourse on same-sex love departed from previous Chinese views of male-male or female-female attraction in multiple ways. Besides the fact that its predominant focus was on the eroticism in modern-style education, the discourse on same-sex love annexed, above all, a supplement of interiority and emotionality to preexisting Chinese terminology for same-sex intercourse and erotic pleasure. In the new discourse, same-sex attraction became something that could be more than carnal and superficial. It was infused with depth, whether pathological or romantic. Another key aspect of its modernity is that women's same-sex love received unprecedented attention as a counterpart of men's. The theoretical inclusion mirrored women's greater participation in social and public life in modern times, but it also signaled the expansion of male scrutiny into a formerly private realm of female experience. Whereas in previous ages, Chinese men were largely content to contain female homoeroticism within women's quarters rather than prohibit it, in the Republican period male intellectuals found that it was no longer possible to contain it within inconsequential domestic seclusion, and that increasingly they had to explicitly criticize, regulate, or inhibit women's same-sex attraction.

Remarkably, Republican Chinese discourse on same-sex love did not make "the homosexual," an identity akin to a racial minority, become the predominant figure standing for same-sex attraction.[51] That is, the idea of there being an extraordinary homosexual nature confined to a small percentage of the population did not become the overruling paradigm for understanding homoerotic desire in Republican China. This might be viewed as surprising, given the fact that late-nineteenth- and early-twentieth-century European sexology is usually credited, in the West, for discovering, and perhaps also creating, the figure of the biologically determined quintessential homosexual. In contrast, many Chinese intellectuals, despite their interest in Western sexology, inclined toward understanding same-sex love as relational and situational. How this divergence may be interpreted is surely open to debate. It seems to me simplistic, however, to see it as Chinese intellectuals' failing as readers and translators—

that is, as their not grasping the West's accurate knowledge about identity—as Frank Dikötter has recently argued.[52] Republican Chinese intellectuals' focus on the relational and situational qualities of same-sex attraction may be reflecting a different but equally valid imagination about human subjectivity, one that sees subjectivity as contextual rather than through the tropes of essence and unchanging continuity. In retrospect, and with the hindsight that one of the trends in contemporary queer movement in the West is precisely to reconceptualize the homosexual identity as a form of "strategic essentialism" or "necessary fiction,"[53] we cannot but wonder whether Republican Chinese intellectuals had some justification all along as they insisted on observing the relational and situational in the homoerotic.

At the heart of the issue is whether one may uncritically embrace "identity" or fixed orientation as the only key to a correct and politically useful understanding of sexuality. Even though early sexology provided certain resources for the conceptualization of gay identity, preference, or orientation in certain circles in the West, for many decades the medical discourse on gay "personhood" was a negative and treacherous one. A telling example is that the American Psychiatric Association listed homosexuality as either a pathological or neurological disorder of personality recommended for treatment until 1973. Medical professionals' horrible treatment of homosexual persons—including aversion therapy, electroshock, castration, vasectomy, lobotomy, psychoanalysis, and hormone medication—in twentieth-century America is well documented by Jonathan Ned Katz in *Gay American History*.[54]

In view of the negative effects of the model of sexual orientation and identity, historian John D'Emilio, among others, has pointed out that Kinsey's findings in the 1950s of the high incidence of homosexual behavior in the general population was conceptually revolutionary and politically liberating. D'Emilio maintains, "The data [presented by Kinsey] disputed the common assumption that all adults were permanently and exclusively either homosexual or heterosexual and revealed instead a fluidity that belied medical theories about fixed orientations." Moreover, "Kinsey . . . used his statistics to suggest that such a common sexual activity ought not to be punished. Resting on the misinformed view that homosexual behavior was confined to a small number of individuals, society's treatment of homosexuals, he argued, was socially destructive."[55] If it is, as Kinsey reminds us, that the capacity for homosexuality is not limited to a minority of people supposedly exceptional in physiological or psychological makeup, but rather widely diffused in the population, not only will lesbian or gay communities have to be conceived as having no fast boundaries, but the stigmatizing of homosexual behavior as unnatural, abnormal, or neurotic will also lose its ostensible foundation in rationality. This is not to dispute the point that the establishment of lesbian/gay identities remains a necessary political project, in that people with predominantly homosexual interests ought to have the freedom to define their own orientation as such without being constantly subjected to invisibility, harassment, restraints, or the pressures of conversion, reform, and treatment.

In light of these tensions, Republican Chinese discussion on same-sex love, with its preponderant attention to the intersubjective and the circumstantial, can be viewed as providing an alternative modern discourse on homosexuality rather than as a deformed version of Western sexology, deficient and falling far behind Western knowledge.[56] No matter how urgent it may seem to some to recuperate the notion of people's consistent natures for legitimating sexual difference, we need to recognize that there has always been resistance to sexual categories, and that the refusal of sexual identity may represent yet another tactic for demanding diversity in a globalizing world.

Notes

1   Magnus Hirschfeld, *Men and Women*, 65.
2   Lydia Liu, *Translingual Practice*, 26.
3   According to Zhang Minyun, a Republican Chinese author who did extensive research on the developments of modern sexual science in Europe, America, and Japan since the nineteenth century, the importation of German sexology to Japan began in the late Meiji period (1868–1912) and reached its peak in the Taisho era (1912–1926). Scientific and quasiscientific publications on sex were especially voluminous in the post–World War I years in the Taisho period and the early Showa period. See Zhang Minyun, *Xing kexue*, 50–51. For a detailed discussion of the development of modern Japanese sexology, see Chizuko Ueno, "Kaisetsu," in *Fuzoku, sei*, 505–50; I am grateful to Tadashi Anno for bringing this source of information to my attention.
4   For the early appearances, differences, and current usage of these terms in Chinese sources, see Tze-lan D. Sang, "The Emerging Lesbian," 96–98, 105–7.
5   See the debates on *xing* between Gao Zi and Meng Zi at the beginning of the *Gao zi shang* chapter of Meng Zi, *Mencius*, 160–65.
6   Tetsuji Morohashi's Chinese-Japanese dictionary, 4410, defines one of the usages of *sei* (the same character as *xing*) as the Japanese translation of "sex" in the sense of gender. According to Zhang Minyun, it was not until the Meiji Restoration that Japanese intellectuals began to use *sei* to mean sex.
7   The Japanese used the classical Chinese expression *lian'ai* to translate "love" in a romantic sense in Western languages. Chinese intellectuals adopted the usage. Some even went so far as to assert that there had been no Chinese term corresponding to the concept of romantic love until *lian'ai* was adopted. For example, Zhang Xichen makes this claim in *Xin xingdaode taolun ji*, 92. Zhang served as the editor of two impor-

tant women's journals in the 1920s, *Funü zazhi* (The lady's journal) and *Xin nüxing* (The new woman). He was also the founder of the influential Kaiming (Enlightenment) Bookstore.

8   See Roxane Witke, *Transformation of Attitudes Towards Women*, for her documentation and discussion of the May Fourth discourse of love as well as marriage reform. See also Zhang Xichen.

   It is noteworthy that May Fourth idealization and promotion of male-female love paralleled the burying of Victorian and puritanical "repression" and the alienation between the sexes that went on in England and America in the 1910s and '20s. Chinese intellectuals saw much merit in such texts as Edward Carpenter's *Love's Coming of Age* (1911) and Marie Stopes's *Married Love* (1918). The Chinese translations of these texts were popular and played a significant role in shaping the ideal of heterosexual love for urban middle-class Chinese youth.

9   The sources are too numerous to list. Some notable essays on love can be found in Zhang Jingsheng, ed., *Aiqing dingze*, and the various issues of *Xin nüxing*.

10   "Same-sex sexual desire" would be *tongxing xingyu*; "same-sex sexual intercourse" would be *tongxing xingjiao*. Neither of the two appeared as the equivalents for the category "homosexuality." The first one is an awkward phrase that has never been used; the second, however, can conceivably be used to talk about sexual intercourse between people of the same sex.

11   See Xu Ke, "Changji lei," in *Qing bai lei chao*, 38:114; Tao Wu, "Mo jing dang," 65–70.

12   John Boswell shows that, unlike English, "many languages fail to distinguish in any neat way between 'friend' and 'lover' " (*Same-Sex Unions*, 4). In light of the examples given by Boswell, and Mao Yibo's argument, to be discussed next in my text, I am tempted to speculate that certain cultures' obsession with keeping separate categories of "friendship" and "love" is coextensive with homophobia, and that challenging the distinction between "friendship" and "love" attacks homophobia at its heart.

13   Mao Yibo, "Zai lun xing'ai yu youyi," 1257–58; my translation. The fascinating first two sentences in the Chinese original reads: "Ren suowei liangxingjian de guanxi, zui miqie de youyi guanxi, ji suowei Sexual friendship, wo chengren na shi youde, erqie buxianyu yixingde, tongxingjian you hechang meiyou yinle xinyang, xingqing, shiye dengdeng zhi xiangtouhe er fasheng zui miqie zui qinren de guanxi de ne?" Unless otherwise noted, all translations from Chinese into English are mine.

14   For a detailed analysis of new women's anxiety about same-sex desire, as seen in May Fourth fiction, see Sang, 143–89.

15   Hu Shi comments in 1918 that the author and characters of the Qing homoerotic novel *Pinhua baojian* (A precious mirror for classifying flowers) did not know that men's having sex with other males could be considered a bad or abominable thing (*buzhi nanse wei e shi*). See Hu Shi, "Lun xiaoshuo ji baihua yunwen," 76. *Pinhua baojian*, which depicts Qing elite men's patronage of boy actors specializing in female operatic roles, is the best illustration of the level of sophistication at which male homoeroticism was socially institutionalized along the class and gender hierarchies in Qing China. Hu Shi's comment is a sobering indicator that male-male intercourse in modernizing China, regardless of the class relation between the sexual partners or their respective symbolic gender roles, had acquired a bad reputation and become viewed as deviant

or morally questionable. About Qing attitudes, see also "The Penetrated Male in Late Imperial China," Matthew Sommer's rigorous study of the Qing substatute against lower-class men subjecting young males of commoner (respectable) status to anal penetration (and thus the humiliating loss of masculinity), but not against all male-male sex or all men's sexual interest in other males per se.

16 Jingqu Houren, *Shu yan lie qi lu*, 51.

17 Shan Zai, "Fünü tongxing zhi aiqing," 36–38. I am thankful to Sylvia Li-chun Lin for providing me with this article.

18 "Shan zai" is a Buddhist term and often used as an exclamation or sigh, comparable to but a bit gentler than "My goodness!" By signing thus, the author indicates that he disapproves of but feels powerless to change female same-sex love.

19 It should be noted that before the New Cultural Movement's advocacy of vernacular literature, some early women's periodicals had already opted for the vernacular as their medium in order to reach a wider female audience since the average level of literacy among educated women was lower than men's. *Beijing nübao* (Beijing women's newspaper, 1905–1909) and *Nüzi baihua bao* (Women's newspaper in the vernacular, 1912–13) are two such examples. See Jiang Weitang et al., eds., *Beijing fünü baokan kao*, 36, 99.

20 Havelock Ellis and J. A. Symonds, *Das konträre Geschlechtsgefühl*.

21 Shan, 36.

22 See Giovanni Vitiello, "Exemplary Sodomites," for an in-depth study of the concept of *nanse* in late Ming fiction. See also Sophie Volpp, "The Male Queen: Boy Actors and Literati Libertines." An oft-cited monograph, Bret Hinsch's *Passions of the Cut Sleeve*, provides an overview of male homoerotic love in premodern China. However, later studies by Vitiello, Volpp, and Sommer, which focus on late imperial China, have pointed out various problems in Hinsch's interpretations. Hinsch's book also seems methodologically unsound, in that large portions of his text correspond to two prior Chinese studies, by Weixing shiguan zhaizhu (1964) and Xiaomingxiong (1984), and make the same mistakes in their sloppy use of classical Chinese sources.

23 Shan, 36.

24 Ibid., 38.

25 Jacqueline Nirvard, "Women and the Women's Press," 47.

26 Shen Zemin, trans., "Tongxing'ai yu jiaoyu," 22/23.

27 Here I quote from Carpenter's English original, *The Intermediate Sex*, 90–91.

28 Ibid., 105.

29 Havelock Ellis, *Psychology of Sex: A Manual for Students*, 220–21.

30 Pen names were common in Chinese newspapers and periodicals during the early half of this century. It is probably not because his or her article deals with homosexuality that the author Yan Shi wanted to use a pen name.

31 Yan Shi, "Nannü de geli yu tongxing'ai," 14–15.

32 The word *bian tai* (perversion, abnormality) was beginning to be used widely in Chinese translations of European and Japanese sexological and psychological writings in the early 1920s. The word was probably directly adopted from *hentai* in Japanese sources.

33 Wei Sheng, trans., "Tongxing'ai zai nüzi jiaoyu shang de xin yiyi," 1065. My English translation is based on the Chinese version.

34 Xie Se, trans., "Nü xuesheng de tongxing'ai," 57–74.

35 Zhang Jingsheng was clearly of a heterosexist bias. He writes against male-male anal intercourse in *Xing shi* (*Sex Histories*): "One can say that the slackness of the vagina indirectly encourages the fondness for sodomy [*zhuzhang hao nanse*]. However the anus is the faecal passage and is dirty. Moreover since there is neither vigorous activity nor electrical functioning, it ordinarily does not constitute a rival to the vagina. Therefore I should like to urge all of my . . . readers to note that through giving full consideration and research to the vagina not only can one bring about a perfection and completeness of intercourse between the sexes, but one can also exterminate the ridiculous game of sodomy [*houting baxi*], a game which is abnormal, dirty, meaningless, inhuman, and not even indulged in by the birds and beasts" (79–80; English translation is quoted from Howard Levy, trans., *Sex Histories: China's First Modern Treatise on Sex Education*, 90–91, with my modification of the words "evil habit" into "ridiculous game" as the translation for *baxi*).

36 For details, see Peng Hsiao-yen, "Xing qimeng yu ziwo jiefang," in *Chaoyue xieshi*, 117–37, as well as other essays. Peng's pioneer studies on Zhang Jingsheng are a source of inspiration for my research on Zhang, though my interpretation of Zhang's ideology about gender departs considerably from Peng's.

37 For Zhang's view that pleasurable male-female intercourse is the precondition for creating normal gender distinctions (i.e., his advocacy of men's virility and women's femininity, and his critique of the Chinese race as weak in sexual intercourse and blurry in gender distinctions), see "Xing mei." For Zhang's theory about the causal connection between female climax, ovulation, and perfect impregnation, see "Disanzhong shui yu luanzhu ji shengji he youzhong de guanxi."

For criticism of Zhang's theories as wild fantasy and Taoist superstition masquerading as modern science, see Zhou Jianren, "Xing jiaoyu yundong de weiji"; Zhou Yizhao, "Ping Zhang Jingsheng boshi *Meide xingyu*"; and Zhang Xichen, "Xin nüxing yu xing de yanjiu." See also Pan Guangdan, "Xin wenhua yu jia kexue—bo Zhang Jingsheng." For objections to *Xing shi* (Sex histories) edited by Zhang Jingsheng, criticizing it as pornography, see Zhang Xichen.

38 Ellis, 369.

39 Ibid., 373.

40 Ibid., 374.

41 Ibid., 379.

42 I have labeled Furuya's essay "affirmative" of same-sex love, but one can put quite the opposite emphasis on the content of the essay. In her monograph on modern Chinese women's desire and writing, Wendy Larson analyzes Furuya's article and detects the presence of a social prohibition on lesbian sex in the essay's denial of physical relationships among women. For Larson, the essay's insistent claims that women's same-sex relationships are pure and nonsexual are evidence that the mere possibility of physical lesbian love breached dominant moral ideology. Larson's analysis also cites examples of Chinese intellectuals in the 1920s strongly arguing against women's singlehood

and same-sex bonds as damaging for women, men, and society. See *Women and Writing in Modern China*, 88–91.

43   Edward Carpenter, "The Homogenic Attachment," in *The Intermediate Sex*, 39–82.

44   Qiu Yuan, trans., "Tongxing lian'ai lun," 526.

45   Pan Guangdan, "Zhongguo wenxian zhong tongxing lian juli," 526–47.

46   For an example of Pan Guangdan's reputation as a forerunner in the study of Chinese homosexuality, see Yang Kun's preface to Li Yinhe and Wang Xiaobo's *Tamen de shijie* (1991), the first in-depth sociological-anthropological study of gay men in contemporary mainland China, in which Pan is the only one named as a precursor in researching Chinese homosexuality and translating Western sexology.

47   In the existing scholarship on Republican China, I have found scanty mention, much less analysis, of the translations of "same-sex love" in the feminist journals of the 1920s. A notable exception is Peng Hsiao-yen, who in her study of Zhang Jingsheng, mentions the appearance of the translation of Ellis's essay on female students' same-sex love by Xie Se in *Xin wenhua*. See Peng, *Chaoyue xieshi*, 130. Also an exception is Wendy Larson's analysis of the essay by Furuya Toyoko in *Women and Writing in Modern China*, 88–89. Michael Siu, who studied history at UC-Berkeley, briefly analyzes three discussions of homosexuality in the sex manuals of Shanghai and *The Lady's Journal* in the 1920s and '30s in his senior seminar paper. But Siu appears unaware that those Republican views of homosexuality were informed by translation. See "Attitudes Towards Women's Sexuality in Shanghai in the 1920s and 1930s: A Selective Analysis of Sex Manuals and *Ladies' Journal*," 9–11, 17, 22–23.

      Frank Dikötter's recent research on the Republican view of homosexuality is limited to medical and quasimedical books for sex education. Furthermore, his judgment of the Chinese medical texts he cites glosses over the crucial role of translation. See *Sex, Culture and Modernity in China*, 137–45. Because he does not mention any of the translations in nonmedical journals that I analyze, he either is unaware of or is deliberately ignoring them.

48   Ellis, 235.

49   Pan Guangdan, translator's n. 36, in *Xing xinli xue*, 325–26.

50   It was common for 1930s Chinese medical texts on sex education to include brief passages on homosexuality, describing it as sexual perversion. See, for example, Yi Bi, "Gao chunü: tongxing'ai," in *Xing dian*, 66. See also the sex education pamphlets cited by Dikötter, 137–45.

51   In her recent theoretical rumination, Ann Stoler argues that Michel Foucault was one of the first to point out the importance of a colonial discourse of race for the modern discourse of sexuality. See *Race and the Education of Desire*. Besides the analogy with race, people with same-sex preference have also been construed as a gender minority; Magnus Hirschfeld's theory of "the third sex" is an early example. Recent scientific studies searching for the gay gene or the gay brain (primarily in gay males) perpetuate similar ways of thinking, which seek to either racialize or assign an intermediate biological gender to gay men. The overall assumption of many of these studies is that the homosexual orientation is produced by a biological factor true of only a minority in the overall population. See Simon LeVay, *The Sexual Brain*, for an example of high-

profile biological study of sexual orientation. See also Timothy Murphy, *Gay Science: The Ethics of Sexual Orientation Research*, for an incisive critique of studies like LeVay's.

52 Dikötter, 137–45.

53 See Diana Fuss, *Essentially Speaking*; Jeffrey Weeks, "Values in an Age of Uncertainty," 397.

54 Jonathan Ned Katz, *Gay American History*, 129–207.

55 John D'Emilio, *Sexual Politics, Sexual Communities*, 35, 37. Among cultures that privilege heterosexuality over homosexuality, the degree of acceptance of bisexual behavior nonetheless varies. Chinese sources in the early Republican period suggest that China was more lax on bisexual behavior (at least male bisexual behavior) than Anglo-American cultures.

56 I am responding to Dikötter's criticism of Republican Chinese intellectuals' treatment of homosexuality in medical pamphlets.

Nancy N. Chen *Translating Psychiatry*

and Mental Health in Twentieth-Century China

The *Diagnostic and Statistical Manual of Mental Disorders* is the primary set of classification codes for the diagnosis of psychiatric disorders used in most contemporary practices, in addition to the *International Classification of Disorders* (ICD).
In the most recent revision (DSM-IV) there were several additions, including
an appendix that outlined steps for the clinical formulation of culture-bound
syndromes of twenty-five recognized phenomena. Three categories were associated with Chinese culture: *shenjing shuairuo* (neurasthenia), *shenkui* (panic
disorder), and *qigong* psychotic reaction. In one sense, the inclusion of these
categories indicates a growing acknowledgment of culture in the experiences
of mental illness and the need for tools that can access mental and social disorders according to different cultural contexts within psychiatry. These categories also reflect processes of diagnosis that are based on shared meanings
among professionals throughout the world. The implementation of uniform
categories such as codes from the DSM-IV reflects a growing acceptance of
equivalence that is necessary in globalizing discourses such as psychiatry.

In this essay I address the development of psychiatry in China, which can be
viewed as a series of translingual practices that have occurred over the past century.[1] Rather than weaving a continuous narrative, the institution of psychiatry
has had several ruptures in its political organization and social meanings of
practice. Such ruptures, however, reveal some of the choices made in translating psychiatry in the Chinese context. As a form of specialized medicine
that was introduced by missionary medical practitioners in the late nineteenth
century, psychiatric institutions eventually became part of a larger program

of national order and discipline in the earlier half of the twentieth century. During this century, the institution of psychiatry evolved with the establishment of asylums, hospitals, teaching schools, journals, nursing associations, and other professional groups. Rather than focusing solely on contemporary psychiatric terms and mental health categories, this essay seeks to situate the practices of Chinese psychiatry within historical frameworks of cultural translation and national discourses of modernity. Terms, categories, and even spatial orders in psychiatry are inextricably linked to the contexts of translation in which meanings and practices are adopted and utilized. Neologisms such as asylum (*fengyuan*), psychiatric institution (*jingshenke bingyuan*), mental hygiene (*jingshen weisheng*), and mental health (*jingshen jiankang*) in particular are simultaneously embedded within Chinese social categories as well as professional definitions. Psychiatry in contemporary China is thus situated at particular intersections between cultural meanings of madness, international and national classification categories for mental illness, and evolving institutional practices. Thinking about psychiatry in cultural context offers opportunities to view the ways in which practice has been transformed by institutional discourses of modernity. Psychiatry has been particularly useful in placing bodies under a centralizing medical gaze. Tracing the transformations of Chinese psychiatry to particular moments of translation reveals how much this profession and its institutions are integral to national platforms for mental health and desires for social order.

Three historical contexts mark the development of psychiatry and have particular salience for the circulation of notions and forms of treatment in China: pre-1949 missionary, Maoist, and post-Mao global psychiatry. These periods are chosen for their use of the asylum and psychiatry in the treatment of mental disorders in quite distinct ways. In each of these periods prevailing political discourse between global institutions and local conditions determined the uses of categories and forms of mental health care. "Modern" psychiatry, particularly what constitutes modern practice, continues to be revised and contested and can be viewed as a microcosm of social relations and power structures in conversation.

The first section of this essay addresses the process of building the profession that also locates it in the national context of state building which was intent on removing the stigma and long-standing "backward" views about madness to focus on making healthy minds and bodies. The shift from mental illness to mental hygiene and health is addressed in the second section. Mental hygiene is viewed as a marker of the socialist enterprise of producing fit subjects in the twentieth century. The third section addresses the culture-bound disorders of neurasthenia and *qigong* deviation that are officially recognized in Chinese psychiatry and continue to be negotiated in clinical practice. Patient narratives of the latter are included in a special subsection on constructing deviation.

Putting Psychiatry in Place

Madness in Chinese folklore and traditional medical writings was recognized early and commonly associated with winds. Shamanic healing by Daoist healers involved a wide range of treatments. Depending on the individual nature of the suffering, these prescriptions included ingesting ashes of spiritual inscriptions, physical exercises, and forms of exorcism. In the *Huangdi Neijing Suwen* (The Yellow Emporer's inner canon of medicine), a classic of state orthodox medicine, madness was differentiated into three main categories of *dian*, *kuang*, and *xian*.[2] Most mental illnesses were associated with excess emotions and the imbalance caused by such excess or deficiency in the internal organs of the body rather than located as a mental symptom. Although mental illness was categorized as a pathological state, the care of patients did not become a public concern until the late nineteenth century, when foreign medical missionaries began to organize support for public clinics. Further, psychiatric institutions in China were not built and did not become systematized until mental health became a massive state campaign under Mao in the 1950s.

The alliance between state building and mental health in China has always been concerned with two long-standing issues: providing for a large population and maintaining social order. Concepts of mental health are composed of complex ideologies that are closely linked to the cultural context of Western missionary medicine in China. In fact, Chinese psychiatry is embedded within missionary encounters of the late nineteenth century when Western-trained physicians campaigned for more "humane" (i.e., Christian) treatment of the insane. The implementation of psychiatry was part of a general concern for the mentality of Chinese people on the part of missionaries. The advocacy of Western medicine by Christian missionaries further intensified during the late nineteenth century and especially during the Republican era of the 1920s and 1930s as these clinics provided the only psychiatric services to the general public. The fusion between Christian humanitarianism and American philanthropy configured with Chinese notions of modernism.

The first psychiatric hospital, the Canton Refuge for the Insane, was opened in 1898 by Dr. Joseph Kerr, an American missionary, who believed in "clinical evangelism" and occupational therapy for patients. Kerr was the designated heir to Dr. Peter Parker, the first Protestant missionary to establish a presence in Canton with his surgery practice.[3] The establishment of the asylum took considerable effort and was a lifelong project of Kerr, who had a distinguished career with the publication of several medical texts and the development of teaching facilities in China. In 1849 a report by Dr. Hobson, who established the Hong Kong Missionary Hospital, mentions the relative infrequency of insanity in China: "Considering the phlegmatic temperament and temperate habits of the Chinese, it might be appreciated that this malady is not of frequent occurrence, and I think further inquiry will prove that insanity prevails to a much less extent in China than in Europe. . . . Lunatic Asylums are unknown in China."[4]

Most medical missionaries emphasized surgery, particularly ophthamalic operations and removals of tumors, which had an abundance of Chinese patients seeking immediate and visible results. Despite Kerr's considerable stature in the profession, there was marked reluctance from fellow missionaries and even more resistance from family members of potential patients to attend such a clinic. It wasn't until Kerr purchased three acres of his own land and sought assistance from private donors that the refuge was built and opened, just three years before his death. In contrast to the charity hospitals run by missionaries, the Kerr refuge was based primarily on revenue generated from patient billing and donors. At the turn of the century, the main source of patients began to be referred from local police and magistrates, who used the hospital as an overflow penal institution and paid for the bills in order to house patients. The mental hospital remained open until 1927, when it closed in the face of continued controversy; it had admitted a total of 6,599 cases over the three decades it had operated.[5] Later, some of the work was continued in other hospitals under the Republican government. Up until the establishment of the People's Republic in 1949, an assortment of private institutions and charities provided the primary source of mental health care available in China. As the use of psychopharmacology was not yet integral to the treatment of patients, the treatment modalities of this time included rest cure, work therapy, and physical restraint for the worst cases. Small psychiatric wards as part of missionary hospitals eventually opened throughout Chinese provinces, but Canton was clearly the first and foremost place where the profession was established.

Most of the missionary doctors had much difficulty convincing Chinese families to bring individuals into the hospital and even greater difficulty in retaining patients, as many tried to run away. This general problem of adherence was due in part to the social stigma of mental illness and also to the fear of being mistreated by foreigners, often referred to as foreign devils. The popular concept of the reformatory was akin to that of prison, where one would be forced to work against one's will. Confining a relative in the attic or banishment to the streets was the preferred mode of treatment rather than allowing someone to be confined by the "Other" or Western doctors. Kerr noted that the failure of especially the well-to-do and middle classes to adhere to new methods, which stemmed from general reluctance to seek help that would make public their family secrets, meant that few Chinese families would utilize the asylum. Only when private offices were established where clients could pay for services in anonymity did more middle-class families come to the refuge.

The frequent occurrence of mad persons who tore off their clothes and danced in the streets added to the chaos associated with the streets. In response, the call for social order brought the role of the police into focus by establishing the streets as an arena of state ideology. In the 1920s Beijing rickshaw pullers and mental deviants alike faced the wrath of the street police.[6] The disturbances of public order by such individuals commonly ended with the street police bringing the mad to the local jails. The relationship between the asylum and the police became even stronger when an agreement was made between local police and the Canton asylum at the turn of the century.[7]

The work therapy model was quite a popular form of treatment in the missionary hospital context, where patients produced small goods for several hours each day. Work was viewed as an antidote to mental instability and believed to promote moral character and hygiene. Such methods remain in use even today as most major institutes incorporate handicraft production as part of weekly therapy.

In sum, practices of psychiatry in the late nineteenth and early twentieth centuries were primarily carried out by Western missionary doctors with Chinese patients who were recruited from the streets or brought in by local authorities. Occasionally Western-educated Chinese physicians were trained and practiced in the asylums. The psychiatric asylum then was a site where notions of social order were integral to the separation of madness from Chinese public spaces with the enforcement of police as well as bringing in patients from the isolation of domestic spaces.

The early socialist period in the mid–twentieth century was transformative with regard to official legislation for mental health and educational programs. In contrast to missionary psychiatry where proponents of this discipline worked closely with authorities to remove disruptive elements from the street, this new phase in Chinese psychiatry seemed to embrace mental health as a platform for developing the minds and hearts of the population. With the inception of the People's Republic of China mental health care became intertwined with the idea of social progress. Mental health care was cited in the first Five Year Plan (1958–1962) as a top priority for a modernizing China focused on socialist revisions of policies and practices. But rather than continuing the institutions established by Western missionaries, a socialist model of mental hygiene (*jingshen weisheng*) embracing Soviet psychological theories and practice was established instead. The emphasis on psychiatry and psychology was based on Soviet public health campaigns during the Great Leap Forward (1957). The highly touted Barefoot Doctor Program even included a segment on diagnosis and treatment of mental illness in the countryside. New centers and hospitals were created so that former missionary centers and practices were deemphasized. The Chinese use of Soviet models of mental health care did not entirely replicate the extreme use of "penal psychiatry," which the Soviet asylums were known to use to control and punish political dissidents. Instead, new theories and modalities of treatment emphasized political engagement with socialist liberation models. The therapeutic system emphasized that mentally ill persons could be retrained to become valuable citizens and model workers for a new society. In this vast social program of psychiatry for the people, there was a shift from the notion of the asylum as a way to confine madness to one of psychiatric clinics and hospitals that rehabilitated those with the debilitating stigma of mental illness. Pathologized states, whether organic or social in origin, were still possible to reform and cure through activity and work, which was a central proponent of Pavlovian theory.

The political activism of the Great Leap Forward and the Cultural Revolution during the 1960s had immense impact on the practice of psychiatry. Again the emphasis was on work as an indicator of moral character and aptitude for socialist principles. While the factories attached to mental hospitals continued to produce socks, staplers, and screws, Pavlovian work therapy incorporated political activity where readings of Mao Zedong's writing were considered crucial to one's mental well-being. Such activities in socialist thought reform reflected larger social transformations outside of the mental hospital, where all citizens were expected to read political works. To choose not to participate indicated one's reluctance to reform and hence madness. In their study of Chinese psychology, Robert and Ai-ling S. Chin document the role of Soviet psychology on transforming notions of Chinese psychiatric practice during this period.[8]

The departure from Western psychiatric practice was most emphasized during the Cultural Revolution (1966–1976). Psychology was viewed as a decadent Western theory and Chinese practitioners who tried to incorporate Freudian theory were made to scrub toilets instead. The discipline of psychology was viewed as having a different intellectual genealogy in China and hence the linkages to work therapy and actual bodies of patients as subjects meant that psychiatry had a different political trajectory from the social sciences. In the years when the Gang of Four ruled, acts of violence throughout rural and urban settings were committed. It was during this time that Red Guards, youthful agents of political thought, were active in the process of control and punishment in the general population and within the hospital units. Deviation from the socialist orthodoxy of the Party became grounds for demotion and transfer of staff members and administrators. Psychiatrists who were senior staff during this period relate that the social madness and turmoil that then surrounded psychiatric institutions was far greater than that contained within the walls. Many psychiatric hospitals closed down as doctors were made to engage in political study. Yet a few psychiatrists managed to secretly counsel old patients and distraught family members who sought them in confidence.

Contemporary mental health care reflects larger social and economic transformations since post-Mao reforms of the late 1970s. Like its counterparts in the rest of the world, Chinese psychiatry is gradually embracing international diagnostic categories and psychotropic treatment with codes of Chinese classification since the 1980s. The development of mental health care began with an outreach by the post-Mao government to Western and overseas Chinese experts.[9] Reforms in mental health care during this period sought to reverse the directions that Maoist thought reform and psychiatric practices had taken in the previous decades.

Mental health remains part of the public health structure but now is once more included in the language of development. In the present state of Chinese psychiatry, "mental hygiene" is intertwined with biomedical practices to underscore a prevailing state discourse on the need for order and normality. The Chinese asylum is the site of several intersecting forces and desires: transnational aid agencies and pharmaceutical corporations, embodiments of socialist modernization, and arenas of negotiation among family members. There is also an ironic twist—the return to the very sites created by missionaries established prior to 1949. A model rehabilitative center in the suburbs of Shanghai is based in the former physical structure of a French charity hospital. Grilled ironwork and gardens are only part of the physical and program restructuring taking place.

Today early Western models of mental health care exist concurrently with recently imported models of biomedicine, where scientific research and psychotropic drugs are increasingly emphasized in the treatment of mental patients. Political reforms introduced in the late 1970s and early 1980s allowed Chinese scholars and psychiatrists to participate in exchange programs abroad and international bodies such as the World Health Organization to open collaborative centers for joint research and training. Along with the import of Western biotechnology, there was a transfer of classification categories from the DSM-IV and ICD-10. Such use of screening tests is intended to align with global psychiatric practices. The Chinese professional community is presently engaged in active translation of the latest Western psychiatric articles and international classification categories into Chinese. These translations of categories in the *Chinese Classification of Mental Disorders* (CCDM-2R) are a critical site of translingual practice. Despite all intentions of conformity with international classification codes, the CCDM-2R is an area where specific additions, deletions, retentions, and variations are clear indicators that cultural meanings and differences are being negotiated.[10] Urban centers are primarily in control of these translations, as the larger research hospitals and majority of professionals are located in cities. In other regions, there is a slight time lag in the adoption of global psychiatric research. Even with the uniform use of the CCDM classifications in China, there remain great regional differences, especially differences in hospital stays between rural patients (average stay 37.2 days) and urban patients (140 days) due to work-unit health packages and insurance in urban regions.

In sum, the establishment of asylums by missionary practitioners in the late nineteenth century introduced new concepts of treatment to deal with madness and deviance. These practices and institutions were quickly assimilated by local authorities to maintain social order. The renewed efforts to develop mental hygiene under the aegis of a broader socialist public health campaign in the mid–twentieth century transformed psychiatric asylums into social institutions that were model units of rehabilitation. The emphasis on Maoist therapies based on Soviet Pavlovian theory demonstrates how translating psychiatry to Chinese institutions was not based solely on Western theories but instead was viewed as an integral process of subject making and hence state building.

Mental Health and Hygiene

Despite interventions in the development of the asylum, the social stigma of mental illness in China remains acutely experienced by individuals and their family members who seek mental health care. Many of the patients and their relatives whom I interviewed in ethnographic fieldwork cited the difficulty of sharing their distress with outsiders. To be open with neighbors or coworkers would entail the loss of face in social situations or even, in some cases, the loss of normal responsibilities at work. Seeking mental health care still involves a great risk and unspoken fear of being found out by one's neighbors or colleagues. Popular images of madness such as divine fools who dare to speak the truth or frenzied *feng zi* (mad persons) who run naked through the streets are often cited by Chinese as examples of those with mental disorders. Such stereotypes resound with past popular images of lunatics. In contrast to this long-standing view, psychiatric institutions continue to be promoted as centers of medical science where mental illness can be treated as a disease and not as a social deviation. The image of psychiatry that is promoted by the state is thus one of scientific objectivity in line with Marxist practice, a necessary part of the grand scheme for a "socialist civilization" (*shehuizhuyi wenming*) that Anagnost documents in her study of the Chinese state.[11] Such an official notion of mental health is also apparent in the term "mental hygiene" (*jingshen weisheng*), which is still used in reference to mental health care.

In the 1990s when I conducted ethnographic research in psychiatric institutions, I was struck by the seeming incongruity between English uses of the term mental health and Chinese uses of the term mental hygiene. The present use of hygiene underscores several genealogies of institutional practice and meaning outlined earlier. First, the use of the term mental hygiene (*jingshen weisheng*) in Chinese rather than mental health (*jingshen jiankang*) indicates the ideological emphasis on hygiene and sanitation in relation to the pathologized category of mental illness. Meanings of hygiene and notions of "cleanliness" have frequently been incorporated by socialist and even Republican health programs that borrowed significantly from missionary disease control campaigns. Hygiene (*weisheng*) has occupied particular prominence in Maoist campaigns for socialist transformations of mental illness, once carried as private burdens, into mental diseases that could be countered with work therapy and political reform. Mental hygiene was thus a part of larger public health initiatives that were simultaneously linked to morality in which both social and political forms of decay would be rehabilitated with socialist values and practice. Ironically, although the socialist health care movement meant to eradicate disease and pestilence, the drive to get rid of decadence also politicized many public health issues, especially mental health, as moral issues.

In the process of updating psychiatric classification codes and practices to be equivalent to international categories in the late twentieth century, little attention is given to the contexts in which the terms mental hygiene and mental health are used. In the ethnographic context, based on observations of weekly team meetings, clinical discussions, and conference proceedings, mental hygiene (*jingshen weisheng*) is more often invoked to refer to programmatic or institutional approaches to mental health, and mental health (*jingshen jiankang*) is used when addressing individual cases. The discipline presently depends on active dialogue among professional committees, state institutions, and international colleagues as well as institutional support. Such engagements are crucial not only in furthering the global discourse of psychiatry but also in critical practices of subject making. The Chinese psychiatric asylum functions as an official site of order and control of the disorderly and chaotic elements that emanate from within an individual rather than the social setting.

Mapping Disorder

The rest of this essay addresses post-Mao practices of psychiatry and two specific categories that illustrate psychiatry as a set of translingual practices and negotiations. Both neurasthenia and *qigong* psychotic reaction are specifically noted in the DSM-IV as included in the CCDM-2R. The inclusion of these categories in both documents indicates a growing tendency to locate culture-bound syndromes in mainstream psychiatry. Further, the acknowledgment of different sources of classification and the efforts to make cross-links reflect an ongoing process of making psychiatry more universal. After situating neurasthenia and the impact of this category in the Chinese profession, I then turn to the more recent classification of *qigong* deviation and the cultural dilemmas of translation that have been part of the discursive construction and experience of this phenomenon.

Shenjing shruairuo, or the clinical diagnosis given for the experience of weak nerves, fatigue, sleeplessness, headache, dizziness, and other complaints, is one of the most recognized and diagnosed categories in Chinese psychiatric clinics today. Causal explanations for this category stem from Soviet theories in which unfavorable conditions cause tensions in the nervous system, thus weakening a person's constitution. In tracing the usage and eventual demise of the diagnosis of neurasthenia in the United States, Arthur Kleinman asserted that the continued experience of this disorder in China rather than the diagnosis of clinical depression reflected importantly upon the cultural meanings of somatization and psychiatric categories.[12] "Neurasthenia" continues to be used as an equivalent translation for shenjing shuairuo even though the frequency of this diagnosis has decreased considerably in recent years. In a collection of essays in the journal *Culture, Medicine, Psychiatry*, Chinese practitioners and scholars argued for the necessity of retaining neurasthenia as a diagnostic concept in China.[13] Whereas Western psychiatrists might diagnose such symptoms as depression, the doctors argued that the category was still prominent in Chinese culture and hence a critical code. The call to retain neurasthenia as an indigenized category reflected an ongoing concern with the high prevalence of sufferers both in and outside clinics. Literary explorations of this condition during the May Fourth movement as well as contemporary social discourses indicate that as a cultural category, neurasthenia remained a powerful signifier of the absence of agency both at the individual level and for the body politic. Debates about neurasthenia and *shenjing shuairuo* illustrate how even with shared diagnostic categories, the uses of these codes and the professional meanings of such symptoms are nonetheless embedded in cultural contexts. Thus, even as psychiatry might be a globalizing discourse, the translation or translatability of symptoms is highly dependent on the professionals who use them and the everyday contexts that encompass their meanings.

Whereas *shenjing shuairuo* stemmed from a specific relation between an environment of social stress and individual responses, the category of *qigong* psychotic reaction is related to the healing practice of *qigong*, which ironically was intended to address one's illnesses. The DSM-IV describes this phenomenon: "A term describing an acute, time limited episode characterized by dissociative, paranoid, or other psychotic or nonpsychotic symptoms that may occur after participation in the Chinese folk health enhancing practice of qi-gong ("exercise of vital energy"). Especially vulnerable are individuals who become overly involved in the practice. This diagnosis is included in the *Chinese Classification of Mental Disorders*, Second Edition (CCDM-2)." [14] In contrast to the term used in DSM-IV, most Chinese psychiatrists continue to refer to this phenomenon as *qigong* deviation (*qigong piancha*). Only occasionally in cases where the patient's behavior warranted the term did psychiatrists ever refer to the terms of *qigong* psychotic reaction or *qigong*-induced mental disorder (*qigong suozhi jingshen zhangai*). Initially, most psychiatrists were reluctant to label the disorder with the new category; instead, patients were admitted with the initial diagnosis of schizophrenia, hysteria, or other mental illness until further observation and response to drug therapy could be obtained. The rationale for this process acknowledges the overlap and sometimes indistinguishable characteristics of *qigong* deviation and other mental illnesses, chiefly hallucinations and delusions. All of the patients I interviewed distinguished themselves from the general patient population with their state of affect, which seemed quite functional. Most patients good-naturedly engaged in animated conversations with me and shared the common experience of other inpatients in telling me that they were not mentally ill, only misunderstood. Though they stood out in appearance and manner at first, gradually the rhythm of existence inside the ward anesthetized them to a daily routine of structured activity, drug therapy, and sleep. The following discussion addresses the social and political contexts of this disorder and the multiple constructions of this category.

In the years following the post-Mao economic reforms, a resurgence of traditional rituals and practices was noted throughout rural and urban areas. *Qigong* began to circulate in the public sphere as a form of traditional healing practice. Articles about *qigong* in Chinese newspapers and journals emerged in the early 1980s. Along with other state enterprises that began to be privatized, most publishing houses also faced the question of survival in the new market economy. One strategy involved publication of best-sellers, which set the stage for how-to books on *qigong* and even *qigong* novels. By the mid-1980s there were not only popular books, magazines, and news articles on *qigong*, but also in the academic realm there were articles and books devoted to scientific aspects of the topic. The writings correlated with the emergence from obscurity (*chu shan le*) of *qigong* masters, who began to teach or heal in the urban centers. Burgeoning audiences included practitioners and the afflicted as well as scientists and even skeptics.

By the late 1980s the stage was set for several charismatic *qigong* masters, who captured the popular imagination with their powers to heal and bring thousands in an audience to states of trance and ecstatic movements. Charmed followers claimed miraculous transformations of illness into well-being and newfound meaning in daily practice. Factory workers and cadres alike paid 35 to 40 yuan (the equivalent of a week's wages) to attend mass sessions of famous *qigong* masters and be the recipients of the master's external (*wai*) qi.[15] Meanwhile, traveling shows of less well-known *qigong* magicians (*mo shu*) adept at mastering feats of external *qi* energy arrived on streets and in work units; their performances included walking on glass and then swallowing the shards, feeling no pain from fire or great blows to the body, and demonstrating paranormal abilities (*te yi gong neng*) such as hearing written characters.

By the 1990s *qigong* was a widespread social phenomenon with a broad base of followers and masters. The proliferation of *qigong* practitioners was especially visible after the Tiananmen demonstrations and before state economic policies began to be renewed. Along with the deregulation of state presses and more entrepreneurial special-interest publications, enterprising *qigong* masters became charismatic cultural producers of healing and even modern-day mystics. Individuals who claimed to be masters of healing opened *qigong* clinics and charged dearly for private sessions. Soon state regulation of *qigong* practice was undertaken to respond to the proliferation of charismatic masters who operated without accountability to any official unit. Citing *qigong* deviation and "false," unscientific practices as reasons for state intervention, steps were undertaken to license masters and prevent popular mass sessions. Yet, even though practitioners and the social context of *qigong* came under scrutiny by state regulatory bureaus, individuals and state officials alike continued to practice the breathing and healing exercises, sometimes in defiance of growing rules or simply with the rationale that their leisure time devoted to self-healing was apolitical.

Although the local context of *qigong* in the PRC was increasingly polarized by official regulations as either scientific or false and unscientific, the practice of *qigong* was nonetheless condoned and exported by the Ministry of Health to promote *Chinese* healing arts to Japan and other countries.[16] Masters who were licensed and had fulfilled all requirements for foreign visas were sent on exchange programs to promote official forms of *qigong*. In addition, individual masters who had clients and private sponsors abroad also managed to travel and so establish growing networks of *qigong* practitioners and clinics of "oriental" medicine.

Individual practices and magical claims about *qigong* in contemporary China existed within the same spaces that were created for post-Mao economic reforms and Chinese modernization. In the late twentieth century, ideologies of Chinese socialist modernization rely heavily on scientific rationality, which emphasizes global economic dominance and orderly citizens who are productive and docile. Yet local and private meanings of this process meant more stresses in everyday life: crowded urban centers, increased costs of living, and imposed order. *Qigong* was readily embraced in this context as it provided the chance to transcend the burdens of everyday life into more personal spheres of meaning. The focus on the body and bodily experiences through *qigong* corresponded with the growing commodification of bodies and evolving consumer culture in 1990s China. As new fashions and cosmetic surgery emphasized external appearances, *qigong* practice offered unique opportunities to experience and refigure bodies as sites of discipline from within oneself. Part of the appeal of *qigong* to initial practitioners was the notion of the good life, where good health and even superhuman abilities come with regular practice. As examples of the body fantastic, masters demonstrated how their own bodies could become an instrument forged by the mind and body together to withstand pain and even heal others. But *qigong* was unusual in that it was believed that *any* illness or ailment, even symptoms of neurasthenia, could be cured with *qigong*. In the 1990s most practitioners cited health reasons for taking up the practice. Even in cases of chronic pain, injury, and disease, many afflicted sought *qigong* for initial relief and eventual transformation of their health status from incurable to healed. Whether for somatized complaints or congenital defects, *qigong* provided a cheaper alternative to the systems of Western medicine and traditional Chinese medicine and was accompanied by sensational changes that seemed almost immediate. Anyone could buy a book on *qigong* or go to the parks to take up the practice. Rather than undergoing many years of training and certification, a novice could easily sense differences in his or her body and experience the movement of qi. Feeling the body, visualizing internal landscapes, and talking about intimate processes of the body were part of the daily ritual in breathing exercises.

The social context of the popular emphasis on healing and self-cultivation made it possible for individuals to meet with other practitioners in times and places that emphasized the rhythms of the body and nature. Most practice took place outside with other devotees. On streets, in front of buildings, and especially in parks in the early morning one could observe qigong practitioners along with other activities such as taiji, wushu, and disco. Many groups adhered to particular forms or schools and yet these groups were not exclusive. Anyone could join who showed genuine interest and made the commitment to practice.

Although daily practice was the most common form of social interaction, qigong devotees would also attend mass qigong sessions where a master would lecture and give qi to the audience. Before 1989, this was the way charismatic masters could address hundreds, sometimes thousands, of followers (and skeptics). Such masters embodied those who could "ride the tiger" (i.e., have real power & control), immerse themselves in chaos, and emerge with true power in health and wealth.

Shortly after the popular rise of qigong practice, individuals complaining of a variety of responses to the practice began to trickle into psychiatric clinics. Their symptoms ranged from mild discomfort or pains from qi to unusual sensations in their bodies to more drastic sensations of hearing voices or being controlled by spirits or other voices. This phenomenon was found in hospitals and other venues such as traditional Chinese medicine clinics throughout China. In a weekly psychiatric inpatient team meeting that I attended in the early 1990s in which two qigong patients were discussed, one senior psychiatrist noted that in a sample study of one hundred qigong patients in Shanghai, 80 percent were male. In contrast, many of the inpatients admitted in Beijing for qigong deviation were female. None of the patients had a prior history of mental illness; however, after practicing qigong, all patients claimed to be able to visualize illness within the body and to cure others with this power.

Patients' descriptions of their experience of qigong deviation seemed to fall into two categories. The first category of symptoms was related to mechanical problems with qi energy unleashed by qigong practice. One husband in his fifties exclaimed, "Ever since I had problems concentrating, my qi has remained in my head, which is painful, so painful I want to kill myself." Another outpatient related how the qi in her stomach area could not be released and consequently she had even greater difficulty with regular digestion and sleep. The second group of symptoms associated with *qigong* deviation involved uncontrollable visions and images with accompanying severe emotional distress, great pain, anger, and fear. One patient described being able to see and communicate with alien beings after his extrasensory perceptions opened with *qigong* (*gongneng tongle*). The visions were welcome at first, but soon he was unable to control when the aliens would contact him and occupy his mind and body. The descriptions of hallucinations and visions by *qigong* deviation patients were similar to those of other mental patients, especially schizophrenic patients. Such similarity led many psychiatrists to question how to diagnose and treat patients whose symptoms corresponded with their practice.

The following three patient narratives (using pseudonyms) explore how differently the emerging disorder was experienced and the dilemmas patients faced from being placed in a new psychiatric category. Focusing on the experiences of family units as well as individuals in response to mental illness, I hope to illustrate the continuum of the illness experience that is managed and constantly negotiated in relation to state institutions in contemporary China. An anthropology of psychiatry and suffering in China cannot be isolated simply in the individual. Whether the illness is acute or chronic, the burden of mental health care lies squarely on the shoulders of family members. Especially in a culture-bound disorder such as *qigong* deviation, even before a person is brought to the psychiatric unit, family members have probably already sought the services of several agents: traditional Chinese medicine practitioners, *qigong* masters, neighbors, friends, and colleagues. Such pluralistic approaches are usually not addressed in the literature on Chinese mental health care, as the focus is usually institutional or in terms of social policy that addresses community resources. Second, I examine how family units and the intricate network of social relations within this web of kinship have reconstituted themselves given the tremendous upheavals in the latter half of this century. The disruptions of political change, separation, and generational differences have immensely impacted the lives and experiences of all families in China such that the relations and narratives of Chinese families in the late twentieth century reveal the flexible and reflexive character of these social and moral worlds.

LIN HUA was a young woman in her late twenties who in 1990 started to practice *qigong* to deal with her headaches. Very soon after learning the basic steps and practicing on her own she started to hear voices, including those of her master telling her that she needed to practice more. As she listened to these commands, the voices became more incoherent and crowded and demanded that she jump off the fifth floor of her elderly parents' apartment building. Fortunately, her older sisters happened to be visiting and noted her strange behavior: being incommunicable, getting up suddenly to run out of the apartment at times, and talking incessantly about her master. They quickly responded by first seeking the aid of her *qigong* master, who told them that she needed to stop practicing *qigong*. Lin Hua stopped attending the *qigong* class but continued to practice in secret. The final episode that brought her sisters to take her for an exam at the mental health center was the night she ran into the street dressed in her pajamas and screaming about horrible voices telling her to kill herself.

In the outpatient clinic, the doctor quickly admitted her as an inpatient. I met Lin first in the ward and later as the weekly case study for the floor residents and nurses. Hers was an unusual case in that her many caregivers held different opinions on the diagnosis. Such debate over the diagnosis and proper treatment of her category would be typical of many other patients that year who initially practiced *qigong* but also had overlapping features of other mental illnesses. Over the eight weeks that she was in the wards, her sisters and sometimes her aged parents came to visit twice weekly. As I gradually came to learn more from Lin and meet with her family, her sisters confided that they felt her condition was really due to her unmarried status rather than *qigong* practice. They believed a cure would be found not in psychopharmaceuticals or *qigong* healing, but in the stability that a family life of her own would bring. In the last weeks of her stay, Lin was ultimately diagnosed with delusional schizophrenia and was soon after released to her sisters. The sisters had negotiated for continued home care between them as the work unit would no longer pay for Lin's hospital bills, nor were their elderly parents capable of taking care of Lin by themselves. The Lin sisters came back each week to the outpatient clinic to check in with the doctors and discuss continued medication. The siblings were her primary caregivers, with the dual responsibility of taking care of Lin's needs in addition to their parents'.

ZHONG MING was another young inpatient with *qigong* deviation symptoms who arrived at the hospital soon after Lin's departure. He was a young man in his late teens who had the distinction of being a student demonstrator who fled to the countryside after June 4th. As the state sought his whereabouts, his family kept in close contact with police, university officials, and other local authorities. Once captured by local police, he spent the days awaiting his hearing by learning *qigong* from another cell mate. Shortly after doing so, he started to have severe hallucinations and was transferred to a forensic psychiatric unit for observation. As soon as Zhong's father realized that his son was in a hospital unit rather than the local jail, he managed to arrange for his transfer to the Beijing psychiatric unit, maintaining that his son needed proper care and rest with family members nearby. Surprisingly, officials agreed to have Zhong transferred to the mental health hospital, where he was analyzed for mental illness. Throughout his six-week stay, Zhong's parents were in constant negotiation not only with the public security bureau and university officials, but also with the hospital over his final diagnosis. His father was concerned that a diagnosis of qigong deviation would not be taken as seriously as schizophrenia by authorities, who would therefore not excuse his son's actions in relation to the student demonstrations. Hence there were frequent meetings and discussions with hospital staff to steer the eventual diagnosis to that of schizophrenia with qigong-related symptoms.

IN THE THIRD CASE, Mr. and Mrs. Tang were both factory workers who stayed in the hospital together. Mrs. Tang originally started practicing qigong to treat her symptoms of neurasthenia. Her husband decided to also learn qigong for increased health after accompanying her to several courses and finding that the lessons brought immediate effects of invigorating energy. One night her husband started to experience loss of sensation in one leg, eventually leading to the entire loss of control in that leg later the next day. As the symptom seemed to be related to qigong, they first sought their qigong master, who tried to restore sensation with qigong healing energy. As this procedure did not bring any results, the Tangs sought several other masters who brought about varying results. In addition, Mrs. Tang decided to bring her husband to acupuncturists and neurologists for second opinions. Throughout this period of several months, Mr. Tang continued his practice, feeling that qigong helped to restore sensation and at least made him feel energetic enough not to worry about his increasing loss of control of one leg.

Mr. Tang finished his daily routine of qigong practice one day to find that not just one leg but both legs began to feel out of control. In my meeting with him, he told me, "My legs were no longer a part of my body. The qi in my body felt quite out of balance, and they [the legs] started to take me out of the house and out onto the street." Mr. Tang's legs continued to make him walk uncontrollably, until eventually street police took him not to jail for disorderly behavior but to the mental hospital when he insisted that an external alien force was controlling his legs. His wife found him at the mental hospital, where she recounted to the psychiatrist their experiences with qigong and the ensuing loss of control. Even though Mr. Tang did not exhibit any other symptoms of mental illness, he was admitted as an inpatient for observation for several days. During this time, his wife slept on a small cot beside him in the observation unit. She helped to provide twenty-four-hour care during this period, thus cutting down immense hospital expenses that would not be paid by his work unit. The Tangs were able to leave within a few days as Mr. Tang did not seem to experience further distress and loss of power over his legs.

The appearance of *qigong* deviation as a psychiatric diagnostic category, its associated behaviors and dramatic symptoms, and the narratives of experiences by patients and family members are a window into the cultural anxieties and concerns that mostly urban residents faced in the 1990s. While these stories of patients and families are quite distinct, their encounters with the mental health care system were based on constant negotiation for diagnosis, treatment, and attention by staff that all families face in the present system. Particularly for those patients diagnosed with the emergent category of *qigong* deviation in the early 1990s, the intervention and involvement of family members were crucial not only for the eventual recovery of the patient but also for the proper institutional responses of hospital staff, work units, neighbors, and even public security. Inside the psychiatric wards, relatives were frequently questioning staff about drug regimens and diagnostic categories while trying to relate to their family members and update them with news of recent events in their lives. In the outpatient clinics there was the continuous search for an elusive diagnosis. In the everyday realm the family had to pick up the pieces and return to routines disrupted by sudden incidences of madness or frequent visits to the mental health center. *Qigong* narratives were compelling because they revealed the startling disjuncture between a traditional health practice and the total therapeutic system to which these patients were submitted by family members. Unsupervised encounters with *qigong* unleashed intense emotional experiences that challenged individuals. Whereas healers had mastered these moments and could move beyond to harmonizing chaotic elements, novices who could not handle the power unleashed through *qigong* practices were unable to maintain a steady path. Rather than finding order and relief from *qigong* healers, these individuals instead faced a totalizing existence inside the psychiatric hospital.

The interviews with patients and family members as well as participant observation with clinicians made me realize the need to compare the experience of inpatients with those who went to the outpatient clinics with *qigong*-related disorders. By the time a person was admitted to the psychiatric ward, his or her mental distress was so advanced that the initial diagnoses of *qigong*-induced mental disorder or psychotic reaction (*qigong suozhi jingsheng zhangai*) was no longer the primary disorder. Rather, this category seemed to be applied for a specific and limited time to patients whose behavior returned to normal once practice discontinued. Those individuals who continued to be unmanageable and have hallucinations or delusions tended to be classified as schizophrenic or as having reactive psychosis. The psychiatric community throughout China were reluctant to adopt the new category unless patient symptoms clearly corresponded with the Chinese classification. The tenuousness of the category is also due to the possibility that many patients themselves were either mentally ill before taking up the practice or, more likely, reluctant to perceive their condition as a mental disorder.

Although the discussion above addressed the emergence of qigong deviation as a psychiatric phenomenon and its consequences for patients, the existence of deviation in breathing exercises was already a known entity by masters and long-term practitioners. The indigenous phenomenon of deviation was referred to as qigong piancha (qigong deviation, in lay terms) and zhouhuo rumo (a form of qigong possession). Rather than being a psychiatric category of mental illness, deviation was a range of possible disorders that was viewed as part of the long road to progress in one's practice. The popular image of qigong healing and masters in the public sphere supported this belief. After delving into the manifestations of disorder inherent in qigong practice, it is necessary to explore the paradox of why qigong remained so popular despite the occurrence of deviation. To do so, it is necessary to look to the social context and individual reasons for taking up the practice.

Initially, practitioners who experienced qigong deviation remained circumspect, seeking healers in confidence or remaining out of sight in the asylum. In contrast to the silence that surrounded the psychiatric disorder, the public realm was saturated with popular folklore, literature, media, even videos on the common practice of healing through qigong. Sanctioned by the state or by party officials seeking cures and longevity themselves, the thousands that thronged to gymnasiums to participate in the lectures of famous masters ensured the popularity of qigong and the continued publications of best-sellers on the subject.

The many definitions of deviation can be found in the richness of linguistic terms used to describe the phenomenon and accompanying experiences. The formal term of qigong-induced psychosis or psychotic reaction (qigong suozhi jingshen zhangai) used in medical records was never used in everyday life. Instead, a whole variety of terms describing the loss of control fell into three categories: mechanical problems, sensory (primarily auditory and visual) problems, and possession. Phrases such as "I have deviated [wo pian le]" were more likely to be heard to describe the phenomenon. Mechanical problems were common phenomena that all practitioners faced initially during practice. After one first learned how to sense qi (both within and around oneself), the next step involved learning how to move qi throughout one's body. If the qi moved chaotically or moved suddenly to the head (similar to a phenomenon in kundalini yoga) during this step, it was necessary to focus on regaining the balance of elements in one's body.

Closely related to the first group of possible problems, the second category of deviation concerned sensory problems. As qigong practice opened the senses (gong neng tong) to the natural and supernatural worlds, it was not uncommon for individuals to hear voices of masters or alien entities communicating with them. Practitioners of specific forms of qigong often spoke of receiving external information or messages (wai xin) from other entities. Unwanted visions or hallucinations were also part of this stage. As one woman in her midfifties remarked, "I was terrified when I saw the tiger in the corner but I closed my eyes and concentrated on my master's instructions and the image disappeared." Like the experience of qi movement in the body, visual and auditory perceptions were part of the ongoing process in everyday practice. Alleviation required strict discipline and working under the guidance of a master. At this stage practitioners describe the extrasensory experiences as a challenge to overcome and a necessary threshold to higher levels of controlling the qi energy in one's body.

The third category of deviation, qigong possession, can be viewed as a continuum of diverse experiences ranging from simply being controlled by qi to being totally controlled by other entities (spiritual, animal, or human). Practitioners often referred to this phenomenon as zhouhuo rumuo (literally, "to deviate and having demons enter") and considered the condition very serious and requiring expert help in resolving the problem. Whereas the first two categories were considered a natural part of learning, this last category was viewed as an internal struggle with power. Learning to manage the boundaries between self and the external world was essential to achieving balance of life forces within oneself.

Whereas psychiatric responses to deviation involved medicalizing the disorder and treatment within a codified therapeutic order, nonpsychiatric means of intervention were syncretic, often including a mixture of methods taken from traditional Chinese medicine, Daoist healing, and folk tradition. In cases of deviation, practitioners commonly sought the advice of the master from whom they had been taking instructions. For those practitioners who learned from a popular publication instead of learning in the traditional way, seeking a healer involved an informal referral system by word of mouth or through masters. In the 1980s there was significant proliferation of qigong clinics at state institutions as well as the development of private specialists who focused on realigning the qi of wayward practitioners. Throughout city streets one could see posters advertising private practices that involved qi healing for disorders ranging from simple ailments to more difficult cases.

Parallel to my clinical observations in the psychiatric ward, I also attended qigong healings of three types: traditional Chinese medical clinics that specialized in qigong treatment, private qigong clinics, and on-the-spot healing sessions. Most masters used the force of their qi to treat patients. In extreme cases of qigong possession, masters not only used qi healing but also incorporated Daoist exorcism practices. Master Ma, an older woman in her midseventies, practiced every day in a Shanghai park. When I approached her, she playfully asked me how old I thought she was. I truthfully replied that she must be in her midfifties. As it turned out, Ma was trained in qigong and traditional Chinese medicine by her father, who was a traditional healer. This was unusual, because most traditional Chinese medical doctors (lao zhongyi) are male, as the knowledge of healing descended along patrilineal lines. She now operated a private clinic as a subcontractor to a traditional Chinese medicine hospital twice a week on Thursday and Sunday afternoons. When I attended the clinic bath, old and new patients came to her for help. After diagnosing their ailments and giving herbal prescriptions, she would massage and then focus on the area with external qi.

In the psychiatric context, patients who spoke of having the ability to heal themselves or others were told by psychiatrists that they suffered from delusions. The official stance toward qigong healing that was being articulated more clearly in state publications took the extreme view that such healing abilities involved suggestion (anshi) rather than scientific means of curing. The lay notion of healing could not be more different: in the everyday context, self-healing through qigong was both the means as well as the end goal. Deviation and sometimes trance were a natural part of the experience of learning to align the rhythms of one's mind and body with the cosmos rather than remaining within the structures of official time and space.

The casting of popular healing and deviation as false and delusional reveals how healing and power are intimately related. When institutionalized as part of official medicine, the state becomes an official healer with power bestowed on selected representatives. However, the state treats popular healing practices as subversive and superstitious. Healing is thus an arena where the desires of the state for a unified body politic conflict with individual desires and imagination of a personal body. Healing is a medium of power sought by both institutions and individuals.

Warnings about deviation were a traditional part of learning *qigong* with a master. Even if one read about *qigong* and practiced without a master, it was still common knowledge that the practice required a peaceful environment and balanced emotions. My informants all repeated these conditions as necessary to their progress in practice.

Given this paradox of deviation as a natural process with the possibilities of further, more serious consequences, how could *qigong* continue to be such a popular phenomenon? Notions of qi energy are found in diverse traditions, suggesting an interconnected web of meanings that link Chinese traditional medicine, martial arts, spiritual practice, and even contemporary science (especially physics and parapsychology). To understand the reason for its popularity, it is important to look at the significance of miraculous healing in a social and political context devoted to modernization. The popular dimension of *qigong* in urban China is intimately related to economic transformations that took place during the 1980s even though the practice harks back to a traditional era.

The popularity of *qigong* continued to grow because individual and social experiences of daily practice were generally beneficial. *Qigong* practitioners benefited from improved health status and noted having more harmonious family relations. However, unforeseen consequences of deviation transformed initial pleasure and autonomy to excruciating pain and associated discomfort, thus returning the individual to a familial and social matrix of order. Families of those practitioners who lost their balance first sought help through alternative healers and traditional Chinese medicines. The last recourse was the psychiatric hospital, which resonated with social stigma.

Conclusion

Viewing psychiatry in its fragmented history and translations is an exercise in viewing notions of modernity. From the very beginning of this discipline with medical missionaries and even with renewed socialist efforts, psychiatry was always part of state making in the quest for modernity. For psychiatry to be fully translated there needed to be professionals with knowledge that could be replicated through training, sites such as hospitals and clinics, a clientele, and ultimately shared diagnostic categories. With the implementation of such codes, it became possible to engage psychiatry not just in state projects of public health and mental hygiene but also in the making of appropriate subjects with healthy minds and bodies. Thus psychiatry depends on continued practices of professionalization and translation in the transformation of disorderly to orderly bodies. In mapping disorder, I traced the development of recent Chinese psychiatric categories as they were contested in multiple contexts—not just in the psychiatric realm but also within families and in public arenas. Thus, in spite of the globalizing discourses of psychiatry, differences still matter and exist within the very structures that try to erase them.

Notes

The author would like to thank Lydia Liu for her encouragement and two anonymous reviewers for their insightful comments.

1   For a full elaboration on the subject, see Lydia Liu, *Translingual Practice*.
2   For detailed studies, see John Jay Kao, *Three Millennia of Chinese Psychiatry*.
3   For Peter Parker, see Larissa Heinrich in this volume.
4   K. Chimin Wong and Lien-Teh Wu, *History of Chinese Medicine*, 361.
5   Ibid., 709.
6   For an informed study, see David Strand, *Rickshaw Beijing*.
7   For a recent study, see Neil Diamant, "China's 'Great Confinement'?"
8   Robert S. Chin and Ai-Li S. Chin, *Psychological Research in Communist China*.
9   Tsung-Yi Lin and Leon Eisenberg, *Mental Health Planning for One Billion People*.
10 See Sing Lee, "Cultures in Psychiatric Nosology."
11 Ann Anagnost, *National Past-Times*.
12 See Arthur Kleinman, *Social Origins of Distress and Disease*.
13 Cited in Yan Heqin, "The Necessity of Retaining the Diagnostic Concept of Neurasthenia."
14 American Psychiatric Association, DSM-IV, 847.
15 See Qiong Zhang in this volume for a study of the earlier interest in the notion of qi shown by the Jesuit missionaries.
16 The labels of "unscientific" or "false" were often met with derision by qigong masters and practitioners. The common reply was that the official forms of qigong were actually false, and that true and authentic forms of qigong were maintained and passed on by masters who did not emerge in public or become licensed.

PART 4

Language and the

Production of

Universal Knowledge

Q. S. Tong   *The Bathos of a Universalism:*

I. A. Richards and His Basic English

I. A. Richards is now remembered primarily as the inventor of "practical criticism," a critical practice that derives its name from his influential book bearing that title. Although subsequent critical developments have called into question its ideology and its methodology, there is little doubt about the importance of Richards as a critic, who almost single-handedly institutionalized critical practice in the first few decades of this century. Perhaps more than anyone else, as Paul Bové says, Richards "deserves the title of 'father' of academic criticism,"[1] whether that title is meant to be an encomium or an irony or anything else. But given this preeminence, it is impossible not to be struck by the conspicuous absence of scholarly attention to his experience of China, as a country as well as a cultural phenomenon, and in particular to his passionate and unflagging efforts to promote and teach Basic English there. A substantial part of his "splendid career," as his student William Empson called it,[2] is bound up with China, an apparently rather odd locale figuring prominently in his intellectual landscape that is at the same time inhabited by, for example, Coleridge.[3] Richards visited China about half a dozen times; the total length of time he spent there is four and a half years, spaced out over a period of half a century from the late twenties to the late seventies, a period in which China went through radical transformations.

This is rather remarkable. No Western man of letters of comparable status, before or after him, has ever visited China so frequently and spent such an extended length of time there.[4] China, for Richards, was not just an imaginary locale, a spatially distanced object suitable only for philosophical meditation, as it had been for a considerable number of prominent thinkers before him in the West. His experience of China, as he himself once said, was "one of the things that shaped my life."[5] That this substantial and important China dimension in Richards's professional and intellectual configuration should have received so little academic attention illustrates how short the historical memories of our profession can be, and how easily moments of history can be effaced or self-effaced for reasons not altogether self-evident.

Richards's abiding interest in China was sustained by his vision of Basic English as a world language. The very idea of world language might make one jittery today, but we must not forget that it was proposed *not* so very long ago, and that between the mid-1930s and the mid-1940s Basic English was an influential movement. Although C. K. Ogden was the "inventor" of Basic, it was Richards who went to China to promote and teach Basic. He was at once an ambassador, a teacher, and a practitioner of Basic English, and his academic standing in those years put him in a position that allowed him to advocate Basic with unique vigor and force. As embodied in those trips he made to China, his passion for the country and his sense of the mission to eliminate misunderstandings in human communication, which, for him, often constituted a direct cause of brutal war and disastrous human self-destruction, inspire respect and admiration. But the very fact that he was unaware of, or unwilling to accept, the ultimate failure of Basic even at the end of his life imparts a sense of him as one who was historically displaced, bearing a striking resemblance to the ethos of the nineteenth century.

How should one understand and describe him? Is he a sinophile or an orientalist? a romantic idealist or a cultural missionary?

Early Encounters

Richards was first brought into contact with Chinese culture by G. L. Dickinson, whose *Modern Symposium* was, Richards tells us, "a sort of Bible" for him. But it was when he was working in collaboration with Ogden and James Wood on *The Foundations of Aesthetics* (1922) that he became attracted to "the multiple potentialities of Chinese phrases." Richards recalled many years later the excitement with which they played with those Chinese phrases: "We compared different translations of them together in a kind of rapture. It was [Wood] who brought the Chung Yung [zhongyong] into our *Foundations*."[6] Although Richards's interest in Chinese culture at this stage was perhaps no more than an intellectual curiosity, arising largely from the exotic appeal of the protean and unpredictable behavior of Chinese thought and language, his subsequent commitment to a study of *Mencius* in Beijing in the late twenties placed China more permanently in his intellectual topography. The result of the study is *Mencius on the Mind* (1932). This work is an extended commentary on the difficulties involved in translating passages from *Mencius* into English, which are attributable to the differences in the mode of thinking between the Chinese mind and its Western counterpart as well as the differences in the ways the Chinese language and Western languages work.

The irony about this *Mencius* project is a familiar one, an irony that characterizes much of the Western intellectual representation of China in the nineteenth century. Like some of his European predecessors such as Humboldt and Hegel, who commented on the relation between thought and language in the Chinese tradition, rather sweepingly and often with that familiar tone of authority derived from a sense of complete self-confidence and self-righteousness, Richards did not have a working knowledge of the Chinese language. Of course, direct contact with Chinese thought and practice in the nineteenth century had been very difficult, but perhaps neither was first-hand knowledge of China considered essential for those thinkers to advance more general arguments and observations. Richards, however, did not hesitate to acknowledge his inadequacy in the Chinese language, and as if to counterbalance this weakness, he actually went to China, working with *Mencius* specialists on the *Mencius* text.[7] For Richards, in fact, this project was not primarily for the purpose of presenting to the Western reader one more text of canonical Confucianism. "Here was I," he tells us, "doing my best to take part in academic activities which illustrated incomprehension—unknown, unrecognized failure of understanding and on such a scale, always hitting you. I felt I must do something."[8] In that sense, the project is, perhaps more than anything else, a statement that difficulties arising from transcultural communication can be overcome and the diversity of cultures can be brought into a harmonious body of knowledge. What mattered for him in the whole experiment was not just the diversity of textual possibilities that were opened up in *Mencius*, but also the personnel diversity represented in the team formed for the project involving himself and four Chinese specialists. Visualizing the scene of Richards working with his Chinese colleagues together in Beijing in the late twenties, one would have a picture capturing an interesting moment in one of the most exciting historical periods in modern China.[9]

Mencius on the Mind, therefore, is at once a demonstration of his research and a statement that emphasizes the importance of bringing into *direct* contact cultures that hitherto have been separated. The publication of the book in 1932 marked an important step in Richards's pursuit of the problem of "the meaning of meaning," presenting, in detail and with specific examples from *Mencius*, the concept of "multiple definition" that had been first formulated in *The Meaning of Meaning*. The principle of multiple definition is, as Richards says, also a "technique" that attempts to grasp the whole range of meanings of a word, a sentence, a paragraph, or even a whole text, which can be juxtaposed for comparison. The *Mencius* project, therefore, may well be appropriately considered an extension of his practical criticism into the area of translation as a form of cross-cultural communication.

It should be noted, however, that despite its apparent liberal spirit, the semantic field that is created with the principle of multiple definition is severely circumscribed. The multiplicity of meaning exhibits ramifications of an underlying totality of truth that can be understood only with a recognition of its formal diversity in the first place. And the recognition of this diversity involves not an insistence on the differences between separate cultural experiences in linguistic terms, but rather a reconfirmation of their fundamental commensurability. Translation, for Richards, is never merely an act that puts one piece of knowledge into a comprehensible linguistic form. His purpose in translating *Mencius*, as mentioned above, is precisely to annihilate communicative barriers that prevent meaningful and productive intellectual interactions between vastly different cultures. What he is concerned with is the question of what a man of letters such as he could do to cancel the linguistic differences in order to reach a thorough cultural understanding. In this sense, Jacques Lacan's satirical dismissal of Richards's experiment with *Mencius* is not all to the point.[10] For Richards, universality of cultures is ontologically veritable, even though they are separated from one another by their own linguistic boundaries. Therefore, for the lofty mission to restore human linguistic conditions to that pristine unity and integrity, a world language would seem not just a dream that many had wished to fulfill, but a necessity that had acquired renewed urgency for the self-definition and self-cultivation of our humanity.

The curse of Babel must be lifted. And the story of Basic English begins.

Basic in China

The genesis of Basic goes back to Richards's first collaboration with Ogden on their influential book *The Meaning of Meaning* (1923). Richards recalled that while they were working on the "Definition" chapter in that book, the same words kept coming up. This suggested to them that "with under a thousand words you can say everything."[11] Basic English, as defined by Richards, is then "English made simple by limiting the number of its words to 850, and by cutting down the rules for using them to the smallest number necessary for the clear statement of ideas."[12] Despite its skeletal structure, and with only 850 words including 18 verbs, Basic English, Richards claims, has "unlimited range" of expression, and "it is ready to hand now for the purposes of business, trade, industry, science, medical works, the arts of living generally, all the exchanges of knowledge, belief, opinion, and news which are man's chief interest."[13] Although Basic was perhaps a chance discovery, a by-product of *The Meaning of Meaning*, Ogden took an obsessive interest in the issue of world language. He read John Wilkins and Leibniz on the subject,[14] and in the making of Basic he was inspired by "suggestions about language made all through the history of English thought from Bacon to Jeremy Bentham."[15] One can imagine the excitement that Richards and Ogden experienced when the idea of Basic as an international language was actually put into an apparently workable system. Indeed, who could resist the idea of such a world language, so simple and so easy to learn, and yet so much more natural than an artificial world language such as Esperanto? We all are probably ready to harbor some utopian illusions from time to time.

Richards's faith in Basic was strong, and his commitment to it was total, so total, in fact, that he would later abandon altogether literature, an area in which he once enjoyed astonishing success and prestige. From 1928 onwards, Richards became increasingly involved in the Basic project. In his academic prime, his rather dramatic decision "to back out of literature, completely, as a subject, and go into elementary education" is profoundly suggestive.[16] What could be a more thorough demonstration of one's faith in and commitment to a course than a complete conversion to it? The Basic project redefined Richards as an educator, or rather, with it he reinvented himself as that.

Favorable and supportive responses to Basic were prompt, in particular from the United States. Basic brought Richards to Harvard in 1939, and the Rockefeller Foundation provided him with an endowment for three years, allowing him to produce "some Basic English texts" and to train "some people" in this field.[17] Richards's most important contribution to Basic is, however, associated with China. It was Richards who almost single-handedly created a Basic movement in China. One might say that Cambridge, England, is the birthplace of Basic; Cambridge, New England, the site of its manufacture; and China the laboratory of its experimental application. Indeed, what could be a more powerful demonstration of Basic's universality than its success in China, a country that had then, as now, the largest population in the world and a language so fundamentally different from European alphabetic languages? "China's one of the few places," Richards once said, "where you could really do something."[18]

Things seemed to be going well at first for Basic in China. Thanks to Russo's well-documented book on Richards, we are able to be a bit more historically specific here, presenting in some detail the story of Basic in China in the mid-1930s.[19] The Orthological (Basic English) Institute of China (Zhonguo zhenzi xuehui, as it is called in Chinese) was established in 1935, and R. D. Jameson, an American professor at Qinghua University, became its first director. The Institute published Richards's *First Book of English for Chinese Learners* in 1938. Prior to that, Y. R. Chao, who met Richards at Harvard in 1916 and later became his colleague for a while at Qinghua University, produced "a textbook of Basic English, for which [he] also spoke, trying to use a non-American accent, for a set of records." This textbook with accompanying records came out in 1934.[20] George Yeh (Ye Gongchao), another colleague of Richards at Qinghua University, reviewed Richards's *Basic in Teaching: East and West* and contemplated possible ways of applying Basic English at the university level.[21]

Between 1936 and 1937, Richards made two visits to China, and these two years were an important time for his Basic mission. Richards demonstrated his amazing administrative abilities and skills in these two visits. He negotiated with Chinese officials, organizing teaching programs, arranging textbooks and other teaching materials to be in place before teaching started, requesting funds from the Rockefeller Foundation in New York for the extension of his stay in China. He designed and mounted a course that aimed at training secondary school teachers of English in the summer of 1936; about one hundred teachers enrolled in the course. In May 1937, Richards "presented his case before a high-ranking government committee meeting in Nanking, with the minister, Wang Shih-chie, presiding." His "program for training middle school teachers in Basic, the start to the much-awaited nationwide experiment," was in effect approved by the Chinese government. This official endorsement was exactly what he wanted. Richards was thrilled and sent his wife, in Beijing at the time, a telegram informing her of the good news: "HAVE EVERYTHING I WANT. SOMETHING MUST BE WRONG." [22]

Both Richards and Ogden had long realized the crucial importance of creating a solid institutional basis and of winning the Chinese government's support for the Basic campaign in China. Ogden, for example, outlined clearly their strategy: "Special attention will be given to the needs of the education authorities in China . . . and Dr. I. A. Richards . . . is pushing forward with suggestions for Middle Schools." [23] The establishment of the Orthological Institute in Beijing in 1935 was the first step toward a more permanent home for Basic in China; to have won the full endorsement of the Ministry of Education of the Chinese government was a tremendous boost to the Basic movement. The Committee on the Teaching of English in Middle Schools, under the Ministry of Education, made specific recommendations for teaching and learning Basic in middle schools and proposed practical ways to implement these recommendations. It is not difficult to see Richards's influence on the Committee's "Resolution." On the general objective of English teaching, the Resolution emphasizes (1) "The modernization of expressional habits with regard to thought, outlook, attitude, feeling, etc."; (2) "Vocational and practical uses"; and (3) "Cultural uses." On a specific point about teaching vocabulary, it decrees: "The selection of words should be limited so far as possible to *picturable* and tangible objects and to acts which can be easily performed by the teacher and learner; and . . . preference should be given to those words which have regular inflection and regular spelling" (my italics). On the issue of personnel training, it recommends that "teachers of good record who have been in service for five years should be released for at least six months, with full pay, to gain refreshment and stimulation through work in designated centers," and that "for the preparation of well-qualified men to serve as future university professors in charge of the training of teachers of English in the middle school . . . they may be sent abroad to carefully chosen centres (such as the Institute of Education, London, England) to receive further professional training." [24]

The acceptance of Richards's proposal for Basic in middle schools by the Chinese government was indeed the climactic moment for Basic in China. However, immediately following the climax came the bathos. Despite the official endorsement of Basic, and despite the strong "moral support" that Richards had received from such prominent scholars as Hu Shi and Y. R. Chao, Basic, after the Sino-Japanese War, never rose to its antebellum glory. Basic English was never practiced on a nationwide level as the Committee recommended. The speed with which Basic disappeared into oblivion from the China scene is as astonishing as its dramatic prewar success.

Time moved on as it does. But the relentless progression of time had made no dent in Richards's faith in Basic. In 1973, he predicted, "In about the next ten years there'll be a need for it, particularly in connection with China, because China's greatest shortage at the moment is capable speakers of even moderate English." [25] To get things moving in China, fifty thousand copies of *English through Pictures* (Books 1 and 2) were shipped to Beijing in 1974.[26] But the response was hardly encouraging. Acknowledging the receipt of the books, the head of the Western Languages Department at Peking University wrote to Richards on 2 July that year: "Your 'English through Pictures,' Books I (23,200 copies) and II (24,700 copies) and the related films, slides and other teaching materials have come to hand. Some of your works and translations have also been received. Both render valuable help to our understanding of the linguistic research you have been engaged in. We take much interest in your work."[27] There is a peculiar irony here: emphasizing their interest in Richards's research in linguistics, instead of responding to Basic English as he was expected to, the department head seemed to have missed the whole point. But that was during the Cultural Revolution. Richards's faith in Basic brought him to China for the last time in 1979. Since then, however, English learning in China has taken entirely new directions, and Basic as an international language or even as a second language in China is no longer a relevant issue.

Language and Modernity

One might say, as Richards did, that the failure of Basic in China was due to the outbreak of the Sino-Japanese War in 1937.[28] However, there had been highly critical voices against Basic well before that. Chen Yuan, a Chinese sociolinguist, was quick to point out the imperialistic overtones of the very label for the movement. Basic is an acronym for five English words: British, American, Scientific, International, Commercial.[29] The whole Basic enterprise, therefore, sounded imperialistic to some Chinese scholars at the time. Chen Yuan recalls that there were articles critical of Basic published in Chinese newspapers as early as 1933, and he himself contributed to this critical campaign against Basic, dismissing it as a pidgin mixture that could only impair the human intellect.[30]

To recapitulate historical debates over the linguistic ramifications of Basic reaches beyond the scope of this paper.[31] The pertinent question here is why Basic failed in China. The question becomes all the more pertinent when it is placed against the intellectual background of the momentous language reform movement in China in the first few decades of this century. What Bertrand Russell once called the "problem of China" in the early twenties is, in the ultimate analysis, a problem of China's modernity. The modernization of the Chinese language, in particular its writing system, is an integral and vitally important part of the intellectual field of discursive events that took place during the May Fourth period and the years following it. But its significance as a prominent thesis of the new cultural movement as a whole at the time has not yet received as much attention as it deserves, in particular in terms of its tremendous impact on the shaping of China's modern consciousness. To some extent, linguistic reform had been in the vanguard of what Richards calls the "Chinese Renaissance";[32] in that sense, the search for a modern China was in the first place a search for a new national language.

As is well-known, the language reform movement was primarily concerned with, among other things, whether or not the Chinese writing system should be phoneticized for a total correspondence between writing and speaking. The transcription of written characters in phonetic symbols is by no means a modern scholarly effort in China. It goes back to Matteo Ricci, who first worked out, in the early seventeenth century, a scheme by which the sound system of Chinese characters could be romanized. Early efforts to phoneticize written Chinese were largely for the purpose of making the study of the Chinese language less daunting for Western missionaries, as born out in the title of the French missionary Nicolas Trigault's book on the romanization of written Chinese characters, *Aids to Listening and Reading for the Western Scholar* (*Xiru ermuzi*, 1626). Toward the end of the nineteenth century, however, the reform of the Chinese language increasingly became part of a much larger intellectual quest for a modern identity for China. As if responding to the repeated critiques of the Chinese language by some major European philologists and philosophers in the nineteenth century, a large number of Chinese intellectuals joined this extraordinary project of language reform.

Radical suggestions were made. Qian Xuantong may be invoked here as a typical voice in the campaign for language reform. His advocacy for a total abolishment of the Chinese language and his recommendation to adopt an alphabetic world language such as Esperanto as a lingua franca in China embody fairly well, on the linguistic front, the general sentiments of the new cultural movement at the time: "To abolish Confucianism and to eliminate Taoism is a fundamental way to prevent the fall of China and to allow the Chinese to become a civilized nation in the twentieth century. But a more fundamental way than this is to abolish the written Chinese language [*hanwen*], in which Confucian thought and fallacious Taoist sayings are recorded. After the abolishment of the written Chinese language . . . in my view, the artificial language Esperanto should be adopted: its grammar is simple, its pronunciation unified, and its etymology pure."[33]

However, when he was later convinced of the possibility and practicability of creating a romanized system of writing, he amended his view and supported the experiment of romanizing the Chinese writing system, suggesting, though, that a foreign language be used in the interim. His recommendation was French.[34] Qian's abhorrence of written characters is extreme but, as mentioned above, not untypical of the general intellectual sentiments of the May Fourth era. Looking back at the language reform movement, one is necessarily struck by the intellectual radicalism displayed in its rejection of the Chinese language, in particular its writing system. Due to the constraints of the space and scope of this paper, it is not possible to evoke more examples, abundant as they are, to exhibit the amazing extent to which written Chinese characters were held to be a major origin of the evil that had brought about the paralysis of Chinese society at all levels at the turn of the century.[35] In comparison with such radicalism, the relegation of the Chinese language to the category of the nonorganic and therefore inferior linguistic system in the discourse of nineteenth-century Western comparative philology, as I have discussed elsewhere, would seem all too gentle a critique.[36]

It is evident that many at that time were either unaware of or unable to come to terms with the complex network of relations between the traditional and the modern, between the Chinese and the Western, which were locked in a dynamic process of "dissolving," "diffusing," and "dissipating" one another.[37] This complexity of relations, both historical and theoretical, calls into question what is meant exactly by the concept of "modernity" itself. It is helpful to recall here de Man's reflection on the issue of "literary modernity." At some moments in history, de Man observes, "the topic 'modernity' might be used just as an attempt at self-definition, as a way of diagnosing one's own present. This can happen during periods of considerable inventiveness, periods that seem, looking back, to have been unusually productive. At such actual or imaginary times, modernity would not be a value in itself, but would designate a set of values that exist independently of their modernity."[38] Modernity therefore is not necessarily a clearly definable category bearing ontological significance, but one that is frequently evoked as a means to self-comprehension and self-definition. Nietzsche's comments, quoted by de Man, are worth repeating in part here:

> [The critical student of the past] must possess the strength, and must at times apply this strength, to the destruction and dissolution of the past in order to be able to live. He achieves this by calling the past into court, putting it under indictment, and finally condemning it; any past, however, deserves to be condemned, for such is the condition of human affairs that they are ruled by violence and weakness. . . . the past is judged critically, attacked at its very roots with a sharp knife, and brutally cut down, regardless of established pieties. This is always a dangerous process, dangerous for life itself. Men and eras that serve life in this manner, by judging and destroying the past, are always dangerous and endangered. For we are inevitably the result of earlier generations and thus the result of their mistakes, their passions and aberrations, even of their crimes.[39]

One of the dangers in denying China a national language indigenous in origin, as some came to realize, would be the further cultural disintegration of the country. Indeed, what has often been less emphasized with regard to the language reform movement in the early twentieth century is its underlying political agenda. In the call for the modernization (more appropriately here, perhaps, Westernization) of the Chinese language, there was the subterranean movement of an uneasy consciousness that national unity was defined, to a great extent, by the linguistic unity of the Chinese language. "Unity of the Country" and "Unity of the Language" were a pair of rubrics that appeared frequently in various language reform proposals at the time. To unify the sound system and to match it with the uniformity of the writing system within the Chinese language were, for some intellectuals at least, not just for the purpose of taming recalcitrant written characters and making them more accessible for the general public. The abundance of dialects in Chinese society seriously threatened the formation of an unmistakable national linguistic identity and undermined the unity of the whole country, which already had been made vulnerable enough with the demise of the Qing Dynasty and increasingly aggressive involvement of foreign powers in China. Speaking about the importance of a unified Chinese language in 1920, Cai Yuanpei had this to say: "Why should we learn Chinese? First for the defense of the country from foreign aggression; second for the unity of the country within its own boundaries. At present, universalism has been gradually getting prevalent, and it seems to some that there is no need for national defense. But ours is a weak country, and there are powerful neighbors, we have to be careful. The fragmentation of the country, such as boundaries among provinces and gaps between South and North, results from the dialects. . . . The disunity between speech and writing has numerous undesirable consequences."[40] The nationalist undertones in this passage are unmistakable. And with this linguistic nationalism emerges the paradox of the language reform movement. Whereas to construct a total correspondence between speech and writing is crucial for the forging and consolidating of China's modern identity, to "modernize" the Chinese language by replacing it with a world language or, to a lesser degree, by phoneticizing its writing system is precisely to resist that identity. It should generate some painful self-reflections for those May Fourth intellectuals to have fully realized the implications of this dilemma.

Although I am not concerned with the issue of the modern Chinese language per se, it is of relevance to observe here that the failure of the campaign for alphabetic writing in China should perhaps be considered in terms of the dilemma the language reform movement found itself in at the very outset. If the alphabetic system of writing, such as *pinyin wenzi*, created from within the Chinese language itself could not replace the existing writing system, it is hard to conceive that a totally artificial language such as Esperanto could uproot the Chinese language, which had been in use for thousands of years. It is still harder to conceive that a foreign language could operate, as Qian Xuantong once suggested, as a secondary linguistic system along with spoken Chinese, whether it were French or (Basic) English.

Richards, with his intellectual sensitivity, saw the problems the new cultural movement had encountered. And his attitude to the radicalism of the "Chinese Renaissance," not surprisingly, was rather ambiguous. For him, the unmediated introduction of Western thought that flooded the Chinese intellectual scene manifested a "pragmatism," which had rather violently sidelined the humanistic tradition that had as its focus of attention the "Pursuit of Truth." [41] Hu Shi's argument that "Chinese Philosophy has nothing to contribute to modern thought, and that it has merely a historical interest," was subtly brushed aside by him.[42] In the domain of linguistic practice, Richards was particularly concerned with the impurity of the vernacular that was replete with the intrusions of foreign linguistic elements. "Since Dr. Sheh [sic, presumably Hu Shi] launched the movement for using the vernacular in place of the literary language," observes Richards, "Chinese has been going through many sudden changes. Styles have been tried which are hardly comprehensible without some understanding of the foreign constructions — English or Russian, for example — they are borrowing." [43] The earlier cacophony in Chinese expression embodies the anxiety of the Chinese language itself, as it fumbled its way toward the formation of its identity.

Richards's solution to this problem is: Gain knowledge of Western ideas, attitudes, and so on, "through some form of Western Language. In practice this means some form of English." He argues that the "only way in which false and misleading *approximations* to Western units of meaning with Chinese 'equivalents' can be avoided is by giving these meanings through, and together with, an apparatus for comparing complex meanings — through an explicit analytic language. Such a language is Basic English." [44] This is in effect a recommendation for a Western language (here Basic English) as a second language, a recommendation that Qian Xuantong had made. What is revealed in Richards's suggestion is not only his conviction, as always, in the importance of Basic, but also an inherent conception that a certain body of knowledge can only be effectively learned in the language in which it was first formulated. Basic can attenuate daunting linguistic difficulties encountered by a foreigner, a Chinese in this case, in his or her experience of the original English text and can smooth his or her way into its world of ideas. At the same time, Basic provides the most economical way to protect the purity of Western knowledge and to prevent it from being distorted when brought into China. What Richards seems to suggest here is precisely the incommensurability of languages in communication, an idea apparently contradictory to his holistic view on human minds. But to look at the issue from a slightly different perspective, we may find that there is no fundamental contradiction here at all. What Richards has attempted is not a universalism in the abstract. It is not, for that matter, a utopian universal framework that is the outgrowth of a groundless romantic fancy. It is a universalism that is grounded in a concretized and practicable linguistic system. Basic, therefore, is not just an expression and manifestation of his universalism, but also a medium in which that universalism is written, comprehended, and practiced.

As Richards diagnosed, embedded in the attempt at a self-definition of China's modernity in the May Fourth movement is a pragmatic attitude toward Western culture. However, what Richards fails to see, or is not ready to admit, is that the overwhelming call for reforming the Chinese language at the time is largely a *strategic* move, and that the acceptance of Western languages, in particular English, as a way toward a full knowledge of the West should be understood in such a pragmatic framework. The universalism of Basic, as that of Esperanto, fundamentally contradicts the May Fourth intellectual pursuit of China's modern identity. Due to its inherent linguistic imperfection derived from its skeletal nature, Basic could not perform the task of transmitting Western knowledge in its full form, which was much needed and desired in China's reinventing of itself. Richards did not see this restriction of Basic that would beset its promotion in China, but his Chinese collaborator T. T. Hsui told him with complete candor that there was no real interest in Basic in China unless it was designed as an introduction to full English. In a letter to Richards dated 11 April 1939, Hsui advised Richards to pay attention to the gap between Basic and general English: "It will be poor policy for us to neglect this problem in China, as in this country there is and will be no one (with the exception of poor lunatics like me) who will even take an interest in Basic for itself, unless it is offered as a better system for beginning the attempt to master the English language."[45] Like Esperanto, Basic could not be instituted as a second language in China, and it is most ironical that it could not even replace normal English as a foreign language, though it might serve as a step toward it. This double failure of Basic in China can hardly be considered the result of unpredictable historical contingencies such as the Sino-Japanese war.

The Politics of Basic

Since the publication of *The Meaning of Meaning* (1923), both Richards and Ogden had been working on the full range of implications suggested in the book. Three years later, the second edition of the book was issued, and along with revisions and amendments, they added a preface. What is particularly notable in this preface is their suggestion that "an Institute of Linguistic Research with headquarters in Geneva, New York, and Peking" should be established.[46] In the preface to the third edition (1930), there is no further mention of it, but it is indicated that Richards's experience in Beijing as visiting professor (1929–1930) made "the need for further work upon," among other things, this Institute of Linguistic Research "appear still more urgent."[47]

This ambitious plan to establish an international Institute of Linguistic Research joining the three continents never materialized. However, Richards's vision of a geolinguistic unity would readily lead to the idea of geopolitical unity; indeed, it would soon catapult his linguistic universalism into the political realm. His postwar book *Nations and Peace* (1947), though largely forgotten now, is an important one, at least for my purpose, and will put the ideology of Basic in perspective. The book is written in Basic English, with typical Richardsian illustrations on almost every page and presented pretty much in the way today's comic books are. But the presentation is in itself a statement. The book was written for two reasons, Richards tells us: "The first is our desperate need to think more clearly about what we are doing. The second has to do with language. We can no longer afford unnecessary misunderstanding. A common second language — easy for all and clear to everybody — has become an obvious part of the campaign against disaster. I wanted to try out an extremely simple form of English on the greatest and most complex current questions."[48]

One of these "greatest and most complex current questions" with which Richards is profoundly concerned is related to the forces that might hold a nation together. He argues that some of the general conditions, such as "common history, language, arts and ways of living," which are usually associated with the formation of national identity are not the defining, or even important, features of a nation. What holds a nation together, according to him, are our feelings of "self-love" and "fear of others" (34–35), which are subject to subtle and skillful exploitation by the totalitarian government of the nation in question and can be readily transformed into a misguided nationalism. Richards does not make any substantive distinction between the notion of nation and nationalism; as a matter of fact, the very notion of nation, he argues, is the product of our own misunderstanding of nation (79). As much of the trouble in the present world is, he claims, rooted in the division of nations, he believes that the ultimate solution to the problem of the fragmentation of the world is to eliminate the boundaries between all nations and to reconstitute the world by dissolving nations into a supernation and establishing a world government, which will oversee the operation of all individual nations.

What Richards envisages is a world organization that, unlike the UN, has the power to make law and to make nations keep the law (109). It will be the "great nations" on earth that will have special responsibility for instituting such a world organization. And what country is more qualified than the United States to lead the way for accomplishing such a task? "The United States has today so much power that it is responsible for guiding all the peoples on earth to World Government. Other nations are waiting" (145). Not only major (primarily Western) countries (excluding, of course, Germany and Japan) such as "Britain, Canada, Australia, New Zealand, France . . . would be ready to go with the United States" in moving forward for this goal, but also China and India would support this "World Government" (146). And all these nations "are waiting for the government of the United States to say the word and make the offer of power to a World Government" (147).

One could easily laugh off all this today. But surely Richards was not the only one to take it seriously half a century ago. And it is in relation to this political globalization that Richards believes Basic would have an important role to play. Basic, for him, is the most suitable candidate for the official language of this world government, its superiority derived from the superiority of the English language itself. The fact that one could not possibly fail to notice, Richards reminds us, is that English was, around 1941, "either the mother tongue or the government language of over 600 million of the world's two billion people. And it [was] a secondary language of many additional millions. No other language [approached] this position." [49] In a sharp reversal of the prevalent nineteenth-century view that the superiority of the Germanic languages lies in their grammatical inflection, Richards claims that the noninflectional system is precisely what makes English a better language: "A richly inflected language like Russian or German—teeming with random case endings and moods and tenses—is far harder for us to learn than a regular uninflected language like English, which does its grammatical work almost entirely through its logical word order." [50] A discernible strand of nationalist feeling slips in here, and the old rivalry between German and English emerges from historical unconsciousness. For it is in this context that Richards mentions Rudolph Hess's "prophesy" in 1940 that when the Nazis won the war, they would see to it that "English [became] no more than an unimportant Germanic dialect." [51] The dominance of the English language in today's world, Richards concludes, "is political and rests finally on the steel shoulders of the British and American fleets." [52]

But there are still more reasons for Basic to be adopted as a world language. English is not just the language of Britain and North America but also the language of science and international commerce. The range of implications of what "Basic" represents—"British," "American," "Scientific," "International," and "Commercial"—is now fully illuminated. It is here that Basic reveals its disturbing side that differs from its self-claimed idealistic origin, and it is also here that Basic starts to open itself up for political appropriation and exploitation. Although there are good reasons to believe that Richards might still be pursuing universal human values in the Western idealistic tradition, Churchill, with his unique political shrewdness, saw a different use of Basic. "The widespread use of [Basic English]," remarked Churchill, "would be a gain to us far more durable and fruitful than the annexation of great provinces. It would also fit in with my ideas of closer union with the United States by making it even more worth while to belong to the English-speaking club." [53] He recommended that a committee of ministers be established to study ways to promote Basic English.[54]

On 6 September 1943, on the occasion of receiving an honorary degree from Harvard, Churchill went public in his speech recommending Basic:

> The gift of a common tongue is a priceless inheritance and it may well some day become the foundation of a common citizenship. I like to think of British and Americans moving about freely over each other's wide estates with hardly a sense of being foreigners to one another. But I do not see why we should not try to spread our common language even more widely throughout the globe and, without seeking selfish advantage over any, possess ourselves of this invaluable amenity and birthright.

He continued, paying compliments to those involved in the Basic project at Harvard:

> I do not wish to exaggerate, but you are the head-stream of what might well be a mighty fertilizing and health-giving river. It would certainly be a grand convenience for us all to be able to move freely about the world—as we shall be able to do more freely than ever before as the science of the world develops—be able to move freely about the world, and be able to find everywhere a medium, albeit primitive, of intercourse and understanding. Might it not also be an advantage to many races, and an aid to the building-

up of our new structure for preserving peace? All these are possibilities, and I say: "Let us go into this together. Let us have another Boston Tea Party about it." [55]

Churchill's speech put Basic English into the international spotlight and made Richards a University Professor at Harvard shortly afterwards.[56] But unlike Richards, who advocated the universal applicability of Basic both at home and abroad, Churchill's idea of Basic was for a more specific use: it was meant for those "who do not have the good fortune to know the English language to participate more easily in our society." [57] What is revealed here is so self-evident that it is perhaps not worth pursuing further. Richards's Basic is now turned into nothing but a political scheme, in a further departure from its self-declared idealistic origin. To some extent, the causes of its degeneration were rooted in its own inherent flaws, both linguistic and ideological, which were ready to be politically appropriated for cultural domination.

Some Reflections

It has been generally recognized that the cultural consequences of Western imperialist expansion have been far more inveterate and enduring than, say, economic and military ones. The end of the Western colonial era has put in sharper focus the consequences of Western cultural expansion that played an active role at an earlier stage of the colonial and imperialist practices. In India, for example, "the Eurocentric literary curriculum of the nineteenth century was less a statement of the superiority of the Western tradition than a vital, active instrument of Western hegemony in concert with commercial expansionism and military action." [58] More generally, however, the extent to which Western cultural resources have been put to use for the purpose of influence and domination has yet to be thoroughly scrutinized. Precisely because cultural domination is more enduring and in its form more evasive, a recognition of the complexities *within* its own discourse becomes more urgent before a meaningful critique of it can be advanced. That Western cultural domination is still an overt force in many parts of our world after the demise of the colonial enterprise must be at least partly attributable to its particular patterns and ways of self-perpetuation and self-propagation. To situate cultural domination indiscriminately in colonial discourse as part of political coercion runs the risk of totalizing discursive colonial practices and confining these practices only to former "colonies."

China stands here as a different case, and Richards and his Basic English in relation to China afford for critical inquiry a unique example of a form of linguistic expansionism. Although embedded in Basic is an ideology that runs fundamentally against true democratic values, it is important to recognize the complexities of Richards's idealism and to make a distinction between the ideology of his linguistic universalism and the political appropriation of that linguistic universalism. The form and pattern this idealism adopts in practice register, at its incipient stage, a beguiled universalism that does not divulge so much an intention of coercive imposition as a self-righteousness about a course considered immeasurably worth pursuing. There is therefore in the whole enterprise of Basic English what de Man would call, in a different context, a "blindness," a blindness that could subject its idealism and universalism to political appropriation and exploitation. Admittedly, it is of vital importance to be fully aware of the implications and potentialities of this unqualified and unchecked form of universalism, for there is no absolute distinction between cultural holism and political totalitarianism. But it is equally important, I argue, to recognize their differences. For one could otherwise assume a transparent and direct passage from an idea to a practice, reducing thereby the complex field of discursive practices that have brought about a certain historical phenomenon to a simple cause-and-effect procedure. The conservative ideology of organic aesthetics, for example, has long been considered an intellectual source, which gave rise, "especially in Germany, to an extremely nationalistic attitude toward their fatherland." [59] But what would be the philosophical origin of British imperialism or the intellectual source of British colonialism? The point here is that all historical forms of intellectual idealism should be considered *historical* products, and they should be studied, examined, and interrogated under the historical conditions that have shaped or influenced or altered their formulations.

At the same time Basic had its early success in China, Chinese society was paralyzed as a result of the combined forces of the decrepitude of its tradition and the aggression of the West. The advent of the issue of China's modernity at the turn of the century was a manifestation of the deeply experienced sense of national crisis resulting from its demoralizing encounters with the West. And what Chinese intellectuals were concerned with at the time was how to Westernize China in the *absence* of an absolutely dominating Western power on the Chinese scene. There was not, therefore, such an issue as decolonization in the true sense of the word. The issue was, one might say, how China could, at an intellectual level at least, *colonize itself* with all the Western cultural resources available, even though some of these resources were made available by way of familiar patterns of Western expansion. The choice of a national cultural identity, for Chinese intellectuals, was still a genuine one, which was not true of some former British colonies.

In this process of constructing a modern identity for China, however, what presented as a most frustrating difficulty was where to situate, within the accepted frame of Western scientific knowledge, the indigenous systems of knowledge. Those Chinese intellectuals, in their pursuit of Western scientific knowledge around the turn of the century, were ensnared a priori in the pervasiveness of traditional discursive practices that were historically constituted. Their concept of "science," for example, "was *jointly* constituted by the philosophical interpretations of Comte, Huxley, Spencer, Russell, Dewey, and others on science, as well as traditional Chinese epistemology, moral philosophy, and the conception of the universe." [60] The constructing of China's modern identity both as an intellectual pursuit and a social practice, therefore, is at once conditioned by the cultural resources imported from without and historical forces generated from within. This is not, one may add, just a paradox of the May Fourth enlightenment project. It is characteristic of much of China's quest for a new self in the twentieth century. The issue of China's modernity, which has been haunting the Chinese consciousness for nearly a century, is embodied in the process of an intense intellectual negotiation between the Chinese and the Western, between the local and the universal, which, however, cannot reach a satisfactory conclusion. On the linguistic front, those various schemes for the introduction or creation of a language that could be at once universal and indigenous fell into this pattern. The case of Richards and Basic English testifies, once again, to all the complexities of what Lydia Liu calls "translingual practice" that China has experienced in its awakening consciousness of its own modern identity in the first few decades of this century.[61]

In his intellectual and academic prime, Richards's dramatic shift into Basic, which subsequently became the most important professional commitment in his life, threw its roots back into his first encounter with Chinese students in Beijing in 1929. "Those students of mine," said Richards, "were the best I've ever had. They make any other students anywhere look silly." But they "were working under the most absurd disabilities, hardly knew the language they were working in with me. . . . So little by little I decided that work towards unifying the planet was worth so much more than any sort of work I'd dreamt of before." [62] In 1979, at the age of 86, Richards made his final trip to China against medical advice. He collapsed during his visit and died shortly after he was flown back to England. Between his first trip to China in 1927 and his last trip in 1979, half a century elapsed. Richards's passions for China and for Basic in China remained unchanged. When asked by his interviewer in 1973 about his short sojourn in China in 1950, Richards recalled his experienced emotions about this new country in a spontaneous overflow of feelings: "1950. It was a wonderful, wonderful moment. 'Bliss was it, in those days, to be alive,' as Wordsworth said about the French Revolution. It was really too beautiful for words, to see the Chinese returning to their natural pride and glory." [63] His emotional involvement was, of course, more manifest on the level of personal friendship. Leo Ou-fan Lee remembers that during his meeting with Richards in the sixties, his mention of the name of the Cambridge-educated poet Xu Zhimo brought tears to Richards's eyes.[64]

In Richards's experience of China, there are certain aspects that, though yet to be crystallized, are profoundly moving. "Looking back now," as Hollingsworth says, "there is no good reason for us not to credit Richards fully for his optimism, his idealism, his sense of personal commitment—all of which can be seen at its fullest in the China theme to be found in his writings." [65] *Mencius on the Mind* is by far Richards's most significant book on "the China theme"; he once described it as a work that was "written out with much of the feeling one has in trying to scribble down a dream before it fades away." [66] Perhaps it was so with the Basic English program. But there are things that last longer than a dream. The emanations of the pathos surrounding the failure of the Basic English project would perhaps constitute, not for sentimental reasons, a more stable source for musing in the years to come.

Notes

I am grateful to Lydia H. Liu for her comments and suggestions. To the anonymous readers of this volume who have suggested useful information in relation to some specific moments in my argument, I am much obliged. All English translations from Chinese are mine.

1   Paul Bové, *Intellectuals in Power*, 40. More recently, Simon During asserts that Richards along with Eliot developed literary criticism as a typical Anglo-American phenomenon. See Simon During, "Literature—Nationalism's Other?", 149.

2   William Empson, "The Hammer's Ring," in R. Brower, H. Vendler, and J. Hollander, *I. A. Richards*, 73.

3   See note 37 below.

4   Except perhaps his student William Empson. Empson's first university appointment in China in 1937 came as a result of Richards's recommendation; he taught in China twice, for seven years altogether. However, Empson's experience of China was, on the whole, a much simpler case: he had been professor of English at Qinghua University before he left China in 1953 for domestic considerations and, apart from teaching, had not been substantially involved in the Basic English movement or any other prac-

tices in China. For more information about his teaching experience in China, see the text of his inaugural lecture at the University of Sheffield in 1954, "Teaching English in Far East and England."

5   I. A. Richards, "Fundamentally, I'm an Inventor," 52.

6   See I. A. Richards, "Beginnings and Transitions," 31.

7   Richards acknowledged that the book "was worked up from notes made between Tsing Hua and Yenching, under the guidance of divers advisers" ("Toward a Theory of Translating," 247). See also note 9 below.

8   Richards, "Beginnings," 32. Around the time he was working on this project, Richards, in an article published in China, said:

> No one who has made any special study of ambiguity can regard translations with anything but suspicion, even in the case of cognate languages; and where languages so different as Chinese and English are concerned, the arguments in favour of a direct comparative study of their resources by the light of modern logical and psychological analysis seem very clear and pressing. Such a comparative survey of Chinese and English would certainly assist the theory of meaning, it would probably make important contributions to psychology and it would help to reduce the great dangers of inaccurate or one-sided translation. . . . This comparative survey would need the close collaboration of at least three students—a Chinese scholar with a taste for exploring impartially the subtleties of Chinese thought and especially the systematic ambiguities of Chinese philosophy; a translator with as free and plastic control of the resources of the two languages as possible, with a taste for definitions, and a cultivated distrust of accepted equivalences; thirdly, a student of meaning whose business it would be to analyse, generalise and classify the linguistic situations which be observed arising in the course of the discussion." (I. A. Richards, "The Meaning of 'The Meaning of Meaning,' " 15)

9   Richards describes their collaboration thus: "I got together a very able team of four and I sat in more or less as secretary. I didn't pretend to any Chinese. I could just distinguish one character from another, but I didn't know anything. I couldn't be sensitive to the terrific, universe-wide, reverberations. And these four people were so sensitive in their various ways, and they did their best to explain to me some of the key things" ("Beginnings," 32).

10 Referring to the logical positivism in The Meaning of Meaning, Lacan writes that Richards "took for his purposes a page from Mong-tse (Mencius to the Jesuits) and called the piece, Mencius on the Mind. The guarantees of purity of the experiment are nothing to the luxury of the approaches. And our expert on the traditional Canon which contains the text is found right on the spot in Peking where our demonstration-model mangle has been transported regardless of cost." "But," Lacan continues in this self-indulgent fashion, "we shall be no less transported, if less expensively, to see a bronze which gives out bell-tones at the slightest contact with true thought, transformed into a rag to wipe the blackboard of the most dismaying British psychologism" (Jacques Lacan, "The Insistence of the Letter in the Unconscious," 117–18 n. 7).

11 Richards, "Beginnings," 34.

12 I. A. Richards, Basic English and Its Uses, 23.

13 I. A. Richards, "Basic English," 89.

14 Richards, "Beginnings," 34.

15 The Orthological Committee, *Notes on Basic English*, 2.

16 Richard Luckett, introduction to I. A. Richards, *Selected Letters*, xvi.

17 Richards, "Beginnings," 35.

18 Richards, "Fundamentally," 53.

19 See John Paul Russo, *I. A. Richards*, in particular chap. 17, "Basic English: The Years in China," 397–429.

20 Y. R. Chao, *Autobiography*, 85.

21 In his review article, Ye expressed his confidence in the value of Basic and his hope that it would be soon adopted in secondary schools and universities throughout the country. See Ye Gongchao, "Review of *Basic in Teaching*," 959. See also Yang Lien-sheng, "Zhuihuai Yeshi Gongchao," 235–36.

22 See Russo, 420.

23 C. K. Ogden, *A Short Guide to Basic English*, 35.

24 A copy of the English version of the Committee's Resolution is in I. A. Richards files, boxed material, box 1, Houghton Library, Harvard.

25 Richards, "Beginnings," 55.

26 See Russo, 670–71.

27 A copy of this letter, unsigned, is in I. A. Richards files, boxed material, box 3, Houghton Library, Harvard.

28 "We had really great success in China with Basic English," says Richards, "but it was pushed out by the Japanese, all lost" (Richards, "Beginnings," 53).

29 Chen Yuan, *Shehui yuyanxue*, 372 n. 13. It is worth noting here that this etymology of the term Basic has been less and less mentioned. In the context of giving a historical account of Basic, Ogden once said that at its early stage, "many special captions or trademarks for the system were suggested, but B A S I C—British American Scientific International Commercial (English)—has been finally adopted" (Ogden, *Basic English*, 12).

30 Chen, 372 n. 13.

31 Chen Yuan was not alone so critical of the artificiality of Basic; it was subject to vigorous criticism in the West as well. See Michael West et al., "A Critical Examination of Basic English."

32 Chow Tse-Tsung argues that to describe the May Fourth movement as a "Chinese Renaissance" is a mismatch of it with the European Renaissance. See Chow Tse-Tsung, *The May Fourth Movement*, 338–42. Richards's term is used here as a rhetorical formulation rather than as a comparison between the two. In fact, Richards himself was aware of their differences: "The phrase 'The Chinese Renaissance' has passed into general use as a description of the modern intellectual movement in China; but the parallels to be drawn with our own Renaissance are few. China is not to-day renewing contact with a past phase of her tradition . . . she is being violently and reluctantly torn from it" (I. A. Richards, *Basic in Teaching*, 22–23).

33 Qian Xuantong, "Zhongguo jinhouzhi wenzi wenti," 354.

34 See Qian Xuantong, "A Reply to Yao Jiren," 543.

35 For a useful introduction to the phonetic writing movement, see Ni Haishu, *Zhonguo*

pinyin wenzi yundongshi jianbian, in particular chap. 5. For more theoretical reflections on the language reform movement at the time, see, among Shen Xiaolong's other works on the subject, *Zhongguo yuyande jiege yu renwen jingsheng* (The structure of the Chinese language and its humanist spirit). I'm grateful to Professor Chen Yangu for drawing my attention to Shen's works.

36   See Q. S. Tong, "Myths about the Chinese Language."

37   Coleridge uses these words in his famous definition of imagination in chapter 13 of *Biographia Literaria*. Coleridge is evoked here deliberately. For, as W. H. N. Hotopf says, "Coleridge and Confucianism were both major influences upon Richards" (*Language, Thought and Comprehension*, 63). More specifically, Richards argues that there are great similarities between passages from *Mencius* and those in Coleridge (see "Beginnings," 32). It should be noted further that Richards places Coleridge firmly in the Platonic tradition. This triad of Confucian ethics, Platonic transcendentalism, and Coleridgean organic aesthetics is a typical formulation of Richards's faith in a more fundamental intellectual universalism, which, however, would require a separate study to deal with.

38   Paul de Man, *Blindness and Insight*, 143.

39   Friedrich Nietzsche, "Vom Nutzen und Nachteil der Historie für das Leben," quoted in de Man, 149.

40   Cai Yuanpei, "Zai guoyu jiangxisuo yanjiangci," 426–27.

41   I. A. Richards, "The Chinese Renaissance," 103.

42   See I. A. Richards, *Mencius on the Mind*, xii–xiii.

43   Richards, "Basic English," 90.

44   Richards, *Basic in Teaching*, 45, 47.

45   The original letter is in I. A. Richards files, boxed material, box 2, Houghton Library, Harvard.

46   C. K. Ogden and I. A. Richards, *The Meaning of Meaning*, xiii.

47   Ibid.

48   See note on the author appended to the text of I. A. Richards, *Nations and Peace*. Page references will be indicated hereafter in parentheses.

49   Richards, "Basic English," 90.

50   Ibid. The apparent simplicity of Basic English has always been considered its most attractive aspect for being an international language. Linguistic simplicity, however, is never just a linguistic matter. Commenting on this, Benjamin Whorf asserts: "Basic English appeals to people because it seems simple. But those to whom it seems simple either know or think they know English—there's the rub! Every language of course seems simple to its own speakers because they are unconscious of structure. But English is anything but simple—it is a bafflingly complex organization, abounding in covert classes, cryptotypes, taxemes of selection, taxemes of order, significant stress patterns and intonation patterns of considerable intricacy. . . . As with Basic English, so with other artificial languages—underlying structures and categories of a few culturally predominant European tongues are taken for granted; their complex web of presuppositions is made the basis of a false simplicity" ("A Linguistic Consideration of Thinking in Primitive Communities," in *Language, Thought, and Reality*, 82–83).

51   Richards, "Basic English," 90. Obviously Richards must have felt very strongly about

Hess's statement. Two years later, in 1943, he mentioned this again in *Basic English and Its Uses* and claimed, quoting Bismarck, that "the most significant event of the nineteenth century was the acceptance of English as the language of North America" (23).

52 Richards, "Basic English," 90.

53 Winston S. Churchill, letter to Sir Edward Bridges, 11 July 1943, in Churchill, *Second World War*, 651.

54 This Committee of Ministers on Basic English later submitted a report, which was "approved in principle by His Majesty's Government." Churchill made a statement, apparently on the basis of the recommendations made by the Committee, on 9 March 1944. It is of relevance and interest to quote parts of his statement here:

> His Majesty's Government have . . . decided on the following steps to develop Basic English as an auxiliary international and administrative language: — (1) The British Council will include among its activities the teaching of Basic English. . . . (2) Diplomatic and commercial representatives in foreign countries will be asked to do all they can to encourage the spread of Basic English as an auxiliary language. (3) It is also intended to arrange for the translation into Basic English of a wider range than is at present available of literature — scientific, technical and general — both from ordinary English and from foreign languages and also to increase the supply of manuals of instruction in Basic English. (4) Some Colonial Governments will be invited to experiment by the issue in Basic English of handbooks for colonial peoples on agriculture, hygiene, etc., and by the use of this simplified language as the medium for some administrative instructions issued by the Government. (5) The British Broadcasting Corporation has been asked to consider a recommendation to include the use and teaching of Basic English in appropriate overseas programmes. . . . It is recognised that such developments as may be practicable must proceed in parallel with the steps to be taken by other agencies. (*The Atlantic Charter, and the Prime Minister's Statement on Basic English of March 9, 1944; in their original form, and in Basic English, for purposes of Comparison*, 3–5)

55 Winston Churchill, *Complete Speeches*, 6825–26.

56 See Richards, "Fundamentally," 53.

57 Winston Churchill, *Onwards to Victory*, 342.

58 Gauri Viswanathan, *Masks of Conquest*, 166–67.

59 Erich Auerbach, "Vico and Aesthetic Historicism," in *Scenes from the Drama of European Literature*, 187.

60 Wang Hui, "The Fate of 'Mr. Science' in China," 69–70; my italics.

61 See Lydia Liu, *Translingual Practice*.

62 Richards, "Fundamentally," 52–53.

63 Ibid., 54. Wordsworth is, of course, misquoted. The line appears in *The Prelude* as follows: "Bliss was it in that dawn to be alive" (9: 108).

64 I am grateful to Professor Leo Ou-fan Lee for sharing this personal experience with me.

65 Alan M. Hollingsworth, "I. A. Richards in China and America," 140.

66 Richards, "Toward a Theory," 247.

Jianhua Chen   *Chinese "Revolution"*

in the Syntax of World Revolution

The classical Chinese compound *geming* was resurrected, reconstructed, and incorporated into the diverse syntax of "world revolution" via the Japanese *kanji* term *kakumei*. Chinese reformers and revolutionaries appropriated and contested the availability of the meaning of "revolution" for what they understood to be the true meaning of *geming* throughout the century. In the last years of the Qing reign, this volatile engagement with *geming* as revolution generated a whole range of historical meanings and activities, from proposals for moderate social reform to calls for a violent overthrow of the Qing government.

Observing a growing trend of revolutionary fervor throughout China, the prominent Chinese intellectual Liang Qichao remarked in 1902: "A few years ago, most people were terrified to hear the word *minquan* [civil rights]. But when the word *geming* [revolution] began to circulate, they no longer felt that way about *minquan* but feared *geming*." [1] Liang himself was responsible for popularizing the new concept of *geming* derived from a Japanese *kanji* translation of the European concept "revolution." The refurbished classical Chinese term took on this new meaning in the writings and speeches of progressive essayists and political activists when many of them, like Liang himself, went into exile in Japan or studied there at the turn of the century. Within a short period of time, *geming* gained extraordinary currency and led to what Benjamin Schwartz has called the "mystique of revolution" in China: "radicalism had won a foothold by the first decade of the twentieth century." [2]

In *Confucian China and Its Modern Fate*, Joseph Levenson suggests that the classical Chinese term *geming* is no longer the same term in the twentieth century but "rather a translation back into Chinese, as it were, of the modern Japanese *kakumei* which had used the 'mandate' characters metaphorically to convey the idea of revolution." [3] Wolfgang Franke holds, however, that the content of the expression of *geming* "unites traditional concepts from the earliest period with modern Western ideas and the Western concept of 'revolution.' " [4] Their insights spotlight different aspects of the cross-cultural translations among *geming*, *kakumei*, and "revolution" and raise the larger question of how one might talk about change, language, and meaning. In a recent study, Prasenjit Duara shows a "semantic conflation" between two different meanings of *geming* in his reading of one of Tao Chengzhang's 1908 texts. He suggests that one of these meanings comes from the Confucian classical text *Yi jing* (*Book of Changes*) meaning "following the people's will and depriving a ruler of the mandate of heaven to rule"; the other meaning is the Japanese neologism for modern revolution, signifying change in societal structure. [5] His point about "semantic conflation" is very relevant to my own research, but a question lingers: When and how did *geming* return from Japan as a neologism?

In *Translingual Practice*, Lydia H. Liu raises the issue of "loanword neologism" as a theoretical problem and explores it with much rigor. In discussing the influx of loanwords and neologisms in recent Chinese history and their implications for understanding modern intellectual history, Liu argues that existing philosophical approaches and analytical categories cannot sufficiently explain how the circulation of theories such as *guomin xing* (national character), *gerenzhuyi* (individualism), and *wenhua* (culture) occurred and generated new meanings in a different language. She develops a notion of "translingual practice" to address the issue and to investigate the broader meanings of translation in cross-cultural contexts. [6]

In the same spirit, I trace the modern origins of Chinese "revolution" in this chapter by analyzing the cross-linguistic and cross-cultural translations of *geming*, *kakumei*, and "revolution" at the turn of the century up to 1904. Of course, revolution does not necessarily start with the use of the word revolution, nor must the study of revolution begin with its usage. In previously published works on Chinese revolution, the word has been treated as a metaphor or, as Crane Brinton writes, "hardly more than an emphatic synonym for 'change,' perhaps with a suggestion of sudden or striking change." [7] The "Chinese Revolution" is simply taken as a modern phenomenon—a response to or a part of the world revolution, since revolution in the West, as Hannah Arendt points out, has carried it with a modern character after the eighteenth century. [8]

In *The Great Chinese Revolution*, John Fairbank describes Chinese revolution as a process of changes under "international influences" of "modern science and technology," albeit an unfulfilled project of modernization.[9]

However, an inquiry into the process of how the classical Chinese word *geming* was revived and transformed through the Chinese and Japanese rendering of global revolution in the modern era may lead to different conclusions.[10] What follows is my analysis of the writings of Wang Tao (1828–1897), Sun Yat-sen (1866–1925), and Liang Qichao, with a focus on their discursive practice centering on the translation and transvaluation of *geming*. This discursive practice goes far beyond literal translations bearing syntactic and contextual restrictions and beyond theoretical polemics of fidelity and translatability. *Geming*, as rendered by the three intellectuals, has come down to us in three distinct genres of writing: the historical, the political, and the literary. Their interpretations of this idea are also determined, among other factors, by their intellectual background, political motivation, and social affiliations. All three aim to universalize their revolutionary acts and nationalist identities but, at the same time, their language is complicated by the Confucian connotations of *geming* signifying dynastic change, the mandate of heaven, popular sovereignty, and the ethics of loyalty. Until the publication of Zou Rong's (1885–1905) *Geming jun* (The revolutionary army) in 1903, the meaning of *geming* in translation had by no means been homogeneous. Its discursive circulation mirrored the translingual conditions of contingency, arbitrariness, and possibility, and was open to interpretation.

The Discourse of Geming in Premodern China and Japan

"Revolution," says Crane Brinton, "is one of the loose words."[11] So do I argue are *geming* and *kakumei*. Each of the words has a history and its meaning has changed over time. Here, instead of defining the meaning of revolution, I will reflect on a definition of revolution given by Liang Qichao in 1904, which should help provide a meaningful historical context for the discussion to follow. In his essay "Zhongguo lishi shang *geming* zhi yanjiu" (A study of revolution in Chinese history), Liang makes a distinction between a "broad" sense of *geming* and its "narrow" meaning. The broad sense encompasses the changes in societal and political structure by either peaceful or violent means, and the narrow meaning refers to military actions specifically aimed at overthrowing the central government. The former, asserts Liang, is born of Western revolutionary experience that brings human history to the modern era; the latter goes back to the rebellious upheavals in China's past. His depiction of peasant rebellions in terms of violence, selfishness, and backwardness suggests an aversion to the contemporary anti-Manchu movement. This is largely attributable to Liang's own changing politics and his ambivalence toward the Manchu regime. Nevertheless, Liang's definition of *geming* took hold on his generation of intellectuals.[12]

Before elaborating on Liang's politics, let us briefly consider the etymological roots of *geming* in the Confucian classical text *The Book of Changes*.[13] *The Book of Changes* describes *geming* as follows: "Heaven and earth undergo their changes, and the four seasons complete their functions. The kings Tang and Wu *overthrew the thrones (geming)* of Xia (2100–1600 B.C.) and Shang (1600–1100 B.C.) in accordance with the will of Heaven, and in response to the wishes of men. Great indeed is what takes place in a time of change."[14] At the core of the statement is an affirmation of dynastic changeability. Tang's and Wu's successful dethronements are legitimized on three levels: they are approved cosmologically by "the will of Heaven," socially by "the will of men," and naturalized by the motion of the seasons. However, this authoritative text is like the sword of Damocles to any throne, for rebels or rivals may use it to proclaim political legitimacy in the name of Heaven and people. By the mid–second century B.C., a serious debate occurred in the Han court on the appropriation of the *geming* text. When a bookish scholar began questioning the establishment of the Han, Emperor Liu Qi stopped the debate and virtually prohibited the discussion.[15] The question revealed a paradox between power and moral justice implicit in the *Yi Jing* text: according to Confucian ethics, Tang's and Wu's disloyalty can by no means be justified. At stake was the case of Liu Bang, who established the Han Dynasty after having destroyed the Qin by his rebellious force.

Most Confucians kept silence on the issue of *geming* or, if unavoidable, would treat it with awe. The debate was nonetheless renewed among twelfth-century neo-Confucianists, this time focusing on another important *geming* theory in *Mencius*. Mencius asserts that both Tang and Wu represent justice in their annihilation of old regimes because they fulfill the ideal of *ren* (benevolence), the highest Confucian moral principle, and embody the people's interests as well. The rise of neo-Confucianism signaled a new wave of reannotating and reinterpreting classical Confucian scriptures, in response to political and cultural crises of the Southern Song period (1127–1279). In 1190, Zhu Xi (1130–1200), one of the leading neo-Confucianists of the time, published *Sishu Zhangju jizhu* (Four books with collected annotations). It included fundamental texts such as *The Analects of Confucius* and *Mencius*, provided with selective annotations by neo-

Confucianists. As an officially approved textbook, it exerted enormous impact on social thought in late imperial China.

In those annotations on the *geming* discourse in *Mengcius*, the neo-Confucian attitude toward *geming* seemed no less paradoxical than that of their predecessors. In general, their concerns were more practical than cosmological; they put more stress on the "will of men" than the "will of Heaven." As Zhang Zai (1021–1077) writes, "It is hard to be distinguished. While the mandate of heaven continues, the different statuses of the monarch and his subjects will remain. Once the mandate of heaven ends, the emperor becomes an autocrat. How does one know when the mandate of heaven ends? It is decided by the people's wishes." [16] This statement tends to judge the mandate of heaven by the result of the punitive expedition rather than by the principle of benevolence. The "people's wishes" seems a vague notion, as it is likely those in power who decide whether it is *geming* or not. Other scholars were more assertive, emphasizing the "will of men." Zhao Qi writes, "The punitive expedition should accord with the people's will. If so, the mandate of heaven is obtained." Echoing this, Zhu Xi says, "When the people all over the country welcome him, he is the Son of Heaven. When all people betray him, he loses his status as the Son of Heaven." [17] Both Zhao and Zhu highly esteem the support of the masses.

The Japanese word *kakumei* was a translation from *geming*. There was no analogous word in Japanese native culture.[18] According to recent scholarship, as early as the eighth century Mencius's *geming* theory began to travel to Japan.[19] However, it took a new course in that country, whose culture was influenced by and yet quite different from China's. As Mizoguchi Yūzō asserts, the difference primarily lies in the differing political and cultural traditions in China and Japan: the former is characterized by dynastic revolutions, the latter by the reign of a single imperial house throughout history.[20] Traveling in this new landscape, Chinese *geming* theory was gradually remolded and made compatible with the Japanese polity.

One particular political event in medieval Japan greatly affected the meaning of *geming*. In 900, Miyoshi Kiyoyuki (847–918), a literary scholar at court, wrote a letter to Sugawara Michizane, the second official in the state, foretelling events of the following year, the year called *shin yu kakumei nen* (revolutionary year of *xinyou*). Drawing on the mystique of calendric calculation, the letter persuaded Sugawara to retire from the height of his official career in order to avoid his political downfall. The theory of the "revolutionary year of *xinyou*" applied by Miyoshi was derived from a part of the Chinese classical annotations of *Yi Jing* that had long been lost in its homeland. Miyoshi actually supported

Fujiwara Mototsune, the highest official in the state, who resented Sugawara's rapid rise as imperial favorite and planned to overthrow him.[21] Sugawara refused to retire. In the following year the court banished him in accordance with Miyoshi prophesy. Thus, the word *geming* generated a new implication in Japan: it was used to reinforce the existing imperial power instead of legitimizing a newborn dynasty. This application of Chinese *geming* theory was conditioned by the characteristics of the Japanese political system.

It was in the Tokugawa period (1603–1868) that Japanese *kakumei* discourse developed a clearer nationalist character. As Morohashi Tetsuji's *Dai Kan-Wa jiten* (Great Sino-Japanese dictionary) notes, "In the Tokugawa period, scholars thought Confucianism unsuitable to our state polity, and thus rejected the *geming* theory." [22] While the study of neo-Confucianism flourished under the Tokugawa family, it took forms for which there was no precedent in China's experience: "First, it focused attention on the question of legitimate imperial rule and the unbroken succession of the reigning house, which ultimately enkindled a new loyalty to the Throne and prepared the way for an imperial restoration; second, it inspired a new study of native religious traditions which contributed to the revival of Shintō." [23] Awakened by nationalist and religious consciousness, the Tokugawa thinkers reconfigured neo-Confucianism for their own purposes. Not surprisingly, Chinese *geming* theory, especially that of Mencius, became a target of their critiques. For example, Yamazaki Ansai (1618–1682), an important advocate of Shintō, wrote an article entitled "On the Tang-Wu Revolution Theory," in which he opposed Mencius's revolutionary ideal, stressing royalty and piety to Japanese imperial sovereignty. His disciple Asami Keizai (1652–1711 or 1712) went even further as he accused Tang and Wu of being "capital criminals who murdered their emperors." [24]

Nevertheless, their critiques of Chinese revolution theory rejected neither Confucianism nor the term *geming*. At the end of the Tokugawa era, when the radical royalists launched a movement of Revering the Emperor and Expelling the Foreigners (*sonno-joi*), the traditional discourse of revolution was reshaped, opposing Tokugawa aristocracy on the one hand, and advocating changing the feudal system under imperial authority on the other. *Geming* was transformed into a reform drive. The pivotal figure who gave the word a modern sense was Yoshida Shōin (1830–1859). Regarded as a great hero of the Restoration movement, he enthusiastically combined Confucian morality, nationalism, and an awareness of the need to learn from the West. In a letter to a friend, he related the meaning of *geming* to ancient calendric myth, recalling the tradition of the revolutionary year of *xinyou* created by Emperor Jimmu, founder of Japan.[25] Although heavily influenced by Mencius's moral ideal, Shōin thoroughly rejected Mencius's revolution theory, which contradicted his notion of emperor worship.

Wang Tao and Sun Yat-sen: From Rebellion to Revolution

After the mid–nineteenth century, perhaps initiated by Xi Jiyu's (1795–1873) *Yinghuan zhilue* (A brief account of the world) in 1848, many books about the history of foreign countries were published in China. Compiled or written by Western missionaries or Chinese intellectuals, these books taught the Chinese to perceive the world as a round globe and China as a nation of nations. Wang Tao's *Chongding Faguo zhilue* (A revised history of France) published in 1890 became one of the most notable. In it, the phrase *Faguo geming*, rendering "the French Revolution," appeared for the first time in China. The book was a compilation based on several Japanese translations of French and world history, and the section on the French Revolution is largely indebted to Okamoto Kansuke's *Bankoku shiki* (An account of world history) published in 1879 in Japan.

According to the guidelines (*reigen*) of *Bankoku shiki*, Okamoto took for reference several Western histories translated by Japanese scholars. Sharing the Meiji enthusiasm for Western learning, he edited the book hoping it would be used in schools as a history textbook. The book shows an ambivalent attitude toward the French Revolution, reflecting the political consensus of it in the Meiji period.[26] When the French Revolution is translated into *Fukkoku kakumei*, it is acknowledged as a great event in human history. Yet at the same time its dark aspects—the mass rebellion, violence, social chaos, and persecution of the monarch—are severely condemned. Okamoto's treatment is worth noticing: the word *Fukkoku kakumei* or *kakumei* is never applied while narrating the process of the revolution, which is instead called *ran* (disaster, or rebellion). Only in the passages about the restoration of the Bourbon Dynasty did *kakumei* appear:

> May 4, 1814, Napoleon was exiled to the island of Elba. The same day Louis XVIII entered Paris and mounted on the throne, hoping to make a peace with the Alliance. In May, the rulers of Russia, Austria, Prussia, and England came to Paris. The territory of France was redefined as a little broader than that before the revolution (*kakumei*).

Later in the same chapter:

> In November 1815, the Alliance agreed on a peace treaty with France. The throne of Louis XVIII was restored. . . . Since the *French Revolution* [*Fukkoku*

kakumei] the whole of Europe suffered war for more than two decades, and now the guns were silenced and the people enjoyed the peace.[27]

The two passages remain almost intact in Wang Tao's *Chongding Faguo zhilue*.[28] This similarity was partly motivated by his eagerness to transmit a universal discourse of the French Revolution through Japanese sources. As a "free-spirited littoral reformer," Wang Tao, like others of the new type of intellectual of his time, believed that Japanese interpretation of Western learning was more advanced. When Wang Tao visited Japan in 1879, he met Okamoto and later praised his newly published *Bankoku shiki* as a "monumental work with everlasting value."[29]

Wang Tao shared Okamoto's ambivalent view of the French Revolution. In his commentaries, formulated according to the Chinese mode of historiography, he portrays the mob and their leaders Robespierre and Danton as fierce, cruel *luanmin* (rebellious mob) and *luandang* (rebellious party). Of the persecution of Louis XVI, he bemoans: "Where is the principle of Heaven? Does not this mean that heaven and earth are upside down, that the noble and the mean are displaced, and that the imperial order is ruined?"[30] Yet turning around, Wang claims that the doomed emperor could only blame himself, for it was not unfair for the maltreated people to rise up and punish him.

The ambiguous term French Revolution (*Faguo geming*) in Chinese writing does blur the boundary of revolution and rebellion, attributing some legitimacy to the latter and thus adding new meaning to the traditional discourse of *geming*. This implication of legitimacy had dangerous political associations when China was undergoing tremendous social upheavals at the time. From early 1850s on, Wang served as a Chinese editor in a Western-style press in Shanghai. But in 1862 he was exiled to Hong Kong on accusation of treason: he had secretly communicated with the Taiping rebels.[31] When he visited France in the late 1860s, he was impressed with the freedom he saw there and admired the French and Parisian life. The changes that had shaped France after the Revolution aroused Wang's political imagination of a free, democratic society for China. He categorized all countries of the world as having three types of political systems: a monarchical state (*zizhu zhi guo*), a democratic state (*minzhu zhi guo*), and a monarchical/democrat state (*jun min gong zhu*). France belonged to the democratic. Using the example of how the French Revolution resulted in Napoleon's hegemony over the European nations and how the Bourbon Dynasty collapsed after losing people's support, Wang Tao emphasized the importance of freedom and democracy in effecting historical change in China.

When the Qing Empire faced political crisis after the 1894 Sino-Japanese war, this revolutionary discourse lurked at the Gate of Heaven, threatening to topple the Manchus. During the Hundred Days Reform of 1898, Kang Youwei (1858–1927), the leading reformer at the time, depicted the French Revolution as a bloody catastrophe. In one of the memorials he submitted to Emperor Guangxu, he warned that the empire would collapse like the Bourbon Dynasty unless political reform was enacted immediately.[32] Another notable reformer, Zhang Binglin (1869–1936), issued a similar warning in *Shiwu bao* (Current news), a reformist journal published in Shanghai. In an essay called "Lun xue-hui you dayi yu huangren, ji yi baohu" (A treatise on the urgent need to protect the learned societies that benefit the yellow people), Zhang proposes promotion of traditional Chinese learning so that nationalist culture can be preserved against the intrusion of Christianity. Toward the end of his essay, however, he shifts the topic to revolution. He explains that the idea of *geming* in the past only related to the "rise and decline of imperial houses," but now "it has been spreading in Western countries. The rebellious parties seek their opportunities in the name of *geming.*" Zhang worried that Chinese people would be influenced by Western revolutionary tendencies and become uncontrollable. He called for an urgent reform from above: "Now our urgent task is to reform our polity to curb a revolution."[33]

The *geming* discourse in Kang's and Zhang's writings infused its traditional connotations with the notion of Western revolution, as did Wang Tao in his own. While condemning revolution to promote their reform agenda, they virtually rejected the Confucian discourse of *geming*, and the ambiguity of the Meiji revolutionary ethos to be found in Wang Tao's book was lost as a result. *Geming* was negatively attributed to the West and, at the same time, it was also detached from its indigenous historical context where it had been used to justify a new dynasty in the name of people and heaven. By questioning the legitimacy of the Qing Dynasty, their use of the translated notion of revolution differed from that in Japan, where the ideas of reform and revolution converged to empower the imperial house in the name of *geming*.

Another origin of modern Chinese revolutionary discourse began with Sun Yat-sen. Whereas the reformers Kang and Zhang denounced revolutionaries as dangerous rebels, Sun used *geming* as a catchword to legitimize his own dissent and effectively arouse antidynastic enthusiasm. According to the accounts given by Chen Shaobai (1869–1934) and Feng Ziyou (1882–1958), Sun began to proclaim himself a revolutionist in 1895.[34] After his Canton revolt failed, he fled to Japan as a refugee and saw a Kobe newspaper labeling him as the leader of a "revolutionary party" (*kakumei to*). Sun said to his follower Chen Shaobai, "The word *geming* is rooted in *Yi Jing*. Kings Tang and Wu made revolutions according to the will of heaven and people. Its meaning is excellent. From now on we can call our party *geming dang.*" Although some scholars questioned the truthfulness of this record,[35] it does reveal the significance of the locale where the meeting of the languages took place. In translating the Japanese "revolutionary party," the Chinese discourse of *geming* gained the modern aura of mass movement and historical progress. The journalistic reportage in this Japanese newspaper, emblematic of modern media power, lent the Chinese rebels an authoritative voice.

As the Kobe episode suggests, Sun Yat-sen had not connected his revolution to the word *geming;* this is also evidenced by Chen Shaobai's reminiscence, which is very similar to Sun's: "Having arrived at Kobe, we bought a newspaper. . . . At a glance, we saw 'the Chinese revolutionary party of Sun Yat-sen,' strikingly presented before our eyes. Previously we thought that only emperors could claim '*geming*' for their legitimacy, and that our actions could only be called *zaofan* (rebellion). Ever since we read this newspaper, the term 'revolutionary party' has been imprinted on our minds." [36] Whereas Kang Youwei and Zhang Binglin rejected the discourse of *geming* for fear of its hindrance to Chinese modernity, Sun and Chen revived the aura of dynastic change in a modern sense by switching from *zaofan* to *geming,* causing an inversion of value within the Confucian discourse of *geming.* Sun and Chen seized the new translation of *geming* as a promise of social change.

Harold Schiffrin argues that, before Sun's 1895 encounter with Japanese *kakumei,* he "had not adopted the term which meant only that the 'ruler's name was changed.'" [37] But whether Sun could have adopted the term or not also depended on the condition of whether the Chinese translation of revolution had been available as *geming* or *zaofan.* In his early years Sun had received Western education in missionary schools and was exposed to the history of the French Revolution and the stories of Napoleon and Washington in his English textbook. According to Paul Linebarger's biography, Sun began his anti-Manchu campaign in the 1880s with the slogan "Tianming wu chang" (Divine right does not last forever) among villagers.[38] The invention of this slogan expressed his desire to overthrow the Son of Heaven, but *geming* was not directly available for his purpose, because traditionally only those who dethroned the previous monarch could use the term favored by the mandate of Heaven. When the Japanese neologistic use of *geming* gave Sun a legitimate claim of social change and new political future, he immediately embraced it. Infusing a borrowed meaning of revolution into *geming,* the Japanese *kanji* translation helped remove some of the classical Chinese connotations of *geming* and turned it into a new word.

Also related to this background was a translation enterprise dominated by

Western missionaries in the nineteenth century. In the 1880s *The Global Magazine* (*Wanguo gongbao*), perhaps the most influential missionary periodical of the time, was rigorously engaged with a reform project, publishing regular articles introducing the educational systems, politics, and history of the West, and criticizing traditional Chinese culture.[39] Revolution or rebellion, in this case, was not encouraged by the missionaries. In occasional news reports of social or political events in China and other countries, the mass turmoil or revolt was condemned as *luan* (chaos, or disasters) and the rebels as *fei* (bandits). The Christian bent was equally shown in Xie Weilou's *Wanguo tongjian* (A chronicle of world history) published in 1882, in which the description of the French Revolution was darker and more terrifying than Wang Tao's *Chongding Faguo zhilue*, and of course the word *geming* was not used.[40]

Sun Yat-sen's English account of how he was captured and imprisoned by Qing government agents in London in 1896 was published under the title *Kidnapped in London*. His use of "reform" and "revolution" in that book mirrors the contemporary use of "revolution" in English in an interesting way. Sun argued that the Young China Party he joined had no intention of subverting the Manchu regime and that its "idea was to bring about a peaceful reform."[41] Two decades later, Sun recalled that he had used the rhetoric of reform in *Kidnapped in London* because he could not reveal his anti-Manchu scheme then. "Though I was in London," said Sun, "there were things I was not supposed to say at the time."[42] But Sun's emphasis on reform seems more than a rhetorical strategy purporting to win over international support. The word revolution did carry the connotation of violence and rebellion in English. As Raymond Williams has shown, "In political controversy arising from the actual history of armed risings and conflicts, *revolution* took on a specialized meaning of violent overthrow, and by the last period (third) of the nineteenth century was being contrasted with *evolution* in its sense of a new social order brought about by peaceful and constitutional means."[43] This should shed some interesting light on Sun's use of "revolution" in *Kidnapped in London*.

The appendix to Sun's book includes an article entitled "The Supposed Chinese Revolutionist," originally published in *China Mail* in Hong Kong. Clearly on Sun's side, the author writes: "Sun Yat-sen, who has recently been in trouble in London through the Chinese Minister attempting to kidnap him for execution as a rebel, is not unlikely to become a prominent character in history." Despite the defensive tone throughout the text, "revolutionist" was used almost synonymously with "rebel." The author says, for example, "In China, any advocate of reform or any foe of corruption and oppression is liable to be regarded as a violent revolutionist, and summarily executed."[44] For example, he also mentions "leaders of abortive revolution" or "the rebellion" being "precipitated in March."[45] In this respect, Feng Ziyou's reminiscence has a special value, for Feng points out that the 1894 manifesto of Sun's *Xingzhonghui* did not contain the word *geming* but, among the numerous translated terms with which Sun had been familiar in Hong Kong, a common Chinese translation of the English revolution had been *zaofan*.[46]

Liang Qichao and the Modernity of Geming Discourse

Liang Qichao was not the first person to revive the word *geming* for revolution in modern China, but he was the first to self-consciously "modernize" this discourse through Sino-Japanese-European translation by introducing a Darwinian notion of evolution into it, thus giving the ideology of revolution a deterministic character in twentieth-century China. Some of the textual details about his theory of revolution have drawn scant scholarly attention so far. I analyze them to add yet a third dimension to my discussion of the revolutionary thinking of Wang Tao and Sun Yat-sen.

After the failure of the Hundred Days Reform in 1898, Liang Qichao fled to Japan. Despite his reformist allegiance, his writings in 1898–1903, most of which appeared in *Qingyi bao* (The China discussion) and *Xinmin congbao* (New citizen journal), helped ferment the anti-Manchu revolutionary climate of the time.[47] Shortly after his arrival in Japan, Liang began to notice that the Japanese called the Meiji period *kakumei jidai* (the revolutionary era) and Yoshida Shōin *kakumei jimbutsu* (a revolutionary figure). He was fascinated by the fact that the Japanese translated English revolution into *kakumei*, making the word mean "changes in all societal affairs." To emulate the Meiji Reformation as a viable alternative to the anti-Manchu movement, Liang began to rework the meaning of *geming* in his writing.[48]

In December 1899, Liang was on a ship from Yokohama to Honolulu, sent by Kang Youwei to seek support from overseas Chinese. In his diary *Hanman lu* (A record of travel), Liang makes what seems to be the first mention of "poetry revolution" (*shijie geming*) that he envisions for China's future. "Although I am not a talented poet," writes Liang, "I will do my best to introduce European spiritual thought, so that it can serve as poetic materials for future poets. In short, the fate of Chinese poetry would be doomed if there were no poetic revolution. However, poetry can never die and a revolution is just around the corner. A Columbus or a Magellan will soon appear on the horizon."[49] *Shijie geming* was Liang's new coinage, in which *geming* certainly connotes a general idea of change. This relation of revolution to the poetic realm signifies the birth of a new type of revolution disenchanted from the mandate of Heaven in traditional political *geming* discourse, and thus opens new possibilities to change in everyday life. Liang himself was fond of this novel verbal combination and, in his diary several days later, he again speaks of a "prose revolution" (*wenjie geming*), praising Tokutomi Sōho (1863–1957) as a forerunner in assimilating European ideas in modern Japan. Liang says, "Tokutomi is one of three chief newspaper editors in Japan. His literary style is as sharp as it is powerful, uniting European thought with Japanese prose writings in a perfect style. He has really created a new prose genre. I admire him very much. If China should have a prose revolution, it must start at this level." [50]

Liang proposes "three principles" for the poetry revolution: "new language, new theme and old style." After a substantial discussion of these principles, he subordinates, at the end of the text, the poetry revolution to the loftier political cause of national salvation; he thus concludes that compared to the "revolutionary army" (*geming jun*) poetry is a "minor matter." This manifesto of poetry revolution expresses his contradictory expectations for contemporary poets: he expects them to be a Columbus or a Magellan in exploring the new poetry world, but he also expects them to join the revolutionary army. The neologism *shijie geming* is paradoxically engaged with *geming* in its sense of political violence. Liang advocates a poetry revolution not solely for aesthetic purposes; rather, he wants to mobilize literary forces to rescue China. Because the national crisis demanded a radical political solution and most Chinese readers were still accustomed to the old meaning of *geming*, the neologism *shijie geming* or *wenjie geming* aroused political revolutionary passion rather than aesthetic feelings.

After advocating a poetry revolution, Liang repeated this slogan in a number of articles; he also developed a column on revolutionary poetics titled "Poetic Remarks from the Studio of an Ice Drinker" in *Xinmin congbao*. Many of his followers and contemporary poets responded to his call and contributed experimental poems to the journal. Most of the poems, infused with Western ideas of freedom, democracy, and revolution, conveyed political messages. Particularly following the tragic Boxer Uprising in 1900, the word *geming* expressed and, in some works, endorsed antidynastic politics. Among them, Jiang Zhiyou's (1865?–1929) "Lu Sao" (Rousseau) was the most widely read. The latter half of the poem says:

> We do our best to pave the way for equality,
> And shed our blood on the flower of freedom.
> The day will come when our words come true,
> And the revolutionary tide sweeps across the world! [51]

Liang Qichao was, however, concerned about the growing trend of revolutionary violence which he attributed to popular misunderstanding of his concept of *geming* and felt compelled to clarify it. In an article entitled "Shi ge" (An explanation of the meaning of revolution) published in late 1902, he explains that the word *ge* implies the dual meanings of reform and revolution. Reform refers to a peaceful and evolutionary change whose nature is good, as in the case of the British Parliament in 1832. Japanese translates it well as *henkaku* (change, reform) or *kakushin* (reform, innovation). Revolution means rejecting one's roots and making a new world, as exemplified by the French Revolution in 1789. Both reform and revolution are necessary for a society to progress; all human affairs, not only the political, are subject to reform or revolution. He further argues that the Japanese translation of the English revolution into *geming* is inappropriate, because the Chinese *geming* comes from *The Book of Changes* and *Shu Jing* (Book of documents) and signifies violent overthrow of dynasties, ultimately distorting the true meaning of revolution.[52]

This reworking of the meaning of *geming* occurred through an interesting slippage in Japanese between *kakumei* (revolution) and *gaikaku* (reform). As a sympathetic reader of *The Nation's News* (*Kokumin Shinbun*) edited by Tokutomi Sōho, Liang shared Tokutomi's perspectives on national reform, as Sōho was one of the architects of Meiji revolutionary ideology. From 1882 to 1887 the latter founded a private school, Oe Academy, in Kumamoto and edited the *Ōe gijuku zasshi* (Journal of Oe Academy), in which he expounded the Western ideas of freedom and revolution with enthusiasm and demonstrated a preference for the English revolution. Tokutomi and his students advocated reform under the aegis of imperial constitutional polity and eulogized the Meiji reform as *ishin dai kakumei* (literally, reformation as great revolution). Hanatachi Saburō has documented the frequent occurrence of *kakumei* (revolution) and *gaikaku* (reform) in this journal and detected almost no difference in the meanings of the two words.[53]

The Japanese slippage reverberates through Liang's own attempt to make a plausible distinction in Chinese. He suggests a new translation of "revolution" as *biange* (change, reform) to replace *geming*. But as we can see, even as Liang tries to pin down the "true" meaning of revolution as *biange*, he cannot but refer back to the word *geming*:

Extinction and change occur not only in political but various other realms of worldly affairs. There are Japanese translated terms, such as religious revolution, moral revolution, academic revolution, literary revolution, custom revolution, and industrial revolution. In the favorite terms of today's youth, revolution can occur everywhere: classics, historiography, prose, poetry, drama, fiction, music, language, and so on. So why can we not call all these *geming* when they have nothing to do with dynastic changes? Those who fear *geming* would do well to know that its real meaning is *bianqe*. *Geming* may sound terrifying, but how can *bianqe* be so?[54]

The assorted phrases associated with *geming* presented in such a flamboyant and hyperbolic manner virtually eclipse Liang's assertion of *bianqe*. Liang's contradictory explanation aroused some debates at the time that caused the meaning of this word to expand, diffuse, and become flexible.

Liang adds a further twist to this debate by linking the idea to Darwinian evolutionism and modern historical consciousness.[55] He takes reform and revolution as an imperative for China's survival in the progressive history governed by the Darwinian principles of natural selection and elimination. He argues: "If the people want to survive, they must effect great change and take action immediately. If the monarch and officials want to survive and win people's favor, they must not fear great change but promote it."[56] Embedded in this appeal is his vision of historical necessity. Such aspiration for "great change" is analogous to what Hannah Arendt calls the "strange pathos of novelty" that emerged in the revolutionary epoch of modern history.[57] Politically it also indicates that the *geming* theory makes a break with the traditional notion of cyclical dynastic change and is incorporated into the universal idea of historical progress.

In this Sino-Japanese-European cycle of translation, *geming* has become a complex discursive terrain on which the idea of revolution is both universalized and localized in nationalist politics. Edward W. Said once remarked that theory traveling between cultures undergoes "four stages": a point of origin, a distance traversed, conditions of acceptance and resistance, and an accommodated idea.[58] The Chinese concept of *geming* seems to have undergone a more complex process of transformation through the mediation of Japanese *kakumei* and presents what I see as a triangular relationship. This is further complicated by what Liang calls the "narrow sense" and "broad sense" of *geming* in his article "A Study of Revolution in Chinese History" published in 1904.[59]

Liang criticizes the "narrow sense" of *geming* because of its suggestion of violence. In embracing its "broader sense," however, he cannot but gloss over the implication of violence in that sense as well. Zou Rong's 1903 pamphlet *The Revolutionary Army* shows eloquently how Liang's propaganda successfully inspired the anti-Manchu nationalist sentiments. Zou instigated racial hatred, proclaiming that Chinese revolution must start with "killing the Manchus," but he equates this same revolution with the "universal principle of evolution," a promise of social change including "freedom of speech, freedom of thinking, freedom of publication," and so on.[60] This promise of modernization echoes Liang's idea that a true revolution brings great change in Chinese society.

As Xiaobing Tang observes, the year 1902 signaled a turning point in Liang's political and intellectual enterprise. Liang saw himself as a "New Historian" and "laid the theoretical foundation for a nationalist rewriting, or creation, of Chinese history."[61] With this new historical imagination, Liang tried to create a nationalist discourse of modernity. The year 1902 witnessed Liang's dilemma about the concept of revolution as he began to doubt its usefulness for the reformist agenda. He argued that the new revolutionary ideology evoked by this catchword seemed to be tainted by its etymological and cultural roots and to carry with it a collective memory of violence from the imperial past.

In spite of Liang Qichao, the word *geming* continued to grow and accumulate meanings as it became more widely disseminated across modern Chinese history. In the process of negotiating with Western ideas and China's own dynastic past, the new meaning of *geming* is no longer identical with its original etymology, but carries a global and universal message with it. While tracing this discursive history of *geming* back to an earlier moment, I find myself recalling the memories of my own experience in the Cultural Revolution and reflecting on the recent disappearance of the word *geming* from the political discourse of Mainland China today. But it seems to me that "revolution" continues to have a hold on the society and exert its influence on the current political and social reality in a different, and now negative, form. One of the current tendencies is to repudiate or escape from *geming*, best exemplified by Li Zehou's expression: "Yes to reform; no to revolution."[62] But as we have seen, such repudiation has always been part of China's complex experience of revolution since Liang Qichao's translations. The use or "misuse" of *geming*, therefore, holds the key to the historicity of Chinese revolution and its global significance.

Notes

Leo Ou-fan Lee and Peiheng Zhang, my mentors at Harvard and Fudan, have encouraged me in this study, which began in the 1980s when I was still in China. Special thanks are due Julie Mallozzi, who gave the essay many readings. I am very grateful to Lydia Liu for her intellectual support and editing. All English translations are mine unless otherwise noted.

1   Liang Qichao, "Jing gao wo tongye zhujun."
2   Benjamin Schwartz, introduction to *Reflections on the May Fourth Movement: A Symposium*, 3.

3   Joseph R. Levenson, *Confucian China and Its Modern Fate: A Trilogy*, 2:119. On the relation of modern Chinese revolution and its cultural origins, Japanese scholarship is valuable. See Ojima Sukema, *Chūgoku no kakumei shisō*, and "Juka to kakumei shisō." Also see Takeuchi Yoshimi and Nomura Kōichi, eds. *Chūgoku — kakumei to dentō.*

4   Wolfgang Franke, *A Century of Chinese Revolution, 1851–1949*, 1.

5   Prasenjit Duara, *Rescuing History from the Nation*, 126.

6   Lydia H. Liu, *Translingual Practice*, 20.

7   Crane Brinton, *The Anatomy of Revolution*, 3.

8   Hannah Arendt, *On Revolution*, 21–52.

9   John King Fairbank, *The Great Chinese Revolution*, 7–8.

10 Tracing modern uses of *geming* helps solve textual problems and use historical data in a more proper way. For example, in the 1920s Liang Qichao in his reminiscences described his "revolutionary" ideas or deeds in his early years, but actually it was after 1899 when he used the word *geming* in a positive sense. Misled by Liang's revolutionary description, literary historians in Mainland China asserted that the "poetry revolution" began in 1897. I pointed out the mistake in my essay "Wan Qing 'shijie geming' fasheng shijian ji qi tichang zhe kaobian." Another typical instance is the original version of "Xingzhonghui zhangcheng," in which there was not the word *geming*. Yet later it was retitled by historians "Xingzhonghui *geming* xuanyan." Feng Ziyou, Republican historian, specifically corrected it in an article. See my essay "Wan Qing 'shijie *geming*' yu piping de wenhua jiaolü — Liang Qichao, Hu Shi yu '*geming*' de liangzhong yiyi."

11 Brinton, 3.

12 *Xinmin congbao* 46–48 (February 1904). In 1905, Qin Lishan wrote a long essay, "Shuo geming" (On revolution), in which he also divides *geming* into the "broad" and "narrow" senses, though slightly different from Liang's. See *Qin Lishan ji*, 114–71. A recent example is Chang P'eng-yuan, "Geming yu xiandaihua jiaozhi xia de jindai Zhongguo." The year 1905 also witnessed a series of debates of revolution theories between reformers and revolutionaries, which made its meaning more mixed with the two senses. See James Hong-yuan Chu, *Revolutionary Theory of T'ung-meng hui: The "Min pao" as a Case Study*.

13 There are two minor themes in the classical Chinese connotation of *geming*. One refers to a legend that the ancient king Yao passed on the throne to his son Yu. Linked with this story, the word *geming* means a peaceful replacement of dynasties (e.g., "Feng Yan zhuan," in Wang Xianqian *Hou Hanshu jishi*, 354). In 1901, when the reformers began to worry about the spread of revolutionary ideas, they tried to interpret *geming* in the above sense to curb the anti-Manchu current, but the article had little effect. See Shuli shanren, "Zun geming" (Respecting *geming*), 5973–75 (the page numbers are according to the reprint of *Qingyi bao* by Taipei Chengwen chubanshe in 1967).

Another theme refers to the word *geming* associated with a system of *ganzhi* (the heavenly stems and earthly branches), a system for calculating years, months, and days in premodern China. During the Han Dynasty (206 B.C.–A.D. 220), the system often served at court to foretell political events. After the Han, this *geming* theory was rejected by Confucianists. In the late nineteenth century, Yoshida Shōin used *geming* in this astronomical origin. See the section on Japanese translation of *geming* in this essay.

14 See James Legge, trans., *The Book of Changes*, 254. I have slightly altered Legge's translation.

15 See Sima Qian, *Shiji*, 3122–23.

16 As quoted in Zhu Xi, *Sishu zhangju jizhu*, 222.

17 Ibid., 222, 221. Zhao is cited by Zhu.

18 The characters of *geming* were originally Chinese. In Japanese there are two ways of reading Chinese characters: one is *kundoku*, reading a character with Japanese sounds; the other is *ondoku*, reading a character with Chinese sounds. A different method is used for the Chinese character *gong* (public), which is read either by *ondoku* as *kō* or by *kundoku* as *ōyake*. *Ōyake* is rooted in Japanese native culture, its meaning different from the Chinese *gong*. As for *geming*, there is no *kundoku* in Japanese. In February 1993, I attended a lecture on Chinese concepts of *si* (private) and *gong* (public) by Professor Mizoguchi Yūzō, who at the time was visiting the University of California, Los Angeles. By interpreting the word *ōyake*, he pointed out different conceptions on the part of the public between Japan and China. This example helps understand the case of *geming*.

19 According to recent research, *The Book of Mencius* was transported to Japan as early as the eighth century. See Noguchi Takehiko, *Ōdo to kakumei no aida*, 5.

20 Mizoguchi Yūzō, "Zhongguo minquan sixiang de tese," 343–61.

21 Tokoro Isao, *Miyoshi Kiyoyuki*, 71–100. Also see G. B. Sansom, *Japan: A Short Cultural History*, 208–9.

22 Morohashi Tetsuji, ed., *Dai Kan-Wa jiten*, 12747.

23 Ryusaku Tsunoda, Wm. Theodore de Bary, and Donald Keene, *Sources of Japanese Tradition*, 308.

24 See Wang Jiahua, *Rujia sixiang yu Riben wenhua*, 202.

25 Naramoto Tatsuya and Sanada Yukitaka, eds., *Yoshida Shōin*, 254–55.

26 The typical Meiji view of the French Revolution is reflected in Mizutani Yoshiaki's *Kokkai no kakin*. The author emotionally condemned the National Assembly's decision to persecute Louis XVI during the French Revolution, but at the same time he regarded this act as a mistake of the National Assembly, rather than negate the National Assembly as well as the principles of freedom and democracy associated with the French Revolution.

27 Okamoto Kansuke, *Wanguo shiji*, 11:6b, 9a; emphasis added.

28 Wang Tao, *Chongding Faguo zhilue*, 6:27a; 7:1a–b. Paul A. Cohen substantially discussed the close relationship between Wang Tao's *Chongding Faguo zhilue* and Oka Senjin's *Furansu shi*, yet he neglected to note that the role of the French Revolution in Wang's work was much indebted to Kansuke's *Wanguo shiji*. See *Between Tradition and Modernity: Wang T'ao and Reform in Late Ch'ing China*, 121–27.

29 Wang Tao, *Manyou sui lu, Fusang youji*, 248.

30 Wang Tao, *Chongding Faguo zhilue*, 5:30b.

31 Cohen has a detailed discussion of Wang Tao as a "traitor." He says, "After the fall of the Taipings, his intellectual rebellion against the prevailing order of things gained progressively momentum, and he became one of China's vocal advocates of far-reaching reform." See *Between Tradition and Modernity*, 56.

32 See Jian Bozan et al., eds., *Wuxu bianfa*, 3:57.
    Huang Zhangjian argued that Kang Youwei's claim that he submitted the memo-
    rials to the Emperor Guangxu during the Hundred Days Reform is problematic. Ac-
    cording to Huang's research, Kang wrote a "fake" memorial during 1909 and 1915 for
    his new constitutional politics. See *Kang Youwei wuxu zhen zouyi*, 503–5.

33 Zhang Binglin, "Lun xuehui you da yi yu huangren ji yi baohu."

34 See Chen Shaobai, *Xingzhonghui geming shiyao*, 12; Feng Ziyou, *Geming Yishi* (Reminis-
    cences of the revolution), 1:1. Also Harold Z. Schiffrin, *Sun Yat-sen and the Origins of the
    Chinese Revolution*, 98–100.

35 Chen Xiqi, ed., *Sun Zhongshan nianpu changbian*, 100–103.

36 Chen Shaobai, 102.

37 Schiffrin, 99.

38 Paul Linebarger, *Sun Yat-sen and the Chinese Republic*, 200–203.

39 See Federico Masini, *The Formation of Modern Chinese Lexicon and Its Evolution Toward a
    National Language: The Period from 1840–1898*, 40.

40 Xie Weilou, *Wanguo tongjian*, 4: sec. 1, 15b–16a; sec. 2, 1b–3b.

41 Sun Yat-sen, *Kidnapped in London*, 13.

42 Sun Yat-sen, "Zhongguo geming shi," 202.

43 Raymond Williams, *Keywords*, 273.

44 Sun, *Kidnapped in London*, 116.

45 Ibid., 117.

46 See Zhonghua minguo kaigo wushi nian wenxian bianji weyuanhui, ed., *Zhonghua
    minguo kaigo wushi nian wenxian*, part 1, 9:278.

47 See Michael Gasster, "Reform and Revolution in China's Political Modernization,"
    67–96. Also see Hao Chang, *Liang Ch'i-ch'ao and Intellectual Transition in China, 1890–1907*,
    167.

48 See Liang Qichao, "Shi ge." At the same time, Kang Youwei was excited about his
    discovery of the new meaning of *geming* in Japan, as evidenced by one of his poems
    dedicated to Shōin and eulogizing the Meiji Reform as "a great revolution in a mil-
    lennium." See *Qingyi bao* 9 (1899): 557.

49 Liang Qichao, *Hanman lu*, 2280–83.

50 Ibid., 2349.

51 In *Xinmin congbao* 3 (1902): 100.

52 Liang, "Shi ge," 1–8.

53 Hanatachi Saburō points out: "Although we now use the two words in their clearly
    different senses, there was no distinction at that time" (*Tokutomi Sōho to Ōe gijuku*, 87).

54 Liang, "Shi ge," 4.

55 See Leo Ou-fan Lee, "In Search of Modernity: Some Reflections on a New Mode of
    Consciousness in Twentieth-Century Chinese History and Literature."

56 Liang, "Shi ge," 7–8.

57 Arendt, 21–52.

58 Edward W. Said, *The World, the Text, and the Critic*, 226–27.

59 Liang Qichao, "Zhongguo lishi shang geming zhi yanjiu."

60 Zou Rong, *Zou Rong wenji*, 41.

61 Xiaobing Tang, *Global Space and the Nationalist Discourse of Modernity: The Historical Thinking of Liang Qichao*, 3.
62 Li Zehou, "Heping jinhua, fuxing Zhonghua—tan 'yao gailiang, buyao *geming*.' " Also see Wu Guoguang, "*Geming* he gaige." Another variation of the dichotomy of revolution and reformation is revolution and modernization. See Chang P'eng-yuan, "Modernization and Revolution in China, 1860–1949," 47.

Wan Shun Eva Lam   *The Question of Culture in*

Global English-Language Teaching:

A Postcolonial Perspective

This essay considers the pedagogical issues of language, knowledge, and cultural encounter in the new global condition of cross-cultural contact within and across national borders, the worldwide circulation of cultural products in commercial forms, and the rise of the notion of a global village facilitated by transnational capitalism and information technology. In particular, it examines what foreign language educators, as a type of "cultural worker"[1] in our own playing field, need to know about the learning and teaching of culture.

The significance of the cultural dimension in foreign-language education has been slowly recognized by the profession in the past two decades. The demands for and difficulties in the teaching of culture in the language curriculum have been observed, and foreign-language educators have begun to reconsider the relations between cultural study and the language classroom. For example, the notion of global competence has gained wide circulation in the European continent in response to increasing integration of the economic systems of the European nation-states in order to stay competitive in the global market.[2] A number of cross-cultural educational programs have been established to "open up national institutions of education and training to their counterparts in other countries, create networks of cooperation and overcome the linguistic and cultural obstacles by educational exchange and study abroad—mobility as *deus ex machina* for the economic, political and cultural integration of Europe."[3] This growing realization of the need to address the cultural dimension of language education is also witnessed by the efforts undertaken by the American Council for the Teaching of Foreign Languages to determine and classify the elements on a scale of cultural proficiencies for the purposes of instruction and assessment.[4]

Yet Kramsch points out that the heavy emphasis on the pragmatic values of education, the transmission or information-processing model of learning, and the striving for immediacy facilitated by electronic media in the American educational culture tend to impede the development of critical understanding of native and foreign cultures.[5] In an article detailing the ways in which foreign-language textbooks reflect the ethnocentric views and ways of the American educational culture, Kramsch arrives at the conclusion that the integrative discourses and culture-learning strategies presented in the majority of textbooks serve to reinforce mainstream American culture, and can be deemed useful only to the extent that they teach linguistic skills and some reified cultural facts.[6]

Indeed, foreign-language educators now realize that the presentation of factual information about foreign cultures serves only to produce the tourist- and holiday-maker type of knowledge, and has little effect on helping students develop cross-cultural sensitivities.[7] Even efforts to teach culture in a comparative/contrastive fashion, as exemplified by the collection of articles in Culture Bound, also fail to promote a higher level of synthesis and critical understanding of cultural facts presented in an anecdotal manner.[8] All of the above point to the need for the development of a theoretical understanding of the role of culture in the foreign-language curriculum. In this essay, I explore four characteristics of cultural identity, knowledge, and encounter in the postcolonial world: the formation of cultural identity in dialectical relationships, culture as historical process, culture as border experiences, and emerging realities. These aspects of cultural study are placed in the context of English-language teaching as an educational endeavor in various countries around the world.

The Question of Culture in English-Language Teaching

Initiated by colonial domination in the past and propelled by commerce, science, and technology in the present, the spread of English in the world has always been facilitated through instruction in the classroom, as witnessed by the rise of the English-Language Teaching (ELT) profession. However, the past two decades have seen an increasingly wide range of criticisms being launched against the teaching of English as a second or foreign language, which has caused many in the profession to reconsider the cultural dimensions of ELT. In the following, I lay out some of the major concerns and arguments regarding the question of culture in ELT: cultural imperialism, native resistance, bilingualism versus biculturalism, and the diversification of linguistic and cultural norms.

The pervasiveness of English in today's world is certainly not new, as is clear in the following statistics published in the *Cambridge Encyclopedia of Language*:

English is used as an official or semi-official language in over 60 countries, and has a prominent place in a further 20. It is either dominant or well established in all six continents. It is the main language of books, newspapers, airports and air-traffic control, international business and academic conferences, science, technology, medicine, diplomacy, sports, international competitions, pop music, and advertising. Over two-thirds of the world's scientists write in English. Three-quarters of the world's mail is written in English. Of all the information in the world's electronic retrieval systems, 80% is stored in English. English radio programmes are received by over 150 million in 120 countries.[9]

A recent article, " 'Cultural Conflict' or 'Cultural Invasion,' " in the popular Hong Kong news magazine *Cheng Ming*, portrays the rather heated debate on cultural imperialism currently taking place in China.[10] This is sparked, in part, by the Westernization of various cultural commodities, such as goods and services in shops, restaurants, hotels, and apartment buildings, whose surface forms include foreign terms and transliterations. Prodromou provides a concrete example of the relation between language and cultural imperialism in his discussion on the phenomenon of the term "supermarket" in the socioeconomic context of Greek society:

The word "supermarket" sums up more than any other what I mean by Granglais as a linguistic phenomenon—but as a cultural and political phenomenon, too. Here are the distinctive features of a Greek "supermarket": (1) "Supermarket" is an English word. (2) It is also a Greek word now (my mother-in-law, who doesn't speak English, does not use the available "Greek" word, but "supermarket" instead). (3) It is an imported concept and institution. (4) It sells lots of desirable goods, both Greek and imported. (5) It is a sign that Greece is a modern consumer society, buying and selling on a large scale. The fact that a large percentage of the goods sold in Greek supermarkets are foreign is, on the one hand, a sign that the country is culturally and economically developing in that it has money to spend on fulfilling a wide variety of material needs which it shares with the Western developed nations that export the goods. But this "development" is ambiguous. The word "supermarket" captures this ambiguity perfectly.[11]

Hence, to call English a "world commodity," as Phillipson has done, is perhaps not too farfetched.[12] The marketing of this world commodity has been actively undertaken by various governmental and private agencies of the major native-English-speaking countries. Some of this is in the form of "aids" to developing countries to expand educational activities, for example, in the setting up of schools and programs, many of which use English as a medium of instruction or include English as a subject of study.[13] A considerable part of the active promulgation of English as a world language is undertaken through sending expatriate English teachers and ELT specialists and spreading ELT methodologies and materials around the globe. For example, in recent years, the communicative pedagogy, which promotes students' verbal expression and group work in the classroom, has been exported to many parts of the world in the forms of curricular materials and teacher-training programs. Both the ideology of human relationships that is endorsed by this current teaching methodology and the instructional activities derived from it are sometimes greatly incongruent with the local cultures of the people adopting it.[14]

Regarding cultural imperialism in general, and educational imperialism in particular, as it is related to English teaching in Hong Kong, a number of educators have criticized the long-practiced colonial policies of creating and maintaining a small group of local elites as "intermediate leaders," educated in a Western or modified-Western system, and denying the validity and competitiveness of educational certification from Taiwan and Mainland China.[15] Although close to 99 percent of the population in Hong Kong are native speakers of Cantonese, a widely used Chinese dialect in the Guangdong Province of southern China, English is an important medium of instruction in the formal education system and is used to various extents by the citizenry in their daily economic activities, especially in academic and business transactions.

British English was instituted as an official language and remained the primary means of oral and written communication in the Hong Kong government since the inception of colonial administration in 1841, even though Chinese was given official status in 1974. English-language education in the early colonial period of this fishing economy began with the educational work of Christian missionaries in the 1840s.[16] These Western schools received small amounts of financial and administrative support from the colonial government. In the following decades, the government set up and assisted in the development of various kinds of elite schools, often called Anglo-Chinese schools, to provide a bilingual and bicultural education, strongly modeled after the Western academic traditions, to a select group of Chinese who could then act as middlemen for the British in their transactions with Mainland China.[17] This initial colonial

Table 1. Chinese vs. English as the Language of Instruction in Hong Kong Middle Schools, in percentages

	Chinese Middle Schools	Anglo-Chinese Schools
1960	42.1	57.9
1965	29.0	71.0
1970	23.3	76.7
1975	21.3	78.7
1980	12.3	87.7
1985	9.5	90.5
1990	8.3	91.7

Source: Kwo and Bray, 1987: 99; Hong Kong Education Department, 1991: 63. Cited in W. O. Lee, "Social Reactions towards Education Proposals: Opting against the Mother Tongue as the Medium of Instruction in Hong Kong," 206.

educational policy was followed by a period of strong promotion of English-language education, until the first half of the twentieth century when there was a growing movement toward the expansion and vernacularization of education in the lower grades and for the grassroots populace.

Even so, there was in actuality little change in the power and prestige of English and the aspiration of the local Chinese to master this language for the economic and educational prospects it provides. Besides being the official language, English was also an important medium of business transactions in the expanding commercial sectors of the colony. For the Hong Kong Chinese, attending university in the People's Republic of China was unrewarding in economic terms and even "dangerous" in the political scenario, and English literacy was a prerequisite for higher education locally or abroad in English-speaking countries. Hence, the language has been considered the key to social mobility and greater political security for the average citizen.[18]

Against this political and economic backdrop, it is not surprising to see the following statistics on the growth of English-medium schools (Anglo-Chinese schools) in comparison with Chinese middle schools where Chinese is the primary medium of instruction and English is taught as a separate subject (see Table 1). With the reversion of Hong Kong to China's sovereignty in 1997, the percentage of English-medium schools is currently reduced to about 25 percent, but English remains prevalent in most tertiary institutions (colleges and universities), which are seen as the city's bridge to the outside world.[19] An important reason for using English as the medium of instruction is to maximize exposure to and thus "mastery" of the English language. However, one could surmise that, in making English the primary medium of instruction, it also becomes inevitable to adopt textbooks written by native-English-speaking authors or English-educated locals, to employ more expatriates as teachers or teacher trainers, and to adhere more closely to a Western academic culture. In recent years, there has been a resurgence of interest in the hiring of expatriate English teachers to provide more "native" models of the language to students whose proficiency in English has been widely considered inadequate in meeting the requirements of higher education and the workplace.[20]

The hegemony of English and the implication of language teaching in the processes of cultural invasion have been met with some resistance in the host countries. One form of resistance can be seen in the ways English is taught and learned in the classroom. In many countries where English is taught as a foreign language—for example, Japan, China, Korea, other parts of Asia, Africa, and Latin America—the focus of language teaching is on the grammatical code rather than on its functional use in cross-cultural communication settings. This has been interpreted by Alptekin and Alptekin as a way to protect the ethnolinguistic identity of students from the need to acculturate to foreign models in a world marked by persistent unequal relationships among cultural groups.[21] In Malaysia, for instance, some Malay Muslims have felt the threat to the values of Islam of Western cultural influences perpetrated through the teaching of English.[22] Yet the acquisition of English is still considered an important tool for personal and national development in a globalized world. Some students seek to reconcile these conflicting feelings by separating language learning from cultural learning. As secondary students in Dan et al.'s study said, "Western culture does not necessarily mean negative culture. We can learn English but not copy the 'Western' way of life. . . . To be influenced by Western values will depend on an individual's personality. Learning the language doesn't mean adopting the culture. . . . In learning English, the Western influence seeps through without us realizing it, but through 'imam' and 'taqwa,' the influence can be obstructed." [23]

In an ethnographic study of English-language teaching in a Sri Lankan classroom among Tamil students, Canagarajah finds that resistance to cultural domination manifests itself in students' disregard for the cultural elements in the reading passages and the learning styles and strategies suggested (or dictated) by the American-language textbooks imported for use in the country.[24] For instance, they wrote disparaging remarks about the text passages in the margins of their books, and some even refused to follow the textbook instructions to engage in the interactive/cooperative group activities with their peers. Yet the students showed great concern for their success in acquiring the language and tended to concentrate on mastering the language code and passing the mandatory English tests in the university system.

Canagarajah interprets the students' focus on grammar as a way for them to resolve the conflict between the threat of cultural alienation and the pragmatic necessity of learning English. Concluding from his research findings, Canagarajah observes:

> Grammar learning enabled the students to be detached from the language and the course, avoid active use of the language which could involve internalization of its discourse, and thereby continue their opposition to the reproductive tendencies of the course. At the same time, this strategy enabled them to maintain the minimal contact necessary with the language in order to acquire the rules of grammar—which in their view was the most efficient preparation for getting through the examination. This strategy while enabling them to preserve their cultural integrity (however tenuously) also enabled them to accommodate the institutional requirement of having to pass English and thus bid for the socioeconomic advantages associated with the language.[25]

The growing resistance to cultural dominance at various levels of society in the host countries of English-language teaching has been one of the critical factors in spurring the efforts of some researchers and practitioners in the ELT profession to eliminate culture from the teaching of language.

Due to its widespread use in international business, communications, academic research, science, and technology, the English language is believed by some to have universalized to the extent that developing proficiency in an international form of the language does not require a concomitant knowledge of the culture of any of the countries where English is used as a national language. In "deculturizing" English (alternatively, de-Anglicizing and de-Americanizing) or promoting an international variety of the language, it is hoped that ELT will rid itself of the stigma of cultural imperialism and still be able to meet the needs of the masses of people around the world for whom the English language is one of the keys to a successful career, or even a necessity for survival in the school system. Alptekin and Alptekin put it this way: "If EFL [English as a Foreign Language] instruction in non-English-speaking countries is to become effective and realistic, care must be taken by the ministry of education of each country not to let it either turn into a tool of Anglo-American sociocultural domination, or take on ethnocentric features in order to isolate itself from such domination. In practical terms, this means that less attention should be paid to teaching models based on native-speaker norms and values, and more to developing 'culturally neutral, non-élitist, and learner-oriented' EFL programs (George 1981: 12)."[26]

In Hong Kong, as mentioned above, where English has long been an official language of the colonial government and remains a key institutional language in many formal arenas of life but has never taken root as a primary language of social/interpersonal communication, popular culture, or ethnic and national identity, some language educators have proposed setting up a policy where the most universal characteristics of formal English would be the target of instruction in order to avoid negative ethnolinguistic reactions.[27] Among them, Johnson has attempted to identify the features of "International English" (IE) with a view to more effective planning and design of "a core curriculum in English for international use, which is clearly differentiated from either an L1 or L2 [first language or second language]."[28] For instance, in terms of sociocultural features, he suggests that IE should exhibit no social distinctions nor a sense of group identity and solidarity. Moreover, it is necessarily learned in classroom settings and symbolizes the condition of "modernity." The textual feature of IE is very much context-reduced and its discourse style largely analytic, both of which correlate well with the primarily ideational and transactional functions that it is expected to fulfill. In other words, it is what is said or written that matters, not interpersonal or communal relationships. Johnson has proposed IE as the norm for English education in Hong Kong, the reason being that this is the language that teachers are competent in teaching and students will find useful in their academic and professional lives.

In a survey of student interests and classification of authentic texts used for reading instruction in English, Crewe and Tong find that many university undergraduate students in Hong Kong exhibit little knowledge and interest in texts that contain foreign cultural themes, topics, and information (i.e., all that is not Hong Kong-, China-, Japan-, or to a lesser extent, U.S.-oriented).[29] Based on the findings, they conclude that reading instruction in the second language would be most effective when carried out with texts that are more culturally neutral or familiar to the students and do not require understanding of a foreign culture. After all, they quote, "The use of English in Hong Kong and China is an economic and political statement of citizens of the world, not a cultural orientation towards Britain or the U.S. (Paulston 1987: 70)."[30]

The proposals to adopt IE and culturally neutral materials for instruction are reminiscent of the efforts behind the spread of Basic English in China merely half a century ago, as seen in Q. S. Tong's essay in this volume. They reveal the tension between global orientation and national identity in the modern era, exemplified in both the contemporary Hong Kong scenario and the clash between the linguistic universalism of Basic English and China's modern national identity. This contradictory logic of modernity shows how the global status/power of a nation is created through the production of universalism and its appropriation, whether as an imperialist agenda or a statement of world citizenship. Any form of universalism encodes its own ideology forged in cross-cultural encounter.[31]

Hence, it is important to note that in stripping English of its cultural baggage, the profession runs the risk of forfeiting the opportunity to help students develop the critical language skills for evaluating the ideology behind the continued flow of information and cultural products wrapped in the English language. Working in Morocco, Hyde rightly points out:

Moroccans, along with people all over the world, are living in an age in which a global information technology revolution is taking place. Information, mostly in English, is flooding the world, through advertisements, magazines, newspapers, books, instruction manuals, satellite television, films and rock music, videos, radio, telephones, the post, fax and telex machines, computers and information technology in general, tourism and migration for economic and educational reasons, and business relations. All of these make it very doubtful that the outside world could be kept out of Moroccan (or any other) society. . . . On the other hand, if it [English teaching] involves focusing students' awareness on the ideology behind English discourse, by developing a critical language awareness in students (Fairclough 1992), it becomes more viable.[32]

In view of the controversy over language and culture in the teaching of English, some educators advocate a local approach to the integration of language and culture, particularly in places where the language has been appropriated or "nativized" to the extent that a distinct indigenous culture of second-language users of English can be found. Braj Kachru is one of the leading scholars in the field of applied linguistics who have elucidated the distinct varieties of English-language forms and uses in what he has termed the norm-developing "Outer Circle," countries that are mostly former British colonies and have adopted English as one of their official languages (e.g., India, Nigeria, and Singapore).[33] In its acculturation to a new context, the English language is modified in its formal features, for example, via nativized lexical items and codes of politeness, to fulfill certain culturally specific communicative functions. Kachru has called attention to the distinctive features of intranational registers of English and the multiple dimensions of creativity they exhibit: mixing language elements from various languages; switching registers within languages and varieties; rearranging high and low styles of language use; and readjusting culturally dependent acts of interaction. In regard to the practicality of adopting local cultural norms for language instruction, he notes, "The strength of English lies in its multicultural specificity, which the language reveals in its formal and functional characteristics, as in, for example, West Africa, South Asia, and the Philippines."[34]

Adaskou, Britten, and Fahsi report a large-scale textbook project that was undertaken to design the cultural content of a new national English course for Moroccan secondary school students. The aim of the project was to make the cultural contexts represented in the English textbooks more relevant to the lives of the students, that is, that involve the kinds of people and settings in which English is actually used in the country. The result was the creation of Moroccan characters who are "educated urban dwellers, mostly students or young professionals—and English-speaking."[35] Even though the characters are not representative of all the secondary students, the researchers assert that "this mise-en-scène presents a world to which Moroccan secondary learners can reasonably aspire and with which they can identify without alienation."[36] In a sense, this project can be seen as a way to create a "national variety" of English-speaking Moroccans through the educational system, as much as it reflects the reality of the use of English in the country.

The need for a local approach to merging culture and language in English teaching has also been proposed by ELT researchers and practitioners in other non-English-speaking countries where there are no recognizable indigenous norms of English use.[37] Instead of emptying language of its cultural components, they suggest that students can most profitably use their developing skills in the language to describe their own culture. Prodromou advocates juxtaposing the local and "target" cultural phenomena when designing pedagogical materials to facilitate comparison between the two cultures.[38] Moreover, to help students become world citizens, he proposes broadening the cultural content of language instruction to include other cultures, and English, being "at the center of international and global culture," is eminently suited for the job.[39]

With the renewed interest in developing pedagogical approaches to address the cultural component of language learning, it is important to heed the call of Kramsch and Byram to develop a theoretical base for the study of culture in foreign-language education.[40] How can the study of culture counteract the threat of cultural imperialism from either side of the encounter, respect the local culture but not be constrained by it, and go beyond the learning of cultural facts or the simple comparison of facts, to engage students in developing the knowledge, skills, and moral responsibilities for cross-cultural understanding and communication that involve critical reflection on the self and other? The question of culture is indeed a large and complicated one. In the rest of this essay, I explore a few ways to rethink the cultural dimension of foreign-language education, particularly in the field of English-language teaching.

A Postcolonial Perspective on Culture and ELT

It is now little disputed that the formation of personal identity is largely a social process, and the "writing" of personal biography requires a considerable amount of joint authorship. The same can be said of ethnicity, gender, and national culture: there are no intrinsic ethnic, gendered, or cultural characteristics that can be objectively described, but understandings or "definitions" of characteristics develop through contact with and in relationship to the *others* around one. The sense of being an Indian in the state of India is radically different from that in the Caribbean.[41] The big waves of historical changes that have swept through the Chinese landscape, which include encounter with Western imperialism, political revolutions, and the Chinese diaspora in the modern era, have produced immense fluidity, ambiguity, and complexity in the definition of Chineseness.[42]

The work of cultural and literary historians has shown us that admitting the interdependence of people or groups of people, or that one's identity is defined in relationship to others, is not an easy process. In the creation of hegemony and racial or cultural superiority, the tendency has been to distance and radicalize others for the sake of legitimating and facilitating the acts of domination. As eminently argued and detailed by Said, the study of Oriental cultures in the West had proceeded as a series of "transformation" of the other that served to produce an alter ego for self-gratification and symbolic and material domination. It is not hard to identify some commonality between the following remarks by Said and the way we study culture in foreign-language education today: "It is perfectly natural for the human mind to resist the assault on it of untreated strangeness; therefore cultures have always been inclined to impose complete transformations on other cultures, receiving these other cultures not as they are but as, for the benefit of the receiver, they ought to be."[43]

However, the reality of the impact of colonialism has spoken otherwise, as witnessed by the different ways Western cultural institutions and practices changed in the history of imperialism. For instance, Pratt argues that the glorification of the natural world by European explorers in the colonized African and Caribbean territories was instrumental in developing the Romantic tradition in Western literature.[44] Moreover, Viswanathan shows that the study of English literature did not become an institution, or an organized cultural and political endeavor, until it was developed as a method by the British Empire to exert moral and social control over its Indian subjects.[45] In regard to both the material realities and the cultural imagination of the metropolis, the processes and consequences of cross-cultural encounter have never been unilateral or unequivocal.

Hence, it is important to conceptualize the study of culture as an engagement between the self and the other in dialectical relationships, where knowledge production becomes a process of constant realization of and battle against the projection of oneself onto the other, the persistent striving to understand more about the other through his or her eyes, and an opening to the discovery of oneself through the eyes of the other. Working in the field of cultural anthropology, Fabian proposes a hermeneutic framework for understanding self and other in the study of culture. This involves a *copresence* of both parties as the subjects for analysis and interpretation and an emphasis on self-reflection: "A praxis that does not include the one who studies it can only be confronted as an image of itself, as a representation, and with that, anthropology is back to the interpretation of (symbolic) forms. . . . More insidious than individual moral failure is a collective failure to consider the intellectual effects of scientific conventions which, by censoring reflexions on the autobiographic conditions of anthropological knowledge, remove an important part of the knowledge process from the arena of criticism."[46]

In the study of culture in foreign-language education, Kramsch has proposed a hermeneutic approach to understanding both the native and the foreign cultural imaginations and realities.[47] The aim of this approach is to help students develop a more comprehensive understanding of another culture by experiencing different levels of interpretation of both cultures; that is, understanding *one's perception of the other culture* (often, images of oneself) and realizing how these perceptions are affected by the *cultural imagination or popular perception of themselves* by the people of each culture. The process of this approach to the study of cultural texts takes into consideration both the native (local) and foreign (original) contexts of reception for the texts and explores how the self-perception of each culture determines how it views the other culture. It is hoped that a more complete understanding of native and foreign cultures would be developed through the confrontation of these layers of interpretation.

However, for English-language teaching in the postcolonial world, it is important not to lose sight of the impact of persistent and new forms of power inequality in cross-cultural relations. The attempt to critique the dominant voices in a cultural text can be a truly agonistic dialectical process. (For example, as a teacher of English to second-language learners in the United States, I sometimes find it difficult to form another perspective on American culture through the eyes of my students when some of them have already taken the dominant American views as the norm.) Hence, to construct the condition for a more equal confrontation of viewpoints and perceptions, it is necessary to encourage a counterdiscursive stance and a wider set of reading and writing practices in relation to cultural texts.[48]

Drawing on Freire's work on critical pedagogy, JanMohammed argues for the "demystification of social-political-cultural structuration," which involves the understanding of how one is culturally encoded under terms of domination.[49] As he notes from Freire's work, "Culture, as an interiorized product that in turn conditions men's subsequent acts, must become the object of men's knowledge so that they can perceive its conditioning power."[50] This critical understanding of culture necessitates a certain amount of interpretive knowledge of the historical processes of cultural formation. I discuss this aspect of culture next.

> We take culture to be the semantic space, the field of signs and practices, in which human beings construct and represent themselves and others, and hence their societies and histories. . . . Culture always contains within it polyvalent, potentially contestable messages, images, and actions. It is, in short, a historically situated, historically unfolding ensemble of signifiers-in-action, signifiers at once material and symbolic, social and aesthetic. — JOHN COMAROFF AND JEAN COMAROFF, Ethnography and the Historical Imagination

Understanding culture through a study of the historical processes in its formation and transformation through contact with other cultures has constituted a new praxis for cultural anthropologists. For instance, in their study of the changes that took place in the sociocultural systems of a number of African societies in the period of colonialism, Comaroff and Comaroff point out the contradictory elements of the inner workings of the societies, and how they interact with the outside forces of the colonial enterprise to produce new fluctuating social orders.[51] They illustrate in detail the dialectical nature of the historical encounter between the local society and the imperial powers, where change was not a one-way process of domination and subjugation of indigenous ways. Instead, the diverging ideologies of the colonizers — embraced variously by the empire state, the industrial-capitalist colonial settlers, and the nonconformist Christian missionaries — entered into contests with each other during the colonial encounter, which resulted in a reconfiguring of the relationships among the different groups of colonizers. In a way, the colonial territory became a field in which the social conflicts inherent in the colonizing country were played out in relation to a subordinated group of people.

The concept of culture as a "shifting semantic field" characterized by the appropriation and reinvention of meanings is explored by Lydia Liu in a different context. In studying the formation of the national culture and literature of China in the past century, Liu remarks that "to draw a clear line between the indigenous Chinese and the exogenous Western in the late twentieth century is almost an epistemological impossibility." [52] Instead, she proposes the following for cross-cultural analysis: "My point can be stated simply: a cross-cultural study must examine its own condition of possibility. Constituted as a translingual act itself, it enters, rather than sits above, the dynamic history of the relationship between words, concepts, categories, and discourses. One way of unraveling that relationship is to engage rigorously with those words, concepts, categories, and discourses beyond the realm of common sense, dictionary definition, and even historical linguistics." [53] In tracing and analyzing the historical process of the formation of the notions of "national character" and "individualism" in early-twentieth-century China, Liu details how these words were borrowed from the West initially through translation, which allowed them to become incorporated into the Chinese language as neologisms. These neologistic constructions were then conceptualized and deployed by the new generation of intellectuals to reform the society. For instance, the concept of "national character" was used by May Fourth writers to create a new narrative voice that was able to analyze and critique the traditional culture. Moreover, the discourse of "individualism" was instrumental in liberating the individual from traditional bonds to the family and relocating him or her in connection to the state.

All of the above illustrate the need to problematize the definition of cultural identity in today's world. In understanding the subject positions of oneself and others in cross-cultural situations, it is important to be aware of the multivalent and global influences in the historical formation of cultural identity. By studying the multiple appropriations of the words and meanings of various cultural constructs, students may become more sensitive to the indeterminacy of meaning and the mutual influences of the different cultures of the world. However, in view of the fact that the construction of meanings in history is saturated with unequal terms of power relationships, it is necessary, as Giroux points out, to have students read alternative historical accounts, which can challenge the sanitized and monologic portrayals of cultural characteristics and help them reconstruct a more comprehensive and critical view of society. [54]

In proposing an ethnographic approach to intercultural education in foreign-language study, Byram and Kane stress the need to gather various kinds of texts and cultural artifacts from the foreign culture for analysis and interpretation, and ultimately to yield a comparative understanding of two or more cultures.[55] As valuable as this "fieldwork approach" or "ethnographic technique"[56] may be in learning the "native" (there is a predominance of the singular native in their discourse) or insider perspective on a foreign culture, this orientation to cultural study is predicated largely on a "national" model of culture and the perception/presentation of cultures as distinct from each other. I would add that one avenue for engaging in a historical analysis of cultural constructs may be located in the "hybrid semantic fields" of cultural contact. This is noted by Comaroff and Comaroff—"global forces played into local forms and conditions in unexpected ways, changing known structures into strange hybrids"[57]—and is constitutive of the third aspect of cultural study discussed here.

A prominent feature of today's global cultural landscape is the intermingling of customs and lifeways and the presence of multiculturalism within national borders. The movement of peoples on a massive scale across territorial boundaries, set forth by the colonial disruption of relatively closed communal living in various parts of the world, has served to problematize the definition of "native" and "authenticity." As Chambers portrays in poignant terms but with an exulting tone, the uprooted "native" cultures and transient nature of the electronic age are characterized to a large degree by a sense of "homelessness" and have transformed the notion of authenticity to "an authentically migrant perspective," which is open to multiple possibilities and transmutations.[58] So where is the "native" in today's world? This is a futile question both for the sinologist who searched feverishly for a "pure" version of national Chinese poetry (uncontaminated by Western influences) and ended by lamenting the loss of the Chinese national heritage, and for the contemporary student of European cultures who still sees as fringes the numerous diasporic communities and the massive "coloring" of the white landscape.[59]

Said has noted that this transmutation and hybridization of cultural identity, and the syncretic perspective that arises from it, can constitute a new space for the study of culture.[60] The colonial subjects, having their precolonial nature unsettled by imperialism, developed a "second nature" in the midst of cultural contact and living under domination. However, neither of these identities fully describes the legacy of colonialism; it is necessary "to seek out, to map, to invent, or to discover a third nature" wherein resides the potential for better understanding the experiences of the postcolonial subjects.[61] In the same vein, Bhabha reacts against the polarization and simplification of culture that recent critical theories dwell on in the binary opposition of self and other, center and periphery, oppressor and oppressed. He uses the metaphor of "a third space" to signify a new frame of reference and process of signification that occurs in *between* cultures as a result of contact and the clash of difference. For Bhabha, there is no simple definition of "nation" in a world where the movement of peoples and cultures has been occurring on a massive scale. Many of us are forever dwelling in the "in-between space" at the margins of nations. For Bhabha, hybridity is never an admixture of established cultures or identities, but the elusive conditions where signs and meanings can be "appropriated, translated, rehistoricized, and read anew."[62]

In recent anthropological thinking, the notion of culture as an analytical concept has been problematized to take into account the destabilized relationships of people, language, space, and culture.[63] Working from a transnational perspective on cultural flows and social networks, these theorists have called into question the comparative approach to culture and proposed that we may better understand cultural identity as the choices of affiliations that people make in their social practices, which often stretch beyond the national boundaries. On this, Appadurai writes, "Culture becomes less what Bourdieu would have called a habitus (a tacit realm of reproducible practices and dispositions) and more an arena for conscious choice, justification and representation, the latter often to multiple and spatially dislocated audiences."[64] Here, Appadurai points to the partial dissolution of the bulwark of national culture in people's imagination and signals the degree of maneuvering within existing sociopolitical structure and changes in the structure, for example, as brought forth by economic globalization.

Hence, it is important to think "across borders" in our attempts to learn about the nature of postcolonial cultures in general, whether in the so-called first or third world, and to understand cultural encounter and the emergence of difference in a deeper sense. The fears that arise in some quarters when faced with the widespread hybridization of culture have motivated some people in positions of power to fuse culture with national identity, citizenship, and patriotism. This describes well what the Mainland Chinese government has been undertaking as a benign way to gain allegiance from the Hong Kong Chinese people in the transitional period both preceding and following the official exchange of colonial sovereignty.[65] This is also why the new spaces of hybrid cultural identities and the shifting borders of race, gender, and ethnicity in the United States have created a certain amount of panic among people whose interests are served by the traditional boundaries.[66] All of this has made it even more critical for us to foster a practice of language learning and cultural study in the *borders of representation*, where intermixing serves as the most legitimate area of inquiry, where multiple voices speak out from history to dialogue with each other, and where difference is not only acknowledged but cultivated in the acts of mixing.

Giroux proposes the notion of "border pedagogy" to represent the educational endeavor to struggle against the dominant powers of representation that tend to normalize structural inequalities by maintaining a sanitized and rigid version of cultural pluralism.[67] Kramsch also points out the need for the study of culture in foreign-language education to become "a systematic *apprenticeship of difference*," [68] and for foreign language study in general to become a form of "boundary study." [69] I suggest that the study of culture in ELT focus on border experiences and identities as important sources for learning about cultural differences, cross-cultural encounters, and the languages of representation. The global spread and indigenization of the English language, together with the ever more pressing need for cross-cultural communication in the "language," necessitate a turning away from the study of the "national cultures" of the metropolises and from simply using the language to describe "local" lifeways. It is the meeting of cultures in the border experiences of many people around the world, be they in the first or the third world, the target or the native country, that should constitute a center of cultural analysis. And it is also in this new center that culture is remade and identity is negotiated and redefined.

> *Every interaction takes place within specific social, institutional, and historical coordinates, all of which color the interaction at the same time as they are reshaped, to a greater or lesser extent, by that interaction.* — BRUCE MANNHEIM AND DENNIS TEDLOCK, *The Dialogic Emergence of Culture*

A number of theorists whose works I cited earlier—John and Jean Comaroff in the field of cultural anthropology, Lydia Liu in literary studies, and Iain Chambers in cultural studies—all point to the generative and open-ended nature of cross-cultural encounter. In studying the history of the colonial enterprises in Africa and the Caribbean, Pratt proposes the concept of a "contact zone" to capture the creative aspects of colonial cultural encounters.[70] Besides domination and subjugation, the contact zone spotted the complexity of new ways of life and cultural categories: an intermingling of lifestyles among settlers and natives, transracial love stories and sexual alliances, and the emergence of autobiographical writings of ex-slaves who inserted themselves into the European print culture with the help of the abolitionist movement in the last decades of the eighteenth century. These early slave autobiographies marked the beginning of African American literature; instead of constituting an authentic native voice, they were characterized by a transcultural and dialogic mode of expression. As Pratt notes, "In very elaborate ways, these early texts undertook not to reproduce but to *engage* western discourses of identity, community selfhood, and otherness. Their dynamics are transcultural, and presuppose relations of subordination and resistance." [71]

The notion of culture as proliferating and always in the making, especially under conditions of contact and confrontation, is taken up by recent theoretical thinking on the methodology of ethnographic fieldwork, which emphasizes the heterogeneity of culture and the discursive nature of its constitution. One form of praxis that has emerged out of this awareness can be found in the work of some anthropologists who seek to integrate insights from anthropology, linguistics, and literary theory. [72] Ethnography is reconceived not only as a form of one-sided data gathering and interpretation, where knowledge is gleaned from the "natives" and interpreted through the expert eyes of the anthropologist, but as an "emergent cultural phenomenon" and "a form of culture making." [73] In their dialogical approach to the study of culture, they aim to relocate both participants in the cultural encounter, or multiple narrators of shared cultural experiences, in the production of ethnographic knowledge. And dialogue becomes a primary means of fostering this multiplicity of voices and their confrontation. As Attinasi and Friedrich point out, for dialogues (and, I would add, joint narration) to lead to the remaking of culture and the transformation of reality, they need to be ruminated on and also interpreted in light of subsequent experiences. [74] Hence the importance of action, reflection, and reinterpretation in the "dialogical emergence of culture."

The potential for an intercultural education in foreign-language study to open up "new horizons" for students has been acknowledged by some in the field, but the notion of "new" tends to remain on the level of existing phenomena waiting to be discovered by students. [75] In other words, the concept of *(re)making* culture in the language classroom tends not to be fully recognized and practiced in the profession. Kramsch proposes the broadening of classroom discourse (i.e., beyond explicit language instruction to develop accuracy or practicing language skills in discussing familiar topics to develop fluency) to exploit its multiple potential for cross-cultural dialogue and confrontation in the increasingly multicultural student population of the U.S. foreign-language classroom. [76] The differences in cultural values and practices, as revealed in students' reasoning and discourse styles, can be pointed out and negotiated through the joint construction of (new) meanings in dialogue.[77]

In the teaching of English as a second or foreign language around the world, the language classroom has also been characterized, in the majority of cases, by students coming from various cultural backgrounds, in terms of ethnicity, gender, class, religion, geographic origin, political views, or differences of another nature. The classroom can thus be seen as an arena in which a cacophony of voices coming from the cultural texts of foreign or local origin, from the different subject positions of the students, and from the teacher as a more experienced intercultural speaker, enter into dialogue with each other for the continual process of (re)interpreting, (re)representing, and (re)making cultural realities.

Conclusion

In this essay, I have addressed the question of culture in English-language teaching by examining the place of postcolonial cross-cultural study in foreign-language education. In view of the many changes that have swept across the globe—the ever increasing need for cross-cultural contact, the inexorable movement toward a greater recognition for difference, the growing hybridization of culture, *and* the constant reemergence of cultural domination in various guises—it becomes all the more important for foreign-language educators in general, and ELT in particular, to critically reevaluate the cultural dimensions of both the theory and practice of our profession. The widespread use of English, in its diverse forms and functions in various parts of the world, need not become a deterrent to the study of culture, thereby relieving us of our political, educational, and ethical responsibilities. Instead, it can be seen as a particularly rich source for inquiry into the relations between language and culture for cross-cultural understanding and communication. In reconceiving culture as constituted in dialectical relationships, historical processes, border experiences, and emerging realities, it is hoped that the teaching of culture will become less of a sheer accumulation of cultural "facts" or a simple comparison of these facts, whether derived from native or foreign countries, and more of a critical engagement with our students to develop the ability to interpret and remake our cultures through language.

What I have proposed and outlined so far is indeed heavily theoretical in nature, and although the theoretical base for cultural study still needs to be strengthened and continually reworked, the *hows* of practice are also urgent questions to be explored, both in light of theory and to inform theory. The everyday practices that the above concepts and ideas seek to capture need to be discovered and created in the field through the collaboration of theorists, practitioners, and students. Cross-disciplinary and cross-cultural forms of teamwork are necessary, where scholars, teacher trainers, teachers, and students can come together to inform and work with each other to create educational curricula. It is here, again, that the confluence made possible by the spread of English can become a place for the exploration and cultivation of difference and respect for one another.

Notes

1   See Henry A. Giroux, *Border Crossings: Cultural Workers and the Politics of Education*, for a discussion of the role of teachers as cultural workers.
2   See, for example, Gisela Baumgratz, "Language, Culture and Global Competence: An Essay on Ambiguity."
3   Ibid., 441.
4   See American Council for the Teaching of Foreign Languages (ACTFL), *Proficiency Guidelines*.
5   Claire Kramsch, "Culture in Language Learning: A View from the United States."
6   Claire Kramsch, "The Cultural Discourse of Foreign Language Textbooks."
7   See, for example, Michael Byram, "Foreign Language Learning for European Citizenship."
8   Joyce Merrill Valdes, ed., *Culture Bound: Bridging the Cultural Gap in Language Teaching*.
9   Cited in Alastair Pennycook, "English in the World/The World in English," 36.
10 B. Wai, " 'Cultural Conflict' or 'Cultural Invasion.' "
11 Luke Prodromou, "English as Cultural Action," 78.
12 Robert Phillipson, *Linguistic Imperialism*.
13 Ibid.
14 See Claire Kramsch and Patricia Sullivan, "Appropriate Pedagogy."
15 See, for example, *Educational News* (Hong Kong), March 1995, 112.
16 See Anthony Sweeting, *A Phoenix Transformed: The Reconstruction of Education in Post-War Hong Kong*.
17 See Bernard H. K. Luk, "Chinese Culture in the Hong Kong Curriculum: Heritage and Colonialism."
18 See W. O. Lee, "Social Reactions towards Education Proposals: Opting against the Mother Tongue as the Medium of Instruction in Hong Kong."
19 See *Educational News* (Hong Kong), December 1997.
20 See Education Commission (Hong Kong), *Education Commission Report No. 6*.
21 Cem Alptekin and Margaret Alptekin, "The Question of Culture: EFL Teaching in Non-English-Speaking Countries."
22 See, for example, W. C. Dan, H. A. Haroon, and J. Naysmith, "English and Islam

in Malaysia: Resolving the Tension?"; and Alastair Pennycook, *The Cultural Politics of English as an International Language.*

23   Cited in Dan et al., 230.

24   A. Suresh Canagarajah, "Critical Ethnography of a Sri Lankan Classroom: Ambiguities in Student Opposition to Reproduction through ESOL."

25   Ibid., 622.

26   Alptekin and Alptekin, 18.

27   See, for example, Nigel Bruce, "EL2-Medium Education in a Largely Monolingual Society: The Case of Hong Kong"; and R. K. Johnson, C. K. W. Shek, and E. H. F. Law, *Using English as the Medium of Instruction.*

28   R. Keith Johnson, "International English: Towards an Acceptable, Teachable Target Variety," 301.

29   William Crewe and Keith S. T. Tong, "Cultural Considerations in the Selection of ESL Reading Texts."

30   Ibid., 54. A problem with this study is the confounding of topical interest and country of origin of the texts used. The researchers tend to make categorical rankings of the countries of origin of the texts chosen to gauge students' interest, without taking due consideration of the variation depending on the topical contents of the texts. For example, two texts about Britain ("A Ms. Is as Good as a Male") and Burma ("Anatomy of a Burmese Beauty Secret"), which lie rather low in the ranking system by country, received unexpectedly enthusiastic reception by the students.

31   See Lydia Liu's introduction and essay in this volume.

32   Martin Hyde, "The Teaching of English in Morocco: The Place of Culture," 297–98.

33   See, for example, Braj B. Kachru, *The Other Tongue: English across Cultures*; "World Englishes and Applied Linguistics"; and "World Englishes and English-Using Communities."

34   Kachru, "World Englishes and Applied Linguistics," 13.

35   K. Adaskou, D. Britten, and B. Fahsi, "Design Decisions on the Cultural Content of a Secondary English Course for Morocco," 9.

36   Ibid.

37   See Alptekin and Alptekin, and Crewe and Tong.

38   Luke Prodromou, "What Culture? Which Culture? Cross-Cultural Factors in Language Learning."

39   Also basing their argument on the "global" nature of the English language, some language educators and researchers have proposed the development of a European variety of English to express a transnational "European culture." See, for example, Margie Berns, "English in Europe: Whose Language, Which Culture?" Bern writes: "An outcome of de-anglicizing and de-Americanizing is a common language useful as an expression of their 'Europeanness' (however defined), and as a means of mutual communication" (26).

40   Claire Kramsch, "The Cultural Component of Language Teaching"; Byram, " 'Background Studies' in English Foreign Language Teaching: Lost Opportunities in the Comprehensive School Debate."

41   See Lee Drummond, "The Cultural Continuum."

42 See, for example, Wei-ming Tu, ed., *The Living Tree: The Changing Meaning of Being Chinese Today.*

43 Edward W. Said, *Orientalism,* 67.

44 Mary Louise Pratt, *Imperial Eyes: Travel Writing and Transculturation.*

45 Gauri Viswanathan, *Masks of Conquest: Literary Study and British Rule in India.*

46 Johannes Fabian, *Time and the Other: How Anthropology Makes its Object,* 137, 95.

47 See Claire Kramsch, *Context and Culture in Language Teaching.*

48 See Bill Ashcroft, Gareth Griffiths, and Helen Tiffin, *The Empire Writes Back: Theory and Practice in Post-Colonial Literatures,* and Pennycook, *The Cultural Politics of English as an International Language,* for discussions on counterdiscursive practices in literary work and language teaching, respectively.

49 Abdul R. JanMohammed, "Some Implications of Paulo Freire's Border Pedagogy," 242–53.

50 Ibid., 245.

51 John Comaroff and Jean Comaroff, *Ethnography and the Historical Imagination,* 27.

52 Lydia Liu, *Translingual Practice,* 29.

53 Ibid., 20.

54 Henry A. Giroux, "Living Dangerously: Identity Politics and the New Cultural Racism," 29–56.

55 Byram; and Lawrence Kane, "The Acquisition of Cultural Competence: An Ethnographic Framework for Cultural Studies Curricula."

56 See Michael Byram, et al., *Teaching-and-Learning, Language-and-Culture.*

57 Comaroff and Comaroff, 5.

58 Chambers, *Migrancy, Culture, Identity,* 14.

59 Chow, *Writing Diaspora: Tactics of Intervention in Contemporary Cultural Studies,* 22.

60 Said, *Orientalism.*

61 Ibid., 226.

62 Homi Bhabha, *The Location of Culture,* 37.

63 See, for example, Arjun Appadurai, *Modernity at Large: Cultural Dimensions of Globalization;* Akhil Gupta and James Ferguson, "Beyond 'Culture': Space, Identity, and the Politics of Difference"; and Ulf Hannerz, *Transnational Connections: Culture, People, Places.*

64 Appadurai, 18.

65 The notions of "national consciousness" and "patriotism" are heavily propagated in the pro-PRC (People's Republic of China) public media in Hong Kong. In the educational arena, there is a movement toward redesigning and expanding the civic education curriculum, and some educators have proposed making "patriotism" a centerpiece in the reform on civic education. See, for example, *Educational News* (Hong Kong), October 1996, 10.

66 See Giroux, "Living Dangerously: Identity Politics and the New Cultural Racism."

67 Giroux, *Border Crossings: Cultural Workers and the Politics of Education.*

68 Kramsch, *Context and Culture in Language Teaching,* 235.

69 Claire Kramsch, "Redrawing the Boundaries of Foreign Language Study," 214.

70 Pratt, *Imperial Eyes: Travel Writing and Transculturation.*

71 Ibid., 102.

72 See, for example, Dennis Tedlock and Bruce Mannheim, eds., *The Dialogic Emergence of Culture*.

73 See ibid., 2, 13.

74 John Attinasi and Paul Friedrich, "Dialogic Breakthrough: Catalysis and Synthesis in Life-Changing Dialogue," 33–54.

75 See, for example, Michael Byram, "Teaching Culture and Language: Towards an Integrated Model"; and Meinert Meyer, "Developing Transcultural Competence: Case Studies of Advanced Foreign Language Learners."

76 Claire Kramsch, "The Dialogic Emergence of Culture in the Language Classroom."

77 See Claire Kramsch, "Rhetorical Models of Understanding," and "Stylistic Choice and Cultural Awareness"; and Claire Kramsch and Linda von Hoene, "The Dialogic Emergence of Difference: Feminist Explorations in Foreign Language Learning and Teaching."

GLOSSARY

aiqing 愛情
Aiqing dingze 愛情定則
anshi 暗示
Asami Keizai 淺見炯齋

Baige changpian 百歌唱片
Bailemen 百樂門
Bankoku shiki 萬國史記
Bankoku kōhō 萬國公法
Beihai changpian 北海唱片
Bi Fangji 畢方濟
Bi Gongchen 畢拱辰
bianchang 變常
biange 變革
biantai 變態
Bo-gui 柏貴
Budeyi bian 不得已辨

Cai Yuanpei 蔡元培
Changcheng changpian gongsi 長城唱片公司
"Changpian de piping" 唱片的批評
"Changpian de shiyong ji baocun fa" 唱片的使用及保存法

Chen Shaobai 陳少白
Cheng Yi 程頤
Cheng Yishan 程宜山
Chen Yuan 陳原
Chongding Faguo zhilue 重訂法國志略
Chong-hou 崇厚
Chu 楚
chu shan le 出山了
chuanju 川劇
Chuanqi 傳奇
Chung Yung (zhongyong) 中庸

Daqing lüli 大清律例
Da xue zhang ju 大學章句
Da zhonghua changpian gongsi 大中華唱片公司
Dai Kan-Wa jiten 大漢和辭典
Deng Yuhan 鄧玉函
dian 癲
Ding Weiliang 丁韙良
Dongfang baidai changpian gongsi 東方百代唱片公司
dongjue zhi qi 動覺之氣
Dong Xun 董恂
dongya bingfu 東亞病夫
doseiai 同性愛

e shi 惡事
Emei changpian gongsi 峨嵋唱片公司
erqi liangneng 二氣良能

Faguo geming 法國革命
Fang Hao 方豪
fei 匪
feilao bing 肺癆病
feng 風
feng zi 瘋子
Feng Ziyou 馮自由
fengyuan 瘋院
Fukkoku kakumei 佛國革命
funü tongxing zhi aiqing 婦女同性之愛情

Funü zazhi 婦女雜誌

Funüshibao 婦女時報

Fu nü yu nü tongxing zhi xiang lian'ai shi tongyu nanzi zhi hao nanse 夫女與女同性
之相戀愛實同與男子之好男色

Furuya Toyoko 古屋登代子

gaige 改革

Gao Yizhi 高一志

Gaoting 高亭

Geguo lüli 各國律例

geming 革命

geming dang 革命黨

Geming jun 革命軍

gerenzhuyi 個人主義

Gong qinwang (Prince Gong) 恭親王（奕訢）

gongfa 公法

Gongfa bianlan 公法便覽

Gongfa huitong 公法會通

Gongfa xinbian 公法新編

gongneng tongle 功能通了

Guan Qiaochang 關喬昌

Guangbo dianshi qiye shi neibu shiliao 廣播電視企業史內部史料

Guangzhou 廣州

Guanzi 管子

gui¹ 歸

gui (ghost) 鬼

gui shen 鬼神

Guo Moruo 郭沫若

guohuo 國貨

guominxing 國民性

Guoyu 國語

Guoyu jiangxisuo 國語講習所

Guoyue changpian 國樂唱片

Haiguo tuzhi 海國圖志

Han Langen 韓蘭根

Hanman lu 汗漫錄

Hanwen zhengshi 漢文正史

Hanying sishu 漢英四書

hao nanse 好男色

haoran zhi qi 浩然之氣

He Luting 賀綠汀

He Yan 何晏

henkaku 變革

hentai 變態

Hesheng changpian 和聲唱片

hong 行

houru 後儒

Hu Qiuyuan 胡秋原

Hu Shi 胡適

"Hua diao" 花凋

hua xiazi 話匣子

Huang Shounian 黃壽年

Huangchao liqi tushi 皇朝禮器圖式

Huangdi neijing 黃帝內經

Huangdi neijing suwen 黃帝內經素問

huangtian shangdi 皇天上帝

huju 滬劇

hun 魂

i (yi) 夷

ishin dai kakumei 維新大革命

Jiang Tie 江鐵

Jiang Zhiyou 蔣智由

Jiaoyu zazhi 教育雜誌

jibing 疾病

jing, shen, hun, and po 精、神、魂、魄

jingqi 精氣

jingshen jiankang 精神健康

jingshen weisheng 精神衛生

jingshenke bingyuan 精神科病院

junmin gong zhu 君民共主

junzi 君子

Kaiming 開明

kakumei 革命

kakumei jidai 革命時代

kakumei jimbutsu 革命人物

kakushin 革新

Kang Youwei 康有為

kanji 漢字

Ke Zhenghe 柯政和

Kokumin Shinbun 國民新聞

Kongji gezhi 空際格致

kuang 狂

kun 坤

Kunlun changpian 昆崙唱片

lao zhongyi 老中醫

li 利

Li Andang 利安當

Li Hongzhang 李鴻章

Li ji, jiaotesheng 禮記郊特牲

Li ji, jiyi 禮記祭義

Li Jinhui 黎錦暉

Li Leisi 利類思

Li Madou 利馬竇

Li Qing 李青

Li Qingming 李慶明

li xue 理學

Li Zehou 李澤厚

Li Zhizao 李之藻

lian'ai 戀愛

Liang Qichao 梁啟超

lianxing changpian 聯星唱片

Lige 麗歌

Lin hua (Lam Qua) 林華

Lin Zexu 林則徐

Ling yan li shao yin 靈言蠡勺引

Lingyan lishao 靈言蠡勺

Liu Bang 劉邦

Liu shu xiyi 六書析義

liufu 六府

Liusheng ji 留聲機

"Liusheng ji de liyong" 留聲機的利用

"Liusheng jiqi de huiyin" 留聲機器的迴音

Liuxing gequ cangsang ji 流行歌曲蒼桑記

Lu Sao 盧騷

Lu Xiangshan 陸象山

luan 亂

luandang 亂黨

luanmin 亂民

lüfa 律法

"Lun xuehui you da yi yu huangren, ji yi baohu" 論學會有大益于黃人，亟宜保護

Lun yu 論語

Lun yu zhu shu 論語注疏

Luo Ka (Law Kar) 羅卡

Mao Yibo 毛一波

Mei Lanfang 梅蘭芳

Meiguo shengli 美國勝利

Mengzi 孟子

mimi zhi yin 靡靡之音

ming 命

Ming qing jian yesu huishi yizhu tiyao 明清間耶穌會士譯著提要

minquan 民權

minzhu zhi guo 民主之國

Miyoshi Kiyoyuki 三善清行

Mizoguchi Yūzō 溝口雄三

mo jing dang 磨鏡黨

Moruo wenji 沫若文集

moshu 魔術

nannü de geli 男女的隔離

Ni Haishu 倪海曙

Nicolas Trigault 金尼閣

Nie Er 聶耳

Nüsheng 女聲

Ōe gijuku 大江義塾

Okamoto Kansuke 岡村監輔

Pan Guangdan 潘光旦

Peikai 倍開

pibao gongsi 皮包公司

po 魄

qi[1] 气
qi 氣
Qi yuan yitan 氣源一探
qi, xue, zhi, qing 氣、血、知、情
qian 乾
Qian Guangren 錢廣仁
Qian Xuantong 錢玄同
qigong 氣功
qigong piancha 氣功偏差
qigong suozhi jingshen zhang'ai 氣功所致精神障礙
Qin Qiming 秦啟明
qing 清
Qingyi bao 清議報
qingyin 清音
qingyu zhi diandao 情慾之顛倒
qixue 氣學
quan 權
quanli 權利

ren 人
Ren Bonian 任伯年
Ren Guang 任光
renquan 人權
Ruan Lingyu 阮玲玉
Ruan Yuan 阮元
Rujiao shiyi 儒教實義

Sanshan lunxue ji 三山論學記
sei 性
Shan Zai 善哉
shangdi 上帝
Shanghai baidai gongsi zhi yange 上海百代公司之沿革
shehui zhuyi wenming 社會主義文明
Shen Fengxi 沈鳳喜
shen xin xing ming zhi xue 身心性命之學
Shen Zemin 沈澤民
shen[1] 伸

shen (divine spirit) 神

Shengli 勝利

shengyang zhi qi 生養之氣

shenjing shuairuo 神經衰弱

shenkui 神虧

shenti, xinzhi, lingjue, shenming 身體、心知、靈覺、神明

"Shi ge" 釋革

shijie geming 詩界革命

shin yu kakumei nen 辛酉革命年

shiren ziran zhi quan 世人自然之權

Shisan jing zhu shu 十三經注疏

Shiwu bao 時務報

"Shouzai paituo" 壽仔拍拖

Shu jing 書經

Shui Jing 水晶

Shuowen jiezi 說文解字

Si shu ji zhu 四書集注

Sishu zhangju jizhu 四書章句集注

Sixing lunlue 四行論略

sonno-joi 尊王攘夷

Sugawara Michizane 菅原道真

Sulian zhi you she 蘇聯之友社

Sun Yat-sen 孫逸仙

Sun Zhang 孫璋

suru 俗儒

ta [fem.] 她

ta [masc.] 他

taiji 太極

Taiping changpian 太平唱片

Taixi renshen shuogai 泰西人身說概

"Tan tan wo guo jiben shuchupin yu xinxing gongye" 談談我國基本輸出品與
新興工業

Tang Ruowang 湯若望

Tao Chengzhang 陶成章

Tao lu 陶錄

Tao shuo 陶説

tao-li 道理

te yi gongneng 特異功能

tian 天

Tian Han 田漢

tianming wu chang 天命無常

Tianxue chu han 天學初函

Tianzhu shilu 天主實錄

Tianzhu shiyi 天主實義

Tianzhu shiyi yin 天主實義引

Tianzhujiao dongchuan wenxian 天主教東傳文獻

Tianzhujiao dongchuan wenxian sanbian 天主教東傳文獻三編

Tianzhujiao dongchuan wenxian xubian 天主教東傳文獻續編

Tixiao yinyuan 啼笑因緣

tixing zhi qi 體性之氣

Tokugawa 德川

Tokutomi Sōho 德富蘇峰

tongxing lian 同性戀

tongxing lian'ai 同性戀愛

tongxing'ai 同性愛

waiqi 外氣

waixin 外信

Wang Fuzhi 王夫之

Wang Tao 王韜

Wang Tingxiang 王廷相

Wang Yangming 王陽明

Wang Zhongmin 王重民

Wang yue: sou bu yuan qian li er lai, yi jiang you yi li wu guo hu 王曰：叟不遠千里而
　　來，亦將有以利吾國乎

Wanguo gongbao 萬國公報

Wanguo gongfa 萬國公法

Wanguo tongjian 萬國通鑒

wangyun 望云

Wei Sheng 薇生

wenhua 文化

wenjie geming 文界革命

Wen-xiang 文祥

"Wo he Mingyue" 我和明月

wo pian le 我偏了

Wong Kee-chee (Huang Qizhi) 黃奇智

"Wu ti" 無題

Wu Xiangxiang 吳相湘

Wukeduo 物克多

wushu 武術

wuxing 五行

Xiru ermuzi 西儒耳目資

xian 癇

Xian Xinghai 洗星海

Xie Se 謝瑟

Xie Weilou 謝衛樓

Xin Ma Shisheng 新馬師生

Xin nüxing 新女性

Xin qingnian 新青年

Xin wenhua 新文化

xin xing daode 新性道德

xin xue 心學

xing 行

xing (nature) 性

xing (sex) 性

xing ai 性愛

Xing Bing 邢昺

xing jiaoyu 性教育

Xing kexue 性科學

xing mei 性美

Xing shi 性史

xing xinlixue 性心理學

xingfa 性法

xingjiao 性交

Xingli zhenglun 性理正論

Xingli zhenquan 性理真詮

xingqi 形氣

Xingshi changpian 醒獅唱片

Xingxue cushu 性學觕述

xingyu 性慾

Xinhua huabao 新華畫報

Xinmin congbao 新民叢報

Xinyue ji 新月集

Xinyue liusheng ji changpian gongsi 新月留聲機唱片公司

Xu Guangqi 徐光啟

Xu Jiyu 徐繼畬

Xu Shen 許慎

Xu Xu 徐訏

Xu Xu quanji 徐訏全集

Xu Zhimo 徐志摩

Xu Zongze 徐宗澤

Xue Juexian (Sit Gok-sin) 薛覺先

Y. R. Chao 趙元任

Yan Shi 晏始

yang 陽

Yang Guangxian 楊光先

Yang Lien-sheng 楊聯陞

yang qi 陽氣

"Yangren da xiao" 洋人大笑

Yao Li 姚莉

Yazhou changpian 亞洲唱片

Ye Gongchao (George Yeh) 葉公超

yi 夷

Yi jing 易經

yi qi guan chuan 一氣貫穿

yimu 夷目

yin 陰

Yinghuan zhilue 瀛環志略

Yinyue jia Ren Guang 音樂家任光

yixing zhijian de ai 異性之間的愛

"Yiyongjun jinxingqu" 義勇軍進行曲

Yoshida Shōin 吉田松陰

youyi 友誼

Yuan Dehui 袁德輝

yueju 越劇

"Yuguang qu" 漁光曲

zaofan 造反

Zhang Binglin 章炳麟

Zhang Changfu 張長福

Zhang Henshui 張恨水

Zhang Jingsheng 張競生

Zhang Minyun 張敏筠

Zhang Xichen 章錫琛

Zhang Zai 張載

Zhao Enrong 趙恩榮

Zhao Qi 趙歧

zheng fanyi guan 正繙譯官

zhengru 正儒

zhengxue 正學

Zhengxue liushi 正學鏐石

Zhongguo gudai yuanqi xueshuo 中國古代元氣學說

"Zhongguo lishi shang geming zhi yanjiu" 中國歷史上革命之研究

Zhongguo Tianzhujiao shi renwu zhuan 中國天主教史人物傳

"Zhongguo wenxian zhong tongxing lian juli" 中國文獻中同性戀舉例

Zhongguo zhengzi xuehui 中國正字學會

zhongxi hebi 中西合璧

Zhongyong 中庸

Zhou Dunyi 周敦頤

Zhou Jianren 周建人

Zhou Yizhao 周燡昭

Zhu Xi 朱熹

zhuo 濁

zhuquan 主權

Zhuzhi qunzhen 主制群徵

Zhuzi yu lei 朱子語類

Zichan 子產

ziran zhi fa 自然之法

zizhu zhi guo 自主之國

Zongli yamen 總理衙門

zouhuo rumuo 走火入魔

Zou Rong 鄒容

Zou Yan 鄒衍

zui qing 最清

Zuozhuan 左傳

BIBLIOGRAPHY

Abbreviations

ARSI Ruggieri, Michele, and Matteo Ricci. *Tianzhu shi yi* (The veritable records of the lord of heaven). 1584. Archivum Romanum Societatis Iesu, Jap. Sin. I, 189.

SSJZS *Shisan jing zhu shu* (Thirteen classics with annotations and subannotations). Ed. Ruan Yuan (1764–1849). 2 vols. Beijing: Zhonghua shuju, 1980.

TXCH *Tianxue chu han* (Heavenly studies—a first collection). Ed. Li Zhizao (1565–1630) et al. Taipei: Taiwan xuesheng shuju, 1965.

TZJDC Xu Guangqi (1562–1633) et al. *Tianzhu jiao Dong chuan wenxian, xu bian* (Documents on the Eastern transmission of Catholicism, second collection). Reprint of Vatican Library edition. Taipei: Taiwan xuesheng shuju, 1966.

XGQJ Xu Guangqi (1562–1633). *Xu Guangqi ji* (Collected works of Xu Guangqi). Ed. Wang Zhongmin. 2 vols. Beijing: Zhonghua shuju, 1963.

Archives and Other Unpublished Sources

British Foreign Office Records, Public Record Office, London.

Chinese Letters of the Board of Foreign Missions of the Presbyterian Church in the United States of America, Philadelphia.

Diary and Consultation of the Council for China. East India Company Factory Records (1595–1840). The British Library, London.

IOR. British Library and India Office Records, London.

NARA. United States National Archives and Records Administration, Washington, DC.

NARA, Office of Finance. United States National Archives and Records Administration, Washington, DC.

NARA, RG [Record Group number]. United States National Archives and Records Administration, Washington, DC.

National Art Library, Auction House Records, London.

Papers of Rev. Peter Parker. Harvey Cushing, John Hay Whitney Medical Historical Library, Yale University, New Haven.

PRO. Public Record Office, Kew Gardens, London.

PRO/WO. Public Record Office, War Office Archives, Kew Gardens, London.

RBFMPC. Records of the Board of Foreign Missions of the Presbyterian Church, Presbyterian Historical Society, Philadelphia.

I. A. Richards Files, Houghton Library, Harvard University, Cambridge.

Royal Engineers Museum, Brompton Barracks, Chatham. Acquisition Records and Collections.

USMHI. United States Military History Institute, Carlisle Barracks, PA.

Victoria and Albert Museum, MSS and Acquisition Records, London.

Published Sources

Aarsleff, Hans. *From Locke to Saussure*. Minneapolis: University of Minnesota Press, 1982.

Adaskou, K., D. Britten, and B. Fahsi. "Design Decisions on the Cultural Content of a Secondary English Course for Morocco." *ELT Journal* 44.1 (1990): 3–10.

Aleni, Julio. *Xingxue cushu* (An outline of the study of human nature). Shanghai cimutang, woodblock ed., 1873.

Allgood, George. *China War 1860: Letters and Journal*. London: Longmans, Green, 1901.

Alptekin, Cem, and Margaret Alptekin. "The Question of Culture: EFL Teaching in Non-English-Speaking Countries." *ELT Journal* 38.1 (1984): 14–20.

Altick, Richard. *The Shows of London*, Cambridge, MA: Belknap Press, 1978.

Amariglio, Jack, and Antonio Callari. "Marxian Value Theory and the Problem of the Subject: The Role of Commodity Fetishism." In *Fetishism as Cultural Discourse*, ed. Emily Apter and William Pietz. Ithaca: Cornell University Press, 1993.

Ament, William. "The Charges against Missionaries." *Independent* 53 (1901): 1051–52.

American Council for the Teaching of Foreign Languages (ACTFL). *Proficiency Guidelines*. Hastings-on-Hudson, NY: ACTFL Materials Center, 1988.

American Psychiatric Association. *Diagnostic and Statistical Manual of Mental Disorders*, 4th ed. Washington, DC: APA, 1994.

Anagnost, Ann. *National Past-Times: Narrative, Representation, and Power in Modern China*. Durham, NC: Duke University Press, 1997.

Andrews, Bridie J. "Tuberculosis and the Assimilation of Germ Theory in China, 1895–1937." *Journal of the History of Medicine and Allied Sciences* 52 (January 1997): 114–57.

Appadurai, Arjun. *Modernity at Large: Cultural Dimensions of Globalization*. Minneapolis: University of Minnesota Press, 1996.

Apter, Emily, and William Pietz, eds. *Fetishism as Cultural Discourse*. Ithaca: Cornell University Press, 1993.

Arendt, Hannah. *On Revolution*. New York: Viking, 1965.

Ariga Nagao. *La Guerre Sino-Japonaise au Point de Vue de Droit International*. (Studies of the nation). Paris: Libraire de la Cour d'Appel, 1896.

———. *Kokkagaku*. (International law and the Japanese-Qing War). Tokyo, 1889.

———. *Nisshin Sen'eki Kokusaihōron*. Tokyo: Rikugun Daigakko, 1896.

Aristotle. *Generation of Animals*. Trans. A. L. Peck. Cambridge, MA: Harvard University Press, 1979.

Arnold, David, ed. *Imperial Medicine and Indigenous Societies*. New York: Manchester University Press, 1988.

Ashcroft, Bill, Gareth Griffiths, and Helen Tiffin. *The Empire Writes Back: Theory and Practice in Post-Colonial Literatures*. New York: Routledge, 1989.

The Atlantic Charter, and the Prime Minister's Statement on Basic English of March 9, 1944; in their original form, and in Basic English, for purposes of Comparison. London: Printed and Published by His Majesty's Stationery Office, 1944.

Attali, Jacques. *Noise: The Political Economy of Music*. Trans. Brian Massumi. Minneapolis: University of Minnesota Press, 1985.

Attinasi, John, and Paul Friedrich. "Dialogic Breakthrough: Catalysis and Synthesis in Life-Changing Dialogue." In *The Dialogic Emergence of Culture*, ed. Dennis Tedlock and Bruce Mannheim. Urbana: University of Illinois Press, 1995.

Auerbach, Erich. *Scenes from the Drama of European Literature*. Manchester: Manchester University Press, 1984.

Ayers, John "The Early China Trade." In *The Origins of Museums: The Cabinets of Curiosities in Sixteenth- and Seventeenth-Century Europe*, ed. O. Impey and A. MacGregor. Oxford: Clarendon, 1985. 259–66.

Bakumatsu/Meiji Shoki ni Okeru Seiyō Bunmei no Yunyū ni Kan Suru Kenkyūkai, eds. *Yōgaku Jishi*. Tokyo: Bunka Shobo, 1993.

Banno, Masataka. *China and the West, 1858–1861: The Origins of the Tsungli Yamen*. Cambridge, MA: Harvard University Press, 1964.

Barnett, Suzanne Wilson, and John King Fairbank, eds. *Christianity in China: Early Protestant Missionary Writings*. Cambridge, MA: Harvard University Press, 1985.

Barrow, George de S. *The Fire of Life*. London: Hutcheson and Co., 1942.

Bartlett, C. J. "Peter Parker, the Founder of the Modern Medical Missions: A Unique Collection of Paintings." *Journal of the American Medical Association* 67 (August 1916): 407–11.

Basu, Dilip. "Chinese Xenology and Opium War." Paper presented at the conference "Empire and Beyond," University of California at Berkeley, 1997.

Baudrillard, Jean. *For a Critique of the Political Economy of the Sign*. Trans. Charles Levin. St. Louis: Telos Press, 1981.

———. *Symbolic Exchange and Death*. Trans. Iain Hamilton Grant. London: Sage Publications, 1993.

Baumgratz, Gisela. "Language, Culture and Global Competence: An Essay on Ambiguity." *European Journal of Education* 30.4 (1995): 437–47.

Beasley, W. G. *Japanese Imperialism 1894–1945*. Oxford: Oxford Clarendon Series, 1991.

Beasley, W. G., and E. G. Pulleybank, eds. *Historians of China and Japan*. London: Oxford University Press, 1961.

Benfey, Theodor. *Geschichte der Sprachwissenschaft und orientalischen Philologie in Deutschland*. Munich: Cotta, 1869.

Benjamin, Walter. *Gesammelte Schriften*. Frankfurt am Main: Suhrkamp, 1980.

———. *Illuminations*. Trans. Harry Zohn. New York: Harcourt, Brace & World, 1968.

Benoit, Pierre, and Roland Murphy, eds. *Immortality and Resurrection*. New York: Herder and Herder, 1970.

Bentham, Jeremy. *An Introduction to the Principles of Morals and Legislation*. New York: Hafner Press, 1948.

Benveniste, Emile. "Catégories de pensée et catégories de langue." *Etudes philosophiques* 4 (October–December 1958). Reprinted in Benveniste, *Problèmes de linguistique générale*. Paris: Gallimard, 1966–74.

———. *Problems in General Linguistics*. Translated by Mary E. Meek. Coral Gables, FL: University of Miami Press, 1971. Originally published as *Problèmes de linguistique générale* (Paris: Gallimard, 1966–74).

Berlioz, Hector. *Evenings with the Orchestra*. New York: Knopf, 1956.

Berman, Antoine. *L'Épreuve de l'étranger: Culture et traduction dans l'Allemagne romantique*. Paris: Gallimard, 1984.

Bernal, Martin. *Black Athena*, vol. 1 New Brunswick, NJ: Rutgers University Press, 1987.

Bernard-Maitre, Henri. "Les Adaptations Chinoises d'Ouvrages Européens: Bibliographie Chronologique depuis la Venue des Portugais a Canton jusqu'a la Mission Française de Pekin, 1514–1688." *Monumenta Serica* 10 (1945): 1–57, 309–88.

———. "Les Adaptations Chinoises d'Ouvrages Européens: Bibliographie Chronologique depuis la Fondation de la Mission Française de Pekin jusqu'a la Mort de l'Empereur K'ien-long, 1689–1799." *Monumenta Serica* 19 (1960): 349–83.

Berns, Margie. "English in Europe: Whose Language, Which Culture?" *International Journal of Applied Linguistics* 5.1 (1995): 21–32.

Berry-Hill, Henry, and Sidney Berry-Hill. *George Chinnery, 1774–1852, an Artist of the China Coast*. Leigh-on-sea, England: F. Lewis, 1963.

Bevans, Charles I. *Treaties and Other International Agreements of the United States of America, 1776–1949*. Washington, DC: U.S. Government Printing Office, 1918–1930.

Bhabha, Homi. *The Location of Culture*. London: Routledge, 1994.

Biagioli, Mario. "The Anthropology of Incommensurability." *Studies in History and Philosophy of Science* 21.2 (June 1990): 183–209.

———. "Stress in the Book of Nature: Galileo's Realism and Its Supplements." Unpublished manuscript.

Bishop, Heber. *The Heber Bishop Collection of Jade and Other Hard Stones*. New York: Metropolitan Museum of Art, 1900.

Bloom, Alfred. *The Linguistic Shaping of Thought: A Study in the Impact of Language on Thinking in China and the West*. Hillsdale, NJ: Lawrence Erlbaum, 1981.

Bodde, Derk. *Chinese Thought, Society, and Science: The Intellectual and Social Background of Science and Technology in Pre-Modern China*. Honolulu: University of Hawaii Press, 1991.

Bohman, James, and Matthias Lutz-Bachmann, eds. *Perpetual Peace: Essays on Kant's Cosmopolitan Ideal*. Cambridge, MA: MIT Press, 1997.

Bond, Michael Harris. *The Handbook of Chinese Psychology*. Hong Kong: Oxford University Press, 1996.

Bonsall, Geoffrey W. Introduction to *George Chinnery: His Pupils and Influence*. Hong Kong: Urban Council and Hong Kong Museum of Art, 1985.

Boodberg, Peter A. "Philological Notes on Chapter One of the *Lao Tzu*." *Harvard Journal of Asiatic Studies* 20 (1957): 598–618.

Bopp, Franz. *Ueber das Conjugationssystem der Sanskrit-Sprache*. Frankfurt: Andreäische Buchhandlung, 1816.

Boswell, John. *Same-Sex Unions in Premodern Europe*. New York: Villard Books, 1994.

Bourdieu, Pierre. *Algeria 1960: The Disenchantment of the World, the Sense of Honour, the Kabyle House or the World Reversed*. Trans. Richard Rice. Cambridge: Cambridge University Press, 1979.

——. "Economics of Linguistic Exchanges." *Social Science Information* 16.6 (1977): 645–68.

——. *Language and Symbolic Power*. Ed. John B. Thompson. Trans. Gino Raymond and Matthew Adamson. Cambridge, MA: Harvard University Press, 1994.

——. *In Other Words: Essays Towards a Reflexive Sociology*. Trans. Matthew Adamson. Stanford: Stanford University Press, 1990.

Bové, Paul. *Intellectuals in Power: A Genealogy of Critical Humanism*. New York: Columbia University Press, 1986.

Brantlinger, Patrick. *Rule of Darkness*. Ithaca: Cornell University Press, 1988.

Breckenridge, Carol. "The Aesthetics and Politics of Colonial Collecting: India at the World Fairs." *Comparative Studies in Society and History* 31.2 (1989): 195–216.

Brieger, Gert. "Sense and Sensibility in Late Nineteenth-Century Surgery in America," in *Medicine and the Five Senses*, ed. W. F. Bynum and Roy Porter. Cambridge: Cambridge University Press, 1993.

Brinton, Crane. *The Anatomy of Revolution*. New York: Vintage Books, 1965.

Brower, R., H. Vendler, and J. Hollander, eds. *I. A. Richards: Essays in His Honor*. New York: Oxford University Press, 1973.

Brower, Reuben A., ed. *On Translation*. Cambridge, MA: Harvard University Press, 1959.

Brown, Arthur J. *New Forces in Old China: An Unwelcome but Inevitable Awakening*. New York: Fleming H. Revell Co., 1904.

Bruce, Nigel. "EL2-Medium Education in a Largely Monolingual Society: The Case of Hong Kong." *HK Papers in Linguistics and Language Teaching* 13 (1990): 9–25.

Buck, David D. "Forum on Universalism and Relativism in Asian Studies: Editor's Introduction." *Journal of Asian Studies* 50.1 (February 1991): 29–34.

Bumb, Heinrich. "The Great Beka 'Expedition,' 1905–6." *Talking Machine Review* 41 (1976).

Burlington Fine Arts Club. *Catalogue of Blue and White Oriental Porcelain Exhibited in 1895*. London: Author, 1895.

——. *Catalogue of Coloured Chinese Porcelain Exhibited in 1896*. London: Author, 1896.

——. *Exhibition of Japanese and Chinese Works of Art*. London: John C. Wilkes, 1878.

Bushell, Stephan W. "Chinese Architecture." In *Smithsonian Museum Annual Report for 1904*. 677–92.

——. *Chinese Art*. 2 vols. London: HMSO, 1904–1906.

——. *Chinese Porcelain before the Present dynasty*. Peking: Pei-t'ang Press, 1886.

——. *Oriental Ceramic Art, illustrated from the collection of W. T. Walters*. New York: D. Appleton and Co., 1897.

Bushell, Stephan W., with William Laffan. *Catalogue of the Morgan Collection of Chinese Porcelain*. New York: Metropolitan Museum of Art, 1907.

Butler, Smedley D. *Old Gimlet Eye: The Life of Smedley Butler as told to Lowell Thomas.* New York: Farrar & Rinehart, 1933.

Buttjes, Dieter, and Michael Byram, eds. *Mediating Languages and Cultures: Towards an Intercultural Theory of Foreign Language Education.* Clevedon, England: Multilingual Matters, 1991.

Bynon, Theodora. *Historical Linguistics.* Cambridge: Cambridge University Press, 1977.

Byram, Michael. " 'Background Studies' in English Foreign Language Teaching: Lost Opportunities in the Comprehensive School Debate." In *Mediating Languages and Cultures: Towards an Intercultural Theory of Foreign Language Education,* ed. Dieter Buttjes and Michael Byram. Clevedon, England: Multilingual Matters, 1991.

———. "Foreign Language Learning for European Citizenship." *Language Learning Journal* 6 (1992): 10–13.

———. "Teaching Culture and Language: Towards and Integrated Model." In Buttjes and Byram.

Byram, Michael, et al. *Teaching-and-Learning, Language-and-Culture.* Clevedon, England: Multilingual Matters, 1994.

Cai Yuanpei. "Zai guoyu jiangxisuo yanjiangci" (Speech at the Institute of the National Language, 13 June 1920). In *Cai Yuanpei quanji* (Complete works of Cai Yuanpei), ed. Gao Pinshu. Beijing: Zhonghua shuju, 1984: 426–31.

Canagarajah, A. Suresh. "Critical Ethnography of a Sri Lankan Classroom: Ambiguities in Student Opposition to Reproduction through ESOL." *TESOL Quarterly* 27.4 (1993): 601–26.

Candidius, George. "A Short Account of the Island of Formosa." In *A Collection of Voyages and Travels.* Ed. Awnsham Churchill and John Churchill. London, 1704.

Carnegie Endowment for International Peace. *Signatures, Ratifications, Adhesions, and Reservations to the Conventions and Declarations of the First and Second Hague Peace Conferences.* Washington, DC: Carnegie Endowment, 1914.

Carpenter, Edward. *The Intermediate Sex.* London: George Allen & Unwin Ltd, 1908.

———. *Love's Coming of Age.* New York: M. Kennerley, 1991.

Carter, W. H. *The Life of Lieutenant General Chaffee.* Chicago: University of Chicago Press, 1917.

The Celestial Empire. Shanghai, 1900.

Certeau, Michel de. *Heterologies: Discourse on the Other.* Trans. Brian Massumi. Minneapolis: University of Minnesota Press, 1986.

Ch'eng Chung-ying. *New Dimensions of Confucian and Neo-Confucian Philosophy.* Albany: State University of New York Press, 1991.

Chamberlain, Wilber. *Ordered to China.* New York: Frederick A. Stokes Co., 1903.

Chan, Wing-tsit. *Source Book in Chinese Philosophy.* Princeton: Princeton University Press, 1963.

Chanan, Michael. *Musica Practica: The Social Practice of Western Music from Gregorian Chant to Postmodernism.* London: Verso, 1994.

———. *Repeated Takes: A Short History of Recording and Its Effects on Music.* London: Verso, 1995.

Chang, Eileen. *Chuanqi* (Romances). Rev. ed. Shanghai: Zhongguo tushu gongsi, 1946.

Chang, Hao. *Liang Ch'i-ch'ao and Intellectual Transition in China, 1890–1907.* Cambridge, MA: Harvard University Press, 1971.

Chang Hsi-tung. "The Earliest Phase of the Introduction of Western Political Science into China (1820–1852)." *Yenching Journal of Social Studies* 5.1 (13 July 1950).

Chang, James. "Short Subjects: A Reconstructive Surgeon's Taste in Art: Dr. Peter Parker and the Lam Qua Oil Paintings." *Annals of Plastic Surgery* 30.5 (May 1993): 468–74.

Chang P'eng-yuan. "Geming yu xiandaihua jiaozhi xia de jindai Zhongguo" (Revolution and modernization in modern China). *Si yu yan* 29 (September 1991): 2–19.

——. "Modernization and Revolution in China, 1860–1949." *Bulletin of the Institute of Modern History, Academia Sinica* 19 (June 1990): 45–60.

Chao, Y. R. *Autobiography: First 30 Years, 1892–1921.* Ithaca, NY: Spoken Language Services, Inc. 1975.

Charcot, Jean-Martin, and Paul Richer. *Difformes et les Malades Dans l'Art.* Amsterdam: B. M. Israel, 1972.

Charme, Alexandre de la. *Xingli zhenquan* (Elucidating the true meaning of nature and principle). 1750. Reprint, Shanghai Cimutang, 1889.

Chen Chun. *Neo-Confucian Terms Explained (The Pei-hsi tzu-i) by Ch'en Ch'un, 1159–1223.* Trans. Wing-tsit Chan. New York: Columbia University Press, 1986.

Chen Jianhua. "Wan Qing 'shijie geming' fasheng shijian ji qi tichang zhe kaobian" (A study of the time and advocate of "Poetry Revolution" in the late Qing). In *Zhongguo gudian wenxue congkao.* Shanghai: Fudan University Press, 1985. 321–40.

——. "Wan Qing 'shijie geming' yu piping de wenhua jiaolü—Liang Qichao, Hu Shi yu 'geming' de liangzhong yiyi" (Late Qing "Poetry Revolution" and anxiety of cultural criticism: Liang Qichao, Hu Shi, and the two implications of the term *geming*). In *Chinese Literary Criticism of the Ch'ing Period, 1644–1911,* ed. John C. Y. Wang. Hong Kong: Hong Kong University Press, 1993. 211–45.

Chen Sen. *Pin hua bao jian* (A precious mirror for classifying flowers). 2 vols. Beijing: Renmin zhongguo chubanshe, 1993.

Chen Shaobai. *Xingzhonghui geming shiyao* (Outline of the revolutionary history of Xing-zhonghui). Taipei: Zhongyang Wenwu gongyingshe, 1956.

Chen Xiqi, ed. *Sun Zhongshan nianpu changbian* (Extended chronology of Sun Yat-sen). Beijing: Zhonghua shuju, 1991.

Chen Yuan. *Shehui yuyanxue* (Social linguistics). Shanghai: Xuelin chubanshe, 1983.

Cheng Yishan. *Zhongguo gudai yuanqi xueshuo* (Theories of the primordial *qi* in ancient China). Wuhan: Hubei Renmin chubanshe, 1986.

Chin, Robert S., and Ai-Li S. Chin. *Psychological Research in Communist China 1949–1966.* Boston: MIT Press, 1987.

Chinese Medical Association. *Chinese Classification of Mental Disorders.* 2d ed. Hunan: Hunan Medical University, 1990.

Chinese Medical Association. *Chinese Classification of Mental Disorders.* 2d ed. rev. Nanjing: Dong Nan University Press, 1995.

Chinese Ministry of Information. *China Handbook, 1937–1943.* New York: Macmillan, 1943.

Chouban yiwu shimo (A complete account of the management of foreign affairs). Photo-lithographic reproduction. Beijing, 1930.

Chow, Rey. *Writing Diaspora: Tactics of Intervention in Contemporary Cultural Studies.* Bloomington, IN: Indiana University Press, 1993.

Chow Tse-Tsung. *The May Fourth Movement: Intellectual Revolution in Modern China.* Cambridge, MA: Harvard University Press, 1960.

Chu, James Hong-yuan. *Revolutionary Theory of T'ung-meng hui: The "Min pao" as a Case Study.* Taipei: Institute of Modern History, Academia Sinica, 1985.

Churchill, Winston. *Complete Speeches, 1943–1949,* vol. 7. New York: Chelsea House, 1974.

———. *Onwards to Victory: War Speeches.* Boston: Little, Brown, 1944.

———. *Second World War: Closing the Ring.* Boston: Houghton Mifflin, 1951.

Clifford, James. *Routes: Travel and Translation in the Late Twentieth Century.* Cambridge: Harvard University Press, 1997.

Clunas, Craig. *Chinese Export Watercolours.* London: Victoria and Albert Museum and Crown Books, 1984.

———. *Pictures and Visuality in Early Modern China.* Princeton: Princeton University Press, 1997.

Cocks, Anna S. *The Victoria and Albert Museum: The Making of the Collection.* London: Windward, 1980.

Cohen, Paul A. *Between Tradition and Modernity: Wang T'ao and Reform in Late Ch'ing China.* Cambridge, MA: Harvard University Press, 1987.

———. *Discovering History in China: American Historical Writing on the Recent Chinese Past.* New York: Columbia University Press, Studies of the East Asian Institute, 1984.

———. Review of *China and the Christian Impact: A Conflict of Cultures,* by Jacques Gernet. *Harvard Journal of Asiatic Studies* 47.2 (December 1987): 674–83.

Coleridge, S. T. *Biographia Literaria.* Ed. James Engell and Walter Jackson Bate. 2 vols. Princeton: Princeton University Press, 1983.

Colombos, C. J. *A Treatise on the Law of Prize.* London: Grotius Society, 1940.

Colquhoun, Archibald. *Overland to China.* New York: Harper & Brothers, 1900.

Comaroff, John, and Jean Comaroff. *Ethnography and the Historical Imagination.* Boulder, CO: Westview Press, 1992.

Commercial Directory of Shanghai. Shanghai: Commercial Press, 1928.

Conte, Pat. "The Fourth World: From Stone Age to New Age." Compact disk liner notes for *The Secret Museum of Mankind, Vol. 1: Ethnic Music Classics, 1925–1948.* Yazoo 7004, 1995.

Covell, Ralph. *W. A. P. Martin: Pioneer of Progress in China.* Washington, DC: Christian University Press, 1978.

Crewe, William, and Keith S. T. Tong. "Cultural Considerations in the Selection of ESL Reading Texts." *Hong Kong Papers in Linguistics and Language Teaching* 11 (1988): 54–69.

Crossman, Carl L. *The Decorative Arts of the China Trade.* Suffolk: Antique Collector's Club, 1991.

Daggett, A. S. *America in the China Relief Expedition.* Kansas City, MO: Hudson-Kimberly, 1903.

Dan, Washima Che, Harshita Aini Haroon, and John Naysmith. "English and Islam in Malaysia: Resolving the Tension?" *World Englishes* 15.2 (1996): 225–34.

Dana, Richard Henry, ed. *Elements of International Law,* by Henry Wheaton. 8th ed. Boston: Little, Brown, 1866.

Davidson, Donald. "On the Very Idea of a Conceptual Scheme." In *Inquiries into Truth and Interpretation*. New York: Oxford University Press, 1984.

Davies, Anna Morpurgo. "Language Classification in the Nineteenth Century." In *Current Trends in Linguistics*, vol. 11, *Historiography of Linguistics*, ed. Thomas A. Sebeok. The Hague: Mouton, 1975.

Davis, John. *History of the Second Queen's Royal Regiment*. 6 vols. London: Eyre and Spottiswoode, 1906.

de Man, Paul. *Blindness and Insight: Essays in the Rhetoric of Contemporary Criticism*. London: Routledge, 1983.

D'Emilio, John. *Sexual Politics, Sexual Communities: The Making of a Homosexual Minority in the United States, 1940–1970*. Chicago: University of Chicago Press, 1983.

Derrida, Jacques. *Of Grammatology*. Trans. Gayatri Chakravorty Spivak. Baltimore: Johns Hopkins University Press, 1974.

———. *Positions*. Trans. Alan Bass. Chicago: University of Chicago Press, 1981.

———. "The Supplement of Copula: Philosophy *before* Linguistics." In *Textual Strategies: Perspectives in Post-Structuralist Criticism*, ed. Josué V. Harari. Ithaca: Cornell University Press, 1979.

DeWitt, Bryce S., and Neill Graham. *The Many-Worlds Interpretation of Quantum Mechanics*. Princeton: Princeton University Press, 1973.

D'Hérrison, Count. "The Loot of the Imperial Summer Palace at Pekin." *Annual Report of the Smithsonian Institution*. Washington, DC: U.S. Government Printing Office, 1901. 601–35.

Diamant, Neil. "China's 'Great Confinement'? Missionaries, Municipal Elites and Police in the Establishment of Chinese Mental Hospitals." *Republican China* 19, no. 1 (November 1993): 3–50.

Dikötter, Frank. *Sex, Culture and Modernity in China: Medical Science and the Construction of Sexual Identities in the Early Republican Period*. Honolulu: University of Hawaii Press, 1995.

Dillon, Edward J. "The Chinese Wolf and the European Lamb." *Contemporary Review* 79 (1901): 1–31.

Dower, John. *War Without Mercy — Race and Power in the Pacific War*. New York: Pantheon, 1986.

Dreyfus, Hubert L., and Paul Rabinow. *Michel Foucault: Beyond Structuralism and Hermeneutics*. 2d ed. Chicago: University of Chicago Press, 1983.

Drummond, Lee. "The Cultural Continuum." *Man* 15 (1980): 352–74.

Duara, Prasenjit. *Rescuing History from the Nation: Questioning Narratives of Modern China*. Chicago: University of Chicago Press, 1995.

Dubarle, Andre-Marie. "Belief in Immortality in the Old Testament and Judaism." In *Immortality and Resurrection*, ed. Pierre Benoit and Roland Murphy. New York: Herder and Herder, 1970. 34–53.

During, Simon. "Literature — Nationalism's Other?" In *Nation and Narration*, ed. Homi K. Bhabha. London: Routledge, 1990. 138–53.

Duyvendak, J. J. L. "Review of Pasquale d'Elia, *Le Origini Dell' Arte Cristiana Cinese (1583–1640)*." *T'oung Pao* 35 (1940): 386–98.

Eastwood, Alexis Dudden. "International Terms: Japan's Engagement with Colonial Control." Ph.D. diss. University of Chicago, 1998.

Eco, Umberto. *Foucault's Pendulum*. Trans. William Weaver. New York: Harcourt Brace Jovanovich, 1988.

Education Commission. *Education Commission Report No. 6*. Hong Kong: Education Department, 1995.

Educational News. Hong Kong: Association of Hong Kong Educators, March 1995, October 1996, December 1997.

Ellis, Havelock. "Appendix: The School-Friendships of Girls." *Sexual Inversion: Studies in the Psychology of Sex, Vol. 2*. 3d ed. Philadelphia: F. A. Davis Company, 1920. 368–84.

———. *The Psychology of Sex: A Manual for Students*. 2d ed. New York: Emerson Books, 1944.

Ellis, Havelock, and J. A. Symonds. *Das konträre Geschlechtsgefühl*. Trans. Hans Kurella. Leipzig: Georg H. Wigand's Verlag, 1896.

Elman, Benjamin. *From Philosophy to Philology: Intellectual and Social Aspects of Change in Late Imperial China*. Cambridge, MA: Harvard University Press, 1990.

Empson, William. "Teaching English in the Far East and England." In *The Strengths of Shakespeare's Shrew: Essays, Memoirs and Reviews*, ed. John Haffenden. Sheffield: Sheffield Academic Press, 1996. 209–19.

Engelfriet, Peter M. "Euclid in China: A Survey of the Historical Background of the First Chinese Translation of Euclid's *Elements* (Jihe Yuanben, Beijing, 1607), an Analysis of the Translation, and a Study of Its Influence up to 1723." Ph.D. diss., Leiden University, 1996.

Esherick, Joseph. "Harvard on China: The Apologetics of Imperialism." *Bulletin of Concerned Asian Scholars* 4.4 (December 1972): 9–16.

Étiemble. *L'Europe chinoise*. Vol. 1, *De l'empire romain à Leibniz*; vol. 2, *De la sinophilie à la sinophobie*. Paris: Gallimard, 1988–89.

Eze, Emmanuel, ed. *Postcolonial African Philosophy*. Cambridge, MA: Blackwell, 1997.

Fabian, Johannes. *Time and the Other: How Anthropology Makes Its Object*. New York: Columbia University Press, 1983.

Fairbank, John King. *The Great Chinese Revolution, 1800–1985*. New York: Cornelia & Michael Bessie Book, 1987.

———. *Trade and Diplomacy on the China Coast: The Opening of the Treaty Ports, 1842–1854*. Cambridge, MA: Harvard University Press, 1953.

———., ed. *The Chinese World Order: Traditional Chinese Foreign Relations*. Cambridge: Harvard University Press, 1968.

Fairbank, John K., and James Peck. "An Exchange." *Bulletin of Concerned Asian Scholars* 2.3 (April–July 1970): 41–61.

Fang Hao. *Zhongguo Tianzhujiao shi renwu zhuan* (Biographies of Catholics in China). Beijing: Zhonghua shuju, 1988.

Feng Ziyou. *Geming Yishi* (Reminiscences of the revolution). Changsha, 1939.

Feyerabend, Paul. *Against Method*. London: Verso, 1988.

———. "Explanation, Reduction, and Empiricism." In *Scientific Explanation, Space, and Time*, ed. Herbert Feigl and Grover Maxwell. Minnesota Studies in the Philosophy of Science, vol. 3. Minneapolis: University of Minnesota Press, 1962.

Fingarette, Herbert. *Confucius—The Secular as Sacred*. New York: Harper & Row, 1972.

Firth, J. R. "Linguistic Analysis and Translation." In *Selected Papers of J. R. Firth 1952–59*, ed. F. R. Palmer. Bloomington: Indiana University Press, 1968.

Fleming, Peter. *The Siege of Peking*. New York: Harper & Brothers, 1959.

Foley, Frederic J. *The Great Formosan Impostor*. Rome and St. Louis: Jesuit Historical Institute and St. Louis University, 1968.

Foreign Office (Japan). *Treaties and Conventions between the Empire of Japan and Other Powers*. Z. P. Maruya & Company, 1899.

Foucault, Michel. *The Archaeology of Knowledge and the Discourse on Language*. Trans. A. M. Sheridan Smith. New York: Pantheon, 1972. Originally published as *L'archéologie du savoir* (Paris: Éditions Gallimard, 1969).

———. *The History of Sexuality: Vol. 1, An Introduction*. Trans. Robert Hurley. New York: Vintage Books, 1990.

———. *Power/Knowledge: Selected Interviews and Other Writings, 1972–1977*. Ed. Colin Gordon. New York: Pantheon, 1980.

Fox, Daniel M., and Christopher Lawrence. *Photographing Medicine: Images and Power in Britain and America since 1840*. New York: Greenwood Press, 1988.

Franke, Wolfgang. *A Century of Chinese Revolution, 1851–1949*. New York: Harper Torchbooks, 1970.

Fu Po-shek. "Framing Identity: Mainland Emigres, Marginal Culture, and Hong Kong Cinema, 1937–1941." Unpublished manuscript, 1994.

Funü zazhi (The Lady's Journal). Shanghai: Shangwu yinshuguan, 1915–1931.

Fuss, Diana. *Essentially Speaking*. New York: Routledge, 1989.

Gaimusho, ed. *Nihon Gaikō Monjo*. (Documents of the foreign ministry). Tokyo: Nihon Kokusai Renmei Kyokai, 1933–56.

Gaisberg, F. W. *The Music Goes Round*. New York: Macmillan, 1942.

Gardner, Daniel K. *Chu Hsi and the Ta-Hsueh: Neo-Confucian Reflection on the Confucian Canon*. Harvard East Asian Monographs, vol. 118. Cambridge, MA: Council on East Asian Studies, Harvard University, 1986.

Gasster, Michael. "Reform and Revolution in China's Political Modernization." In *China in Revolution: The First Phase, 1900–1913*, ed. Mary Clabaugh Wright. New Haven: Yale University Press, 1968.

Gelatt, Roland. *The Fabulous Phonograph, 1877–1977*. New York: Macmillan, 1977.

Gernet, Jacques. *China and the Christian Impact: A Conflict of Cultures*. Trans. Janet Lloyd. New York: Cambridge University Press, 1985. Originally published in French as *Chine et christianisme: action et réaction* (Paris: Éditions Gallimard, 1982).

———. "Christian and Chinese Visions of the World in the Seventeenth Century." *Chinese Science* 4 (September 1980): 1–17.

———. "The Encounter between China and Europe." *Chinese Science* 11 (1993–94): 93–102.

Gibson, Tom. *The Wiltshire Regiment*. London: Leo Cooper, 1969.

Gilman, Sander L. *Disease and Representation: Images of Illness from Madness to AIDS*. Ithaca: Cornell University Press, 1988.

———. "Lam Qua and the Development of a Westernized Medical Iconography in China." *Medical History* 30.1 (January 1986): 57–69.

Giroux, Henry A. *Border Crossings: Cultural Workers and the Politics of Education.* New York: Routledge, 1992.

———. "Living Dangerously: Identity Politics and the New Cultural Racism." In *Between Borders: Pedagogy and the Politics of Cultural Studies,* ed. Henry A. Giroux and Peter McLaren. New York: Routledge, 1994.

Giroux, Henry A., and Peter McLaren, eds. *Between Borders: Pedagogy and the Politics of Cultural Studies.* New York: Routledge, 1994.

Goodman, Howard L., and Anthony Grafton. "Ricci, the Chinese, and the Toolkits of Textualists." *Asia Major,* 3d ser., 3.2 (1990): 95–148.

Goodrich, L. Carrington, and Nigel Cameron. *The Face of China as Seen by Photographers and Travelers, 1860–1912.* Millerton, NY: Aperture Press, 1978.

Goodrich, L. Carrington, and Chaoying Fang, eds. *Dictionary of Ming Biography, 1368–1644.* New York: Columbia University Press, 1976.

Goody, Jack. *The Logic of Writing and the Organization of Society.* New York: Cambridge University Press, 1986.

Graham, A. C. " 'Being' in Western Philosophy Compared with *shih/fei yu/wu* in Chinese Philosophy." *Asia Major* 7 (1959): 79–112.

———. *Disputers of the Tao: Philosophical Argument in Ancient China.* La Salle, IL: Open Court, 1989.

Granger, Gilles. *La théorie aristotélicienne de la science.* Paris: Aubier Montaigne, 1976.

Greene, Marc T. "Shanghai Cabaret Girl." *Literary Digest,* 23 October 1923.

Gronow, Pekka. "The Record Industry Comes to the Orient." *Ethnomusicology* 2.25 (May 1981): 251–84.

———. "The Record Industry: The Growth of a Mass Medium." *Popular Music* 3 (1983): 53–76.

Guide to China's Foreign Trade: Import and Export Annual 1933. Shanghai: Bureau of Foreign Trade of the Ministry of Industry, 1933.

Gulick, Edward V. *Peter Parker and the Opening of China.* Cambridge, MA: Harvard University Press, 1973.

Guo Moruo. *Moruo wenji* (Collected works of Moruo). 17 vols. Beijing: Renmin wenxue chubanshe, 1957.

Gupta, Akhil, and James Ferguson. "Beyond 'Culture': Space, Identity, and the Politics of Difference." *Cultural Anthropology* 7.1 (1992): 6–23.

Hanatachi Saburō. *Tokutomi Sōho to Ōe gijuku* (Tokutomi Sōho and Ōe Academy). Tokyo: Penkan sha, 1982.

Hannerz, Ulf. *Transnational Connections: Culture, People, Places.* New York: Routledge, 1996.

Hansen, Chad. *Language and Logic in Ancient China.* Ann Arbor: University of Michigan Press, 1983.

Harbsmeier, Christoph. *Wilhelm von Humboldts Brief an Abel Rémusat und die philosophische Grammatik des Altchinesischen.* Stuttgart/Bad Cannstatt: Frommann-Holzboog, 1979.

Harootunian, Harry. "The Samurai Class During the Early Years of the Meiji Period in Japan, 1868–1882." Ph.D. diss. University of Michigan, 1957.

Hart, Robert. *These from the Land of Sinim.* London: Chapman & Hall, 1901.

Hart, Roger. "On the Problem of Chinese Science." In *The Science Studies Reader,* ed. Mario Biagioli. New York: Routledge, 1999.

———. "Proof, Propaganda and Patronage: The Dissemination of Western Studies in Seventeenth Century China." Manuscript in progress.

Harvey, David. *The Condition of Postmodernity.* Cambridge, MA: Basil Blackwell, 1990.

Haswell, Jock. *The Queen's Royal Regiment (West Surrey).* London: Hamish Hamilton, 1967.

Havens, Thomas. *Nishi Amane and Modern Japanese Thought.* Princeton: Princeton University Press, 1970.

Hegel, Georg W. F. *Hegel's Philosophy of Nature.* Trans. Michael John Petry. London: George Allen & Unwin, 1970.

———. *The Philosophy of History.* Trans. J. Sibree. New York: Dover, 1956.

———. *Vorlesungen über die Geschichte der Philosophie.* Ed. Karl Ludwig Michelet. Berlin: Duncker & Humblot, 1833.

———. *Werke in zwanzig Bänden.* Frankfurt am Main: Suhrkamp, 1980.

Herbert, Trevor, and Margaret Sarkissian. "Victorian Bands and Their Dissemination in the Colonies." *Popular Music* 16.2 (1997): 165–79.

Herder, Johann Gottfried. *Abhandlung über den Ursprung der Sprache: Text, Materialien, Kommentar.* Ed. Wolfgang Pross. Munich: Hanser, 1978.

———. *On the Origin of Language.* Trans. John H. Moran and Alexander Gode. New York: Ungar, 1966.

Hevia, James. "The Archive State and the Fear of Pollution: From the Opium Wars to Fu-Manchu." *Cultural Studies* 12.2 (1998): 234–64.

———. *Cherishing Men from Afar.* Durham, NC: Duke University Press, 1995.

Hill, Boyd H. "The Grain and the Spirit in Medieval Anatomy." *Speculum* 40 (1965): 63–73.

Hinsch, Bret. *Passions of the Cut Sleeve: The Male Homosexual Tradition in China.* Berkeley: University of California Press, 1990.

Hippocratic Writings. Trans. J. Chadwick and W. N. Mann. Ed. with an introduction by G. E. R. Lloyd. New York: Penguin Books, 1983.

Hirschfeld, Magnus. *Men and Women: The World Journey of a Sexologist.* Trans. O. P. Green. New York: G. P. Putnam's Sons, 1935.

Hollingsworth, Alan M. "I. A. Richards in China and America." In *R.O.C. & U.S.A.: 1911–1981,* ed. Tung-hsun Sun and Morris Wei-hsin Tien. Taipei: American Studies Association of the Republic of China, 1982. 125–40.

Hollis, Martin, and Steven Lukes, ed. *Rationality and Relativism.* Cambridge, MA: MIT Press, 1982.

Holmes, R. *Naval & Military Trophies & Personal Relics of British Heroes.* London: John C. Nimmo, 1896.

Hotopf, W. H. N. *Language, Thought and Comprehension: A Case Study of the Writings of I. A. Richards.* London: Routledge & Kegan Paul, 1965.

Hsü, Immanuel C. Y. *China's Entrance into the Family of Nations: The Diplomatic Phase, 1858–1880.* Cambridge, MA: Harvard University Press, 1960.

Hu Sheng, *Cong yapian zhanzheng dao wusi yundong* (From the Opium War to the May Fourth movement), vols. 1–2. Beijing: Renmin chubanshe, 1981.

Hu Shi. "Lun xiaoshuo ji baihua yunwen" (On fiction and vernacular verse). *Xin qingnian* (New youth) 4.1 (1918): 75–79.

Huang, Philip. "Theory and the Study of Modern Chinese History: Four Traps and a Question." *Modern China* 24.2 (April 1998): 183–208.

Huang, Ray. *1587, A Year of No Significance: The Ming Dynasty in Decline*. New Haven: Yale University Press, 1981.

Huang Zhangjian, ed. *Kang Youwei wuxu zhen zouyi* (Kang Youwei's true memorials in 1898). Taipei: Zhongyang yanjiuyuan lishi yanjiusuo, 1974.

Humboldt, Wilhelm von. *Sur l'origine des formes grammaticales*. 1823. Reprinted, Bordeaux: Ducros, 1969.

———. *Wilhelm von Humboldts Gesammelte Schriften*. Ed. Albert Leitzmann. Berlin: Behr, 1907.

Hutcheon, Robin. *Chinnery, the Man and the Legend*. Hong Kong: South Chinese Morning Post, 1975.

Hyde, Martin. "The Teaching of English in Morocco: The Place of Culture." *ELT Journal* 48.4 (1994): 295–305.

Impey, O. *Chinoiserie*. London: Oxford University Press, 1977.

Impey, O., and A. MacGregor, eds. *The Origins of Museums: The Cabinets of Curiosities in Sixteenth- and Seventeenth-Century Europe*. Oxford: Clarendon, 1985.

Inoue Haruki. *Ryojun Gyakusatsu Jiken* (Port Arthur massacre). Tokyo: Sakuma Shobo, 1995.

Inoue Tetsujiro et al. *Tetsugaku Jii* (Dictionary of philosophical terms). Tokyo: 1881.

Iriye, Akira. *China and Japan in a Global Setting*. Cambridge, MA: Harvard University Press, 1992.

Ito Hirobumi. *Marquis Ito's Experience*. Trans. Teizo Kuramata. Nagasaki: Gwaikokugo Kyojusho, 1904.

———. *Report of Count Ito Hirobumi, Ambassador Extraordinary to His Imperial Majesty the Emperor of Japan of His Mission to the Court of China, 18th Year of Meiji / Ito Tokuha Zenken Taishi, Fuku Meisho*. Tokyo: Foreign Ministry, 1885.

Ito Hirobumi and Hiratsuka Atsushi, eds. *Hisho Ruisan: Chōsen Kōshō Shiryō* (Classified collection of the private office: Documents pertaining to Korean affairs). Rev. ed. 3 vols. Tokyo: Hara Shobo, 1969.

Ito Hirobumi Kankei Bunsho Kenkyukai, ed. *Ito Hirobumi Kankei Bunsho* (Materials relating to Ito Hirobumi). Tokyo: Hanawa Shobo, 1974.

Jakobson, Roman. *Language in Literature*. Cambridge, MA: Harvard University Press, 1987.

Jan Mohammed, Abdul R. "Some Implications of Paulo Freire's Border Pedagogy." In *Between Borders: Pedagogy and the Politics of Cultural Studies*, ed. Henry A. Giroux and Peter McLaren. New York: Routledge, 1994.

Jami, Catherine. Review of *Histoire des mathématiques chinoises* by Jean-Claude Martzloff. *Historia Scientiarum* 41 (November 1990): 59–62.

———. "On Linguistic Aspects of Translation." In *On Translation*, ed. Reuben A. Brower. Cambridge, MA: Harvard University Press, 1959.

Jefferys, W. Hamilton, and James L. Maxwell. *The Diseases of China, including Formosa and Korea*. Philadelphia: P. Blakiston's Son & Co., 1910.

Jensen, Lionel M. *Manufacturing Confucianism: Chinese Traditions and Universal Civilization*. Durham, NC: Duke University Press, 1997.

Jespersen, Otto. *Progress in Language: With Special Reference to English.* 1894. Reprinted, Amsterdam: Benjamins, 1993.

Jian, Bozan, et al., eds. *Wuxu bianfa* (One hundred day reform). Shanghai: Renmin chubanshe, 1957.

Jiang Tie. *Liusheng ji* (The phonograph). Shanghai: Commercial Press, 1932.

Jiang Weitang et al., eds. *Beijing funü baokan kao, 1905–1949* (An examination of Beijing women's press, 1905–1949). Beijing: Guangming ribao chubanshe, 1990.

Jingqu Houren. *Shu yan lie qi lu* (Writing about the erotic and hunting for the unusual). Shanghai: Fengxing chubanshe, 1940.

Johnson, R. Keith. "International English: Towards an Acceptable, Teachable Target Variety." *World Englishes* 9.3 (1990): 301–15.

Johnson, R. Keith, Cecilia K. W. Shek, and Edmond H. F. Law. *Using English as the Medium of Instruction.* Hong Kong: Longman, 1993.

Jones, Andrew F. "Popular Music and Colonial Modernity in China, 1900–1937." Ph.D. diss., University of California at Berkeley, 1997.

Joshi, G. N. "A Concise History of the Phonograph Industry in India." *Popular Music* 7.2 (May 1988): 147–56.

Josyph, Peter. *From Yale to Canton: The Transcultural Challenge of Lam Qua and Peter Parker.* Exhibition catalogue. Smithtown, NY: Smithtown Township Arts Council, 1992.

———. "The Missionary Doctor and the Chinese Painter," *MD* 36, 8 (August 1992): 46–58.

Jowett, Benjamin, trans. *The Dialogues of Plato.* Oxford: Clarendon Press, 1871.

Julien, Stanislas. *Meng Tseu vel Mencius.* Paris, 1824.

Jusdanis, Gregory. *Belated Modernity and Aesthetic Culture: Inventing National Literature.* Minneapolis: University of Minnesota Press, 1991.

Kachru, Braj B. "World Englishes and Applied Linguistics." *World Englishes* 9.1 (1990): 3–20.

———. "World Englishes and English-Using Communities." *Annual Review of Applied Linguistics* 17 (1997): 66–87.

———, ed. *The Other Tongue: English across Cultures.* Rev. ed. Urbana: University of Illinois Press, 1992.

Kajima, Minorosuke. *The Diplomacy of Japan 1894–1922.* Tokyo: Kajima Institute of International Peace, 1976.

Kane, Lawence. "The Acquisition of Cultural Competence: An Ethnographic Framework for Cultural Studies Curricula." In *Mediating Languages and Cultures: Towards an Intercultural Theory of Foreign Language Education,* ed. Dieter Buttjes and Michael Byram. Clevedon, England: Multilingual Matters, 1991.

Kant, Immanuel. *Kant's Political Writings.* Ed. H. Reiss. Cambridge: Cambridge University Press, 1970.

Kao, John J. *Three Millennia of Chinese Psychiatry.* New York: Institute for Advanced Research in Asian Science and Medicine, 1979.

Kato Shuichi and Maruyama Masao, eds. *Honyaku no Shisō; Nihon Kindai Shisō Taikei* (Translation philosophies; collection of Modern Japanese thought). Vol. 15. Tokyo: Iwanami Shoten, 1991.

Katz, Jonathan Ned. *Gay American History: Lesbians and Gay Men in the U.S.A.* Revised ed. New York: Meridian, 1992.

Ke Zhenghe. "Changpian de piping" (Record criticism). *Yinyue zazhi* 1.10 (February 1932): 17.

———. "Changpian de shiyong ji baocun fa" (The use and preservation of records). *Yinyue zazhi* 9 (January 1930).

———. "Liushengji de liyong fa" (How to use the phonograph). *Yinyue chao* 1.5 (December 1927): 7–10.

Keenan, Thomas. "The Point Is to (Ex)Change It: Reading *Capital,* Rhetorically." In *Fetishism as Cultural Discourse,* ed. Emily Apter and William Pietz. Ithaca: Cornell University Press, 1993.

Kellner, Douglas. *Jean Baudrillard: From Marxism to Postmodernism and Beyond.* Stanford: Stanford University Press, 1989.

Kenwood, A. G., and A. L. Lougheed. *The Growth of the International Economy, 1820–1960.* London: Allen and Unwin, 1971.

Kida Junichiro. *Nihongo Daihaku Butsukan, Akuma no Bunji to Tatakatta Hitobito* (The repository of Japanese and the people combating the nightmarish script). Tokyo: Jyasuto Shisutemu, 1994.

King, Gail. "The Family Letters of Xu Guangqi." *Ming Studies,* no. 31 (1991): 1–41.

King's Regulations and Orders for the Army. London: HMSO, 1901.

Kiparsky, Paul. "From Paleogrammarians to Neogrammarians." In *Studies in the History of Linguistics,* ed. Dell Hymes. Bloomington: Indiana University Press, 1974. 331–45.

Kirk, G. S., et al. *The Presocratic Philosophers: A Critical History with a Selection of Texts.* 2d ed. Cambridge: Cambridge University Press, 1983.

Kirshenblatt-Gimblett, B. "Objects of Ethnography." In *Exhibiting Cultures,* ed. I. Karp and S. Lavine. Washington, DC: Smithsonian Institution Press, 1991. 386–443.

Kleinman, Arthur. *Rethinking Psychiatry: From Cultural Category to Personal Experience.* New York: Free Press, 1988.

———. *Social Origins of Distress and Disease: Depression, Neurasthenia, and Pain in Modern China.* New Haven: Yale University Press, 1986.

———. *Writing at the Margin: Discourse between Anthropology and Medicine.* Berkeley: University of California Press, 1995.

Knollys, Henry. *Incidents in the China War of 1860 compiled from the private journals of General Sir Hope Grant.* Edinburgh: William Blackwood and Sons, 1873.

Krafft-Ebing, Richard von. *Psychopathia Sexualis.* Stuttgart: Verlag von Ferdinand Enke, 1892.

———. *Psychopathia Sexualis.* Trans. F. J. Rebman. New York: Rebman Company, 1906.

Kramsch, Claire. *Context and Culture in Language Teaching.* Oxford: Oxford University Press, 1993.

———. "The Cultural Component of Language Teaching." *Language, Culture and Curriculum.* 8.2 (1995): 83–92.

———. "The Cultural Discourse of Foreign Language Textbooks." In *Towards a New Integration of Language and Culture,* ed. Alan Singerman. Middlebury, VT: Northeast Conference, 1988. 63–88.

———. "Culture in Language Learning: A View from the United States." In *Foreign Lan-*

guage Research in Cross-Cultural Perspective, ed. K. de Bot, R. Ginsberg, and C. Kramsch. Amsterdam: J. Benjamins, 1991. 217–40.

————. "The Dialogic Emergence of Culture in the Language Classroom." In Language, Communication and Social Meaning, ed. James E. Alatis. Washington, DC: Georgetown University Press, 1993. 465–88.

————. "Redrawing the Boundaries of Foreign Language Study." In Language and Content: Discipline- and Content-Based Approaches to Language Study, ed. M. Krueger and F. Ryan. Lexington, MA: D.C. Heath, 1993. 203–17.

————. "Rhetorical Models of Understanding." In Functional Approaches to Written Texts: Classroom Applications, ed. Thomas Miller. Paris: USIS, 1995. 61–78.

————. "Stylistic Choice and Cultural Awareness." In Challenges of Literary Texts in the Foreign Language Classroom, ed. Lothar Bredella and Werner Delanoy. Tübingen: Gunter Harr, 1996. 162–84.

Kramsch, Claire, and Linda von Hoene. "The Dialogic Emergence of Difference: Feminist Explorations in Foreign Language Learning and Teaching." In Feminisms in the Academy, ed. Domna Stanton and Abigail Stewart. Ann Arbor: Michigan University Press, 1995. 330–57.

Kramsch, Claire, and Patricia Sullivan. "Appropriate Pedagogy." ELT Journal 50.3 (1996): 199–212.

Krausz, Michael, ed. Relativism: Interpretation and Confrontation. Notre Dame, IN: University of Notre Dame Press, 1989.

Kuhn, Thomas S. "Second Thoughts on Paradigms." In The Structure of Scientific Theories, ed. Frederick Suppe. Urbana: University of Illinois Press, 1974.

————. The Structure of Scientific Revolutions. 2d ed., enlarged. Chicago: University of Chicago Press, 1970.

Kurokawa Mayori. Yokobunji Hyakunin Isshu. Tokyo: Bunendo, 1873.

Lacan, Jacques. "The Insistence of the Letter in the Unconscious." Yale French Studies, nos. 36–37 (1966): 112–47.

Landor, Henry Savage. China and the Allies. 2 vols. New York: Charles Scribner's Sons, 1901.

Lapham, Claude. "Looking at Japanese Jazz." The Metronome (June 1936): 13–39.

Larson, Wendy. Women and Writing in Modern China. Stanford: Stanford University Press, 1998.

Lattis, James M. Between Copernicus and Galileo: Christoph Clavius and the Collapse of Ptolemaic Cosmology. Chicago: University of Chicago Press, 1994.

Lau, D.C., trans. Mencius. Hong Kong: Chinese University Press, 1979.

Lee, Leo Ou-fan. "In Search of Modernity: Some Reflections on a New Mode of Consciousness in Twentieth-Century Chinese History and Literature." In Ideas Across Cultures: Essays on Chinese Thought in Honor of Benjamin Schwartz, ed. Paul Cohen and Merle Goldman. Cambridge, MA: Harvard University Press, 1990.

Lee, Sing. "Cultures in Psychiatric Nosology: The CCDM-2-R and International Classification of Mental Disorders." Culture, Medicine, and Psychiatry 20 (1996): 421–72.

Lee, W. O. "Social Reactions towards Education Proposals: Opting against the Mother Tongue as the Medium of Instruction in Hong Kong." Journal of Multilingual and Multicultural Development 14.3 (1993): 203–16.

Legge, James, trans. *The Book of Changes.* Toronto: Bantam Books, 1986.

——. trans. *Hanying sishu* (Chinese-English edition of the Four Books). Corrected by Liu Zhongde and Luo Zhiye. Chongsha, PRC: Hunan chubanshe, 1992.

——, trans. *The Works of Mencius.* In *The Chinese Classics.* 1861–72. Reprinted, Taipei: Southern Materials Center Publishing, 1991.

Leonard, Lloyd. *Catalogue of the United States Military Academy Museum.* West Point, NY: United States Military Academy Printing Office, 1944.

Leslie, N. B. *Battle Honours of the British and Indian Armies, 1695–1914.* London: Leo Cooper, 1970.

LeVay, Simon. *The Sexual Brain.* Cambridge, MA: MIT Press, 1994.

Levenson, Joseph R. *Confucian China and Its Modern Fate: A Trilogy.* Berkeley: University of California Press, 1968.

——. *Liang Ch'i-ch'ao and the Mind of Modern China.* Harvard Historical Monographs, vol. 26. Cambridge, MA: Harvard University Press, 1953.

Levy, Howard, trans. *Sex Histories: China's First Modern Treatise on Sex Education,* by Zhang Jingsheng. Yokohama: Author, 1967.

Li, Jinhui. "Wo he Mingyue she" (The Bright Moon ensemble and myself). *Wenhua shiliao* 3.4 (1985–86).

Li Qing et al. *Guangbo dianshi qiye shi neibu shiliao* (Internal historical documents on the history of the broadcasting and television industries). Shanghai: Zhongguo chang-pian gongsi, 1994.

Li Qingming and Huang Yuren. " 'Qi' yuan yitan" (Inquiry into the origins of [the conception of] qi). *Zhongguo renmin daxue shubao ziliaoshe fuyin baokan ziliao,* no. 8 (1985): 22–26.

Li Yinhe and Wang Xiaobo. *Tamen de shijie: Zhongguo nan tongxinglian qunluo toushi* (Their world: Looking into the gay male communities in China). Hong Kong: Tiandi tushu youxian gongsi, 1991.

Li Zehou. "Heping jinhua, fuxing Zhonghua—tan 'yao gailiang, buyao *geming*' " (Peaceful progress to restore China—"We want reform, not revolution"). *China Times Weekly* (3–9 May 1992): 42–45; (10–16 May 1992): 44–47.

Liang Qidiao. Hanman lu. *Qingyi bao* 35, 36, 38 (February 1900): Reprinted, 2275–83; 2343–50; 2473–79. Taipei: Chengwen chuban gongsi, 1967.

——. "Jing gao wo tongye zhujun" (A reverent speech to my colleagues). *Xinmin congbao* 17 (October 1902): 1–7.

——. "Shi ge" (An explanation of the meaning of revolution). *Xinmin congbao* 22 (February 1902): 1–8.

——. "Zhongguo lishi shang geming zhi yanjiu" (A study of revolution in Chinese history). *Xinmin congbao* 46–48 (February 1904): 115–31.

Lieber, Francis. *Instructions for the Government of the Armies of the United States in the Field.* New York: D. Van Nostrand, 1863.

Lin, Tsung-Yi. "Neurasthenia Revisited: Its Place in Modern Psychiatry." *Culture, Medicine and Psychiatry* 13.2 (1989): 105–30.

Lin, Tsung-Yi, and Leon Eisenberg, ed. *Mental Health Planning for One Billion People—A Chinese Perspective.* Vancouver: University of Columbia Press, 1985.

Lin, Tsung-Yi, Wen-Tsing Tseng, and Eng-Kung Yeh, eds. *Chinese Societies and Mental Health.* Hong Kong: Oxford University Press, 1996.

Linebarger, Paul. *Sun Yat-sen and the Chinese Republic.* New York: Century Co., 1925.

Liu, Lydia H. *Translingual Practice: Literature, National Culture, and Translated Modernity— China, 1900–1937.* Stanford: Stanford University Press, 1995.

Luk, Bernard H. K. "Chinese Culture in the Hong Kong Curriculum: Heritage and Colonialism." *Comparative Education Review* 35.4 (1991): 650–68.

Lun yu zhu shu (Confucian analects, with annotations and subannotations). Compilation of annotated editions by He Yan (190–249) and Xing Bing (932–1010). In SSJZS.

Lutz, Jessie G. "Karl F. A. Gützlaff: Missionary Entrepreneur." In *Christianity in China: Early Protestant Missionary Writings,* ed. S.W. Barnett and J.K. Fairbank. Cambridge, MA: Harvard University Press, 1985.

Lynch, George. *The War of Civilizations.* London: Longmans, Green, 1901.

Lyons, John. *Semantics.* Cambridge: Cambridge University Press, 1977.

MacDonnell, John. "Looting in China." *Contemporary Review* 79 (March 1901): 444–52.

Mackerras, Colin. *Western Images of China.* Hong Kong: Oxford University Press, 1989.

MacLeod, Roy, and Milton Lewis, eds. *Disease, Medicine, and Empire: Perspectives on Western Medicine and the Experience of European Expansion.* New York: Routledge, 1988.

Mao Yibo. "Zai lun xing'ai yu youyi" (Yet again on sexual love and friendship). *Xin nüxing.* 3.11 (1928): 1248–58.

Martin, W. A. P. *A Cycle of Cathay: or, China, south and north.* 1897. New York: Fleming H. Revell, 1900.

———. *Gongfa bianlan* (An overview of public law). A translation of *Introduction to the Study of International Law,* by Theodore Dwight Woolsey. Beijing 1878.

———. *Gongfa xinbian* (A new compilation of public law). A translation of *A Treatise on International Law,* by W. E. Hall. Beijing, 1903.

———. *The Siege of Peking.* New York: Fleming H. Revell Co., 1900.

———. *Wanguo gongfa* (Public law of all nations). A translation of *Elements of International Law,* by Henry Wheaton. Beijing, 1864.

Martzloff, Jean-Claude. "La compréhension chinoise des méthodes démonstratives euclidiennes au cours du XVIIe siècle et au début du XVIIIe." In *Actes du IIe colloque international de sinologie: Les rapports entre la Chine et l'Europe au temps des lumières.* Paris: Les Belles Letters, 1980.

———. "Eléments de réflexion sur les réactions chinoises à la géometrie euclidienne à la fin du XVIIe siècle: Le *Jihe lunyue* de Du Zhigeng vu principalement à partir de la préface de l'auteur et de deux notices bibliographiques rédigées par des lettres illustrés." *Historia Mathematica* 20.2 (May 1993): 160–79.

———. "La géometrie euclidienne selon Mei Wending." *Historia Scientiarum* 21 (September 1981): 27–42.

———. *A History of Chinese Mathematics.* Trans. Stephen S. Wilson. New York: Springer, 1997. Originally published as *Histoire des mathématiques chinoises* (Paris: Masson, 1987).

———. "Matteo Ricci's Mathematical Works and Their Influence." In *International Symposium on Chinese-Western Cultural Interchange in Commemoration of the 400th Anniversary* of the Arrival of Matteo Ricci S.J. in China. Taibei, Sept. 11–16, 1983. Taibei: Furen daxue chubanshe, 1983.

———. "Space and Time in Chinese Texts of Astronomy and Mathematical Astronomy in the Seventeenth and Eighteenth Centuries." *Chinese Science* 11 (1993–94): 66–92.

Marx, Karl. *Capital: A Critique of Political Economy*. Vol. 1. Trans. Ben Fowkes. New York: Vintage, 1977.

———. *Grundrisse: Foundations of the Critique of Political Economy*. Trans. Nicolaus Martin. New York, 1973.

Masini, Federico. *The Formation of Modern Chinese Lexicon and Its Evolution Toward a National Language: The Period from 1840–1898*. Berkeley: University of California, Berkeley, Project on Linguistic Analysis, 1993.

Matheson, James. *The Present Position and Prospect of Our Trade with China*. London, 1836.

McCloskey, Donald N. *The Rhetoric of Economics*. Madison: University of Wisconsin Press, 1985.

McFarland, Earl. *Catalogue of the Ordnance Museum, United States Military Academy*. West Point, NY: United States Military Academy Printing Office, 1929.

Meyer, Meinert. "Developing Transcultural Competence: Case Studies of Advanced Foreign Language Learners." In *Mediating Languages and Cultures: Towards an Intercultural Theory of Foreign Language Education*, ed. Dieter Buttjes and Michael Byram. Clevedon, England: Multilingual Matters, 1991.

———. "English in the World/The World in English." In *Power and Inequality in Language Education*, ed. James W. Tollefson. New York: Cambridge University Press, 1995.

M'Ghee, R. J. L. *How We Got to Peking*. London: Richard Bentley, 1862.

Mitchell, Timothy. *Colonising Egypt*. New York: Cambridge University Press, 1988.

Mizoguchi, Yūzō. "Zhongguo minquan sixiang de tese" (The characteristics of Chinese thoughts on civil rights), in *Zhongguo xiandaihua lunwen ji* (Essays on Chinese modernization), ed. Zhongyang yanjiuyuan jindaishi yanjiusuo. Taipei: Institute of Modern History, Academica Sinica, 1990. 343–61.

Mizutani Yoshiaki. *Kokkai no kakin* (The defect of the parliament). Tokyo: Kobun sha, 1892.

Montesquieu. *Persian Letters*. Trans. C. J. Betts. London: Penguin, 1973.

Morohashi, Tetsuji, ed. *Dai Kan-Wa jiten* (Morohashi's Chinese-Japanese dictionary). 12 vols. Tokyo: Daishukan shoten, 1955.

Morrill, Samuel. *Lanterns, Junks and Jade*. New York: Frederick A. Stokes Co., 1926.

Müller, Max. *Lectures on the Science of Language*. New York: Charles Scribner's Sons, 1884.

Mungello, David E. *Curious Land: Jesuit Accommodation and the Origins of Sinology*. Studia Leibnitiana Supplementa, no. 25. Stuttgart: Steiner, 1985.

———. *Leibniz and Confucianism: The Search for Accord*. Honolulu: University Press of Hawaii, 1977.

Murdoch, John E. "Editions of Euclid." In *Dictionary of Scientific Biography*, ed. Charles Coulston Gillispie. New York: Scribner, 1970–.

Murphy, Timothy. *Gay Science: The Ethics of Sexual Orientation Research*. New York: Columbia University Press, 1997.

Nah, Seoung. "Language and the Ultimate Reality in Sung Neo-Confucianism: The Nature and Inevitability of Ch'i." Ph. diss., Harvard University, 1993.

Naikaku Kanpōkyoku. *Hōrei Zensho* (Complete laws and ordinances). Reprint. Tokyo: Harushobo, 1974.

Naramoto Tatsuya, and Sanada Yukitaka, eds. *Yoshida Shōin.* Tokyo: Kadokawa Shoten, 1976.

Needham, Joseph. *The Grand Titration: Science and Society in East and West.* London: George Allen & Unwin, 1969.

Needham, Rodney. *Exemplars.* Berkeley: University of California Press, 1985.

Nettl, Bruno. *The Western Impact on World Music.* New York: Schirmer Books, 1985.

Ni Haishu. *Zhongguo pinyin wenzi yundongshi jianbian* (A brief history of the phonetic writing movement in China). Shanghai: Shubao chubanshe, 1948.

Nicholls, Bob. *Bluejackets and Boxers: Australian Naval Expedition to the Boxer Uprising.* Sidney: Allen & Unwin, 1986.

Nirvard, Jacqueline. "Women and the Women's Press: The Case of the Ladies' Journal (*Funü zazhi*) 1915–1931." *Republican China* 10.1b (November 1984): 37–55.

Nishi Amane. "Yōji wo motte Kokugo o Kaku Suru Ron." *Meiroku Zasshi* (Journal of the Meiji Six Society), no. 1 (March 1874).

Noguchi Takehiko. *Ōdo to kakumei no aida* (Between the ways of kingship and revolution). Tokyo: Chikuma shobo, 1986.

Norman, E. H. *Origins of the Modern Japanese State — Selected Writings of E. H. Norman.* Ed. John Dower. New York: Pantheon, 1975.

Ogden, C. K. *Basic English: International Second Language.* New York: Harcourt, Brace & World, 1968.

———. *A Short Guide to Basic English.* Cambridge: The Orthological Institute, 1937.

Ogden, C. K., and I. A. Richards. *The Meaning of Meaning.* New York: Harcourt, Brace and Company, 1936.

Ojima Sukema. *Chūgoku no kakumei shisō* (The thought of revolution in China). Tokyo: Chikuma shobo, 1967.

———. "Juka to kakumei shisō" (Confucianism and revolutionary ideas). *Shinagaku* 2.3 (November 1921): 198–210; 2.4 (December 1921): 271–80.

Okamoto Kansuke. *Wanguo shiji* (An account of world history). Huaguotang ed., reprint in China, 1990.

Okubo Toshiaki, ed. *Nishi Amane Zenshū* (Complete works of Amane Zenshū). Tokyo, 1961.

Okubo Yasuo. *Nihon Kindaihō no Chichi — Bowasonaado* (Boissonade: Father of modern Japanese law). Tokyo: Iwanami Shinsho, 1977.

The Orthological Committee. *Notes on Basic English (A short account of the system).* No. 1 (October 1940). Cambridge, MA: Author, 1940.

Osatake Takeki. *Kinsei Nihon no Kokusai Kannen no Hattatsu* (The development of the international ideal in early modern Japan). Tokyo: Kyoritsusha, 1932.

Ots, Thomas. "The Silent Body, the Expressive Leib: On the Dialectic of Mind and Life in Chinese Cathartic Healing." In *Embodiment and Experience: The Existential Ground of Culture and Self,* ed. Thomas Csordas. Cambridge: Cambridge University Press, 1991. 116–36.

Otsuki Fumihiko. *Mitsukuri Rinshō kunden* (Biography of Mitsukuri Rinshō). Tokyo: Maruzen, 1907.

Owen, Stephen. *Readings in Chinese Literary Thought.* Cambridge, Mass: Harvard University Press, 1992.

Pan Guangdan. "*Xin wenhua yu jia kexue — bo Zhang Jingsheng*" (New culture and fake science — a refutation of Zhang Jingsheng). In *Pan Guangdan wenji* (The writings of Pan Guangdan). 2 vols. Beijing: Beijing daxue chubanshe, 1993. 1: 401-6.

———. "*Zhongguo wenxian zhong tongxing lian juli*" (Examples of homosexuality in Chinese historical documents). In *Xing xinli xue.* Beijing: Sanlian shudian, 1987. 516-47.

———. *Xing xinli xue.* A translation of *The Psychology of Sex,* by Havelock Ellis. Shanghai, 1946. Beijing: Sanlian shudian, 1987.

Pang Zhenggao. "*Dongyi jiqi shiqian wenhua shilun*" (A study of the prehistory of Eastern *yi* culture). *Lishi yanjiu* 3 (1987): 54-65.

Pearce, Nick. " 'From the Summer Palace': The Creation of an Imperial Style." Paper presented at the International Convention of Asian Scholars, Leiden, 1998.

Pearson, Veronica. *Mental Health Care in China: State Policies, Professional Services and Family Responsibilities.* London: Gaskill, 1995.

Peck, James. "The Roots of Rhetoric: The Professional Ideology of America's China Watchers." *Bulletin of Concerned Asian Scholars* 2.1 (October 1969): 59-69.

Peng Hsiao-yen. *Chaoyue xieshi* (Beyond realism). Taipei: Lianjing, 1993.

———. "The New Woman: May Fourth Women's Struggle for Self Liberation." *Zhongguo wenzhe yanjiu jikan* (Journal of the Institute of Literature and Philosophy) 6 (1995): 259-338.

———. "*Wusi de 'xin xing daode': nüxing qingyu lunshu yu jiangou minzu guojia*" (The 'new sexual morality' of the May Fourth era: Female sexuality and nation-building). *Jindai zhongguo funüshi yanjiu* (Study of modern Chinese women's history) [Taipei] 3 (1995): 77-96.

Pennycook, Alastair. *The Cultural Politics of English as an International Language.* London: Longman, 1994.

———. "English in the World/The World in English." In *Power and Inequality in Language Education,* ed. James W. Tollefson. New York: Cambridge University Press, 1995. 34-59.

Perkins, John F., Alan Kelly, and John Ward. "On Gramophone Company Matrix Numbers 1898 to 1921." *The Record Collector* 23 (1976).

Peron, Rene. "The Record Industry." In *Communication and Class Struggle,* ed. Armand Mattelart and Seth Siegelaub. New York: International General, 1979. 292-97.

Peterson, Willard J. "Western Natural Philosophy Published in Late Ming China." *Proceedings of the American Philosophical Society* 117.4 (August 1973): 295-322.

Phillips, Michael. "Strategies Used by Chinese Families Coping with Schizophrenia." In *Chinese Families in the Post Mao Era,* ed. Deborah Davis and Stevan Harrell. Berkeley: University of California Press, 1993.

Phillipson, Robert. *Linguistic Imperialism.* New York: Oxford University Press, 1992.

Pietz, William. "The Problem of the Fetish." Parts 1, 2, and 3a. RES 9 (spring 1985): 5-17; 13 (spring 1987): 23-45; 16 (autumn 1988): 105-23.

Plotnitsky, Arkady. *Complementarity: Anti-Epistemology after Bohr and Derrida.* Durham, NC: Duke University Press, 1994.

Pollard, David. "Ch'i in Chinese Literary Theory." In *Chinese Approaches to Literature from Confucius to Liang Ch'i-chao*, ed. Adele Austin Rickett et al. Princeton: Princeton University Press, 1978. 43–66.

Pomian, Krzysztof. *Collectors and Curiosities: Paris and Venice 1500–1800*. Cambridge: Polity Press, 1990.

Porter, Whitworth. *The History of the Corps of Royal Engineers*. 7 vols. London: Longmans, Green, 1889.

Postone, Moishe. *Time, Labour, and Social Domination: A Reinterpretation of Marx's Critical Theory*. New York: Cambridge University Press, 1993.

Pratt, Mary Louise. *Imperial Eyes: Travel Writing and Transculturation*. New York: Routledge, 1992.

Prodromou, Luke. "English as Cultural Action." *ELT Journal* 42.2 (1988): 73–83.

———. "What Culture? Which Culture? Cross-Cultural Factors in Language Learning." *ELT Journal* 46.1 (1992): 39–50.

Psalmanazar, George. *A Historical and Geographical Description of Formosa*. 2d ed. London, 1705.

Purcell, Rosamond Wolff. *Special Cases: Natural Anomalies and Historical Monsters*. San Francisco: Chronicle Books, 1998.

Purchas, Samuel, ed. *Hakluytus Posthumus, or Purchas His Pilgrimes, Containing a History of the World in Sea Voyages and Lande Travells by Englishmen and Others*. Vol. 12. Glasgow: James MacLehose and Sons, 1906.

Qian Guangren. "Tantan woguo jiben shuchupin yu xinxing gongye" (A discussion of China's basic import-export goods and newly emergent industries). *Xinyue ji* 2 (September 1930).

Qian Xuantong. "A Reply to Yao Jiren." *Xinqingnian* (New youth) 5.5 (November 1918): 542–43.

———. "Zhongguo jinhouzhi wenzi wenti" (The problem of written Chinese characters in the future). *Xinqingnian* (New youth) 4.4 (April 1918): 350–56.

Qin Lishan. *Qin Lishan ji* (The collective works of Qin Lishan). Beijing: Zhonghua shuju, 1987.

Qin Qiming, ed. *Yinyue jia Ren Guang* (Musician Ren Guang). Hefei: Anhui wenyi chubanshe, 1988.

Qiu Yuan (Hu Qiuyuan). "Tongxing lian'ai lun" (On same-sex romantic love). A translation of "The Homogenic Attachment," by Edward Carpenter. *Xin nüxing* 4.4 (April 1929): 513–34; 4.5 (May 1929): 605–28.

Queen's Regulations and Orders for the Army. London: HMSO, 1868.

Quine, Willard V. O. "Meaning and Translation." In *On Translation*, ed. Reuben Arthur Brower. Cambridge, MA: Harvard University Press, 1959.

———. "On the Very Idea of a Third Dogma." In *Theories and Things*. Cambridge, MA: Harvard University Press, 1981.

———. "Two Dogmas of Empiricism." In *From a Logical Point of View*. 2d ed. rev. Cambridge, MA: Harvard University Press, 1961.

Reid, Gilbert. "The Ethics of Loot." *Forum* 31 (1901): 581–86.

———. "The Ethics of the Last War." *Forum* 32 (1902): 446–55.

Reischauer, Edwin O., John K. Fairbank, and Albert M. Craig. *A History of East Asian Civilization.* Boston: Houghton Mifflin, 1960–65.

Reisman, W. Michael, and Chris T. Antoniou, eds. *The Laws of War—A Comprehensive Collection of Primary Documents on International Laws Governing Armed Conflict.* New York: Vintage, 1994.

Report of the Commissioners appointed to inquire into the realisation and distribution of Army Prize; with Minutes of Evidence and Appendix. 1864. London: HMSO.

Ricalton, James. *China through the Stereoscope.* New York: Underwood & Underwood, 1901.

Ricci, Matteo. *China in the 16th Century: The Journal of Matthew Ricci 1583–1610.* Trans. Louis J. Gallagher. New York: Random House, 1953.

———. *Fonti Ricciane: Documenti Originali Concernenti Matteo Ricci e la Storia della Prime Relazioni Tra L'Europa e la Cina (1579–1615).* Edited with commentaries by Pasquale M. D'Elia. Roma: La Libreria Dello Stato. 1942–49.

———. *Opere Storiche del P. Matteo Ricci S.I.* Edited with commentaries and notes by P. Pietro Tacchi Venturi. 2 vols. Macerata: Premiato Stabilimento Tipografico, 1911, 1913.

———. *Tianzhu shi yi* (The true meaning of the Lord of Heaven, ca. 1596). In TXCH. Translated into English as Matteo Ricci, *The True Meaning of the Lord of Heaven* (T'ien-chu shih-i).

———. "*Tianzhu shi yi yin*" (Introduction to *The true meaning of the Lord of Heaven*). In TZSY. In Ricci, *Lord of Heaven.*

———. *The True Meaning of the Lord of Heaven* (T'ien-chu shih-i). Translated with introduction by Douglas Lancashire and Peter Hu Kuo-chen. A Chinese-English edition. Taipei: The Ricci Institute, 1985. Also in an edition by Edward J. Malatesta, S.J. Series 1: Jesuit Primary Sources in English Translations, no. 6. St. Louis: Institute of Jesuit Sources, 1985.

Richards, I. A. "Basic English." *Fortune,* June 1941.

———. *Basic English and Its Uses.* New York: Norton, 1943.

———. *Basic in Teaching: East and West.* London: Kegan Paul, Trench, Trubner & Co., 1935.

———. "Beginnings and Transitions: I. A. Richards Interviewed by Reuben Brower." In *I. A. Richards: Essays in His Honor,* ed. R. Brower, H. Vendler, and J. Hollander. New York: Oxford University Press, 1973. 17–41.

———. "The Chinese Renaissance." *Scrutiny* 1.2 (September 1932): 102–13.

———. "Fundamentally, I'm an Inventor." I. A. Richards interviewed by Jane Watkins. *Harvard Magazine* 76 (September 1973): 50–56.

———. "The Meaning of 'The Meaning of Meaning.'" *Qinghua xuebao* (Qinghua academic journal) 6.1 (1930): 11–6.

———. *Mencius on the Mind.* London: Kegan Paul, Trench, Trubner & Co., 1932.

———. *Nations and Peace.* New York: Simon and Schuster, 1947.

———. *Selected Letters of I. A. Richards.* Ed. John Constable. Oxford: Clarendon Press, 1990.

———. "Toward a Theory of Translating." In *Studies in Chinese Thought,* ed. Arthur F. Wright. Chicago: University of Chicago Press, 1953. 247–62.

Robinson, Deanna Campbell, Elizabeth B. Buck, Marlene Cuthbert, and the International Communication and Youth Consortium. *Music at the Margins: Popular Music and Global Cultural Diversity*. Newbury Park: Sage Publications, 1991.

Ronan, Charles E., and Bonnie B. C. Oh, eds. *East Meets West: The Jesuits in China, 1582–1773*. Chicago: Loyola University Press, 1988.

Ronan, Colin A., ed. *The Shorter Science and Civilisation in China*, by Joseph Needham. Abridged, vol. 1. Cambridge: Cambridge University Press, 1978.

Ruan Yuan, ed. *Shi san jing zhushu* (Commentaries on the thirteen classics). Vol. 2. Yangzhou, PRC: Jiangsu guangling guji keying she, 1995.

Russo, John Paul. *I. A. Richards: His Life and Work*. Baltimore: Johns Hopkins University Press, 1989.

Ryusaku Tsunoda, Wm. Theodore de Bary, and Donald Keene, eds. *Sources of Japanese Tradition*. New York: Columbia University Press, 1961.

Said, Edward W. *Culture and Imperialism*. New York: Vintage Books, 1993.

———. *Orientalism*. New York: Random House, 1979.

———. *The World, the Text, and the Critic*. Cambridge, MA: Harvard University Press, 1983.

Sambiasi, F. "Ling yan li shao yin" (Preface to "A preliminary discussion of anima"). In TXCH.

Sambiasi, F. (d. 1649), and Xu Guangqi. "Ling yan li shao" (A preliminary discussion of anima). In TXCH.

Samoyault-Verlet, Colombe. *Le Musée chinois de l'impératrice Eugénie*. Paris: Editions de la Réunion des musée nationaux, 1994.

Sang, Tze-lan D. "The Emerging Lesbian: Female Same-Sex Desire in Modern Chinese Literature and Culture." Ph.D. diss., University of California, Berkeley, 1996.

Sansom, G. B. *Japan: A Short Cultural History*. New York: Appleton-Century-Crofts, 1962.

Saussure, Ferdinand de. *Course in General Linguistics*. Trans. Roy Harris. La Salle: Open Court, 1983.

Saussy, Haun. "The Prestige of Writing: Wen, Letter, Picture, Image, Ideography." *Sino-Platonic Studies* 75 (1998).

———. *The Problem of a Chinese Aesthetic*. Stanford: Stanford University Press, 1993.

Scaglione, Aldo. *The Classical Theory of Composition*. Chapel Hill: University of North Carolina Press, 1972.

Schall, Johann Adam. *Zhuzhi qunzheng* (A host of evidence that God rules). In *Tianzhujiao dongchuan wenxian xubian*, ed. Wu Xiangxiang. Taipei: Taiwan xuesheng shuju, 1966, 2: 497–615.

Schiffrin, Harold Z. *Sun Yat-sen and the Origins of the Chinese Revolution*. Berkeley: University of California Press, 1968.

Schlegel, August Wilhelm von. *Observations sur la langue et la littérature provençales*. Paris, 1818.

Schlegel, Friedrich von. *Über die Sprache und Weisheit der Indier*. Heidelberg: Mohr & Zimmer, 1808.

Schleicher, August. *Die Sprachen Europas in systematischer Uebersicht*. Bonn: H. B. König, 1850.

Schwartz, Benjamin. "The Limits of 'Tradition Versus Modernity' as Categories of Explanation: The Case of Chinese Intellectuals." *Daedalus* 101.2 (spring 1972): 71–88.

————. *In Search of Wealth and Power: Yen Fu and the West.* Cambridge, MA: Harvard University Press, 1964.

————. *The World of Thought in Ancient China.* Cambridge, MA: Harvard University Press, 1985.

————, ed., *Reflections on the May Fourth Movement: A Symposium.* Cambridge, MA: Harvard University Press, 1972.

Seiyōbunmei no Yunyū Kenkyūkai, ed. *Yōgaku Jishi* (The formation of Western learning), by Sawa Omi. Tokyo: Bunka Shobo Hakabunsha, 1993.

Shan Huaihai. "Qigong Piancha Yu Kuan Wenhua Jingshen Yixue" (Qigong deviation and cross-cultural mental health study). *Jiankang Bao* (Health news), 16 May 1990.

Shan Zai. "Funü tongxing zhi aiqing" (Same-sex erotic love between women). *Funü shibao* (Women's times) [Shanghai] 1.7 (June 1911): 36–38.

Shanghai Hong List. Shanghai: Investigation Bureau of Commerce & Industry, 1940.

Shell, Marc. *Money, Language, and Thought: Literary and Philosophic Economies from the Medieval to the Modern Era.* Baltimore: Johns Hopkins University Press, 1993.

Shen Xiaolong. *Zhongguo yuyande jiege yu renwen jingsheng* (The structure of the Chinese language and its humanist spirit). Beijing: Guangmingribao chubanshe, 1988.

Shen Yucun. *Jingshenbingxue* (Psychiatry). Beijing: Renmin Weisheng Chubanshe (People's Health Press), 1980.

Shen Zemin. "Tongxing'ai yu jiao yu" (Same-sex love and education). A translation of "Affection in Education," by Edward Carpenter. *Jiaoyu zazhi* (Chinese educational review) [Shanghai] 15.8 (1923): 22115–24.

Shigeno Yasutsugu. *Bankoku Kōhō* (International law). Kagoshima. 1869.

Shisan jing zhu shu (Thirteen classics with annotations and subannotations). Ed. Ruan Yuan (1764–1849). 2 vols. Beijing: Zhonghua shuju, 1980.

"Shouzai paituo" (Shouzai goes dating). *Xinyue ji* 1 (September 1929).

Shui Jing. *Liuxing gequ cangsang ji* (A record of the vicissitudes of popular song). Taipei: Dadi chubanshe, 1985.

Shuli shanren. "Zun geming" (Respecting geming). *Qingyi bao* 94 (October 1901): 5973–75.

Sima Qian. *Shiji* (Historical records). Beijing: Zhonghua shuju, 1959. 3122–23.

Simpson, Bertram L. *Indiscreet Letters from Peking.* 1907. Reprinted, New York: Arno Press and New York Times, 1970.

Siraisi, Nancy. *Avicenna in Renaissance Italy: The Canon and Medical Teaching in Italian Universities after 1500.* Princeton: Princeton University Press, 1987.

Sirr, Henry-Charles. *China and the Chinese, Vol. I: Their Religion, Character, Customs, and Manufactures: The Evils Arising from the Opium Trade: With a Glance at Our Religious, Moral, Political, and Commercial Intercourse with the Country.* London, 1849; reprinted by Southern Materials Center, Taiwan, ROC.

Siu, Michael. "Attitudes toward Women's Sexuality in Shanghai in the 1920s and 1930s: A Selective Analysis of Sex Manuals and *Ladies' Journal.*" Unpublished essay, 1991.

Sivin, Nathan. "Why the Scientific Revolution Did Not Take Place in China—Or Didn't It?" *Chinese Science* 5 (June 1982): 45–66.

Skidmore, Eliza. *China the Long-Lived Empire.* New York: Century, 1900.

Smith, Arthur H. *China in Convulsion.* 2 vols. New York: Fleming H. Revell, 1901.

Smith, Judson. "The Missionaries and Their Critics." *North American Review* 172 (1901): 724–33.

Sommer, Mathew. "The Penetrated Male in Late Imperial China: Judicial Constructions and Social Stigma." *Modern China* 23.2 (1997): 140–80.

———. *Sex, Law and Society in Late Imperial China.* Ph.D. diss., University of California, Los Angeles, 1994.

Soyinka, Wole. *Aké.* London: Arrow, 1983.

Spence, Jonathan. *The Memory Palace of Matteo Ricci.* New York: Viking Penguin, 1984.

———. *The Search for Modern China.* New York: Norton, 1990.

Spivak, Gayatri Chakravorty. *In Other Worlds.* New York: Methuen, 1987.

Stafford, Barbara. *Body Criticism: Imaging the Unseen in Enlightenment Art and Medicine.* Cambridge, MA: MIT Press, 1994.

Standaert, Nicolas. "Science, Philosophy and Religion in the 17th-Century Encounter between China and the West." *Synthesis Philosophica* 7 (January 1989): 251–68.

Stanton, Domna, ed. *Discourses of Sexuality.* Ann Arbor: University of Michigan Press, 1992.

Statutes of the United Kingdom of Great Britain and Ireland. London: HMS., 1814, 1821, 1832.

Steel, Richard. *Through Peking's Sewer Gate.* New York: Vintage, 1985.

Stendahl, Krister, ed. *Immortality and Resurrection: Four Essays by Oscar Cullmann, Harry A. Wolfson, Werner Jaeger, and Henry J. Cadbury.* New York: Macmillan, 1965.

Stern, John Peter. *The Japanese Interpretation of the "Law of Nations," 1854–1874.* Princeton: Princeton University Press, 1979.

Stewart, Norman. *My Service Days.* London: John Ouseley, 1908.

Stewart, Susan. *Crimes of Writing: Problems in the Containment of Representation.* Oxford: Oxford University Press, 1991.

Stoler, Ann. *Race and the Education of Desire: Foucault's History of Sexuality and the Colonial Order of Things.* Durham, NC: Duke University Press, 1995.

Stopes, Marie Carmichael. *Married Love.* 1918. Reprinted, New York: G. P. Putnam's Sons, 1931.

Strand, David. *Rickshaw Beijing: City People and Politics in the 1920's.* Berkeley: University of California Press, 1989.

Sun Yat-sen. *Kidnapped in London.* London: Bristol, 1897.

———. "Zhongguo geming shi" (A history of Chinese revolution). In *Zhonghua minguo kaiguo wushi nian wenxian,* ed. Zhonghua minguo kaiguo wushi nian wenxian bianji weiyuanhui. Taipei: Zhongyang wenwu gongying she, 1963. Part 1, vol. 9, 191–202.

Sweeting, Anthony. *A Phoenix Transformed: The Reconstruction of Education in Post-war Hong Kong.* Hong Kong: Oxford University Press, 1993.

Swiderski, Richard M. *The False Formosan: George Psalmanazar and the Eighteenth-Century Experiment of Identity.* San Francisco: Mellen Research University, 1991.

Swift, Jonathan. *A Modest Proposal for preventing the children of poor people from being a burthen to their parents, or the country, and for making them beneficial to the public.* Dublin: Harding, 1729.

Swinhoe, Robert. *Narrative of the North China Campaign of 1860.* London: Smith, Elder and Co., 1861.

Takahashi, Sakuyé. *Cases on International Law During the Chino-Japanese War.* Cambridge: Cambridge University Press, 1899.

Takeuchi Yoshimi, and Nomura Kōichi, eds. *Chūgoku—kakumei to dentō* (China: revolution and tradition). Tokyo: Chikuma shobo, 1967.

Tang, Xiaobing. *Global Space and the Nationalist Discourse of Modernity: The Historical Thinking of Liang Qichao.* Stanford: Stanford University Press, 1996.

Tao Wu. "Mo jing dang" (The mirror-rubbing gang). In *Shanghai funü nie jingtai* (A mirror of Shanghai women's sin), ed. Zhonghua tushu jicheng bianjisuo (The editorial staff of Zhonghua tushu jicheng gonsi). Shanghai: Zhonghua tushu jicheng gongsi, 1918. 4:65–70.

Tao Xiang, ed. *Sheyuan mocui* (The gems of painting and calligraphy). Beijing, 1929.

Taussig, Michael. *Alterity and Mimesis: A Particular History of the Senses.* New York: Routledge, 1993.

Taylor, Rodney L. *The Religious Dimension of Confucianism.* Albany: State University of New York Press, 1990.

Tedlock, Dennis, and Bruce Mannheim, eds. *The Dialogic Emergence of Culture.* Urbana: University of Illinois Press, 1995.

Temkin, Owsei. *Galenism: Rise and Decline of a Medical Philosophy.* Ithaca: Cornell University Press, 1973.

Teng, Ssu-yü, John K. Fairbank, E-tu Zen Sun, and Chaoying Fang. *China's Response to the West: A Documentary Survey, 1839–1923.* Cambridge, MA: Harvard University Press, 1954.

Terrenz, Johann. *Taixi renshen shuogai* (Theories of the human body in the Far West). Chinois 5130. Paris: Bibliotheque Nationale, 1643.

Thiriez, Regine. "The Rape of the Summer Palace." Paper presented at the International Convention of Asian Scholars, Leiden, 1998.

Thomas, Nick. "Licensed Curiosity: Cook's Pacific Voyages." In *The Cultures of Collecting*, ed. R. Cardinal and J. Elsner. London: Reaktion Books, 1994.

Thomson, John. *China and Its People in Early Photographs: An Unabridged Reprint of the Classic 1873–4 Work.* New York: Dover, 1982.

Tianxue chu han (Heavenly studies—a first collection). Ed. Li Zhizao (1565–1630) et al. Taipei: Taiwan xuesheng shuju, 1965.

Tiffany, Osmond, Jr., *The Canton Chinese, or the American's Sojourn in the Celestial Empire.* Boston: James Monroe & Co., 1849.

Ting, Joseph S. P. *Gateways to China: Trading Ports of the 18th and 19th Centuries.* Hong Kong: Hong Kong Museum of Art, Urban Council, 1987.

———. *Hong Kong: The Changing Scene. A Record in Art.* Hong Kong: Urban Council, 1980.

———, ed. *Late Qing China Trade Paintings.* Hong Kong Museum of Art, presented by the Urban Council, Hong Kong. Catalogue to exhibition of 7 September 1982–22 August 1982.

Toby, Ronald. *State and Diplomacy in Early Modern Japan: Asia in the Development of the Tokugawa Bakufu.* Stanford: Stanford University Press, 1991.

Tokoro Isao. *Miyoshi Kiyoyuki.* Tokyo: Kōbunkan, 1970.

Tomlinson, John. *Cultural Imperialism.* Baltimore: Johns Hopkins University Press, 1991.

Tong, Q. S. "Myths about the Chinese Language." *Canadian Review of Comparative Literature* 20.1–2 (1993): 29–47.

Treaties, Conventions, etc., Between China and Foreign States. 2d ed. 2 vols. Shanghai: Statistical Department of the Inspectorate General of Customs, 1917.

Tsiang, T. F. "Bismarck and the Introduction of International Law into China." *The Chinese Social and Political Science Review* 15 (April 1931).

Tsukatani Akihiro. *Nihon Shisō Taikei* (Collection of Japanese Thought). Tokyo: Iwanami Shoten, 1973.

Tsutsumi Koshiji. *Bankoku Kōhō Yakugi* (International law in translation). Tokyo, 1868.

Tu, Wei-ming. *Centrality and Commonality: An Essay on Confucian Religiousness.* Albany: State University of New York Press, 1989.

———. "A Confucian Perspective on Embodiment." In *The Body in Medical Thought and Practice*, ed. Drew Leder. Dordrecht: Kluwer Academic Publishers, 1992. 87–100.

———, ed. *The Living Tree: The Changing Meaning of Being Chinese Today.* Stanford: Stanford University Press, 1994.

Tulloch, A. B. *Recollections of Forty Years' Service.* Edinburgh: Blackwood, 1903.

Twain, Mark. "To My Missionary Critics." *North American Review* 172 (1901): 520–34.

———. "To the Person Sitting in Darkness." *North American Review* 172 (1901): 161–76.

Twitchett, Denis, and John K. Fairbank, eds. *The Cambridge History of China.* Cambridge: Cambridge University Press, 1978–.

Ueno, Chizuko. "Kaisetsu" (Commentary). In *Fuzoku, sei* (Customs and sexuality), ed. Shinzo Ogi, Isao Kumakura, and Chizuko Ueno. In *Nihon kindai shiso taikei* (Collected documents on modern Japanese thought). Tokyo: Iwanami, 1990. 23: 505–50.

Unschuld, Paul U. *Medicine in China: A History of Ideas.* Berkeley: University of California Press, 1985.

U.S. Government, Office of Finance. *Ledgers of Emergency Fund Account, 1898–1909.*

Vagnoni, Alphonso. *Kongji gezhi* (Investigation into the Material Compositions of the [sublunary] space). In *Tianzhujiao dongchuan wenxian sanbian*, ed. Wu Xiangxiang. Taipei: Taiwan xuesheng shuju, 1972. 2:841–1030.

Valdes, Joyce Merrill, ed. *Culture Bound: Bridging the Cultural Gap in Language Teaching.* New York: Cambridge University Press, 1986.

Vinograd, Richard. *Boundaries of the Self: Chinese Portraits 1600–1900.* New York: Cambridge University Press, 1992.

Viswanathan, Gauri. *Masks of Conquest: Literary Study and British Rule in India.* New York: Columbia University Press, 1989.

Vitiello, Giovanni. "Exemplary Sodomites: Male Homosexuality in Late Ming Fiction." Ph.D. diss., University of California, Berkeley, 1994.

Volpp, Sophie. "The Male Queen: Boy Actors and Literati Libertines." Ph.D. diss., Harvard University, 1995.

Wai, B. " 'Cultural Conflict' or 'Cultural Invasion.' " *Cheng Ming* April 1996, 86–87.

Waley, Arthur. *The Opium War Through Chinese Eyes.* London: Allen & Unwin, 1958.

Waley-Cohen, Joanna. "China and Western Technology in the Late Eighteenth Century." *American Historical Review* 98.5 (December 1993): 1525–44.

Walker, Brett. "Reappraising the Sakoku Paradigm: The Ezo Trade and the Extension of Tokugawa Political Space into Hokkaido." *The Journal of Asian History* 30.2 (1996).

Walrond, Theodore, ed. *Letters and Journals of James, Eighth Earl of Elgin*. London: John Murray, 1872.

Wang Hui. "The Fate of 'Mr. Science' in China." In *Formations of Colonial Modernity in East Asia*, ed. Tani E. Barlow. Durham, NC: Duke University Press, 1997. 21–81.

Wang Jiahua. *Rujia sixiang yu Riben wenhua* (Confucian thought and Japanese culture). Hangzhou: Zhejiang renmin chubanshe, 1990.

Wang Tao. *Chongding Faguo zhilue* (A revised general history of France). Shanghai: Songyinlu edition, 1890.

———. *Manyou sui lu, Fusang youji* (Record of my wanderings, and Travels in Japan). Changsha: Hunan renmin chubanshe, 1982.

Wang Xianqian. *Hou Hanshu jijie* (The collective annotations of the history of the latter Han Dynasty). Beijing: Zhonghua shuju, 1984.

War Office. *Manual of Military Law*. London: HMSO, 1884, 1887, 1893, 1899, 1907, 1914.

Weber, Hans-Reudi. "Biblical Understanding: A Mediating Body for the Christ." *Religion and Society* 19.4 (1972): 5–15.

Weber, Max. *The Religion of China: Confucianism and Taoism*. Trans. Hans H. Gerth. Glencoe, IL: Free Press, 1951.

Weeks, Jeffrey. "Values in an Age of Uncertainty." In *Discourses of Sexuality*, ed. Domna C. Stanton. Ann Arbor: University of Michigan Press, 1992. 389–411.

Wei Sheng, trans. "Tongxing'ai zai nüzi jiaoyu shang de xin yiyi" (The new meaning of same-sex love in women's education), by Furuya Toyoko. *Funü zazhi* 11.6 (1925): 1064–69.

Wei xing shiguan zhaizhu. *Zhongguo tongxinglian mishi* (The secret history of homosexuality in China). Hong Kong: Yuzhou chubanshe, 1964.

Weinreich, Uriel. *Languages in Contact: Findings and Problems*. The Hague: Mouton, 1968.

Welch, Walter L., and Leah Brodbeck Stenzel Burt. *From Tinfoil to Stereo: The Acoustic Years of the Recording Industry, 1877–1929*. Gainesville: University Press of Florida, 1994.

West, Michael, et al. "A Critical Examination of Basic English." *Bulletin* no. 2. Toronto: University of Toronto Press, 1934.

Westman, Robert S. "The Copernicans and the Churches." In *God and Nature*, ed. D. C. Lindberg and R. Numbers. Berkeley: University of California Press, 1986.

Wheaton, Henry. *Elements of International Law: With a Sketch of the History of the Science*. Philadelphia, 1836.

———. *Elements of International Law*. 1863. Boston: Little, Brown, 1866.

———. *Elements of International Law*. Oxford: Clarendon Press, 1936.

Whitney, William Dwight. *Language and the Study of Language*. New York: Charles Scribner & Company, 1868.

Whorf, Benjamin Lee. *Language, Thought, and Reality: Selected Writings of Benjamin Lee Whorf*. Ed. John B. Carroll. Cambridge, MA: MIT Press, 1956.

Williams, Frederick W. *Anson Burlingame and the First Chinese Mission to Foreign Powers*. New York, 1912.

Williams, Raymond. *Keywords*. New York: Oxford University Press, 1985.

Wilson, James H. *China*. New York: D. Appleton and Co., 1901.

Witke, Roxane Heather. "Transformation of Attitudes Towards Women During the May Fourth Era of Modern China." Ph.D. diss., University of California, Berkeley, 1970.

Wolseley, Garnet J. *Narrative of the War with China in 1860.* 1861. Reprinted, Wilmington, DE: Scholarly Resources Inc., 1972.

———. *The Story of a Soldier's Life.* 2 vols. New York: Charles Scribner's Sons, 1904.

Wong, J. Y. *Anglo-Chinese Relations 1839–1860: A Calendar of Chinese Documents in the British Foreign Office Records.* Oxford: Oxford University Press, 1984.

Wong, K. Chimin, and Lien-Teh Wu. *History of Chinese Medicine: Being a Chronicle of Medical Happenings in China from Ancient Times to the Present Period.* 2d ed. Shanghai: National Quarantine Service, 1936. Reprinted, Taipei, 1977.

Wong Kee-chee. "Shanghai Baidai gongsi de yange" (Pathé: The evolution of a record company). In *Mandarin Films and Popular Songs, 40's–60's: Program of the 17th Hong Kong International Film Festival,* ed. Law Kar. Hong Kong: Urban Council, 1993. 91.

Wu Guoguang. "Geming he gaige" (Revolution and reform). *Minzhu Zhongguo* 4 (October 1990): 57–68.

Wu Hung. "Emperor's Masquerade—'Costume Portraits' of Yongzheng and Qianlong." *Orientations,* 26, no. 7 (July–August 1995).

Wu, Kuang-ming. "Counterfactuals, Universals, and Chinese Thinking—A Review of *The Linguistic Shaping of Thought: A Study in the Impact of Language on Thinking in China and the West.*" *Philosophy East and West* 37.1 (January 1987): 84–94.

Wu Xiangxiang, ed. *Tianzhujiao dongchuan wenxian* (Collection of documents related to the spread of Catholicism to the East). Taipei: Taiwan xuesheng shuju, 1965. *Xubian* (second collection), 1966. *Sanbian* (third collection), 1972.

Xiaomingxiong. *Zhongguo tongxing'ai shilu* (The history of homosexuality in China). Hong Kong: Fenhong sanjiao chubanshe, 1984.

Xie Se. "Nü xuesheng de tongxing'ai." A translation of "The School-Friendships of Girls," by Havelock Ellis. *Xin wenhua* 6 (October 1927): 57–74.

Xie Weilou. *Wanguo tongjian.* In *Xiguo fuqiang congshu xuancui* (Selected books on the Western countries of wealth and power), ed. Zhang Yinhuan. Taipei: Guangwen shudian, 1972.

Xu Guangqi. *Xu Guangqi ji* (Collected writings of Xu Guangqi). Ed. Wang Zhongmin. 2 vols. Beijing: Zhonghua shuju, 1963.

Xu Guangqi et al. *Tianzhujiao dong chuan wenxian, xu bian* (Documents on the Eastern transmission of Catholicism, second collection). Reprint of Vatican Library edition. Taipei: Taiwan xuesheng shuju, 1966.

Xu Ke. *Qing bai lei chao* (Classified notes of Qing dynasty unofficial historical material). 48 vols. Shanghai: Shangwu yinshuguan, 1917.

Xu Shen. *Shuowen jiezi* (Explaining the [etymology] of terms and characters). Beijing: Zhonghua shuju, 1963.

Xu Xu. *Xu Xu quanji* (Complete works of Xu Xu). Taipei: Zhengzhong, 1967.

Xu Zongze. *Ming qing jian yesu huishi yizhu tiyao* (Summary of the publications by the Jesuits during the Ming and Qing). Taipei: Zhonghua shuju, 1957.

Yan Heqin. "The Necessity of Retaining the Diagnostic Concept of Neurasthenia." *Culture, Medicine, Psychiatry.* 13 (1989): 139–45.

Yan Shi. "Nannü de geli yu tongxing'ai" (The segregation between the sexes and same-sex love). *Funü zazhi* 9.5 (1923): 14–15.

Yanabu Akina. *Honyaku no Shisō—Shizen to Nature* (Translation thought: "Shizen" and nature). Tokyo: Chikuma Gakuei Bunko, 1995.

———. *Honyakugo Seiritsu Jijo* (The formation of translated terms). Tokyo: Iwanami Shinsho, 1995.

Yang Kun. Xu (Preface) to *Tanien de shijie: Zhongguo nan tongxinglian qunluo toushi*, by Li Yinhe and Wang Xiaobo. Hong Kong: Tiandi tushu youxian gongsi, 1991.

Yang Lien-sheng. "Zhuihuai Yeshi Gongchao" (Remembering my teacher Ye Gong-chao). In *Ye Gongchao qiren qiwen qishi* (Ye Gongchao: his personality, his writing, and his life), ed. Qin Xianci. Taipei: Zhuanji wenxue chubanshe, 1983. 234–44.

Yasuoka Akio. *Nihon Kindaishi* (Modern Japanese history). Tokyo: Geirin Shobo, 1996.

Ye Gongchao (George Yeh). "Review of *Basic in Teaching: East and West*." *Qinghua xuebao* (Qinghua academic journal) 10.4 (1935): 957–62.

Yi Bi. "Gao chunü: tongxing'ai" (A warning for virgins about homosexuality). In *Xing dian* (A dictionary of sex). Shanghai: Qizhi shuju, 1930. 66.

Young, John D. *East-West Synthesis: Matteo Ricci and Confucianism*. Hong Kong: University of Hong Kong, 1980.

Young, Robert. *Colonial Desire*. London: Routledge, 1995.

Yuanyang zhenren. *Huangdi neijing* (The Yellow Emperor's inner canon [of medicine]). N.p.: xinan shifan daxue chubanshe, n.d.

Yule, Henry, and A. C. Burnell. *Hobson-Jobson*. London: John Murray, 1903.

Zhang Binglin. "Lun xuehui you da yi yu huangren ji yi baohu" (A treatise on the urgent need to protect the learned societies that benefit the yellow people). *Shiwu bao* 19 (March 1897): 3–6.

Zhang Henshui. *Tixiao yinyuan* (Fate in tears and laughter). Taiyuan: Beiyue wenyi chu-banshe, 1993.

Zhang Jingsheng. *Aiqing dingze* (The rules of love). Shanghai: Meide shudian, 1928.

———. "Disanzhong shui yu luanzhu ji shengji he youzhong de guanxi" (The relation-ships between the third kind of water, the egg, the vital moment, and eugenics). *Xin wenhua* 1 (1927): 104–8.

———. *Sex Histories: China's First Modern Treatise on Sex Education*. Trans. Howard Levy. Yokohama: Levy, 1967.

———. "Xing mei" (Sexual beauty). *Xin wenhua* 6 (1927): 45–56.

———. *Xing shi* (Sex histories). Shanghai: Meide shudian, 1926.

Zhang Minyun. *Xing kexue* (Sexual science). Shanghai: Shanghai wenyi chubanshe, 1988. Originally published as *Weiwulun xingkexue* (The sexual science of materialism). (Shanghai: Shidai shuju, 1950).

Zhang Qiong. "Translation as Cultural Reform: Jesuit Scholastic Psychology in the Transformation of the Confucian Discourse on Human Nature." In *The Jesuits: Cul-ture, Learning and the Arts, 1540–1773*, ed. G. A. Bailey et al. Toronto: University of Toronto Press, 1999.

Zhang Xichen. "Xin nüxing yu xing de yanjiu" (*New Woman* and the study of sex). *Xin nüxing* 2.3 (1927): 237–41.

———, ed. *Xin xingdaode taolun ji* (Discussions on new sexual morality). Shanghai: Liangxi tushuguan, 1925.

Zhonghua minguo kaiguo wushi nian wenxian bianji weiyuanhui, ed. *Zhonghua minguo kaiguo wushi nian wenxian* (The documents on the history of the Republic of China, 1911–1961). Taipei: Zhongyang wenwu gongying she, 1963.

Zhou Jianren. "Xing jiaoyu yundong de weiji" (Crisis in the movement of sex education). *Xin nüxing* 2.2 (1927): 135–39.

Zhou Yizhao. "Ping Zhang Jingsheng boshi *Meide xingyu*" (A review of Dr. Zhang Jingsheng's *The Sex Drive of Beauty*). *Xin nüxing* 2.5 (1927): 543–52.

Zhu Xi. *Da xue zhang ju* (The great learning, separated into chapters and sentences). In *Sishu zhangju jizhu* (Four books, separated into chapters and sentences, with collected annotations). Beijing: Zhonghua shuju, 1983. Translated in Gardner, *Chu Hsi and the Ta-Hsueh*.

———. "Gui shen" (Ghosts and spirits). In *Zhuzi yu lei* (Conversations with master Zhu, arranged topically). Beijing: Zhonghua shuju, 1986.

———. *Sishu zhangju jizhu* (The four books with collected annotations). Beijing: Zhonghua shuju, 1983.

———. *Zhuzi yu lei* (Assorted sayings of master Zhu). Beijing: Zhonghua shuju, 1986.

Zou Rong. *Zou Rong wenji* (The collected works of Zou Rong). Ed. Zhou Yonglin. Chongqing: Renmin chubanshe, 1983.

Zürcher, Erik. "The Jesuit Mission in Fujian in Late Ming Times: Levels of Response." In *Development and Decline of Fukien Province in the Seventeenth and Eighteenth Centuries*, ed. E. B. Vermeer. New York: E. J. Brill, 1990.

Zürcher, Erik, et al. *Bibliography of the Jesuit Mission in China (ca. 1580–ca. 1680)*. Leiden: Centre of Non-Western Studies, Leiden University, 1991.

INDEX

Abolitionist movement, 392

Acquaviva, Claudio, 75

Air. *See* Qi

Aleni, Giulio, 98, 99, 105n

Alibert, Jean-Louis, and medical illustration, 250, 259

Allgood, George, 197

American Board of Commissioners for Foreign Missions, 207; and prime directive, 255

American Council for the Teaching of Foreign Languages, 375

American culture, electronic media and education in, 376

Amputation: Chinese proscription of, 261; in Lam Qua's paintings, 259–264

Anatomy, early Jesuit translations of, 98–100

Anima, 61

Anthropology, 1, 15, 386, 390, 392

Anthropomorphization of China, 46. *See also* Sick Man of Asia

Appadurai, Arjun, 218, 219, 221; on Bourdieu, 390

Arai Hakuseki, 167

Area studies: and "broad-sampling method" in transnational studies, 5; and East Asia, 4, 5, 129. *See also* Sinology

Arendt, Hannah, 356, 369

Ariga Nagao, 177; and creation of perception of legality for Japan's military victories, 184, 185

Aristophenes, 110

Aristotle, 50; and the four elements, 93–97; *Meteorologica*, 93, 94; translations of Aristotelian philosophy, 60, 75, 84, 87, 88, 98

Arrow War, 142

Art market, growth of and knowledge about Chinese, 193, 200–203

Authenticity, 16, 18; in Chinese and Western commercial art, 244; and looted art objects, 198–202; and state legislation of *qigong*, 316, 317; and transmission of the Confucian Way, 83

Authorship, 16; and coauthorship in circulation of meaning, 21, 36

Autopsy: Chinese proscription of, 261; and Peter Parker's patient, 265, 266

Bhabha, Homi, 390

Barbarian, and Tokugawa regime, 167,

linguists and, 108–120; perceived absence of grammar in, 108, 111–114, 118; question of a national language for, 338, 340, 341; and writing system, 338–340, 341

Chinnery, George, 243, 244

Chosen Incident, 177

Christianity: doctrinal disputes within, 57, 58; and English-language education by missionaries, 378, 387; Matteo Ricci's presentation of, 81; translations of theological terms, 60, 61; and W. A. P. Martin, 137, 141, 156. *See also* Jesuits; Missionaries; Parker, Peter; Ricci, Matteo

Chukwudi, Emmanuel, 20, 21

Churchill, Winston: on Basic English, 346, 354n

Civil rights: Liang Qichao on, 355

Clavius, 53, 54

Clifford, James, 38n

Cohen, Paul, 65n

Coleridge, Samuel, 331, 353n

Colonialism: and colonial economics of record-companies, 225, 227, 231; and colonial historiography, 128–131, 134; discourse of, 347; and encounter of languages and cultures, 19; and gramophone as target of anti-colonial resistance, 220, 227–230; historical processes of, 3, 19, 387–389; and new urban media culture, 228; and process of global circulation, 3, 128; and Romantic tradition in Western literature, 385, 386; and spread of English, 376, 378, 379

Comaroff, Jean, and John Comaroff, 387, 389, 391

Commensurability: cultural, 152, 153, 156; and I. A. Richards, 333; and languages, 13; in translation theory, 13, 47, 64, 67n; under colonialism, 34, 35. *See also* Gernet, Jacques; Incommensurability

Commercial art: Chinese mastery of Western styles in, 244, 252, 253, 258

Commissioner Lin. *See* Lin Zexu, Imperial Commissioner

Confucianism: and Catholicism, 74, 80, 82, 83; Jesuit borrowing of terms from, 61; and qi, 77–80, 84, 85; and translated legal terms, 153. *See also* Neo-Confucianism

Connoisseurship, of Chinese objects, 200–203

Conquer Korea Debates, 170

Copula, 46, 49–51, 54, 66n, 68n, 70n; and claims of conceptual incommensurability, 54

Cook, Captain James, 21; expeditions, 198

Crucifixion of Jesus: Jesuit failure to mention in translation, 60, 71n, 72n. *See also* Jesuits: translation strategies of

Culture: as analytical concept, 390; and cultural imperialism, 377; and cultural relativism, 6, 47, 58; and electronic media, 376; and global influences on cultural identity, 388, 389; heterogeneity of, 392; in language curricula, 375; "national" model of, 389; and power inequality in cross-cultural relations, 386, 387; teaching and learning of in the language-teaching profession, 375–397

Culture Bound, 376

Cultural translation. *See* Translation

Cumming, Dr. William Henry, 265

Curiosities: global discourse on, 198, 199; historical significance of, 198

Dana, Richard, 167

Darwin, Charles: and Darwinian understanding of race, 242, 253, 271; and the discourse of *geming* ("revolution"), 366, 369

Davidson, Donald, 46, 52, 54, 68n

de Certeau, Michel, 18, 19, 21

de la Charme, Alexandre, 97

de Man, Paul, 340

Defoe, Daniel, 17

Derrida, Jacques: and Baudrillard, 40n; and critique of Benveniste, 46, 51, 54;

Derrida, Jacques (*continued*)
    and critique of the myth of transcen-
    dental signified, 19; and Western
    metaphysics, 13, 14
Deus, 61. *See also* God
D'Hérrison, Count, 194, 206, 209n
*Diagnostic and Statistical Manual of Mental
    Disorders*, 9, 305; as a site of translingual
    practice, 312. *See also Chinese Classifica-
    tion of Mental Disorders*; Psychiatry
Dickinson, Lowe, 332
Difference: and deconstruction, 3; his-
    torical understanding of, 19; and the
    Other, 64; and spread of English, 394;
    and translation, 13, 58
Dikötter, Frank, 297, 298, 303n
Ding Weiliang. *See* Martin, W. A. P.
Diseases of China, 271
Doctrine of the Mean, 78, 87, 89
Domesticity: and music, 217, 218, 232n,
    233n
Dower, John, 184
"Dr. Sex." *See* Zhang Jingsheng
Duara, Prasenjit, 356

East-West encounter, 4, 5, 7, 75, 129, 340.
    See also China/West divide; Identity:
    Chinese
Edison, Thomas Alva, 215
Element: Western concept of, rendered in
    Chinese, 94–96
Elements of International Law, 139, 155, 167,
    187n; in Chinese, 136, 139, 142; Chinese
    reception of, 143–145, 148; editions of,
    127, 128, 157, 168, 169, 204; in Japanese,
    136, 169; comparison of terms used in
    Chinese and Japanese translations, 173
Ellis, Havelock, 9, 276, 280–283; on
    female homosexuality, 286; translations
    into Chinese, 286, 289–297
Empson, William, 350n
English: hegemony of and resistance to,
    380–38; as a medium of business trans-
    actions, 379; prestige of in Hong Kong,
    379; promulgation of English as a world

language, 378, 379, 381. *See also* Basic
    English
English Language Teaching (ELT), 10, 11,
    376; and border experiences and iden-
    tities, 391–392; cultural imperialism
    in, 376–385; to educate middlemen
    for the transactions of the British in
    China, 378, 379; English-medium and
    Chinese-medium schools in Hong
    Kong, 379, 380; and "local" approach
    to integration of language and culture,
    383, 384; and Moroccan secondary
    school students, 384
Equivalence: between Chinese and En-
    glish, 148, 152, 153; conceptual, 41n;
    and gender, 36; and "homosexuality"
    as a category, 300n; hypothetical, 37,
    137, 187n; linguistic, 5, 75; and Marx's
    theorizing of the universal equivalent,
    6; paradox of, 37; in psychiatry, 305;
    and reciprocity in translation, 34, 35.
    See also Commensurability; Incommen-
    surability; Translation
Esperanto, 10, 335, 339
Ethnography, 16, 389, 392
Eucharist, 71n
Euclid, 47, 49; and translation of terms in
    Euclidean geometry, 60, 67n, 71n
Eugénie, Empress, 194
Evolution, and theory of human emotions,
    288. *See also* Darwin, Charles
Existence, problems in translation to
    Chinese, 54–57, 70n
Extraterritoriality, 166, 176

Fairbank, John King, 47
Family: as site of resistance to medical
    missionary practice, 266, 267, 269, 270;
    as target for marketing of gramophone,
    217, 218. *See also* Domesticity
Fang Hao, 63, 72n
Female sexual beauty, 289, 290. *See also*
    Zhang Jingsheng
Feminine pronoun. *See* Third-person
    pronoun

Feng Ziyou, 363, 364, 366

Fetish: and Kant, 20–22; problem of, 20

Feyerabend, Paul, 52, 53, 69n

Fine Arts Club of Burlington House in London, 203

Fontenay, Father, 17

Forgery: modern notion of, 15, 18. See also Authenticity

Formosa: fictitious alphabet, 16; fictitious currency, 16. See also Psalmanazar, George

Foucault, Michel: and "dispositifs" of power, 181; and "existing discourses," 188n; and modern obsession with disfigurement, 240, 303n; and post-colonial studies, 4

Franke, Wolfgang, 356

French Revolution, 119; and geming ("revolution"), 361, 362, 363, 365, 372n

Freud, Sigmund, 9, 276; and Chinese practitioners, 310

Fryer, John, 161n

Fung Sun, 127

Furuya Toyoko, as translated by Wei Sheng, 288–289, 293

Gaisberg, F. W., 220, 221, 233n

Galen, 99

Galileo, 59, 71n

Gay gene, 303n

Geming. See Revolution

Gender: modernity as a homogenizing force in, 288, 289; translation of the category into Chinese, 279. See also Third-person pronoun

Gernet, Jacques, 6, 47–59; and the copula, 66n; and theories of commensurability, 61, 63, 66n, 67n, 70n

Gilman, Sander: and Lam Qua's medical portraiture, 250, 253, 271

Gimu. See Obligation

Giroux: and "border pedagogy," 391

Global circulation: after the Cold War, 1; and difference/alterity, 1; and local culture, 5; and information technology, 375; and international law, 128; and media culture, 2; and meaning value, 21; and Protestant missionaries, 138. See also Colonialism

Global village, notion of, 375

God: and translation, 58–62, 60, 64, 72n, 72n

Goethe, 109, 110

Gong, Prince, 136, 143–145, 148, 158, 161n

Graham, A. C., 50

Gramophone in China: early appearance of, 214; expansion of industry, 221, 222; first records in India, 231n; in pop literature, 232n; and proliferation of indigenous music, 217; and preservation of individual performances, 217; and technical constraints, 216, 217; as symbol of domestic felicity, 217, 218

"Grand titration." See Needham, Joseph

Grant, Hope (General), 195, 196, 198, 210n

Great China Records, 223, 225, 226; and Sun Yat-sen, 225

Greek, and Chinese, 49, 50, 60, 61

Gronow, Pekka, 221, 233n, 234n

Grotius, Hugo, 153, 166

Guo Moruo, 227

Gützlaff, Karl, 133, 134, 154, 155

Habermas, Jürgen, 150, 151

Hague Convention, 204–209

Hall, W. E., 136, 140, 150, 158

Hallek, Henry W., 154

Halley, Edmund, 38n

Harris, Townsend, 171

Hart, Robert, 139, 143, 161n, 162n

Heaven and hell, 88, 89

Hegel, G. W. F., 117, 333

Heidegger, Martin, 51

Herbert, Sidney, 196

Heuskins, Harry, 171

Hevia, James, 41n, 129, 159n

Hirschfeld, Magnus, 276

Hinsch, Bret, 300n

Medhurst, Walter Henry, 133

Medical illustration, 241, 250

Meiji School of Law, 169

Meiji Six Society, 165

Mei Lanfang, 224

Meirokusha. See Meiji Six Society

Mencius: and *geming* ("revolution"), 358–361; and *qi*, 77, 78, 109, 111; Richards on, 333; on sex and human nature, 278, 279

Mental health in China. *See* Psychiatry

Metaphysics, 14, 88

Minquan. See Civil rights

Missionaries: and Boxer Uprising, 200; and English-language education, 378, 387; and looting, 207; and medicine, 101, 138, 307, 308; and publication of books, 361, 364, 365. *See also* Jesuits; Ricci, Matteo; Christianity

Mitsukuri Genpo, 169

Mitsukuri Rinsho, 169, 170, 187n

Miyoshi Kiyoyuki, 359, 360

Modernity: and "belated modernity," 218–220; as identity for China, 349; gramophone as an emblem of, 220; and discourse of homosexuality in China, 295, 298, 299; and "literary modernity," 340; and proposals to adopt International English, 382, 383

Montauban, General, 194

Montesquieu, Guy de, 153, 154

Mori Arinori, 165

Moriyama Shigeru, 173, 174

Morrison, Robert, 132, 133, 138

Müller, Max, 118

Music industry: and Cantonese folk melodies, 227; management of, 224, 225; notation and non-Western music, 216; for overseas populations, 223; transnational character of, 215; and women's magazines, 233n. *See also* Gaisberg, F. W.; Gramophone; Record Industry

Mutsu Horikichi, 181

Mutsu Munemitsu, 181, 182, 190n

Napier, Lord, 132, 133

Napoleon III, 194, 361

"Native": in ethnographic discourse, 389, 392

Natural law, 152–154, 156

Nature: Chinese term for, 80, 94, 100, 278, 279

Needham, Joseph, 47, 65n

Neo-Confucianism, 74, 79; and *geming* ("revolution"), 358, 359; and Jesuits, 6, 74, 80, 82; and *qi*, 84, 85; and the soul, 85; and spirituality, 79, 80. *See also* Confucianism

Neologisms: and international legal terms, 148–152; and the Jesuits, 60, 64. *See also* Translation

New Culture, 289. *See also* Zhang Jingsheng

New Moon Records, 226, 232n, 235n

Newton, Isaac: and George Psalmanazar, 38n

Nie Er, 228, 229

Nietzsche, Friedrich, 340

Nishi Amane, 165, 171

Norman, E. H., 183

Obligation, in Japanese, 170

Oe Academy, Journal of, 368

Ogden, C. K., 332, 334–336, 344

Okamoto Kansuke, 361, 362

Opium War, 132, 141, 142, 154, 157, 162

Orientalism, 123n; and I. A. Richards, 332. *See also* Said, Edward

Orthological Institute of China, 336

Osatake Takeki, 173

Oyama Iwao, 185

Pan Guangdan, 286; and *Psychology of Sex*, 294, 295, 302n

Parker, Peter, 9, 307; and the Chinese "temper," 251, 252; and individual medical cases painted by Lam Qua, 256–270; and the medical mission to Canton, 239, 245, 248; and translation of Vattel, 140, 141, 155

Paris Universal Exposition, 170

Pascal, Blaise, 97
Patriotism: in Hong Kong education, 396n
Peking opera, 214, 224
Peking Oriental Society, 202
Peng Hsiao-yen, 302n, 303n
Phillipson, Robert, 378
Phonography: constraints of, 216
Pietz, William, 20
Plato, 87, 88, 93, 99
Pneuma. See qi
"Pocket-book" record companies, 224, 225, 229, 235n
Popular songs: American music in Shanghai, 234n; and Filipino musicians, 225; and profitability on the urban record market, 216; and Shanghai corner stores, 232n; Tin Pan Alley, 225
Porcelain, 202, 203
Positive law, 152–156, 166
Pratt, Mary Louise, 385–386, 391–392
Primitivism, 208, 209
Prodromou, Luke, 377, 384
Proselytizing: and Protestant missionaries, 138. *See also* Missionaries; Jesuits; Parker, Peter; Translation
Psalmanazar, George, 15–19, 21, 38n; and Edmund Halley, 38n; and Isaac Newton, 38n; and Swift, 38n
Psychiatry: and culture-bound syndromes, 305; and early Western medical missionaries, 307–311, 315; and hygiene, 312–314; and institutions in China, 305–309; literary explorations of, 314, 315; neurasthenia, 305, 314, 315, 317; nonpsychiatric means of intervention, 324, 325; panic disorder, 305; and patient narratives, 319–322; in present public health structure, 307, 311, 312, 313, 325; *qigong* psychotic reaction; 305, 314–319, 323, 324, 327n, social stigma of mental illness, 309, 312, 313, 326; in traditional medical writings, 307. See also *Diagnostic and Statistical Manual of Mental Disorders*
Puffendorf, Samuel, 166

Qi: and anatomy, 98–100; in Confucian and neo-Confucian thought, 77–80, 89–91; earliest written records, 76–77; Jesuit translations of, 75, 76, 97; and reinterpretation as Aristotelian elements, 75, 91; as *spiritus* or *pneuma*, 98–100; in Vagnoni, 93–97
Qian Guangren, 226, 227
Qian Xuantong, 339
Qin burning of books, 64, 81, 104n
Qiu Yuan, 293–295
Quanli. See Right
Queue: as Chinese cultural difference, 265, 266, 272, 273
Quine, W. V. O., 69n; and translation, 46, 52, 54

Record industry: decentralization, 234n; market statistics, 234n; and Pathé-EMI, 222–226, 229; and RCA-Victor, 223–225; in Shanghai, 218–220. *See also* Gaisberg, F. W.; Gramophone; Music Industry
Relativism, 47, 58, 64, 66n; conceptual, 68n
Ren Bonian, 259
Ren Guang, 228–230, 236n
Revolution, 10; discourse of *geming*, 357; early etymology of, 358, 371n; Liang Qichao on, 355; in medieval Japan, 359, 360; and neo-Confucianism, 358, 359; as neologism from Japan, 356; and "poetry revolution," 366, 367
Ricci, Matteo, 138; and Euclid, 49, 66n; on interpretation of Confucian doctrine, 81–89, 102n, 104n; and qi, 6, 74–76, 83, 84; on romanization of Chinese language, 339; and translation of concepts of God and spirits, 53, 55–57; and *Zuozhuan*, 86, 87
Richards, I. A., 10, 331; and Basic English, 332–350; intellectual influences, 353n; and principle of multiple definition, 334
Right: translations of, 148, 153, 170
Rites Controversy, 61

Third-person pronoun: and gendering in modern Chinese, 28, 29, 34, 36, 40n

Tian, in Chinese high antiquity, 80. *See also* God

Tianjin Convention. *See* Treaty of Tianjin

Tokugawa: and Chinese lexicon, 168; *geming* ("revolution") theory during, 360; and international law, 167; and "the West," 166

Tokugawa Akitake, 170

Tokutomi Soho, 367

Tongwen guan. See Imperial College

Translation: and Buddhism and Confucianism, 60, 61, 64; cultural translation, 1, 34; as invention, 278; as Jesuit strategy, 60, 64, 74, 75, 101; and legal terms, 148–152; "literal," 109; as means of legitimation, 61, 62; mistranslation approach, 169; pidgin, 110–112, 114; of psychiatric symptoms, 305–309, 315; and reciprocity, 34, 38n; and I. A. Richards, 351 n. 8; theory of, 5, 6; and "translatability," 14, 15, 28, 29, 34, 35, 137; and translator, 128, 276, 277; and transliteration, 60; unidiomatic, 110; and Western missionaries, 364, 365; word-for-word, 109, 112; and world history, 14. *See also* Jesuits: strategies of translation; Meaning-value; Quine, W. V. O.

Translingual practice: and Chinese "same-sex love," 278; and loanword neologism, 356; and "national character" and individualism in China, 388. *See also* Liu, Lydia

Transliteration. *See* Translation

Transnational culture: and the gramophone, 218–222, 227; and cultural flows, 390

Treaty of Beijing, 201

Treaty of Kanghwa, 178

Treaty of Peace and Friendship between Meiji and Yi Governments, 175

Treaty of Shimonoseki, 181–183, 190n

Treaty of Tianjin, 131–133, 178–180

Trigault, Nicolas, 92, 104n, 339. *See also* Romanization

Trinity: and omission in Jesuit translations, 60

Triple Intervention, 183

Tsuda Mamichi, 171

Tsutsumi Koshiji, 171, 173

Uchida Yasutoshi, 172

Ukawa Morisaburo, 177

Universalism: of Basic English, 343, 383; and *competing universalisms*, 19; dialectic of universal and particular, 19; of English language, 381; historical making of, 128, 146–148, 155; in international law, 127–129, 148–159; linguistic, 334, 342, 348; and the masculine pronoun, 36; and Western cultural imperialism, 276, 277; in translation, 1, 169

Universal equivalent, and Marx, 22–23

Urase Hiroshi, 173, 174

Vagnoni, Alphonso, and translation of Aristotelian theory of four elements, 93–97, 99

Vattel, Emmerich, 138–141, 155, 162n, 204; and Peter Parker, 140, 141, 155

Victoria and Albert Museum, 197, 203, 210n

Vissering, Simon, 171

Vitiello, Giovanni, 300n

Volpp, Sophie, 300n

Wade, Thomas, 133, 160n

Waley, Arthur, 162n

Wang Tao, 10, 357; and democratic society for China, 361–363, 365

Wanguo Gonfa. See Elements of International Law

War: and Japan, 183–186, 190n; and international legal terms, 159

Ward, John, 139

Wen-xiang, 142

CONTRIBUTORS

JIANHUA CHEN is a Ph.D. candidate in the Department of East Asian Languages and Civilizations at Harvard University. NANCY N. CHEN is Assistant Professor of Anthropology at the University of California, Santa Cruz. She is the author of "Urban Spaces and Experiences of Qigong," (in *Urban Spaces: Autonomy and Community in Post-Mao China*, Deborah Davis, ed.) and "Speaking Nearby": A Conversation with Trinh T. Minh-ha," (in *Visualizing Theory*, Lucien Taylor, ed., and in *Visual Anthropology Review* 8). ALEXIS DUDDEN is Sue and Eugene Mercy Assistant Professor of History at Connecticut College. ROGER HART is a National Endowment for the Humanities fellow at the School of Historical Studies at the Institute for Advanced Study in Princeton. He is completing work on a book manuscript "Proof, Propaganda, and Patronage: A Cultural History of the Dissemination of Western Studies in Seventeenth-Century China" and an edited volume "Cultural Studies of Chinese Science, Technology, and Medicine." LARISSA N. HEINRICH is a Ph.D. candidate in the Department of East Asian Languages, University of California at Berkeley. JAMES HEVIA is Associate Professor of History at the University of North Carolina, Chapel Hill, and the author of *Cherishing Men from Afar*. ANDREW F. JONES is Assistant Professor of Chinese at the University of California, Berkeley. He is the author of *Like a Knife: Ideology and Genre in Contemporary Chinese Popular Music* and translator of Yu Hua, *The Past and the Punishments*. WAN SHUN EVA LAM is a Ph.D. candidate in language, literacy, and culture, Graduate School of Education, University of California at Berkeley. LYDIA H. LIU is Associate Professor of Chinese and Comparative Literature at the University of California, Berkeley. She is the author of *Translingual Practice: Literature, National Culture, and Translated Modernity—China, 1900–1937*. TZE-LAN DEBORAH SANG is Assistant Professor of Chinese at Stanford University and the author of a forthcoming book, "The Emerging Lesbian: Female Same-Sex Desire in Modern Chinese Literature and Culture." HAUN SAUSSY is Associate Professor of Chinese and Comparative Literature at Stanford University and the author of *The Problem of a Chinese Aesthetic.* Q. S. TONG is Associate Professor in the English Department at the University of Hong Kong and is the author of *Reconstructing Romanticism: Organic Theory Revisited.* QIONG ZHANG is Assistant Professor of History at Western Connecticut State University. She is the author of "About God, Demons, and Miracles: The Jesuit Discourse on the Supernatural in Late Ming China," *Early Science and Medicine* 4 (February 1999), and is finishing a book manuscript, "Making a Difference: The Cultural Politics of Miracles and Learned Discourse in the Jesuit Mission to Late Ming China."

Library of Congress Cataloging-in-Publication Data
Tokens of exchange : the problem of translation in global circulations /
edited by Lydia H. Liu.
p. cm. — (Post-contemporary interventions)
Includes bibliographical references and index.
ISBN 0-8223-2401-6 (cloth : alk. paper).
ISBN 0-8223-2424-5 (pbk. : alk. paper)
1. Translating and interpreting—Social aspects. 2. Translating and interpreting—China. 3. Intercultural communication. I. Liu, Lydia He.
  II. Series.
P306.2.T65 1999
418'.02—dc21 99-28628 CIP